MANAGEMENT
A PROGRAMMED APPROACH
WITH
CASES AND APPLICATIONS

MANAGEMENT
A PROGRAMMED APPROACH
WITH
CASES AND APPLICATIONS

FOURTH EDITION

Leonard J. Kazmier

Arizona State University

McGraw-Hill Book Company
New York St. Louis San Francisco Auckland Bogotá Düsseldorf
Johannesburg London Madrid Mexico Montreal New Delhi
Panama Paris São Paulo Singapore Sydney Tokyo Toronto

To Lorraine

Library of Congress Cataloging in Publication Data
Kamier, Leonard J
　Management, a programmed approach with cases and applications.

　Third ed. published in 1974 under title: Principles of management.
　Includes bibliographies and index.
　1. Management—Programmed instruction. I. Title.
HD31.K36　1980　　658.4'007'7　　79-17132
ISBN 0-07-033453-6

MANAGEMENT: A PROGRAMMED APPROACH WITH CASES AND APPLICATIONS

Copyright © 1980 by McGraw-Hill, Inc. All rights reserved. Formerly published under the title of PRINCIPLES OF MANAGEMENT: A PROGRAMMED-INSTRUCTIONAL APPROACH, copyright © 1974, 1969, 1964 by McGraw-Hill, Inc. All rights reserved. Printed in the United States of America. No part of this publication may be reproduced, stored in a retrieval system, or transmitted, in any form or by any means, electronic, mechanical, photocopying, recording, or otherwise, without the prior written permission of the publisher.

3456 HDHD 898

This book was set in Times Roman by A Graphic Method Inc. The editors were John F. Carleo and Frances A. Neal; the designer was Craigwood Phillips, A Good Thing, Inc.; the production supervisor was Richard A. Ausburn.

CONTENTS

PREFACE	xiii
TO THE STUDENT	xvii

PART 1 INTRODUCTION

1	**THE DEVELOPMENT OF MANAGEMENT CONCEPTS**	3
	Taylor's Scientific Management	4
	Fayol's General Principles of Management	7
	Influences of Behavioral Science on Management Concepts	11
	The Systems and Quantitative Approach to Management Concepts	15
	The Cultural Framework of Management	18
	The Contingency View of Management	21
	Review	23
	Discussion Questions	25
	References	26
	Case Study: Consultants' Reports	28
	Case Study: The Old-Line Foreman	29
	Applications Reading: "Some Basic Trends Affecting Management in the Future," Keith Davis	31
	Questions on Reading	37
2	**THE FUNCTIONS OF THE MANAGER**	39
	The Functional Approach to Management	40
	Planning	43
	Organizing	45

	Directing	47
	Controlling	49
	Coordinating	50
	Review	51
	Discussion Questions	54
	References	54
	Case Study: The New Manager	55
	Case Study: Selection of a Senior Buyer	56
	Applications Reading: "How to Manage Your Boss," Peter F. Drucker	57
	Questions on Reading	63
PART 2 PLANNING	**3 ORGANIZATIONAL OBJECTIVES AND PLANNING PREMISES**	**67**
	Types of Objectives	68
	Management by Objectives	74
	The Environment of Planning	76
	Social Responsibility and Governmental Regulation	82
	Sales Forecasting and Planning	83
	Review	88
	Discussion Questions	90
	References	91
	Case Study: Planning in a Staff Department	93
	Case Study: A Decline in Government Contracts	94
	Applications Reading: "A Long-Range Approach to MBO," Richard Babcock and Peter F. Sorensen, Jr.	95
	Questions on Reading	102
	4 POLICIES, PROCEDURES, AND METHODS	**103**
	Policies	104
	Procedures and Methods	109
	Decision Making	111
	Review	115
	Discussion Questions	116
	References	117
	Case Study: Krueger Metal Products Corporation	118

	Case Study: A Wage and Salary Policy Problem	118
	Applications Reading: "Making Policy Readable," E. K. Lybbert	119
	Questions on Reading	124
	5 QUANTITATIVE DECISION-MAKING TECHNIQUES	**125**
	Management Science	126
	Illustration of a Model	128
	Some Quantitative Techniques	131
	An Illustrative Application of Linear Programming	135
	Illustrative Applications of Statistical Decision Analysis	142
	Review	147
	Discussion Questions	150
	References	151
	Case Problem: Pliable Plastics Corporation	152
	Case Problem: Choice of Investments	153
	Case Problem: A Franchise Opportunity	153
	Applications Reading: "Treading Softly with Management Science," Roger D. Eck	154
	Questions on Reading	161
PART 3 ORGANIZING	**6 ORGANIZATION STRUCTURE**	**165**
	Departmentation	166
	Vertical and Horizontal Growth in the Organization	172
	Span of Management	174
	Decentralization and the Overall Organization	177
	Review	182
	Discussion Questions	184
	References	185
	Case Study: Lesner's Department Store	186
	Case Study: A Question of Managerial Authority	187
	Applications Reading: "A Contingency Approach to Decentralization," Howard M. Carlisle	189
	Questions on Reading	198

7 LINE AND STAFF RELATIONSHIPS — 199

Line and Staff Functions — 200
Advisory Staff Authority — 202
Service Staff Authority — 204
Control Staff Authority — 205
Functional Staff Authority — 206
Line-Staff Friction — 211
The Personal Staff — 213
Review — 214
Discussion Questions — 215
References — 216

Case Study: Noncooperative Line Managers — 216
Case Study: A Choice of Job Offers — 218
Applications Reading: "Using Central Staff to Boost Line Initiative," Edward C. Schleh — 219
Questions on Reading — 225

8 THE ORGANIZATION AS A SOCIAL SYSTEM — 227

Status — 228
Role — 232
Functions of the Informal Organization — 235
Charting the Informal Organization — 238
Power and Politics — 241
Review — 244
Discussion Questions — 246
References — 246

Case Study: Conflict among Mangers — 248
Case Study: A Proposal for Product Redesign — 249
Applications Reading: "Rules of the Road: Doing Something Simple about Conflict in the Organization," Donald G. Livingston — 251
Questions on Reading — 256

9 STAFFING THE ORGANIZATION — 257

Organizational Planning for Executive Needs — 258
Use of Interviewing in Selection — 263
Appraisal of Managerial Performance — 267
Management Development — 276
Review — 282
Discussion Questions — 285
References — 285

Case Study: A Management Development
    Program   288
Case Study: An Irresistible Job Offer   289
Applications Reading: "The Annual
    Performance Review Discussion—Making
    It Constructive," Herbert H. Meyer   291
Questions on Reading   298

PART 4 DIRECTING

10 ADMINISTRATIVE COMMUNICATION   **301**
Basic Concepts   302
Symbols in Communication   305
Barriers to Communication   307
Communication Networks   311
Communication Patterns in Small Groups   314
Review   317
Discussion Questions   318
References   319

Case Study: A Problem in Listening   321
Case Study: The Misinformed Supervisor   321
Applications Reading: "How to Be a Better
    Listener," Sherman K. Okun   323
Questions on Reading   327

**11 HUMAN MOTIVATION:
    BASIC FINDINGS**   **329**
Introduction   330
Categories of Motives   331
Multiple Motivation and the Conflict of
    Motives   336
Reactions to Frustration and Conflict   342
Review   346
Discussion Questions   347
References   348

Case Study: Professional Employee
    Motivation   348
Case Study: The Reluctant Supervisor   350
Applications Reading: "Understanding
    Frustration-Instigated Behavior,"
    Paul L. Wilkens and Joel B. Haynes   350
Questions on Reading   356

12 MOTIVATING PEOPLE AT WORK 357
Motivation, Morale, and Productivity 358
McGregor's Theory X and Theory Y 362
The Motivation-Maintenance Theory 367
Review 377
Discussion Questions 379
References 379

Case Study: Junior Managers at Universal Systems 381
Case Study: Transfer to Another Department 383
Applications Reading: "Behavior Modification: A Contingency Approach to Employee Performance," C. Ray Gullett and Robert Reisen 384
Questions on Reading 394

13 LEADERSHIP 395
Leader-Oriented Approaches to Studying Leadership 396
The Organizational Climate 400
Leadership Styles 403
The Contingency View of Leadership 410
Managerial Power and Disciplining 414
Review 417
Discussion Questions 419
References 420

Case Study: A Change of Supervisors 423
Case Study: A Matter of Overtime 424
Applications Reading: "Leadership Styles: Which Are Best When?" Alan Weiss 426
Questions on Reading 432

14 EFFECTIVE SUPERVISION 433
The Role of the First-Level Supervisor 434
Supervisory Effectiveness 440
The Managerial Grid 446
Overcoming Resistance to Change 450
Review 455
Discussion Questions 457
References 457

Case Study: A Change of Supervisory Philosophy at Triflex 459

	Case Study: An Analysis of Operating Procedures	460
	Applications Reading: "Rethinking the Supervisory Role," David S. Brown	462
	Questions on Reading	469
PART 5 **CONTROLLING**	**15 THE CONTROL PROCESS**	**473**
	General Concepts	474
	Budgetary Control	478
	Other Control Devices	484
	Human Reactions to Centralized Control Procedures	488
	Toward Effective Controls	490
	Review	492
	Discussion Questions	494
	References	494
	Case Study: Western Office Equipment and Supply Company	496
	Case Study: Control of In-Process Inventory	497
	Applications Reading: "Zero-Base Budgeting: Where to Use It and How to Begin," Peter A. Pyhrr	499
	Questions on Reading	507
	16 PROGRAM EVALUATION AND REVIEW TECHNIQUE (PERT)	**509**
	Systems-Oriented Techniques in Controlling	510
	Elements of the PERT Network	514
	Using the PERT Network	524
	Review	531
	Discussion Questions	533
	References	534
	Case Problems: Program Evaluation and Review Technique	534
	Case Study: An Unsuccessful Application of PERT	536
	Applications Reading: "Management Rediscovers CPM," George J. Berkwitt	537
	Questions on Reading	541

PART 6
SYSTEMS CONCEPTS

17 THE SYSTEMS APPROACH TO MANAGEMENT — 545
Systems Concepts and Management — 546
Program Management — 556
Computer Information Systems — 561
Review — 567
Discussion Questions — 569
References — 570

Case Study: A First Experience with Program Mangement — 572
Case Study: A Systems-Oriented Manager of Data Processing — 573
Applications Reading: "Project Management — A New Style for Success," Richard A. Jacobs — 575
Questions on Reading — 584

INDEX — 585

PREFACE

This book has been designed as an effective aid to understanding the major functions of management and the skills that lead to managerial success, be it in business firms or other kinds of organizations. The study of the process of management is based on the assumption that there are common skills that lead to managerial success in a wide variety of fields and in various kinds of organizations. These concepts and techniques serve as the foundation for the topics covered in this book.

Several distinct approaches have been developed for studying and describing the practice of management. Although the organization of this book follows the management process approach by analyzing the principal management functions of planning, organizing, directing, and controlling, an introduction to the quantitative and behavior approaches to studying managerial activity is included. For example, both the basic findings in the area of human motivation and the application of these findings are discussed in some detail in Part 4 on directing. Similarly, the quantitative decision-making techniques are described in Part 2 on planning, and the systems-oriented Program Evaluation and Review Technique (PERT) is included in Part 5 on controlling. Whereas the behavioral, quantitative, and systems-oriented approaches to management have stimulated productive research and the development of managerial techniques, the functional approach is particularly suited for presenting these concepts and techniques in an orderly and understandable way. This book recognizes that effective management does not result from rigid application of particular techniques. Rather, the managerial approaches that make best sense are contingent upon the environment in which they are to be applied.

This fourth edition has been updated to include recent developments. Specific changes include the new sections on the contingency view of management in Chapter 1, on social responsibility in Chapter 3, and on the contingency view of leadership in Chapter 13. Beyond such specific changes, the inclusion of applications-oriented readings represents a major addition for this edition of the book. These readings have been chosen to be complementary to the chapter coverage and to provide examples of specific real-world applications of management concepts and techniques. By intention, the programmed section of each chapter is designed to cover the terminology and concepts of management on a general level. The discussion questions, case studies, and applications readings then round out the coverage by requiring the reader to focus on the practical application of management concepts and techniques.

The Use of This Book In academic programs, this book has been developed for use in undergraduate courses in management or for those graduate students who do not have an undergraduate background in management or administration. By covering the basic terminology, concepts, and techniques in an effective self-instructional manner, the book prepares the student for more meaningful class participation directed toward the application of management concepts and techniques. Thus, more class time can be devoted to such activities as analysis of case studies, discussion of readings, and participation in such training techniques as role playing and business simulation. Essentially, the format of this book makes it possible for the instructor to devote less time to lecturing the class about management concepts and more time to class activities concerned with the application of management concepts and techniques.

Because this book is oriented toward applications,

the previous editions have been widely used in management development programs. The addition of the applications readings should enhance such use. After the first two chapters, which include a historical and conceptual overview of the development of management principles, the chapters can be covered in any desired order because they have been designed to be as independent of one another as possible. One technique that has been used successfully in management development programs is to have program participants prepare additional short case studies for group discussion. Such activity helps to establish better understanding of the concepts in each chapter as well as to focus the applications on matters of specific interest to the program participants.

Acknowledgment As for the previous editions of this book, I owe a debt of gratitude to the students at Arizona State University, at the University of Notre Dame, and to the individuals in management development programs who participated in the field testing of the preliminary versions of the programmed sections of this book. Similarly, I express gratitude to the companies which made available the descriptions that serve as the basis for the case studies and to the business journals which gave their permission to reprint the applications articles included in this book. Of course, all company and individual names used in the case studies are fictitious. Finally, I owe special thanks to William A. Clarey, Bradley University; David Kelley, Iowa State University; Ronald C. Semone, U.S. Civil Service–Bureau of Training; and Arthur V. Wolfe, Texas A & M University, who gave generously of their time to recommend changes for this edition.

Leonard J. Kazmier

TO THE STUDENT

The format of this book is different from that of a typical textbook in that each section of the chapter is made up of a series of short paragraphs, called *frames*, which not only present you with some information but also require you to answer key questions about the material. The answers to these questions are provided along the left margin of each page. Please cover these answers until you have tried to answer each question on your own, and then compare your answer with the one given in the margin. By following this recommended procedure you will gain two advantages that will increase your learning effectiveness: having independent practice, and being able to check on whether you understand the concepts and remember important facts as you do your reading.

The questions in the introductory chapters will probably seem easy to you. However, the development of the material in this book is relatively fast-moving and comprehensive, with little repetition, and so you will find that close attention on your part is necessary. If you do not understand why the answer given in the margin differs from yours, place a question mark in the margin as a reminder to ask for clarification of the concept during class discussion. A review section is included at the end of each chapter. You can use this as an overall self-test after completing the chapter, as well as for later review. Each frame in the review section refers to the frame numbers with which it is related in that chapter. If you have any difficulty answering the questions in the review, consult the referenced frames immediately, while the problem is still fresh.

Best success in your study of management, and in your application of the concepts and techniques included in this book!

Leonard J. Kazmier

Introduction

In Chapter 1 four important influences on the development of management concepts are first described: Taylor's scientific management movement, Fayol's general principles of management, the application of the behavioral sciences, and the systems and quantitative approach to management. We conclude this chapter by considering the cultural framework within which management principles are applied, and then describe the contingency approach to management, by which the several diverse approaches to the development of management concepts can be unified.

Chapter 2 is devoted to a description of the so-called "functional approach" to the study of management concepts. This approach also is often referred to as the management process approach, and is concerned with the principal functions, or activities, that are performed by managers in all types of organizations. The managerial functions that are described in Chapter 2 are those of planning, organizing, directing, and controlling. Whereas the historical influences on management concepts described in Chapter 1 have been concerned with the development of a better understanding of managerial concepts, the functional approach, with its orientation toward managerial activities, is a convenient basis by which the management concepts can be organized for the purpose of study and application. It is for this reason that the functional approach to management serves as the principal basis for organizing the contents of this book.

Part 1

THE DEVELOPMENT OF MANAGEMENT CONCEPTS

- Taylor's Scientific Management
- Fayol's General Principles of Management
- Influences of Behavioral Science on Management Concepts
- The Systems and Quantitative Approach to Management Concepts
- The Cultural Framework of Management
- The Contingency View of Management
- Review
- Discussion Questions
- References
- Case Study: Consultants' Reports
- Case Study: The Old-Line Foreman
- Applications Reading: "Some Basic Trends Affecting Management in the Future" Keith Davis
- Questions on Reading

The attempt to formulate general management concepts is based on the assumption that there is a common set of principles underlying successful managerial performance in a diversity of fields. The purpose of this chapter is to review the major influences on the development of management concepts that have occurred during this century. From the standpoint of the history of human managerial activity, these are admittedly relatively recent influences. However, it has been during the twentieth century that the development of large-scale complex organizations and the need for managerial concepts has been particularly apparent. An understanding of these historical influences will help you to recognize their respective contributions to contemporary management concepts and techniques as described in the remainder of this book.

Taylor's Scientific Management

Frederick W. Taylor is generally acknowledged to be the founder of the scientific management movement. His overall goal was higher industrial efficiency, in the form of higher productivity and lower unit cost. What distinguishes scientific management from other approaches is not so much its goal, but the basic assumptions, specific objectives, and techniques by which industrial efficiency is to be achieved. The techniques of scientific management reflect Taylor's belief that the *planning* of tasks needs to be separated from the *doing*. His book, *The Principles of Scientific Management,* was first published in 1911.

1   One of the assumptions underlying scientific management is that the application of the *methods of science* to problems of management will lead to high industrial efficiency. It was in this sense that Frederick **Taylor** _____ believed management should be "scientific."

2   Observation, measurement, and experimental comparison are among the principal methods of **science** _____ that can be applied to problems of **management** _____.

3   A second basic assumption is that the incentive of high wages will promote the mutuality of interest between workers and managers that will result in high industrial _____. **efficiency (or productivity, etc.)**

Taylor's Scientific Management • 5

4 Thus two basic assumptions underlying the techniques of scientific management are that industrial efficiency can be improved through the application of the methods of _____ and the payment of [high / low] wages.

science
high

5 Several specific objectives are included in the scientific management approach to improving industrial efficiency. One is the *standardization of working conditions*. Determining the best temperature and humidity for achieving productivity has to do with the standardization of _____ _____.

working conditions

6 The provision for work breaks of optimum duration and frequency is another example of standardization of _____ _____ to achieve higher industrial _____.

working conditions
efficiency

7 Closely related to the objective of standardizing working conditions is the *standardization of work methods*. Determining the best procedure for doing a job is an example related to standardization of _____ _____.

work methods

8 *Motion study* is the observation of all the motions that compose a particular job and the determination of the best set of motions that leads to the greatest efficiency. Therefore, _____ _____ is a technique used to attain the specific objective of standardizing work methods.

motion study

9 Taylor concentrated on observing and measuring the performance of high producers in order to discover and develop standardized _____ methods for particular jobs.

work

10 The use of motion-picture cameras to record worker movements and work methods is included in the technique of _____ _____.

motion study

11 In addition to the standardization of _____ _____ and the standardization of _____ _____, Taylor believed

working conditions
work methods

6 • Chapter 1 • The Development of Management Concepts

that the planning of a *large daily task* promotes industrial efficiency.

work methods
daily task

12 Just as motion study is a technique related to the standardization of _____ _____, *time study* is related to the planning of a large _____ _____ for each worker.

time study

13 The use of a stopwatch is related to the technique of _____ _____.

time study

14 Determining the appropriate production standard for a particular job can be accomplished by using the technique of _____ _____.

motion study

15 On the other hand, observing the detailed job performance of a number of workers in order to discover the best way to do a job is related to the technique of _____ _____.

high

low

16 Another specific objective of scientific management is that encouragement to stay in a job should be given to [high / low] producers, whereas encouragement to transfer to a different job should be given to [high / low] producers.

higher (Note that not only overall pay but also per-unit pay is higher.)

17 Accordingly, for those producing above standard the per-unit pay under the Taylor Differential Piecework Plan is [higher / lower] than it is for those producing below standard.

discouraged

encouraged

18 As a result, job transfers for employees producing above standard are [encouraged / discouraged] by the use of the Taylor Differential Piecework Plan, whereas job transfers for those producing below standard are [encouraged / discouraged].

science; high wages

19 Thus two basic assumptions of scientific management are the industrial efficiency can be attained through the application of the methods of _____ and the payment of _____ _____.

20 Of the techniques of scientific management, stud-

Fayol's General Principles of Management

working conditions ies of rest breaks, lighting, and the like are related to the objective of defining standardized _____ _____.

work methods **21** Motion study is related to the objective of defining standardized _____ _____.

stay in the job (etc.)
transfer to another job (etc.) **22** The use of the Taylor Differential Piecework Plan is related to the objective of encouraging high producers to _____ while encouraging low producers to _____.

time study **23** The production standard to be used in a wage incentive system can be determined by using the technique of _____ _____.

management **24** Although the historical connection is not direct, recent work in operations research, which emphasizes the application of the methods of science to managerial decision making, is a modern development of one of the operating assumptions of Taylor's scientific _____.

Fayol's General Principles of Management

In contrast to Taylor's primary emphasis on management techniques applicable at the working, or operative, level, Henri Fayol's approach to developing management concepts is oriented toward the higher levels of the organization. The so-called "functional approach" to the study of management is a direct outgrowth of Fayol's work. Because all of Chapter 2 is devoted to describing the functional approach to management, our coverage of Fayol's work in this chapter is restricted to providing a brief exposure to the overall framework that Fayol followed in his development of management concepts.

Henri Fayol was a French industrialist who published his observations about general management principles in 1916 in French, under the title *Administration Industrielle et Générale*. However, this monograph was not translated into English until 1929 and was not published in the United States until 1949.

25 Fayol identified six activities which he believed

financial

had to be accomplished in all organizations. Referring to Figure 1.1, the organizational activity concerned with the optimum use of capital is the _____ activity.

1. Technical
2. Commercial
3. Financial
4. Security
5. Accounting
6. Managerial

Figure 1.1 Fayol's identification of the activities to be accomplished in all organizations.

commercial

26 Continue referring to Figure 1.1 for the following frames. The buying, selling, and exchange functions in an organization are related to the _____ activity.

technical

27 Production would be classified as a _____ activity in Fayol's analysis.

accounting

28 The determination of present financial position is included in the _____ activity.

security

29 Protection of property would be included in the _____ activity.

managerial

30 Finally, Fayol identified the functions of planning, organizing, commanding, coordinating, and controlling as being included in _____ activity.

managerial

31 Most of Fayol's analysis of organizational activities was devoted to the area listed in the preceding frame, i.e., the analysis of _____ activity.

top

32 Fayol held that the importance of managerial ability increases as one goes up the chain of command. Consequently, one would expect that managerial skill is the most important component of job performance in [first-level / top] management positions.

33 Fayol also identified a number of principles of

Fayol's General Principles of Management

management, listed in Figure 1.2, which apply in varying degrees in all managerial situations. We consider some of these principles briefly in the frames that follow, in order to illustrate his approach to managerial problems. These fourteen concepts, then, are considered to be the most important principles of **management** _____.

1. Division of work
2. Authority and responsibility
3. Discipline
4. Unity of command
5. Unity of direction
6. Subordination of individual interest to general interest
7. Remuneration of personnel
8. Centralization
9. Scalar chain
10. Order
11. Equity
12. Stability of tenure of personnel
13. Initiative
14. Esprit de corps

Figure 1.2 Fayol's general principles of management.

34 *Remuneration of personnel* concerns the importance of the remuneration system being fair and affording maximum satisfaction to employee and employer. This principle is similar to one of the basic assumptions underlying the field of **scientific management** _____, which we described in the preceding section of this chapter.

35 The *scalar chain* refers to the chain of superiors from the highest to the lowest rank, which should be short-circuited only when scrupulous following of it would be detrimental. This principle suggests, for example, that an employee [should / **should not**] feel free to contact his immediate superior's superior.

36 The *unity of command* principle suggests that an employee should receive orders from [**only one** / several] superior(s).

37 *Initiative* is conceived of as the thinking out and execution of a plan. Fayol suggests that since it is one of the "keenest satisfactions for an intelligent man to experience," managers should "sacrifice personal vanity" in order to permit subordinates to exercise it. Fayol thus appears to suggest that managers should share some of their decision-making authority with their _____.

subordinates

38 The principle of *division of work* suggests that specialization within an enterprise leads to a higher level of _____.

efficiency (or productivity, etc.)

39 "A place for everything (everyone) and everything (everyone) in its (his or her) place" concerns the principle of *order*. The use of a formal organization chart in a company would be [consistent / inconsistent] with the objective of this principle.

consistent

40 *Stability of tenure of personnel* suggests that high employee turnover is [advantageous / detrimental] to an organization.

detrimental

41 In concluding his description of management principles, Fayol stated that he had tried to present only those that he had the most occasion to use in his career as a manager. Thus the principles [were / were not] regarded as being exhaustive.

were not

42 In addition to his description of organizational activities and principles of management, Fayol considered the specific *functions,* or elements, of management. These universal elements, or _____, constitute the essence of the managerial job.

functions

43 Although we make only brief reference to this aspect of Fayol's work in this section, it constitutes a major part of his writing. Planning, organizing, commanding, coordinating, and controlling were identified by Fayol as being the _____ of management.

functions (or elements)

44 Throughout Fayol's writings there is an emphasis on the generality of management functions and principles. Therefore, he believed that political, religious, philanthropic, and other organizations [would / would not] all be able to apply his principles.

would

complementary (the principles and techniques used are not contradictory)

45 Because their interests were directed toward different aspects of managerial work in organizations, the methods and principles developed by Taylor and Fayol are typically considered to be [conflicting / complementary].

Influences of Behavioral Science on Management Concepts

The behavioral science approach to management concerns the application of the methods and findings of psychology, social psychology, and sociology for the purpose of understanding organizational behavior. Historically, the first significant use of the behavioral science approach to management problems occurred in the famous series of studies in the Hawthorne Plant of the Western Electric Company during the late 1920s and early 1930s; the studies are usually referred to as the *Hawthorne studies.* The researchers began these studies with the intention of investigating the relationship between physical conditions of work and employee productivity. However, they found that the social variables were more important than the physical variables as factors affecting productivity. As a result, their research had an unexpected outcome.

46 The development of the field of *human relations,* which is the study of human behavior at work for the purpose of developing higher levels of productivity and personal satisfaction, was a direct result of the _____ studies.

Hawthorne

47 Several people made significant contributions to the studies in the Hawthorne Plant. However, Elton Mayo, a principal consultant in the Hawthorne studies, is generally considered to be the founder of the field called _____ relations.

human

48 To Taylor, human relations problems stood in the way of production and should be removed. To _____ [name], human relations became a broad new area of study in order to improve morale and productivity, and was not considered simply as a "problem."

(Elton) Mayo

49 For example, in the Hawthorne Plant, Mayo

found that the piecework systems in use led to extensive conflicts between workers and time-and-motion-study experts. Thus employee reactions to piecework systems [were / were not] those desired by Taylor.

were not

50 The Hawthorne studies provided evidence that, in addition to being a formal arrangement of functions, an organization is a social system whose success depends on the appropriate application of _____ science principles.

behavioral (or social)

51 Early human relations research tended to focus on employee satisfaction and morale, the implicit assumption being that high morale leads to [high / low] productivity.

high

52 Later research has indicated that the initial assumption about the relationship between morale and productivity was oversimplified. Futhermore, because the scope of organizational application has increased, most writers now prefer the term "behavioral science approach to management" in place of the term "human _____."

relations

53 The area of *employee motivation* continues to be of prime interest in the _____ _____ approach to management.

behavioral science

54 A determination of the factors that lead to high productivity as well as to high morale in an organization is included in the study of employee _____.

motivation

55 Another area of behavioral science research is the study of the organization as a *social system*. Studies of role, status, and status symbols are included in viewing the organization as a _____ system.

social

56 Studying the functions of informal groups and their effect on organizational success is also consistent with viewing the organization as a _____ _____.

social system

57 Increasingly, the area of *leadership* and its rela-

Influences of Behavioral Science on Management Concepts • 13

behavioral   tionship to organizational success have been included in _____ science research.

58 The problem of distinguishing between successful and unsuccessful managerial behavior is included in the study of leadership. Since the study of leadership includes consideration of environmental factors that

includes   affect a leader's success, it [includes / does not include] more than the study of the individual leader.

59 In addition to studying employee

motivation   _____, viewing the organization as a

social   _____ system, and studying the process of

leadership   _____, the behavioral science approach to management directs attention to *communication* and its relationship to organizational success.

60 The study of the factors related to achieving understanding in two-person situations is included in the

communication   behavioral interest in _____.

61 Furthermore, consideration of the best structuring and use of the channels of contact in an organiza-

communication   tion is included in the study of _____.

62 The four areas of application of the behavioral science approach to management discussed so far

motivation;   have been employee _____, considering

social system;   the organization as a _____ _____,

leadership;   _____, and _____.

communication

63 Finally, an interest in *employee development* is

behavioral science   included in the _____ _____ approach to management theory.

64 Studying and applying the principles leading to efficiency in learning are included in the area of

development   employee _____.

65 A study of the factors leading to appropriate application of what has been learned to a new situation

employee   is also included in the interest in _____

development   _____.

communication

66 Reviewing this section briefly, the area of behavioral science application that emphasizes the importance of common understanding and its assessment is _____.

motivation

67 The area of behavioral science research that focuses on the personal factors underlying high productivity, as well as high morale, is the area of employee _____.

social system

68 Charting the informal pattern of relationships in an organization is included in the research perspective which views the organization as a _____.

leadership

69 The area having to do with identifying personal characteristics and situational factors leading to managerial success is that of _____.

development

70 The area concerned with the continued upgrading of employee skills, including managerial skills, is that of employee _____.

**motivation;
social system;
leadership;
communication;
development**

71 The five areas of managerial application of behavioral science methods and findings which have been introduced in this chapter are employee _____, viewing the organization as a _____, _____, _____, and employee _____.

72 As we have indicated, the Hawthorne studies marked the beginning of the human relations field and the subsequent interest in applying behavioral science methods and principles in the study of managerial problems. In the book that serves as a comprehensive report of these studies, Roethlisberger and Dickson summarized one of the studies by reporting:

> The study of the bank wiremen showed that their behavior at work could not be understood without considering the informal organization of the group

and the relation of the informal organization to the total social organization of the company.[1]

Of the five areas of behavioral science application which have been considered, the one that is represented in this excerpt is that of viewing the organization as a _____ _____.

social system

The Systems and Quantitative Approach to Management Concepts

Historically, the systems approach is a recent contributor to management theory and techniques. As is also true for the other contributions which have been described, certain ingredients included in this approach can be traced to early historical antecedents, but they have undergone recent significant development resulting in a distinct approach to organization and management. In this case, the significant historical event is represented by the development of operations research (OR) in the British military services during World War II. In this section we introduce the general characteristics of the systems approach that was stimulated by the development of OR, consider the associated use of mathematical models and quantitative methods, and discuss the role of communication and decision processes in the systems orientation.

73 In general, a *systems approach* indicates a primary interest in studying whole situations and relationships, rather than organizational segments. In this sense, if product design, manufacture, and marketing were largely accomplished independently of one another by specialized managers, the procedure used would be [consistent / inconsistent] with the systems approach.

inconsistent

74 The general characteristics of the systems viewpoint are described in some detail in Chapter 17, where this approach is used as the basis for summarizing some of the major concepts in this book. As indicated by the above example, even though specialized

---

[1]F.J. Roethlisberger and William J. Dickson, *Management and the Worker*, Cambridge, Mass.: Harvard University Press, 1939, p. 551.

knowledge is still considered to be important, the application of the systems approach results in the need to develop people who are [technical specialists / generalists].

generalists

75 In the case of a business organization the term "system" could mean "social system" and thus have a behavioral orientation, or it could apply to functional relationships and decision processes and thus have a relatively impersonal orientation. The systems approach associated with operations research concerns the identification of appropriate mathematical models as the basis for determining best decisions, and therefore it is relatively [behavioral / impersonal] in its orientation.

impersonal

76 Thus, whereas the continued development of the behavioral science applications since the Hawthorne studies has mainly led to developments in such areas as [employee motivation / decision-making techniques], the continued development of the systems approach stemming from operations research has led to developments in [employee motivation / decision-making techniques].

employee motivation

decision-making techniques

77 The techniques associated with operations research are described further in Chapter 5. For now we can observe that, as an overall approach, the most important characteristic of OR is its orientation toward [whole systems / particular problems].

whole systems

78 Even though the systems orientation of OR is its most important contribution to management theory, the quantitative techniques have come to be widely used in many specialized problem areas, such as production and distribution. Therefore, many people think of the collection of such techniques as linear programming, queuing methods, and computer simulation as constituting the definition of _____ research.

operations

79 As it has continued to develop in recent years, the systems approach not only includes an interest in mathematical models and the quantitative techniques associated with operations research, but it has also resulted in viewing the organization as a communication and decision-making system. In the context of the systems approach "communication" refers to [channels provided for information flow / factors influencing changes in behavior].

channels provided for information flow

80 From this standpoint, whereas many of Fayol's general principles of management were concerned with [division of formal authority / communication structure], the systems approach to management tends to view any organization as representing a _____ _____.

division of formal authority

communication structure

81 The Program Evaluation and Review Technique (PERT) is a planning and controlling method which represents the systems approach in its orientation and is extensively used in the construction and aerospace industries. Described in detail in Chapter 16, this technique [cuts across / closely conforms to] the established specialized departments in a firm.

cuts across (and thus has a wholistic orientation)

82 The systems approach to management shares a number of characteristics with Taylor's earlier work in that both are relatively impersonal in orientation, emphasize the use of the methods of science, and have resulted in contributions to the planning process. As if to highlight this similarity, the quantitative systems approach has frequently been called "management science," as contrasted to Taylor's _____ _____.

scientific management

83 However, the scope and techniques associated with these two contributions to the practice of management are quite different. The approach oriented toward study of entire situations with identification of best organizationwide decisions is _____ _____, whereas the approach oriented toward identifying best methods of work within an established system is _____ _____.

management science (or systems approach)

scientific management

84 Another development that has added fuel to growing interest in the systems approach is the use of

processing of information for general management use

electronic data processing in commercial applications beginning in the early 1950s. The applications particularly relevant to the systems approach are those that are concerned with [rapid sequences of computations, such as in payroll / processing of information for general management use].

85 The full potential of the computer is represented when it is used to develop information for more effective decision making, rather than when it is simply used as a rapid calculator. To the extent that current procedures associated with "instructing" the computer through computer programs can be simplified, the use of such equipment in conjunction with the systems approach to management will be [curtailed / enhanced].

enhanced (since the need to write individual programs limits computer use when the problem is nonrepetitive)

The Cultural Framework of Management

The coverage in the preceding sections of this chapter has been concerned with management as an internal process, and this is also the main orientation of the entire book. By "internal" we mean that the focus is on the things that managers should do within the organization to achieve organizational objectives. However, in addition to the internal process the cultural framework within which the organization exists represents the external process which may (and should) influence the specific decisions made by managers. Of course, the cultural factors which exist in different countries are likely to differ. But the point particularly developed in this section of the chapter is that a manager needs to be aware of changing cultural influences in our own society in order to be effective in applying the principles of management developed in this text.

86 The general manager of a steel mill in Sweden can analyze organizational objectives and apply principles of management in a manner similar to an American counterpart. However, because the mill is located in a different (socialistic) political system, the

cultural (or external)	_____ influences are likely to be quite different.
management	**87** Even within the context of a particular country, cultural changes take place which influence the appropriateness of particular managerial actions. Managerial alertness to cultural changes is therefore a prerequisite to the successful application of the principles of _____ presented in this book.
No These developments have resulted in governmental legislation (etc.).	**88** In the remainder of this section we consider four external, or cultural, factors that have been particularly important in the United States during the past twenty years: the internationalization of business, the increase in minority group participation, the concern for the ecology, and the rise in individual self-expression. Given the nature of these cultural influences, has it been possible for a business firm or other type of organization to ignore these developments? [Yes / No] Why or why not? _____ _____ _____
on a global scale	**89** Of course, the four areas of development which are considered do not cover all of the changes taking place in our society, but indicate the kinds of developments that should be given attention by managerial personnel. The first development, the *internationalization of business*, identifies the fact that both United States and foreign firms have been increasingly active [within their own countries only / on a global scale].
internationalization	**90** Not only has trade among countries increased, but business firms have increasingly established subsidiaries in other countries. Thus, this multinational orientation is what we have in mind when we speak of the _____ of business.
	91 The multinational scope of business activities has also opened the door to a number of problems, including the existence of different political systems, chang-

20 • Chapter 1 • The Development of Management Concepts

ing monetary exchange rates, and different ways of "doing business" in different countries. But given the mutual opportunities to develop new markets, such difficulties [have / have not] prevented the internationalization of business in the past twenty years.

have not

92 A second important external factor influencing organizations in this country during the past twenty years is the movement toward greater *minority participation* in our society. These concerns have resulted in specific government regulations to increase employment opportunities for such groups as blacks, Mexican-Americans, women, and older citizens. As a result, the use of such established personnel selection methods as employment tests [has / has not] been affected.

has (since some of these tests have been judged to include a cultural bias)

93 Thus, two external factors that have had a profound effect on the organizational perspective of managers during the past twenty years are the _____ of business and the increase in _____ group participation.

internationalization

minority

94 A third cultural influence has been the increasing *concern about the ecology* of our country. Some years ago it was considered entirely acceptable for a steel mill to dispose of wastes in the local environment, both in the air and in adjoining streams and rivers. Such a managerial attitude is now [unlikely / impossible].

impossible (since federal and state legislation now exists with respect to such activities)

95 Outside the area of waste disposal as such, managers today are likely to be very much aware of the visual and cultural impact of company facilities and the necessity of replenishing natural resources where possible. All such concerns are reflective of the manager's awareness of the national interest in our _____.

ecology

96 Finally, a fourth area of development in our culture during the past twenty years, and one that is more difficult to pin down, concerns the increased interest in individual *self-expression*. In an era in which there is less conformity to specific modes of dress, Taylor's emphasis on having all workers do a given job in the identical ("one best") way is likely to be viewed as providing [sufficient / insufficient] opportunity for self-expression.

insufficient

97 The increased emphasis in many organizations in setting objectives and then allowing organizational members to choose their own work methods, within some limits, provides greater opportunity for _____ by the people employed in that organization.

self-expression

98 If the management of a company or an industry chooses to ignore cultural developments, the effects nevertheless eventually occur in one way or another. For example, minority group participation was formalized through governmental legislation. However, if business and other organizations are to provide a leadership role in our society, then they [should / should not] wait for such external actions as governmental legislation to take place.

should not

99 Aside from the legislative aspects of cultural change, historically it can be observed that organizations which recognized the implications of technological developments achieved greater success. Similarly, organizations which recognize the implications of such cultural developments as the increasing desire for individual self-expression are [more / less] likely thereby to achieve greater organizational success.

more

The Contingency View of Management

The cultural factors considered in the preceding section of this chapter serve to illustrate the fact that management concepts are not universal in the sense that a given technique or solution is correct under all circumstances. Rather, the overall *environment* within which the management techniques are used has to be considered. The *contingency* view of management has developed in recent years as a method by which the various concepts and techniques associated with the functional, behavioral, and systems approaches to management can further be studied and refined in terms of their application.

contingency

100 The view, or approach, to developing management concepts which holds that the environment within which the concepts are to be applied has to be considered is the _____ view of management.

101 From the standpoint of the contingency view of management, such factors as the structure, processes, and technology in a firm constitute the *internal environment,* while such factors as the social, technical, economic, and political/legal constitute the external

environment

_____.

internal; external

102 Thus, the environment within which management concepts are applied can broadly be classified as being _____ or _____.

103 On the simplest level, the contingency view of management states that whether or not a given management technique is appropriate depends on the situation. Certainly, most operating managers have long been aware of this fact. But the contingency view extends beyond this observation to present a framework by which the environmental factors can be considered, thereby improving appropriate applications of

management techniques (or concepts, etc.)

_____ _____.

104 The framework for considering the environmental factors is an "if-then" approach, by which the various environmental factors, such as the structure of the firm, are the "if," and the applicability of various management techniques is the "then." The goal of the contingency view of management is to carry out specific studies by which many such relationships can be established. Thus, a particular management technique is not universally appropriate, but depends on the organizational _____, both internal and external.

environment

105 Although adherents to the various approaches to management historically seemed to claim that their principles were universally applicable, throughout this text it is recognized that particular techniques are appropriate for particular types of situations, thereby incorporating the _____ view of management.

contingency

Review

106 The approach founded by Frederick Taylor that has the major objective of attaining higher industrial efficiency by separating the planning from the doing of tasks is called _____ _____. (Frames 1 to 24)

scientific management

107 Two assumptions underlying the specific objectives and techniques of scientific management are that industrial efficiency can be attained through the application of the methods of _____ and the payment of _____ _____. (Frames 1 to 4)

science
high wages

108 Studies of the relationship between employee productivity and such physical factors as lighting, temperature, humidity, and rest pauses concern the objective of defining standardized _____ _____. (Frames 5, 6, and 20)

working conditions

109 Standardized work methods can be determined by applying the technique of _____ study, whereas setting the production level to be used as the standard for a wage incentive system can be accomplished by the application of the technique of _____ study. (Frames 7 to 24)

motion

time

110 In contrast to Taylor's work in studying first-level management, Henri Fayol centered his attention on _____ management. (Frames 25 to 45)

higher-level (etc.)

111 The organizational activity with which most of Henri Fayol's writings are concerned is the _____ activity. (Frames 25 to 31)

managerial

112 In Fayol's analysis, planning, organizing, com-

functions (or elements)   manding, coordinating, and controlling are considered to be the _____ of management. (Frames 30 to 32, 42 to 45)

113 Fayol also listed and described fourteen general principles of management, ranging from "division of work" to "esprit de corps." He believed that these principles, based on his own experiences as a manager, represented a(n) [complete / incomplete] listing. (Frames 33 to 41)

incomplete

114 The third important influence on management concepts is the application of the methods and results of the _____ _____ approach. (Frames 46 to 72)

behavioral science

115 The famous studies that led to widespread application of behavioral science principles to problems of management were the _____ studies. (Frames 46 to 52)

Hawthorne

116 The area of behavioral science application that is concerned with determining employee goals is employee _____, whereas studying the influence of informal groups on individual performance is related to viewing the organization as a _____ _____. (Frames 53 to 56, 72)

motivation

social system

117 Attempting to discover the basis for the success or failure of individual managers involves the area of research in _____. (Frames 57 and 58)

leadership

118 Determining the factors related to conveying understanding has to do with _____, whereas improving the performance of organizational members involves the matter of employee _____. (Frames 59 to 71)

communication

development

119 The systems approach to management traces its recent growth to the development of _____ research during World War II. (Frames 73 to 85)

operations

120 As applied in business organizations, the sys-

information and decision processes
tems approach to management has resulted in particular interest being given to [behavioral factors / formal authority / information and decision processes]. (Frames 73 to 85)

cultural
121 The appropriateness of particular managerial actions is influenced by societal, or _____, influences, as well as by managerial principles as such. (Frames 86 to 88)

internationalization

minority
122 The multinational scope of activities of firms in all countries in recent years is a cultural development which has been referred to as the _____ of business, while a cultural development in our own country has been the increasing participation of _____ groups in organizations. (Frames 89 to 93)

ecology

self-expression
123 Increasing national concern about pollution and about the quality of our environment is included in the concern about the _____, while designing jobs so that an individual is required to do a repetitive task in an automated fashion may run counter to the increased desire for individual _____ in our society. (Frames 94 to 99)

contingency
124 The view of management which holds that management concepts and techniques are situational, and not universal, is the _____ view. (Frames 100 and 105)

environment
125 With respect to the contingency view of management, the appropriateness of particular management techniques is dependent on the internal and external _____ of the organization. (Frames 101 to 104)

Discussion Questions

1. Do you think that there are general principles of management that affect the success of, for example, sales managers as well as production managers?
2. Describe the kind of work done for the purpose of improving industrial ef-

ficiency that would be an application or development of Taylor's scientific management.
3. In what respect have Fayol's general principles of management resulted in contributions to management methods that are different from the techniques of Taylor's scientific management?
4. What are some major areas of behavioral science research that have had an impact on management concepts?
5. How is the term "system" generally defined in the systems approach to management? Discuss the similarities and differences between this approach and each of the other historical influences which are described in this chapter.
6. Since a manager's job is concerned with achieving organizational objectives as efficiently as possible, why should factors outside the organization, such as the concern for minority rights, influence a manager's decisions?
7. The use of Taylor's scientific management during the 1920s was frequently accompanied by managerial abuses of the approach, in that the techniques of the system were often used without the overall philosophy of gaining worker cooperation and sharing the gains associated with the system. Consider the possible relationship between such abuses and events in United States industry during the 1930s.
8. Fayol's conclusion that management principles are general, and apply to many areas of managerial endeavor, was considered to be a controversial position at the time he made his observations at the turn of the century. Today there is little question about the generality of management concepts. Why the difference? Is it because a science of management has been developed based on managerial principles that have been tested and proved?
9. Some writers and researchers in the area of management principles believe that the contingency view of management holds great promise for determining the appropriate application of various types of management techniques, whether these techniques stem from a behavioral science or a systems approach. Consider some reasons why this belief might be correct.
10. In conjunction with the preceding question, it has also been suggested that no matter what viewpoint or approach to developing management concepts proves to be productive during the next decade, the functional approach to management will continue to be the most popular method by which to summarize and communicate management concepts. Consider some reasons why this belief might be correct.

References

Chase, W. H. "Adjusting to a Different Business/Social Climate." *Administrative Management*, vol. 40, no. 1, January 1979.

Connell, J. J. "How Your Job Will Change in the Next 10 Years." *Administrative Management,* vol. 40, no. 1, January 1979.
Cooper, M. R., et al. "Changing Employee Values: Deepening Discontent?" *Harvard Business Review,* vol. 57, no. 1, January-February 1979.
Fayol, H. *General and Industrial Management.* New York: Pitman, 1949.
Galbraith, J. K. "Defense of the Multinational Company." *Harvard Business Review,* vol. 56, no. 2, March-April 1978.
George, C. S., Jr. *The History of Management Thought,* 2d ed. Englewood Cliffs, N.J.: Prentice-Hall, 1972.
Greenwood, W. T. "Future Management Theory: A 'Comparative' Evolution to a General Theory." *Academy of Management Journal,* vol. 17, no. 3, September 1974.
Hackett, D. W. "Facts and Fallacies about International Business." *Advanced Management Journal,* vol. 41, no. 1, Winter 1976.
Johnson, R. A., F. E. Kast, and J. E. Rosenzweig. *The Theory and Management of Systems,* 3d ed. New York: McGraw-Hill, 1973.
Koontz, H. "The Management Theory Jungle." *Academy of Management Journal,* vol. 4, no. 3, December 1961.
Longenecker, J. G., and C. D. Pringle. "The Illusion of Contingency Theory as a General Theory." *The Academy of Management Review,* vol. 3, no. 3, July 1978.
Lorsch, J. W. "Making Behavioral Science More Useful." *Harvard Business Review,* vol. 57, no. 2, March-April 1979.
Luthans, F. "A Contingency Theory of Management: A Path Out of the Jungle." *Business Horizons,* vol. 16, no. 3, June 1973.
Luthans, F., and T. I. Stewart. "A General Contingency Theory of Management." *The Academy of Management Review,* vol. 2, no. 2, April 1977.
Luthans, F., and T. I. Stewart. "The Reality or Illusion of a General Contingency Theory of Management: A Response to the Longenecker and Pringle Critique." *The Academy of Management Review,* vol. 3, no. 3, July 1978.
Mayo, E. *The Human Relations of an Industrial Civilization.* Cambridge, Mass.: Harvard, 1933.
Miller, D. W., and M. K. Starr. *Executive Decisions and Operations Research.* Englewood Cliffs, N.J.: Prentice-Hall, 1960.
Negandhi, A. R., and D. Robey. "Understanding Organizational Behavior in Multinational and Multicultural Settings." *Human Resource Management,* vol. 16, no. 1, Spring 1977.
Peterson, R. B. "A Cross-Cultural Perspective of Supervisory Values." *Academy of Management Journal,* vol. 15, no. 1, March 1972.
Pfeffer, J. "Beyond Management and the Worker: The Institutional Function of Management." *The Academy of Management Review,* vol. 1, no. 2, April 1976.
Preston, L. E., and J. E. Post. "The Third Managerial Revolution." *Academy of Management Journal,* vol. 17, no. 3, September 1974.

Roethlisberger, F. J., and W. J. Dickson. *Management and the Worker.* Cambridge, Mass.: Harvard, 1933.
Shepard, J. M., and J. G. Hougland, Jr. "Contingency Theory: 'Complex Man' or 'Complex Organization'?" *The Academy of Management Review,* vol. 3, no. 3, July 1978.
Simon, H. A. *Administrative Behavior.* New York: Free Press, 1976.
Taylor, F. W. *The Principles of Scientific Management.* New York: Harper, 1911.
Wren, D. A. *The Evolution of Management Thought.* New York: Ronald, 1972.
Zeira, Y., and E. Harari. "Managing Third-Country Nationals in Multinational Corporations." *Business Horizons,* vol. 20, no. 5, October 1977.

CASE STUDY: Consultants' Reports

The Corby Manufacturing Company is a manufacturer of industrial power tools located in the Midwest. During the last five years, since the appointment of Phillip Sherman to the presidency, the company has been particularly successful in broadening its product lines and achieving technological improvements in existing products. Although a controller and a personnel manager are included in the top management group, the large majority of the company's middle and top management have a background in professional engineering, reflecting the nature of the company's products and customers.

Although the company is considered to be one of the most successful in its field, Sherman has taken special notice of the fact that profits did not keep pace with advances in sales during the past year, even with external factors considered. As Sherman perceives the situation, the very success that the company has enjoyed has also created operating difficulties at the management level. He finds, for example, that he can no longer keep tabs on all the areas of managerial activity in the firm. Where five years ago there were twenty managers at the departmental level and above, there are now thirty-five managers, resulting in greater difficulties in coordinating sales, manufacturing, and shipment of the various products. Sherman does not consider the situation to be serious now, but he is concerned about the possibility that, as the firm continues to grow, this symptom of a developing organization problem will become more serious.

In order to obtain an objective diagnosis of the company's situation as a basis for developing a plan of action, Sherman retained two consultants, representing two different management consulting firms, to carry out a diagnostic survey of company operations at the managerial level. Very briefly, the first consultant reports that there is a basic need to develop a greater awareness of the managerial skills among company executives. Among his specific recommendations he proposes a series of conferences, to include all levels of management, aimed at defining organization objectives and leadership and decision-making skills. He suggests that the company needs to determine what factors really motivate managers and employees, and to make use of this knowledge in organizing work groups as well as in evaluating the financial compensation system itself.

The second consultant reports that areas of authority and responsibility are not clearly designated and that the formal organization structure does not reflect present organizational needs. Accordingly, he proposes that a major company reorganization at this point in company growth is desirable. The objective of this reorganization will be to define the principal functions being carried out in the company and to group operating activities according to these functions at all organizational levels. Of course, this reorganization will have to be accomplished with complete top management participation, and the resulting organization structure should not only better serve present needs, but should also provide the framework for further organizational growth.

Mr. Sherman had planned to take immediate remedial actions in areas where both consultants agreed and to further study their other observations and recommendations. Upon reading their reports, however, he finds it diffcult to find any area of agreement between the two analyses.

1. Given that both consultants studied the same firm, why are their results so different?
2. In what respects are the consultants in implicit agreement?
3. Which report do you believe provides the better basis for further action? Why?

CASE STUDY: The Old-Line Foreman

John Norris has worked for United Electric Company since 1956, when he was released from military service after the Korean war. Following several years' experience as a production worker he was promoted to foreman of a manufacturing section in 1963. By 1970 he was promoted to general foreman of an entire department. The performance of his department was so exceptional that in 1975 he was considered for promotion to assistant plant manager. However, the fact that his formal education did not include any work at the college level led to some question about whether his preparation for such a position was adequate, particularly since as a matter of policy the company wants assistant plant managers to be qualified for promotion to plant manager. Further, John Norris himself indicated that he preferred to remain in the type of managerial position in which the human relations factors are the primary ones affecting job performance. From this standpoint, he enjoyed working close to the operative level at which the "work was really being done" in the company.

During the past few years the department headed up by John Norris has continued to do well, but George Malcolm, the plant manager, has taken note of the fact that the department does not have the exceptional quality and cost performance it once exhibited. He recognizes that an individual, or a department, cannot be at a "peak" all of the time, but his review of the performance statistics of the past several years now indicates a downtrend that, if continued, will soon lead to performance at an unacceptable level. During the annual appraisal interview, therefore, Mr. Malcolm decided that it would be well to discuss this apparently deteriorating situation in some detail with John Norris.

As usual, George Malcolm first reviewed the areas of departmental strength and the areas of possible improvement with John during the appraisal conference. Then, in a broader vein he indicated overall satisfaction with John's work, but expressed his concern about the deterioration in performance in recent years. He asked John what his thoughts were about why his department no longer displayed the exceptional levels of performance that were once typical of those areas working under his supervision. John's immediate reaction to this question made it obvious that he was indeed very much aware of the decline, and that it had distressed him.

"You're right, George," he replied. "The people in my department are performing adequately, but nothing like the way they were a few years ago. And it's all because of the kind of people that we've been hiring lately. I'm as much for equal rights as the next man, but I also know that if I'm going to be responsible for the work in my department then I should have the authority to choose the kind of people who I think will work well for me when they're sent to me by the personnel department. Over the years I've found that young fellows whose fathers have skilled trades jobs in manufacturing plants work out best for me, because they've usually got a good background in mechanical things and also understand about discipline in a production situation. But, as I say, during the past few years the personnel department has said that because of equal opportunity reasons, I can't follow my own standards anymore. These minority group people just don't seem to follow directions the same way. What's worse, even the other young fellows they've been sending me don't seem any better. Instead of following through and doing the job as instructed, they start asking 'why' and talk about 'doing their own thing.' I'll tell you, until we get another depression to remind these fellows what it's all about, we can forget about getting much out of them except minimum performance. You know what I'm talking about, don't you George?"

1. In what respects is John Norris correct in his diagnosis of the developing problem in his department?
2. In what respects is John's diagnosis incorrect?

3. What should George Malcolm do to achieve some corrective and remedial results?
4. What should George Malcolm do in the broader context of his responsibilities as plant manager?

APPLICATIONS READING:

Some Basic Trends Affecting Management in the Future

Keith Davis
Professor of Management
Arizona State University

There are many recognized potential problems facing business and our other institutions during the next ten years. A variety of difficulties have appeared, and more are sure to come. Today the struggle is with such problems as consumerism, ecology and environment, business and public ethics, oppressive regulation, protest groups, and assorted other developments.

One way to deal with these problems is the firefighting approach: wait until a problem occurs and then try to do something with it. It may be possible to muddle through by fighting fires, but a better approach is to cut through all the details and try to understand the fundamental issues that cause many of these developments. It is necessary to see the big picture in order to come up with the right answers.

The discussion that follows focuses on certain major developments that are at the root of many of the changes that are beginning to occur. The influence of these developments fans out through the whole society; it affects the entire social system. It is necessary to understand these developments in order to deal intelligently with problems that will occur in the future. As the saying goes, "You cannot solve a problem until you can find it." The best made plans are no good if they attack the wrong problem.

This article will address four fundamental trends. These ideas are not offered with the proposal that this is the way society *ought to go*, but merely that this is the way society *is going*. The ideas presented here relate to the future, and the future often is seen darkly; but certain long-run trends appear quite evident today.

Source: From *Arizona Business,* vol. 23, no. 9, November 1976. Reprinted by permission of the Bureau of Business and Economic Research, College of Business Administration, Arizona State University.

A Service Economy

The first trend is toward a *service economy*. In the 1960s the United States became the world's first service economy. This means that the majority of labor hours in the economic system became employed in services such as retailing, banking, insurance, and education, rather than in direct production of material goods such as manufacturing, farming, and construction.

At first glance this development may not sound important, but it is. Most of the population of the world today still lives in an agrarian economy, meaning that the majority of labor hours are employed in production of food to prevent hunger among their people. That necessity creates a society entirely different from that provided by an industrial or service economy. The society of the United States was dramatically changed when this country moved from an agrarian to an industrial economy in the late 1800s and early 1900s. Cities grew, factories with large labor forces developed, labor gained power, and a host of other changes occurred.

In one century the United States has moved from an *agrarian* to an *industrial* to a *service* economy! The changes that are occurring from this shift to a service economy are just as vast and significant as they were when this country shifted to an industrial economy.

Dislocations are magnified because the pace of change to a service economy is very fast. The change is fast because the industrial economy has been so successful that it has released large numbers of workers to enter service work. Law and Pereira state that service workers now make up 60 percent of the labor force, and by 1980 seven of ten workers will be in the service area.[1] Service work will dominate society, and production of material goods will use a relatively small portion of the labor force.

One point should be made clear. As far as is known, no nation in history has ever become a service economy. This country is the first; it has moved into uncharted waters. There are no real guidelines from the experience of others, so the situation must be handled with care. Although there is no way to be certain what will happen, a few developments can be forecasted.

One result of the service economy is that the rate of productivity growth is likely to be slower. Productivity could even become stagnant or decline. Productivity growth is not the same as economic growth. Economic growth is the net increase in total economic output, and for a number of reasons some people want a stable, no-growth economy. However, productivity growth relates to output in relation to input. It is a measure of how effectively society uses its resources, regardless of that society's level of economic output. Quite simply, lack of productivity is a measure of how badly a society wastes its existing resources, so practically no one favors less productivity.

There are many reasons for the slower productivity growth of a service economy, but a principal one is that service work is labor intensive and often difficult to mechanize. Although services employ 60 percent of the labor force, the

---

[1] Law and Pereira, *Management Review*, March 1976, p. 28.

output of services is only 38 percent of the gross national product.[2] As this country's growth slows, other nations that are in an industrial or an agrarian economy should begin to catch up with U. S. productivity, because productivity increases in those types of economies are easier to accomplish. However, their progress toward catching up will depend partly on how well they can keep their birth rate under control.

Another result of a service economy is that it may lead to further moves into suburbs and smaller towns. Service industries tend to have rather small and decentralized operating units compared with manufacturing. No longer does this nation need, from an economic point of view, the large cities and giant factories that led to increased crowding of people into small pieces of expensive urban real estate. People and their employers may opt for an easier life style in less crowded areas. Central cities are likely to face increasing problems; and the value of real estate in some of them may continue to decline. People will have more of an open option regarding which life style they want. In any case, the service economy will lead to a changing character for cities.

Another result of the service economy is the requirement for more white-collar rather than blue-collar workers. Among the white-collar workers, an increasing proportion will be professional people. Even though service work includes many food handlers and custodians, it generally requires a higher proportion of professional workers. Employers will need to prepare their people for these changes, if they are to maintain a stable and satisfied labor force.

Another need of the service economy is for more managers and supervisors, particularly at the lower levels. Statistics consistently show that for a number of reasons service work has a smaller span of management than industry or agriculture, so it requires more managers for each hundred workers. This development forecasts a continuing shortage of capable management talent. If the required proportion of managers increases by just one percentage point during the next decade, such as from 10 percent of the labor force to 11 percent, about one million new managers and supervisors will be required. Considering the fact that many retiring managers will have to be replaced, it is unlikely that enough competent managers can be prepared in the time available. The result will be a continuing shortage of managers. Existing managers will be overloaded, and there will be raiding by other employers. Organizations will need to recruit more widely among minorities, women, community college graduates, and younger persons. There will be more competition for managers and more mobility among them.

A Knowledge Society

A second key development is that the nation is becoming a *knowledge society*. A knowledge society is one in which the majority of the labor force performs work based on knowledge rather than on manual skill. Examples are accountants,

[2]Ibid.

computer programmers, and teachers. Even the surgeon, who must have a delicate manual skill, is primarily working from knowledge and from an intellectual base. In the 1970s it is estimated that the United States has become the world's first knowledge society. Because no society has ever been there before, there are few guidelines; but its effects will be felt throughout the whole society, in the life styles of people, in their motivation, in education, and in the business-education interface.

One major result of the knowledge society will be further changes in the motivational patterns of workers. Motivation of knowledge workers is more complex and difficult than for manual workers. For example, autocratic methods can virtually require a person to load a truck or operate a machine, but an intellectual worker cannot be forced to be creative or to make effective plans. These kinds of activities must be internally motivated by a much more sophisticated management that is able to appeal to the intellectual worker's higher-order needs. These needs are complex, variable, and difficult to determine.

The knowledge society also requires a larger proportion of knowledge oriented, educated citizens. Increasing proportions of people must attend colleges and universities in order to be prepared to assume a useful role in society. No longer are U. S. colleges educating a self-motivated, elite 10 percent of younger persons. Now they have the upper 50 percent, many of whom are less motivated and less prepared for intellectual work. Many of these less motivated students feel imprisoned in an educational cycle of fourteen, sixteen, or more years before they are ready to enter full-time productive work. They biologically mature before they occupationally mature, so they do not have a feeling of social usefulness and accomplishment at the time they mature. (This compares with fifty years ago when young people had perhaps ten years of schooling, allowing them to enter the world at about the time they matured.) The result of these developments is a high degree of psychological dissonance of students. When they cannot resolve it, there is increasing unrest, frustration, and alienation from the system. Some withdraw from society into their own little circle of alienated friends, while others simply criticize society, often without constructive proposals to alleviate the dissonance.

A number of approaches have been helpful in reducing this alienation. One is for students to work part time while finishing advanced education, thereby maintaining a feeling of occupational usefulness. Another approach is to introduce more career oriented educational programs, particularly in community colleges. A third approach is to improve instructional systems in education so that they are more experiential, participative, and self-motivating.

A further effect of the knowledge society is that it requires a more active and a closer interface between employers and higher education. Employers need intellectually prepared workers, and educational institutions need to educate people who can fill useful roles in life. Twenty-five years ago educators kept close to their ivory towers and had little interaction with the world of work. Employers kept close to their own practical world and had little to do with educators in their ivory towers. Today, there is a much closer interface through active consulting by educators, mutual attendance at professional meetings, interchanging of ideas, and interest in the same type of literature.

A Socially Concerned Humanistic Society

A third major development is that the country has become a *more socially concerned, humanistic society*. Values are being reexamined and many of them are changing. People are becoming concerned with the broad and complex quality of life, instead of primarily material gain. Employers who do not realize this fact need to take a crash course to understand what is happening, because it affects all that they do. For example, it affects a firm's markets, stockholder relations, employee relations, public relations, and just about everything else a business does.

One result of the humanistic society is a trend away from the traditional work ethic in which the person's job is that person's central life interest, toward a less-defined social ethic in which social values become more central and work less central. Studies show that the work ethic in the United States has been declining consistently for the last fifteen years or more. For an employer this often means more difficult motivational problems, because employees are less internally motivated. For some of them, money plays a declining role as they become more concerned with human and social values.

Another result of the humanistic society is more variety and independence in life styles as employees and customers try to achieve their individual self-satisfying way of life. Company loyalty is harder to build, and turnover tends to increase as employees leave for seemingly insignificant reasons. Those who do stay insist on a more participative system in which concern for people ranks equally with concern for production.

A major result of all this concern with quality of life and humanistic values is an emphasis on the social accountability of all organizations, public and private. For example, business was formerly viewed as an independent system that could pursue its own interest as long as it obeyed the law. Now business is considered as a system within a large social system. Business must be concerned about its social outputs as well as its economic outputs. Examples of major areas of concern are equal employment opportunity, urban issues, and ecology.

Ecology has been a particularly difficult and costly adjustment for business. Formerly air and water were considered free public goods that anyone including business could use. Any amount could be used and polluted in the quest for economic efficiency. The result was that the costs of pollution were externalized by the business; that is, passed on to the community. Now that quality of life is paramount, critics are insisting that business internalize its social costs of production; that is, that it bear those costs as part of its basic cost structure. Essentially, economic efficiency as an end in itself tends to be downgraded when it comes into conflict with quality of life.

Trends toward social accountability are fundamental and are not likely to change, but they do have certain effects, at least in the short run:

1. A large number of value-disoriented people who are upset and unsure of themselves because they are in a condition of value change. This condition complicates the employment relationship because employers have a variety of points of view to satisfy.
2. An increase in economic costs for business and all other institutions, thereby adding fuel to inflationary fires. Quality of life, particularly ecological improvement, is economically very costly. Its large costs have just started to be felt at the consumer level.
3. More government intervention in business and personal life for social purposes. The formerly well-defined public policy of economic efficiency is being replaced by a vague policy of social justice that is easily subject to the whims and personal prejudices of politicians and government bureaucrats. There will be an immense amount of government administrative controls and meddling that may be counterproductive, further encourage inflation, and eventually lead to a public backlash.

A Fast-changing, Unstable Society

A fourth major development, which in a way overlays all the others, is a *fast-changing, unstable society*. This kind of society is one in which a vast amount of change is taking place, allowing people only short-term stability. The result is that people are placed under stress as they face instability in family life, occupations, values, and almost everything else. This is truly the "age of discontinuity" that Peter Drucker named it. It is, indeed, a cause for "future shock" as seen by Alvin Toffler. It is a major social revolution. And an upsetting fact is that while earlier revolutions tended to take a century or more, this one seems to be headed for major change in only twenty-five to fifty years.

For example, one study showed that about forty million persons in the United States change their residences every year. Many of these also change their cities, their jobs, and their children's schools. But the changes are not just geographical. They are also technological, educational, organizational, and so on. It all adds up to a king-sized headache in the short run, even if the long-run results are likely to be better. The learning curve for change is costly in its early stages, regardless of its eventual favorable results.

One effect of the large amount of change is more pressures on management and more pressure groups interacting with management. Management will need to be more sophisticated. It must have more system understanding and more insight into the role that social values play in the whole system.

A related development is more emphasis on the boundary mediation activities of managers. A manager's ability to interface with other groups will become primary evidence of managerial competence. People with different values, both inside and outside the firm, will make conflicting demands that must somehow be mediated successfully. For example, the environmentalists and the economic efficiency advocates cannot both have their way. Mediation is necessary with consumers, minorities, social activists, government bureaucrats, moralists, and others. In a similar manner internal mediation must be achieved with unions, skilled and unskilled workers, engineers and production specialists, and others.

Another effect of the unstable society will be more instability in the organizational system. There will be more ad hoc temporary teams, more project organization, and more transfers across organizational lines. Organizational development (OD) programs, which are a way to deal with planned change, are likely to become more, rather than less, common.

An additional result will be a requirement for continuous lifelong learning, both for management and employees. Just as accountants have had to learn computers and lathe operators have had to learn numerically controlled machines, future workers will need to learn new occupations. They may actually have two or three different ones during their working life. Continuing education will become the rule, rather than the exception. Most persons will be "going back to school" frequently, either in their employer's training program or in an educational institution. Lifelong learning will be a necessity.

Among professionals, many of them will train to become biprofessionals or multiprofessionals. That is, they will prepare themselves in two or more occupations so that they can be more useful in their jobs and more flexible as society changes. An example of a biprofession is accounting and law, or engineering and management. Employers will want to encourage the development of more biprofessionals through part-time education because they never know when it may be needed among their employees.

Conclusion

The developments discussed are fundamental. They will have far-reaching consequences throughout the business and social system during the next decade or two. No business or other organization will escape their effects. These developments suggest that future managers need to be better prepared than ever. They will need more behavioral, social, political, and system understanding. They, as well as their employees, will face lifelong learning as they attempt to deal constructively with all the changes that are taking place.

Although some managerial stress and disorientation will occur, managers will have an exciting, challenging job. They will work not for perfection (because that is impossible in an uncertain world), but for a high degree of accomplishment. The best of their intellectual abilities will be required to achieve results that meet human expectations. There will be disappointments, but also successes. The future is an opportunity, not a problem.

Questions on Reading

1. Identify the four basic trends in society which Professor Davis believes are affecting management.

2. Consider some of the major effects associated with the United States having become a predominantly service economy.
3. Identify some of the results associated with the development of a knowledge society.
4. Describe some of the effects associated with the nation having become a socially concerned, humanistic society.
5. What are some of the results associated with a fast-changing, unstable society?

2 THE FUNCTIONS OF THE MANAGER

- The Functional Approach to Management
- Planning
- Organizing
- Directing
- Controlling
- Coordinating
- Review
- Discussion Questions
- References
- Case Study: The New Manager
- Case Study: Selection of a Senior Buyer
- Applications Reading: "How to Manage Your Boss" Peter Drucker
- Questions on Reading

Stemming from the work of Henri Fayol, the functional approach to management focuses upon the managerial *activities* that have to be carried out in order to achieve organizational objectives. In this chapter we consider the characteristics of the major management functions of *planning, organizing, directing,* and *controlling.* There is no universal agreement regarding which activities constitute the major management functions, but these four are listed by the large majority of writers in the field. Along these lines, some have added the function of "staffing" to this list. Fayol himself identified a fifth function he called "coordinating," and in the last section of this chapter we examine why coordinating is better considered an objective of management rather than a function of management. The four major functions described in this chapter serve as the principal basis for organizing the topics in the remainder of this book, and therefore the ideas introduced in this chapter are more fully developed in later chapters.

The Functional Approach to Management

In addition to focusing upon what managers do, the functional approach to the study of management emphasizes the general applicability of the functions. Thus, whether in a small business firm, a governmental agency, or a large corporation, whether on the general management level or in a specialized area of work, all managers are involved in carrying out the functions of planning, organizing, directing, and controlling.

functional

1   General, or broad, applicability and the focusing upon what managers do is descriptive of the _____ approach to studying the process of management.

organizational

management

2   *Management* functions should not be confused with *organizational* functions. Thus finance, production, and sales are examples of _____ functions, whereas planning, organizing, directing, and controlling are _____ functions.

Yes

3   Is a manager whose area of activity is restricted to one organizational function, such as production, nevertheless concerned with the several management functions? [Yes / No]

4   Figure 2.1 illustrates the relationship between some representative organizational functions and the management functions. The figure indicates, for ex-

The Functional Approach to Management • 41

ample, that a manager who has a primary assignment in the organizational function of production can effectively carry out this assignment by appropriate use of the management functions of _____, _____, _____, and _____.

planning;
organizing;
directing;
controlling

Representative organizational functions

Management functions	Production ↓	Sales ↓	Finance ↓	Personnel ↓
Planning →				
Organizing →				
Directing →				
Controlling →				

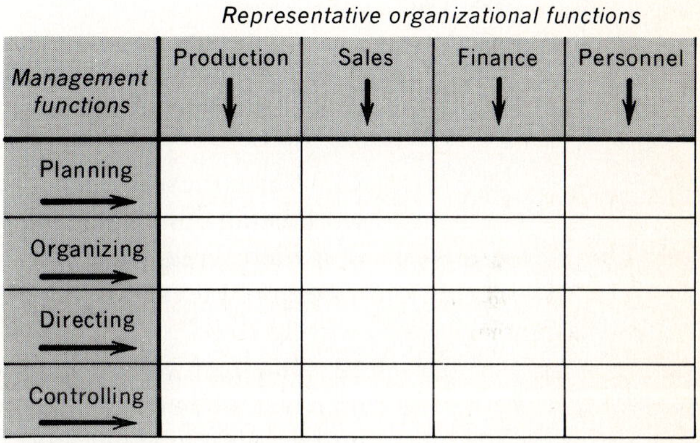

Figure 2.1 The relationship between organizational functions and management functions.

5 Viewed from the other standpoint, Figure 2.1 indicates that effective planning for a firm as a whole requires planning for each of the _____ functions represented in that firm.

organizational

6 Therefore, the relationship between organizational and management functions is such that a manager should typically [choose to do one or the other / give attention to both].

give attention to both

7 In addition to the difference between organizational and management functions, another distinction that needs to be made is between *managerial* and *technical* activities. To the extent that an executive is carrying out the functions of planning, organizing, directing, and controlling, he or she is involved in _____ activities.

managerial

8 On the other hand, to the extent that a manager

technical	does not delegate nonmanagerial tasks but carries them out personally, he or she is involved in _____ activities.
managerial technical	**9** A senior accountant who directs the efforts of a group of junior accountants is performing _____ work. A senior accountant who audits certain records or reports is doing _____ work.
No	**10** Therefore, is all of a manager's time necessarily spent carrying out management functions? [Yes / No]
first-level	**11** Since these managers are closest to the technical work being done, the time spent on technical activities is usually greatest at the [top / middle / first-level] managerial level.
management	**12** In effect, we are suggesting that a manager is *not* a manager when doing technical work. Similarly, an employee who does not have a managerial title is in fact working as a manager when he or she has responsibility for any of the _____ functions.
misleading	**13** Therefore, the absolute distinction between managers and nonmanagers that is implied by position titles is generally [accurate / misleading].
managerial	**14** Just as the time spent on managerial and technical activities varies with managerial level, the proportion of time spent on planning and organizing, as contrasted to directing and controlling, also varies with the _____ level.
planning and organizing	**15** Top managers, who need to be concerned about the future position of the organization, are likely to spend relatively more time on the functions of [planning and organizing / directing and controlling].
	16 On the other hand, first-level managers, whose prime responsibility is to see that work already scheduled is accomplished, are likely to spend more

Planning • 43

directing and controlling time on the functions of [planning and organizing / directing and controlling].

17 Though he included coordinating in his analysis, Fayol had difficulty in distinguishing coordinating **functions** from the other management _____. In this chapter we regard coordinating not as a function, but as an objective related to all of the functions.

18 In the following sections of this chapter, we briefly consider the descriptions of the four management functions of _____, **planning;** _____, _____, and **organizing;** **directing;** _____. More complete development for **controlling** each of these functions takes place in later chapters.

Planning From the standpoint of logical progression, the function of planning precedes activities in organizing, directing, and controlling. And within planning, the first logical and necessary step is the identification of the organization's objectives. Following the identification of objectives, necessary policies, procedures, and methods can then be determined.

19 In considering organizational objectives, we cannot ignore the fact that the groups of people associated with an organization have their own personal objectives that affect the organization's success. The owner and employee groups, for example, are considered to **within** be [within / outside] the firm, whereas suppliers and **outside** customers are [within / outside] the firm.

20 From this standpoint, equitable distribution of economic gains to the various groups associated with **enhances** an enterprise [enhances / diminishes] the likelihood of long-run success.

21 However, an organization can also be viewed as an entity with its own objectives. In their search for a universal organizational objective, management theorists have considered three general objectives: profit, growth and survival, and the product or service

profit

objective. Of these, the objective most frequently associated with privately owned firms is _____.

22 For a number of reasons to be considered in Chapter 3, most writers in management identify the production of an economic value in the form of a product or service as being the universal objective of all organizations. This objective assigns particular importance to the influence of [owners / employees / customers] on organization success.

customers

23 As part of the process of defining specific operating objectives, such factors as expected demand, technological changes, and governmental fiscal policy have to be considered. These factors have been called *planning premises* because they [are / are not] subject to the firm's direct control.

are not

24 The determination of *policies,* which are general statements that guide decision making in the organization, typically follows the identification of the organization's specific operating _____.

objectives

25 In contrast to the needs of top management personnel, a first-level manager needs relatively [specific / broad] policy statements for guidance in decision making.

specific

26 Accordingly, policies are often classified according to the _____ level affected.

managerial (or organizational)

27 It is also useful to classify policies according to the organizational function involved. An example of the latter would be the company's _____ policies.

finance (or production, sales, etc.)

28 Whereas a "general guide for decision making" defines a _____, a *procedure* specifies the sequence of steps to be taken to attain an objective.

policy

29 On the other hand, a *method* specifies how some one step of a procedure should be performed, and is

Organizing

policy
procedure
thus more detailed than either a _____ or a _____ .

methods
30 Overall, the identification of the organization's objectives and the formulation of policies, procedures, and _____ are all components of the planning process.

planning
31 Though the skill of *decision making* is involved in all management functions, it is especially important in determining the manager's effectiveness in carrying out the function of _____ .

decision
32 In addition to research interest in creativity, there has been extensive application of quantitative methods to improve managerial skill in _____ making.

quantitative
33 Some of the techniques of operations research (OR) are presented and described in Chapter 5. The development of OR has resulted in expanded application of _____ methods in managerial decision making.

Organizing The organization chart, which is a kind of model representing the formal organization, indicates the grouping of activities, authority relationships, and formal communication channels. As such, the organization chart represents the result of the management function of organizing. The function itself consists of determining the activities to be performed in an organization, grouping these activities, and assigning managerial authority and responsibility to people employed in the organization.

chart
34 As indicated in the introduction above, the results of the process of organizing are typically represented by means of an organization _____ .

activities (etc.)
35 *Departmentation,* which is the grouping of _____ , in a business enterprise can be done on the basis of several different factors.

36 For example, grouping of activities according to

such factors as sales, finance, production, and the like is departmentation based on organizational _____.

functions

37 Grouping of activities according to the number of people, type of product, territory, type of customer, and the process involved are other bases for _____.

departmentation

38 As an organization expands, growth may take place in either a vertical or a horizontal direction. The addition of more levels of management represents _____ growth, whereas the addition of more organizational functions, with the number of levels held constant, represents _____ growth.

vertical

horizontal

39 Determining the ideal *span of management,* i.e., the number of employees whose work can be effectively supervised by one manager, has been a long-standing problem related to the management function of _____.

organizing (Of course, this also becomes a directing problem.)

40 Whereas classical writers tended to search for an ideal span of _____ for all situations, contemporary writers emphasize the importance of such factors as the organization level involved, the type of activity, the type of personnel, and the type of organization.

management

41 Overall organizational structure is greatly affected by whether the enterprise tends toward a philosophy of managerial *centralization* or *decentralization.* Concentration of authority at top management levels is reflective of managerial _____.

centralization

42 On the other hand, wide dissemination of authority in the organization is reflective of a managerial philosophy of [centralization / decentralization].

decentralization

43 Identification of *line* and *staff* activities, and definition of the authority relationships between the two,

Directing

organizing — constitutes another dimension of the management function of _____.

staff — 44 Activities that are *directly* concerned with attaining company objectives are classified as line activities, whereas those that have an indirect relationship are classified as [line / staff] activities.

line — 45 There are various ways in which the staff gives assistance in attaining the organization's objectives, sometimes involving even staff control of _____ activities.

in addition to — 46 Further, the manager needs to be aware that in every enterprise an *informal social organization* exists [instead of / in addition to] the formal one defined and constructed by the manager.

faster — 47 The informal organization serves as an additional communication medium, making possible [faster / slower] flow of information within an enterprise, though the information may or may not be accurate.

No — 48 From what you know about the tendency of people to communicate and get together outside formal organization channels, would you expect it to be possible to eliminate the informal organization in an enterprise? [Yes / No]

organizing — 49 Finally, an organization has to be staffed, which includes the determination of personnel needs and the selection, appraisal, and training of the people who are required. Therefore, such personnel functions can also be considered an inherent part of the management function of _____.

Directing — The function of directing involves guiding and supervising the efforts of subordinates toward the attainment of the firm's goals. Through research in human motivation, leadership, communication, and employee development, the behavioral sciences have contributed substantially to our understanding of this function in recent years.

50   In contrast to the classic economic-man assumption, which suggested that the amount of pay is the only factor determining worker productivity, recent findings emphasize the diverse motives underlying employee behavior, thus resulting in [more / less] complex motivational models which are [more / less] realistic.

more
more

51   The fact that an individual has a number of different motives, and that these motives are not necessarily compatible with one another, suggests that a person must often make a choice about which _____ to attempt to satisfy.

motives

52   The supervisor has the choice of using *positive* or *negative* motivational methods, or a combination of these two methods. Motivating people by threatening to reduce their current levels of satisfaction involves _____ motivation.

negative

53   On the other hand, the promise of increased satisfaction involves _____ motivation.

positive

54   Since *communication skill* is related to a supervisor's effectiveness in guiding people's behavior, it is also directly related to effectiveness in the management function of _____.

directing

55   The passing of information and understanding from one person to another defines the process of _____.

communication

56   In a communication situation involving two people, the channel is relatively simple. On the other hand, a formal organization can be viewed as being made up of a number of decision centers interconnected by communication _____.

channels

57   In addition to the areas of motivation and communication, studies by behavioral scientists in the area of *leadership* have increased our understanding of the management function of _____.

directing

58   Classic studies of leadership success tended to be

Controlling • 49

leader focused exclusively on the characteristics of the principal person in the situation, that is, the _____.

increasing **59** However, contemporary studies of leadership have included consideration of the situational factors that affect the appropriateness of specific leadership methods, thus [increasing / reducing] the number of factors that have to be included in studies of leadership.

directing **60** Finally, one of the practical difficulties faced by managers at all levels is *resistance to change*. Therefore, the methods by which such resistance can be overcome are also relevant to carrying out the management function of _____.

Controlling The fourth management function, that of controlling, is concerned with evaluating performance in an organization and applying necessary corrections. The control process includes the steps of establishing standards, comparing actual results with the standards, and taking corrective action.

late **61** To define standards only for the culmination of a process, rather than for points along the way, results in errors or discrepancies being detected relatively [early / late] in the process. For this reason, *strategic control points*, which are used as focal points for control action *within* a process, are typically established.

strategic control **62** Rather than inspect every unit of work in process, it is typical to select only a portion of inspection at a _____ _____ point.

standards **63** The standards with which results are compared may be of several types. Quantity, cost, time use, and quality measurements are four types of _____ which are described in Chapter 15 on the control process.

control **64** On the other hand, budgets, statistical control reports, and break-even-point analysis are among the *control devices* used to achieve effective management _____.

cost 65   Of the classical control devices, the budget is by far the most frequently used, and it is particularly associated with control in respect to [cost / time].

time 66   On the other hand, PERT, which is described in detail in Chapter 16, is particularly associated with control in respect to [cost / time].

No 67   Managers who rely on the use of formal control systems frequently assume that people will automatically correct their behavior when informed of a discrepancy from defined standards. Is this necessarily true? [Yes / No]

resist 68   The tendency to want to avoid unpleasant facts, failure to accept the organization's goals, and objection to "outside" staff groups are among the reasons why individuals might [cooperate with / resist] a formal control system.

Yes 69   In American industry there has been a general movement toward emphasizing the advantages of self-control in contrast to centralized control of individuals and organizational units. Is it possible that this approach might *not* be successful in another country at this time? [Yes / No]

Coordinating   Contemporary writers in the field of management regard coordinating as an objective of management, rather than as a function in itself. Thus, successful coordination of activities results from effectively carrying out the functions of planning, organizing, directing, and controlling.

planning 70   One reason for a lack of coordination between two departments might be that their respective objectives, policies, procedures, or methods are not consistent across departmental lines. In this case, the lack of coordination can be traced to a failure to carry out the management function of _____.

71   On the other hand, a failure to define authority relationships so that they are similarly understood by the various organizational units and personnel

organizing

involved would signify a failure in the _____ function.

directing

72   The failure of a unit or of specific personnel to carry out assigned functions according to schedules previously agreed upon reflects a lack of coordination probably related to management weakness in the function of _____ .

controlling

73   Finally, in the case in which one segment of an organization considers an output to be acceptable whereas another does not, the discrepancy in defining the standard involves difficulty in the management process of _____ .

**planning;
organizing;
directing;
controlling**

74   Thus, a successfully coordinated enterprise results from effectively carrying out the management functions of _____ , _____ , _____ , and _____ .

function

75   When a lack of coordination is detected, the appropriate action is to identify the management _____ requiring improvement.

planning

controlling

76   Throughout this chapter we have always listed the management functions in the same order so as to highlight their sequential relationship. As shown in Figure 2.2 on the following page, the first function requiring managerial attention is _____ , while the last one in the sequence, which culminates in the attainment of organization objectives, is _____ .

masked

77   Of course, managers are typically involved in all of the management functions on a continuing basis as a result of overlaps in company projects. Because of this, the sequential relationship among the functions that is described in Figure 2.2 tends to be [masked / highlighted] in operating situations.

Review

78   The approach to developing management concepts that focuses on general management activities is

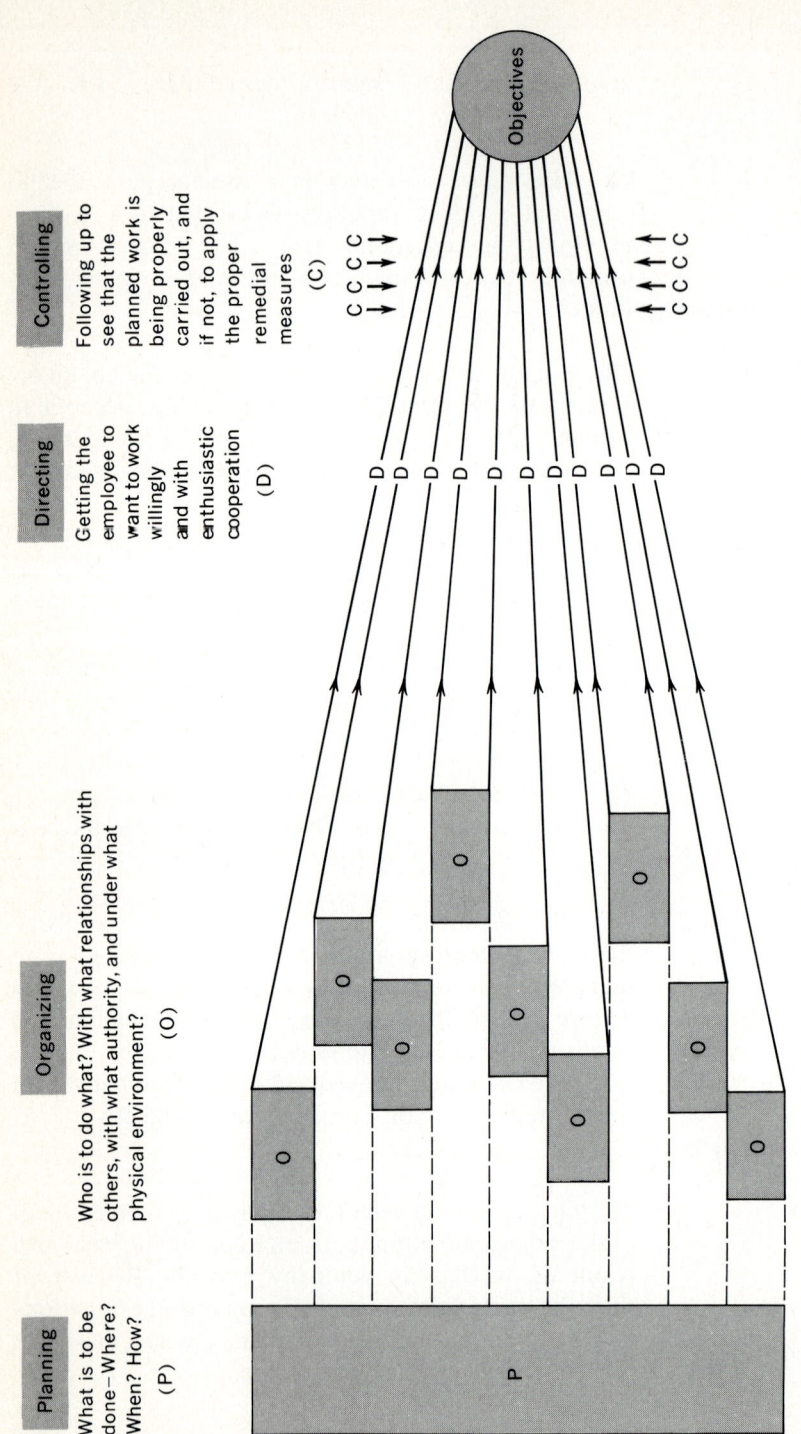

Figure 2.2 The sequential relationship among the functions of management. (Adapted from George R. Terry, *Principles of Management*, 7th ed., Richard D. Irwin, Inc., Homewood, Ill., 1977, p. 34. Reproduced with permission.)

Planning
What is to be done—Where? When? How?
(P)

Organizing
Who is to do what? With what relationships with others, with what authority, and under what physical environment?
(O)

Directing
Getting the employee to want to work willingly and with enthusiastic cooperation
(D)

Controlling
Following up to see that the planned work is being properly carried out, and if not, to apply the proper remedial measures
(C)

Review 53

functional — the _____ approach. (Introduction to the chapter)

organizational
management

79 Production is an example of an _____ function, whereas controlling is an example of a _____ function. (Frames 1 to 6)

No

80 Is it true that, by definition, all the things that a manager does are considered managerial activities? [Yes / No] (Frames 7 to 10)

technical

81 As compared with those at other managerial levels, top managers usually spend the largest portion of their working time carrying out managerial activities, rather than carrying out nondelegated, or _____, activities. (Frames 11 to 13)

Top
First-level

82 Which level of management generally is most involved in the function of planning? [Top / First-level] In the function of directing? [Top / First-level] (Frames 14 to 18)

planning

83 The identification of organizational objectives and the formulation of policies, procedures, and methods make up the _____ process. (Frames 19 to 33)

organizing

84 The determination and grouping of activities and the definition of authority relationships in the organization are involved in the management function of _____. (Frames 34 to 49)

directing

85 Guiding and supervising the efforts of subordinates toward the attainment of the organization's goals describes the function of _____. (Frames 50 to 60)

controlling

86 Establishing standards, comparing actual results with standards, and taking corrective action are the steps included in the process of _____. (Frames 61 to 69)

87 A coordination problem within an enterprise signifies that there has been a failure in performing at

functions least one of the management _____.
(Frames 70 to 75)

88 In terms of their sequential relationship, the four functions of management are appropriately identified in the following order: _____, _____, _____, and _____. (Frames 76 and 77)

**planning;
organizing;
directing;
controlling**

Discussion Questions

1. What are management functions, as contrasted to management "skills," for example?
2. What is the relationship between the management functions and the organizational functions in a firm?
3. When is a manager a manager? When is a manager a technical specialist?
4. We have always listed the management functions in a particular order in this chapter. Why?
5. Why is "coordinating" properly considered a management objective rather than a management function?
6. The use of many managerial techniques is associated with more than one of the functions. For example, budgeting is considered to be a planning tool as well as a controlling device. Does this indicate that the functional approach to management is not really descriptive of the actual practice of management?
7. Should employees who are nonmanagers be concerned about management concepts and techniques? Why?
8. As indicated in the introduction to this chapter, there is no universal agreement about which functions represent *the* functions of management. For example, an alternative listing to the one used in this book is: planning, organizing, staffing, directing, and controlling. Another is: planning, organizing, activating, controlling. A third is: planning, organizing, motivating, communicating, and controlling. Do these differences suggest that the "functional approach to management" is too diverse from the standpoint of being considered a common approach?

References

Barnard, C. I. *The Functions of the Executive*. Cambridge, Mass.: Harvard, 1938.
Davis, R. C. *The Fundamentals of Top Management*. New York: Harper, 1951.
Fayol, H. *General and Industrial Management*. New York: Pitman, 1949.

Mintzberg, H. "The Manager's Job: Folklore and Fact." *Harvard Business Review,* vol. 53, no. 4, July-August 1975.

Shetty, Y. K., and N. S. Peery. "Are Top Executives Transferable across Companies?" *Business Horizons,* vol. 19, no. 3, June 1976.

Urwick, L. F. *The Elements of Administration.* New York: Harper, 1944.

Wetzler, R. T. "Management Theory Can Produce a Continuing Bottom Line Impact." *MSU Business Topics,* vol. 24, no. 1, Winter 1976.

CASE STUDY: The New Manager

After two years in the research and development department of the Altec Company, a manufacturer of electrical components, Bill Jeffries gained a reputation as an innovator and idea man who worked well with the other members of the fifteen-man department. In addition to his generally superior performance, two of his projects resulted in patents of significant competitive value. With the retirement of Joe Stephenson, the former department manager, several of the senior department members were considered likely candidates for the job. However, because of Bill's record of achievement and in order to boost the level of overall departmental performance, the president of Altec asked Bill Jeffries to assume the duties of department manager. Bill accepted the appointment and felt highly complimented at the level of confidence in him that the promotion implied.

After six months as manager of the research and development department, however, Bill Jeffries has begun to question the wisdom of his decision to accept the appointment. Worse, he now wonders whether the president also questions the wisdom of the decision to offer him the position. Although no official comment has been made thus far, he is well aware that no significant product improvement has come out of the R&D department in the last six months. Although he has publicly taken the position that it is too early to assess the results of the work during this period, he doesn't in fact see any significant improvement resulting from the work now under way.

There appears to be no motivational or morale problem in the department, for the other members accepted Bill's appointment almost immediately, unexpected though it was, and have been enthusiastic about the research freedom that they have had under his leadership. As one of the department members commented, "I've finally had a chance to look into some technical problems that I haven't been able to get to during the past couple of years." Generally, the department members believe that Bill is too impatient for results, considering the nature of their work. And because of his obligations concerning departmental correspondence, executive meetings, and various personnel functions relating to the department, Bill has not found the time to extend his earlier research in the directions he believes would result in further patents of competitive advantage to the firm.

1. Why was the position of the department manager offered to Bill Jeffries? What is your evaluation of the president's approach to this executive assignment decision?
2. In what ways might the company president's approach to executive selection and development be improved?
3. If the present condition of nonproductivity continues, should Bill Jeffries be relieved of the responsibility for managing the department?
4. In his position as department manager, what can Bill do to "find time" and make progress in the research areas he judges to be promising?

CASE STUDY: Selection of a Senior Buyer

As manager of purchasing in a large merchandising service, Bill Perkins faced the necessity of replacing his senior buyer, George Carlson, who was leaving the company. The logical choice was T. J. Smith, because he had the greatest number of years of experience in the department. Further, because of his excellent record as a buyer and his many good merit reviews he was the highest paid of the fifteen buyers in the department.

After determining that Mr. Smith was in fact interested in the position, Mr. Perkins began holding individual conferences with each of the buyers in the department to keep them informed about the likely appointment and to determine if there might be any adverse reaction to such appointment. Three of the first six men with whom he talked expressed their regrets with his choice for senior buyer based on doubts they had about Mr. Smith's managerial ability. Further, each of the three buyers thought that he was better qualified than Smith for the position, and they went so far as to hint that they would look for other positions if Mr. Smith was promoted to the supervisory post.

In order to maintain maximum harmony in the purchasing department, Perkins began looking outside the department for a person to appoint as senior buyer. He finally found a woman, Ruth Peterson, who was in a supervisory position in the purchasing department of the state government and who was very interested in the position. He appointed Ms. Peterson to the position and introduced her to the other buyers as a person who had successfully supervised such operations in her previous job.

Although Ruth Peterson took charge immediately and began studying all of the various aspects of the product lines with which the buyers were involved, her attempts to supervise the buying activities were largely ineffective. Invariably, the buyers in the department gave her industry-related reasons why her suggested procedures could not be followed. Instead of following the directives of their new senior buyer, they kept doing things the old way or devised new procedures of their own to take care of new types of buying problems. After about four months it was obvious that Ruth Peterson was being systematically bypassed, and the buyers were doing things increasingly on their own. Consequently, there was an absence of any actual leadership in the buying department, and at this late date Bill Perkins again began looking for another person to head up the buyers.

1. From the information given in the case description, why do you think Ruth Peterson failed in her appointment as senior buyer?
2. Should Bill Perkins have consulted his men with respect to his original intention of appointing Mr. Smith to the supervisory position? Should he have stuck with that decision?
3. Was the decision to appoint someone from outside the company as the senior buyer appropriate, or should it have been the most qualified person from within the company?
4. What should Mr. Perkins do now?

APPLICATIONS READING:

How to Manage Your Boss

Peter F. Drucker
Clarke Professor of Social Science and Management
Claremont Graduate School

If there's one problem most of us talk about, grumble about, but do nothing about, it's the boss. Every manager I know finds managing the boss the most difficult task he has. Very few even try.

How you handle the problem of your boss can be quite revealing. For example, it is one of the few indicators we can rely on to tell which of the younger people in an organization are going to go places and which are going nowhere. Those who only talk about how incompetent and impossible the boss is and complain about how much they suffer are not going anyplace. On the other hand, you can spot the comers because they do something about managing the boss—and I don't necessarily mean buttering him up or polishing the apple. It's really quite simple. What you do almost depends on the boss himself.

- The first thing to recognize is that the boss is neither a monster nor an angel; he's a human being who insists on behaving like one. Bosses, therefore, have to be treated like human beings, like individuals. So for some bosses, then, you do polish the apple; for others, that's the worst thing you can do.

Source: From *Management Review*, Vol. 66, No. 5, May 1977; adapted from *The "How to" Drucker, A Practicing Manager's Day-to-Day Guide*, © 1977 by Peter F. Drucker, a cassette program produced and distributed by AMACOM, a division of American Management Associations. Reprinted by permission of Peter F. Drucker.

- The second thing to know is that no matter how able and competent the boss is, he is not a mind reader. You have to make sure he understands what you're trying to do.
- The third thing to remember is that although he does not give you enough of his time, he gives more, as a rule, than he should—more than he has to give. So it's up to you to manage that time and to ensure that it's productive time.
- Finally, remember that it's more dangerous to underrate the boss than to overrate him. The most serious mistake you can make is to underrate the boss and be caught doing it.

What Makes the Boss Tick

I'm always amazed that almost nobody ever seems to recognize that bosses, like most people, can be divided into "readers" and "listeners," the same way people can be divided into right-handers and left-handers. So the first thing you do is figure out whether your boss is one or the other.

If you have a reader for a boss—like an Eisenhower or a Kennedy—don't just go into his office and talk to him about a problem or a project. Write it up first, make sure you have something for him to read; then you can start to talk.

If you have a listener—someone like Franklin Roosevelt or Harry Truman—don't send in a memorandum. Go in and talk about it first; then you can leave the memo.

If your boss likes a little reassurance, a little flattery, or if he wants facts and figures or a page of recommendations, then that's what he should get. Give him 150 pages out of a statistical abstract. Accept the fact that he's a human being, that he's set in his ways and unlikely to be changed by you, and that it's up to you to get him to respond to your need. Those who want to manage the boss should first find out who it is they want to manage. In the final analysis, however, one doesn't really manage a boss; you work with a human being. And if you learn to do this, your batting average is going to be a great deal better than if you don't.

Word Magic

Now this may strike you as trivial, but be sure to learn about word magic. That is, know which are good words and which are bad words when talking with your boss. One of the ablest men I ever worked with—an engineer who was also an autocrat and a pedant—couldn't stand the word "control." Instead of control, we had to learn to say "measurement." The rule was never say "control." If you did say it, his mind snapped shut, and for the next six weeks, he delivered sermons on why "control" was a bad, bad word.

In any case, it's your job to work with the boss—he's your resource.

Resources have to be worked the way they are, not the way you want them to be. Now that may sound manipulative, but it's manipulation in the sense of adapting yourself to the way an individual is put together.

No Surprises

Many people assume their bosses are mind readers. That's only natural—children assume it about their parents, parents about their children, teachers about their students, and students about their teachers. Apparently, a very difficult thing to accept is the first insight of modern psychology, which started around 1880 with the startling discovery that *what is obvious to me, nobody else can see at all.* Very few people accept this, particularly in dealing with the boss. But you'd better keep it in mind.

It's your job to make sure the boss knows what you are trying to do, what you need, what you expect from him. If you just blithely go ahead, assuming that what you're doing is so obvious that any fool can see it, why then does everybody wonder just what is it you are doing?

Think through what you're trying to do, including those things you'd rather the boss didn't know about. Then make certain that the fellow on whom you depend so heavily—the fellow in that office next door, the boss—understands. Maybe not necessarily approves, but understands so that he isn't surprised. There's really no such thing as a pleasant surprise.

Don't baffle the boss. Go to him, or write a memo, saying: "This is what I am going to do." Or, "This is what I'm not going to do." Let him know that you are aware, say, of that problem with the branch office in England, but that you're not going to tackle it now because you think that if you leave it alone, they'll work it out. Of course, you say, you'll keep checking it, and if London doesn't solve the problem in six months, then you'll come down on them like a ton of bricks.

The idea is not to let him wonder why *you* don't seem aware of the mess in the London office. Let him know you have made a decision—that you are giving London another six months to straighten out, and if they don't, you'll have to tackle it.

That's a decision. But don't make the mistake of thinking it's obvious. It isn't. Mind readers exist only in science fiction novels. You won't find them in executive offices.

Never Hide an Elephant

In many instances, then, you don't have to tell the boss what you're going to do; you tell him what your objectives are and how you're proposing to achieve those objectives. But how you handle it really depends on the boss. With some bosses, you tell them exactly what you are going to do—others you ask for their advice. It depends on how the boss works, not on what you like.

One thing you never do is hide problems. Never try to brush an elephant under the rug. Hiding problems is unfair to the boss. It's also very unfair to you.

I wish every young man or woman could have the same good fortune I had in my early twenties when a wise old man, a senior partner in the firm I worked for, called me in and said:

"Mr. Drucker, you've been an awful fool again. You've been hiding a problem. You've done it twice, and if you do it a third time, I'll make damn sure that you go to work for the competition."

I never did it again. But I needed to be spanked hard. I was a conceited pup and needed rough treatment—and I got it. It was a lesson most young people still need to learn. Their instinctive reaction to a problem is to hide it because, they think, maybe it will go away. Well, maybe it will, maybe it won't, and if it won't, you're in trouble.

Better to handle the situation by thinking through how to warn the boss of an impending problem. Anyone working for me had better come in and tell me what he plans to do about a problem. On the other hand, anyone working for a certain friend of mine had better go in to him and say something like this: "There's a cloud on the horizon, but I think I know how to deal with it. If it gets any bigger, I'll let you know."

My friend doesn't want to know how you propose to do your job; he feels that's your business—and he may be right. But other bosses want to be part of the problem, so you say to them: "Look, I see this coming, and I thought I might impose on your time to get your advice." The boss in this kind of situation is a person who believes that a superior should be a coach, a problem-shooter.

So look at the individual. It isn't important whether you crow about successes or try to minimize mistakes. They are fairly unimportant. Again, what is terribly important is the rule: no surprises. It's your job to make sure that your boss is never going to be surprised. He has a boss, too, you know—someone who probably takes a dim view of being hit by a storm that's been brewing for six months without anyone telling him about it—until he learns of it from the outside.

Take a situation where an account, say an old customer, is having trouble, perhaps going delinquent. It may well be that you can repair the situation. But if you can't, and six months later you've had an acrimonious correspondence filling several file folders, it's *your* fault if the relationship is destroyed.

But if you see your boss promptly and tell him what's happening, he might be able to straighten things out then if you can't. And if necessary, he can mobilize his boss in time to help repair any damage. But if you wait six months, *you* have lost that account. Indeed, you have.

Managing the Boss's Time

Many things are kept from bosses because their subordinates know how busy they are and mistakenly hesitate to impose on them. You've got to balance conflicting demands; you shouldn't monopolize the boss's time. At the same time, however, you are entitled to his advice.

A wise, old German peasant proverb says, "Don't go near your prince unless he calls for you at least twice." There's something to be said for not being too much in the limelight. On the other hand, almost every manager complains that his boss doesn't have enough time for him and that his own subordinates take too much of his time. He's right on both counts.

The responsible and intelligent manager thinks through how to use the boss's time. Again, look at the boss as a human being, not as an abstraction. Remember that you're looking at a person—a man, a woman.

One boss may work by sitting down with a subordinate (though very rarely) for three full hours. In between sessions, he may not want to see anybody. Another boss may prefer ten-minute ad hoc meetings (which some people, by the way, consider a total waste of time). You have to adjust to the way a boss manages, or mismanages, his time. There's very little you can do about how he manages.

Do Your Homework

Never go into the manager's office unless you have done your homework. There's a sound old rule: It takes ten minutes of preparation for each minute of interview time.

There's no need to overdo this advance work, however. It's impossible to have every fact and figure. It's more important to know what you are going in for, to think through what you expect to come out with. Do you want a decision? Advice? Do you want to advise the boss that down the line you might come to him with this or that? Be sure he understands.

The military has some good advice for this kind of situation: The first rule of warfare is to control the battlefield. This means that *you* must set the stage by doing your homework. But at the same time take into account that the boss already is complaining that his subordinates take too much of his time. That's why you must make your occasion with him productive—for him and yourself.

Follow-up is important. Sit down afterward and tell the boss in writing, "This is what happened in our meeting this morning..." Remind him that he decided that Carter should be pulled off his present assignment and put on the redesign of the water cooler as soon as he returns from his trip, and that you'll let him know when Carter is being reassigned. This ensures that there will be no doubt later about what was decided.

Doing this gives him a chance—since people are not infallible—to remember prior commitments that may conflict with any promises he made to somebody else. For example, he may look at the memo and say, "Oh, my god, I forgot that only the day before yesterday, I promised the president that he can have Carter for that meeting in Washington." Or the big boss may call him and ask when Carter is coming back from that trip to the Near East—"I want to put him right to work on a study of that question we discussed at the last board meeting." Your memo keeps the boss from going too far out onto thin ice.

When to Abandon Ship

Rating the boss is a function of your own native intelligence, not of your relationship with him. It's just stupid to underrate the boss, yet very bright young people do it all the time.

You risk nothing, as a rule, by overrating a superior. And if it turns out that you haven't overrated him at all, then you have an ally, a supporter. The worst that can happen is that you've been too pushy.

But if you systematically lose because you overestimate the boss, get out. One of the first things to learn about managing anything is when to abandon it—even a boss. There's no better prescription for success than to have a boss who is going places, and there is no more certain prescription for frustration and failure than to work for an incompetent.

Another time to change jobs is when the boss is corrupt. He doesn't have to have his hand in the till—that's only one form of corruption. A more serious form of corruption is when the boss has values and standards that are ethically and morally unacceptable to you. Never work for a boss whose standards demean you—you become corrupt yourself, you become contemptuous of yourself, you begin to loathe yourself.

When it becomes obvious that you are working for an incompetent or corrupt boss, I think you have to say, "All right, I like the company, but this isn't going to work out." Abandon the job and look for something else—within the company or outside it.

You also have a problem if the boss is a paragon. It's possible to stay too long with a paragon or near-paragon for the good of your career. Staying makes it too easy to become just an "assistant to" rather than your own man.

There's still a great deal of fear—though less now than ten years ago—of becoming the organization man, someone whom the organization uses as a servant. There has never been enough emphasis on the opposite, however; that is, looking upon the organization as *your* tool.

Size up your job from two viewpoints: (1) What can I contribute to it? and (2) What can it contribute to me? Also ask yourself, "What has it done for me lately?" and "What is it likely to do for me in the future?"

If you are in a position where you have gotten as much out of the job, the boss, and the company as they will ever give you and if you are still below late middle age and have given all you are likely to give, then it's time to move on. Don't move out too often, however, and don't rush. Remember there is a time limit, and keep in mind that a person moves out because of success as much as failure.

Accountability

In today's society, everybody has a boss. Even the company president and the chief executive officer are accountable to stockholders and to outside regulatory and other agencies just as a hospital administrator is accountable to the community and the president of the United States to the voters and to the Congress.

You don't have to like and admire your boss, nor do you have to hate him. You do have to manage him, however, so that he becomes your resource for achievement, accomplishment, and—let's be candid about it—personal success as well.

Questions on Reading

1. What are the implications of identifying a boss as a "reader" vs. a "listener"?
2. What does Drucker have in mind when he states, "There is no such thing as a pleasant surprise"?
3. In the military, the first rule of warfare is to control the battlefield. How does this concept relate to subordinate/boss relationships?
4. Under what circumstances does Peter Drucker suggest that it is best to leave a job?

Planning

The process of planning includes the determination of organizational objectives and the selection of policies, procedures, and methods designed to lead to the attainment of these objectives. Success in the managerial function of planning requires recognition of the social environment of the firm or organization, the stimulation of creativity to encourage new ideas and imaginative approaches to the challenges of management, and an understanding of quantitative decision-making techniques and their appropriate use.

Chapter 3 is concerned with the types of objectives associated with organizational activity, with special attention given to the concept of management by objectives. The presentation on the environment of planning includes consideration of the external planning premises that affect the planning function, with a separate section devoted to social responsibility and governmental regulation. The final section contains an overview of sales forecasting and its role in the planning process.

Chapter 4 includes a description of types of organizational policies, and the formulation of the general policies and the specific procedures which are directed toward the achievement of the objectives of the organization. A separate section on decision making is included in this chapter because this area of skill is important in planning.

Chapter 5 begins with a general description of management science as a systems-oriented method of planning which is based on the use of mathematical models. Following an overview of several types of quantitative decision-making techniques, illustrative examples of the application of linear programming and statistical decision analysis are presented.

Part 2

3 ORGANIZATIONAL OBJECTIVES AND PLANNING PREMISES

- Types of Objectives
- Management by Objectives
- The Environment of Planning
- Social Responsibility and Governmental Regulation
- Sales Forecasting and Planning
- Review
- Discussion Questions
- References
- Case Study: Planning in a Staff Department
- Case Study: A Decline in Government Contracts
- Applications Reading: "A Long-Range Approach to MBO" Richard Babcock and Peter F. Sorensen, Jr.
- Questions on Reading

The first step in the planning process is that of determining the objectives of the organization and identifying the environmental factors that determine the scope of opportunities and limitations affecting planning. In this chapter we begin by considering the types of group and organizational objectives which serve as the basis for individual and group activity. This orientation with respect to objectives is then extended in the section on management by objectives, which is a management concept affecting planning at all levels in an organization.

The environment of planning includes the external factors that influence the planning process, and these factors as well as the related topic of social responsibility are covered in the following two sections of this chapter. The final section of the chapter includes a description of sales forecasting and its role in planning.

Types of Objectives

Organization objectives have been described by economists and management theorists both in terms of the firm as a whole and in terms of the groups of people who have an interest in the performance of the firm. In this section we first consider the particular objectives of the several groups of people within and outside the firm. The identification of the groups is not intended to be exhaustive, but it should illustrate the extent to which the management of a company needs to consider the different group objectives which affect overall organizational effectiveness. Following this, we consider the organization as an entity and evaluate several approaches that have been used in the attempt to identify the universal organizational objective, i.e., the objective held in common by all firms and organizations. In this context the profit objective, the survival and growth objective, and the product or service objective are described.

1 People associate themselves with an organization in order to satisfy their own objectives. Therefore, before considering the objectives of a firm as such, it is useful to identify some of the groups of people associated with a firm and to consider their objectives. For our purposes we consider *owners* (or investors), *managers,* and *employees* as examples of groups that

within are located [within / outside] the firm. On the other hand, we consider vendors, customers, and govern-
outside ment as groups that are [within / outside] the firm.

2 With respect to the economic objectives for the groups within the firm, we can describe the owners as being oriented toward earning a ———— **profit**, whereas the managers and the employees are described as being oriented toward earning a ———— **salary (or wage, etc.)**.

3 For the groups outside the company, vendors look to the firm as a customer and thus as a source of sales revenue; governmental units at the local, state, and federal levels look to the firm as a source of tax revenue (as well as having broader considerations); and customers look to the firm as a supplier of ———— **products (or services)**.

4 In exchange for the economic benefits or values obtained from the firm, each of the groups we have considered contributes to the firm's effectiveness. Thus, vendors provide the firm with raw material, employees devote their services to the firm, and owners (investors) provide the firm with ———— **capital**.

5 Although each group is in an interchange with the firm, each may view itself as competing with one or more of the other groups for the economic gains generated by the firm's activity. Thus, employees may take the attitude that the amount of money available for wages and salaries is reduced by profits paid to ———— **owners (or investors)**.

6 Figure 3.1 portrays these relationships. It indicates that each group contributes to the firm's effectiveness, represents a demand upon the firm's resources, and may in this particular case consider itself in competition with as many as ———— [number] **five** other groups for those resources.

7 Without the contribution of each group represented in Figure 3.1, the existence or effectiveness of the firm would be threatened. Therefore, one of the primary tasks of company management is to allocate available resources so that a balance is achieved among the competing interests of the several groups represented. For example, what would be the likely ef-

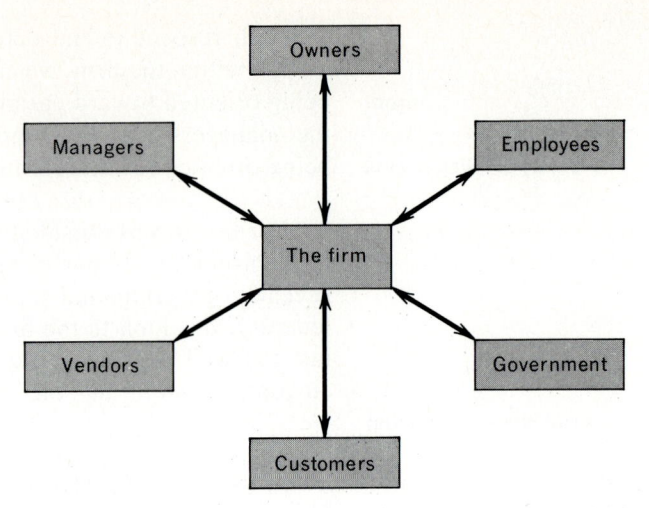

Figure 3.1 Some of the groups associated with a firm's activities.

fect of reducing the salaries of professional employees in the company?

Many competent employees would be likely to leave the company, thus impairing its effectiveness.

_____
_____
_____
_____

8 Thus, from the standpoint of the presentation thus far, organizational objectives might be studied by considering the objectives of the several competing _____ that have interchange with the organization.

groups

9 In addition to the objectives of the specific groups, an overall organization objective would seem to be desirable to provide a direction for the firm's activities. Within the framework of the free enterprise system, for example, it might be said that the one objective all business firms share is the desire to earn a _____.

profit

10 Although all the groups associated with a firm are jeopardized in the absence of profitable operations, the group most directly and immediately affected is the _____ group.

owner (or investor)

11 Therefore, one possible disadvantage of identifying *profit* as the principal goal of all organizations is

Types of Objectives • 71

organization (or firm) — that we may be confusing the objectives of a specific group, namely, the owners, with the principal objective of the _____.

12 Another disadvantage of identifying profit as a universal organizational objective is that any management theory based on this premise could not be readily applied to nonprofit organizations. Yet an underlying assumption that has stimulated the development of management concepts and principles is that such principles are applicable [only in profit-oriented enterprises / in all types of organizations].

in all types of organizations

13 In considering organization objectives some writers in the field have concluded that the objective of *organizational survival and growth* characterizes all formal organizations. This viewpoint also assumes that the groups that make up the organization as contrasted to the organization as such [can / cannot] be considered distinct and separate entities.

can

14 The viewpoint that all organizations have the common objective of survival and growth is particularly applicable to business firms whose form of ownership is the [sole proprietorship / partnership / corporation].

corporation

15 When the ownership of a business enterprise is other than corporate, the firm legally ceases to exist with the death of an owner or co-owner. Thus, the general objective of survival and growth does not appear to apply very well to a firm that is legally organized as a _____ _____ or a _____.

sole proprietorship
partnership

16 Important as each may be in its own right, neither the profit objective nor the objective of survival and growth fully qualifies as a universal objective for all organizations, whether publicly or privately owned and regardless of legal form or ownership. Therefore, some writers in this field have suggested that the ultimate objective of any formal organization can be identified as a *product* or *service*. In our description of the groups of people associated with company activities,

customer

we particularly identified an interest in the product or service with the _____ group.

17 Thus, just as profit might be criticized as a general objective because it is too closely associated with a particular group of people, so also might an orientation toward a product or service be criticized. However, unlike profit, the product or service objective can be used to study the operations of [privately owned firms only / either private or public organizations].

either private or public organizations

customer

18 Another advantage of focusing on a product or service as the "reason for existence" of any organization is portrayed in Figure 3.2. The ultimate source of funds used to finance the activities of an organization is associated with the _____.

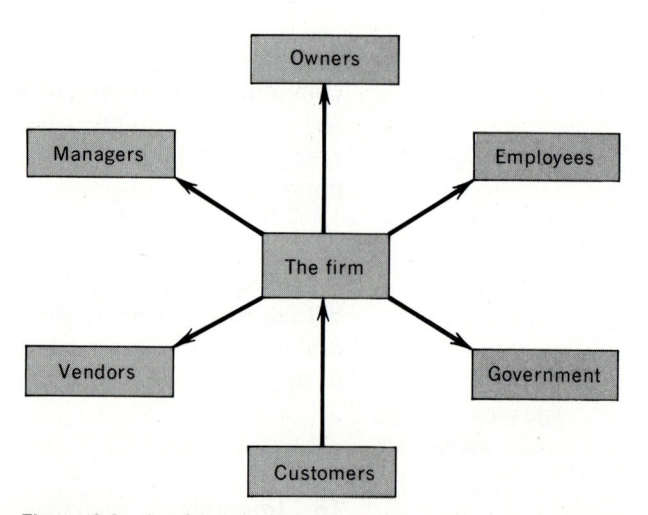

Figure 3.2 A schematic diagram representing the flow of funds in the operation of an established firm.

19 Whether the output is in the form of a product or a service, every firm or organization exists to create something of economic value. From this standpoint, the principal objective of the Chevrolet Divi-

automobiles
merchandise for sale (etc.)

sion of General Motors is to manufacture _____. The principal objective of Sears Roebuck is to provide _____ _____.

20 Since profit is what is "left over" after the demands of every group except those of the owners have presumably been satisfied, it is a convenient basis for measuring the firm's effectiveness in providing a

product; service

_____ or a _____ desired by consumers.

21 Thus, although profit may be an indicator of a firm's success or failure, it does not specifically identify the *basis* for that success or failure. In a free enterprise system, the economic value of a firm's products or services is ultimately decided by the

customer

_____ group.

22 In the case of public organizations and monopolies, profit as such may be nonexistent or inapplicable as a way of evaluating organizational performance. Nevertheless, the size of the agency or firm and its continued existence are still decided by consumers (though indirectly) in their activities as citizens and voters. For example, charitable organizations depend directly on public contributions and support. Government programs depend on ultimate support by the electorate. Thus, all organizations, whether private or public, share the common primary objective of provid-

product; service

ing a _____ or a _____ of economic value.

23 Identifying the product or service objective as the universal objective of all organizations provides us with the basis for evaluating the activities of both public institutions and privately owned firms. Furthermore, since a firm's profitability is dependent on customer decisions, careful identification of a company's

more

product or service goals makes it [more / less] likely that the firm will earn a profit as the result of its operations.

Management by Objectives

As indicated in the preceding section, the ultimate objective of an organization as an entity is the creation of economic values in the form of products or services. The individual divisions and departments in a firm may not be producing completed products or services, but all should be contributing to the creation of these economic values. In a sense, the concept of *management by objectives* (MBO) is an extension of the product or service objective to the operating units within the firm. This concept suggests the need for a hierarchy of compatible objectives within the organization and suggests further that these objectives identify the economic contribution of each segment of the organization in measurable terms.

24   The management-by-objectives approach focuses on the economic contribution of each of the operating units in the firm. In order to achieve the firm's product or service objective effectively, the specific objectives of the operating units that make up the firm need to be

compatible   [identical / compatible].

25   Since each organizational unit has a different mission, specific objectives will not be identical, but they do need to be compatible. One way of achieving this compatibility throughout the organization is to ascertain that in each of the several functional areas of work the objectives at each organizational level contribute to those at the next higher organizational level. The outcome, then, is referred to as a hierarchy of

objectives   _____.

26   Figure 3.3, on the following page, illustrates the hierarchy of objectives for a selected segment of an organization. The overall objective of this company is

a product   identified as being [profit / a product / a service].

27   In Figure 3.3 the hierarchy of objectives within the personnel and industrial relations division is identified. In addition to the division objective, objectives are also identified at the levels of the

department; section   _____ and _____.

28   Further, note that at each of the organizational levels the objective is defined in terms of [detailed

measurable goals   procedures / measurable goals].

Management by Objectives • 75

```
                        ┌─────────────────────┐
                        │ Clariair Corporation│
                        └─────────────────────┘
Organization objective:   Manufacture emission-control
                          devices for motor vehicles
```

| Sales division | Personnel and industrial relations division | Manufacturing division | Finance division |

Division objective: Contribute to human effectiveness in the organization through assistance in the recruitment, selection, training, and compensation of personnel

| Employment department | Training department | Wage analysis department | Performance evaluation department |

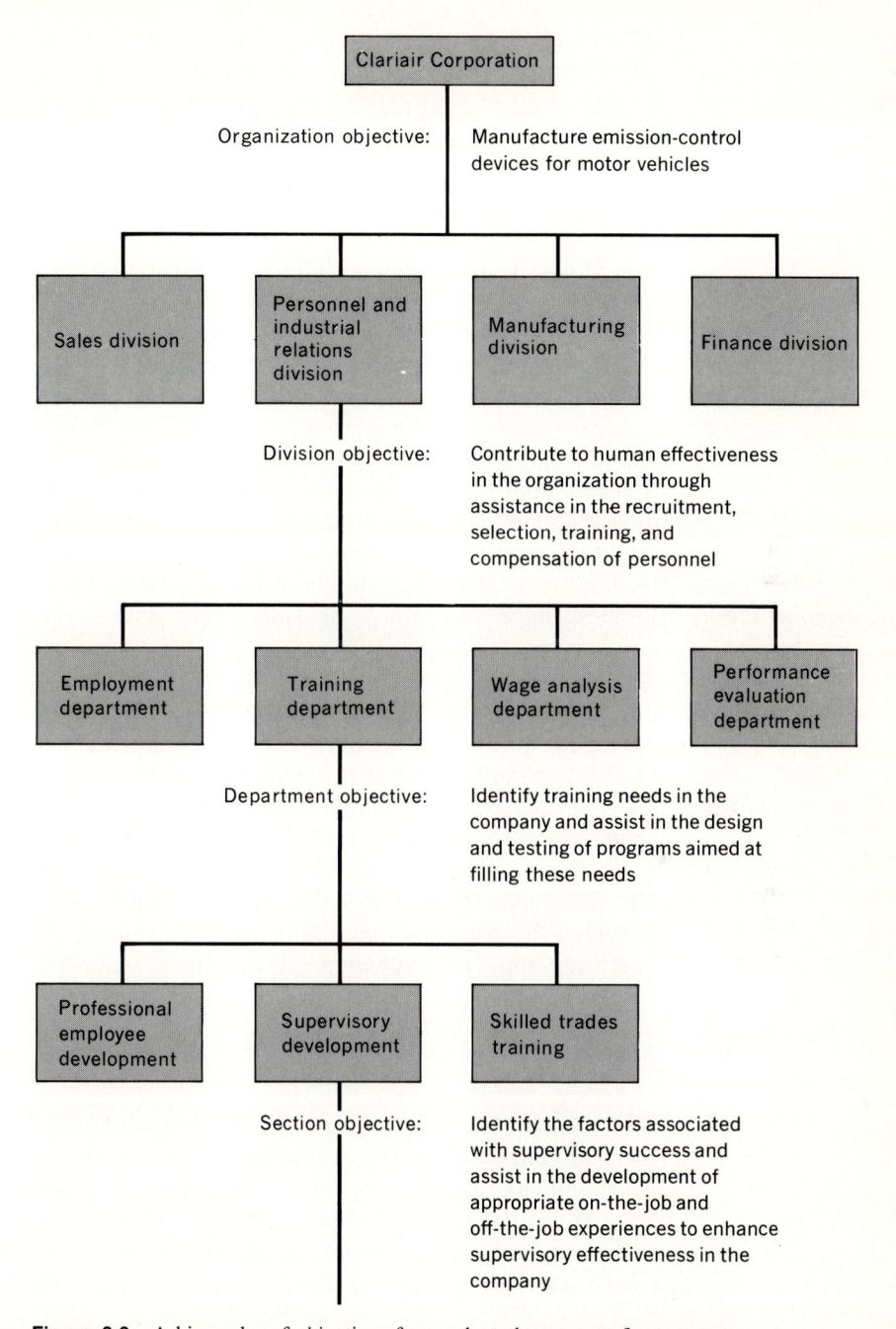

Department objective: Identify training needs in the company and assist in the design and testing of programs aimed at filling these needs

| Professional employee development | Supervisory development | Skilled trades training |

Section objective: Identify the factors associated with supervisory success and assist in the development of appropriate on-the-job and off-the-job experiences to enhance supervisory effectiveness in the company

Figure 3.3 A hierarchy of objectives for a selected segment of a company.

29 Thus, the philosophy of *management by objectives* requires that for the several organizational levels a _____ of objectives be identified and that these objectives be specified in the form of measurable _____.

hierarchy

goals

30 The approach that focuses on defining *measurable goals* and ascertaining that these goals *contribute to the overall product or service objective* of the organization (rather than focusing on the particular methods and procedures to be followed in the organization) is called _____.

management by objectives

31 The identification of objectives constitutes the first essential step in the managerial process of planning. Since management by objectives has a direct influence on methods of organizing, directing, and controlling, as well as on planning, it has become a basis for describing and improving [planning / managerial activity as a whole].

managerial activity as a whole

32 Because personal commitment to the goals of an operating unit makes it more likely that those goals will be accomplished, individual participation in defining these goals is typically [encouraged / discouraged].

encouraged

33 The management-by-objectives approach also provides the basis for evaluating the performance of operating units and individuals in the organization by comparing the goals specified for a particular time period with the goals actually _____ during that period.

achieved (etc.)

34 Finally, since performance evaluation within the management-by-objectives approach is oriented toward objective work goals rather than employee characteristics and personal traits, needed changes in employee and managerial performance are [more / less] easily achieved by this approach.

more

The Environment of Planning

As indicated in the preceding section, the process of planning begins by designating organizational and unit objectives. In addition, we must consider the various

The Environment of Planning • 77

possible strategies or courses of action that will lead to the achievement of these objectives. Since the organization does not exist in a vacuum, managers have the responsibility of assessing the various external factors that either limit the company's action possibilities or provide the opportunity for action aimed at accomplishing objectives. In this section we identify some of the major environmental factors and describe their effect on the planning process. Because these factors represent external constraints on planning, some writers in the field of management have referred to these factors as *external planning premises.*

35 Although the order in which we consider the environmental factors does not imply an order of importance, it is certainly true that the level of *political stability* is one of the most important factors affecting the planning process. In the absence of a politically stable environment, business planning tends to be limited to the [long / short] run.

short

36 The factor of political stability has been particularly important for firms engaged in international operations. For example, one of the important factors affecting managerial planning in South American countries is the relatively high level of political [stability / instability].

instability

37 On the other hand, firms engaged in business operations in Western Europe in recent years have been able to carry out the planning function in a climate of political [stability / instability].

stability

38 Although international illustrations provide particularly vivid contrasts in political stability, this is a factor that operates on our domestic scene as well. Other factors being equal, business firms prefer to locate in states and municipalities with an [established / emerging] pattern of political stability.

established

39 Similarly, we would predict that during periods of political uncertainty at the national level, such as at the inauguration of a new President, long-range planning commitments by business firms tend to [increase / decrease].

decrease

40 Closely associated with the factor of political stability is the nature of *government fiscal and monetary policy, regulations,* and *controls.* The fiscal and monetary policy affects the overall economic environment within which planning takes place. For example, if a business owner believes that interest rates are likely to decline in the near future, the owner is [more / less] likely to apply for a capital improvement loan at the present time.

less

41 Specific fiscal and monetary policies may affect some types of firms more than others and may indirectly benefit one industry at the expense of another. For example, if interest rates on home mortgages were to be maintained at a high level while excise taxes were removed from airline fares, the [construction / airline] industry would tend to benefit by such a policy.

airline

42 *Governmental regulations and controls* also tend to affect firms in some industries more than in others. As compared with electronics firms, for example, railroads operate under a relatively [high / low] level of governmental regulation and control.

high

43 With the growth of our industrial system, the extent of control and regulation by all levels of government has been generally on the [increase / decline].

increase

44 Occasionally, however, reductions in government regulation and control have taken place when such reductions are considered to be of benefit to the public. As compared with the 1970s, for instance, airline scheduling is now [more / less] subject to government control.

less

45 Another factor in the environment of planning is the overall *trend in employment, productivity, and income.* Unless a company finds itself in a declining industry, as these statistics tend upward, the overall demand for products and services tends to [rise / fall / stabilize].

rise

46 Incidentally, if a firm is in a declining industry,

managerial action in regard to objectives is certainly necessary. For example, with the decline in birthrate in the United States a firm that has specialized in the manufacture of baby food might well consider expanding its product offerings to include [infant wear / dietetic foods].

dietetic foods

47 In a country in which the prospects for continued increases in employment, productivity, or income become bleak, long-range commitments by business firms are likely to [increase / decrease].

decrease (thereby adding to the poor prospects)

48 The factor of *changing price levels* is another influence on the planning process. The situation which leads to the greatest difficulty in planning is the one in which prices in an industry are [slowly increasing / slowly declining / subject to change in unanticipated ways].

subject to change in unanticipated ways

49 Of course, the general movement of prices in the economy is associated with the nature of governmental fiscal policy. At least since World War II, federal fiscal policy has resulted in a general and continuing price [rise / decline].

rise

50 Price movements in particular industries do not necessarily follow general price movements in the economy. During the past fifteen years, for example, electronic calculators have generally declined in price. Thus if a manager concludes that a general price increase of 6.5 percent for consumer goods is likely during a planning period, the assumption that the selling price of his firm's products can be increased by about 6.5 percent is [warranted / unwarranted].

unwarranted

51 All of the environmental factors that we have considered thus far seem to presume unchanging engineering concepts. But the fact that *technological changes* are likely is itself a factor that affects planning. Again, this factor may be more important in some industries than in others. For example, of the following two industries the factor of technological change is especially important as a planning factor in the [automobile / aerospace] industry.

aerospace

52 But the very example we have just cited indicates the increasing importance of technological change in all industries, since even the relatively stable automobile industry has experienced major technological improvements in manufacturing techniques and automobile weight reduction, and may be even more drastically affected by the possible development of [more safety features / **different power systems**].

53 By hindsight, the impact of the technological changes that have already occurred appears obvious, and business history is abundant with examples of firms that failed to recognize the planning implications of such technological developments as the jet engine in aircraft propulsion. At the point of planning, however, these implications are, of course, uncertain. For example, during the 1960s the Chrysler Corporation invested substantially in the development of a turbine-powered car. On the basis of later developments, this investment appears to have been [warranted / **unwarranted (This is the author's conclusion based on the absence of any subsequent developments in turbine-powered cars. But work on trucks has continued.)**].

54 Thus far we have considered political stability; governmental fiscal policy; trends in employment, productivity, and income; price levels; and technological change as environmental factors that constitute important planning premises. An additional external factor that would be given first consideration by many managers is the *expected demand* for the kind of product or service provided by the company. Studies and reports published by various governmental agencies and trade associations are most useful for forecasting the level of expected sales for a particular [company / **industry**].

55 We consider sales forecasting as a technique for predicting a particular company's sales in the final section of this chapter. At this point, however, we might

The Environment of Planning

observe that as a firm grows, the likelihood that the sales forecast is based on detailed studies conducted by the firm itself [increases / decreases].

increases

56 Finally, a group of external planning premises that has to do with the acquisition of goods and services by the firm has been referred to as the "factor market." This includes consideration of the availability of *land, labor, raw materials and parts, and capital* in a given geographic area. These factors are particularly relevant for planning activities directed toward [level of production / location of facilities].

location of facilities

57 The availability of land is one of the factors affecting plant or company location. In this context, "land" refers to [available acreage as such / acreage with necessary transportation facilities and utilities].

acreage with necessary transportation facilities and utilities

58 In terms of the *labor* factor, firms often locate their facilities in an area where people with the needed skills already live. From this standpoint, an industrial machinery manufacturer is most likely to find people with needed skills in the [Midwest / West], whereas people with aerospace experience are most likely to be located in the [Midwest / West].

Midwest

West

59 To the extent that a manufacturer is dependent on certain *raw materials or parts*, he will tend to locate his facilities close to the source of supply. For example, the early development of the steel industry in and around Pittsburgh was influenced by the availability of _____ in that area.

coal

60 As is true for the other environmental factors affecting planning, the source of raw materials or parts may be of relatively less importance in some industries because of their transportability. Thus, of the following two types of companies, the one that is less affected by the location of raw materials and parts is the [lumber company / electronic equipment manufacturer].

electronic equipment manufacturer

61 Finally, and in some cases most importantly, a

firm's planning alternatives are affected by *capital availability*. Along these lines, studies indicate that the two principal causes for the bankruptcy of small business establishments are lack of management skill and shortage of capital. However, even a large firm's ability to obtain financing for new ventures is limited, especially if it has experienced recent product [suc-

failures cesses / failures].

Social Responsibility and Governmental Regulation

Historically, professional managers in business firms have tended to view their primary obligation as being to the owner or stockholder group. This has often led to profit being considered as the only relevant measure of organizational success. During the past decade, however, increased support has been given to the view that business firms have broader responsibilities in our free enterprise system. Further, the tendency to ignore social needs in the past has led to governmental regulations that have specifically mandated such responsibilities.

62 Prime examples of areas of social responsibility are minority employment, urban renewal, environmental protection, and support of education and the arts. If one takes the position that a business firm exists to produce a product or provide a service as efficiently as possible, and with the associated objective of maximizing profit for the owners or stockholders,

should not then managers of the firm [should / should not] be expected to devote company resources to social service projects.

63 Those who favor the so-called "profit ethic" do not necessarily do so for any narrow or selfish reasons. They point out that it is not right for executives to spend the stockholders' money on projects of their own choice, that such expenditures may increase prices and put the firm in financial jeopardy, and that such activities put too much power in the hands of business executives in our society. From this viewpoint, if one type of power-generating plant is lower priced than another type of plant but results in more pollution, then given that both plants satisfy minimum legal standards the manager should always invest in the [lower-cost / higher-cost] facility.

lower-cost

64 Those who favor greater social responsibility believe that people now expect business firms to accept broader responsibilities beyond the traditional product or service objective. They argue that the historical profit ethic may be effective in the short run but not in the long run. For example, nonconcern about the physical and cultural environment of the community may maximize short-run profitability. But if the area in which the firm is located comes to be regarded as an undesirable place to live, the company will have to increase wage rates and salaries to attract competent employees to the area, thus [increasing / decreasing] payroll costs.

increasing

65 Proponents of social responsibility also point out that when business firms have neglected such responsibilities historically, the result has often been government regulation. Business firms are now burdened with the procedural work associated with environmental impact statements and affirmative action programs because of previous [responsiveness to / neglect of] such responsibilities.

neglect of

66 In our modern pluralistic society power is widely distributed among many institutions and organized groups of people. This has resulted in [simplification / greater difficulty] in defining corporate responsibility and business objectives.

greater difficulty

Sales Forecasting and Planning

Since the anticipated revenues associated with a sales forecast determine the economic limitations with which plans have to conform, the forecast represents an important influence on the planning process. In this final section of the chapter we consider the general nature of sales forecasting and then describe the principal methods that have been used for arriving at such forecasts: the jury of executive opinion method, the sales force composite method, the users' expectation method, and the statistical methods.

67 The sales forecast provides a company with the basis for determining anticipated revenues and for planning associated investments and other expenditures. Because of these significant uses, the final decision regarding forecasted sales is the responsibility of [technical specialists in this field / the top management of a company].

the top management of a company

68 The *jury of executive opinion* is the oldest and simplest of the sales forecasting methods. By this method the opinions of all members of top management are pooled in order to arrive at an overall sales estimate. One advantage of this method is that it may force all key executives to obtain information relevant to the forecast, thus [increasing / decreasing] their awareness of market factors that affect company success.

increasing

69 Furthermore, since the sales forecast has a direct effect on the planned budgets for the various operating divisions of an enterprise, the participation of key executives in sales forecasting makes general acceptance of the budgets [more / less] likely.

more

70 However, the jury of executive opinion method may result in combining poorly founded hunches and opinions, thus resulting in an overall forecast with [high / low] reliability.

low

71 Further, since no one individual or department has the primary responsibility for collecting and analyzing the data necessary for the forecast in the jury of executive opinion method, improvement of forecasting techniques from one period to the next is [likely / unlikely].

unlikely

72 The first method of sales forecasting we have described, which represents an attempt to pool the best judgments of the company's key executives, is the _____ method.

jury of executive opinion

73 The *sales force composite method* also represents a combination of the opinions of a number of people but in a way quite different from the jury of executive opinion. In the jury of executive opinion method each manager submits a forecast for [a particular segment of the market / the entire market].

the entire market

74 On the other hand, in the sales force composite method each participating individual submits a forecast for only a particular segment of the market. Typically, sales representatives are asked to forecast sales for their districts, and then these are reviewed by regional sales managers and higher-level executives. This method of sales forecasting has the advantage of being based on the judgment of those people in the company who are [closest to the consumer market / experts in sales forecasting].

closest to the consumer market

75 Furthermore, participation in sales forecasting by those who have to "make good" on the forecasts may provide a sales incentive during the period of forecast. However, this factor is also a major source of weakness of the sales force composite method. When forecasts are used to set sales quotas, the original forecasts by sales personnel tend to be [optimistic / pessimistic].

pessimistic

76 A further difficulty of the sales force composite method is that the individual sales representatives tend to give undue weight to present market conditions and cannot, after all, include consideration of company or competitor product developments unknown to them. From this standpoint their sales forecasts tend to be [too high / too low / either high or low].

either high or low

77 Thus, the sales forecasting method that has the advantage of being based on close contact with the consumer and the weakness of not including enough consideration of future economic and product developments is the _____ composite method.

sales force

78 Like the jury of executive opinion method and the sales force composite method, the *users' expectation method* is also based on a composite of individual judgments or opinions. As the name implies, however, in this method the opinions are those of the potential _____.

users (or customers, etc.)

79 The users' expectation method is particularly useful when there are only a few customers. This is most likely to be true for products or services supplied to [consumers in general / industrial customers].

industrial customers

80 If there are a large number of customers, the use of sampling techniques becomes necessary in the _____ expectation method.

users'

81 A weakness of this technique is that a firm may rely too heavily on opinions that are themselves not well founded. Thus, the composite sales forecast obtained can be no more reliable than the sum of the collective customer opinions that are obtained by the _____ method.

users' expectation

82 Thus far in our description of sales forecasting we have considered the jury of executive opinion method, the sales force composite method, and the users' expectation method. Finally, the *statistical methods* represent the last group of methods we consider. As the name implies, this includes application of [a particular technique / a number of possible alternative techniques].

a number of possible alternative techniques

83 Among the most popular of the statistical techniques is *trend analysis,* by which the historical trend in the sales of a company's products is projected for the purpose of predicting sales during the planning period. Thus, the use of trend analysis is based on the assumption that the factors that have influenced changes in sales volume in the past [will / will not] continue to operate in the future.

will

84 Some of the more sophisticated statistical methods, such as *correlation analysis,* are directed at identifying the underlying causes affecting previous changes in sales volume. However, both trend analysis and correlation analysis are dependent on the availability of [current / historical] data.

historical

85 The use of a *mathematical model* represents still another step in sophistication, since in this case the analyst attempts to incorporate all known causative variables in one mathematical formulation. The model might, for example, require use of consumer income figures, consumer debt, and present sales level in a **sales** _____ forecast for the planning period.

86 Through careful analysis of historical data, influences on the company's sales volume that are not otherwise obvious might be detected by one of the **statistical** _____ methods.

87 On the other hand, by the use of the statistical methods the effect of new products or marketing developments [can / **cannot**] be readily determined.

88 In total, we have discussed the strengths and weaknesses associated with four approaches to sales forecasting: the _____ **jury of executive** opinion method, the _____ **sales force** composite method, the _____ **users'** expectation method, and the _____ **statistical** methods.

89 In practice, a company typically uses a combination of these methods (rather than just one of them) in arriving at a final sales forecast. For example, Figure 3.4 portrays a situation in which _____ [number] **three** independent forecasts of sales are forwarded to a management committee for final consideration.

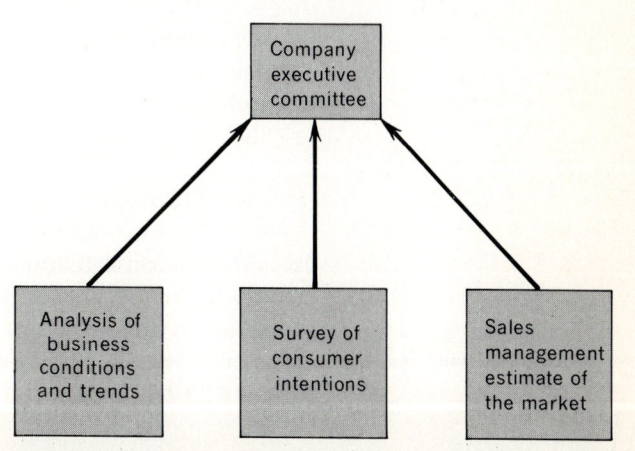

Figure 3.4 Example of the use of several independent sources of information for the sales forecast.

90 As we indicated at the outset of this section, the implications of the sales forecast are so great that final responsibility for the forecast is typically assigned to the company's _____.

top management

Review

owners, managers, or employees

vendors, customers, or government

91 Several different groups can be identified as having an interest in the activities of a firm and achieving certain goals by their interaction with it. An example of such a group within the company is the _____, whereas an example of a group outside of the company is the _____. (Frames 1 to 8)

92 In considering the underlying common objectives of all organizations as entities, an objective that may be more of a "measuring stick" of success than the objective as such is _____. (Frames 9 to 15)

profit (The objective of survival and growth might also be so regarded.)

93 The general organization objective that highlights the "reason for existence" for business firms, as well as for other organizations, and also takes cognizance of the ultimate source of the funds that contribute to profit and make survival and growth possible is the objective of _____ or _____. (Frames 16 to 23)

product; service

94 The approach to planning, as well as to the management functions in general, which represents a type of extension of the firm's product or service objective to the operating units of the firm is called _____.

management by objectives

(Frames 24 to 28)

95 An important feature of the management-by-objectives approach is the requirement that within the organization a hierarchy of objectives be defined in terms of [designated procedures / measurable results]. (Frames 29 to 34)

measurable results

96 Of the environmental factors affecting planning, the factor of political stability has particularly influenced firms in their [domestic / international]

international

Review

domestic — operations, whereas concern about government fiscal and monetary policy has been most prevalent on the [domestic / international] scene. (Frames 35 to 44)

97 With good prospects for continued growth in employment, productivity, and income, business firms are more likely to make [short- / long-] term commitments. The situation in changing price levels which leads to the greatest difficulty is the one in which prices are _____ _____. (Frame 45 to 50)

long

changing in unanticipated ways (etc.)

98 The factor of technological change as a planning premise affects [only a few / virtually all] industries today. The expected demand for the kind of products or services provided by the company is still another [internal / external] planning premise. (Frames 51 to 55)

virtually all

external

99 The so-called "factor market," which includes consideration of the availability of land, labor, raw materials or parts, and capital, is the final environmental factor we considered. As far as labor is concerned, the typical need nowadays is for [unskilled / skilled] personnel. Overall, the factor market as an environmental factor is most relevant for planning [volume of production / location of facilities]. (Frames 56 to 61)

skilled

location of facilities

100 Those who believe that business firms have the responsibility to provide a service or produce a product as efficiently as possible generally [do / do not] favor devoting company resources to social service programs. (Frames 62 and 63)

do not

101 Proponents of corporate social responsibility have argued that such programs maximize profitability in the long run, and that corporate neglect of such responsibilities has led to an increase in regulation by _____. (Frames 64 to 66)

the government (etc.)

102 The method of sales forecasting which is generally least sophisticated when used alone, and which represents a pooling of top management opinion, is the _____ method.

jury of executive opinion

(Frames 67 to 72)

103 The method by which the judgments of field representatives and sales personnel are first reviewed and then combined in order to arrive at a sales forecast is the _____ method. (Frames 73 to 77)

sales force composite

104 The method of sales forecasting based on combining customer reports regarding their buying intentions during the planning period is the _____ method. (Frames 78 to 81)

users' expectation

105 Finally, the methods that include such quantitative and analytical techniques as trend analysis, correlation analysis, and the use of mathematical models are the _____ methods. (Frames 82 to 88)

statistical

106 In practice, the sales forecasts developed by business firms tend to be based on the use of [a particular method in preference to others / a combination of methods]. (Frames 89 and 90)

a combination of methods

Discussion Questions

1. Is it useful to consider the objectives of the several groups of people associated with a firm's activities? Why or why not?
2. What do you think is the "real" objective of business firms?
3. In response to a question posed by a financial analyst at a public meeting, a corporate officer in a conglomerate (multiproduct) firm has stated that it is the objective of the company to earn a fair profit in each fiscal period, considering the required investment of resources and business risks involved. Comment on this statement.
4. In what respects are the "product or service" objective and "management by objectives" related?
5. Discuss the impact of management by objectives on the way the functions of planning, organizing, directing, and controlling are carried out.
6. What is the particular factor associated with management by objectives which often represents an advantage over an approach which specifies the *way* that departmental functions are to be carried out?
7. Consider and discuss the implications of the statement, "Only large firms can afford programs concerned with social responsibility, because small firms necessarily must be concerned about profitability and survival in the short run."

8. Is it unrealistic to expect top managers to become involved in the details of sales forecasting?

References

Ackerman, R. W. "How Companies Respond to Social Demands." *Harvard Business Review,* vol. 51, no. 4, July-August 1973.

Banks, L. "The Mission of Our Business Society." *Harvard Business Review,* vol. 53, no. 3, May-June 1975.

Bhatia, M. L. "MBO in Government Organizations." *Journal of Systems Management,* vol. 29, no. 9, September 1978.

Calhoun, R. E. "Results: Five Years with MBO." *Training and Development Journal,* vol. 31, no. 10, October 1977.

Carroll, S. J., and H. L. Tosi, Jr. *Management by Objectives: Applications and Research.* New York: Macmillan, 1973.

Chambers, J., et al. "How to Choose the Right Forecasting Techniques." *Harvard Business Review,* vol. 49, no. 4, July-August 1971.

Davis, K. "Five Propositions for Social Responsibility." *Business Horizons,* vol. 18, no. 3, June 1975.

Decker, P. G., H. Weinrich, and S. D. Wood. "Does MBO Enhance or Inhibit Creativity?" *Arizona Business,* vol. 24, no. 6, June-July 1977.

DeFee, D. T. "Management by Objectives: When and How Does It Work?" *Personnel Journal,* vol. 56, no. 1, January 1977.

Drucker, P. F. *The Practice of Management.* New York: Harper, 1954.

Hollman, R. W. "Supportive Organizational Climate and Managerial Assessment of MBO Effectiveness." *Academy of Management Journal,* vol. 19, no. 4, December 1976.

Hollman, R. W., and D. A. Tansik. "A Life Cycle Approach to Management by Objectives." *The Academy of Management Review,* vol. 2, no. 4, October 1977.

Humble, J. "A Practical Approach to Social Responsibility." *Management Review,* vol. 67, no. 5, May 1978.

Jantsch, E. "Forecasting and Systems Approach: A Frame of Reference." *Management Science,* vol. 19, no. 12, August 1973.

Kearney, W. J. "Behaviorally Anchored Rating Scales—MBO's Missing Ingredient." *Personnel Journal,* vol. 58, no. 1, January 1979.

Kirchoff, B. A. "MBO: Understanding What the Experts Are Saying." *MSU Business Topics,* vol. 22, no. 3, Summer 1974.

Lea, G. R. "An MBO Program for All Levels: One Company's Success Story." *Advanced Management Journal,* vol. 42, no. 2, Spring 1977.

Levinson, H. "Management by Whose Objectives?" *Harvard Business Review,* vol. 48, no. 4, July-August 1970.

Likert, R., and M. S. Fisher. "MBGO: Putting Some Team Spirit into MBO." *Personnel,* vol. 54, no. 1, January-February 1977.

Lodge, G. C. "Business and the Changing Society." *Harvard Business Review*, vol. 52, no. 2, March-April 1974.
Mohn, N. C., and C. L. Hubbard. "How to Reduce Uncertainty in Sales Forecasting." *Management Review*, vol. 67, no. 6, June 1978.
Morrisey, G. L. *Management by Objectives and Results for Business and Industry*. Reading, Mass.: Addison-Wesley, 1977.
Odiorne, G. S. "How to Succeed in MBO Goal Setting." *Personnel Journal*, vol. 57, no. 8, August 1978.
Owens, J. "The Values and Pitfalls of MBO." *Michigan Business Review*, vol. 26, no. 4, July 1974.
Owens, J. "Business Ethics: Age-Old Ideal, Now Real." *Business Horizons*, vol. 21, no. 1, February 1978.
Preston, L. E., F. Rey, and M. Dierkes. "Comparing Corporate Social Performance: Germany, France, Canada and the U.S." *California Management Review*, vol. 20, no. 4, Summer 1978.
Salton, G. J. "The Focused Web-Goal Setting in the MBO Process." *Management Review*, vol. 67, no. 1, January 1978.
Sherwin, D. S. "Management *of* Objectives." *Harvard Business Review*, vol. 54, no. 3, May-June 1976.
Shuster, F. E., and A. F. Kindall. "Management Objectives: Where We Stand—A Survey of the Fortune 500." *Human Resource Management*, vol. 13, no. 1, Spring 1974.
Simmons, W. W. "A Strategic Planning Program for the Next Decade." *Advanced Management Journal*, vol. 41, no. 1, Winter 1976.
Slusher, A., and H. Sims. "Commitment through MBO Interviews." *Business Horizons*, vol. 18, no. 4, August 1975.
Weihrich, H. "MBO in Four Management Systems." *MSU Business Topics*, vol. 24, no. 4, Autumn 1976.
Weihrich, H. "Getting Action into MBO." *Journal of Systems Management*, vol. 28, no. 11, November 1977.
Werther, W. B., Jr., and H. Weihrich. "Refining MBO through Negotiations." *MSU Business Topics*, vol. 23, no. 3, Summer 1975.
West, G. E. "Bureaupathology and the Failure of MBO." *Human Resource Management*, vol. 16, no. 2, Summer 1977.
Winning, E. A. "MBO: What's in It for the Individual?" *Personnel*, vol. 51, no. 2, March-April 1974.

CASE STUDY: Planning in a Staff Department

As manager of the training department in the Clariair Corporation, Mary Anderson has been assigned responsibility for determining training and development needs within the company and presenting the results of such studies, along with recommended courses of action, to her immediate superior, who is a vice president in charge of personnel and industrial relations. Further, Mary's department has responsibility for implementing the decisions of the company's administration committee by designing and conducting training and development programs that are used as prototypes for programs conducted in the company's geographically decentralized facilities.

The training department contains three sections, each specializing in a particular type of job represented in the company. Thus the department includes sections whose principal work concerns professional employee development, supervisory development, and skilled trades training.

During Ms. Anderson's regular weekly meeting with her section supervisors, the topic of department and section objectives came up for discussion. Specifically, some section supervisors defined their objectives in terms of providing *requested* training services, whereas other included the *discovery* of training needs in the objectives. As a result of the diversity of views expressed in the meeting, Mary Anderson recognized the need to devote further departmental attention to this area, and therefore posed the following question to her section supervisors: "What are the objectives that guide the activities in your section?"

She has requested that the answer to this question be included in a report to be submitted to her by each supervisor within the next two weeks.

1. What immediate positive results are likely to come from Mary Anderson's request?
2. In what respects is her request incomplete?
3. What are the weaknesses, if any, in her overall approach to the task of defining objectives?
4. What would be the most effective way of proceeding after the written reports are submitted by the section supervisors?

CASE STUDY: A Decline in Government Contracts

The Rolamar Electronics Company was established in 1965 and experienced rapid growth during the 1960s and 1970s through its success in bidding on and being awarded government contracts for the development and manufacture of military electronics equipment. As would be expected, the company is heavily oriented toward research and development, and the electronic components developed by the company have always been at the forefront of state-of-the-art developments, By the beginning of the 1980s, however, the growth in government contracts peaked and thereafter began to decline. Funding for the associated area of space communication systems, particularly in regard to manned space flights, was also reduced by the government. The company had assembled a top-caliber engineering team, and Elroy McMann, the founder and company president, would like to see the research group kept intact. If government funding of space programs were to be again increased, for example, the company would be in a favorable position to obtain government contracts with the present research and development team. However, with the expiration of a major contract in eight months the company cannot maintain the present work force without other sources of revenue.

Mr. McMann discussed this situation at some length with his top executives. As the result of this discussion, Richard Sloan, who is manager of the research and development group, has proposed a specific product area that the company might enter as some of the military electronics work is reduced. He suggests that the engineers who have been involved in developing the electronics components for military applications have the capability of developing amplifier systems, stereo systems, and radio receivers that would be technologically much superior to systems now commercially available. Richard Sloan was particularly aware of this opportunity because many of his engineers have built "sound systems" of various kinds for their own homes and apartments. "All we have to do is to tap this capability," said Sloan, "and within a year we can have a sound system on the market that is superior to anything now available to the general consumer."

1. If the proposal presented by Mr. Sloan is accepted, what is the implication from the standpoint of the company's objectives?
2. Given the technological capability of the research and development personnel, what are some reasons for caution with respect to the proposal?
3. If the proposal were successfully implemented, what would be the probable effect on the president's desire to maintain the technological team intact?
4. What other types of products or service opportunities might the company consider as government contracts are reduced?

APPLICATIONS READING:

A Long-Range Approach to MBO

Richard Babcock
Visiting Associate Professor
DePaul University

Peter F. Sorensen, Jr.
Director of Graduate Studies in Administration and Organizational Behavior
George Williams College

Many strategies for implementing a management-by-objectives program require immediate, total introduction of major MBO components. These strategies imply that organizations and their managers, having weathered the shock of sudden immersion in the MBO process, will adjust over time to their new organizational environment as program improvements and modifications are introduced.

But companies too often underestimate the risks and overall costs of all-out, immediate implementation of MBO; managers should think twice before plunging headlong into a total program. Mounting evidence suggests that many companies would be better served by utilizing an MBO strategy based on the concept of implementing the program in stages extending over periods of from three to seven years.

Gradual introduction and spacing of MBO elements into organizational life heighten prospects for effective and lasting benefits from MBO techniques and enhance opportunities for a final, secure linking of MBO processes with longer-term goals and strategic planning. This stage model of MBO implementation also offers three other basic advantages:

- A low level of risk to the firm. The adverse effects of failure to adjust immediately to new planning techniques are minimized.
- A minimum of organizational disruption.
- The possibility of a do-it-yourself process with a minimum of outside help.

The major impetus for this alternative style of MBO implementation also is three-fold. It has emerged from the authors' consulting and research experience; feedback from MBO seminars that have included managers from a variety of large firms in various stages of implementation of MBO; and significant issues that have been documented or raised by other analysts of management techniques and organizational behavior.

Source: Reprinted, by permission of the publisher, from *Management Review*, vol. 65, no. 6, June 1976; © 1976 by AMACOM, a division of American Management Associations. All rights reserved.

Supporting Observations

1. The success of MBO is closely related to and is dependent upon the support of top management This observation has been documented by a number of empirical studies. Plentiful data suggest that this support must be maintained over time inasmuch as the initial support for a comprehensive MBO program may be difficult to sustain as MBO becomes more routine. On the other hand, gradual implementation—the addition of features over an extended period—conveys the impression of growing support as MBO expands and grows.

2. Failure to institutionalize the MBO process contributes to the failure of MBO Studies have shown that institutionalization of MBO calls for the integration of MBO with existing organizational systems (that is, budgeting, performance appraisal, management development, and compensation). It also requires managers to conceptualize their jobs in terms of ends or objectives rather than activities or means.

3. MBO is positively perceived as contributing to planning, goal clarification and understanding, and role expectations; it also assists in the appraisal process For example: Clarification of expectations, the focusing of planning, and setting target dates were the most frequently cited advantages in a study of managers' reactions to MBO by Henry L. Tosi, Jr. and Stephen J. Carroll in the *Journal of Management Studies*. One of the authors of this article (Babcock) made similar observations in his work with utility, aerospace, and consumer firms.

4. A major change effort such as MBO causes significant organizational "disruption" This area has been relatively neglected in the study of MBO, but it represents an important consideration. Indeed, the question of whether or not the strengths of MBO are worth the "cost of jolting the organization with massive and simultaneous changes" is a point well taken. MBO is an additional activity superimposed upon employees' existing activities and may well add to problems of organizational dislocation.

5. Different environmental conditions affect the applicability of MBO This area of concern also needs further exploration. One point of view holds that MBO is most, or perhaps only, applicable in stable environments. Another suggests that differential goal-setting strategies are called for.

Our experience in several institutional settings suggests that the high cost and risk involved in the extensive change required in MBO may well be a critical consideration. But coupling this factor with the need for institutionalization of MBO through integration of multiple existing systems creates a dilemma for those who wish to implement MBO. Integration with other systems is essential, but we also believe that advocates of a total initial approach to introducing MBO considerably underestimate the shock such an effort has on the organization. Levels of tension are raised considerably, and the probability of resistance and failure also is increased. These factors are eliminated, or at least mitigated, by the alternative

Stage I	Stage II	Stage III	Stage IV
Clarification of strategic purposes	Complete network of enterprise and manager objectives	Integration of MBO with management systems	Integration with strategic planning
Top-management goal setting	Informal review sessions	Horizontal integration of objectives	Linking MBO with monetary reward system
	Specific MBO training	Training focused on integration	Training for total integration

Figure 1 Sequential Model of MBO Implementation.

strategy of MBO implementation suggested here: *gradual integration* of MBO by stages into the existing management functions.

The Alternative Model: Sequential Introduction

Figure 1 illustrates a sequential introduction strategy designed to take into consideration the need for organizational learning and the maintenance of adequate levels of risk taking. Thus the extent of new concepts and processes presented in an MBO program is limited in any one period of time.

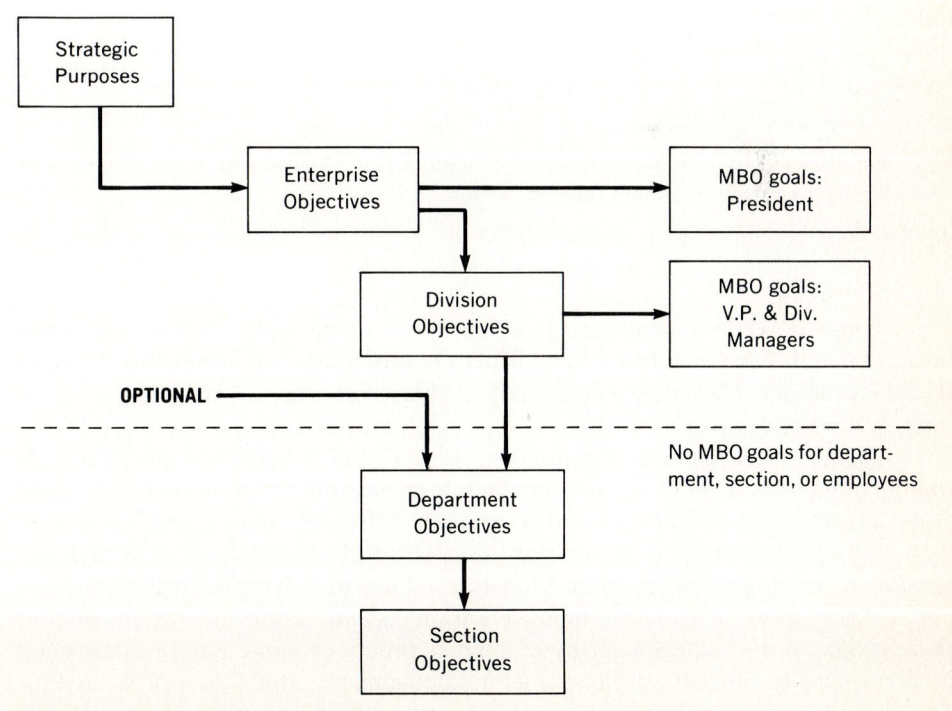

Figure 2 Implementation for Stage I.

Stage I. Organizational preparation This stage prepares the organization for MBO. The main focus is on goal setting by top management and MBO training for all personnel with special emphasis on rewording and clarification of the firm's strategic goals. Inclusion of top management in the initial process provides the requisite visible top-management involvement; and centering the early MBO activities at top-management levels minimizes organizational disruption. The organizational units and levels of management that would be included in Stage I are indicated in Figure 2.

The second objective of Stage I is the development of an organizational climate receptive to the implementation of MBO by subordinate managers. This objective can be accomplished through introductory sessions in the philosophy and methods of MBO and the policies and procedures that will guide implementation in the second stage.

We also have observed two other forms of training: One revolves around the use of T groups to facilitate the development of an open climate to encourage the establishment of goals that are real, substantive, and challenging rather than safe and unimaginative; the second centers on the development of an achievement-oriented climate through the use of achievement-motivation training that centers around developing abilities to set and work toward realistic goals.

It is our experience, however, that the natural working through of the MBO process itself facilitates a climate of real, rather than superficial, goal setting.

Before moving to Stage II of implementation, the firm should achieve the following results:

1. Development of well-written operational and organizational objectives.
2. An understanding of MBO by top-level managers.
3. Demonstration by top-level managers of their support for the MBO program through direct involvement in writing their individual job objectives.
4. An overall understanding of basic MBO philosophy and methods by all managers who will subsequently participate in the MBO program.

Stage II. Overall goal setting and review Once top-level managers have become familiar and comfortable with MBO, subordinate managers are brought into the program. The latter establish their objectives, and informal appraisals of their performances begin.

In this phase the most common options for writing MBO objectives are: (1) writing objectives level by level, with each level serving as the basis for the next layer; (2) directing all managers to write their MBO objectives simultaneously, with only a loose attempt at integration; and (3) having all managers draft their objectives within a framework of previously established enterprise objectives.

This phase of MBO implementation is the point at which institutionalization of the management-by-objectives process begins, and for that reason it is especially important. The major mechanisms through which institutionalization occurs are intermediate reviews, coaching, and progress-report sessions. Individual sessions are preferred, but we have found that group sessions also work effectively. Because persons just learning the MBO process usually need help in adjusting from an activity-oriented to a planned goal-oriented perspective, frequency in review sessions is vital. Monthly reviews are the preferable format, with quarterly sessions about the longest satisfactory time frame.

It is important that reviews be scheduled regularly and that data on goal performance be recorded on MBO review forms. Care also must be taken to ensure that the appraisal sessions are constructive and that the results of performance against goals are not made a basis for judging a manager's overall performance. Thus the summary forms should not be placed in personnel files, but should be retained by the subordinate manager and his boss.

Specific training in MBO goal setting and review is the supportive adjunct to the appraisal sessions. The training should center on writing verifiable objectives and conducting constructive appraisal sessions. The benefits of MBO in these early stages are centered on improved planning and clarifying roles, and the success of the program should be judged in terms of achieving these objectives.

It has been our experience that one reaction to the positive impact of MBO on planning and role expectations is a sharp increase in "psychic" income that provides a strong base for later stages of MBO development. Limiting these initial stages considerably decreases the shock effect and the risk of introducing new management systems. It provides more learning time, particularly in practice and risk taking around goal setting. The staff also benefits from having more freedom to experiment with goal flexibility and time frames consistent with organizational and environmental constraints.

At the end of Stage II the following results can be expected:

1. A network of objectives (possibly integrated) as goal setting is extended throughout the enterprise and managerial levels.
2. Managerial ability to write MBO-style goals and to appraise performance constructively.
3. Improved planning and role understanding.
4. A beginning toward the institutionalization of MBO.

Stage III. Initial systems integration The third stage marks the point at which MBO starts to impact on other management systems. Changes can be expected in budgeting, management information, and performance appraisal systems.

Financial constraints can impinge on the types of goals that are set, and it must be recognized that unless adequate funds are budgeted, it may be impossible to set many desirable objectives (especially those relating to problem solving, innovative activities, and goals).

The management-information and forecasting systems must reflect on the program and provide backup data for result areas in which goals were not previously established. This requirement may well mean the development of new data sources and use of new forecasting procedures.

Systematic appraisal of performance, with review sessions held and recorded, closes the integrative loop of the MBO process.

In this stage it becomes important to write horizontally consistent goals and to adjust the time cycle for reviews. There is no magic formula for writing managers' goals that are consistent in lateral functional areas. But it is our experience that managers do so informally as they see they are progressing with difficulty while trying to achieve their MBO goals. We know of one company that appraises performance monthly in Likert-type link-pin committees where inherent visibility provides the basis for removing these inconsistencies.

Stage III focuses first on a review and appropriate modification, strengthening, and tightening of the planning process. Secondly, the MBO process is integrated with other management systems (such as budgeting, forecasting, and information with performance appraisal) but not, for the time being, with compensation.

The MBO process in Stage III is still very much a learning activity, and the latitude for learning and experimentation must be maximized. Although MBO training in this phase emphasizes integration with other management systems, a linkup with the organizational reward system should be delayed. The intrinsic satisfaction of achieving the explicit MBO goals is sufficient to continue the growth of the MBO program.

Stage IV. Mature systems integration MBO training in this final phase emphasizes the difficult problems of total integration as well as a review and updating of the MBO processes. At the same time, it moves into murky areas, uncharted waters marked by controversy.

Because the refinements of the previous stages make it possible to write more accurate and precise goals, the final stage moves toward developing a link between MBO and the monetary reward systems. However, MBO goal setting and appraisal are not and will not become a precise science—the luck factor will continue to influence goal accomplishment. The best system we have seen links MBO with a bonus plan while continuing to appraise the manager on his job of managing. In this way salary levels do not become locked into past goals and past performance. Managers must eventually see their pay as a measure of their contribution.

Little empirical research has been published on the question (and problems) of linking merit compensation to management by objectives. Available findings, however, indicate that this tie-in is positively associated with perceptions of the worth of MBO, role clarity, feelings of accomplishment, and enhancement of subordinate development and performance. In our opinion, any positive perceptions will tend to reinforce earlier stages of the MBO process, and organizational learning will further minimize possible disadvantages.

A premature focus on the reward system, however, sharply increases the probability of generating a number of dysfunctional consequences that include the perception of high risks associated with MBO, encouragement of organizational game playing, selection of safe, low-return objectives, and numbers manipulation. The gradual implementation process described here should curtail these tendencies; therefore, any tie-in to compensation should be delayed until MBO becomes firmly institutionalized as an organizational way of life.

Strengthening the linking of MBO with strategic and long-term planning initiated in Stage I is the final step in the sequential implementation of an MBO program. It is important to develop a systematic relationship between program or process goals and the firm's longer-run objectives and strategic plans. We have seen too many processes started and never completed. For example, one MBO program to reduce juvenile crime developed numerous goals over a five-year period, but juvenile crime rates rose anyway. The organization never got to measuring the end-result objective—to reduce juvenile crime.

Setting a Timetable

The timing of implementation strategy presented here can easily be controlled. Both resources and commitment to MBO can be introduced when an evaluation of progress indicates it is appropriate to move into the next phase. Definite times for evaluation should be set, however.

Because of this latitude, this MBO model is basically a low-risk strategy that permits the development of internal skills to implement the program, with outside consultants brought in to handle specific training and development assignments.

A basic timetable for completing this format of MBO implementation covers a minimum of a little over two and one-half years to a maximum of seven years:

	Optimistic	Pessimistic
Stage I	2-6 months	1 year
Stage II	6 months	1-2 years
Stage III	1 year	1-2 years
Stage IV	1-2 years	1-3 years

Assessment of the Program

In summary, the introduction of MBO over an extended period with defined stages of integration with various other management systems provides these basic advantages over "total" implementation programs:

1. It minimizes the "shock" effect and decreases anxiety, frustration, and resistance that accompany large-scale change efforts.
2. It builds on the positive impact of MBO on planning and clarification of roles and expectations.
3. It delays the more difficult task of integration with the compensation system until the organization has had sufficient learning time to provide a realistic basis for linking individual MBO programs with reward systems.

4. It provides learning time for experimentation and risk taking in determining the appropriate goal-setting strategy appropriate to the organization's environment.
5. It provides on-going systematic reinforcement by top-level management.

Questions on Reading

1. Why do the authors argue against a total initial implementation of MBO into an organization?
2. Outline the principal stages in Babcock and Sorensen's sequential introduction of MBO into an organization.
3. Identify the results that should be achieved by the end of Stage I of introducing MBO.
4. Identify the results that should be achieved by the end of Stage II of introducing MBO.
5. What is the timetable suggested by the authors for completing the sequential introduction of MBO into an organization?

4 POLICIES, PROCEDURES, AND METHODS

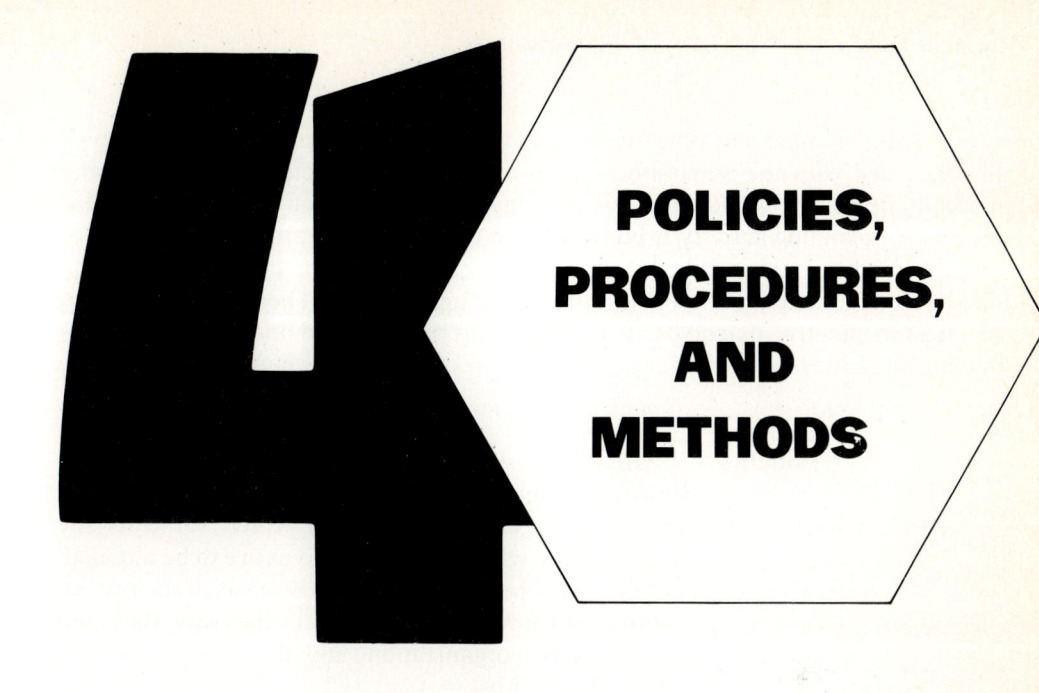

- Policies
- Procedures and Methods
- Decision Making
- Review
- Discussion Questions
- References
- Case Study: Krueger Metal Products Corporation
- Case Study: A Wage and Salary Policy Problem
- Applications Reading: "Making Policy Readable" E. K. Lybbert
- Questions on Reading

After organization objectives have been identified, the function of planning is concerned with the selection and definition of the policies, procedures, and methods necessary to achieve overall organizational objectives. Each of these "levels" of planning activity is considered in turn in this chapter. Whether it be at the level of determining policies, procedures, or methods, the process of decision making is an essential component of the planning function. Therefore, the factors that lead to effective diagnosis, discovery of alternatives, and analysis in decision-making situations are considered in the last section of this chapter.

Policies Whereas objectives are necessary to give direction to individual and group efforts in the organization, policies are general statements which serve as the guidelines by which these objectives are to be attained. Policies have been classified on the basis of the organizational level which they affect, the way they are formed in the organization, and the area of work to which they apply.

1   A business firm may have the specific objective of attaining greater market penetration in its product field; relying on price competition to achieve this objective would be an example of a business _____.

policy

2   Policies have been defined as general statements or understandings that guide decision making by subordinates in the various departments of an enterprise. By this definition, do such statements have to be set down in writing in order to be considered policies? [Yes / No]

No

3   Whether or not they have been written down, policies serve as broad, comprehensive guides for _____ _____ in the organization.

decision making

4   Policies may be classified in several ways. One classification that is useful is based on the organizational level of the managers affected. Thus *basic, general, and departmental policies* identify the organizational _____ of policy application.

level

5   The *basic policy,* which is very broad in scope and affects the organization as a whole, is used mainly by [top / middle / first-level] managers.

top

Policies

basic

6 A policy of marketing a competitive product for each one offered by a major competitor is an example of a _____ policy.

middle

7 The *general policy,* which is more specific, typically applies to large segments of the organization but usually not to all of it. It is used mainly by [top / middle / first-level] managers.

general

8 A policy that purchasing agents should work with local contractors whenever possible is an example of a _____ policy.

first-level

9 The *departmental policy* is most specific in nature and applies to everyday activities at the departmental level. It is used mainly by [top / middle / first-level] managers.

departmental

10 The policy that employees are expected to call when they are going to be absent because of illness is a _____ policy.

basic; general; departmental

11 In summary, there are three types of policies, based on the scope and managerial level affected. These are _____, _____, and _____ policies.

middle
first-level;
top

12 The general policies relate primarily to the activities of _____ managers, the departmental policies are of most concern to _____ managers, and basic policies affect _____ managers most directly.

formed

13 Another classification of policies is based on the way they are formed in the organization. *Originated policy, appealed policy,* and *imposed policy* are three types of policy based on the way they are _____.

is

14 An *originated policy* is one initiated by the managers of a company for the purpose of guiding themselves and their subordinates. Typically, the relationship between originated policy and organizational objectives [is / is not] fairly close.

Chapter 4 • Policies, Procedures, and Methods

originated

15 The decision to promote the sale of service contracts with equipment sales to ensure that customers maintain the equipment properly is an example of _____ policy.

appealed

16 An *appealed policy* is also formulated by a company manager. The distinction is that the appealed policy comes into existence from the appeals by managers to their superiors about handling exceptional cases; this is the basis for its being called _____ policy.

Yes

17 Since appealed policy is based on the handling of individual cases, which may each involve special circumstances, is there any danger that such policy will be incomplete, uncoordinated, and perhaps inconsistent? [Yes / No]

appealed

18 In the absence of a previously specified policy, a manager asks his superior what to do about an overdue account receivable. The superior's decision constitutes the formulation of _____ policy.

originated

19 When managers find themselves continually occupied in formulating appealed policy, it indicates that not enough attention had been given to formulating the type of policy we previously described, that is, _____ policy.

increasing

20 *Imposed policy* is formed as the result of some external influence on the organization, such as action by a governmental unit, trade association, or labor union. In general, the importance of imposed policy has been [increasing / decreasing] with the development of industrialization.

Yes (since they are subject to the same governmental, trade association, and union pressures)

21 Would you expect that the imposed policy in General Motors would be very similar to the imposed policy in the Ford Motor Company? [Yes /No]

22 A policy of equipment depreciation that is formulated because of Air Force contract requirements is an example of _____ policy.

imposed

23 Based on the way they are formed in the organization, we have discussed three types of policies: _____, _____, and _____.

originated; appealed; imposed

24 The type of policy which would be similar for different companies within the same industry is _____ policy.

imposed

25 The policy specifically formulated to establish guidelines needed to achieve organizational objectives before any problems have been encountered is _____ policy.

originated

26 The type of policy whose abundance indicates a lack of appropriate managerial attention to anticipating needed guidelines for decision making is _____ policy.

appealed

27 Finally, another classification of policies is based on the *area of work* to which the policies apply. Although a number of categories could be discussed, we consider *sales, production, finance,* and *personnel* as major areas of _____ in business firms.

work

28 *Sales policies* have to do with such decisions as the selection of the product to be manufactured, its pricing, the sales promotion to be carried out, and the selection of distribution channels. Since these are interdependent areas of decision making, close coordination of these efforts [is / is not] essential.

is

29 A decision to restrict the distribution of a certain brand of beer to the Midwest area constitutes a _____ policy.

sales

30 *Production policies* include such decisions as whether or not to make or buy a needed component, the location of production facilities, the purchase of production equipment, and the inventories to be maintained. Can production policies be formulated without

108 • Chapter 4 • Policies, Procedures, and Methods

No

regard to the sales policies of the enterprise? [Yes / No]

production

31 The decision to locate new plants within a certain distance from a major market area constitutes a _____ policy.

would

32 *Finance policies* are concerned with such matters as capital procurement, depreciation methods, and the use of available funds. As such, they [would / would not] directly affect all other areas of policy formulation.

finance

33 The decision to lease rather than buy needed warehouse space is an example of a _____ policy.

Yes

34 *Personnel policies* concern personnel selection, development, compensation, morale development, and union relations. Is it important that these policies be consistent throughout the company? [Yes / No]

personnel

35 The decision that applicants should be placed in an apprentice program primarily on the basis of ability tests is an example of a _____ policy.

**sales;
production; finance;
personnel**

36 The four types of policies based on area of work that have been discussed above are the _____, _____, _____, and _____ policies.

managerial (or organizational); way (method, etc.); work

37 Obviously, any given policy can be described in terms of each of the three major classification systems we have discussed: the _____ level involved, the _____ in which the policy was formed, and the area of _____ affected.

**general
appealed**

38 The employment manager of a company has informed his superior that he is unable to hire certain technical personnel in the local community, and, as a result, the industrial relations director decides that these personnel should be recruited in a distant city. From the standpoint of managerial level, this is a _____ policy; from the standpoint of the way it was formed, it is an _____ policy; and

Procedures and Methods • 109

personnel

from the standpoint of the area of work, it is a _____ policy.

39 The top managers of a company decide that the firm will concentrate its merchandising efforts in the electronic equipment field. This can be described as a _____, _____, and _____ policy.

basic; originated; sales

40 Because of the requirements of a union-management contract, foremen are directed to use only certain time-study methods in determining production standards. This can be described as a _____, _____, and _____ policy.

departmental; imposed; production

Procedures and Methods

A statement of *procedure* is more specific than a policy statement in that it enumerates the chronological sequence of steps to be taken in order to achieve an objective. A *method*, on the other hand, specifies how some one step of a procedure is to be performed.

41 A description of how each of a series of tasks is to take place, when it will take place, and by whom it is to be accomplished is normally included in a statement of a _____.

procedure

42 A set of specific instructions for processing orders, which may include activities in the sales, accounting, and production departments, is an example of a specified _____.

procedure

43 Figure 4.1 shows an example of a procedure. In this case, an _____ procedure is described.

employment

1. Preliminary (screening) interview
2. Application form
3. Aptitude tests
4. Check of references
5. Employment interview
6. Approval by the supervisor
7. Physical examination
8. Orientation

Figure 4.1 Outline of a typical employment procedure.

Chapter 4 • Policies, Procedures, and Methods

less

44 As compared with policies, procedures allow [more / less] latitude in managerial decision making.

method

45 In contrast to a procedure, a description of how some one step of a procedure is to be performed is called a _____.

Yes

46 Is it possible that a method would involve just one department and just one person in that department? [Yes / No]

method

procedure

47 The specified technique to be used in administering an aptitude test is a _____, whereas the sequence of steps involved in the employment function shown in Figure 4.1 makes up a _____.

methods improvement

48 *Methods improvement* refers to improvements in the manner of performing specific tasks. Historically, replacement of manual methods by mechanical means has been a popular approach to _____.

procedures

49 From a broader point of view, *work simplification* applies to efforts to make a particular task, or a whole series of tasks, more efficient and economical. Therefore, work simplification can apply to changes in either methods or _____.

work simplification (The effect is usually broader in scope than methods improvement.)

50 In recent years, electronic equipment has been importantly involved in achieving _____.

b

51 Which do you think is more likely? [a / b]
   a. A change in a particular method will dictate a change in overall procedure.
   b. A change in overall procedure will affect the need for a particular method.

procedures

52 Since a change in procedure may make certain steps, and hence methods, in that procedure unnecessary, it follows that work simplification should begin with a study of the existing [methods / procedures].

Decision Making ● 111

methods;
procedures

53 Unless the work simplification is itself planned, however, it is easier to achieve improvement and simplification in _____ than in _____.

easier

54 For example, as compared with simplification of the overall personnel selection procedure, which may involve several departments, improvements in the method of administering and interpreting an aptitude test are [easier / more difficult].

policies;
procedures; methods.

55 In summary, in the first two sections of this chapter we have described three levels of planning that are related to achieving organizational objectives. These are the determination of _____, _____, and _____.

procedure

method

56 A chronological description of the steps to be taken in attaining an objective is a _____, whereas the specification of how a particular step should be carried out is a _____.

work simplification

57 Improvements and simplification in either procedures or methods are referred to as _____.

Decision Making

Decision-making skill is the key to successful planning at all levels. This involves more than the selection of a plan of action, for at least three phases—*diagnosis*, *discovery of alternatives*, and *analysis*—have to be completed before a choice can be made.

diagnosis

58 The sequence of decision-making activities is of considerable importance. Successful analysis of alternatives depends on previous discovery of appropriate alternatives, and this phase, in turn, depends on accurate _____.

diagnosis

59 The function of the first phase in decision making, that of _____, is to identify and clarify a problem.

60 An accurate diagnosis depends on a *definition of*

organizational objectives with which present results are compared. This is consistent with our previous observation that objectives are the focal point for the managerial function of _____.

planning

objectives

61 After organizational _____ are identified, diagnosis then involves *identifying major obstacles* to their attainment. Along these lines, it should be observed that describing a problem [does / does not] necessarily identify the obstacles.

does not

62 For example, identifying a problem as involving the marketing function is at the level of a description, whereas locating specific failures in the within-company communication system constitutes an identification of _____.

obstacles

63 In addition to the definition of organizational _____ and the identification of major _____, the diagnosis phase of decision making usually involves recognizing the factors in the situation that cannot be changed. Would the latter action tend to increase or decrease the number of possible solutions to the problem? [Increase / Decrease]

objectives;
obstacles

Decrease

64 In the diagnosis phase of decision making, care should be taken to avoid "blocking out" alternatives that are in fact possible. For example, the marketing executive who accepts the present product distribution system as a fixed factor is [likely / unlikely] to consider an obvious alternative system.

unlikely

65 The first phase of the decision-making process, which we have just described, is that of _____. This phase is followed by the discovery of *alternative courses of action*.

diagnosis

66 It is in this second phase of discovering _____ courses of action that the element of creativity is especially important.

alternative

67 Are there marked individual differences among people in regard to creative thinking? [Yes / No]

Yes

68 Granting the importance of individual differences in creativity, there are several organizational variables that affect the likelihood of creativity. One obvious, but often overlooked, factor is that rewarding creative behavior makes it [more / less] likely to occur.

more

69 Thus the manager who brushes aside novel suggestions with little consideration does not encourage the development of _____ on the part of his subordinates.

creativity

70 Another factor affecting creativity is the level of stress in the environment. Although some stress is stimulating, psychological research in this area indicates that high stress leads to either behavioral disruption or behavioral rigidity, neither one of which is conducive to creativity. Accordingly, people in a "high-pressure" organization are [more / less] likely to be creative; although they may be productive in routine tasks.

less

71 In comparing successful research organizations with successful production organizations, we would therefore expect to find less emphasis on day-to-day schedules in the [research / production] organizations.

research

72 Finally, creative thought and new solutions cannot take place without allowing *time* for acquiring and considering the necessary factual material. This suggests that "thinking time," during which no overt progress is obvious, [is / is not] time productively spent.

is

73 Thus there are at least three factors that affect the creativity climate. Creativity is enhanced when it is _____, when the level of _____ is appropriate, and when adequate _____ is available for considering the problem.

rewarded; stress (etc.)
time

74 Following diagnosis and the discovery of alternatives, the final phase of the _____ process is that of *analysis,* which involves comparing

decision-making

the possible courses of action and choosing one of the alternatives.

75 To the extent that a manager bases decisions on hunches or inner feelings, the process of choice is based on intuition. In a totally intuitive approach, the third phase of decision making, that of _____, might appear to be virtually absent.

analysis

76 That the basis for the choice of an alternative is not clear, even to the decision maker, is one weakness or disadvantage of relying on _____ in making decisions.

intuition

77 As an alternative to the intuitive approach, the method of *factual analysis* requires that the factors or reasons underlying hunches be identified and evaluated, thus increasing the extent to which the analysis process is [personal / public].

public

78 Identifying, and possibly listing, the advantages and disadvantages related to each of the alternatives is one example of the method of _____.

factual analysis

79 Would you expect that it would often be useful to quantify the various factors involved in the factual analysis? [Yes / No]

Yes

80 A method of analysis that relies on the quantification of all factors, and that has been found useful in decision making, is management science. One of the features of this approach to analyzing decision-making situations is the construction of a model for the situation. Consistent with the quantitative orientation of management science, the model used is typically a [physical / mathematical] model.

mathematical

81 Thus management science, which is described in greater detail in Chapter 5, places emphasis on the importance of identifying and quantifying all variables involved in a decision-making situation and constructing a _____ model to represent the situation.

mathematical

Review
objectives

82 As the first step in planning, organizational _____ must be identified. (Frame 1)

policies; procedures;
methods

83 Following the identification of objectives, the planning process includes the selection and definition of _____, _____, and _____. (Introduction to the chapter)

84 Policies, which serve as general guides for decision making by managers, can be classified in several ways. On the basis of the organizational level of the managers directly affected, policies are described as

basic; general;
departmental

being _____, _____, or _____. (Frames 2 to 12)

85 For example, the type of policy that applies to large segments of an organization but not to all of it, and which is of greatest concern to middle managers,

general

is the _____ policy. (Frames 7 and 8)

86 There are also three types of policies, based on the way they are formed in the organization. These

originated; appealed;
imposed

are _____, _____, and _____ policies. (Frames 13 to 23)

87 A great deal of which type of policy formulation indicates that top managers have not successfully anticipated the policy needs of the organization?

Appealed

_____ policy. (Frames 16 to 26)

88 The third classification of policies we considered is based on the area of work to which they apply. On

sales; production;
finance; personnel

this basis, there are _____, _____, _____, and _____ policies. (Frames 27 to 36)

89 The decision to lease rather than purchase retail sales outlets is an example of the formulation of

finance

_____ policy. (Frames 32 and 33)

90 Any policy can be described from the standpoint of all three classification systems we have described. The decision that all first-level supervisors in the company are to be held accountable for the development

Chapter 4 • Policies, Procedures, and Methods

departmental; originated; personnel

of their subordinates can be classified as a _____, _____, and _____ policy. (Frames 37 to 40)

procedure

91 A description of how each of a series of tasks is to take place, when it will take place, and by whom it is to be accomplished is normally included in a statement of _____. (Frames 41 to 44)

method

92 By contrast, the detailed specification of how some one step of a procedure is to be performed is a statement of _____. (Frames 45 to 57)

diagnosis; discovery of alternatives; analysis

93 The selection of a plan of action represents the culmination of the decision-making process. The process itself is made up of at least three phases: _____, _____, and _____. (Frames 58 to 78)

rewarded; stress time

94 In the discovery of alternative courses of action creativity is particularly important in decision making. Creative behavior is made more likely when it is _____, when the level of _____ is appropriate, and when adequate _____ is available for considering a problem. (Frames 66 to 73)

management science

95 The extension of factual analysis, which is based on mathematical model building and which has been found to be useful in decision making, is called _____ _____. (Frames 79 to 81)

Discussion Questions

1. The term "strategies" is frequently used to denote specific courses of action that can be taken to achieve an organization's goal, usually in the context of a competitive environment. How does this definition relate to the definition of "policies" given near the beginning of this chapter?
2. A manager states that in his organization most policies are defined as the result of an appeal rather than being originated, and that this has the advantage of having policies where they are most needed and avoiding unnecessary policy statements. Do you agree with him?
3. In what ways does effective planning on the departmental level in an organization depend on actions taken "higher up" in the organization?

4. Policies have been classified in various ways. Why is a single classification system not sufficient?
5. Consider the difference between methods improvement and work simplification. Why is the latter approach to be preferred in most instances?
6. We have suggested that several distinct types of activities make up the decision-making process. Discuss these, indicating the probable consequences associated with omitting any of the activities.
7. What is the role of creativity in planning? Do you think individual creativity can be developed, or is it inborn?
8. Though some managers believe that "experience is the best teacher," others hold that "experience is a dangerous basis for decision making." Can you reconcile these two views?

References

Ackoff, R. L. *A Concept of Corporate Planning.* New York: Wiley-Interscience, 1970.
Baldridge, J. V., and R. A. Burnham, "Organizational Innovation: Individual, Organizational, and Environmental Imports." *Administrative Science Quarterly,* vol. 20, no. 2, June 1975.
Barrett, F. D. "Guideposts to Creativity and Innovation." *Advanced Management Journal,* vol. 38, no. 4, October 1973.
Beach, L. R., and T. R. Mitchell. "A Contingency Model for the Selection of Decision Strategies." *The Academy of Management Review,* vol, 3, no. 3, July 1978.
Cleland, D. I., and W. R. King. "Organizing for Long-Range Planning." *Business Horizons,* vol. 17, no. 4, August 1974.
Hayashi, K. "Corporate Planning Practices in Japanese Multinationals." *Academy of Management Journal,* vol. 21, no. 2, June 1978.
Mockler, R. J. *Business Planning and Policy Formulation.* New York: Appleton-Century-Crofts, 1972.
Paul, R. N., N. B. Donavan, and J. W. Taylor. "The Reality Gap in Strategic Planning." *Harvard Business Review,* vol. 56, no. 3, May-June 1978.
Raudsepp, E. "Are You a Creative Executive?" *Management Review,* vol, 67, no. 2, February 1978.
Reif, W. E., and J. L. Webster. "The Strategic Planning Process." *Arizona Business,* vol. 23, no. 4, April 1976.
Steiner, G. A., and J. B. Miner. *Management Policy and Strategy.* New York: Macmillan, 1977.
Tushman, M. L. "Special Boundary Roles in the Innovation Process." *Administrative Science Quarterly,* vol. 22, no. 4, December 1977.
Vancil, R. F., and P. Lorange. "Strategic Planning in Diversified Companies." *Harvard Business Review,* vol. 53, no. 1, January-February 1975.

CASE STUDY: Krueger Metal Products Corporation

The Krueger Metal Products Corporation specializes in the installation of heating and air conditioning equipment in a metropolitan area of about one million people. Although the company usually installs nationally known equipment, it engages in limited manufacturing of certain components used with the heating and cooling systems, particularly for commercial installations. Since it was established some thirty years ago, the company has earned a reputation for quality work.

Gerald Carter has been with the company as sales representative for two years. During this period he believes that the company has missed a number of opportunities to obtain lucrative contracts because of the conditions under which he is forced to operate. Particularly in the case of commercial installations, he does not have the authority to make any decisions or commitments during preliminary contract negotiations; he has to withhold discussion of price, completion time, and credit arrangements until after each of the technical experts in these areas has reviewed the job and made formal commitments. By this time, a competing firm has frequently already completed negotiations and obtained the contract. Mr. Carter considers this a continuing problem, and feels hamstrung in that he sees himself as "selling the product," but without authority to specify how, when, for how much, and under what conditions.

1. In what respects do you think Mr. Carter is justified in his complaint?
2. In what respects is he perhaps not justified?
3. What can he do to improve his situation?
4. If this is something of an organizational problem, rather than one confined to Gerald Carter, what should be done on a companywide basis to improve the situation?

CASE STUDY: A Wage and Salary Policy Problem

The Conklin Manufacturing Company is a medium-sized firm located in the Midwest and involved in the manufacture of valves and related metal fittings. The company has had the policy of paying above-average wages to its employees and expecting in return an above-average commitment to producing quality products. For several years, one particular group of inspectors has been supervised by Ed Haley. Ed's philosophy has been to give his people what he considered to be adequate, but not extravagant, increases in salary at the time of each annual salary review. As a result of this philosophy, many of the inspectors have now reached the top classification grade and the top salary within that grade.

Recognizing that the cost-of-living adjustments to the salary scales, which are also made annually, do not provide an opportunity for any real improvement in income, Ed Haley has consulted with George Nowak, the wage and salary administrator, about the problem. Nowak has refused to authorize either higher grades for the inspectors or higher top salaries for the existing grades. His position is that the company's wage scale is in line with and in fact exceeds the wage scales of comparable companies in the same area, and he has wage survey data which support his position.

Several of the inspectors have been at top salary for over two years, and the absence of any merit increases is becoming a major morale problem in the department. Because Ed Haley is within two months of retirement, his designated successor, Bill Reilley, has also been approached by several of the inspectors about the problem. Bill has responded by consulting with the plant manager about the situation. The answer he received is that all possible avenues for a solution have been explored and that there is no alternative to consistent application of the company wage and salary policies.

1. From the standpoint of the inspectors, in what respect is their complaint justified and in what respect is it not justified?
2. Should the company policy regarding maximum pay in grade be made more flexible? Why or why not?
3. How might Ed Haley have prevented the present problem from developing?
4. If this problem is in fact occurring throughout the organization, what change should the company consider in its wage and salary policies?

APPLICATIONS READING:

Making Policy Readable
E. K. Lybbert

Few people like to read policies and procedures, and almost nobody likes to write them. Yet around school and college offices, governmental offices, banks, corporate offices—wherever people have to do business with each other and account for what they do and how they do it, policy and procedure manuals are as universal as in-baskets and paper-clips. The fact is that policies and procedures are nearly indispensable to the proper functioning of many kinds of organizations.

Source: Republished with permission from *Administrative Management*, vol. 39, no. 2, February 1978, copyright © 1978 by Geyer-McAllister Publications, Inc., New York.

But their usefulness to any organization is limited in part by their readability, and most policies and procedures, heaven help us, are not as readable as they could be.

The Long Way

Policy makers don't set out to make their policies wordy, dull, and unreadable. They strive mightily for comprehensiveness and precision, because they know others are going to try to find holes, to challenge their accuracy. This is part of the game—and the serious business—of policy and procedures. But the methods most writers use to eliminate holes are almost always exactly the methods that work best for killing interest, making the way long and deadly dreary for the reader.

Authors of policy, like any other authors, should have their ultimate purpose and audience clearly in mind as they write. They must be sensitive to the readability of the policy they create, while they who lose sight of their ultimate audience and aims will not be so sensitive. Consider the following specimen:

> A lead worker's compensation is comprised of base pay for the normal job activities plus a differential for performance of lead duties. The differential is an additional percent of the hourly rate which is paid to the lead worker for each hour reported (e.g., regular work hours, vacation, sick leave, holidays). The percentage rate will be established by line management at a level consistent with pay policies approved by the personnel director.

This passage is taken directly from an actual policy and procedures manual. It is dull reading by any standard, though it could be worse.

To a reader, such a passage begs for translation in plain English:

> Pay lead workers more than others; check with the personnel director about how much more.

But it is necessary to point out that this translation is more readable than the original not just because it is so much shorter. The crucial difference between the two versions is that the original blurs the focus on people and their actions while the revision sharpens it. And while the original version, which uses a legalistic, definitional style, is more comprehensive and precise, the revision, in simple imperative style, can easily be rendered more precise:

> Pay lead workers base pay for normal job activities, and, for lead duties, an additional percent for each hour reported (e.g., regular work hours, vacation, sick leave, holidays).

A compromise between the ponderous formality of legalese and the informality of imperative style would be narrative style:

> Lead workers receive base pay for normal job activities plus an additional percent for each hour reported. Line management establishes the rate, consistent with pay policies of the personnel director.

There are yet other styles that writers of policy use. But the three we have mentioned (legalese, imperative style, and narrative style) are basic, and most other styles are merely combinations of them. When supplemented judiciously by necessary charts and tables, any combination of these three styles can be used to good effect, depending on the policy maker's aims and ultimate audience.

One cannot read the minds of the authors of the original policy on lead worker compensation. Perhaps there were reasons for using a stilted legalistic/definitional style. Perhaps part of the intent was to make sure that the policy would be legally defensible. But such an aim should not be accepted as an excuse for dull writing.

The format of policy and procedure statements varies a good deal from one organization to another, but a typical maximum sort of structure is as follows:

- Heading (title, number, subject, date, effective date)
- Purpose
- General (background)
- References
- Policy
- Procedures
- Attachments/exhibits (forms)
- Endorsements/approvals.

Not all of these sections are always necessary, but of the eight sections, the one policy makers tend to gloss over most lightly is "purpose." Yet it is the one they should dwell on most carefully in order to assure the readability of their policies. In fact, until the process becomes intuitive and automatic, a "purpose checklist" such as the following should be used, to draw out implicit aims and force authors to state them explicitly:

- Why is this policy necessary? (What does it attempt to accomplish?)
- Who will read it and why? (Whom does it affect? What action, if any, will/should those who read it take as a result of reading it?)
- Is there any reason this policy cannot be couched in either imperative or narrative style?

- If it must be couched in legalistic style, is there any reason it cannot be humanized, by direct reference to the (classes of) people involved and the actions they should take?

Another specimen policy may help to illustrate the utility of such a checklist. It is from a college's policy statement on past due financial obligations of employees, and is given verbatim:

> Commensurate with the privileges afforded individuals upon employment with the College, an employee has a financial responsibility to the College for legitimate financial obligations owed to the College that he has incurred during the course of his employment. Therefore, except as provided in paragraph "C" below, following 30 days notice to the employee, the College may deduct from the net remuneration owed to the employee by the College for the particular pay period, the amount of any or all fees, charges, debts, fines, or other financial obligations owed to the College which shall include, but is not limited to, the following:
>
> 1. Overpayment of salary
> 2. Bookstore debts...
> 15. Personal telephone tolls charged to a college number.

It is clear that the author of this atrociously written policy was trying to make it sound imposing and "legal." After a couple of readings its meaning also becomes clear:

> If an employee owes the college money for any reason the controller must give 30 days notice before deducting the amount of the debt from the employee's net remuneration, except as provided in paragraph "C" below.

It is hard to believe that this more concise statement loses any legal force, and that it is really necessary to list specific types of employee obligations.

Again, it is impossible to know exactly what the writer of the original policy had in mind beyond the obvious purpose of creating a handy collection procedure for employee debts, but the revision does assume certain answers to the "purpose checklist" questions posed above. For example, it is assumed that the policy is necessary to provide fair advance warning to employees and to instruct college officials regarding the actions they can and should take. It is therefore further assumed that the main readership of the policy will be employees who owe the college money and college officials in the controller's group (probably accounts receivable and payroll). (The policy could be made both more precise and more readable if it were known exactly which officers should take what actions.)

We said earlier that the methods most people use to eliminate holes in the policies they write tend to kill reader interest. Consider lists, for example, or outlines, lists of lists. Both are great tools for one whose task is to cover all the bases in an orderly fashion. But they can be deadly to readers, especially if used without care. Policy statements are a form of exposition, and as such involve no strategy of "keep-away" (holding back some surprises) as does storytelling. Exposition is all "giveaway," and lists and outlines can be excellent giveaway tools. But the problem is that in addition to eliminating surprises, lists and outlines tend to discourage specific reference to people. The result is often a compact, comprehensive, but dull document. Consider the following not entirely fictional case:

A traveling salesman, one of his company's best, is about to quit the company because getting reimbursement for travel expenses is such a hassle. His sales manager makes an urgent request to the controller for a credit card in the company's name to be issued to his salesman. The controller, doubtful of the need and worried about setting a precedent, contacts the company president for direction. The president tells him that if the sales vice president authorizes the card's issuance to the salesman, he will go along with it. He also asks the controller to research the matter and develop a general policy for handling such requests. The controller contacts the vice president, obtains approval, issues the card through the sales manager, and comes up with the following first rough sketch of a policy:

Credit Card Policy

A. Requests
  1. Initiation at any level
  2. Submittal only by management
B. Authorization
  1. Departmental verification of need
  2. Vice presidential signature
C. Issuance by company.

Before the card ever reaches the salesman, his wife divorces him and he quits his job to go to work for his brother, who owns a ski resort in Alberta, Canada.

Now, not only does the policy not reflect the unexpected ending of the little drama that spawned it, but its very form probably will continue to keep the people in the drama submerged and obscure. For when the controller resorted to an outline to portray the whole matter as comprehensively and compactly as he could, he was unwittingly setting up a pattern for succeeding versions that almost always leads to gobbledygook. The president will probably ask him to "flesh out" the outline, and he will arrive at something like this:

A. Requests for credit cards—The initiation of a request for a company credit card may occur at any level, but actual submittal of requests to the company should be performed by management.

B. Authorization—Full departmental need verification must be supplied.

The people in the drama have been ignored almost completely in the policy, and the result is unreadable verbiage. The cure, of course, is not necessarily to scrap the outlines, but to put the people back into the policy.

A. Requests for credit cards—Any employee may request a credit card, but only through a manager.
B. Authorization—If the manager verifies the employee's need for the card, the vice president may authorize its issuance.
C. Issuance—Upon receiving authorization, the controller will issue the card to the employee through the manager who submitted the request.

Questions on Reading

1. What is the main reason for policies being written in a long and dreary style in many organizations?
2. What style of writing is a compromise between the formality of the legalese style and the informality of the imperative style of writing policy statements?
3. What are the eight sections that the author considers as the maximum structure for a policy format?
4. What is Mr. Lybbert's principal suggestion to make policy readable?

5 QUANTITATIVE DECISION-MAKING TECHNIQUES

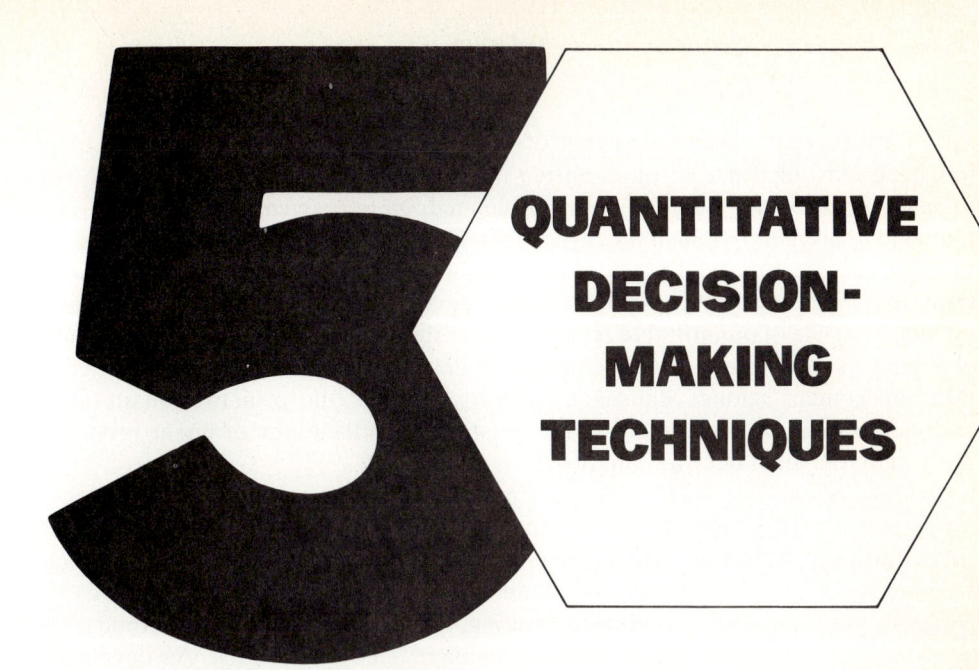

- Management Science
- Illustration of a Model
- Some Quantitative Techniques
- An Illustrative Application of Linear Programming
- Illustrative Applications of Statistical Decision Analysis
- Review
- Discussion Questions
- References
- Case Problem: Pliable Plastics Corporation
- Case Problem: Choice of Investments
- Case Problem: A Franchise Opportunity
- Applications Reading: "Treading Softly with Management Science" Roger D. Eck
- Questions on Reading

Particularly since the advent of the computer as a managerial tool, there has been expanded use of quantitative methods of analysis aimed at improving managerial decision making. Broadly defined, *management science* is a systemwide approach by which all variables in a decision situation are quantified for the purpose of analysis. This approach evolved from the development of operations research (OR) in the British military services during World War II, which included the use of quantitative techniques for the purpose of studying operational problems in the military. In this chapter we describe the general steps required in the management science approach, identify some of the principal quantitative techniques that are used, and provide illustrative applications of linear programming and statistical decision analysis.

Management Science Management science includes more than the application of quantitative, or mathematical, methods to decision making, although quantitative methods are largely the "language" of the approach. As developed in operations research, there are several general components, or steps, included in management science. These are:

1. A systemwide, or enterprisewide, orientation
2. Specific identification and measurement of the goals of the system
3. Specific identification and measurement of all variables that affect goal attainment
4. Construction of a mathematical model to represent the situation being studied

1 In its approach to decision making, management science emphasizes the use of a [departmental / systemwide] point of view.

systemwide

2 A synonym for "entire system," as it would apply in a business firm, would be _____.

the entire firm (or the entire organization, etc.)

3 On this basis, would you expect management science studies to be departmental, that is, within particular departments of an enterprise, or interdepartmental? [Departmental / Interdepartmental]

Interdepartmental

4 Of course, even though a systemwide point of view is encouraged, a particular problem may involve just specific functions within the enterprise. Thus, if an inventory problem is being studied, the entire enterprise [is / is not] necessarily involved.

is not

5 Once a problem or activity of interest has been identified, the first thing that would be done by the management science approach would be to identify the _____ of the process or activity.

goals (or objectives)

6 What might be one goal of a medical supply warehouse?

Not running out of supplies, minimum inventory, minimum spoilage, etc.

_____
_____
_____

7 Thus an overall objective for a firm might involve several subgoals. However, merely identifying the goals is not enough. We must also be able to _____ their attainment.

measure (or quantify)

8 After identifying goals and determining how they should be measured, we then identify the _____ that affect goal attainment in the process.

variables (factors, etc.)

9 And after these variables are identified, the way in which they are to be _____ must also be determined.

measured (or quantified)

10 After the goals and all variables involved have been identified and quantified, study of the system of relationships then "sets the stage" for constructing or choosing the appropriate _____ model.

mathematical (or quantitative)

11 A "good" mathematical model is one that accurately represents the pattern of relationships in a system. Therefore, the complexity of the mathematical techniques used [does / does not] necessarily indicate the adequacy of the model.

does not

12 Which of the following is the better statement? [a / b]
   a. The mathematical model must fit the problem of interest.

a

b. The problem must fit an available mathematical model.

13   Therefore, consistent use by an analyst of a particular mathematical technique, such as linear programming, to the exclusion of other techniques, suggests that either the study is of just particular types of organizational activities or the _____ _____ are often inappropriate.

mathematical models

14   Summarizing the steps in management science, we see that the _____ of the activity are first identified and quantified, then the _____ that affect goal attainment are identified and quantified, and finally a _____ _____ is chosen or constructed.

goals
variables

mathematical model

15   In general, the application of management science is more appropriate in which of the following two situations? [a / b]
a. A large number of decisions are to be made involving different problems.
b. A large number of decisions are to be made in the same problem area.

b (since a common mathematical model could then be used in conjunction with repeated decisions)

Illustration of a Model

A mathematical model can involve the use of any of a number of mathematical or statistical tools. In order to make our discussion of mathematical models more meaningful, an algebraic model utilizing the technique of differential calculus in its solution is illustrated in this section. An understanding of calculus is not necessary to appreciate the role this technique serves in the model.

16   As a simplified example, suppose that the rated quality of customer service in a particular type of department store increases with number of employees only up to a point, and then actually decreases. In this example, the quality of customer service (one of the goals of the store) is a function of what variable? _____

Number of employees

17   Incidentally, can you think of any reason why the

quality of customer service might decrease beyond some point of adding personnel?

The employees get too involved with one another instead of serving the customers (etc.). _____
_____
_____
_____

18 Assuming that we have been able to quantify the relationship between the variable and the goal in this particular problem, illustrate the *general form* of this relationship on the following graph.

19 The graph above can be considered a symbolic model for this problem. Suppose that this relationship can be represented by the equation $Y = 14X - 0.5X^2$.

mathematical The equation, then, is the _____ model representing the situation being studied.

20 Referring to the graph shown in Frame 18, what does the X represent in the equation $Y = 14X - 0.5X^2$?

Number of employees _____

21 Referring to the graph shown in Frame 18, what does the Y represent in the equation $Y = 14X - 0.5X^2$?

Quality of customer service _____

22 The optimum, or best, solution for this simplified problem is to find that value of X for which Y is a

maximum [minimum / maximum] value.

23 One way in which the value of X resulting in the maximum value of Y could be found is by taking different values of X and calculating the effect on the value of Y. Given that $Y = 14X - 0.5X^2$, what is the quality of customer service associated with having six employees in the store? Do your calculations below.

$Y = 14(6) - 0.5(6)^2$
$Y = 84 - 0.5(36)$
$Y = 84 - 18$
$Y = 66$

24 Refer to Figure 5.1. The table and graph indicate the value of Y associated with each of several values of X. At what value of X is Y maximized? $X =$ ____

14

Quality of customer service

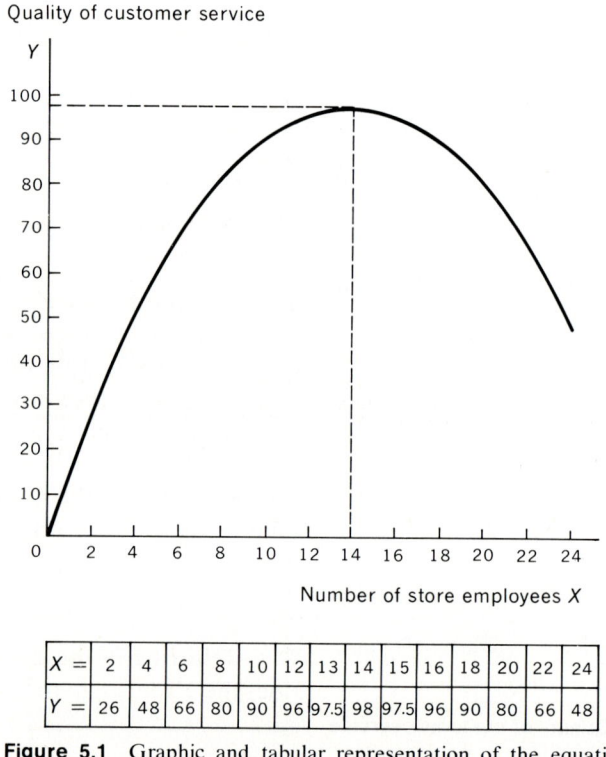

$X =$	2	4	6	8	10	12	13	14	15	16	18	20	22	24
$Y =$	26	48	66	80	90	96	97.5	98	97.5	96	90	80	66	48

Figure 5.1 Graphic and tabular representation of the equation $Y = 14X - 0.5X^2$

25 At fourteen employees, what is the quality of customer service? $Y =$ ____

98

26 In the figure, note that with either fewer or more than fourteen employees the quality of customer service is [increased / decreased].

decreased

27 The same solution could have been achieved more quickly through the application of differential calculus. On the graph in Figure 5.1, note the value of Y with respect to changes in the value of X first increases and then decreases. The optimum solution in this case is at the point where the *rate of change* for Y is zero, because at this point Y is at its [minimum / maximum] value.

maximum

28 For illustrative purposes, the solution to this problem using differential calculus is presented below. If you have not studied calculus, you need not be concerned about the specifics of this solution.

$Y = 14X - 0.5X^2$ basic mathematical model

$dY/dX = 14 - X$ rate of change of Y with respect to X

$0 = 14 - X$ point of optimization, where rate of change equals zero

$X = 14$ value of X at point of optimization

29 For our illustrative example, the optimum solution was that of attaining a maximum value of Y, the goal. Give an example of a goal for which we would want to attain the minimum value possible.

Amount of waste, waiting time, cost, etc.

_____

_____

minimum; maximum

30 Thus the optimum solution can be the attainment of either a _____ or a _____, depending on the type of goal involved.

Some Quantitative Techniques

In the section just concluded, we had an illustration of the use of calculus in finding the optimum solution in a decision-making situation. In this section, we briefly describe the use of several additional techniques of quantitative analysis in management science.

31 Calculus, probability analysis, queuing theory, the simulation method, and linear programming are among the quantitative techniques used to find

_____ solutions in decision-making situations.

optimum

32 The application of *probability analysis* is appropriate whenever the value of one or more variables in the model cannot be definitely specified, but the likelihood of the value being at various levels is [known / unknown].

known

33 If a manager knows that "there is only a 5 percent chance that consumer demand for January will be less than 10,000 units," has the risk been removed from decision making? [Yes / No]

No

34 If the specific probabilities associated with various events have been determined, a manager can act to [minimize / maximize] the overall risk associated with decision acts.

minimize

35 In many situations, not only the degree of risk but also the expected gain, or expected monetary value, associated with each possible _____ can be ascertained.

decision (or decision act)

36 Expected monetary values can be determined for sequential acts as well as individual acts. Because this method of analysis has been given increasing attention in recent years, the final part of this chapter is devoted to illustrating the computation of expected monetary values. In general, when expected monetary values are determined, that decision act is best for which the expected value is [minimized / maximized].

maximized

37 In contrast to the use of probability analysis, *queuing theory* is applicable to waiting-line situations, such as may be involved when several departments use a centrally located computer. When departments or individuals must wait for service of some kind, the delay in service represents a cost in the organization. Is there also a cost involved in reducing or eliminating waiting lines? [Yes / No]

Yes

38 Thus balancing the cost of bottlenecks against the cost of idle capacity is the principal characteristic of the type of problem to which _____ theory can be applied.

queuing

Some Quantitative Techniques ● 133

39 A facility that is too small incurs high costs of waiting by customers, whereas a facility that is too large incurs high idle-time costs. The optimum solution to this type of problem is the one that [minimizes / maximizes] the sum of the two types of cost.

minimizes

40 In what decision-making area might queuing theory be applied in a self-service department store? _____
_____

Determining the number of checkout stands to be provided (etc.)

41 In our endeavor to achieve an optimum solution to organizational problems, we have thus far considered the use of three quantitative decision-making techniques in this chapter: _____, _____ analysis, and _____.

calculus; probability; queuing theory

42 *Linear programming* is another technique used to maximize a gain or minimize a loss. This technique of analysis has been applied extensively, and is useful when there are several variables that affect the attainment of a desired goal and the problem is to choose the best combination of values for these variables. As the name of this technique implies, the relationship between each one of the variables and the goal must be [linear / nonlinear]. That is, a constant change in a variable results in a constant change in goal attainment.

linear

43 For example, a hat manufacturer who wants to determine the quantity of each of several types of hats to manufacture in order to maximize revenue could attempt a mathematical analysis of the problem using the technique of _____ _____.

linear programming

44 Suppose that the hat manufacturer finds that the markup for certain hats gets progressively smaller as production of that type of hat is increased. Because of the nonlinear relationship between production volume and revenue, this problem [does / does not] lend itself to the use of linear programming.

does not (But if the relationship is linear for a certain range of values, the technique can be used within that range.)

45 Despite the requirement that relationships must be approximately _____, the technique of linear

linear

programming has had extensive application in production, transportation, and inventory problems. Because of this, a relatively detailed example of the application of linear programming is included in the following section of this chapter.

46 The four quantitative techniques which have been

calculus;
probability analysis;
queuing theory;
linear programming

thus far described in this chapter are _____, _____, _____, _____, and _____.

47 Finally, the last technique we consider is the *simulation method*. This method incorporates features common to both mathematical models and probability analysis. It is particularly useful when there are several variables affecting results, and further, when these variables are themselves uncertain and subject to probability analysis. Therefore, the simulation method is useful in decision situations that are relatively

complex

[simple / complex].

48 The value of some outcome, such as the inventory level for a particular item at a future point in time, is dependent on such uncertain factors as level of sales, delivery time, and spoilage or inventory loss. Since there are several factors involving a different probability distribution for each factor, the probabilities associated with the several possible inventory levels can

simulation

be determined by application of the _____ method.

49 When the simulation method was first developed it was called the *Monte Carlo method,* because a modified roulette wheel was used to simulate the outcome of each variable affecting the result. The use of this name also indicated that the outcome itself is [de-

probabilistic

terministic / probabilistic] in nature.

50 Instead of manually operated roulette wheels, computers are now used to generate the results of a large number of "trial runs" when the

simulation

_____ method is used.

51 By way of summary, let us review some applications of the five quantitative decision-making methods which have been briefly described. In a particular company, it has been found that product development per dollar spent on research and development increases up to a particular point of expenditure and then decreases; that is, the relationship is curvilinear. The mathematical technique that might be useful to determine the optimum research and development expenditure in this case is _____.

calculus

52 The problem of determining how many machine repairmen to have on call so as to minimize the combined cost of the repairmen's idle time and the machine idle time lends itself to the use of _____ _____.

queuing theory

53 Given the situation in which each of a number of transportation routes has a direct relationship to total transportation cost and in which the objective is to find that combination of routes which minimizes the total cost, the applicable mathematical technique would be _____ _____.

linear programming

54 Making an investment decision on the basis of considering the possible losses and gains associated with each act and the likelihood of each loss or gain involves the application of _____ _____.

probability analysis

55 Finally, given a situation in which the development time for a new product depends on the time required to complete several major project segments, each of which requires an uncertain amount of time, the probabilities that the total required time will be at various levels can be determined by using the _____ method.

simulation

An Illustrative Application of Linear Programming

Because of the extensive application of linear programming to decision-making situations, an example of its use in a production planning problem is given in this section.

56 Suppose that a furniture manufacturer specializes in just two types of products, tables and hutches, which we refer to as products A and B, respectively.

Referring to Figure 5.2, what is the gross revenue associated with producing each unit of product A? ____
Of B? ____

$60
$80

Product	Gross revenue per unit	Process 1: cutting and trimming	Process 2: assembling	Process 3: finishing
A (Tables)	$60	1.8 h	3.0 h	1.5 h
B (Hutches)	$80	2.0 h	2.0 h	4.0 h

Figure 5.2 Process times for two products.

57 In Figure 5.2, each table requires 1.8 hours of cutting and trimming, 3.0 hours of assembling, and 1.5 hours of finishing, for a total of 6.3 hours. Similarly, each hutch involves ____ hours of cutting and trimming, ____ hours of assembling, and ____ hours of finishing, for a total of ____ hours.

2.0
2.0; 4.0
8.0

58 Assuming a market for as many tables and/or hutches as can be produced, what are we trying to optimize through the application of linear programming in this particular problem?
_____

Gross revenue (see next frame)

59 In this decision-making situation, the optimum solution is that level of production for A and for B that results in the highest gross revenue. Referring to Figure 5.2, we can state this objective in the form of an equation as

80   Maximize: $60X_A + $ ____ X_B

where X_A and X_B represent the number of units of each product to be produced.

60 In the language of linear programming, *constraints* represent the limitations that affect the values of one or more of the variables. In a product-mix problem, the fact that production capacity is limited by

An Illustrative Application of Linear Programming

the existing facilities represents a major source of constraints. For each of the three production processes, we assume the availability of just 1800 working hours per month. Thus for process 1, $1.8X_A + 2X_B \leq 1800$; that is, the hours of process 1 devoted to producing units of product A plus the hours devoted to producing product B must be less than or equal to 1800 hours per month. In view of this constraint, can we plan to produce 500 tables and 500 hutches per month (refer to Figure 5.2)? [Yes/ No] Why or why not?

No. The total number of required hours for process 1 would equal 1900 hours, which exceeds the capacity in that department.

61 In view of the constraint $1.8X_A + 2X_B \leq 1800$, can we plan to produce 900 hutches and no tables? [Yes / No] _____

Yes, the constraint does not demand that we produce both products.

62 Similarly, how would you state the constraint, or restriction, of having just 1800 hours per month available for process 2 (refer to Figure 5.2)?

3; 2
$$\_\_ X_A + \_\_ X_B \leq 1800$$

63 State the 1800-hour constraint for process 3 in the form of an equation.

$1.5X_A + 4X_B \leq 1800$

64 For this problem, the objective function is

$$\text{Maximize:} \quad 60X_B + 80X_B$$

subject to the constraints:

$$1.8X_A + 2X_B \leq 1800$$
$$3X_A + 2X_B \leq 1800$$
$$1.5X_A + 4X_B \leq 1800$$

Are there any other constraints imposed in this problem? [Yes / No]

Yes (see next frame)

65 There is an additional category of constraints that is

138 • Chapter 5 • Quantitative Decision-Making Techniques

perhaps so obvious that we hardly think of it in these terms. This constraint is that neither X_A nor X_B can be negative in value (which is, of course, impossible in the practical sense, since we cannot produce a negative quantity of something). Therefore, the quantities of products A and B to be produced must be greater than or equal to zero. Symbolically, the nonnegativity constraint for A is $X_A \geq 0$, and for B it is _____.

$X_B \geq 0$

66 We now proceed to solve this linear programming problem by the graphic method. There are algebraic methods of attaining the optimum solution, which we briefly consider later. In that the solution can be visually portrayed by the graphic method, this method of solution is [the least / among the more] complex.

the least

67 The first step in the graphic solution to a linear programming problem is to chart the constraints on the graph. The first restriction, for the available time in process 1, is $1.8X_A + 2X_B \leq 1800$. If we were to produce only tables and use the full 1800 hours of process 1, how many tables would be manufactured? _____ Similarly, how many hutches would be produced if only hutches were manufactured? _____

1000
900

68 Refer to Figure 5.3. The line on the graph represents the equation _____ + _____ = _____. Note that the values of X_A and X_B at which this line intersects each axis are equal to the values just computed in the previous frame.

$1.8X_A$; $2X_B$; 1800

69 Since the constraint stated "less than or equal to," the feasible-solution area is the entire shaded area below the line of constraint. Why doesn't the feasible-solution area extend below or to the left of the two axes of the graph? _____

Because of the nonnegativity constraints for X_A and X_B (because neither X_A nor X_B can have a negative value).

70 In the graphic solution of a linear programming problem, the area of the graph whose values conform

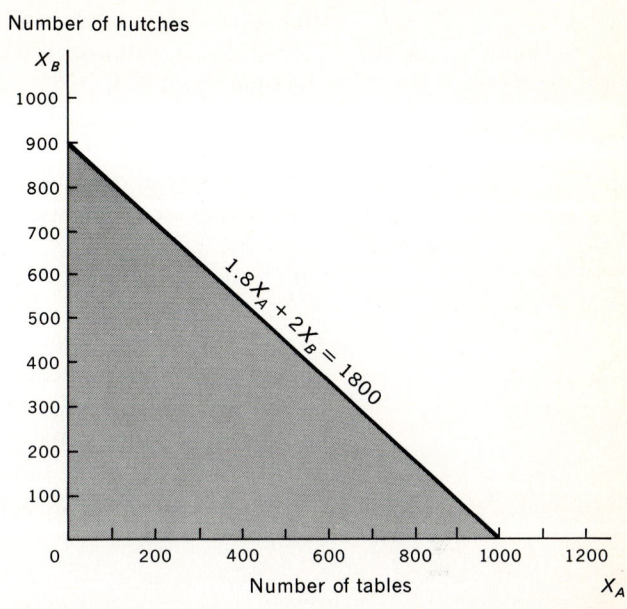

```
            Number of hutches
            X_B
       1000
        900
        800
        700
        600
        500      1.8X_A + 2X_B = 1800
        400
        300
        200
        100
          0    200   400   600   800  1000  1200
                    Number of tables              X_A
```

Figure 5.3 The graphic representation of a constraint in linear programming.

feasible-solution to, or satisfy, the constraints in the problem is called the _____ area.

71 Suppose the production restriction for process 1, which is portrayed in Figure 5.3, were the only constraint in this problem, other than the nonnegativity constraints. How many feasible solutions to this problem would there be (not necessarily all optimum)?

A great number are possible because all combinations of values for X_A and X_B in the shaded area qualify as possible solutions.

72 As far as the *constraints* in this problem are concerned, is the decision to produce no tables and no hutches within the feasible-solution area? [Yes / No]

Yes

73 Many solutions are possible, but there is only one optimum solution. Looking back at Figure 5.2, and recalling that our objective is to maximize $60X_A + 80X_B$, what is the optimum solution with only

140 • Chapter 5 • Quantitative Decision-Making Techniques

0; 900

the one major constraint involved? Produce _____ [number] tables and _____ [number] hutches.

$72,000

optimum

74 At the production level of 900 hutches and no tables, the gross revenue, which is _____, has been maximized; that is, this production plan represents the _____ solution to the problem with only the one major restriction.

75 Of course, the solution we have just described is not the final solution, because only one constraint was considered. Refer to Figure 5.4. We have now entered the two remaining constraints on the graph. Is the feasible-solution area now larger or smaller than before we added the remaining two constraints?

Smaller

[Larger / Smaller]

Number of hutches

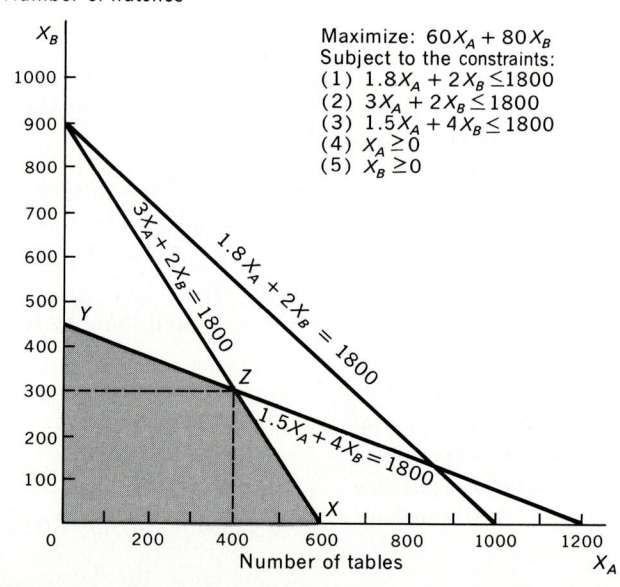

Maximize: $60X_A + 80X_B$
Subject to the constraints:
(1) $1.8X_A + 2X_B \leq 1800$
(2) $3X_A + 2X_B \leq 1800$
(3) $1.5X_A + 4X_B \leq 1800$
(4) $X_A \geq 0$
(5) $X_B \geq 0$

Number of tables

Figure 5.4 The graphic solution of a linear programming problem.

1

76 In Figure 5.4, the feasible-solution area is such that we cannot possibly use the full 1800-hour capacity for process _____.

77 Since we want to maximize gross revenue, the op-

An Illustrative Application of Linear Programming ● 141

timum solution lies somewhere along the line *YZX* in Figure 5.4, and, specifically, it is at point *Y*, *Z*, or *X*. No point within the shaded area could maximize gross revenue because all these points involve unnecessary idle capacity in processes ___ and ___.

2; 3

78 Using the data from Figure 5.4, complete the following chart:

	TABLES (A)		HUTCHES (B)		
Point on graph	No. of units	Revenue per unit	No. of units	Revenue per unit	Total revenue
Y	0	$60	450	$80	$36,000
Z	___	$60	___	$80	$___
X	___	$60	___	$80	$___

400; 300; 48,000
600; 0; 36,000

79 The optimum solution to this problem, then, is to produce ___ [number] tables and ___ [number] hutches. At these productions levels all the constraints are satisfied, and gross revenue is maximized; that is, no other product mix within the feasible-solution area would yield a higher gross-revenue figure.

400; 300

80 In this example two variables affected the goal of maximizing gross revenue, the number of units of products A and B, and thus a two-dimensional graph was required in the solution. Since each additional variable, or product, would add another dimension to the graph, the graphic method of solving a linear programming problem is useful when only ___ [number] variables are involved in the problem.

two
(Conceivably, a three-dimensional graph could also be constructed.)

81 An algebraic technique for solving more complex linear programming problems is the simplex method. There are actually several variations to the technique, but it is particularly applicable whenever a [small / large] number of variables is involved in the problem.

large

82 The optimum product mix in a plant capable of producing twelve different products in ten different departments, with different production times involved, could be determined by applying the ___ method of solving a linear programming problem.

simplex

83 A simplified version of the simplex method, which was developed specifically for problems involving the movement of products from several sources to several destinations, has been referred to as the *transportation method*. Would this technique apply to the kind of linear programming problem that we used to illustrate the graphic method? [Yes / No]

No (since ours was a product-mix problem)

84 Suppose that we have four factories producing similar mechandise and seven warehouses that are geographically dispersed. Determining how much of the production of each factory should be shipped to each warehouse could be done by using the _____ method of solving the linear programming problem.

transportation (also by the more involved simplex method)

85 Of the three methods that we have described for solving linear programming problems, the mathematically most complex is the _____ method, the least complex is the _____ method, whereas intermediate in complexity is the _____ method.

simplex
graphic
transportation

Illustrative Applications of Statistical Decision Analysis

Probability analysis plays a role in a number of quantitative methods. The method of analysis by which economic consequences as well as probability values are considered for the purpose of determining the best decision act has been referred to as *statistical decision analysis*. In the context in which a final commitment by the choice of some one decision act is required, the analysis typically begins by constructing a table of conditional economic consequences, or a *decision table*. When a sequence of decision acts is required, a *decision tree* typically is constructed to aid in the analysis. In this section we illustrate the application of statistical decision analysis in these two types of situations using relatively simple examples.

86 Suppose a manufacturer faces the decision of whether or not to manufacture and market a particular product. The possible decision acts are "manufacture" or "don't manufacture." For the purposes of our simplified example we classify the possible levels of market demand as being "low," "moderate," or "high" at the required price level. Therefore, if the decision table to be constructed is to include a row for each possible decision act and a column for each possible state, then in this case the decision table will have ___ [number] rows and ___ [number] columns.[1]

2
3

87 The basic framework for the decision table is presented below. The next step is to enter the economic consequences in the cells of the table. For example, if the product is not manufactured then the economic consequence would be zero gain no matter what the state, since there can be no gain (or loss) if the product is not marketed. Therefore, enter the appropriate values in the second row of the table below.

	STATE		
Decision act	S_1 (Low demand)	S_2 (Moderate demand)	S_3 (High demand)
D_1 (manufacture)			
D_2 (don't manufacture)			

0; 0; 0

88 Now, in order to complete the first row of the decision table we need to know more about the risk situation. Suppose that the capital investment which is required is such that if demand is low there will be a net loss of $300,000 (gain of −$300,000), if demand is moderate there will be a gain of $50,000, and if demand is high there will be a gain of $250,000 (all in present dollar values). Accordingly, enter these values in the appropriate cells of the table in Frame 87.

In row 1: −300,000; 50,000; 250,000

89 In constructing the decision table, or payoff table, for a decision situation, we identify every possible decision act and every possible economic con-

---

[1] Some textbooks in decision analysis follow the opposite convention and designate the possible states in the rows of the decision table and the available acts as column headings. Therefore, the reader should be alert to this possible difference when referring to different books.

sequence depending on the state that occurs. For example, referring to the table in Frame 87, we see that the consequence associated with manufacturing the product and moderate market demand developing is a _____ [gain / loss].

$50,000; gain

90 Since statistical decision analysis includes the use of probability values as well as economic consequences, the next step is to determine the probability of each state (of demand, in this case). On the basis of previous experience with similar products as well as a market study, suppose that the probability values associated with low, moderate, and high market demand are determined to be 0.20, 0.50, and 0.30, respectively. Enter these values in the table below.

0.20; 0.50; 0.30

	STATE		
Decision act	S_1 (Low demand) (P = ___)	S_2 (Moderate demand) (P = ___)	S_3 (High demand) (P = ___)
D_1 (manufacture)	−$300,000	$50,000	$250,000
D_2 (don't manufacture)	0	0	0

91 The final step leading to the identification of the best act is to determine the expected monetary value (EMV) for each possible act. Mathematically, this is simply the sum of the products of each conditional value for an act multiplied by the respective probability. In this case, three products are summed for each of the two acts. Therefore, for the illustrative decision problem the expected monetary values are:

−300,000
50,000; 250,000; 40,000

$$\text{EMV}(D_1) = 0.20\ (\underline{\qquad}) + 0.50\ (\underline{\qquad}) + 0.30\ (\underline{\qquad}) = \underline{\qquad}$$

0; 0
0; 0

$$\text{EMV}(D_2) = 0.20\ (\underline{\ }) + 0.50\ (\underline{\ }) + 0.30\ (\underline{\ }) = \underline{\ }$$

92 Comparing the expected monetary values for the available decision acts, the best decision in this case is [D_1 / D_2]. Is it possible that the "best act" will turn out to be the incorrect one in a particular decision situation? [Yes / No] What is the probability of this occur-

D_1

Yes

0.20 (which is the probability of experiencing a loss) ring in our illustrative problem? $P = $ _____.

93 Thus, the choice of the "best act" in statistical decision analysis does not assure the correctness of each decision, but is oriented toward optimizing the average economic result over the long run, when many such decisions are made. As contrasted to the situation above, frequently the decision problem is more complicated in that the first decision to be made leads sequentially to the necessity of making other decisions based on intermediate results. For example, the first decision may be whether or not to develop a product, and then the second decision may be concerned with the level of manufacturing if the product is in fact successfully developed. This type of problem is portrayed in Figure 5.5. As indicated in this figure, the type of graph used to analyze a decision problem involving

decision tree sequential decisions is the _____.

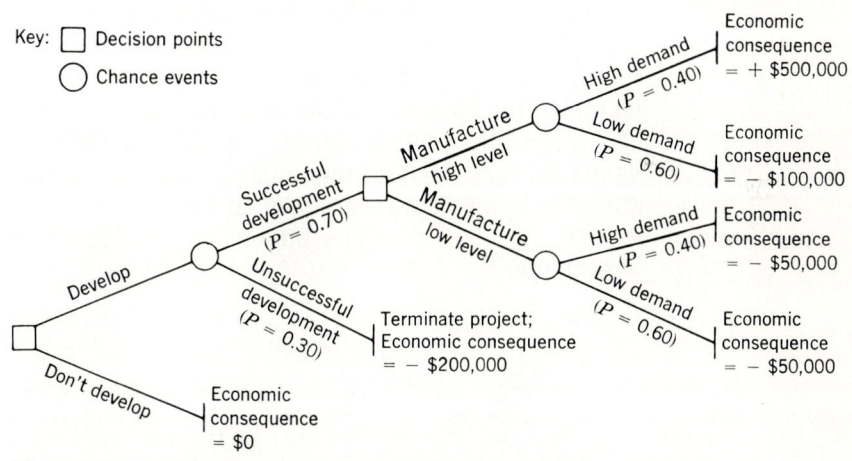

Figure 5.5 Decision tree for the sequential decision problem.

94 The decision tree portrays all decision acts and the states that can occur in their sequential order of occurrence. In Figure 5.5, note that the points of
☐ required decision are designated by the symbol ___,
while the points at which chance events occur are
○ designated by the symbol ___.

95 In Figure 5.5 two points of decision are identified: first, whether or not to _develop_ the product, and then if the product is successfully developed, the level of _manufacturing_ of the product.

96 The value of decision tree analysis is that it permits the decision maker to "look ahead" to the implications of an initial decision. In this case, we would not want to begin development of the product if later market prospects did not look good. For this reason, illustrated in the following frames, the computational analysis using a decision tree proceeds from right to left, rather than left to right. In terms of "looking ahead," one observation we can make by referring to Figure 5.5, even without any further calculation at this point, is that the decision to develop the product will prove to be the right one only if (1) the product [can / cannot] _can_ be developed and (2) subsequent demand for the product is [high / low]. _high_

97 The determination of the best act at each decision point is similar to decision table analysis, in that the act with the largest EMV is designated as the best act. Figure 5.6 repeats the decision tree with EMV values identified for all acts. To illustrate that these values have been calculated as before, note that the EMV of $140,000 for "Manufacture high level" was determined by summing two products as follows:

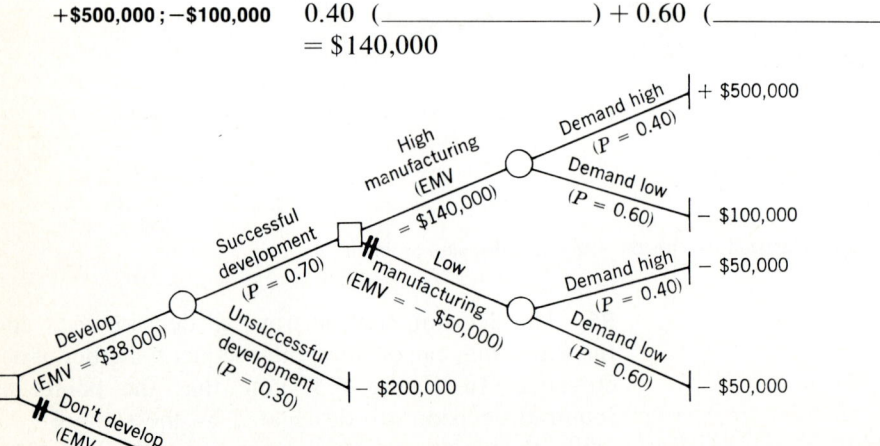

+$500,000 ; −$100,000   0.40 (_____) + 0.60 (_____) = $140,000

Figure 5.6 Decision tree for the sequential decision problem with expected monetary values (EMV) included.

Review ● 147

98 Therefore, given sucessful product development (and working right to left in terms of the decision points in this problem) the two decision acts available are to manufacture at a high level, with an associated EMV of $_____, or to manufacture at a low level, with an associated EMV of $_____. Therefore, given successful product development the best act is to manufacture at a [high / low] level.

$140,000
−$50,000

high

99 It is common practice to eliminate nonpreferred acts on the decision tree by a double bar (//) as is done in Figure 5.6. Now we move left to the next decision point, which is in fact the initial decision point in this problem. Because the monetary values associated with branches that are eliminated are ignored in any further analysis, we can observe that if we choose to develop the product then two economic consequences are possible: the product will be successfully developed, leading to an EMV of $140,000, or the product will not be developed, leading to a loss of $200,000. Therefore:

$140,000
−$200,000; $38,000

EMV (develop) = 0.70 (_____)
+ 0.30 (_____) = _____

100 With respect to the first decision point, then, we have the choice of developing the product, with an associated EMV of $_____, or not developing the product, with an associated EMV of $__. Therefore, the best act is to [develop / not develop] the product.

$38,000
$0
develop

101 Following this "best decision," if product development is in fact unsuccessful the decision process is terminated with a $_____ loss. If development is successful then the best decision with respect to the production level is to manufacture at a [high / low] level.

$200,000

high

Review

goals (or objectives)

102 The first step in the management science approach is the identification and quantification of the _____ of the system. (Frames 1 to 7)

variables

103 Following the identification and measurement of the goals of the system, the _____ that affect goal attainment are identified and measured. (Frames 8 and 9)

104 Having identified and quantified all goals and variables in a decision-making situation, the next step is to select or construct the appropriate _____ _____ to represent the system of relationships. (Frames 10 to 15)

mathematical model

105 Throughout, the orientation of management science is [departmental / systemwide]. (Frames 1 to 4)

systemwide

106 In general, on what basis should a mathematical technique be chosen? (Frames 16 to 30)

Appropriateness to the situation; representativeness of the way the variables actually interact, etc.

107 Considering now the specific quantitative techniques which have been described, the method that is appropriate when costs associated with idle capacity must be balanced against costs of waiting is _____ _____. (Frames 37 to 41, 52)

queuing theory

108 The total cost of detecting output of poor quality first decreases and then increases as personnel are added to a particular inspection department. The mathematical method that can be used to find the point of minimum cost in this case is _____. (Frames 27 to 30, 51)

calculus

109 The manager who attaches quantitative estimates of the likelihood of various events as an aid to decision making is utilizing _____ _____. (Frames 31 to 36, 54)

probability analysis

110 An estimate of the probabilities that various numbers of employees will leave company employment during the coming year, based on probabilities of departure for each of several categories of reasons, can be determined by the application of the _____ method. (Frames 47 to 50, 55)

simulation

Review ● 149

linear programming

111 The mathematical method that is appropriate when we want to determine how many units of each of a number of products should be manufactured within departmental capacity limitations so as to maximize revenue is _____ _____. (Frames 42 to 45, 53, 56 to 85)

constraints (or restrictions)

112 The first step in the graphic solution to a linear programming problem is to construct a graph representing the quantities of the two variables and to chart, or enter, the _____ on this graph. (Frames 56 to 68)

feasible-solution

113 The area on the graph whose values satisfy the constraints in the problem is called the _____ area. (Frames 69 to 73)

optimum

114 Within the feasible-solution area, that combination of values for the two variables which results in the _____ solution is chosen. (Frames 74 to 80)

simplex

115 When a linear programming problem includes more than two variables, such as product quantities, the method of solving the linear programming problem which is more appropriate than the graphic solution is the _____ method. (Frames 81, 82, and 85)

transportation

116 A simplified version of the simplex method, which is applicable to such problems as minimizing shipment costs when several sources and destinations are involved, has been called the _____ method. (Frames 83 to 85)

decision act;
state (either order)

117 When a decision table is used for the purpose of statistical decision analysis, each value in the body of this table represents the economic consequence associated with a particular _____ and a particular _____. (Frames 86 to 89)

expected monetary value (EMV)

118 The "best act" in statistical decision analysis is the one that has the highest _____ _____. (Frames 90 to 92)

119 When sequential decisions are involved, the type of graph frequently used in conjunction with statistical decision analysis is the _____ _____. (Frames 93 to 95)

decision
tree

120 The first decision point subjected to analysis is the decision point located in the extreme [left / right] portion of the decision tree. (Frames 96 to 101)

right

Discussion Questions

1. What is the relationship between the managerial function of planning and the use of quantitative decision-making techniques?
2. Discuss the major steps included in the management science approach. Is there any importance to the sequence of these steps?
3. For what type of decision-making situations is the construction of a mathematical model feasible and worthwhile?
4. Give examples of problems to which calculus, queuing theory, and the simulation method could be appropriately applied.
5. Discuss linear programming from the standpoint of the major assumption of this technique and the type of decision-making situations in which it can be used.
6. At what level or levels in the organization should managers have familiarity with the concepts and techniques of management science?
7. Describe the basic procedure followed in statistical decision analysis, in terms of what factors need to identified, what values need to be determined, and the basis used for determining the "best decision."
8. In the case of sequential decision analysis, describe the logic of working from right to left in the decision tree analysis, rather than the left-to-right orientation that might seem to be more natural in terms of the actual sequence of decision acts and events.
9. Refer to the sequential decision problem illustrated in this chapter. If you were the manufacturer, would you choose to adopt the "best act"? In answering this question, consider the probabilities associated with the events that follow this decision as well as the EMV associated with the decision.
10. Some managers have argued that quantitative decision analysis may be appropriate in certain technical areas of decision making, but that it is inappropriate in the broader decision areas in which managerial ingenuity is impor-

tant. In what respects may such an opinion be correct? In what respects is it incorrect?

References

Anderson, D. R., D. J. Sweeney, and T. A. Williams. *An Introduction to Management Science.* St. Paul, Minn.: West, 1976.

Anderson, J. C., and T. R. Hoffman. "A Perspective on the Implementation of Management Science." *The Academy of Management Review,* vol. 3, no. 3, July 1978.

De Serpa, A. C., S. D. Gerking, and W. J. Boyes. "Linear Programming and the Value of Resources." *Arizona Business,* vol. 22, no. 6, June-July 1975.

Eck, R. D. *QM: An Introduction to Quantitative Methods for Business Application.* Belmont, California: Wadsworth, 1979.

Fuller, J. A., and R. M. Atherton. "Fitting in the Management Science Specialist," *Business Horizons,* vol. 22, no. 2, April 1979.

Green, T. B., W. B. Newsom, and S. R. Jones. "A Survey of the Application of Quantitative Techniques to Production/Operations Management in Large Corporations." *Academy of Management Journal,* vol. 20, no. 4, December 1977.

Heinze, D. *Management Science: Introductory Concepts and Applications.* Cincinnati, Ohio: South-Western, 1978.

Hillier, F. S., and G. J. Lieberman, *Operations Research,* 2d ed. San Francisco: Holden-Day, 1974.

Hocking, R. T., and J. M. Hocking. "The Evolution of Decision Systems." *MSU Business Topics,* vol. 24, no. 3, Summer 1976.

Hora, S. C. "A Path to Better Decision Making." *Arizona Business,* vol. 22, no. 2, February 1975.

Kazmier, L. J. *Business Statistics.* New York: McGraw-Hill (Schaum's Outline Series), 1976.

Kazmier, L. J. *Statistical Analysis for Business and Economics,* 3d ed. (a programmed text). New York: McGraw-Hill, 1978.

Kazmier, L. J. *Basic Statistics for Business and Economics.* New York: McGraw-Hill, 1979.

Lapin, L. *Statistics for Modern Business Decisions,* 2d ed. New York: Harcourt Brace Jovanovich, 1978.

Leavitt, H. J. "Beyond the Analytic Manager." *California Management Review,* vol. 17, no. 3, Spring 1975.

Levin, R. I., and C. A. Kirkpatrick. *Quantitative Approaches to Management,* 3d ed. New York: McGraw-Hill, 1975.

McKenney, J. L., and P. G. W. Keen. "How Managers' Minds Work." *Harvard Business Review,* vol. 52, no. 3, May-June 1974.

Miller, D. W., and M. K. Starr. *Exective Decisions and Operations Research.* Englewood Cliffs, N.J.: Prentice-Hall, 1960.
Oxenfeldt, A. R. "Effective Decision Making for the Business Executive." *Management Review,* vol. 67, no. 2, February 1978.
Pappas, J. L., and D. W. Wichern. "On the Selection of Critical Values in Sequential Decision Problems." *Decision Sciences,* vol. 8, no. 2, April 1977.
Rue, J. "Techniques and Administration of Sampling Projects." *Arizona Business,* vol. 23, no. 8, October 1976.
Savin, R. K. "Elicitation of Subjective Probabilities in the Context of Decision Making." *Decision Sciences,* vol. 9, no 2, January 1978.
Sullivan, W. G., and W. W. Claycombe. "The Use of Decision Trees in Planning Plant Expansion." *Advanced Management Journal,* vol. 40, no. 1, Winter 1975.

CASE PROBLEM: Pliable Plastics Corporation

The Pliable Plastics Corporation is organized into four manufacturing departments with the process-time availability per month indicated in the table below. The company has just been presented with the opportunity to produce either a toy dump truck set or a doll to the extent of the company's full capacity, or to produce any combination of the two items, for a national distributor. The dolls and trucks are to be packed in boxes containing one dozen of either one or the other item. The manufacturing manager estimates that each box of one dozen dolls will require 1.5 hours of molding, 2.0 hours of assembly, 2.0 hours of artwork, and 1.0 hours of packaging. She estimates that each box of a dozen trucks will require 2.5 hours of molding time, 1.0 hours of assembly, 0.5 hours of artwork, and 1.0 hours of packaging. The distributor will pay $80 for each box of dolls and $50 for each box of trucks. How many boxes of dolls and/or trucks should be scheduled for production next month so as to maximize gross revenue? Why might company management decide not to take advantage of this opportunity?

Department	Hours of process time (per month)
Molding	2000
Assembly	1500
Art	1000
Packaging	1500

CASE PROBLEM: Choice of Investments

An individual wishes to invest $50,000 in one of three ways during the coming year: in an insured savings account, a mutual common-stock fund, or in common-stock options. Funds put into a savings account are assured of a $5\frac{1}{2}$ percent rate of return (ignore the compounding of interest for the purposes of this problem). The return on the other investment opportunities depends on the state of the economy during the coming year, however. After reviewing several economic forecasts, the investor decides that the probability that the economy will be in an expansion is 0.30, that it will be stable is 0.60, and that it will be in a recession is 0.10. The mutual fund investment will result in an approximate gain of $7500 if the economy is in an expansion, $2500 if the economy is stable, and −$10,000 if there is a recession. Similarly, investments in stock options will result in an approximate gain of $50,000 if the economy is in an expansion, −$10,000 if the economy is stable, and −$30,000 if there is a recession. Construct the decision table and determine the best decision act for this investment situation. Consider any implications of adopting the "best act."

CASE PROBLEM: A Franchise Opportunity

An investor is considering placing a deposit of $10,000 to reserve a franchise opportunity in a new residential area for one year. There are two areas of uncertainty associated with this sequential decision situation: whether or not a prime franchise competitor will decide to locate an outlet in the same area and whether or not the residential area will develop to be a moderate or large market. Overall, then, the investor must first decide whether to deposit the initial $10,000 as a down payment for the franchise. Then during the one-year period the decision of the competing franchise system will be revealed, and the investor estimates that there is a 30 percent chance that the competing franchise system will also develop an outlet. After the decision of the competing system is known, the investor must then decide whether or not to proceed with constructing the franchise outlet. If there is competition and the market is large, the net gain during the relevant period is estimated as being $15,000; if the market is moderate, this will be a net loss of $10,000. If there is no competition and the market is large, the net gain will be $30,000; if the market is moderate, there will be a net gain of $10,000. The investor estimates that there is about a 60 percent chance that the market will be large. Using decision-tree analysis, determine whether or not the initial deposit of $10,000 to reserve the franchise opportunity should be made.

APPLICATIONS READING:

Treading Softly with Management Science

Roger D. Eck

Associate Professor
Arizona State University

Management science—known also as operations research, operations analysis and systems analysis—was a *cause célèbre* of the early 1960s. The prevailing opinion was that a blend of computers, science, and sophisticated mathematical techniques would bring dramatic changes to the executive suite. Now, after two decades of gestation, we are discovering that management science is not living up to its advanced billing.

Organizations that employ computer specialists, management scientists, operations analysts, and other technical specialists have been, or soon will be, urged to reevaluate the role of such specialists. Three questions are pertinent: (1) In what respect has management science failed? (2) Why has management science failed? (3) What are appropriate organizational responses to management science? It is to these issues that this article is addressed.

As a foundation for discussion, it is useful to distinguish between the roles that have been historically assumed by the manager and by the management scientist.

Manager/Management Science

The *manager* has been traditionally concerned with planning, directing, coordinating, and controlling organizational activities. Of primary concern is the realization that managers state (subject to the approval of higher boards) organizational objectives and select the programs that will be employed to attain the objectives. The manager is held responsible for goal attainment, and managers quite reasonably consider a good decision to be a decision that attains the prescribed objectives. Because managers make decisions in an environment where a lack of information and risk predominate, the decision-making procedures that executives use incorporate historical experiences, intuition, thumbrules, and luck.

The management scientist normally serves as an advisor to the manager, and is most often found in a staff position or in a consulting capacity. The management scientist has been traditionally concerned with attempts to make the

Source: From *Arizona Business,* vol. 22, no. 1, January 1975. Reprinted by permission of the Bureau of Business and Economic Research, College of Business Administration, Arizona State University.

decision-making process more systematic. For example, the management scientist might attempt to specify the factors that should be (not "are") considered in selecting a new plant site. To the management scientist, a good decision is a decision that, irrespective of the final outcome, is made in a logical manner. Management scientists make extensive use of computers, statistical procedures, and other mathematical devices.

The charges against management science concern the extent to which management scientists have been able to assist managers.

Criticisms

C. West Churchman charges that the preparation for dealing with "textbook uncertainty" that is afforded by such disciplines as management science has little to do with preparation for "executive uncertainty."[1] C. Jackson Grayson argues that "the impact of management science has been extremely small" and asserts that management science "appears to be unable to assist in a dynamic decision-making environment."[2] Herbert A. Simon suggests that science-oriented disciplines demand a commitment to knowledge creation that detracts from the advancement of an ability to use knowledge in the actual decision-making processes of organizations.[3]

Underlying Problems

The implications of such charges are that management science does not directly confront the executive function, falls far short of providing the pragmatic insights that are needed for effective top-level management, and, in a dynamic environment, management science has a tendency to produce solutions for yesterday's problems.

The author, a management scientist, is of the opinion that the charges are well founded. Further, the author can find no substantial evidence to suggest that many of the shortcomings of management science will be rectified within the next few years. To understand why the charges against management science are valid, and, more importantly, to comprehend appropriate organizational responses, it is instructive to consider some of the problems that perplex management scientists.

Objectives

Most management science methods that are available at this time assume that organizational objectives can be clearly stated in a manner that is amenable to quantification. Further, the majority of successful applications of management science are found in contexts where there is a prepotent objective. When organizations are faced with multiple, potentially conflicting objectives, the management scientist can proceed only if it is possible to quantify the extent to which the organization would prefer greater attainment of one objective at the expense of lesser attainment of other objectives. The difficulties are further compounded when there is a conflict of interest among the participants who hold a claim on an organization (shareholders, creditors, management, labor, customers, suppliers, and so forth). Management scientists are typically unable to provide means of arriving at a "fair" compromise when there are conflicts of interest.

Problems related to the specification of organizational objectives are important for two reasons. First, it must be acknowledged that the specification of suitable organizational objectives is the most basic executive obligation. Until objectives have been formulated that motivate the continued support of various interested parties, there is no need to "manage." At this time organizational objectives seem to be established by an intuitive and little-understood process. The speciousness of statements of corporate goals that appear in annual reports need not necessarily be accidental. One thing that is clear is that today's management scientist is ill eqipped to contribute to the formulation of organizational objectives. Management scientists tend to enter the picture after objectives have been formulated and attempt to specify the best means of meeting given objectives.

The second objective-related problem is that management scientists have had little success when the objectives are not fully quantifiable. In the face of "fuzzy" specifications as to desired tradeoffs among conflicting objectives, the management scientist is typically impotent.

Probability

When the eventual consequences of an organization's actions can not be foretold with certainty, management science techniques often assume that probabilistic assessments can be obtained. The type of assessments that are required by management scientists have a close connection to the requirements of mathematical probability theory. Two factors seem to introduce a gulf between the manager and the management scientist when uncertainty looms large. First, mathematical probability theory is abstract and often produces results that are countraintuitive. Therefore, the executive who attempts to cooperate with the management scientist can find himself faced with a request to implement a course of action that not only offends his common sense, but that was arrived at by an incomprehensible line of reasoning. Second, by asking the manager to make probability assessments and to act on the basis of such assessments, the management scientist is, in effect, asking the manager to document and assume responsibility for something that might eventually prove to be catastrophic. Even though the *logic* of such a request might be unassailable, there are strong behavioral motivations for ignoring logic. At this time the management scientist tends to respond by attempting to train the practicing manager in the fundamentals of probability theory. It is not at all clear that this response is sufficient for fruitful applications of management science in contexts where uncertainty is a major issue.

Models and Data

Management science methods assume that it is possible to mathematically state how attainment of an organization's objective(s) is (are) influenced by executive actions and other uncontrollable factors. If the "influence mechanism" is known and can be articulated, and if data are available to gauge the relative strengths of various influences, then model building and testing can be a relatively fast exercise. Unfortunately, many of the "influence mechanisms" are either not well known or organizations do not typically maintain the type of records that facilitate the model building and validation process. As a case in point, consider how little is known about the extent to which a two-column ad in the *New York Times* really influences profits.

Management science procedures are, at this time, based on models. Accordingly, management scientists are frequently unable to contribute to urgent concerns due to an inability to build an appropriate model. This is especially true when answers must be extracted from models in a compressed span of time.

Communications

Perhaps the most perplexing problem faced by contemporary management scientists is the problem of communication. By "communication" we mean an efficient and effective *two-way* rapport between the specialist and the manager. Unless both parties are more than minimally acquainted with the cognitive apparatus and *modus operandi* of the other party, errors of omission and oversimplication lead to breakdowns in communication. It is the opinion of many management scientists that management scientists can, and will, learn to think like managers. It is not at all clear that managers will learn to think like management scientists. The difficulty in developing this second direction in the communications process is that a good working grasp of management science seems to require extensive academic preparation. As an informal outline of the type of preparation that management scientists would like to find in the executive suite, it can be proposed that managers have one university-level course in each of the following areas: probability theory, classical statistics, Bayesian decision theory, operations research, and computer programming. It is not at all clear that it is possible for managers to obtain such an extensive background, and it is not at all clear that managers are eager to try.

A Balance Sheet for Management Science

From the preceding admittedly terse and by no means exhaustive list of unsolved problems in management science, there is ample cause for finding the charges of Churchman, Grayson, Simon, and others to be valid. On the other hand, it must be noted that the unsolved problems of the management scientist are also unsolved problems of the manager. Managers do not claim to know how to set good, feasible objectives, and managers do not claim to be infallible decision makers in the face of uncertainty. In large measure, the charges against management science are statements of disappointment. It had been hoped that management science would shed *more* light on the problems that confront and perplex executives.

It should also be recognized that management science *has* made contributions. The fact that statistical tests, simulation, linear programming, inventory formulas, PERT, and other management science tools are being used by a large number of organizations is presented as evidence of the contributions of management science. In view of the historical slowness of business to adopt new quantitative procedures—for example, Neil W. Chamberlain reports that it required about twenty years for a clear majority of our largest corporations to replace "payback" methods of investment analysis with more sophisticated "present worth" methods—the track record of management science cannot be considered to be totally inconsequential.[4]

Some Corporate Responses

This brings us to the point where it is time to consider appropriate organizational responses. With respect to the question, "Should we just ignore management science?" the consensus of responsible opinions appears to be an emphatic negative. The motivation for this response is that in the proper circumstances, management science has made important contributions and has paid for itself.

Current thinking is directed towards efforts to assure that management science will be applied in "proper circumstances" and with reasonable expectations. The following clearly contradictory suggestions can be gleaned from recent issues of such vehicles of emerging trends as the *Harvard Business Review:*

- Confine management science inquiries to the well-structured problems.
- Management scientists should stop refining approaches to already solved problems.
- Management scientists should be held responsible for implementing solutions.
- Management science should be regarded as being a provider of information inputs.
- Management science should pay its own way.
- It is unrealistic to evaluate the contributions of management science in terms of short-run accomplishments.
- The management scientist should hold a high-level staff position where he is privy to the corridors of power.
- The management scientist should be integrated into line units where he will experience operational problems.

To make sense out of such seemingly contradictory suggestions, it would be prudent for an organization to first ask "Can we afford to support management science activities that might not, in the near future, lead to results that cover expenses?" Many smaller firms will probably have to answer "no" to this question. If this is the case, then management science activities should be directed to those areas where management science has had a historical record of success. This area is found at the lower "operating" levels of the organization where organizational entities have clear, unconflicting goals such as "increase product reliability," "increase product output," and "reduce downtime."

Lower Operating Levels

The fruitful areas for immediate results will be areas where the data that are needed for decision making can be gleaned from extant records, such as production records, the existing cost accounting system, specifications provided by the purchasing department, requirements provided by the marketing department, and so forth.

It should be noted that by directing attention to the lower operating levels of the organization, issues of uncertainty tend to be diminished. For example, a burning issue in the executive suite might be "What should our product line be?" but on the production line that uncertainty has been resolved.

Short-Run Payoff

There is a further motivation for confining attention to the lower levels of the organization when it is imperative that management science pay for itself in the short run. It is in the lower operating levels that we find the engineer, the accountant, the computer specialist, and the financial analyst who habitually work with, and make recommendations based on, computational procedures. Here one would anticipate that effective communications could most easily be established.

It is reasonable to anticipate that in lower-level operating positions, problems that are amenable to resolution by readily-available management science techniques would not appear on a daily basis. If the management scientist is to pay his own way, he might have to do so by engaging in activities not strictly "management science." This realization suggests that the management scientist be integrated in a line position where he fully understands the operational aspects of a problem, is responsible for (limited) results, and need apply management science only when conditions are "perfect."

Long-Term Program

For the organization that can afford a long-term program of introspection and upgrading of executive capabilities, there seems to be a different set of appropriate responses. Because management science is poorly equipped to provide answers to the immediate problems that confront top executives, it could be autistic to suggest that management scientists be privy to the chambers of power for immediate purposes (other than the edification of the management scientist). Before the management scientist can become a consistent provider of executive-level answers, many current difficulties will have to be resolved.

By suggesting that management scientists who work at the higher corporate levels *not* be held responsible for implementing programs and demonstrating results, we differ sharply from the suggestions of others—most notably, Grayson. The main reason for differing with Grayson is the belief that, given current abilities, the only way that a management scientist can adequately function in the role of practicing top-level executive is by adopting the *modus operandi* of practicing executives—that is, by largely abandoning management science. Stated another way, it is suggested here that if an executive is needed, an executive should be hired.

This does not mean that it would be unreasonable to support a high-level management science activity. Quite the contrary! The management scientist is particularly well qualified to serve in the capacity of an in-house student of an organization.

Perhaps the most valuable—albeit, intangible—contribution of management science is to provide an alternative perspective of the management process. An investment in high-level management science could be viewed as analogous to purchasing an insurance policy to guard against executive complacency and organizational atrophy. Before dismissing this role for the management scientist, the executive is asked to count the number of critics of the organization who are both knowledgeable and on the side of the executive.

It is to be hoped that the management scientist will eventually be able to make positive contributions to the executive function. Because the actual implementation of management science findings in high-level, unstructured problem areas can be expected to be a long-run proposition, management scientists would be well advised to pay particular attention to executive concerns that are not likely to disappear in the near future. The budgeting process, cash management, dividend policy, standards of performance, the requirements for future management information systems, and the development of criteria for R & D management appear to be promising candidates for high-level, long-term investigation.

It is doubtful that any management scientist is fully knowledgeable in all of the many subfields of management science. If management scientists are to contribute by, first, learning more about the practice of management and, second, by developing and pioneering the application of science to top-level executive decision making, it is reasonable to anticipate that some form of group effort will be required. By turning to a high-level staff *group* of management scientists, the organization can take steps to foster an environment where: (1) management scientists can become more aware of the needs of executives, and (2) the contributions of the management scientist need not be restricted by the limitations of the isolated management scientist. The high-level management science staff group can be, in part, justified as a corporate resource for other management scientists who have been integrated into operating (line) positions.

Conclusion

As we tread softly with management science, we (managers and management scientists) have an opportunity to maximize hope. That, if the author understands Churchman, is progress.

References for Applications Reading

1. C. West Churchman, "Management Education: Preparation for Uncertainty," *Organizational Dynamics* (Summer, 1972).
2. C. Jackson Grayson, Jr., "Management Science and Business Practice," *Harvard Business Review,* LI, 4 (July-August, 1973), 41–48.
3. Herbert A. Simon, "The Business School: A Problem in Organizational Design," *The Journal of Management Studies,* IV, 1 (February, 1967), 1–16.
4. Neil W. Chamberlain, *The Firm: Micro-Economic Planning and Action* (New York: McGraw-Hill, 1962).

Questions on Reading

1. What is the role that historically has been assumed by the management scientist as contrasted to the manager?
2. Describe the four main categories of problems that have impeded the application of management science in organizations.
3. What are some advantages associated with applying management science techniques at the operating levels of the organization, rather than at the higher corporate levels?
4. What does Roger Eck believe to be the proper role of management science with respect to the higher corporate levels of management?

Organizing

There are several facets to the function of organizing that need to be considered in any attempt to develop an overall understanding of this function and its importance in the process of management. In the first place, the formal organization structure needs to be considered, including the basis used for setting up departments, the type of organizational growth, the span of management in the structure, and the effect of managerial decentralization on the structure. These topics are covered in Chapter 6.

Furthermore, a formal set of organizational relationships that has considerable impact on how smoothly a firm functions is that involving line and staff. In Chapter 7, we consider the nature of line and staff activities and the types of authority that can be assigned to those carrying out staff activities.

An organization is not just a structure or a set of formal relationships; it is a social system as well. Accordingly, in Chapter 8 we consider the status and role implications of formal organizational assignments and the nature of the informal organization and its functions, including the use of power and politics.

Finally, an organization is a functional entity by the fact that people are appointed to positions in the organization. Chapter 9 therefore is concerned with staffing the organization, particularly in regard to managerial personnel. The topics covered include the determination of executive needs and the selection, appraisal, and development of managerial personnel.

Part 3

ORGANIZATION STRUCTURE

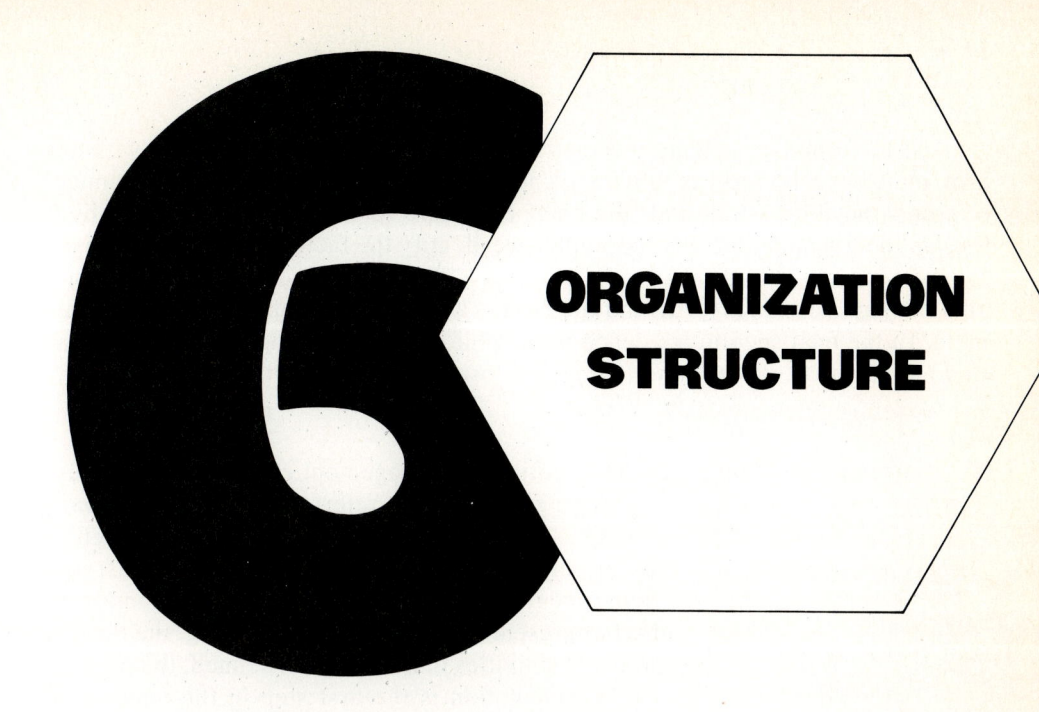

- Departmentation
- Vertical and Horizontal Growth in the Organization
- Span of Management
- Decentralization and the Overall Organization
- Review
- Discussion Questions
- References
- Case Study: Lesner's Department Store
- Case Study: A Question of Managerial Authority
- Applications Reading: "A Contingency Approach to Decentralization" Howard M. Carlisle
- Questions on Reading

The formal organization chart represents the division of activities within a firm, indicates who reports to whom, and serves to describe the vertical channels of communication which link the chief executive to the working, or operative, level in the organization. In this chapter we identify the factors that serve as bases for grouping activities in an organization, the difference between vertical and horizontal organizational growth, and the factors affecting the proper span of management. In the final section we describe the philosophy of managerial decentralization and its effect on the functioning and formal structure of the organization.

Departmentation In the literature on management concepts, the process of grouping activities is referred to as *departmentation*. Thus, departmentation is the grouping of activities at any level in the organization, not just the "departmental" level alone. Because the organization chart represents the relationship among the formal groups of activities that have been defined, the process of departmentation is the first step in the managerial function of organizing.

departmentation

1 Several different bases for the grouping of activities, that is, for _____, can be used. The basis of *number* simply involves assigning an equal number of people at random to each organizational unit.

2 Departmentation on the basis of number alone has fallen into disuse with the growth in complexity of organizations. Is this basis compatible with the need to establish specialized organizational units? [Yes / No]

No

3 Since departmentation based on number is primarily useful when undifferentiated manpower is to be grouped, this basis for departmentation [was / was not] generally applicable in medieval armies.

was

4 The most important and most widely used practice is departmentation according to *function*, or work to be done. Departmentation by function [is / is not] compatible with the need for occupational specialization.

is

5 Although a variety of work has to be accomplished in the modern enterprise, three categories of activi-

function

ty—production, sales, and finance—have been given special attention when departmentation is on the basis of _____.

finance

6 In manufacturing firms, the departments carrying out the functions of production, sales, and _____ have often been called the "major functional departments."

major

7 Although other departments are also important for the firm's continued existence, those departments whose functions are particularly vital to the operation and survival of the firm are called the _____ functional departments.

production

sales

finance

8 The creation of utility in the form of goods or services concerns the _____ function, the exchange of these goods or services for purchasing power constitutes the _____ function, and the allocation of funds in the firm concerns the _____ function.

is

9 No matter what level of the organization is involved, the grouping of activities by function is based on the work to be done. Therefore in large organizations, which include a wide variety of job activities, the basis of function [is / is not] widely used.

function

10 Thus the purchasing and accounting departments within a firm are examples of the grouping of activities according to _____.

function

11 Similarly, the finishing, painting, and inspection departments in a manufacturing plant are examples of departmentation by _____.

number; function

12 Thus far we have described the two bases for grouping activities in an organization: departmentation based on _____ and _____. In addition, activities can also be grouped by *product,* or product line.

13 In departmentation based on product, a plant or division executive has extensive authority over the

is not

manufacture, sale, and service of a given product. Whether the plant or division in question is located near other company facilities [is / is not] necessarily relevant.

14 Two plants of the same company located side by side may have separate sales departments for their particular products. In General Motors, the Buick, Cadillac, and Chevrolet divisions are examples of departmentation by _____.

product

15 Full development of all product lines and the development of specialized product knowledge by engineering and sales personnel are [advantages / disadvantages] of departmentation by product, whereas coordination difficulties and possible undue growth in power of specific product divisions are [advantages / disadvantages].

advantages

disadvantages

16 Departmentation by *territory* is a fourth basis for grouping activities in an enterprise. In this case, physical or geographical location [is / is not] necessarily relevant.

is

17 When nearness to local conditions makes for economies of operation, either in producing or in selling, departmentation based on _____ tends to be used.

territory

18 The desire to adapt to local market conditions is generally a [good / poor] reason for departmentation by territory, whereas doing so because of difficulties in communication within the company is usually considered a [good / poor] reason.

good

poor

19 Establishing sales districts, each headed by a local manager, is an example of departmentation by _____.

territory

20 Thus far we have discussed four bases for departmentation: by _____, _____, _____, and _____.

number; function; product; territory

Departmentation ● 169

customer

21 Departmentation by *customer* is another basis for organizing activities. When the major emphasis is on being better able to serve different categories of buyers of the firm's products, departmentation by _____ deserves serious consideration.

advantage

disadvantage

22 Catering to the specific needs of different types of customers is a(n) [advantage / disadvantage] of departmentation by customer, whereas possible underemployment of facilities because of the changing importance of different customer groups is a(n) [advantage / disadvantage].

customer

23 The Teen Shop in a department store is an example of departmentation by _____.

process

24 Finally, departmentation of a firm's activities may be based on the *process,* or type of equipment, involved. Grouping all punched-card keypunching machines in one area, even though several departments are served, is an example of departmentation by _____.

work

25 Note that departmentation by process is really a special case of departmentation by function. In both cases, activities are grouped according to the _____ being done.

process

26 However, whenever work that would otherwise be done in several different locations in an enterprise is done in one place because of the special equipment used, departmentation by _____ is involved.

process

27 Heavy specialized equipment, or a need for serial use of different types of equipment, makes departmentation by _____ desirable.

function

number

28 In all, six bases for departmentation have been described. The most important basis is by _____. The basis of least importance in modern organizations is departmentation by _____. Other bases are by

product; territory;
customer; process _____, _____, _____, and _____.

29 It is quite typical to find that a different basis for departmentation is used at different organizational levels in a firm. *Primary, intermediate,* and *ultimate*
levels *departmentation* refer to the organization _____ involved.

30 *Primary departmentation* is the grouping of activities at the level immediately below the chief executive officer of the organization. Refer to Figure 6.1. The basis for primary departmentation in this case is by
function _____.

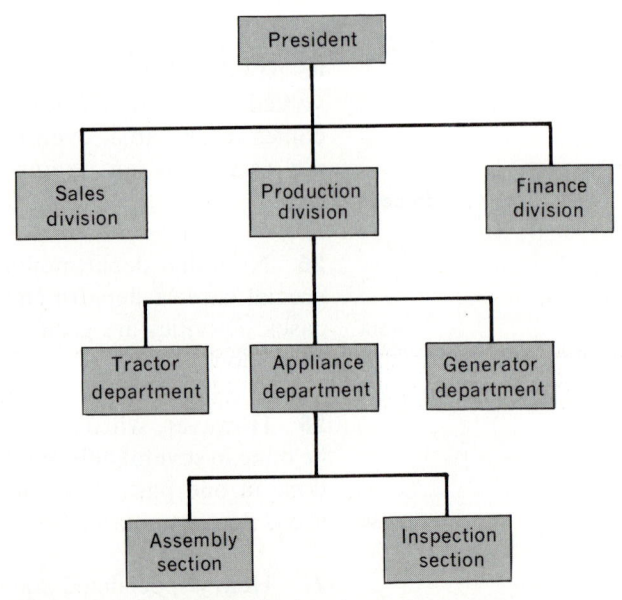

```
                    President
        ┌──────────────┼──────────────┐
      Sales        Production       Finance
    division        division        division
              ┌────────┼────────┐
           Tractor   Appliance  Generator
         department department department
                  ┌──────┴──────┐
               Assembly     Inspection
               section       section
```

Figure 6.1 Partial organization chart.

31 *Intermediate departmentation* includes all the grouped activities in the organization structure below
primary the _____ departments and above the departments at the base of the structure.

32 Because all activities below the primary level of departmentation and above the departments at the base of the organization structure are included, more

Departmentation • 171

intermediate than one organizational level can in fact be involved in _____ departmentation.

33 In Figure 6.1, what is the basis for intermediate departmentation in the production division?
Product _____

34 *Ultimate departmentation* is departmentation at the base of the organization structure, that is, below
primary; intermediate the _____ and _____ departments.

35 In Figure 6.1, what is the basis for ultimate departmentation in the appliance department?
Function _____

36 Refer to Figure 6.2. What level of departmenta-
Intermediate tion is by territory? _____

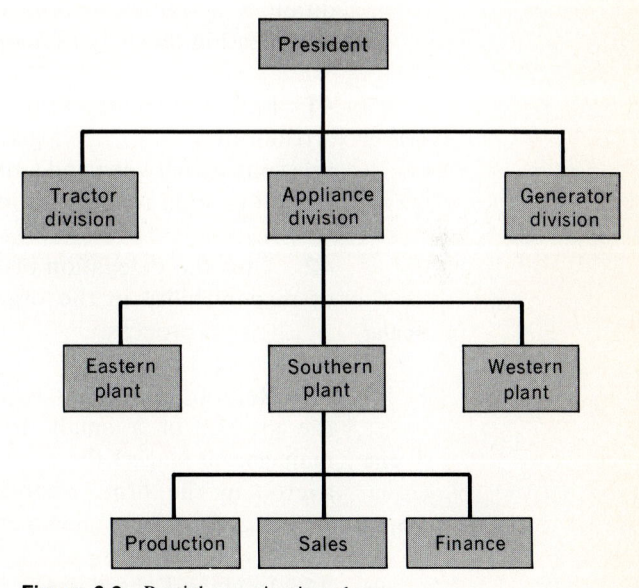

Figure 6.2 Partial organization chart.

37 In Figure 6.2, what level of departmentation is by
Primary product? _____

38 What level of departmentation is by function in
Ultimate Figure 6.2? _____

Chapter 6 • Organization Structure

<blockquote>ultimate;
function</blockquote>

39 Compare Figures 6.1 and 6.2. At what level do the two organization charts follow a common departmentation basis, and what is that basis? In both charts, departmentation at the _____ level is based on _____.

<blockquote>function (or occasionally process, which is a special case of departmentation by function)</blockquote>

40 As is the case in this example, it is almost invariably true that departmentation at the lowest, or ultimate, organizational level is on the basis of _____.

Vertical and Horizontal Growth in the Organization

As an enterprise grows, the organization structure tends to expand both vertically and horizontally. Addition of levels to an organization structure is *vertical growth,* whereas the differentiation of functions or addition of activities without increasing the number of organization levels is *horizontal growth.*

<blockquote>vertical</blockquote>

41 Levels are added to the organization structure as a result of _____ growth. A description of the relationship between and among the levels in an organization is often referred to as the *scalar process.*

<blockquote>scalar</blockquote>

42 Thus the delegation of authority and assignment of responsibility in the organization are part of the _____ process.

<blockquote>one

three</blockquote>

43 Refer to Figure 6.3, which identifies two stages in the growth of a small firm. Counting the owner-manager, at stage I there is (are) ___ [number] manager(s) in the firm, whereas at stage II there are _____ [number] managers.

<blockquote>two

three</blockquote>

44 In stage I there are ___ [number] levels in the organization (counting the owner-manager as a level), whereas at stage II there are _____ [number] levels.

45 Stage II also represents a differentiation of activity as compared with stage I. Whereas the owner-

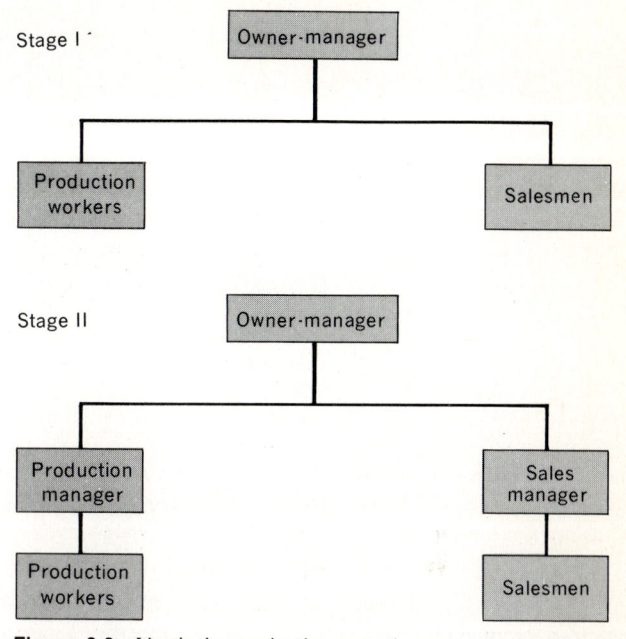

Figure 6.3 Vertical organization growth.

                manager directly supervised the operative employees in stage I, in stage II he has assigned supervisory authority to two subordinate managers. Therefore, changes in the scalar process result in [vertical / horizontal] changes in the organization.

vertical

46 Just as the growth in the vertical dimension concerns the _____ process, the *functional process* affects developments in the horizontal dimension of the organization.

scalar

47 Figure 6.4 represents a third stage in the development of a small firm. The difference from stage II does not concern authority changes within a particular functional area of work, such as production or sales. Rather the change involves the differentiation of an additional *function* at an established organization level. It is for this reason that horizontal changes are associated with the so-called _____ process.

functional

48 At stage II, shown in Figure 6.3, there are _____ [number] levels in the organization and

three

Stage III

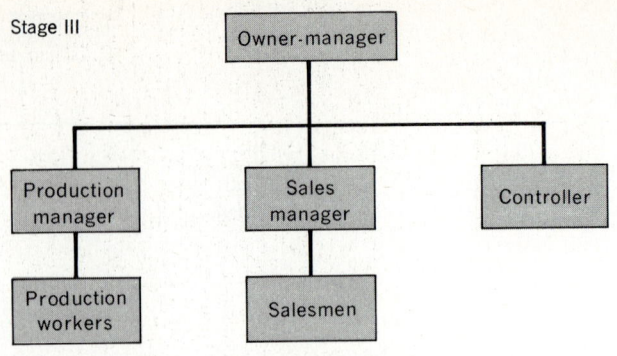

Figure 6.4 Horizontal organization growth.

two (production and sales)	_____ [number] separately identified areas of functional activity.
three; three (production, sales, and controller)	**49** At stage III, shown in Figure 6.4, there are _____ [number] levels in the organization and _____ [number] separately identified areas of functional activity.
horizontal	**50** Thus, functional differentiation, that is, the establishment of a new functional department, typically results in [vertical / horizontal / both vertical and horizontal] organizational growth.
vertical levels horizontal functions	**51** Overall, then, changes in the scalar process are associated with changes in the [vertical / horizontal] dimension and affect the number of organizational [functions / levels]. On the other hand, changes in the functional process are associated with the _____ dimension and affect the number of organizational _____ that are separately identified.
Span of Management	The *span of management* is also called the "span of supervision" and the "span of control." The concept has to do with identifying the number of subordinates whose work a superior can effectively manage. Although early writers in management tried to identify the ideal span of management for all organizational circumstances, the results of studies in this area indicate

that no universal ratio is meaningful. As part of the function of organizing, the characteristics of each situation have to be considered before determining the span of management that is appropriate.

52 The *organizational level,* the *kind of activity* being supervised, the *kind of personnel* being supervised, and the *kind of organization* are all factors that help determine the ideal span of _____ applicable in a particular situation.

management (or supervision, or control)

53 At the lowest organizational level, where responsibility is delegated for performing specific tasks, would you expect a relatively broad (many subordinates) or narrow (few subordinates) span of management to be appropriate? [Broad / Narrow]

Broad

54 Although the differences in span of management at the various organizational levels have not been definitely determined, it is generally true that the span of management at the level of ultimate departmentation is broader than at either the _____ or the _____ level.

primary; intermediate

55 The *kind of activity* supervised also affects the span of management. In general, the more varied the activities in the jobs being supervised, the [broader / narrower] the ideal span of supervision.

narrower

56 Other things being equal, a greater variety of job activity necessitates closer supervision. On the other hand, jobs that follow a fixed routine allow for a [broad / narrow] span of management.

broad

57 For example, as compared with a foreman on a continuous assembly-line operation, we would expect a foreman in a job shop to have [more / fewer] subordinates.

fewer

58 Another factor that influences the span of management, in addition to the organizational _____ and the kind of _____ supervised, is the kind of personnel involved.

level; activity

176 • Chapter 6 • Organization Structure

broad

59 Aside from the amount of routine or varied activity involved, occupations in which individuals traditionally work independently tend to have a [broad / narrow] span of management.

broad

60 For example, for professional salespeople, research scientists, and college professors one would expect a relatively [broad / narrow] span of management, even though the work may involve a great deal of variety.

organizations

61 Finally, the *kind of organization* helps to determine the span of management that is appropriate. The terms "centralized" and "decentralized," or some degree of either in terms of delegation of authority, are descriptions of kinds of _____.

Higher

62 A *centralized* organization is one in which detailed and comprehensive planning is done by the chief executive or by a small group of key managers. Therefore, at what organizational levels are most decisions made in a centralized organization? [Higher / Lower]

narrow

63 Centralized organizations tend to encourage close supervision of subordinates at every level in order to assure that established policies, procedures, and methods are followed. Therefore, the typical result of following the centralized philosophy is that the span of management is relatively [broad / narrow].

More

64 On the other hand, in a *decentralized* organization operating decisions are pushed down to the lowest level possible. If a manager, by company policy, is to give greater "freedom of action" to his subordinates, should he have relatively more or fewer subordinates? [More / Fewer]

broad

65 Therefore, a company that is decentralized from the standpoint of delegation of authority tends to encourage a [broad / narrow] span of management.

66 In summary, then, we have considered four factors that influence the appropriate span of manage-

level; activity; personnel; organization	ment for a particular situation: the organizational _____, the kind of _____, the kind of _____, and the kind of _____.
broad	**67** Work at the ultimate organizational level, routine activity, and a decentralized organization all tend to make the appropriate span relatively [broad / narrow].
centralized narrow	**68** On the other hand, higher organizational levels, varied activity, and a _____ organization all tend to make the appropriate span [broad / narrow].
span of management	**69** In any particular managerial situation some factors may dictate a narrow span, whereas others indicate that a wide span is appropriate. Therefore a manager must consider and balance all relevant factors in deciding on the appropriate _____.

Decentralization and the Overall Organization

Managerial decentralization affects not only the span of management, but also the number of managers and the number of levels in the organization structure. Thus the philosophy of encouraging the delegation of authority to the lowest level possible leads to overall organizational effects, and some of these effects are described in this final section of the chapter.

four eight	**70** Refer to Figure 6.5. In company A each manager has _____ [number] subordinates, whereas in company B each manager has _____ [number] subordinates.
Four Three	**71** What is the number of organization levels in company A (counting the chief executive as a level)? _____ [number]; in company B? _____ [number]

72 A *flat* organization structure is one that has relatively few levels and a large number of subordinates per level, whereas a *tall,* or *pyramidal,* structure has a

Company A:

[Organization chart showing Chief executive → Manager → Assistant manager → Operative employee, with (Total number of operative employees = 64)]

Company B:

[Organization chart showing Chief executive → Manager → Operative employee, with (Total number of operative employees = 64)]

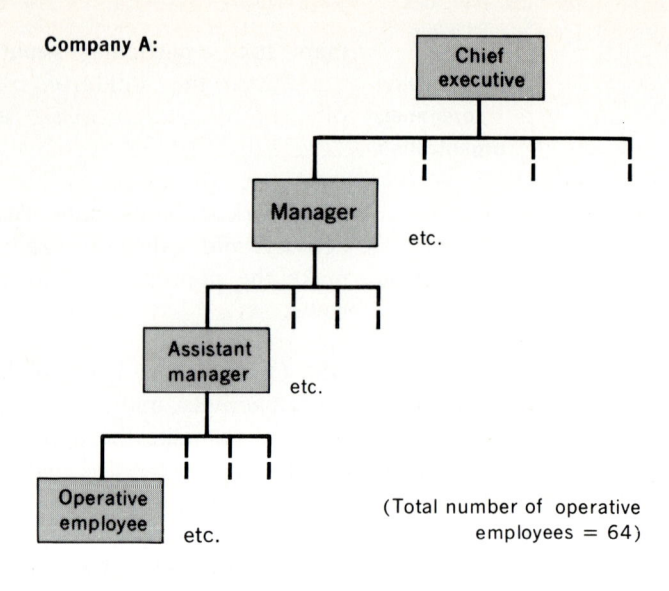

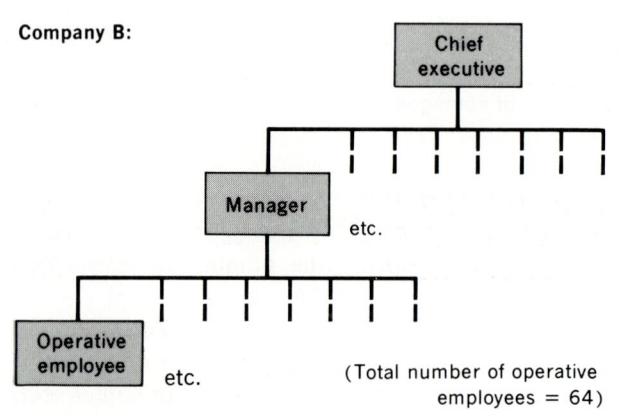

Figure 6.5 Partial organization charts for two companies using different spans of management.

B / A

greater number of levels. In Figure 6.5, company ___ appears to have a relatively flat organization structure, whereas company ___ has a tall structure.

flat

73 Because managerial decentralization encourages a broader span of management, it tends to lead to the development of a [flat / tall] organization structure.

74 Once again, refer to Figure 6.5. In company A, a directive from the chief executive has to go through

Decentralization and the Overall Organization • 179

two   ____ [number] intermediate level(s) before reaching the operative employees, whereas in company B it goes through ____ [number] level(s).

one

75 Thus the flat, or decentralized, organization struc-
shorter   ture results in [longer / shorter] lines of communication in the organization.

76 What is the total number of managers in company A; that is, how many employees are above the opera-
Twenty-one   tive level in company A? _____
Nine   [number] In company B? _____ [number]

77 Therefore, managerial decentralization leads to a
broad; flat;   [broad / narrow] span of management, a [flat / tall] or-
shorter;   ganization structure, [longer / shorter] lines of com-
fewer   munication, and [more / fewer] executives.

78 Conversely, managerial centralization leads to a
narrow; tall;   [broad / narrow] span of management, a [flat / tall] or-
longer;   ganization structure, [longer / shorter] lines of com-
more   munication, and [more / fewer] executives.

79 Which type of organization leads to a closer working relationship between supervisors and subor-
Centralized   dinates and to tighter executive control? [Centralized / Decentralized]

80 Because of the opportunity to make managerial decisions (and mistakes) at lower organization levels, which type of organization is superior in providing the opportunity for executive development [Centralized /
Decentralized   Decentralized]

81 Because of the success associated with the introduction of the managerial philosophy of decentralization at General Motors beginning in the 1920s, this approach to management and organization has gained many adherents in American industry. In his testimony before the Senate Subcommittee on Anti-Trust and Monopoly in 1955, Harlow Curtice, then president of General Motors, gave major credit for the company's success to the application of the philosophy of

decentralization   _____ .

82 In his testimony Mr. Curtice identified Alfred P. Sloan, Jr., who assumed the company presidency in 1921 when the company was in financial difficulty, as being the first executive to apply the concept in General Motors. Exhibit 6.1 is a brief exerpt from Mr. Curtice's testimony. As indicated, Mr. Sloan's organizational innovations led to [complete centralization / complete decentralization / **a blend of centralization and decentralization**].

Exhibit 6.1 *Excerpt from "The Development and Growth of General Motors," by Harlow Curtice.*

(From testimony before the subcommittee on Anti-Trust and Monopoly of the United States Senate Committee on the Judiciary, December 2, 1955, pp. 5–12.)

Even before the crisis of 1920 materialized, Mr. Sloan was very conscious of the need in General Motors for a new and clearly defined concept of management philosophy. He had observed that much time was being consumed in solving detailed administrative problems and in meeting the critical situations which were constantly arising. He recognized that too great a concentration of problems upon a small number of executives limited initiative, caused delay, increased expense, reduced efficiency and retarded development.

He realized that centralization, properly established, makes possible directional control, coordination, specialization, and resulting economies. He also realized that decentralization, properly established, develops initiative and responsibility; it makes possible a proper distribution of decisions at all levels of management, including the foreman—with resulting flexibility and cooperative effort, so necessary to a large-scale enterprise. His objective was to obtain the proper balance between these two apparently conflicting principles of centralization and decentralization in order to obtain the best elements of each in the combination. He concluded that, to achieve this balance so necessary for flexibility of operation, General Motors management should be established on a foundation of centralized policy and decentralized administration. Mr. Sloan's concept of the management of a great industrial organization, expressed in his own words as he finally evolved it, is "to divide it into as many parts as consistently as can be done, place in charge of each part the most capable executive that can be found, develop a system of coordination so that each part may strengthen and support each other part; thus not only welding all parts together in the common interests of a joint enterprise, but importantly developing ability and initiative through the instrumentalities of responsibility and ambition—developing men and giving them an opportunity to exercise their talents, both in their own interests as well as in that of the business."

83 Harlow Curtice also credited the growth of our country and of the automobile industry itself as factors contributing to the growth of General Motors. However, following Mr. Sloan's managerial innovations the company grew much more rapidly than its competitors, who tended to follow a highly centralized management philosophy. Whereas General Motors has consistently accounted for the largest percentage of new car sales in the United States in recent years, in 1921 its percentage of industry sales, as indicated in Figure 6.6, was about ___ percent.

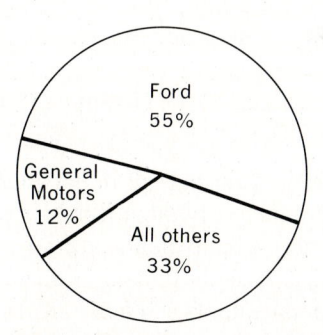

12

Figure 6.6 Percent of industry motor vehicle sales in 1921.

84 Since the 1920s the large majority of firms in the United States have incorporated the philosophy of decentralization into their approach to management and organization. For example, Sears-Roebuck pioneered the application of this philosophy in the field of retailing during the 1930s. In noting the virtues of managerial decentralization, we should also note the

182 • Chapter 6 • Organization Structure

control (and coordination)

principal danger associated with carrying it too far, which is possible loss of managerial _____ (refer to Exhibit 6.1 if you wish).

centralization;
decentralization

85 Before World War II most firms in the United States were relatively centralized and thus found that the benefits associated with more delegation of authority and assignment of responsibility to subordinate managers far outweighed the risks. The current problem in most firms, however, is that of finding the proper balance between the contrasting managerial philosophies of _____ and _____.

Review
departmentation

86 The grouping of activities in order to form organizational units is called _____. (Frame 1)

function

number

87 In all, six bases for departmentation were described. The most extensively used basis is departmentation by _____, whereas the basis that is of least importance when job specialization is involved is departmentation by _____. (Frames 2 to 12)

product; territory;
customer; process

88 The other four bases for departmentation are by _____, _____, _____, and _____. (Frames 13 to 28)

production; sales;
finance

89 Although all departments are established to help achieve organizational objectives, the activities of three departments are so vital to the survival of the firm that they have been called the "major functional departments." These are the departments performing the functions of _____, _____, and _____. (Frames 5 to 8)

primary

ultimate

90 In terms of the organizational level involved, the grouping of activities at the level immediately below the chief executive is referred to as _____ departmentation, the grouping at the base of the organization structure is referred to as _____ departmentation, and the grouping at the level(s) in between

Review ● 183

intermediate is referred to as _____ departmentation. (Frames 29 to 37)

91 The basis for grouping activities at the level of ultimate departmentation is almost invariably by
function _____. (Frames 38 to 40)

92 Levels are added to the organization structure
vertical during _____ growth. The related delegation of authority and assignment of responsibility in the or-
scalar ganization is referred to as the _____ process. (Frames 41 to 45)

93 Just as the pattern of assigning authority in the vertical dimension of the organization chart is referred to as the scalar process, so the division of activities in the horizontal dimension is referred to as the
functional _____ process. (Frames 46 to 51)

94 The number of subordinates for whose work a superior is responsible is referred to as the
span of management _____. (Frame 52)

95 The appropriate span of management depends on
level; the organizational _____ involved, the kind
activity; of _____ supervised, the kind of
personnel; _____, and the kind of
organization _____. (Frames 53 to 69)

96 From the standpoint of delegation of authority, an organization in which top managers do detailed and comprehensive planning can be described as being
centralized _____, whereas the organization in which operating decisions are pushed down to the low-
decentralized est level possible is _____. (Frames 61 to 64)

97 A managerial situation involving a higher organizational level, varied activity, and a centralized organization would tend to result in the appropriate span of
narrow management being [broad / narrow]. (Frames 65 to 69)

98 As compared with centralization, managerial

broad; flat; shorter; fewer	decentralization leads to a relatively [broad / narrow] span of management, a [flat / tall] organization structure, [longer / shorter] lines of communication, and [more / fewer] executives. (Frames 70 to 78)
centralized decentralized	**99** Closer superior-subordinate relationships and closer executive control are typical in the [centralized / decentralized] organization, whereas greater opportunity for the development of management skills is typical in the [centralized / decentralized] organization. (Frames 79 and 80)
General Motors	**100** The introduction of the managerial philosophy of decentralization in American business during the 1920s is generally credited to Alfred P. Sloan, Jr., who was at that time president of _____ _____. (Frames 81 to 85)

Discussion Questions

1. What are the advantages of constructing and using a formal organization chart in a company?
2. For each of the six bases for departmentation, give an example of its appropriate application in a business firm.
3. Why is it logical that departmentation at the ultimate level in the organization should be defined on the basis of function?
4. The direct result of adding people tends to be vertical growth in the organization, while adding functions tends to result in horizontal growth. Why? Why is it likely that both types of growth will occur as a firm expands in size?
5. What is the ideal span of management?
6. In practice, as contrasted to analyzing the factors discussed in this chapter, how is the span of management likely to be determined for a particular situation? Consider the implications of using the alternative approaches.
7. What is the relationship between geographic decentralization of a company and managerial decentralization?
8. What is the philosophy of, and what are the organizational implications of, managerial decentralization?
9. In considering the types of decisions that should be centralized as contrasted to those that should be decentralized, how has the development of computer-based information systems tended to make a higher degree of centralization possible, and perhaps even desirable?

10. It has been said that although a manager can delegate authority, the associated responsibility, or accountability, is assigned but not delegated. Discuss the implications of this statement.

References

Aldrich, H., and D. Herker. "Boundary Spanning Roles and Organizational Structure." *The Academy of Management Review*, vol. 2, no. 2, April 1977.

Atherton, R. M. "Centralization Works Best When Managers' Jobs Are Improved." *Human Resource Management*, vol. 16, no. 2, Summer 1977.

Carlson, H. C. "Organizational Research and Organizational Change: GM's Approach." *Personnel*, vol. 54, no. 4, July-August 1977.

Davis, K. "Trends in Organizational Design." *Arizona Business*, vol. 20, no. 9, November 1973.

Drucker, P. F. "New Templates for Today's Organizations." *Harvard Business Review*, vol. 52, no. 1, January-February 1974.

Ford, J. D., and J. W. Slocum, Jr. "Size, Technology, Environment and the Structure of Organizations." *The Academy of Management Review*, vol. 2, no. 4, October 1977.

Gannon, M. J., and F. T. Paine. "Unity of Command and Job Attitudes of Managers in a Bureaucratic Organization." *Journal of Applied Psychology*, vol. 59, no. 3, June 1974.

Ghiselli, E. E., and J. P. Siegel. "Leadership and Managerial Success in Tall and Flat Organization Structures." *Personnel Psychology*, vol. 25, no. 4, Winter 1972.

Hayes, R. H., and R. W. Schmenner. "How Should You Organize Manufacturing?" *Harvard Business Review*, vol. 56, no. 1, January-February 1978.

House, R. J., and J. B. Miner. "Merging Management and Behavioral Theory: The Interaction between Span of Control and Group Size." *Administrative Science Quarterly*, vol. 14, no. 3, September 1969.

Hrebiniak, L. G. "Job Technology, Supervision, and Work-Group Structure." *Administrative Science Quarterly*, vol. 19, no. 3, September 1974.

Ivancevich, J. M., and J. H. Donnely, Jr. "Relation of Organizational Structure to Job Satisfaction, Anxiety-Stress, and Performance." *Administrative Science Quarterly*, vol. 20, no. 2, June 1975.

Jones, H. R., Jr. "A Study of Organization Performance for Experimental Structures of Two, Three, and Four Levels." *Academy of Management Journal*, vol. 12, no. 3, September 1969.

Koontz, H. "Making Theory Operational: The Span of Management." *The Journal of Management Studies*, vol. 3, no. 3, October 1966.

Laurent, A. "Managerial Subordinacy: A Neglected Aspect of Organizational Hierarchies." *The Academy of Management Review*, vol. 3, no. 2, April 1978.

Lustiger, R., and K. M. Jenkins. "Toward a Contingency Theory of Authority." *Arizona Business*, vol. 25, no. 6, June-July 1978.

McCaskey, M. B. "An Introduction to Organizational Design." *California Management Review*, vol. 17, no. 2, Winter 1974.

McMillan, C., et al. "The Structure of Work Organizations across Societies." *Academy of Management Journal*, vol. 16, no. 4, December 1975.

Mansfield, R. "Bureaucracy and Centralization: An Examination of Organizational Structure." *Administrative Science Quarterly*, vol. 18, no. 4, December 1973.

Negandhi, A. R., and B. C. Reimann. "Correlates of Decentralization: Closed and Open Systems Perspectives." *Academy of Management Journal*, vol. 16, no. 4, December 1973.

Ouchi, W. G. "The Relationship between Organizational Structure and Organizational Control." *Administrative Science Quarterly*, vol. 22, no. 1, March 1977.

Ouchi, W. G., and J. Dowling. "Defining the Span of Control." *Administrative Science Quarterly*, vol. 21, no. 3, September 1974.

Reinharth, L. "The Missing Ingredient in Organization Theory." *Advanced Management Journal*, vol. 43, no. 1, Winter 1978.

Sathe, V. "Institutional versus Questionnaire Measures of Organizational Structure." *Academy of Management Journal*, vol. 21, no. 2, June 1978.

Sokolik, S. L., and I. L. Richardson. "Preparing Organization Charts with a Computer." *Personnel Journal*, vol. 56, no. 10, November 1977.

Stevens, R. I. "Principles of Organization Planning." *Journal of Systems Management*, vol. 28, no. 5, May 1977.

Tsaklanganos, A. A. "The Organization Chart: A Managerial Myth." *Advanced Management Journal*, vol. 38, no. 2, April 1973.

Urwick, L. F. "The Manager's Span of Control." *Harvard Business Review*, vol. 43, no. 3, May-June 1965.

Urwick, L. F. "V. A. Graicunas and the Span of Control." *Academy of Management Journal*, vol. 17, no. 2, June 1974.

Van Fleet, D. D., and A. C. Bedeian. "A History of the Span of Management." *The Academy of Management Review*, vol. 2, no. 3, July 1977.

Wolf, H. A. "The Great GM Mystery." *Harvard Business Review*, vol. 42, no. 5, September-October 1964.

CASE STUDY: Lesner's Department Store

Although his department store is small compared with two large national chain stores located in the same city, Abe Lesner is proud of his ability to judge local demand and to merchandise a variety of goods through his varied promotional efforts. Over the years, he has probably used every promotional technique known in retailing. He has been in the business for thirty years and has seen the store develop to the point where he now has an assistant store manager and three department managers, each of whom is responsible for the buying and retailing of different categories of merchandise.

Mr. Lesner considers himself semiretired in that he no longer spends more than forty hours per week in the store. In fact, he'd like to cut down even more on the hours he spends at work but has concluded that it is just impossible. For one thing, the assistant store manager, who happens to be his son-in-law, makes no decisions without first consulting him, and so he finds that if he's not there, decisions affecting overall operations of the store are just not made. The department managers do tend to operate more independently, but even here he finds it necessary to prod them into the good merchandising practices that they otherwise seem to ignore. And if he had more time to review the department manager activities, Lesner is sure he could further improve performance and profitability. But since Mr. Lesner is approaching his seventieth birthday and feels that he has earned the right to slow down, he would really prefer to reduce the number of hours he spends in managing the business without jeopardizing its continued success.

1. What would happen if Mr. Lesner simply stopped coming to the store? Are his fears realistic?
2. To what extent has the concept of managerial decentralization been applied? How might its use be extended?
3. How might fuller development of his subordinate managers be achieved?
4. Can Lesner's Department Store, as Mr. Lesner knows it, really survive without his active management?

CASE STUDY: A Question of Managerial Authority

Bill Chambers has worked for the Goodwin Manufacturing Company for a number of years, and for the last four years he has been general foreman in charge of the assembly line. His departments have always been rated high with respect to efficiency, cost, and schedules, and Bill is personally respected by his subordinate foremen and by members of the service organizations.

A week ago a new supervisor, Ed Whittaker, was transferred into the area from another division whose operations were discontinued. Ed had been a general foreman in the other division and carried the same title in his new assignment. When the superintendent introduced Ed Whittaker to Bill Chambers and the foremen in the department he made no mention of Ed's specific duties. However, in an earlier conversation in his office the superintendent informed Ed Whittaker that he would be responsible for all subassembly areas while Chambers would be responsible for the final assembly areas. The superintendent did not mention the details of this assignment to Bill Chambers because he was hard pressed to complete some overdue reports. He assumed that the two men could work things out, and in any event he planned to review their respective areas of responsibility again at the end of the week.

The day after his transfer into the area Ed Whittaker began making changes in the existing system and giving instructions to various supervisors in the subassembly areas in order to implement changes which he felt were desirable. The supervisors reacted with dissatisfaction to the proposed changes and immediately went to Bill Chambers to ask what was going on and to inquire who was in charge of the department. Chambers could not furnish any specific information but told the supervisors to do as Whittaker instructed until he could discuss the matter with the plant superintendent.

1. What did the plant superintendent do that was incorrect? How can he correct the situation?
2. When Ed Whittaker received his assignment, did he handle the situation correctly?
3. Do you think that Bill Chambers did the right thing in having the men do as Whittaker had instructed? Should Chambers talk to Whittaker before discussing the matter with the superintendent?
4. Overall, what kinds of reasons may be involved in the superintendent's decision to assign an additional general foreman in the assembly area? Should the reason be communicated to the supervisors in the area?

APPLICATIONS READING:

A Contingency Approach to Decentralization

Howard M. Carlisle
Head, Department of Business Administration
Utah State University

One of the themes that is coming to dominate management theory and practice is referred to as the contingency approach, also known as situational theory or situational management. The gist of this approach is that management concepts are not universally applicable but are only appropriate if the right conditions exist in a given situation. Different situations call for the application of different concepts, and thus the utilization of any specific concept is contingent upon the situation.

Contingency theory first found its expression in studies of leadership. As early as 1948 Ralph Stogdill stated that it "becomes clear that an adequate analysis of leadership involves not only a study of leaders but also of situations." Gradually the situational approach to leadership gained increased support culminating in the landmark *Harvard Business Review* article of Robert Tannenbaum and Warren H. Schmidt in 1958 entitled "How to Choose a Leadership Pattern." In this article they identified certain forces in the manager, in subordinates, and in the situation that called for different types of leadership.

By 1960 this approach was widely accepted, but it had a meager research base. Substantial research support was provided by Fred Fiedler when he published his leadership studies in 1967 in a book entitled *A Theory of Leadership Effectiveness*. Fiedler used the term "contingency" to represent his approach and it has tended to displace prior situational terminology. In the past few years many other studies have been developed supporting the notion that leadership is situational, highlighted by the recent publication of the studies of Victor H. Vroom and Philip W. Yetton in a book entitled *Leadership and Decision-Making*.

The rise in popularity of contingency theories of leadership led to the exploration of the usefulness of this concept in other areas of management. Jay W. Lorsch and Paul R. Lawrence led a group at Harvard that conducted a series of studies in the 1960s that tended to validate the same contingency concepts in organization structure and other areas of management. Many others were also finding empirical support for the value of this analytical framework in viewing management theory and practice. One noted observer, Fred Luthans, predicts that by 1980 the contingency approach "may be the one that leads management out of the existing jungle of theories."

Source: Reprinted, by permission of the publisher, from S.A.M. *Advanced Management Journal*, vol. 39, no. 3, July 1974, © 1974 by Society for Advancement of Management, a division of American Management Associations. All rights reserved.

Characteristics of Contingency Theory

It is still too early to state the exact postulates that comprise the theoretical base of contingency theory. As it has evolved to this period in time, however, six general themes appear to comprise the thrust:

1. There is a strong emphasis on pragmatism. "Using what works" is recognition of an appropriate match between specific concepts and techniques and the variables of a situation.

2. Relativism is also basic to the philosophy. The direction of management study since the beginning of this century has centered on the search for universal principles and concepts that can be used by all administrators. It has been a search for the "one best way" to lead, plan, and organize. However, relativism rejects absolute principles, universal applications, or black and white solutions. All management concepts have desirable and undesirable features. These concepts are appropriate in some situations but not in others. Furthermore, the benefits of any such principles are relevant to the particular situation. Participative management may be extremely useful in one set of circumstances but only of minor advantage in another.

3. Contingency theory holds that any management condition or problem results from a variety of relationships among a number of variables that predominate in a particular situation. Management analysis in the past has been too superficial and too descriptive. Management situations are made up of complex relationships. These need to be understood if the situation is to be comprehended. Contingency theory places primary emphasis on understanding relationships among variables, which is a legacy from systems theory.

4. Contingency theory emphasizes the complexity of managing organizations or making decisions. Too often in the past we have attempted to make decisions based on only one or two factors because of a tendency to simplify a situation that has many inherent complexities. As Morse and Lorsch state, "The strength of the contingency approach...is that it begins to provide a way of thinking about this complexity rather than ignoring it."

5. Contingency theory holds that the primary skill of the manager is to be able to select appropriate concepts and strategies based on the particular situation at hand. Management is thus a challenge in making effective decisions through matching appropriate concepts and strategies with the demands of a situation.

6. The last central theme of contingency theory is based on the premise that even though there are few usable absolutes in management affairs, there are commonalities among certain classifications of situations, and that an understanding of these needs to be developed. Each situation a manager faces is not so unique that guides cannot be developed for related circumstances. The search is therefore to classify situations and variables into common types so that conclusions can be reached regarding appropriate application of management concepts given these circumstances.

Situational Methodology

Contingency theory as it relates to management practice consists of four areas of understanding:

1. A manager needs to be familiar with the various concepts and techniques of management that are available. If a manager is facing a planning problem he should be familiar with the various planning methodologies and systems; if he is reorganizing his unit he needs to be familiar with the appropriate organization concepts.
2. The manager should not just be aware of the concepts and techniques but should be knowledgeable of the trade-offs involved when he selects any particular concept or technique. Since different concepts will bring different results, the specific advantages and drawbacks associated with any particular concept need to be understood.
3. The manager needs to know the context of the situation he is facing. He needs not only to be familiar with the resources involved but also with the attributes and relationships of the people, tasks, technology, organization structure, and external factors such as markets, economic conditions, political conditions, and other such variables that tend to be dominant in situations. Being able to size up a situation through an understanding of the basic factors or forces at work is equally as important as knowing management concepts and techniques.
4. The ultimate goal of situational methodology is for the manager to have sufficient understanding to skillfully match the trade-offs of management concepts with the needs and demands of particular situations. Contingency theory is a challenge in decision making involving matching concepts to situations. Just as the golfer must select the appropriate club given his particular lie on the course, so the manager must apply the appropriate concepts given the particular problem at hand.

Management theory and practice have concentrated primarily on the first two understandings relating to knowing concepts, with the result that we have only limited knowledge of the latter two areas relating to knowing situations.

Contingency Methodology and Decentralization

In very few instances to date have attempts been made to establish a complete contingency model for any particular management concept. This would involve the trade-offs associated with the concept and a list of the situational factors or conditions that would dictate the desirability or lack of desirability for the application of the concept. Vroom and Yetton came the closest to this when they established seven rules based on different situational factors for the application of participative leadership styles. As Vroom himself notes, we need to direct our "efforts toward identifying the properties of situations in which different decision-making approaches are effective rather than wholesale condemnation or deification of one approach."

In this analysis, decentralization will be utilized as an example of how a complete contingency model is established. Decentralization is selected because in the 1950s and 1960s there were many misapplications of the concept resulting from proponents who were guilty of the "deification" referred to by Vroom. Also, decentralization is selected because it is a widely understood concept. Decentralization, as the term is used here, is defined as a condition in an organization when the authority to make decisions is broadly delegated to lower-level units. Centralization is the opposite condition where the upper hierarchy of the organization retains most decision-making authority. Decentralization is an appropriate example of relativism since no organization is completely decentralized or centralized, and each organization exists somewhere between these two theoretical extremes.

The Trade-offs of Centralization and Decentralization

Certain advantages are associated with decentralization that tend to be the corresponding limitations of centralization. The reverse is also true with centralization having certain benefits that are lost through decentralization. The trade-offs, constituting seven of the most well known advantages of each approach, are briefly explained below.

Advantages of centralization:
- The most common argument in favor of centralization is that it is a means of achieving conformity and coordination. If all decisions are made at one point it is easier to integrate the activities of subunits or individuals or to establish a coordinated program such as advertising.
- Top managers generally have the most experience and are proven executives. Based on this experience and knowledge, they should be in a position to make better decisions than less experienced individuals at lower levels in the organization.
- From their position in the organization, the top level executives have a broader perspective of what is taking place. Accordingly, they are better situated to make decisions giving consideration to the interests of the entire organization. This avoids suboptimal decisions at lower levels where individuals make decisions that are optimal for their subunit but suboptimal for the entire organization.
- One of the primary problems in an organization is achieving balance in its activities. If the production, marketing, research and development, and financial functions are not kept in relative balance, the organization is likely to suffer. Centralized decision making relating these functions to each other is a means of insuring this balance.
- One of the disadvantages of decentralization is that it can result in a duplication of efforts or resources if similar activities are carried on independently by different organizational elements. Central control tends to avoid such duplication.

- Centralization at the top permits the pulling together of sufficient resources to employ staff experts in those areas where it is desirable. In instances where procurement, planning, or personnel functions are dispersed throughout the organization, no unit typically has sufficient resources to provide specialized competence in these areas.
- The final advantage of centralization is that it is consistent with the need for strong leadership in the organization. Centralization provides power and prestige to the executive, which may be necessary in time of crisis or when momentum is needed to exert an all-out effort to accomplish a particular objective. It is also consistent with the ego needs of executives who seek status and power in the organization.

Advantages of decentralization:
- Decentralization tends to reduce the workload on overburdened executives. The typical American executive works 55 to 60 hours per week and even with this often does not get at matters that require his attention. Decentralization can relieve this burden and make the organization function more effectively by leaving the executive more time for policy matters.
- Decentralization has been strongly supported by behavioralists because of the motivational effects it has on lower-level supervisors. Individuals generally seek a feeling of recognition, status, and accomplishment in the work they perform. The opportunity to make decisions and be involved in management activates strong drives within individuals that result in greater commitment to the organization and greater individual productivity. It is hard to get a feeling of competence when a supervisor makes all decisions that relate to a subordinate's job.
- As indicated above, it has long been argued that people are more productive when they have a high degree of individual freedom and control over their jobs. Other situational factors could, of course, alter this, such as the individual who does not accept the organization's goals, or positions involving tasks where there is a large degree of interdependence with other employees.
- Management is still primarily an art where one learns by doing. Accordingly, when lower level supervisors are permitted to make decisions they rapidly assume their role as managers and learn through this experience. Profit decentralization has proven valuable to many organizations such as General Motors in developing "general" managers. When a supervisor is given responsibility for the entire operation of a plant he rapidly becomes a generalist in balancing the many interests and functions of the organization.
- Decentralization leads to quicker decisions at the lower levels of the organization since decisions do not have to be referred up the hierarchy. If, when a problem arises, the individual immediately associated with the problem has the authority to make the decision, issues can be rapidly resolved.
- The individual immediately associated with the problem will normally be more aware of local conditions or of other related situational factors than an individual at higher levels in the organization who is more remote. Accordingly the man on the spot will in this respect make better decisions.

- Through establishing relatively independent units where supervisors are responsible for their own operations, decentralization results in improved controls and performance measurements. Costs can be identified with output, and responsibility is much more specific. Profit decentralization is an example where semi-autonomous units are established and local management is given independence as long as the unit meets the profit standards. Often, parallel units are set up to compare productivity and encourage competition.

Situational Variables

Contingency theory holds that organization structure is normally a dependent variable and other factors in the situation are independent variables. Accordingly the assumption is that there are a number of conditions relative to an organization that determine whether centralization or decentralization will be effective in any particular circumstance. Management practice and research studies point to 13 variables as being primary in determining the need for a centralized or decentralized structure:

1. The basic purpose and goals of the organization.
2. The knowledge and experience of top level managers.
3. The skill, knowledge, and attitudes of subordinates.
4. The scale or size of the organizational structure.
5. The geographical dispersion of the structure.
6. The scientific content or the technology of the tasks being performed.
7. The time frame of the decisions to be made.
8. The significance of the decisions to be made.
9. The degree to which subordinates will accept and are motivated by the decision to be made.
10. The status of the organization's planning and control systems.
11. The status of the organization's information systems.
12. The degree of conformity and coordination required in the tasks or operations of the organization.
13. The status of external environmental factors such as governments, labor unions, etc.

Before examining these factors, it should be recognized that they are not present in all situations, and their significance will vary from situation to situation. Also, it is the composite interrelationship of the variables in a situation that determines the relative need for a particular type of organization structure. All 13 factors in a situation will not under normal circumstances unanimously display conditions that call for the same type of structure. Accordingly, any decision on structure can only be made after a comprehensive evaluation of all factors in a particular situation. For instance, the president of the organization may be the most knowledgeable in a policy area, but if he is already overburdened and if the decisions are relatively inconsequential, the authority to make these decisions should still be delegated to someone else.

The purpose and goals of the organization Certain organizations committed to open, democratic relationships—such as universities—will be required to maintain a power-sharing structure based on decentralization. Because the purpose and goals of a small business such as a drug store are different, its structure may be more centralized. A corporation that seeks to become a conglomerate will have to decentralize more because of the diverse product lines than an organization committed to one product line.

The knowledge and experience of top-level managers As noted, if top managers are much more knowledgeable and have more experience than lower level subordinates, it creates a condition that tends to favor centralization.

The skill, knowledge, and attitudes of subordinates Obviously, one of the prime prerequisites for decentralization is to have trained, knowledgeable subordinates who are committed to the goals of the organization. If these conditions do not exist then it is much more risky to decentralize.

The size of the organization structure The larger an organization is, the more difficult it is for any one executive or set of executives to have the knowledge to make all major decisions. Large structures force delegation of authority in order to keep the processes of the organization functioning.

The geographical dispersion of the structure The more geographically dispersed a structure is, the more difficult it is for any one individual to know what is going on in other areas. Individuals in more remote locations are better situated to make decisions relating to their activities, because they are familiar with the local conditions and the context of the immediate situation.

The technical complexity of the tasks One of the factors that has forced organizations to become more decentralized in recent years has been the technical complexity of the tasks undertaken. The structural hierarchy of an organization today represents much less of a knowledge hierarchy than it did prior to World War II. The extreme example is the research scientist. It is difficult for anyone else to make technical decisions regarding the scientist's project because no one knows as much about it as he does. As the tasks in organizations have become specialized and sophisticated, operational decision making relating to these tasks has of necessity been delegated to the functional experts.

The time frame of decisions The time frame within which different decisions must be made is different. A quarterback, sergeant, and control tower dispatcher make decisions under different time constraints than a long-range planning committee or a deliberative group attempting to establish policy. Where quick, on-the-spot decisions must be made, the authority to make them needs to be delegated. Decisions not subject to these constraints can be referred to higher levels.

The significance of the decision Perhaps the most standard criterion for delegating authority has been the significance of the decision: If the decision has a minimal cost impact it can be delegated. Decisions of more primary responsibility that have greater consequences for the organization, however, should be retained by the individual in charge.

Requirement for subordinates to accept and be motivated by the decisions Letting subordinates be involved in or actually make decisions has been recognized as an important means of gaining their acceptance of the decisions. When acceptance of the decision is extremely important, such as the case where subordinates must implement the decision, there is a greater need to delegate authority. In those decisions where subordinate acceptance is not as significant (such as decisions made in relation to outside groups), decision making can be more centralized.

Status of the organization's planning and control systems If decision making is more structured because of existing procedures (standing plans) in relation to an issue, or if clear cut goals and objectives exist, the supervisor is more willing to let others make decisions because he can predict with a greater certainty how they will be made. However, if few goals or planning guidelines exist in relation to the decision area, there is more risk in delegating this authority.

The status of the organization's information systems As indicated, the individual with the most accurate and current information on a problem should make the decision. This has been one of the basic arguments for decentralization. As electronic data processing has introduced real time systems, however, the conditions for centralization of many decisions have become more favorable. Many writers have predicted that this would permit a reverse trend towards centralization. A management information system creates the feasibility for doing this but not necessarily the desirability, since it is only one factor of many that influence this situation.

The conformity and coordination required in the tasks of the organization If the many activities of the organization require precise integration, it is easier to do this from one central point. Such orchestration is seen in centralized units such as production control. Tasks that tend to be more independent, such as selling, can be subject to greater decentralization.

External factors As an organization relates its activities to those of outside groups, it finds that it is often desirable to centralize these points of contact. Dealing with labor unions, major customers, and community officials are examples. It is normally easier to decentralize decisions relating to internal operations than it is to external.

Applying Contingency Theory

Theoretically, in attempting to determine whether to decentralize an organization structure, the manager should evaluate the status and significance of all 13 of the variables in his situation, and on that basis develop the information to make the correct decision. Without using this approach a manager would, through trial and error, experiment with different types of structures until he arrived at one that appeared to be satisfactory. In this trial-and-error process it is the condition of the 13 variables that would determine whether the revised structure was effective. If an administrator attempted to centralize certain decisions in an organization strongly committed to decentralization, it would not take long for the rumblings to get back to him. Also, if a supervisor delegated certain decision making to an individual who had an insufficient background or was not committed to the goals of the organization, it would soon become apparent that he had made a mistake. Clearly understanding the trade-offs involved and being familiar with the conditions that are favorable to centralization or decentralization can avoid many at least temporary errors, and it provides a useful framework for approaching managerial decision making.

The current conditions found in American industry support the validity of the 13 variables enumerated. Generally, operational decisions are decentralized, and major financial and personnel decisions are centralized. In profit decentralization a manager is normally given fairly complete control over his operations as long as he achieves specific profit goals. Nevertheless, he is subject to financial constraints relating to capital investment and budgeting. Technical decisions relating to the operations of the organization are decentralized, because the operating supervisors are generally more familiar with the activities taking place. Also, these are decisions that need to be made quickly, and the decisions tend to be more structured. Major financial and personnel staffing decisions are centralized because of their cost significance and because they are basic controls that top-level managers use to balance the total activity of the organization.

Again many of the applications are obvious. In situations where an organization has weak controls, a lack of direction, few policies, a high degree of integration in its tasks, and undertrained lower-level supervisors, the need for centralization is obvious. In companies with overburdened executives, dispersed operations, diversified products, complex tasks, knowledgeable subordinates, and low morale because little freedom of action is provided, more decentralization is mandatory. Normally, however, decisions on organization structure are not so apparent. It is under these circumstances that contingency methodology becomes valuable because it forces a thorough consideration and weighting of the significant variables in the situation. Also, it establishes a framework where the advantages and limitations of different management concepts must be related to specific conditions in the situation. This way of thinking and method of analysis offers an effective means for dealing with the complexity of managerial decision making.

Questions on Reading

1. What are the principal characteristics of contingency theory?
2. Describe the four areas of understanding in management practice from a contingency theory viewpoint.
3. What are the principal trade-offs of centralization vs. decentralization.
4. Identify and discuss the situational variables which determine whether centralization or decentralization will be effective in a given organization.
5. Generally, what types of decisions are centralized and what types of decisions are decentralized in American industry? Discuss.

7 LINE AND STAFF RELATIONSHIPS

- Line and Staff Functions
- Advisory Staff Authority
- Service Staff Authority
- Control Staff Authority
- Functional Staff Authority
- Line-Staff Friction
- The Personal Staff
- Review
- Discussion Questions
- References
- Case Study: Noncooperative Line Managers
- Case Study: A Choice of Job Offers
- Applications Reading: "Using Central Staff to Boost Line Initiative" Edward C. Schleh
- Questions on Reading

The line activities in an organization are those that are directly concerned with attaining the company's product or service objectives, whereas staff activities exist in order to help make line activities more effective. The authority relationships between those engaged in line activities and those engaged in staff activities, which can follow several patterns, is the major topic of this chapter. Near the end of the chapter we also consider some of the frictions that sometimes develop because of the need to use functional staff experts in organizations.

Line and Staff Functions   In a manufacturing firm, production, sales, and finance are typically considered to be line activities, whereas such areas of work as personnel relations and purchasing are examples of staff activities. Although the level of performance of line activities very quickly affects the overall success of a firm, this does not suggest that staff activities are therefore less important to the long-run survival of the firm.

objectives (or goals)   1   Line activities in an organization are those activities that are *directly* concerned with attaining the firm's _____ .

through   2   The function of staff activities, on the other hand, is to help attain organizational objectives [independently of / through] improved effectiveness of line activities.

Line   3   Insofar as organizational success is concerned, there is a time differential between the effects of line and staff activities. Which type of activity affects organizational success sooner? [Line / Staff]

immediate

longer   4   A failure in the production function has [immediate / long-run] implications with respect to a product objective, whereas a failure to provide for effective employee training and development affects overall organizational success in the [longer / shorter] run.

line   5   The particular activities that are considered to be line (as contrasted to staff) activities are dependent on the type of organization involved. In a manufacturing firm, production, sales, and finance are typically identified as _____ activities.

staff   **6** In manufacturing firms, purchasing, personnel relations, and accounting are examples of _____ activities.

No   **7** Would the line activities in a hospital or university be the same as those in a manufacturing firm? [Yes / No]

line   **8** Once the activities that are directly concerned with attaining the organization's goals, that is, the _____ activities, are identified, the staff functions that help make the line more effective are then established.

is not   **9** The relationship between line and staff activities in most organizations is quite complex. Contrary to what one might expect, for example, the staff [is / is not] invariably subordinate to the line organization.

personal   **10** There are two general categories of staff activity: *specialist* and *personal*. Whereas a specialist staff serves various components of the line organization, that staff which works only for a particular executive is the _____ staff.

personal   **11** An "administrative assistant" or "assistant-to," who may help a particular executive by carrying out some of the routine functions of his office or by investigating special problems for him, belongs to the category of _____ staff.

specialist   **12** On the other hand, a group of experts in a particular field who work with a number of line managers in order to promote greater organizational effectiveness constitute a [personal / specialist] staff.

specialist   **13** The relationship between a specialist staff and line managers can be such that the staff may have *advisory, service, control,* or *functional* authority with respect to line activities. In the sections of this chapter that follow we consider each type of staff authority in turn, thus giving primary attention to the role of the [personal / specialist] staff in the organization.

Advisory Staff Authority A staff group with advisory staff authority offers suggestions and prepares plans in its area of specialty for consideration by line managers; but as the name of this type of authority implies, line managers are in no way obligated to follow staff advice in this case.

14 A "management development department" that serves department managers in a company by investigating problems in supervisory development and recommending possible courses of action to requesting line managers can be described as having _____ staff authority.

advisory

15 Is line authority in effect restricted by the existence of a specialist staff that has been assigned advisory authority? [Yes / No]

No

16 It has been said that a good portion of an advisory staff manager's job is to sell, not tell. Since the line manager need not accept advisory staff recommendations, would this seem to be an accurate description of the authority relationship? [Yes / No]

Yes

17 Development of a complete recommended solution should be the staff person's goal. Often referred to as the concept of *completed staff work*, it makes development of the staff person's own ideas [more / less] likely.

more

18 The pitfall in which a staff specialist simply "writes up" the ideas of line managers can be avoided by following the concept of completed _____ _____.

staff work

19 On the other hand, does the concept of completed staff work suggest that the staff specialist should entirely refrain from discussing the problem or his own tentative solutions with line personnel? [Yes / No]

No

20 Staff solutions arrived at without consultation with affected line personnel are more likely to be [practical / impractical]

impractical

21 But does the staff man appropriately fulfill his

No

function if he bases his written recommendations primarily on line-manager suggestions? [Yes / No]

22 Thus the objective of having the advisory staff specialist submit complete proposals that reflect the specialist's own ideas is included in the concept of

completed staff work _____ _____ _____. To be practical, however, discussion with line personnel to be affected by the proposals is necessary.

23 In many multidivision companies, the central personnel staff conducts studies of the various personnel activities of the divisions, such as training and development, and submits proposals for program changes to the division managers. Of the four kinds of staff au-

advisory thority, this is an example of _____ staff authority.

24 Furthermore, in many companies the division requesting and receiving advisory staff service is billed for the cost involved in conducting the study. Under such circumstances, line managers are likely to

major request staff advice for relatively [minor / major] problems.

25 When a budgetary charge is made for utilizing the advisory staff, the staff recommendations are likely to

seriously be treated [lightly / seriously].

26 When line managers must pay for staff advice, is the size of the staff organization likely to increase beyond the value of its contribution to company effec-

No tiveness? [Yes / No]

27 Thus, imposing a charge for advisory staff recommendations ensures that (1) line managers [do / do

do not; not] request staff advice for every minor problem, (2)
are the staff recommendations [are / are not] seriously
is considered, and (3) advisory staff size [is / is not] consistent with its contribution to overall company effectiveness.

28 Of course, one hazard associated with imposing a

204 • Chapter 7 • Line and Staff Relationships

            infrequently budgetary charge for the advisory activities of a specialist staff is that line managers may request needed advice too [frequently / infrequently].

29 Whether or not a budgetary charge is involved, one approach by which top management tries to make certain that specialist advice is considered by line managers is that of *compulsory staff advice*. Since this refers to advisory authority, does the word "compulsory" indicate that line managers *must* follow the staff recommendations in this case? [Yes / No]

    No (continued in next frame)

30 The word "compulsory" in the context of advisory staff authority indicates that the specialist advice must be sought before a line decision in particular areas is made, *not* that the advice in question must be followed. Again, this is a way of assuring that specialist staff advice will at least be considered by _____ managers.

    line

Service Staff Authority   As the name once again implies, a staff group with service authority is one that carries out some area of activity that has been separated from the line job as a service to the line. However, unlike the situation for advisory staff authority, if the activity in question is to be carried out, the line manager must do it through the staff organization, and is not free to do it himself.

31 Using the area of purchasing as an example, does a line manager typically have the authority to decide what items need to be purchased for the department? [Yes / No]

    Yes

32 Once the line manager has identified the necessary purchases, must he work through the company purchasing agent, or is he free to negotiate purchases on his own, if he wishes?

    In most companies, he is obliged to work through the purchasing agent.

33 Thus, a purchasing department typically can be described as having _____ staff authority.

    service

34 Is line authority restricted to some extent by the existence of service staff authority? [Yes / No]

Yes (The line must use the staff service.)

35 On the other hand, is a line manager likely to do a better job in a particular area of work than the staff personnel specializing in that type of work? [Yes / No]

No

36 For example, the person who is likely to know more about sources of materials and supplies is the [line manager / purchasing agent].

purchasing agent

37 Furthermore, certain economies of centralized operation make it important that the service staff be used. In the case of the purchasing function, assigning this activity to a staff group makes the availability of quantity discounts [more / less] likely.

more

38 Thus, uniformity in procedures, generally more effective work, and economies of centralized operation result from the [voluntary / compulsory] use of service staffs by line managers.

compulsory

Control Staff Authority

A staff group with control staff authority actually has the responsibility for controlling certain aspects of line performance. The staff unit involved usually acts as an agent for a higher line manager.

39 In the preceding sections, we have considered two types of specialist staff authority. They are _____ staff authority and _____ staff authority.

advisory;
service

40 In contrast to these types of staff authority, a department manager who assigns the departmental inspection function to one unit has in effect assigned _____ staff authority to that inspection unit.

control

41 Is operating line authority restricted by the existence of control staff authority? [Yes / No]

Yes (At least it is at the organization levels below the control staff.)

helped

42 On the other hand, higher-management control of operations is [helped / hindered] by the assignment of control staff authority.

43 Control staffs also help achieve a higher caliber of performance by line units. For example, rejection of a marginal product is more likely to be done by [an employee of the manufacturing department / a member of an "outside" inspection unit].

a member of an "outside" inspection unit

44 The operating supervisor may see himself as being in the position of receiving "control" instructions from a higher-level line manager as well as from one or more staff specialists or staff groups with control authority, thus resulting in apparent [compliance with / violation of] the classical management principle of *unity of command*.

violation of

45 But the violation of the unity-of-command principle may be more apparent than real in this case, since the decisions being enforced by the specialists with control authority were made [by the specialists themselves / by a higher line manager].

by a higher line manager

Functional Staff Authority

Functional authority is said to exist whenever an individual is given decision-making authority outside the formal chain of command, and for specified activities only. The manager who is assigned functional authority is a specialist in the area of activity involved, but he may be either a line or a staff manager. As contrasted with control authority, the individual with functional authority has the authority to determine the appropriate standards in that area of speciality, as well as having the authority to enforce these standards.

46 The authority of the safety director to issue instructions regarding installation and use of safety equipment involves the assignment of _____ authority to a staff manager.

functional

47 On the other hand, in addition to the departmental assignment, the finance manager in a company may be given authority to specify the format of financial

line

records kept by other departments. This is an example of the assignment of functional authority to a _____ manager.

Two

48 Refer to the partial organization chart in Figure 7.1. How many of the managers have been assigned functional authority for specified activities? _____ [number]

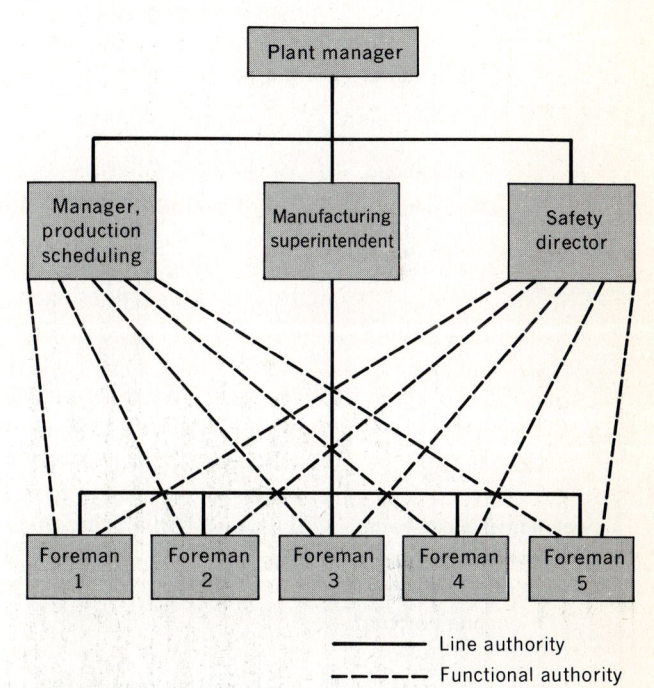

Figure 7.1 Partial organization chart illustrating functional authority as contrasted to line authority.

Five

49 Over how many managers does the safety director have functional staff authority? _____ [number]

line

50 More than any other type of staff authority, the assignment of functional staff authority restricts the authority of the _____ managers affected.

51 For example, in matters of personnel discipline, production scheduling, use of safety equipment, and

No	the like, does the typical production manager have complete decision-making authority? [Yes / No]
diminished	**52** When the company personnel manager requires plant managers to follow seniority in making layoffs, the authority of the plant managers has been [enhanced / diminished].
diminished	**53** Similarly, when the controller requires periodic budgetary reports from company sales offices, the authority of the company sales manager has been [enhanced / diminished].
enhanced	**54** On the other hand, in the last example the authority of the controller has been [enhanced / diminished] by the assignment of functional authority.
Three	**55** Referring once again to Figure 7.1, from how many individuals does each supervisor receive instructions? _____ [number]
violation of (since each supervisor is getting directives from more than one person)	**56** Again, the principle of unity of command states that every individual in an organization should receive instructions from just one superior. The use of functional authority tends to result in [compliance with / violation of] this principle.
Yes	**57** Therefore, is it conceivable that extensive assignment of functional authority could seriously damage or destroy organizational departmentation and the basis for line authority? [Yes / No]
essential	**58** On the other hand, the requirements of companywide coordination of activities and the necessity of common procedures because of governmental and labor-union influences make the assignment of functional authority [essential / unnecessary].
minimize	**59** Because of the organizational effects of the extensive assignment of functional authority, it is considered good practice to [maximize / minimize] the assignment of functional authority.

Five

60 One way of limiting the undesirable organizational effects of functional authority is by specifying that the functional authority of any manager shall not extend beyond one organizational level. Refer to Figure 7.2. How many organizational levels are there in all? _____ [number]

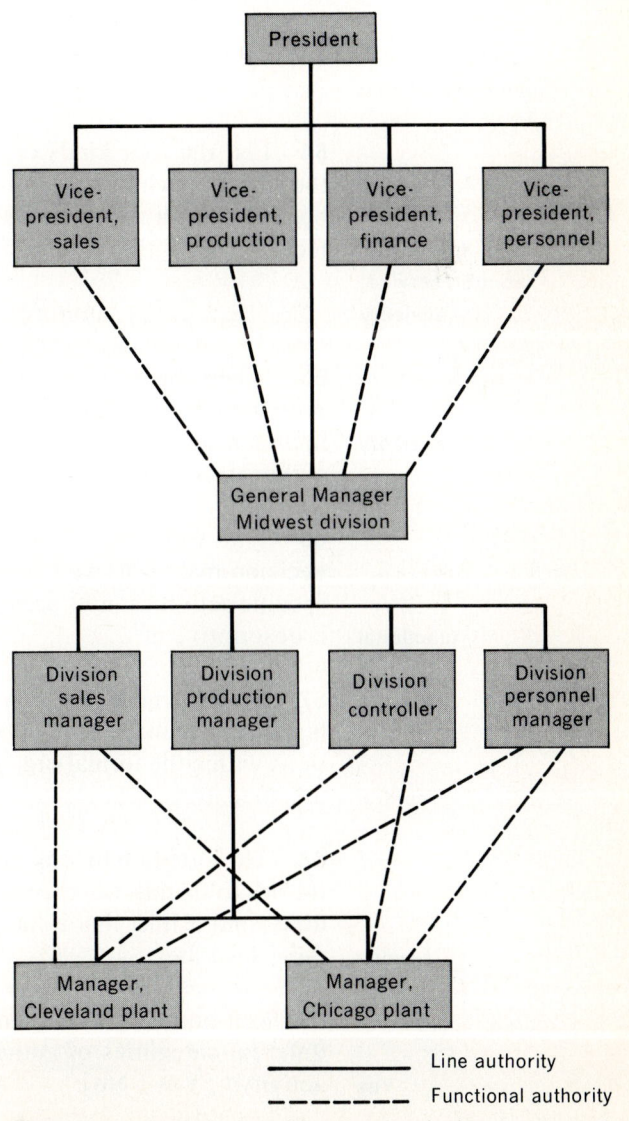

Figure 7.2 The limitation of functional authority to one organizational level.

61 How many organizational levels are directly affected by the functional staff authority of the vice president in charge of personnel? _____ [number]

One

62 How many organizational levels are directly affected by the functional staff authority of the division controller? _____ [number]

One

63 In summary, we have described four kinds of authority relationships between the specialist staff and the line organization: advisory, service, _____, and _____.

control; functional

64 List the four kinds of staff authority in order of the extent to which line authority is thereby restricted, beginning with the relationship involving the most effect on the line: _____, _____, _____, and _____ authority.

functional; control; service; advisory

65 When the staff serves the line by investigating problems and recommending courses of action for line-manager consideration, _____ staff authority is involved.

advisory

66 The situation in which the staff is assigned decision-making as well as enforcement authority over specific activities in its area of specialized competence is descriptive of _____ staff authority.

functional

67 A staff whose function it is to act as an agent of higher line management by supervising specific operations within the formal organization structure has been assigned _____ staff authority.

control

68 The situation in which a line manager has the authority to decide whether or not an activity should be done, and if it is, that it must be carried out by a staff unit, describes _____ staff authority.

service

69 Is it possible for the same staff unit to be assigned different categories of authority for different areas of activity? [Yes / No]

Yes

70 For example, a personnel department may serve the function of advising managers in the areas of executive development and of screening applicants to fill personnel needs. In this case, the personnel unit has been assigned _____ and _____ authority, respectively.

advisory; service

71 Overall coordination of company activities and the formulation of procedures by functional experts are [enhanced / impeded] by the growth of staff authority in an organization.

enhanced

72 Clear authority relationships in the organization and simplification of the organization structure are [enhanced / impeded] by the growth of staff authority.

impeded

Line-Staff Friction

Since the utilization of functional experts in organizations has resulted in the various authority relationships described in this chapter, it should not be surprising to find that some degree of friction sometimes accompanies the necessary activities of technical staff units. In this section it is not our intention to propose solutions, but rather to identify the source of such conflict by describing some of the criticisms that each group directs toward the other group. In part, the solution to such friction lies in clearer authority assignments and in better communication, the latter being the content of Chapter 10. On the other hand, a certain amount of intergroup friction and rivalry is normal in any organization and indicates that people are at least interested enough to compete.

73 From the line point of view, staff people are often seen as *assuming too much authority, taking credit for good ideas, failing to keep line personnel informed,* and *seeing problems only from a specialized and narrow viewpoint.* The line manager who states, "The staff should realize that its job is to help us, not to tell us what to do," is in effect suggesting that staff people assume too much _____.

authority

74 The line comment, "We get blamed for the

212 ● Chapter 7 ● Line and Staff Relationships

          credit   problems in every new program until we get the bugs ironed out, after which every staff department claims it did the job," represents the line complaint that staff often takes _____ for successful programs.

75   The line observation, "Staff people keep significant facts to themselves so as to keep us off balance," is an example of the complaint that staff personnel fail

            line   to communicate with _____ personnel.

76   "The directions I get from the quality assurance department take care of my quality problems all right, but at the expense of problems in scheduling and personnel assignment," illustrates the point that a staff

        narrow   may have a [narrow / broad] conception of problems and solutions.

77   On the other hand, staff people perceive the source of difficulty in line-staff relationships quite differently. They feel, for example, that *the line doesn't make proper use of staff, the line resists new ideas,* and *the line doesn't give the staff enough authority.* When the line managers make decisions in specialized areas without consulting with them, staff people feel that

        are not   their services [are / are not] being appropriately used.

78   The staff comment, "People in the line don't like to be involved with us because they'd rather do things as they always have," indicates that some staff people

       ideas (etc.)   see line personnel as resisting new _____.

79   "We have been hired to bring our specialized knowledge and skill into the organization, but we are then restricted to an advisory role only," suggests that staff people often feel that they have not been assigned

        authority   sufficient _____.

80   Through this presentation we do not mean to suggest that line-staff conflict represents a serious problem in most organizations. For one thing, line and staff personnel frequently have broad areas of mutual and compatible interest, and for another, many organizational conflicts are not at all a matter of line versus staff. For example, friction between the manufacturing

line	and sales divisions of a firm involves conflict between two groups typically considered as being [line / staff] in nature.
	81 When people develop identifications with specialized work groups, some intergroup conflict is probably inevitable. Organizational action to reduce such frictions is desirable, however, when they become [competitive / disruptive] in nature.
disruptive	

The Personal Staff

Whereas a specialist staff serves several components of the line organization, a personal staff, such as the assistant-to, works only with a single line manager.

82 Answering correspondence for the line manager, studying and recommending alternative courses of action, and acting as a liaison with other departments are typical duties of a member of a _____ staff.

personal

83 Other titles in place of assistant-to include "staff assistant" and "administrative assistant." Would the title "assistant manager" also suggest that a staff assistant position is involved? [Yes / No]

No (This title would usually be used for a line executive subordinate to the manager.)

84 Therefore an "assistant manager" is typically a [line / staff] manager.

line

85 In military organizations, a "general staff" consists of a staff of experts who advise a particular senior line commander. Therefore, a general staff is also an example of a _____ staff.

personal

86 The authority of a line manager [is / is not] diminished because of the existence of a personal staff.

is not

87 Through the assistance provided by one or more staff personnel directly subordinate to him a line manager is able to investigate organizational problems and proposed solutions more thoroughly, thereby [increasing / decreasing] his ability to manage a broad scope of operations.

increasing

88 On the other hand, from the viewpoint of subordinate line managers, it may not be clear when a senior executive's staff assistant is speaking "for himself" as contrasted to speaking "for the boss." Thus, a typical consequence of the extensive use of staff assistants is that the decision-making authority of these individuals [is / is not] clearly understood by others in the organization.

is not

Review

line

staff

89 Activities that are directly concerned with attaining company objectives are regarded as _____ activities, whereas those that are indirectly related to attaining company objectives are _____ activities. (Frames 1 to 9)

specialist; personal

90 There are two general categories of staff activity: _____ and _____. (Frames 10 to 13)

Advisory

91 What type of specialist staff authority leads to the danger that staff recommendations will be altered to please line managers and perhaps will even amount to a "writing up" of line ideas? _____ (Frames 14 to 30)

completed
staff work

92 That advisory staff personnel should develop complete proposals for action, rather than partial solutions, is called the concept of _____ _____ _____. (Frames 17 to 22)

Yes

93 Once a manager has decided to take certain action, such as hiring additional personnel, must he do this through the unit having service staff authority in the area? [Yes / No] (Frames 31 to 38)

control

94 A staff group, such as an inspection unit, which acts as an agent for a higher line manager has had _____ staff authority assigned to it. (Frames 39 to 45)

functional

95 Whenever a manager is given decision-making authority outside the formal line structure, and for specified activities only, _____ authority is involved. (Frames 46 to 72)

Yes   **96** Can functional authority be assigned to line as well as to staff personnel? [Yes / No] (Frames 46 and 47)

violation of   **97** The use of functional authority results in apparent [compliance with / violation of] the principle of unity of command. (Frames 55 to 59)

one   **98** In order to limit the undesirable organizational effects of functional authority, it is often specified that such authority shall not extend beyond ____ [number] organization level(s). (Frames 60 to 62)

service;   **99** Of the four types of specialist staff authority described in this chapter, list those that result in some restriction of line authority: _____,
control; functional   _____, and _____. (Frames 34, 41, and 50)

staff   **100** From the line point of view, the cause of any friction between the line and staff components in an organization is often ascribed to too much authority being given to the [line / staff]. (Frames 73 to 81)

personal   **101** In contrast to a specialist staff, the type of staff that works with a particular line manager rather than with a number of line components is the _____ staff. (Frames 82 to 88)

Discussion Questions

1. Since staff groups in a manufacturing firm do not directly produce or sell the product or arrange financing, why are they created?
2. Granted the need for staff advice and assistance, why should members of a staff group ever be given control or functional authority over line activities?
3. When a difference of opinion about how particular work should be done exists between a line manager, such as a production foreman, and a staff specialist, what advantages does the foreman have in this controversy?
4. In a controversy between a production supervisor and a member of a specialist staff, what advantages does the staff person possess?
5. Contrast the organizational position and possible functions of a personal staff with those of a specialist staff.

6. Discuss the difference between control staff authority and functional authority, and describe the characteristics of the situation in which each would appropriately be used.
7. In a firm with geographically dispersed operations, consider the implications of your applying for a position entitled "assistant to the branch manager" as contrasted to "assistant branch manager."
8. If a large firm with production facilities located throughout the country tends toward a philosophy of managerial centralization, how is this likely to affect the formation of specialist staff groups in terms of (*a*) the location of such groups and (*b*) the extent of their development?

References

Atchison, T. J. "The Fragmentation of Authority." *Personnel,* vol. 47, no. 4, July-August 1970.
Browne, P. J., and C. C. Cotton. "The Topdog/Underdog Syndrome in Line-Staff Relations." *Personnel Journal,* vol. 54, no. 8, August 1975.
Browne, P. J., and R. T. Golembiewski. "The Line-Staff Concept Revisited: An Empirical Study of Organizational Images." *Academy of Management Journal,* vol. 17, no. 3, September 1974.
Coleman, C., and J. Rich. "Line, Staff, and the Systems Perspective." *Human Resource Management,* vol. 12, no. 3, Fall 1973.
Dale, E., and L. F. Urwick. *Staff in Organization.* New York: McGraw-Hill, 1960.
Henning, D. A., and R. L. Mosely. "The Authority Role of a Functional Manager: The Controller." *Administrative Science Quarterly,* vol. 15, no. 4, December 1970.
Pettigrew, A. "The Influence Process between Specialists and Executive." *Personnel Review,* vol. 3, no. 1, Winter 1974.
Phillips, V. F., Jr. *The Organizational Role of the Assistant-To.* New York: American Management Association, 1971.
Simon, J. R., C. Norton, and N. J. Lonergan. "Accounting for the Conflict between Line Management and the Controller's Office." *S.A.M. Advanced Management Journal,* vol. 44, no. 1, Winter 1979.

CASE STUDY: Noncooperative Line Managers

As manager of personnel and industrial relations, Clyde Schoen was assigned principal authority and responsibility for personnel selection and training, and additional authority and responsibility to coordinate the company personnel practices in such areas as discipline and wage and salary management so as to assure a consistency throughout the company. In announcing Schoen's appointment to the newly established position several months ago, the company president indicated the advantages of a centralized personnel function at the present stage of the company's growth, and he urged all managers and supervisors to give the new department their full cooperation.

The president's directive notwithstanding, most line managers have failed to give Clyde Schoen very much cooperation. For example, when sending requests that new employees be hired, many supervisors are still not submitting associated job descriptions, which Schoen has requested be provided as a matter of routine. As a result, the personnel department cannot determine the required applicant qualifications in such instances but rather is forced to send the applicants to the department concerned for preliminary screening as well as final selection. Of the eight employee dismissals that have taken place since Schoen assumed his duties, in only two instances did the supervisor request the action through the personnel department. In the other cases the supervisor simply sent a memo informing the personnel department of the action, with little, if any, explanation given. Realizing the necessity of working with rather than against line management, Clyde Schoen has tried to be diplomatic in reminding line managers of the necessity of clearing such actions with the personnel department, without much apparent success.

Most recently, Schoen spent several weeks devising a supervisory development program, originally suggested as an area of need by the company president at the time of Schoen's appointment. The program was scheduled for the last two working hours of each Monday, and the ten meetings were to be oriented toward a discussion of basic management principles. In the directive to the managers and supervisors Mr. Schoen emphasized the importance of the program and the president's expressed interest in it. When he entered the conference room for the first meeting, however, he found only nine of the company's thirty-eight management personnel in attendance.

Feeling both embarrassed and infuriated, Schoen has decided that the time for a confrontation with line management has come. He believes that either he must make an issue of this failure to comply with his directive or see his departmental functions degenerate. Accordingly, arming himself with a copy of the memo that was sent to each supervisor informing him of the supervisory development program, he presents his case to the company president with the request that either line managers be instructed to comply with such personnel directives or that the president accept his resignation as manager of the personnel and industrial relations department.

1. Was line-management response to the actions and requests of the personnel department predictable? Why or why not?

2. How might Clyde Schoen have handled his relations with the managers differently?
3. What is the company president likely to do in response to Mr. Schoen's request? What should he do?

CASE STUDY: A Choice of Job Offers

Carol Stander is scheduled to complete her bachelor's degree in business administration in June, with a dual major in economics and finance. In her course work she has particularly enjoyed the analytically oriented courses, and included several courses in statistics and accounting among her electives. By the end of March she was interviewed by a number of companies at the placement center on campus, and as a result of interviews at company locations she has three offers to which she has to respond by April 15.

One position which has been offered is as a labor economist in the industrial relations department of a large aerospace company. The general nature of the position involves analysis of labor markets to determine equitable wage rates, appropriate location of new company facilities, and possible participation by the company in technical training.

The second position involves appointment to the management intern program of a large regional bank. In this program each participant spends the first year in various assignments in the central offices of the bank and is then assigned as the assistant manager in a branch bank in the second year.

The third position involves appointment to the finance staff of a large manufacturing company which is diversified in terms of products manufactured. The function of the group is to determine the methods by which the company's financing needs can be satisfied and to evaluate alternative investment opportunities. The entry salary level for each of the three positions is about comparable, considering differences in the cost of living at the respective places of work.

While Carol feels fortunate in having three good job offers, the existence of opportunities that are so diverse has created a decision-making problem for her at this time.

1. What professional, or type-of-work, factors should Carol Stander consider in comparing the three job offers?
2. What personal factors should Carol consider in comparing the three opportunities?
3. How could you describe the three positions in terms of line/staff activities?
4. If one of Carol Stander's objectives is to "get into top management some day," how do the three positions relate to this objective?

APPLICATIONS READING:

Using Central Staff to Boost Line Initiative

Edward C. Schleh

President
Schleh Associates, Inc.
Palo Alto, California

Twenty chief executive officers were spiritedly discussing utilization of central staff. Approximately half of them were decentralizing and minimizing central staff; the others were centralizing and strengthening it. Yet none had based the transitions on any strong principles, and no matter what stage their companies were in, all were dissatisfied and therefore moving in the opposite direction.

Unfortunately, these CEOs did not realize that their problems were much more fundamental than deciding whether to centralize or decentralize. The question each really faced was: How does a company increase the value of its central staff without strangling line initiative?

Why the increased interest in central staff? First, great improvements in transportation, communications, and computer technology have enabled companies to direct operations at many different locations. At the same time, government has insinuated controls into the management process at almost every turn. In addition, the increasing availability of knowledge in almost every kind of discipline and subdiscipline has created an apparent need for experts in many more subspecialties than ever before.

Paradoxically, however, central staff tends to overkill, or overemphasize, its specialties to the detriment of the problems it presumably tries to correct. This, in turn, sharply reduces the spirit and enthusiasm of line managers.

Wanted—Expertise

In many companies, central staff employees either are inexperienced or are castoffs. Either type hinders sound staff-line cooperation because central staff members must be recognized as experts by line managers. Thus top management should not attempt to develop "comers" by giving them a two-year tour of duty in key corporate staff positions; they are unlikely to become overnight experts. A new merchandise manager, for example, won't be accepted right away. Other

Source: Reprinted, by permission of the publisher, from *Management Review*, vol. 65, no. 5, May 1976, © 1976 by AMACOM, a division of American Management Associations. All rights reserved.

marketing people will think they know more about merchandising than he or she does. The merchandise manager must be an expert who has been on the job long enough, say three or four years, in order to win the respect of others.

If central staff employees are to act as experts, they must understand all line operations, especially at the first level. But central staff members often are young M.B.A.s who have never worked at the first level; consequently, they do not fully appreciate what is happening there. Management development plans must ensure that central staff members get experience at lower-level or staff jobs first. International firms face an even greater problem because central staff members must also understand different cultures in order to make practical suggestions.

Staff vs. Line

Executives often believe that line managers make decisions on a seat-of-the-pants basis. They argue that if line managers would use more of the expert knowledge available in various staff disciplines, they would be able to do their jobs better.

One way to encourage line managers to use central staff expertise is to require that the staff develop methods and train local staffs or line managers to carry on the work wherever possible. Central staff should not continually mastermind current problems. Instead of being a hot-problem solver, for example, a labor relations specialist should help managers in plants improve their labor relations skills.

Furthermore, central staff should act as a helper to the line, not a tale carrier to the top. Obviously, no line manager wants to consult staff employees who view themselves primarily as informers to top management.

A CEO may favor a strong central staff when he finds it difficult to keep up with the multitude of problems that must be faced, especially as the company expands and operations become more complex. But, when central staff people are used in this way, they tend to advise on all problems. Line operations often slow down because no one wants little "errors" brought to the attention of higher executives.

Thus central staff ordinarily should advise higher executives on general problem areas only. They should report to the appropriate chief executive overall data that indicate a need for a general policy change or a shift in direction, but should not report detailed information on a section and thereby cause a line to run scared. Top management will find this approach much more comfortable in the long run. A CEO will be able to avoid involvement in minor problems and will not continually have to arbitrate squabbles between central staff and line divisions.

One company, for example, greatly improved staff-line relations by switching responsibility of a group of analysts from the controller's office who had been assigned to report on activities in various plants to the home office. Instead, they were directed to help the plants develop better systems and report on improvements after implementation of these systems.

Central staff must be made accountable for line results if line managers are to rely on it. Line managers frequently complain that central staff does not really care about line problems. Take, for example, a central scheduling department of a paint company. It concentrated on long runs in order to lower costs. In practice, however, costs were often higher because of local machine problems, material supplies, traffic conditions, and so forth. To correct the problem, top management made the scheduling department accountable for the difference between the net cost to manufacture and the estimated cost.

Likewise, line managers must be accountable for results to problems on which central staff is working. Otherwise, central staff may encounter difficulties similar to those of a market research director who developed an excellent plan for promoting Product A. When implemented, the plan failed because district and regional managers were told to emphasize Products B, C, D, and E.

Line managers often believe that the need to consult central staff requires following its specialized advice, even if total line results are reduced. Staff thus tends to run the line. To counteract overcontrol by staff, line managers should be allowed to reject advice they believe does not fit their problems.

In a consumer products firm, home-office merchandise managers were practically running the sales force through their programs. Consequently, many salesmen could not do the necessary sales and service work in their territories because they were hesitant about opposing the merchandisers. To correct this problem, each salesman was allowed to accept or reject any program if he believed it did not apply to his territory. The salesmen not only benefited more by the programs that they did accept and apply but also did the necessary servicing in their territories. Sales effectiveness increased greatly, and, as a sidelight, the merchandisers began to check territories to determine why their programs did not apply, thereby gaining a more realistic assessment of their markets.

CEOs often want central staff to help evaluate divisions or functions. But this is a questionable practice. The basic job of central staff should be to *help* divisions. Central staffs who believe their job is to evaluate line managers tend to run the line, and, as noted before, line managers often let them do it. They simply try to satisfy central staff rather than doing their jobs, subtly transferring accountability from operating units back up to the corporate staff (which usually is not accountable for balanced results anyway). The process kills not only line enthusiasm but also commitment to results, the major management requirement in any operation.

Preventing Major Deviations

A CEO needs a good central staff in order to prevent major deviations from the overall direction he has planned for the company or its divisions. Thus he charges central staff with setting up appropriate watchdog procedures to ensure that his policies are followed. However, difficulties arise when top management does not differentiate between functions that should be controlled and those that do not need to be controlled.

For example, in one company a central purchasing department did practically all the buying for its plants. Each requisition required extensive documentation and was critically analyzed by central purchasing and engineering personnel. Not only was it difficult to get quick deliveries in the field, but also much needless communication was created. When top management allowed individual plants to do all routine buying, either directly or under blanket agreements, deliveries improved; plants took less time to place orders than when they had to satisfy the central purchasing department. Central purchasing made more blanket contracts and cut its staff by two-thirds. In addition, the central engineering department cut its staff.

Because control work puts central specialists closer to top management, it often becomes their primary task, even though it usually is less creative than development of better methods for helping the line. Only top management can prevent this.

Making line managers accountable in a balanced way for all areas for which they are responsible can improve operations and decrease deviations. For example, a medical supply firm gave location managers full control of salary administration (outside of setting ranges) after establishing managers' bonuses weighing profit, growth, and inventory. In a sense, each was in business for himself—balanced delegation. It was to the advantage of each manager to pay adequately but not excessively to get work done.

Legal problems are among the deviations that can lead to major catastrophes. Thus CEOs often establish central legal groups with very strong authority. But, in doing so, they may also inhibit much creative action. Even an attorney should be expected to ask line managers what they wish to accomplish and then determine how to accomplish it with acceptable risk.

How should corporate and divisional legal functions differ? Legal staffs tend to believe they are accountable for preventing any untoward actions but not for long-range corporate building, which presumably is the responsibility of general managers. Legal staffs may be more inclined to help, however, if they have to report directly to general managers. In addition, parameters for legal problems that must be controlled on the corporate level should be broad wherever possible, and even then the corporate legal staff should be sensitive to the negative effects of its advice on the business. In effect, legal functions are like any other central staff function. Their purpose is to help solve problems, not to create additional ones.

When central staff assumes that its job is to prevent deviations, it works toward uniform procedures. First-level problems have great variability, however. Most procedures should be made voluntary except for those few that are absolutely necessary to keep people within broad policy. For instance, a chart of accounts may be specified to fit financial data into company statements, but much operating and cost data may vary between operations to fit specific operating needs.

Uniformity Isn't a Virtue

One way to make central staff sensitive to the losses created by uniformity is to make central staff members accountable for the negative effects of their procedures. A small shoe company had to rely on poor credit risks in order to remain in business. When the credit manager was made accountable for sales losses created by tight credit, he took a more balanced view of credit versus sales losses.

Uniformity that reduces costs at the expense of accomplishments is an illusion. In a bank chain, a corportate accounts-receivable expert (backed by the president) established rigid controls that reduced losses. The expert was not accountable, however, for the considerable loss of profitable accounts-receivable business that resulted in the branches. In addition, the bank lost many customers with large growth potential. The line's creative needs should always be weighed against any cost saving by standard staff procedures.

Not breaking down central staff into minute specialties can help prevent excessive uniformity. Wherever possible, specialties should be combined by a desired result. In other words, if two or three specialists affect one result, perhaps one person can be trained to handle all of them adequately.

Every central staff person imposes impacts on the line, but line managers can effectively handle only four to six staff contacts. A marketing department consisting of 18 product managers, for example, was so large that salespeople and district managers could not keep up with all their programs. Reducing the staff to only four product managers solved the problem.

Effective Long-Range Planning

Executives often feel more comfortable about major proposals, especially those involving expensive capital outlays, if they know they are based on the best staff thinking. But this can be a false sense of security if central staff groups are not accountable for line results.

Central staff employees often face no risk if they prevent an action, only if they help take an action. To circumvent this difficulty, one electronics company made its product development department accountable for developing designs that met time schedules and resulted in the product quality and unit cost expected when they were produced in volume. Product development engineers became much more sensitive to the manufacturing practicality of their designs. Redesign for manufacture dropped 50 percent, and bickering between product development and manufacturing was considerably reduced.

Central staff should be made accountable for implementing its plans. If central staff develops a plan and the results expected of the plan are not realized, it has failed. Central staff members should have to face up to accountability just as line managers.

To ensure that a plan does work, line managers should be consulted early-on in the planning process. Asking them to provide data to central staff for it to manipulate does not satisfy this requirement. Line managers should also be asked to give input on practicality.

In order to get manufacturing know-how considered from the beginning stages of the design, central engineering of a chemical company brought various manufacturing people into the equipment design studies very early. Not only were designs much more practical but also the manufacturing staff better understood the rationale and was more committed to the final design.

Central staff engaged in long-range planning often complains that line managers "just don't care." Line managers, too, must be accountable for the long range. Yet most line accountability systems focus on the short range. For example, executive compensation plans rarely emphasize long-range results. Even bonuses for managers of business divisions are usually based on profit, a short-range measurement. This problem is greater in companies that encourage management promotions and transfers. One company eliminated this problem by making managers of businesses accountable for the results of their businesses five years out. When this philosophy was incorporated into its compensation plan, the managers became more interested in carefully developing and implementing long-range plans.

Even central staff often deemphasizes long-range work simply because it is combined organizationally with short-range projects and instead tends to emphasize hot current problems. Medium-size companies where research and product development are combined are especially prone to putting research on the back burner; only current development and application is done. It often helps to break up the R&D department and set up a research group separately from the group developing variations in product for the current line. But, needless to say, the long-range group must be accountable in some way in order to successfully implement any long-range plans.

Long-range groups must also be in tune with operating practicalities. Having long-range experts work on particularly sticky current problems can be effective. In one firm, for example, a facilities planning director had to straighten out a particularly bad plant machine problem each year. This kind of problem kept him in touch with the action.

A Word of Caution

Top executives often resort to organizing a central staff because they believe it is more efficient and will prevent divisions from duplicating services. Computer services, for example, are often centralized in the name of efficiency.

But centralized computer services do not always serve the specific needs of the line or its timing. In addition, every central group tends toward empire building, often greatly increasing central costs beyond expectations. At the same time, line managers surreptitiously add extra people to give them information not provided by the central service.

Careful evaluation of these projects should be conducted after they are installed, adding up all the additional costs incurred by the line and weighing in any reduced service to the line. For example, find out whether each plant still receives information on product runs prompt enough for it to take corrective action. If central staff must account for the net effect of its installations, it will be more careful about making proposals for the future.

Efficient use of central staff is a difficult objective to attain, especially as organizations become more and more complex. But by applying the abundance of knowledge drawn from many disciplines, the return can be well worth the effort. Even when top management makes perceptive use of central staff, the CEO must keep alert to the danger of strangling line initiative. In the long run, companies rise or fall by the strength of their line drive. The basic function of central staff, therefore, should be to help top management increase the effectiveness of line initiative.

Questions on Reading

1. Why has there been increased interest in the use of central staff?
2. How should the central staff personnel and line managers interrelate on a day-to-day basis?
3. Should the objective of central staff be uniformity of procedures throughout the organization? Discuss.
4. How can central staff personnel be made accountable for the implementation of their plans when it is in fact the line managers who do such implementing?

8 THE ORGANIZATION AS A SOCIAL SYSTEM

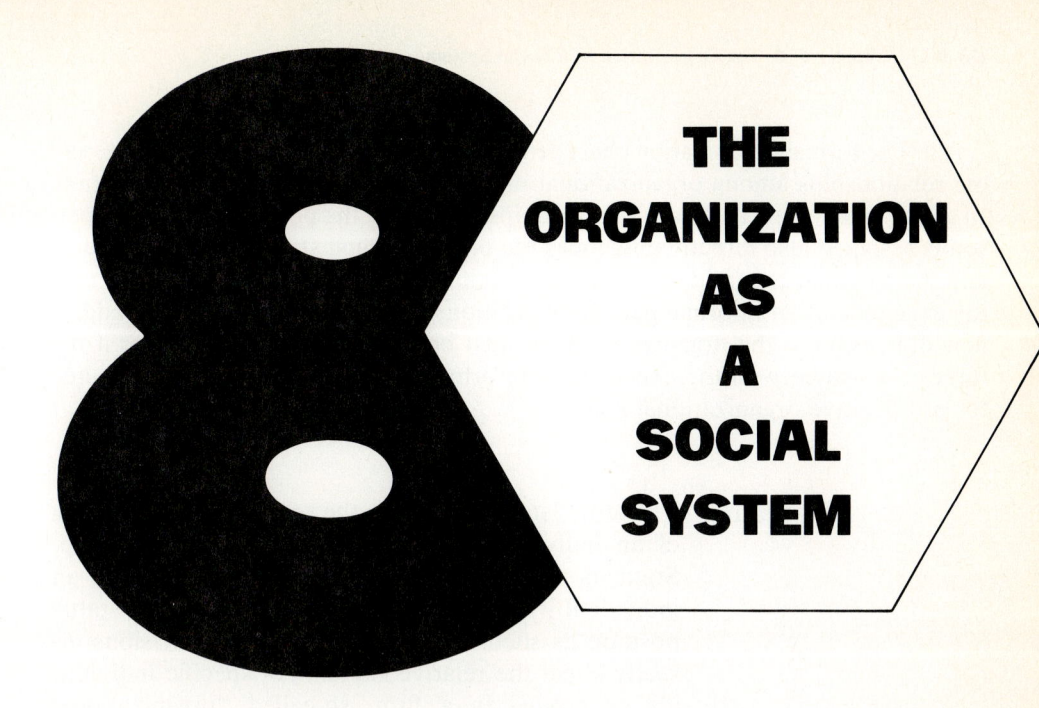

- Status
- Role
- Functions of the Informal Organization
- Charting the Informal Organization
- Power and Politics
- Review
- Discussion Questions
- References
- Case Study: Conflict among Managers
- Case Study: A Proposal for Product Redesign
- Applications Reading: "Rules of the Road: Doing Something Simple about Conflict in the Organization" Donald G. Livingston
- Questions on Reading

The formal organization chart defines areas of authority, responsibility, and the relationships among organizational units and individuals in the organization. In addition to formal authority relationships, however, the position to which a person is assigned also directly influences the organizational status of that individual and the role that the individual strives to fulfill in the organization. Beyond this, the existence of an informal pattern of relationships in every organization adds a new dimension to the organization that must be understood by a manager if the forces associated with the existence of informal social groups are to be directed toward positive organizational goals.

Status The term "status" refers to the relative social standing of an individual compared with others in a group. Status is assigned by group consensus, and hence an individual living in isolation would not have a status position as such. Since many executive decisions directly affect the relative standing of specific individuals or groups in a firm, so-called "organizational problems" often are really status problems.

supported

resisted

1 We would generally predict that a decision that enhances the status of a group in the company will be [supported / resisted] by that group, whereas a decision that lowers the status of a group will be [supported / resisted] by that group.

more

2 There are several factors that determine the status of people in an organization. The most important factor in determining a person's status is that individual's level in the managerial hierarchy, or *scalar status*. From this standpoint, a vice president generally has [more / less] scalar status than a department manager.

scalar

3 The authority to direct the activities of others is the essential feature of _____ status.

functional

4 As contrasted to scalar status, *functional status* is based on a person's job or area of activity in the organization. Although all the vice presidents in a company are equal in scalar status, they do not have equal amounts of _____ status.

5 In a given organization, some work is bound to be considered more important than other work. The

	type of status based on the importance of one's area of work in the firm, as judged by others, is
functional	_____ status.

6 For example, in a manufacturing-oriented organization the industrial engineer would probably have [higher / lower] functional status than a sales representative.

higher

7 Thus, an individual's rank in an organization determines his _____ status, whereas the kind, or area, of work he does determines his _____ status.

scalar
functional

8 In Figure 8.1, would you expect the overall status of the treasurer or the controller to be higher? Why?

Treasurer;
because that individual has
higher scalar status

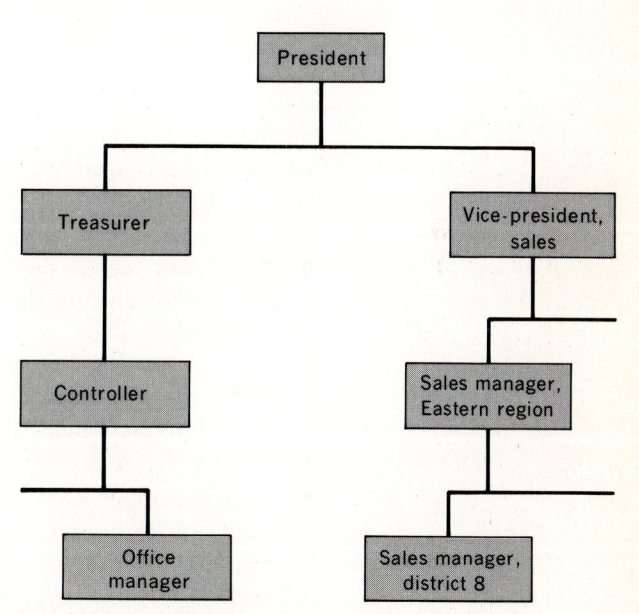

Figure 8.1 A partial organization chart.

9 In Figure 8.1, would a district sales manager or an office manager be higher in overall status?

Uncertain (See
next frame.)

10 Thus, although scalar status can be inferred from the organization-chart structure, this is not the case for _____ status, which also influences a person's overall status in a group.

functional

11 *Status symbols* are used in all organizations as indicators of relative standing. Perhaps the most formalized use of such symbols takes place in military organizations, in which the insignias of rank directly indicate relative _____.

status

12 However, even in nonmilitary organizations, there are numerous indicators of the relative standing of individuals. The size of an office, the presence or absence of carpeting, and the type of desk are all _____ symbols among executives.

status

13 In many large companies, these status symbols follow a formalized system, so that all managers at a given organization level have similar offices, for example. Exhibit 8.1 on pages 232–233 presents a classic and humorous, but not entirely fictional, description of a system of status symbols in business. Note that most of these "visible appurtenances" are such that they are arranged for, or supplied, by [the individual / the organization].

the organization

14 The fewer formal designators of rank that exist, the more important are the visible appurtenances, or status symbols. Thus, when the system of job titles used in a company quite clearly indicates the person's position in the management hierarchy, the status symbols are relatively [high / low] in importance.

low

15 Concern about status is not limited to the executive levels of an organization. Among operative employees, the location of the workplace, the type of clothing worn on the job, and whether or not the tools are owned by the worker can all be _____.

status symbols

16 As organizations have become more complex and people have become more mobile in our society, the

increased	reliance on status symbols has generally [increased / decreased].
status symbols	17 Thus, many of the things we own are valued as much for their prestige value as for their utility. From this standpoint, high-priced cars, clothing that is "in style," and even certain foods all represent _____.
clear	18 Even though the status system serves as a source of organizational problems, it also serves as a coordinating influence. Status systems facilitate cooperative behavior by conferring insignia and titles of office, thus making authority relationships [clear / ambiguous].
less	19 Status systems also affect communication. The use of formal titles of office in business communication results in [more / less] disruption of communication channels with a personnel change in that office.
encouraging	20 Furthermore, the existence of a status system can have motivational consequences in that expectancy of attaining status can serve as an incentive for individuals in an organization, thus [encouraging / discouraging] higher productivity.
negative	21 On the other hand, undue concern regarding one's current status leads to *status anxiety,* or fear of lowered organizational status, which may have [positive / negative] effects on job performance.
anxiety (or reduction, etc.)	22 The failure of a manager to consider the significance of such "minor" factors as the office locations assigned to subordinates is likely to lead to status _____ for some of them.
status symbols	23 Thus, by making authority relationships clearer, by minimizing the effects of changes in personnel, and by serving as incentives, _____ facilitate the attainment of organization goals.
	24 However, when people become worried and preoccupied about their current status, the resulting

Exhibit 8.1 *Status Symbols*

Visible Appurtenances	Top Dogs	V.I.P.'s	Brass
Briefcases	None—they ask the questions	Use backs of envelopes	Someone goes along to carry theirs
Desks, office	Custom made (to order)	Executive style (to order)	Type A, "Director"
Tables, office	Coffee tables	End tables or decorative wall tables	Matching tables, type A
Carpeting	Nylon—1-inch pile	Nylon—1-inch pile	Wool-twist (with pad)
Plant stands	Several—kept filled with strange exotic plants		Two—repotted whenever they take a trip
Vacuum water bottles	Silver	Silver	Chromium
Library	Private collection	Autographed complimentary books and reports	Selected references
Shoe-shine service	Every morning at 10:10	Every morning at 10:15	Every day at 9:00 or 11:00
Parking space	Private—in front of office	In plant garage	In company garage—if enough seniority

Source: From Morris S. Viteles, "What Raises a Man's Morale?" *Personnel,* January 1954, p. 305. Reproduced with permission.

anxiety status _____ can reduce their effectiveness in the organization.

Role The sociological concept of role concerns the set of behavioral expectations that apply to a particular position in a group. In a business organization, the formal position description is generally the most important, but not the only, factor in determining the individual's

Exhibit 8.1 *Status Symbols (continued)*

No. 2's	Eager Beavers	Hoi Polloi
Carry their own—empty	Daily—carry their own—filled with work	Too poor to own one
Type B, "Manager"	Cast-offs from No. 2's	Yellow oak—or cast-offs from Eager Beavers
Matching tables, type B	Plain work table	None—lucky to have own desk
Wool-twist (without pad)	Used wool pieces—sewed	Asphalt tile
One medium-sized,—repotted annually during vacation	Small—repotted when plant dies	May have one in the department or bring their own from home
Plain painted	Coke machine	Water fountains
Impressive titles on covers	Books everywhere	Dictionary
Every other day	Once a week	Shine their own
In company properties—somewhere	On the parking lot	Anywhere they can find space—if they can afford a car

role. The informal organization and decisions made by the individual also have a hand in determining the role definition for a particular position.

25 The behavioral expectations that affect a particular position constitute the forces that determine the **role** ⎯⎯⎯⎯⎯ for that position.

26 The individual is influenced by two major sources

of role expectation in a business organization: those
formal spelled out by the company, or the [formal / informal]
organization, and those determined by the groups with
informal whom the individual works, or the [formal / informal]
organization.

27 As a result of these formal and informal influences, the individual attempts to structure the social situation and to define his or her place in it. This pro-
role cess is called _____ definition.

28 Thus the expected behavior for a given position, as interpreted and defined by the person in that posi-
role definition tion, becomes the _____ for that position.

29 At least three factors, or forces, influence the structuring of a role definition: the individual's self-
formal concept, the expectations of the _____ organi-
informal zation, and the expectations of _____ groups.

30 *Role conflict* results when an individual is faced with two or more role expectations that are incompati-
cannot ble. The individual in question [can / cannot] satisfy both role expectations simultaneously.

31 The nature of the situation and the personality of the individual involved both determine the seriousness
role of _____ conflict.

32 From the standpoint of the situation, the more rigidly incompatible expectations are enforced, the
more [more / less] prevalent role conflict is likely to be.

33 From the standpoint of the personality of the individual, the greater the ability to ignore some of the role
less expectations, the [more / less] severe that individual's role conflict is likely to be.

34 Role conflict can have its source in any of the three forces that influence role definition, namely, the
self-concept; formal individual's _____, the _____ or-
informal ganization, and the _____ organization.

role formal	**35** The foreman who faces incompatible demands for productivity from the line supervisor and for quality from a quality-control staff is in a _____ -conflict situation stemming from expectations of different parts of the _____ organization.
role-conflict informal	**36** A newly appointed supervisor who is faced with incompatible behavioral expectations by fellow supervisors as compared with former coworkers is faced with a _____ situation stemming from expectancies in the _____ organization.
formal; informal	**37** On the other hand, the employee who must choose between satisfying management's expectations regarding performance and alternative pressures from fellow employees is in a role-conflict situation that involves both the _____ and the _____ organization.
formal self-concept	**38** A conflict between company job expectations and the individual's objectives in occupational development involves a conflict between the expectancies of the _____ organization and the individual's _____.
formal informal self-concept	**39** In summary, a role-conflict situation is minimized and an individual's effectiveness maximized when there is compatibility in the role expectations associated with the _____ organization, the _____ organization, and the individual's _____.

Functions of the Informal Organization

In addition to the formal, or planned, pattern of relationships, there is a network of personal and social relationships among the people that make up any organization. Although activities in the informal organization are not under direct managerial control, they have an important influence on how well the organization as a whole functions.

positions	**40** The emphasis of the formal organization is on the [people / positions] in the organization, whereas the

people

emphasis of the informal organization is on [people / positions] and their relationships.

above

below

41 Authority in the informal organization is given by those following the leadership of a particular individual, rather than by organizational assignment. Thus, it can be said that formal authority flows from [above / below], whereas informal authority flows from [above / below].

resist

42 Since people generally prefer to maintain stable formal and informal group relationships, informal groups tend to [promote / resist] changes in either the formal or the informal organization.

maintain

43 Accordingly, in fulfilling the function of *helping group members to attain specific personal objectives,* informal groups typically strive to [maintain / change] the status quo.

informal

44 Therefore, managers who are planning to institute an organizational or procedural change need to consider the reactions to that change in the _____ organization.

status (recognition, social satisfaction, etc.)

45 A second function of informal groups is that of *providing social satisfaction to group members.* Individuals who have little or no formal status in the organization may gain such _____ in the informal group.

status

46 For example, the informal group leader who is consulted for advice by other group members thereby attains a measure of _____ in the organization, although it may not derive from his formal job assignment.

communication

47 A third function of the informal organization, in addition to helping individuals attain specific objectives and providing social satisfaction, is *communication.* The "grapevine" is made up of the channels of _____ that are outside the formal system.

Functions of the Informal Organization • 237

grapevine

48 Because it is often successful in disseminating information more rapidly or broadly than the formal communication system, the _____ is a phenomenon in all larger organizations.

grapevine

49 *Rumor* is the content of the grapevine that is not authenticated. In order to eliminate all rumor, the _____ itself would have to be eliminated.

rapidly (etc.)

50 Not only is elimination of the grapevine impossible, it is not even desirable. Although the grapevine transmits invalid rumors, it also helps to transmit valid information more _____, thus making the organization more effective.

attitudes (or anxieties, etc.)

51 Futhermore, even though rumors may be untrue, the content of these rumors provides significant information regarding employee _____ to the alert manager.

rumors

52 It has been found that attempting to eliminate or track down informal communication channels does little to dispel erroneous beliefs in the organization, but it may actually aggravate them. On the other hand, prompt publication of relevant facts is the most effective method of refuting invalid _____.

refute

53 It is generally preferable that the rumor itself not be described when releasing facts to refute it. Repeating the rumor can result in its being as well remembered as the facts that _____ it.

would

54 For example, if a recent company purchase of land in another locality has led to inaccurate rumors about production facilities being moved, prompt release of the facts (involving, perhaps, company expansion plans) [would / would not] tend to dispel the rumor.

weaken

55 However, discussing the rumor along with the contradicting facts might [strengthen / weaken] the effectiveness of the facts in refuting the rumor.

objectives; social communication

56 The fourth function of informal groups, in addition to helping individuals to attain specific _____, providing _____ satisfaction, and serving as a _____ medium, is *social control* of behavior.

social

57 The _____ control practiced by an informal group can be either internal or external in terms of the organizational location of those persons who are affected by such group pressures.

internal

58 When group pressure is directed toward making members of the group itself conform to group expectations, _____ social control is involved.

external social control

59 On the other hand, in attempts to control the behavior of those outside the social group, _____ _____ is involved.

external

internal social control

60 The informal work-group activities designed to "keep the foreman in line" are an example of _____ social control, whereas "kidding" a work-group member about the unsuitability of his or her work clothes involves _____ _____.

formal; informal self-concept

61 Essentially, we have in this case another example of the influence of the informal group on role definition. In our description of role, we concluded that the three forces which influence role definition are the _____ organization, the _____ organization, and the individual's _____.

objectives; social communication; social control

62 In summary, the four major functions of informal groups consist of helping individual group members attain specific _____, providing _____ satisfaction, serving as a _____ medium, and serving as the agency for _____ _____ of behavior.

Charting the Informal Organization

Company organization charts are used to depict the formal organization, but the informal organization typically is not charted in business firms. One reason is that the system of relationships among the members of an organization is always changing, so that any such chart would soon be too outdated for any managerial use. For those doing organizational research covering a particular span of time, however, it is useful to have a charting of both the formal and the informal organizations in order to more fully understand the dynamics of the firm being studied.

63 There are two general methods of charting the informal relationships in an organization. The first, the *sociogram,* is based on analyzing the attraction among members of a small group. Therefore, the sociometric technique works best for studying the informal relationships within a [division / department / section].

section

64 Sociometric analysis is appropriate for studying informal relations in a small group. Typically, each individual in the group is asked for personal preferences regarding assignment with work companions, or the actual pattern of contacts in the group is observed. The subsequent charting of these preferences results in the construction of a _____.

sociogram

65 Refer to Figure 8.2. How many people are there in the small group being studied? _____ [number]

Eight

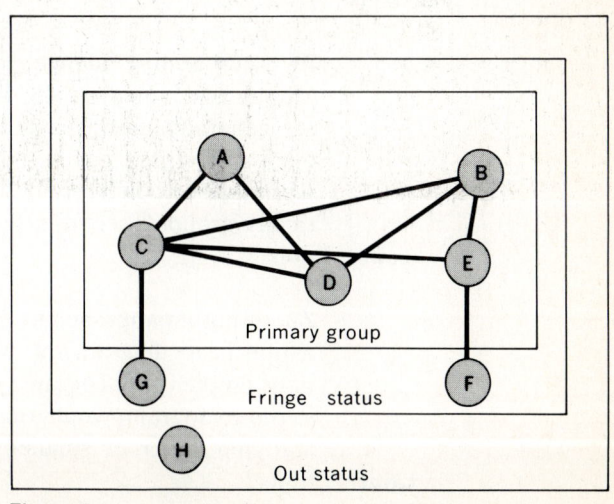

Figure 8.2 A sociogram.

66 Which person has the greatest number of direct relationships with others in the group and thus may be in the position of being the informal group leader, or
C group spokesman? ___

67 *Primary-group* membership involves being completely accepted by the other group members. How
Five many individuals are in the primary group? ___ [number]

68 The *fringe status* is unstable in that this is marginal membership which leads to either membership in the primary group or complete separation. Identify the individual(s) who are in a fringe status in
G and F Figure 8.2. ___

69 Finally, the *out status* is made up of people, often called "isolates," or "loners," who are not members of the informal group, even though they are members of the formal organization being studied. How many
One isolates are there in this figure? ___ [number]

70 Fill in the answers without referring to the figure: The three categories of group membership from the standpoint of sociometric analysis are the
primary group; _____, _____,
fringe status; and _____.
out status

71 Research evidence indicates that small work groups assembled on the basis of sociometric choice are generally more productive than those assembled on an arbitrary basis. Would we generally expect within-group conflict to be higher or lower in sociometrically grouped sections than arbitrarily grouped sec-
Lower tions? ___

72 Another approach to charting the informal organization is to diagram the pattern of informal interactions on the formal organization chart itself. Compared to the sociogram, would this method be appropriate for studying larger or smaller segments of the organiza-
Larger tions? ___

formal; informal

73 Refer to Figure 8.3. The chart depicts both the _____ and the _____ patterns of relationships in the organization.

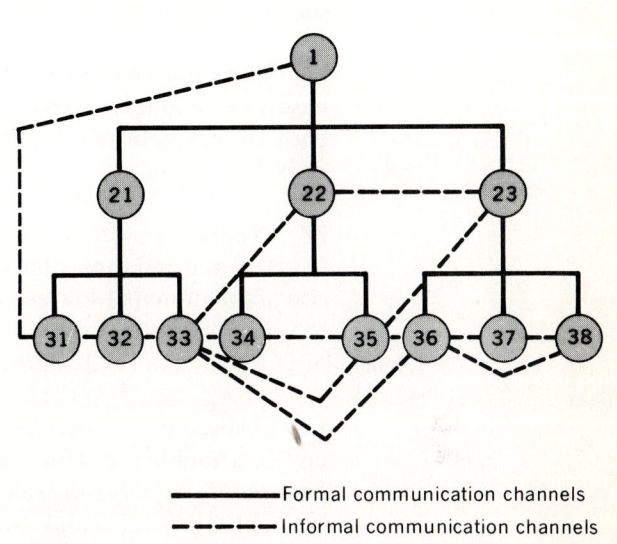

Figure 8.3 Formal and informal patterns of relationship in part of an organization.

———— Formal communication channels
– – – – Informal communication channels

Three (1–31, 22–33, and 23–35)

74 How many of the communication channels in the figure "violate" the formal pattern in that an individual has continuing contact with someone else's superior or subordinate? _____ [number]

No; too rigid (or slower communication, etc.)

75 Would you expect that the organization with no deviation from the planned formal pattern of relationships would be more effective than one in which some deviation occurs? [Yes / No] Why or why not?
_____
_____

Power and Politics

From the standpoint of classical organization theory, the *power*, or influence, possessed in the organization should be directly equivalent to the amount and type of formal authority assigned to an individual. Upon inspection of the actual patterns of influence in all formal organizations, however, we would have to conclude that a number of other sources of organizational power exist. In this section we identify some of these additional sources of power and briefly consider their implications in company politics.

power

76 The total amount of influence that an individual has in an organization, that is, the total ability to influence the behavior of other people, is referred to as his or her _____.

formal

77 Whereas power is the total capacity to apply effective force and thus influence the behavior of others, one of the principal sources of this power is that which has been institutionalized and assigned by delegation of [formal / informal] authority.

knowledge

78 However, in addition to the formal source of power a number of informal sources exist, such as *knowledge, ability to reward, place in the communication system,* and *uniqueness of skill.* For example, because of possessing information about salary levels at competing firms, a personnel manager is likely to have more influence than others as a member of the salary committee. In this case, the source of this additional authority is associated with having specialized _____.

ability to reward

79 Indeed, it might well be said that "knowledge is power" in most organizations. Further, a group with formal service authority may have additional organizational power because it can choose to give priority to some requests. The additional authority in this case is essentially related to the group's [uniqueness of skill / ability to reward].

uniqueness of skill

80 An employee who is difficult to replace because of a combination of talents particularly suited to the requirements of the position has a power source based principally on that employee's [place in the communication system / uniqueness of skill].

81 The factor of *knowledge* as a source of power usually refers to information that the individual has collected or brought into the organization. On the

Power and Politics • 243

communication system

other hand, an individual who is in a position to selectively filter information passing through an office, may gain power as a result of his or her place in the _____.

82 The informal sources of power that we have reviewed have been given as examples, and not as an exhaustive listing. In addition to the relatively impersonal factors that we have described, others involving power gained through personal association might also be considered. In that all such sources of power are distinct from formal authority as such, they are classified as representing _____ sources of authority.

informal

83 The term "playing politics" is often used to refer to the use of informal sources of power for the purpose of attaining certain objectives outside the organization's standard operating procedure. In addition, the term implies that the objective is personal gain, although many writers in this area would not limit the definition in this way. Thus, a methods analyst who is able to "sell" a manager on changing the work procedure in the department through a combination of coercion, compromise, and concession might be described as having gained in his or her objectives by the use of informal sources of power, or playing _____.

politics

84 Unless a purely personal and selfish objective is involved, political activity may well be constructive in nature. Whether organizationally constructive or destructive, the term "political" always indicates that objectives are being attained [within / outside] planned organizational patterns.

outside

85 Almost inevitably, patterns of alliances in the organization develop in conjunction with the use of political methods, with certain groups finding themselves in a position of "natural" conflict. In a manufacturing company, for example, those involved in the production function and maintenance function often find themselves in a position of [alliance / conflict] with one another.

conflict

No (continue in next frame)

86 In addition to conflicts and alliances among the line functions, other areas of conflict and politics include competition between individual managers, between supervisors and subordinates, between line and staff, between staff activities, and between union and management. Should it be an organizational goal that all such conflicts be eliminated, or at least minimized? [Yes / No]

informal

87 The very existence of conflict can stimulate productive activity, and only when it becomes disruptive and destructive is it desirable to curtail such competition. Faced with the presence of conflicting views, political methods often provide the principal approach by which a manager can accomplish organizational objectives by the use of [formal / informal] sources of power.

Review
scalar

88 An individual's level in the managerial hierarchy determines the relative amount of _____ status attached to that individual's position. (Frames 1 to 3, 8 to 10)

functional

89 The importance of a person's area of work in a firm, as judged by others, determines the amount of _____ status attached to that individual's position. (Frames 4 to 10)

status symbols

90 Indicators of relative rank, such as the type of office and its location, are called _____ _____. (Frames 11 to 17)

clear
fewer

encourage

91 Status symbols tend to make authority relationships in an organization [clear / ambiguous], lead to [more / fewer] disruptions in communication associated with personnel changes, and when used as incentives, they [encourage / discourage] higher productivity. (Frames 18 to 20)

status anxiety

92 A continuing concern regarding one's current status which tends to have disruptive effects is called _____ (Frames 21 to 24)

Review • 245

formal
informal
self-concept

93 At least three forces influence the structuring of the role definition: the _____ organization, the _____ organization, and the individual's _____. (Frames 25 to 29)

role conflict

94 When an individual is faced with two role requirements that are incompatible, _____ often results. (Frames 30 to 39)

above

below

95 Leadership authority in the formal organization flows from [above / below], whereas leadership authority in the informal organization flows from [above / below]. (Frames 40 and 41)

objectives (etc.)
social
communication
social control

96 Informal groups help individuals in the group attain their _____, are a source of _____ satisfaction, serve as a _____ medium, and are the agency for _____ of behavior. (Frames 42 to 62)

internal social control

97 The control that informal groups exert over the behavior of members of the group itself is called _____. (Frames 56 to 61)

sociogram

98 A chart that depicts the informal set of relationships within a small group is called a _____. (Frames 63 to 71)

formal organization

99 The other method of charting informal relationships, usually used for larger segments of the organization, makes use of the _____ chart. (Frames 72 to 75)

power

100 The total amount of influence that an individual has in an organization, whether formally or informally derived, is referred to as the individual's level of _____. (Frames 76 to 82)

101 The use of power to accomplish individual or organizational objectives outside the formal channels, often accompanied by alliances with some groups and

politics   conflict with others, is referred to as the use of _____. (Frames 83 to 87)

Discussion Questions

1. How is the sociological concept of "status" differentiated from the concept of "role"?
2. Why are status symbols important in organizations? What are some examples of such symbols in modern business enterprises?
3. Consider the statement, "An individual has many roles, depending on the situation." Do you agree? Illustrate.
4. Why do informal groups exist in every organization? What functions do they fulfill for the individual and for the organization?
5. From the standpoint of sociometric analysis, three degrees of informal group membership can be described. What is there about the "fringe status" that tends to make this degree of membership unstable and short-lived? Exemplify.
6. When used in addition to a formal organization chart, what charting methods give a more complete picture of the organization? How are these techniques usually used?
7. Pressures from the formal organization have been blamed by some observers for a tendency toward overconforming behavior in corporations. Do you agree that the formal organization is the principal source of such pressures?
8. Should an executive be permitted to "get ahead" in a company by playing politics? Consider the pros and cons.

References

Alexander, C. N., Jr. "Status Perceptions." *American Sociological Review,* vol. 37, no. 6, December 1972.
Badawy, M. K. "Bureaucracy in Research: A Study of Role Conflicts of Scientists." *Human Organization,* vol. 32, no. 2, Summer 1973.
Berger, J., B. P. Cohen, and M. Zelditch, Jr. "Status Characteristics and Social Interaction." *American Sociological Review,* vol. 37, no. 3, June 1972.
Burke, R. J., W. Tamara, and G. Duncan. "Informal Helping Relationships in Work Organizations." *Academy of Management Journal,* vol. 19, no. 3, September 1976.
Davis, K. *Human Behavior at Work: Organizational Behavior,* 5th ed. New York: McGraw-Hill, 1977.

Filley, A. C. "Committee Management: Guidelines from Social Science Research." *California Management Review*, vol. 13, no. 1, Fall 1970.

Graham, G. H. "Interpersonal Attraction as a Basis of Informal Organization." *Academy of Management Journal*, vol. 14, no. 4, December 1971.

Greene, C. N. "Relationships among Role Accuracy, Compliance, Performance Evaluation, and Satisfaction within Managerial Dyads." *Academy of Management Journal*, vol. 15, no. 2, June 1972.

Hinings, C. R., et al. "Structural Conditions of Intraorganizational Power." *Administrative Science Quarterly*, vol. 19, no. 1, March 1974.

House, R. J. "Role Conflict and Multiple Authority in Company Organizations." *California Management Review*, vol. 12, no. 4, Summer 1970.

Izraeli, D. N. "The Middle Manager and the Tactics of Power Expansion: A Case Study." *Sloan Management Review*, vol. 16, no. 2, Winter 1975.

Jackson, J. *Norms and Roles: Studies in Systematic Social Psychology*. New York: Holt, 1976.

McFillen, J. M. "Supervisory Power as an Influence in Supervisor-Subordinate Relations." *Academy of Management Journal*, vol. 21, no. 3, September 1978.

McMurry, R. N. "Power and the Ambitious Executive." *Harvard Business Review*, vol. 51, no. 6, November-December 1973.

Mayes, B. T., and R. W. Allen. "Toward a Definition of Organizational Politics." *The Academy of Management Review*, vol. 2, no. 4, October 1977.

Morris, J. H., R. M. Steers, and J. L. Koch. "Influence of Organizational Structure on Role Conflict and Ambiguity for Three Occupational Groupings." *Academy of Management Journal*, vol. 22, no. 1, March 1979.

Murray, J. A. "A Sociometric Approach to Organizational Analysis." *California Management Review*, vol. 13, no. 1, Fall 1970.

Petticrew, A. M. "Towards a Political Theory of Organizational Intervention." *Human Relations*, vol. 28, no. 3, April 1975.

Reif, W., et al. "Perceptions of the Formal and the Informal Organization." *Academy of Management Journal*, vol. 16, no. 3, September 1973.

Rizzo, J. R., R. J. House, and S. L. Litzman. "Role Conflict and Ambiguity in Complex Organizations." *Administrative Science Quarterly*, vol. 15, no. 2, June 1970.

Rogers, D. L., and J. Molnar. "Organizational Antecedents of Role Conflict and Ambiguity in Top-Level Administrators." *Administrative Science Quarterly*, vol. 21, no. 4, December 1976.

Schein, V. E. "Individual Power and Political Behaviors in Organizations: An Inadequately Explored Reality." *The Academy of Management Review*, vol. 2, no. 1, January 1977.

Stogdill, R. "Group Productivity, Drive and Cohesiveness." *Organizational Behavior and Human Performance*, vol. 8, no. 1, August 1972.

Summers, D. B. "Understanding the Process by Which New Employees Enter Work Groups." *Personnel Journal*, vol. 56, no. 8, August 1977.

Tichy, N. "An Analysis of Clique Formation and Structure in Organizations." *Administrative Science Quarterly,* vol. 18, no. 2, June 1973.

Tusi, H. "Organizational Stress as a Moderator of the Relationship between Influence and Role Response." *Academy of Management Journal,* vol. 14, no. 1, March 1971.

Whyte, W. F. *Men at Work.* Homewood, Ill.: Irwin/Dorsey, 1961.

Zaleznik, A. "Power and Politics in Organizational Life." *Harvard Business Review,* vol. 48, no. 3, May-June 1970.

CASE STUDY: Conflict among Managers

The president of Amplex Mills sat at his desk in the hushed atmosphere so typical of business offices after the close of working hours. Again he had spent a great deal of his time with the managers of the purchasing and production functions, and he now tried to compare today's particular problem with others that had occurred in order to find a common thread. Yet the basic difficulty was not entirely obvious, unless it had to do with Dick Corbett, the manager in charge of purchasing, and his ability to work with other managers in the firm.

When the purchasing department was established two years ago, all the managers concerned agreed with the need to centralize this function and place a specialist in charge. As George Morton, the manufacturing manager, saw it, it would free his supervisors from detailed ordering activities that could be better done by someone else. Wil Jorgesson, manager of marketing and sales, voiced the opinion that the flow of materials into the firm was important enough to warrant a specialized management assignment. Yet since the purchasing department began operation, it has been precisely these two managers—of production and marketing—who have had a number of confrontations with the new purchasing manager, and occasionally with one another, in regard to the way the purchasing function is being carried out.

From Morton's point of view, instead of simplifying his job as production manager by taking care of purchasing for him, the purchasing department has developed a formal set of procedures that has resulted in as much time commitment on his part as he had previously spent in placing his orders directly with vendors. Further, he is especially irritated by the fact that his need for particular items or particular specifications is constantly being questioned by the purchasing department. When the department was established, George Morton assumed that the purchasing manager was there to fill his needs, not to question them. After all, the company's principal objective is the manufacture of textile products, and all other activities within the firm, including purchasing, should contribute to this manufacturing objective, not detract from it.

As Wil Jorgesson sees it, the purchasing function is an integral part of the marketing function, and the two therefore need to be jointly managed as a unified process. Effective management of the procurement function implies a concern with the exchange function of buying and selling goods and services and cannot therefore be separated from a firm's overall marketing strategy. However, Dick Corbett has attempted to carry out the purchasing function without regard for this obvious relationship between his responsibilities and those of Wil Jorgesson, thus making a unified marketing strategy impossible.

In his previous position Dick Corbett had worked in the purchasing department of a firm considerably larger than Amplex. Before being hired, he was interviewed by all the top managers, including George Morton and Wil Jorgesson, but it was the president himself who negotiated the details of the job offer. As Corbett sees it, he was hired as a professional to do a professional job. Both Morton and Jorgesson have been distracting him from this goal by presuming that he is somehow subordinate to each of them, which he believes is not the case. The people in the production department, who use the purchasing function most, have complained about the detail that he requires on their requisitions. But he has documented proof that materials are now being purchased much more economically than they were under the former decentralized system. He finds Jorgesson's interests more difficult to understand, since he sees no particular relationship between his responsibilities for efficient and effective procurement and Jorgesson's responsibilities to market the firm's products.

The president has been aware of the continuing conflict among the three managers for some time, but on the theory that a little rivalry is healthy and stimulating, he has felt that it was nothing to be unduly concerned about. With all three managers tending to be strong-willed by temperament, it would have been rather surprising if there were no conflict at all. But now that so much of his time is being taken up by much of what he considers to be petty bickering, the time has come to take some positive action.

1. Is George Morton's view of the situation realistic? Why? Why not?
2. How do you evaluate Wil Jorgesson's position?
3. How might this conflict be associated with factors in the formal organization? With power and politics?
4. What should the president of Amplex Mills do now?

CASE STUDY: A Proposal for Product Redesign

Tom Malone is the Los Angeles field marketing representative for the Chicago Division of Acme Electronics, a multidivision aerospace firm. As a recently retired Army officer, he has many contacts in the military, and was hired to seek and develop markets for portable microwave communications equipment.

In this capacity, he reports on a line basis to Bob Howard, division marketing manager, but on a staff basis to Tom Andrews, microwave product manager, whose products Malone is to market. Both Howard and Andrews are located in Chicago.

Malone approached his new civilian marketing assignment with enthusiasm. He contacted many of his former Army associates about portable microwave communications equipment. While these acquaintances were happy to see Malone when he visited them, only two had any need for microwave equipment. However, the equipment that they needed would require development. Malone believed that a catalog Acme microwave set could, with considerable redesign, meet the requirements for the two potential customers, and he prepared a report recommending that the division undertake the redesign. The report was replete with facts and sales projections indicating the redesign costs could be amortized and a high profit returned to the company in about eighteen months. This was based on a price of $30,000 per set, which Malone's contacts indicated would fit within their budgets. The funds for the redesign would have to be allocated from either the product manager's (Andrews') budget, or from funds under control of the division engineering department.

A meeting was arranged in Chicago at which Tom Malone presented his proposal to Howard, Andrews, and the manager of the division engineering department. These men, Malone learned, were at the same level in the organization. The following viewpoints were expressed at the meeting:

Bob Howard felt that the program should be pursued as proposed by Malone. (The business would fill a void in Howard's division sales forecast eighteen months from now. Howard's forecast was, he felt, a personal promise to management. The forecast had been prepared six months before.)

Tom Andrews was highly opposed to expending his funds for a project that would not generate sales in the current year. (Andrews' product sales for the current year were lagging behind his forecast to management made three months earlier.)

The manager of division engineering was in favor of developing a product, but not on the basis suggested by Malone. Engineering believed that a different, new-design approach incorporating integrated circuits should be adopted instead of redesigning a catalog item. The new design would employ the latest state-of-the-art techniques and would sell for $46,000. (Engineering had previously promised management that a new design incorporating integrated circuits would be released this year.)

As the meeting continued with no apparent progress toward a decision that would be acceptable to all three managers, Malone pondered whether he should have become involved with the proposal at all, or should have restricted his efforts to the sale of catalog items.

1. Should Tom Malone have restricted his efforts to catalog items, rather than developing a new product proposal?

2. How has the organizational position of each person in this situation affected his viewpoint?
3. How can, or should, the conflicting viewpoints be resolved? In what way may the present organizational design be inadequate with respect to such product decisions?

APPLICATIONS READING:

Rules of the Road: Doing Something Simple about Conflict in the Organization

Donald G. Livingston
Vice-President, Industrial Relations
Electronic Associates, Inc.
West Long Branch, New Jersey

Managers' methods for dealing with conflicts within their organizations, as Gardner Murphy suggested in another political context, run from persuasion and cajolery to violence. The last is applied, he wrote, when all other methods fail—"as they will!" In a corporate setting, "violence" can range from the familiar knocking of heads to discharge, with neither extreme really uncommon as the unsatisfactory solution of an exasperated chief.

Organization development techniques developed over the last dozen years for the prevention and resolution of conflict require considerable intervenor skill, internal preparation of the organization, and time. These methods—team building, confrontation sessions, and so on—are considerably more permanent in their positive effects than the one described. But this technique—besides being reasonably quick and usable by relatively inexperienced conflict resolvers—has in common with more comprehensive methods the fact that learning about new methods of resolving conflict can take place in the manager's organization. Once it has been carried out, companies are likely to use the method in one or another form in a variety of conflict settings.

It was all too obvious that marketing and engineering were at swords' points right up to the hilts. The two department heads spoke only by memo or with eyes-averted antagonism at staff meetings. As disciples will, junior members of

Source: Reprinted, by permission of the publisher, from *Personnel*, vol. 54, no. 1, January-February 1977, © 1977 by AMACOM, a division of American Management Associations. All rights reserved.

the departments worked together only when necessary and then with undisguised friction.

No one liked the situation. Most members of the departments complained that work wasn't getting out, that morale had zeroed, and so on. When asked what should be done about the situation, each group answered unanimously: "If *those* people don't start running *their* department right, the president ought to fire their boss, shake 'em up a little."

The president had come to the same conclusion; but he had firing both managers in mind. This was difficult, however; it surely wouldn't make him look very good to the board, nor would it help the company with its customer community. But whatever he had tried seemed to have so little effect that he feared he would be seen as weak or indecisive himself.

Managerial Control: A Narrow Span

To the consultant who was finally summoned to try to head off the impending collision, the interesting feature of the reports from the participants was their insistence that *they* (the other side) had to get squared away, that *they* were at fault, and so on. Out of experience in labor productivity, the consultant knew that a manager can't do much about *their* behavior; in fact, most labor troubles stem from managers' unrewarding efforts to control *them*.

The only thing managers really control is their own behavior and a limited number of processes within their organization, such as its general structure, value enforcement, some aspects of compensation, and so on, which derive chiefly from the manager's own attitudes and competences.

Development of the "Rules"

One can't simply request, however, that the participants in a conflict look at their own contributions to the fray any more than one can ask the parties in the middle of divorce to be so dispassionate. A vehicle is needed to bring out what can in fact be controlled, but must do so in a way the participants can safely accept as a basis for solution of their common problem.

Thus a "Rules of the Road" meeting was arranged. Rules of the road, as every sailor soon learns, have a specific purpose: to avoid collisions. They always place the burden of responsibility only where it can lie: on each skipper, who alone controls his own ship, handling it always in relation to what other craft are doing.

Two simple rules of the road are easily established:

1. Skipper your own ship.
2. Stick to what is happening now, not yesterday or tomorrow.

(OD people will quickly recognize the second rule, as will anyone else who has found it impossible to deal with differences in remembered hurts or projected wrongs.)

Assembling the Adversaries

The Rules were printed on a large sheet of paper, which hung at the head of the off-site long table to which key marketing and engineering managers were invited. ("Bring everybody who can make a difference in how your departments get along" was the instruction given to each department head when they were briefed on the purpose and content of the meeting. "But no more than 12." Each side brought 12.) Operating instructions for the meeting went like this:

Each group will have 30 minutes in another room to put down on paper five things the other department does that make life more difficult for your own department. Engineering, for example, will put down on paper the five specific things marketing does that make it harder for engineering to do its work. Marketing will do the same thing for engineering.

But you are not to tell the other group how to run its department. Rule of the Road No. 1 says you skipper only your own ship, and I will draw a line through any comment that even so much as hints that you're telling the other department how to conduct its business. You can say only what they do that causes you problems, not why or what they ought to do about these things.

Rule of the Road No. 2 says something else to bear in mind: Put down on your list only what the other department is doing *now*. Forget the things they did yesterday or last year. I'm inclined to tell you that several of us in this room won't be around to speculate on tomorrow's management unless we get these problems resolved.

Select some member of your group to be spokesperson. This person will present your list to the other department when you return. Make sure he or she understands the problems well enough to present them meaningfully.

One final thing before you go. Put your items in one-to-five priority order.

The two groups took their jobs very seriously, though each, somewhat to its surprise, found it difficult to list even as many as five specifics. (Examples of typical listings are on the following page.)

Engineering's Complaints

What marketing does that causes us problems:

1. Changes product manager assignments without telling us who is in charge of what.
2. ~~Gave inadequate cost data on the Widget M-6 last year, making us re-do design work~~
2. Cost data format is inconsistent. We do not understand why some costs are budgeted against us rather than warranty.
3. Changes its mind on customer specs after we're told design is frozen; specs are sometimes incomplete and only added later.
4. Makes commitments to customers for delivery or performance specs we cannot meet.
5. Phasing of new orders makes work balancing very difficult.

[Author's note: First No. 2 item above was deleted as a violation of Rule 2.]

Marketing's Complaints

What engineering does that causes us problems:

1. Changes organization so often that we don't know who's in charge of some projects.
2. Doesn't always tell us when it makes a design change that affects customer acceptance; for example, the cover on a new widget.
3. Takes engineers off projects without telling us that there may be a delay in completion so that we can get back to customer.
4. Contacts customers without anyone in marketing or sales knowing about it.
5. ~~Should have better management of R&D budget to stop overruns.~~
5. R&D budget overruns catch us by surprise.

[Author's note: First No. 5 item above was deleted as a violation of Rule 1. It also isn't very helpful as a basis for change.]

Assessing Results

Shortly before the time was up, the consultant visited each group. "Before you come back," he said, "take a few more minutes to make up another list. Put down on another sheet of paper, but keep it hidden when we get back, a list of what you think they are going to say your department is doing that causes trouble for them."

When the two groups reassembled, the consultant asked each side to select another person, a "whistle-blower." The function of the whistle-blower was to signal whenever it was believed the other team transgressed the rules—that is, when the other side was telling its adversary how to run its own department or when old grievances or imagined futures were being offered as current issues. It was also made clear that clarification *should* be requested of each other's items, but that argument about the validity of items was not permitted.

As the spokesperson on each side proceeded through the specifics, tension visibly relaxed and serious inquiry began. In this group (as in all subsequent conflict groups with whom the Rules method has been applied), both sides:

1. Had nearly identical lists of what "the other guy" did that caused them problems.
2. Were able to predict with great accuracy what "the other guy" was going to say they did that caused problems.

Thus it became clear that both sides were attempting to deal with the same issues and that both were frozen in a mutually inappropriate pattern of interaction. And with that, the central aspect of the Rules of the Road meeting emerged.

The groups were then asked to return to their breakaway rooms, but to return this time with written commitments and timetables for changing what they did that caused problems for the other side or reasons why a change could not be made. These presentations were to be made by the head of each department. (If the question arose whether the commitments and timetables were to be given to the president, the choice was left with the participants. None has yet chosen to do so.)

The proposed timetable each presented had to be formally accepted by the other group, and follow-through dates set in accordance with the timetables. Meetings were to be convened if either side was dissatisfied with the rate of change back in the workplace.

(All six of the adversary pairs that used the Rules of the Road procedure chose to follow through by memoranda distributed to all participants. One pair met for updating on progress and then turned the update meeting into a discussion of current issues involving a new-product development.)

Why the Rules Work

The Rules procedure provides a way out of the commonplace "frozen" conflict in industry in which all participants are wearily familiar with the relative contributions of each, but are unable to mobilize for unilateral change. Meetings are kept to the point of the issues, defensive behaviors are minimized, the people who can do something about the causes of conflict commit publicly to doing that something (with the support of their subordinate doers), and the process of follow-up is monitored without the need for additional recrimination. Since change is mutual, monitored, and parallel, neither side—so reminiscent of international relations—has much to fear of the other's political advantage.

The conditions for the effective use of the Rules procedure are fairly simple:

1. Ordinary means of conflict resolution, however ineffective, are not available or must be withheld.
2. The changes that are necessary must be within the control of the groups themselves; that is, they must be relationships or processes they can do something about without the concurrence of, or a change in, a higher power figure. The leading figures of each group must be able to publicly commit to future action and to agree to monitoring.
3. The two Rules *must* be scrupulously observed: Neither group can (or has the right to) tell the other how to operate; and only what is happening in the workplace *now* is relevant to discussion. The meetings procedure as described has built-in alarms for deviation from these rules.
4. There must be awareness of the need for change at all levels of participation, including that of the manager to whom both groups report. The chief roles of this manager are to insist upon conflict resolution and to invest the resolution procedure with his or her own authority if need be ("You agreed to report back; now what are your plans?")

The consultant's role, like the marriage counselor's, is on the side of the union. A person not identified with either of the antagonists can serve the role of process supervisor most easily but actually has relatively little to do once the procedure is set in motion except to insist upon adherence to the Rules and to check whether follow-up is proceeding.

The emerging study of management by relationships (MBR) seems to have something in common with the Rules; both ask "What am *I* doing that *I* can control that is causing problems between us?" Both the Rules and MBR procedures are, then, rooted in making objective—and therefore often reducible—the events that help produce conflict.

Questions on Reading

1. What are the two "Rules of the Road" presented by Donald Livingston and what is their basic purpose?
2. Describe the general procedure by which the Rules of the Road can be applied to resolve conflict in an organization.
3. What are the conditions for the effective use of the Rules procedure?

9 STAFFING THE ORGANIZATION

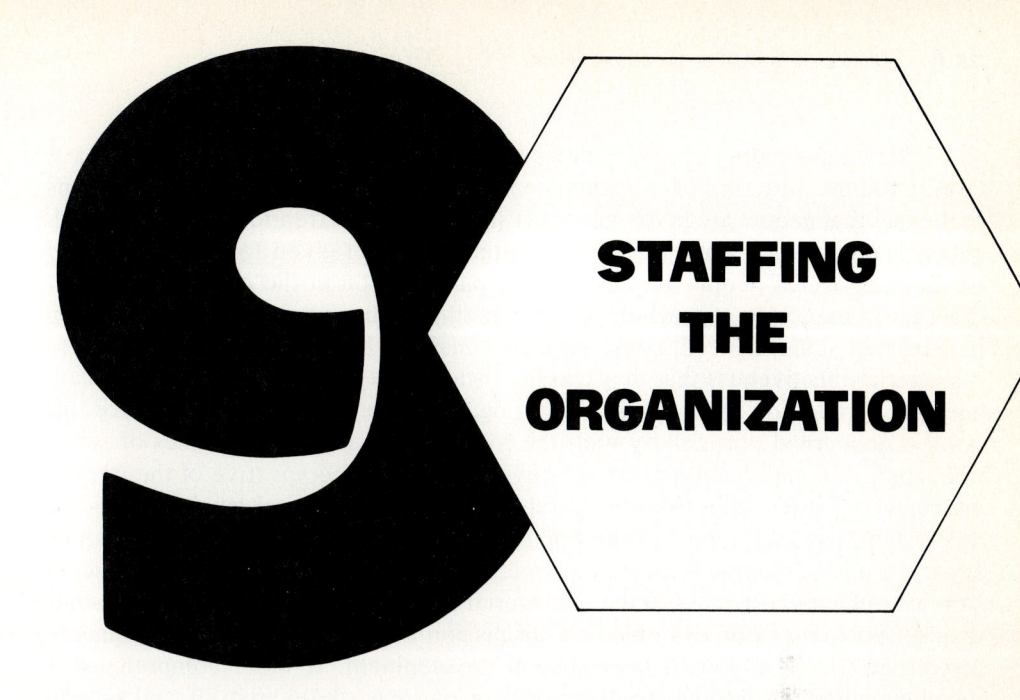

- Organizational Planning for Executive Needs
- Use of Interviewing in Selection
- Appraisal of Managerial Performance
- Management Development
- Review
- Discussion Questions
- References
- Case Study: A Management Development Program
- Case Study: An Irresistible Job Offer
- Applications Reading: "The Annual Performance Review Discussion—Making It Constructive" Herbert H. Meyer
- Questions on Reading

Chapter 9 • Staffing the Organization

In the preceding chapters devoted to the function of organizing we have considered the structure of a business enterprise and the behavioral implications of the fact that people are involved in this structure. Our attention to the human element is incomplete, however, if some attention is not given to the process and methods by which people are selected for participation in the organization, how their performance is appraised, and the methods that can be used to develop higher-level skills. Indeed, some authors consider this process so important to managerial effectiveness that they classify "staffing" as a separate function of management, in addition to planning, organizing, directing, and controlling. Since this book is concerned particularly with the role of the manager, the topics of selection, appraisal, and development are covered from the perspective of the operating manager, rather than from the perspective of the personnel manager. It is for this reason that such topics as the reliability and validity of personnel techniques and the use of personnel tests are not included in this chapter. Further, the discussion of staffing is restricted to the managerial positions in the organization, rather than all positions. For example, the discussion of developmental techniques is concerned specifically with management development. A more comprehensive development of these topics would require an entire textbook in itself, and several such textbooks are included in the references at the end of this chapter.

Organizational Planning for Executive Needs

In order to provide the basis for determining what kinds of managers should be recruited and selected and the kinds of management development activities that should be carried on, it is necessary to identify the present status of managerial staffing and the projected need for additional managers. Therefore, in this section of the chapter we consider the general activities directed toward the objective of determining managerial needs and begin our coverage by describing the management inventory, which is a systematic procedure by which the present status of managerial talent can be assessed.

does not

1 A *management inventory* should include not only a listing of presently assigned managerial personnel, but also their areas of professional interest and major accomplishments to date. In some companies, employees who already qualify for appointment to managerial positions are also included in the inventory. Thus, a management inventory [does / does not] need to be restricted only to those already occupying managerial positions.

Organizational Planning for Executive Needs • 259

Yes 2 In fact, in some companies it is the practice to include all salaried employees above a designated salary level in the management inventory. Given the nature of such an inventory, is it likely that the information contained therein would need to be updated periodically? [Yes / No]

managerial 3 In order to simplify the updating of the inventory and its use, a summary record is often prepared for each individual, as illustrated in Exhibit 9.1 on the following page. Of course, this information could also be entered on punched cards or magnetic tape, thereby facilitating computer analysis of the management data. As indicated in Exhibit 9.1, in addition to containing certain categories of personal data the record form is concerned with the type of _____ position that the individual can fill.

management inventory 4 As indicated throughout the above presentation, the overall procedure by which the number and kinds of managerial personnel available in the organization can be determined is called the _____ _____.

personnel loss 5 Having established the current status of managerial staffing through the development and maintenance of a management inventory, such needs can be projected for the future by considering the rate of *personnel loss* and the likely level of *organizational expansion* (or possibly contraction). Of these two factors, the one which is particularly related to the characteristics of present managers, such as their ages, is that of _____.

historical 6 Personnel losses due to retirement and because of known physical disabilities can be predicted fairly accurately. On the other hand, losses of managerial personnel due to resignations or because of individual desires to transfer to nonmanagerial positions are not as predictable on an individual basis. Therefore, for the latter types of losses an analysis of [personal / historical] data would be most appropriate.

(Front Side)

James A. Miller

Birth date: 3/16/40   Service date: 9/15/75

Family status: Married, 2 children

Company experience: **Assistant controller, 1980–present**
Cost analyst, 1975–1980

Previous employment: **Cost analyst, Hays & Co., 1970–1975**
Financial analyst, Ford Motor Company, 1967–1970

Military service: Ensign and Lt. (J.G.), U.S. Navy Supply Corps, **1962–1965**

Education: M.B.A., University of Michigan, 1967
B.S. (accounting), Wayne State University (Detroit), 1961

(Back Side)

James A. Miller

Professional interests: Financial analysis, budgeting, long-range planning, formulation of control systems

Outside interests: Boy Scouts, Kiwanis, professional groups in financial administration

Health: Excellent

Summaries of recent appraisals:
  1982   Exceptional technical performance; some human relations training recommended
  1981   Has mastered fundamentals of the position of Assistant Controller and performing at acceptable level
  1980   Exceptional performance as analyst; promotion recommended
  1979   Exceptional performance as analyst; qualified for promotion
  1978   Above average performance in the analyst group

Exhibit 9.1   Sample management inventory record.

7   Overall, then, personnel losses due to such factors as retirement can be determined by reference to the personal data in the management inventory. On the other hand, the rate of loss due to resignations can be determined by reference to historical data in the company. Of course historical experience is not necessarily predictive of future losses due to such reasons as resignations, terminations, transfers, leaves, and deaths, but such data provide the foundation for a judgment about the future loss rate. In formulating such a judgment, such industry studies as the projected market demand for various categories of mana-

should   gerial personnel [should / need not] also be considered.

8 The projection of the need for managerial personnel should be based not only on personnel losses but also on the predicted expansion of the organization. Again, an analysis of historical data provides information of value for this purpose. Should such a forecast also include consideration of long-range organizational plans that have already been formulated but not yet
Yes   implemented? [Yes / No]

9 Thus, we have indicated that two principal factors should be considered in projecting the need for managerial personnel in an organization. One is the antici-
loss   pated rate of personnel _____ and the other is the
expansion (or growth)   predicted _____ of the organization.

10 Most major corporations attempt projection of managerial needs at least several years into the future, with five-year projections being quite common. It is important that managerial needs be forecast as far in advance as can be done reliably because of the rela-
long   tively [short / long] time period required for management development.

11 In considering managerial positions as contrasted to managerial personnel, the development of *position descriptions* for all such positions would be useful for all three personnel functions of selection, appraisal, and development. As contrasted to the job descriptions prepared for operative positions in the organization, one difficulty associated with managerial position
less   descriptions is that such positions are [more / less] structured.

12 Because managerial positions do not have the repetitive ingredient associated with most operative positions, the traditional basis of describing jobs in terms of physical activities is not applicable. For this reason, some firms hold the view that such positions cannot really be described by a formal and standardized position description. However, it is the viewpoint in this text that such positions can be described in terms of the responsibilities associated with the principal *management functions,* these being the functions of _____, _____,

planning; organizing
directing; controlling
_____, and _____.

13 In addition to identifying managerial responsibilities, such a position description should also include the specific organizational objectives associated with the position and should identify any areas of technical skill or knowledge that are required. As indicated by the "common elements" included in Table 9.1, therefore, at least _____ [number] areas of information should be included in any managerial position description.

six

Table 9.1 | **Common Elements to Be Included in All Managerial Position Descriptions**

1. Organizational objectives. What are the principal objectives of the organizational unit associated with this management position?
2. Planning. What are the areas of planning activity in terms of scope and time?
3. Organizing. To what extent is the person in this position involved in restructuring work groups, and what are the personnel selection, appraisal, and development responsibilities associated with this position?
4. Directing. How many employees are supervised directly and what types of motivational situations are involved?
5. Controlling. What kinds of control systems are associated with this position? To what extent are they a part of centralized control systems and to what extent do they need to be locally developed?
6. Technical responsibility. What technical areas of responsibility are included in this position, including technical knowledge required for successful management of the organizational unit?

14 In summary, the managerial position description provides the basis for carrying out the personnel functions of _____, _____, and

selection; appraisal
development
_____ for such positions. In addition to describing the type and extent of managerial responsibilities with respect to the functions of planning, organizing, directing, and controlling, each position description should include an identification of the organiza-

objectives (or goals)
technical
tional _____ associated with the position and the areas of _____ knowledge or skill that are required.

Use of Interviewing in Selection

Particularly from the standpoint of the manager as contrasted to that of the personnel department, a primary basis for selecting individuals for an organizational unit is the personal interview. Of course, such factors as previous job experience, previous levels of performance and present availability serve as the basis for determining who will be interviewed for a position opening. In this section we consider the objectives of the selection interview, the principal types of interviewing methods which can be used, and common pitfalls in using interviews for the purpose of selection.

15   A selection interview is a discussion between two (or more) persons oriented toward possible job placement. Though it might thus appear that *personnel selection* is the only objective of such an interview, in the broader sense it is one of three general objectives. In addition to the employer choosing an employee, the prospective employee is also choosing an employer. To do so the prospective employee needs appropriate *information*, and therefore the second objective of a personal interview is that of providing _____ about the organization and its policies.

information

16   Whether or not a mutual job commitment is made, it is to the long-run benefit of the organization that the candidate leave the interview with a positive attitude toward the organization. *Developing a positive attitude* toward the organization and its personnel practices is the third objective of a selection interview. Whereas a description of the organization's promotion policies and fringe benefits would be associated with the objective of _____, sincere attention devoted to the applicant's skills and potential would be associated with the objective of _____.

providing information

developing a positive attitude

17   Thus, the three principal objectives of selection interviewing are _____, _____, and _____.

personnel selection
providing information
developing a positive attitude

several

18 The four types of interviewing methods which we now consider are the patterned interview, the depth interview, the nondirective interview, and the stress interview. We choose to use the terminology "types of interviewing methods" rather than "types of interviews" because of the fact that [only one / several] of these methods can be used within a single interview.

executive

19 The *patterned interview method* is one in which the specific areas of information which the interviewer is to obtain are identified beforehand and are included on a standard form. The interviewer uses the form as a guide during the interview. Exhibit 9.2 on the following page presents the first page of a standardized patterned interview form. Such forms generally differ according to the type of job, or position. The form in Exhibit 9.2 is intended for use in interviewing candidates for _____ positions.

depth

20 Whereas a patterned interview is largely oriented toward standard areas of information, the depth interview method is directed toward an in-depth exploration of the applicant's skills and the personal motives underlying his interest in the position and in the organization. For example, when a sales manager asks an applicant his opinion about particular marketing and pricing practices in order to determine the extent of his knowledge, he can be described as using a _____ interview method.

nondirective

21 Thus far we have considered the patterned and depth interview methods. A third type is the *nondirective interview method*. As used in the context of selection interviewing, a nondirective interview is one in which the interviewer asks very broad questions and leaves it up to the applicant to choose the direction of the answer. *What* the applicant chooses to talk about can be very informative in judging his motives and deciding how he will fit into the organization. "What have you learned or gained in your present position?" would be an example of the type of question used in the _____ interview method.

PATTERNED INTERVIEW FORM — EXECUTIVE POSITION

Date _____ 19 ___

SUMMARY

Rating ☐1 ☐2 ☐3 ☐4 Comments: _____
In making final rating, be sure to consider not only what the applicant can do but also his/her stability, industry, perseverance, loyalty, ability to get along with others, self-reliance, leadership, maturity, motivation, and domestic situation and health.

_____
_____
_____

Interviewer: _____ Job considered for: _____

Name _____ Date of birth _____ ; Phone No. _____
The age discrimination in the employment act and relevant FEP Acts prohibit discrimination with respect to individuals who are at least 40 but less than 65 years of age.

Present address _____ City _____ State _____ How long there? _____

Were you in the Armed Forces of the U.S.? Yes, branch _____ Dates _____ 19 __ to _____ 19 __
(Not to be asked in New Jersey)
_____ 19 __ to _____ 19 __

If not, why not? _____

Were you hospitalized in the service? _____

Are you drawing compensation? Yes ___ No ___

Are you employed now? Yes ☐ No ☐ (If yes) How soon available? _____
What are relationships with present employer?

Why are you applying for this position? _____
Is his/her underlying reason a desire for prestige, security, or earnings?

WORK EXPERIENCE. Cover all positions. This information is very important. Interviewer should record last position first. Every month since leaving school should be accounted for. Experience in Armed Forces should be covered as a job (in New Jersey exclude military questions).

LAST OR PRESENT POSITION

Company _____ City _____ From _____ 19 __ to _____ 19 __

How was job obtained? _____ Whom did you know there? _____
Has applicant shown self-reliance in getting jobs?

Nature of work at start _____ Starting salary _____
Will applicant's previous experience be helpful on this job?

In what way did the job change? _____
Has applicant made good work progress?

Nature of work at leaving _____ Salary at leaving _____
How much responsibility has applicant had? Any indication of ambition?

Superior _____ Title _____ What is he/she like? _____
Did applicant get along with superior?

How closely does (or did) he/she supervise you? _____ What authority do (or did) you have? _____

Number of people you supervised _____ What did they do? _____
Is applicant a leader?

Responsibility for policy formulation _____
Has applicant had management responsibility?

To what extent could you use initiative and judgment? _____
Did applicant actively seek responsibility?

Form No. EP-302-R

Copyright, 1977, The Dartnell Corporation, Chicago, Illinois 60640. Printed in U.S.A.
Developed by The McMurry Company

Exhibit 9.2 A patterned interview form (first page only). Published by the Dartnell Corporation, Chicago. Reproduced with permission.

22 Finally, the *stress interview method* is a type of procedure designed to place the applicant under planned stress and, logically, a stress situation with ingredients common to the stresses included in the position itself. An example of using such a method would be to say to a sales applicant "So you want to be a salesperson. Let's see you sell me this desk pen." Recall the three objectives of a selection interview. The objective that might be well served by this method is that of _____. The one that might be particularly adversely affected is that of _____.

personnel selection

developing a positive attitude

23 Thus, the type of interview procedure which is designed to put the applicant "on the spot" and which requires skillful use so as not to create ill will toward the organization is the _____ interview.

stress

24 Overall, the four types of interviewing methods that have been described are the _____, _____, _____, and _____ methods.

patterned; depth; nondirective; stress

25 Having considered the objectives of selection interviewing and the principal types of interviewing methods which can be used, we now consider some common pitfalls in selection interviewing. These include the halo effect, bias, and the failure to listen. The *halo effect* describes the situation in which a single prominent characteristic of the applicant dominates the interviewer's overall judgment of him. Thus, a neat and alert appearance can lead to a [positive / negative] halo effect while arriving late (or even arriving too early) for an interview can lead to a _____ halo effect.

positive

negative

26 It is of course entirely appropriate to consider specific characteristics of the applicant as being either positive or negative factors with respect to the requirements of the position. But when the interviewer allows some one characteristic to dominate the overall evaluation of the applicant, then a _____ effect is said to have occurred.

halo

27 Somewhat related to the halo effect is the factor of interviewer *bias*, in that the accuracy of the interviewer's perception of the applicant is again involved. Bias, however, is concerned with the interviewer allowing personal preferences rather than position requirements to determine the standards by which applicants are evaluated. When an interviewer has a discussion with an applicant whose interests and values are similar to his or her own, a [positive / negative] evaluation is more likely to be made.

positive

28 The implicit (rather than explicit) nature of personal preferences and their role in selection can be so pervasive that if managerial attention is not directed toward this factor, the organization can come to be staffed only with people who have similar backgrounds and values. The resulting organizational homogeneity can be stifling to diversity and creativity and is certainly contrary to the philosophy of staffing the organization on the basis of skills rather than extraneous factors. For these reasons, interviewers should be particularly concerned about the problem of _____ in the selection process.

bias

29 Finally, a third pitfall in interviewing is the *failure to listen*. Many a manager who is supposed to be conducting an interview finds it only too easy to do almost all the talking. If the manager identifies areas of information to be obtained before the interview, he or she is more likely to ask questions which require the applicant to respond and which consequently require the interviewer to _____ to the applicant.

listen

30 We have identified and discussed three common pitfalls which an interviewer should be aware of in the interview process. These are the _____, _____, and the _____.

halo effect; bias; failure to listen

Appraisal of Managerial Performance

Once individuals have been placed in an organization, their continued performance and progress should be monitored in some systematic way. Performance appraisal occurs whether or not a formal system is established for such a purpose. However, the validity of appraisals and their usefulness for making retention decisions, determining who is best qualified for promotion, and determining training needs is dependent on establishing a planned program for appraisal. In this section we first consider several traditional systems of appraisal and then consider recent trends in appraisal systems, including the so-called "goal-oriented approach."

31 The term "merit rating" is the traditional term used to describe the process by which employees are evaluated. Although the term is still used, there has been a general shift toward rating or appraising the "performance" of an individual, rather than his "merit" as such. Therefore the term _____ appraisal generally has come to be preferred to the term _____ .

performance
merit rating

32 Three possible approaches can be used to evaluate performance, as follows:

a. An unplanned and casual appraisal

b. The traditional and systematic evaluation of (1) employee personality characteristics or (2) employee performance

c. The goal-oriented approach, which often includes involvement of the individual in the goal-setting process.

As indicated in the introduction to this section, the results of an appraisal program are not only useful for the obvious purposes of determining employee retention and promotion, but should also be useful for determining _____ needs in the organization.

training

33 An *unplanned and casual appraisal* may be adequate for determining employee retention, but it is certainly not analytical enough to yield reliable data useful for promotion and training decisions. On the other hand, a formal and planned appraisal system should yield such data. Further, we can also observe that a systematic plan also yields the type of data whereby the performance of individuals [can / cannot] be more readily compared.

can

34 Most appraisal systems used today are based on the *traditional approach* to appraisal. Within this approach, the emphasis may be on the individual per se (employee personality characteristics) or on what the individual does (employee performance). The traditional methods have shifted over the years toward greater emphasis on evaluating the employee against job standards and requirements, and therefore have increasingly emphasized the evaluation of [employee characteristics / employee performance].

employee performance

35 Table 9.2 lists several traditional methods of performance appraisal that have been developed and used. The first method listed, that of *ranking,* is the oldest and simplest system of appraisal. As implied, by this approach a manager ranks subordinates according to their level of worth or their performance in the organization. Suppose that a manager observes that different subordinates have distinctly different areas of strength and weakness. From this standpoint the manager would find it [easy / difficult] to rank the individuals in terms of their performance.

difficult

Table 9.2 **Some Traditional Methods of Performance Appraisal**

Ranking
Forced distribution
Graphic scales
Checklist
Critical incidents method

36 Other than the difficulty involved in ranking individuals who have different areas of strength and whose jobs may also be somewhat different, we can also observe that the results of such an appraisal system [provide / do not provide] data relevant to determining individual training and development needs.

do not provide

37 Because of the weaknesses associated with the ranking method of appraisal, another approach which has been developed is the *forced distribution method.* By this approach, several categories of worth are established in advance, such as quality of work, punctuality, and dependability. The "forced distribution" aspect of the system stems from the fact that five grade levels are established for each characteristic, and a designated percentage of employees are to be assigned to each grade level. Typically, 10 percent are to be placed in the top grade for each characteristic, followed by percentages of 20, 40, 20, and 10 for the remaining grades. Therefore, the subordinates being rated are essentially being [ranked / independently evaluated] with respect to each characteristic.

ranked

38 If all employees happened to be very competent with respect to a particular characteristic, would the forced distribution system indicate this fact? [Yes / No] Would the results of such a rating program be useful for determining training needs? [Yes / No]

No
No

39 The forced distribution rating system is predicated on the assumption that the subordinates being rated are approximately normally (symmetrically) distributed in regard to each characteristic. Therefore, to the extent that the system is useful at all it is more suitable for relatively [small / large] work groups.

large (With small work groups the percentage assumptions are difficult to apply.)

40 Thus, the appraisal system which is more analytical than a simple overall ranking, and by which the individual's general ranking with respect to each of several characteristics is indicated by the rater, is the _____ system.

forced distribution

41 Because of inherent weaknesses associated with the ranking and forced distribution methods of appraisal, neither type of system is now used very much. The most widely used system of performance appraisal is that of establishing scales for each identified factor to be rated, that is, the *graphic scales system.* Figure 9.1 presents an example of a graphic rating scale factor. In this example, note that each individual who is rated would be [ranked / independently evaluated] in relation to other individuals.

independently evaluated

42 Unlike the ranking and forced distribution methods, the evaluations entered on a graphic rating

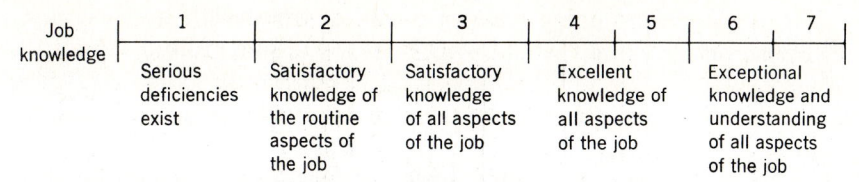

Job knowledge	1	2	3	4	5	6	7
	Serious deficiencies exist	Satisfactory knowledge of the routine aspects of the job	Satisfactory knowledge of all aspects of the job		Excellent knowledge of all aspects of the job		Exceptional knowledge and understanding of all aspects of the job

Figure 9.1 An example of a graphic rating scale factor.

scale represent evaluations with respect to position standards, rather than with respect to other people as such. Thus, if the majority of those being rated are relatively weak in some factor, such as "organization of work," such a situation [would / would not] be obvious as a training need in the appraisal results.

would

43 A graphic rating scale can be made up of a series of boxes or as a continuous scale, as is the case in Figure 9.1. One of the problems with graphic scales is that most ratings tend to be clustered toward the higher end, thus resulting in poorer capability of differentiating the performance levels of different people. Notice that in Figure 9.1 an attempt to gain better discrimination is made by "splitting" the rating categories at the [lower / higher] end of the scale.

higher

44 It is the general practice to sum the ratings for the several factors being rated and to use this total as an indicator of the general level of performance for the person being rated. However, the meaning of such a total is questionable, since being rated high on "dependability," for example, does not really counterbalance being rated low on "job knowledge." Therefore, it is our viewpoint in this text that the useful part of a graphic rating is [the rating on each individual characteristic / the sum of the ratings].

the rating on each individual characteristic

45 Though the graphic scales appraisal method appears very analytical and exact, it is rather difficult to use because it requires that many judgments be made by the rater. There is, therefore, the danger that the rater may simply "fall back" on rating a given employee consistently above (or consistently below) average on all factors without regard to the different area of performance represented by each factor. As far as de-

be of little value

termining training needs is concerned, the resulting ratings would [still be of value / be of little value].

46 Because of the problem cited above, the *checklist method* has been developed as an alternative to the use of graphic scales. A checklist is made up of a series of descriptive statements about the performance of the employee, and the rater checks (or indicates a "yes") for those statements that apply to the person being rated, as indicated in Figure 9.2. Therefore, from the rater's standpoint the checklist requires **describe** that the rater [describe / evaluate] the individual's performance.

		Yes	No
28.	Completes reports on schedule.	___	___
29.	Follows through on areas of administrative difficulty.	___	___
30.	Tends to seek advice too soon when new problems develop.	___	___
31.	Does an appropriate amount of planning.	___	___
32.	Anticipates and corrects difficulties in achieving organizational objectives.	___	___
33.	Has a positive attitude toward the organization.	___	___
34.	Frequently needs to be motivated.	___	___

Figure 9.2 Sample items from a checklist appraisal form.

47 Even though the descriptive statements imply an evaluation, the rater's task is simply to determine whether each statement applies or does not apply to the person being rated. He can of course still choose to bias the rating. But since the levels for a factor are not **less** "lined up" along a scale he is [more / less] likely to introduce rating bias because of a failure to read the individual items carefully.

48 The items included in a checklist are weighted with preestablished values in order to arrive at a total rating. This indicates that the relationship of each descriptive statement to overall performance is deter- **before** mined [before / after] such a form can be used.

Appraisal of Managerial Performance • 273

              49 Therefore, a considerable amount of effort is required to develop a valid checklist form. In terms of using the results of the appraisal for a postappraisal discussion between supervisor and employee, of the following appraisal methods the one that lends itself best to a constructive interview is the [graphic rating scale / checklist].

graphic rating scale

              50 Thus, whereas the checklist is generally easier to use than the graphic scale, it tends to [increase / reduce] costs associated with the development of the appraisal system, to [increase / reduce] the bias included in the appraisals, and it is [more / less] useful for appraisal interview purposes.

increase

reduce

less

              51 Finally, the last of the traditional methods of appraisal which we describe is the *critical incidents method*. By this approach, instead of working with predesignated factors or statements the manager is required to be alert to particular areas of performance (or nonperformance) on the part of each employee on a continuing basis. These "critical" incidents are recorded by the rater and serve as the basis for the appraisal interview. Thus the critical incidents method is principally oriented toward [employee characteristics / job performance].

job performance

              52 Further characteristics of the critical incidents method are that it [does / does not] readily provide an overall quantitative rating for each employee and that it [is / is not] useful for identifying needed areas of training or development.

does not

is

              53 Since the identification and timely recording of critical incidents is crucial to the success of such a rating system, some training and motivation of the managers who are to use the system is required: Whereas use of the technique requires much more of the rater's time, as compared with a standard graphic rating form, the performance areas included by this approach are [more / less] likely to be those that are important in the particular job situation.

more (This is the key idea in identifying "critical" incidents.)

              54 In this section we have described the ranking,

forced distribution, graphic scales, checklist, and critical incidents methods as examples of traditional approaches to performance appraisal. Note that in describing the strengths and weaknesses of each system we [have also / **have not**] identified one of the systems as being the best one for all circumstances.

55 A relatively recent development in the area of performance appraisal is *goal-oriented appraisal*. From the standpoint of this approach, all the traditional appraisal methods are viewed as placing the rater in the role of evaluating and criticizing individuals from a position of superiority. A typical feature of the goal-oriented approach is the mutual establishment of job-oriented goals before the start of the performance period, and a performance review directed toward how these goals have or have not been achieved. When the establishment of the goals is a cooperative endeavor, the approach is predicated on the assumption that the employee being appraised [**is** / is not] oriented toward organizational achievement and that the appraisal is made on a(n) [standardized / **individualized**] basis.

56 The characteristics of the goal-oriented approach are such that it is more appropriate for use with employees in [operative / **managerial**] positions.

57 A primary strength of the goal-oriented approach to appraisal is that of [obtaining standardized evaluations / **stimulating self-improvement**] while a principal weakness of this approach is that of [**obtaining standardized evaluations** / stimulating self-improvement].

58 Any appraisal system that does not provide a comparative evaluation thereby provides less information for decisions involving retention, merit increases, and promotion. But in positions that are not tightly structured, and in which self-improvement and personal commitment are important factors, the _____ **goal-oriented** approach has been found to be useful as the basis for performance appraisal.

59 No matter what approach to appraisal is used, the appraisal interview is a typical aspect of most such systems. When the traditional approach to appraisal is used, the appraisal interview tends to be oriented toward [job objectives / evaluation]. When the goal-oriented approach is used the interview tends to be oriented toward [job objectives / evaluation].

evaluation

job objectives

60 The formal meeting and discussion between the rater and the employee, which is held in conjunction with a periodic appraisal of performance, is called the _____.

appraisal interview

61 Over the years, there have been systematic trends and shifts in performance appraisal. As indicated in Table 9.3, such appraisals have increasingly come to be used for [promotion decisions / self-development], they have increasingly focused on [performance / personal traits], and they have come to involve [more / less] emphasis on quantitative comparisons.

self-development

performance

less

Table 9.3   Changing Emphasis in Performance Appraisal over the Years

Item	Former Emphasis	Present Emphasis
Terminology	Merit rating	Employee appraisal Performance appraisal
Purpose	Determine qualification for wage increase, transfer, promotion, layoff	Development of the individual; improved performance on the job
Application	For hourly paid workers	For technical, professional, and managerial employees
Factors rated	Heavy emphasis upon personal traits	Results, accomplishments, performance
Techniques	Rating scales with emphasis upon scores; statistical manipulation of data for comparison purposes	Management by objectives, mutual goal setting, critical incidents, group appraisal, performance standards, less quantitative
Post-appraisal interview	Supervisor communicates his rating to employee and tries to sell his evaluation, seeks to have employee conform to his views	Supervisor stimulates employee to analyze himself and set own objectives in line with job requirements: supervisor is helper and counselor

Source: Reprinted with permission of The Macmillan Company, New York, from *Personnel: The Management of People at Work*, 3d ed., p. 336, by Dale S. Beach. Copyright © 1975 by Dale S. Beach.

Management Development

In this final section of the chapter we are concerned with two categories of activities associated with training and development: those that take place on the job and those that take place off the job. The on-the-job methods which are described are coaching, position rotation, special projects, and committee assignments. Off-the-job activities include special training courses, management games, role playing, and sensitivity training. These are not all the methods and activities that are used, but they represent a sampling of the more important techniques. The off-the-job activities can be carried out within or outside the organization, as in university-sponsored management seminars. Formal courses that are specific to an organization, such as courses in organization policies and personnel practices, are appropriately conducted as in-house programs.

every manager (since each manager is responsible for "coaching" his subordinates)

62 *Coaching* is a frequently used method of on-the-job development. This approach is based on the viewpoint that day-to-day performance, with the aid of expert guidance, is a proper foundation for self-development as a manager. The use of this method of development places a particular responsibility for training on [the personnel manager / every manager] in the organization.

more
less

63 Of course, every supervisor is responsible for guiding and evaluating the performance of his subordinates in any event. But as compared with the guidance included in performance appraisal, for example, the term "coaching" implies a guidance that is [more / less] frequent and [more / less] formal.

manager

64 One difficulty associated with coaching as a method of on-the-job development is that the manager may neglect the area of responsibility in favor of matters that seem more urgent. Thus the success of coaching as a training method is particularly dependent on the attitude of the _____.

65 Another on-the-job developmental method is

known as *position rotation*. Whereas coaching implies the development of knowledge and skill in [one / several] job(s), rotation implies a development of skill and knowledge in [one / several] job(s).

> one
>
> several

66 Generally, position rotation is used with relatively younger employees as part of a management development program. One of the advantages of position rotation is that by experiencing managerial responsibilities in several areas of the organization the junior-level manager has an opportunity to develop a [specialized / broad] understanding of the organization.

> broad

67 Two weaknesses of position rotation are the possibility of disruptive effects associated with transferring a number of people on a periodic basis and the attitude of the individual toward a job that represents a temporary assignment. One way of minimizing the latter problem is to ascertain that the individual is assigned [specific / general] responsibilities in conjunction with each position.

> specific

68 Thus far we have considered two on-the-job methods of development: _____ and _____.

> coaching
> position rotation

69 A third method of on-the-job training is assignment to *special projects*. A special project involves an assignment outside the scope of the person's routine areas of responsibility. In order to avoid any disruptive organizational effects, such projects usually are assigned [in lieu of / in addition to] the routine areas of responsibility.

> in addition to

70 Of course, when the special project is assigned in addition to the regular job responsibilities, the regular responsibilities [should / should not] be such that they require full-time attention.

> should not

71 By participating in a special project, as for example studying the reliability and validity of a personnel selection procedure used in the organization, the individual has the opportunity to develop various areas of knowledge and to demonstrate analytical ability in a variety of situations. In this respect, the developmental experience has some similarity to [coaching / position rotation].

position rotation

72   For projects that are particularly extensive, several individuals may be assigned from different functional areas to form a task group, and the assignment may even be on a full-time basis for the life of the project. Such interaction would help the participants develop a [specialized / broad] understanding of the organization.

broad

73   The last method of on-the-job development we describe is *committee assignments*. Such assignments have a similarity to the special projects considered above, but differ in that such committees usually exist on a continuing basis and require less time commitment than special projects. For example, a cost control committee might include members of several departments in the organization and meet periodically to coordinate cost control efforts. In order to stimulate meaningful participation on such committees it [is / is not] desirable that member contributions be made known to each person's supervisor.

is

74   Unless it is clear that contribution to the committee's assigned objectives is a part of each member's job responsibility, such participation generally will be neglected in favor of the person's "regular" job assignment. Again, active participation in interdepartmental problems contributes to the development of a _____ understanding of the organization.

broad

75   We have considered four methods of on-the-job development. The one that is concerned with the development of specialized skills in a particular job is _____, and the method that involves formal job transfers within the organization is _____.

coaching
position rotation

76   The on-the-job method of development which involves temporary, and usually part-time, assignment to work on a particular task is _____, while the method that

special projects

Management Development ● 279

committee assignments includes meeting with a group composed of individuals from several departments on a continuing but part-time basis is _____.

77 The four off-the-job developmental methods which we now describe are special training courses, management games, role playing, and sensitivity training. *Special training courses* is the broadest of these categories and such courses are usually concerned with specific areas of knowledge or skill. Thus, the required knowledge and skill to use a new budgeting procedure might be developed by means of a

special training course _____.

78 The method of instruction used in a special training course would depend on the areas of knowledge and skill being developed. If the course is concerned with informing managers about specific budgetary

lecture procedures, then the [lecture / case method] is likely to be used. If the course concerns the development of general problem-solving ability, then the [lecture /

case method case method] is likely to be used.

79 As is true for all the off-the-job methods, special training courses can be offered within the organization or employees may participate in outside programs, such as those sponsored by universities. For such areas as the study of employee motivation it is often felt that awareness of what other companies are doing is better developed by participation in a program

outside [within / outside] the organization.

80 The second method of off-the-job training which we consider concerns the use of *management games*. A management game, or simulation, typically involves the assignment of individuals to teams which interact as competing companies in a simulated industry. Each team makes decisions concerning such factors as production level, capital allocation, and marketing expenditure for each simulated time period. Thus, the training objectives of business games are principally concerned with the development of [human relations /

decision-making decision-making] skills.

81 Although the development of decision-making skills based on analysis is a predominant feature of business games, the interaction of individuals within each team and the necessity of "selling" team members on the appropriateness of certain decisions also has relevance for the development of _____ skills.

human relations

82 The calculations that are carried out to determine the success of each team are quite complex in that they are based on assumed mathematical relationships among such factors as marketing efforts, price, and competitor's strategies. Therefore, the results in each simulated period of play are generally determined by [the teams themselves / a computer program].

a computer program

83 What is learned by the experience of participating in a business game is also related to the type of debriefing discussion that follows the last simulated period of decision making. Rather than being preoccupied with "who won," particular management practices should be given attention. For example, it has been observed that teams that make specialized job assignments for team members (such as production manager) frequently perform better because of the resulting division of labor. Such an observation provides the opportunity for highlighting the importance of the managerial function of _____ in team success.

organizing

84 Whereas business games are concerned principally with the development of decision-making skills, *role playing* is concerned principally with the development of human relations skills, that is, the skills involved in dealing with _____.

people (etc.)

85 As the name of the method implies, in role playing each of two or more individuals is asked to assume a particular role and to interact orally in a human relations problem situation. In effect, the method gives participants a chance to try out problem-solving methods in a [real / laboratory] situation.

laboratory

86 For example, one participant might take the part of an employee whose work has been slipping lately while another takes the part of the manager in an ap-

Management Development • 281

praisal interview. While the two participants interact based on their assigned positions (but placing *themselves* in the roles, rather than following stereotypes) other participants observe the appraisal interview and then discuss its strengths and weaknesses. Such a training session would be called a _____ _____ session.

role-playing

87 Because a participant in a role-playing session has an opportunity to learn how his behavior affects other people, this technique, as contrasted to the techniques of lectures and discussions, can have a particular influence on the participant's [attitudes toward people / knowledge about human relations concepts].

attitudes toward people

88 The last of the off-the-job methods which we consider is *sensitivity training*. Whereas role playing may have an effect on an individual's attitudes toward other people, sensitivity training is particularly concerned with self-awareness and self-knowledge as the key to developing social sensitivity. Therefore, of the training methods which we have considered this method is the most [skills / psychologically] oriented.

psychologically

89 A complete description of sensitivity training is beyond the scope of this text. In general, it involves participation in a small group—called a T (training) group—within an unstructured social situation and with an open and frank discussion of the behavioral traits of the participants. In general, therefore, the trainer acts more like [an observer / a teacher].

an observer

90 Although the trainer plays an outwardly passive role, he needs a thorough knowledge of human behavior so as to introduce subtle guidance to the group's activities during the several days in which such a group typically interacts. Furthermore, because of the nature of the interaction it is desirable that the trainer be an experienced [manager / psychologist].

psychologist

91 The psychological aspects of sensitivity training and the personal nature of the involvement have resulted in considerable controversy regarding its use. We include this method in our coverage not because of the extent of its use, which is rather limited, but because of the attention that has been given to such psychologically oriented techniques in recent years. Because of the type of involvement required in sensitivity training, such sessions are generally held [within / outside] company premises and are carried out on a [one-evening-per-week / live-in] basis.

outside
live-in

92 Of the four methods of off-the-job training which we have considered, the method best suited to covering specific areas of knowledge is _____, and the method that places the participants in a simulated and competitive business environment is _____.

special training courses

business games

93 The training method that is concerned with developing human relations skills by providing the opportunity to practice such behavioral skills is _____, and the method that has been designed to help an individual to "know himself," and thereby also to know others better, is _____.

role playing

sensitivity training

Review

94 The listing of present and potential managers, along with an identification of their areas of interest and organizational achievements to date, is called a _____.(Frames 1 to 4)

management inventory

95 The two principal factors that should be considered in projecting the need for managers into the future are the anticipated rate of personnel _____ and the predicted _____ of the organization. (Frames 5 to 10)

loss (or turnover)
growth

96 A managerial position description should include an identification of the organizational _____ associated with the position and the technical skills required. Beyond this, the activities in the position might very well be described in terms of the four managerial functions, these being the functions of _____, _____, _____, and _____. (Frames 11 to 14)

goals (or objectives)

planning; organizing; directing; controlling

Review

97 The three main objectives of selection interviewing are _____,
_____, and
_____.
(Frames 15 to 17)

<small>personnel selection;
providing information;
developing a positive
attitude</small>

98 The type of interview method that is concerned with obtaining specific areas of information is the _____ interview, while the one by which particular matters are explored and discussed in some detail is the _____ interview. The method by which the applicant has considerable latitude in choosing what to discuss is the _____ interview, while the method by which the applicant may feel he or she is being put under duress is the _____ interview method. (Frames 18 to 24)

<small>patterned

depth

nondirective

stress</small>

99 Three common pitfalls in interviewing which were described are the situation in which the interviewer allows a single prominent characteristic to lead to a _____ effect, allowing personal preferences to influence the evaluation in terms of interviewer _____, and the tendency of some interviewers to do most of the talking and thereby failing to _____ to the applicant. (Frames 25 to 30)

<small>halo

bias
listen</small>

100 The traditional method of appraisal whereby the rater lists the employees according to level of performance is called _____. The method in which the relative percentage ranking of each employee is indicated with respect to each factor, rather than on an overall basis, is the _____ system. (Frames 31 to 40)

<small>ranking

forced distribution</small>

101 The method of appraisal in which the employee is rated with respect to a quantitative scale for each factor is the _____ method. The method in which the rater indicates which statements in a prepared list are descriptive of the employee or his performance is the _____ method. (Frames 41 to 50)

<small>graphic scales

checklist</small>

102 The method of appraisal in which the rater is required to keep a record of notable instances of job success and failure for each employee during the rating critical incidents — period is the _____ method. (Frames 51 to 54)

103 A relatively recent development in the area of performance appraisal by which the performance review is oriented toward job objectives that are often mutually established, and which is therefore particularly useful as a way of stimulating self-improvement, is the _____ approach. (Frames 55 to 58)

goal-oriented

104 The formal discussion between the rater and subordinate which takes place in conjunction with the performance appraisal is called the _____. (Frames 59 to 61)

appraisal interview

105 Of the on-the-job methods of development, the method which is widely used and which concerns the development of knowledge and skill in a particular job is _____. The method in which there is a planned series of assignments to different positions in the organization is _____. (Frames 69 to 76)

coaching

position rotation

106 The on-the-job method of development which involves assignment to additional research studies or tasks that are not part of the usual job routine is called _____. The method that involves periodic group meetings with personnel from other functional areas in the organization is _____. (Frames 69 to 76)

special projects

committee assignments

107 Of the off-the-job methods of training and development, the method most frequently used to convey specific areas of knowledge is known as _____. The method in which the participants are placed in a simulated competitive environment and operate as executive teams is _____. (Frames 77 to 83)

special training courses

business games

108 The developmental method in which participants have the opportunity to learn human relations

role playing skills in a laboratory setting is _____.
The method in which participants meet as a group for a relatively extended period for the purpose of achieving better self-knowledge and awareness of social interac-
sensitivity training tion is _____. (Frames 84 to 93)

Discussion Questions

1. What are the advantages of including all personnel above a given salary level in a management inventory, as contrasted to including in it only those who have actually been assigned to management positions? What are the disadvantages?
2. Position descriptions for operative positions frequently are concerned with the physical activities performed on the job. How does this relate to the appropriate content for a managerial position description?
3. Describe some of the interviewing methods that can be used by a manager and indicate the principal use of each method.
4. Differentiate the occurrence of a halo effect in an interview from that of interviewer bias.
5. What is implied by the term "merit rating" as contrasted to "performance appraisal"? What are the general advantages associated with using the latter term?
6. What are the basic differences between the traditional approach to performance appraisal and the goal-oriented approach? Which approach is most widely used today?
7. What off-the-job developmental methods are likely to be found most useful for the purpose of upgrading technical skills?
8. In what ways are role playing and sensitivity training similar? In what ways do these training methods differ?

References

Atkin, R. S., and E. J. Conlon. "Behaviorally Anchored Rating Scales: Some Theoretical Issues." *The Academy of Management Review*, vol. 3, no. 1, January 1978.

Beach, D. S. *Personnel: The Management of People at Work*, 3d ed. New York: Macmillan, 1975.

Bray, D. "Management Development Without Frills." *The Conference Board Record*, vol. 12, no. 9, September 1975.

Brown, R. J., and J. D. Somerville. "Evaluation of Management Development Programs...An Innovative Approach." *Personnel,* vol. 54, no. 4, July-August 1977.
Brown, R. S. "A Systems Approach to Management Development." *Financial Executive,* vol. 38, no. 4, April 1970.
Burack, E. H., and R. D. Smith. *Personnel Management.* St. Paul, Minn.: West, 1977.
Cummings, L. L., and D. P. Schwab. "Designing Appraisal Systems for Information Yield." *California Management Review,* vol. 20, no. 4, Summer 1978.
Decotiis, T., and A. Petit. "The Performance Appraisal Process: A Model and Some Testable Propositions." *The Academy of Management Review,* vol. 3, no. 3, July 1978.
Dyer, W. G. "What Makes Sense in Management Training?" *Management Review,* vol. 67, no. 6, June 1978.
Elkins, A. "Some Views on Management Training." *Personnel Journal,* vol. 56, no. 6, June 1977.
English, J., and A. R. Marchione. "Nine Steps in Management Development." *Business Horizons,* vol. 20, no. 3, June 1977.
Figler, H. R. "How to Hire an Executive—Intelligently." *Personnel Journal,* vol. 56, no. 7, July 1977.
Flippo, E. B. *Principles of Personnel Management,* 4th ed. New York: McGraw-Hill, 1976.
Ford, R. C., and K. M. Jennings. "How to Make Performance Appraisals More Effective." *Personnel,* vol. 54, no. 2, March-April 1977.
Foulkes, F. K. "The Expanding Role of the Personnel Function." *Harvard Business Review,* vol. 53, no. 2, March-April 1975.
Guyot, J. F. "Management Training and Post-Industrial Apologetics." *California Management Review,* vol. 20, no. 4, Summer 1978.
Haffey, B. T. "Developing the People Who Can Replace You." *Administrative Management,* vol. 40, no. 3, March 1979.
Hanson, M. C. "Career Development Responsibilities of Managers." *Personnel Journal,* vol. 56, no. 9, September 1977.
Haynes, M. G. "Developing an Appraisal Program." *Personnel Journal,* vol. 57, no. 1, January 1978.
Jobe, E. D., W. R. Boxx, and D. L. Howell. "A Customized Approach to Management Development." *Personnel Journal,* vol. 58, no. 3, March 1979.
Kearney, W. J. "Management Development Programs Can Pay Off." *Business Horizons,* vol. 18, no. 2, April 1975.
Kearney, W. J. "The Value of Behaviorally Based Performance Appraisals." *Business Horizons,* vol. 19, no. 3, June 1976.
Keeley, M. "A Contingency Framework for Performance Evaluation." *The Academy of Management Review,* vol. 3, no. 3, July 1978.
Lawler, E. E., III. "For a More Effective Organization—Match the Job to the Man." *Organizational Dynamics,* vol. 3, no. 1, Summer 1974.

Levitt, T. "The Managerial Merry-Go-Round." *Harvard Business Review*, vol. 52, no. 4, July-August 1974.

Locher, A. H., and K. S. Teel. "Performance Appraisal—A Survey of Current Practices." *Personnel Journal*, vol. 56, no. 5, May 1977.

McMaster, J. B. "Designing an Appraisal System That is Fair and Accurate." *Personnel Journal*, vol. 58, no. 1, January 1979.

Mills, T. "Human Resources—Why the New Concern?" *Harvard Business Review*, vol. 53, no. 2, March-April 1975.

Miner, J. B. "Implications of Managerial Talent Projections for Management Education." *The Academy of Management Review*, vol. 2, no. 3, July 1977.

Miner, J. B., and M. G. Miner. *Personnel and Industrial Relations: A Managerial Approach*. New York: Macmillan, 1977.

Morse, J. J., and F. R. Wagner. "Measuring the Process of Managerial Effectiveness." *Academy of Management Journal*, vol. 21, no. 1, March 1978.

Patton, A. "Does Performance Appraisal Work?" *Business Horizons*, vol. 16, no. 1, February 1973.

Patz, A. L. "Performance Appraisal: Useful but Still Resisted." *Harvard Business Review*, vol. 53, no. 3, May-June 1975.

Pigors, P., and C. A. Myers. *Personnel Administration: A Point of View and Method*, 8th ed. New York: McGraw-Hill, 1977.

Reeser, C. "Executive Performance Appraisal—The View from the Top." *Personnel Journal*, vol. 54, no. 1, January 1975.

Sayles, L. R., and G. Strauss. *Managing Human Resources*. Englewood Cliffs, N.J.: Prentice-Hall, 1977.

Schein, E. H. "How 'Career Anchors' Hold Executives to Their Career Paths." *Personnel*, vol. 52, no. 3, May-June 1975.

Schmuckler, E. "Management Development: A Joint Venture." *Personnel Journal*, vol. 55, no. 1, January 1976.

Schneider, B. *Staffing Organizations*. Pacific Palisades, Calif.: Goodyear, 1976.

Sikula, A. F., and J. P. Sikula. "Rethinking Present Appraisal Systems." *Supervisory Management*, vol. 24, no. 3, March 1979.

Sullivan, J. F. "Trends in University-Based Continuing Management Education." *Training and Development Journal*, vol. 31, no. 3, March 1977.

Tagliaferri, L. E. "How Performance Appraisal Can Improve the Appraiser's Performance." *Training and Development Journal*, vol. 32, no. 3, March 1978.

Walker, J. W. "Individual Career Planning." *Business Horizons*, vol. 16, no. 1, February 1973.

Wallace, L. "Nonevaluative Approaches to Performance Appraisals." *Supervisory Management*, vol. 23, no. 3, March 1978.

CASE STUDY: A Management Development Program

The Roscoe Company began an extensive management development program several years ago. Supervisors at all levels participated in the in-company program, and in addition they were also encouraged to improve their skills by taking night courses at local colleges and universities at company expense. At the time the program was initiated and at subsequent management development meetings, the supervisors were advised by top management that the management development program was designed to improve the supervisors as managers and to qualify them for future promotions within the company.

Ann Davis, a section supervisor, has been with the company for over ten years. She has diligently participated in the company management development program and has completed several night courses at a university in order to improve her knowledge of her job functions and the functions of her superior. However, twice during the last two years the company has hired outsiders to fill managerial vacancies within Ann's department. In each case Ann and other section supervisors in the department had applied for the vacancy and felt that their experience with the company plus the additional knowledge gained through the management development program made them better qualified than the outsider who was hired. Ann and her fellow supervisors question whether the management development program is worthwhile if vacancies are filled by outsiders.

At a recent appraisal interview Ann brought up the problem for discussion with her department manager. She was told that in many cases no supervisor within the company is considered to be qualified for the managerial opening. Ann expressed the opinion that the company management development program is a waste of time for the supervisors if the knowledge and experience gained are not recognized by higher-level management. Ann's supervisor explained that it takes time to develop the supervisor for higher-level responsibility, but that individuals are rewarded for their self-improvement efforts by extra merit salary increases associated with the annual performance appraisals.

1. Should the company have given emphasis to the promotional opportunities which are to be associated with participation in the management development program?
2. How might the placements of the two managers who were hired from outside the company have been handled differently?
3. What is likely to be the effect of the response which Ann's supervisor gave to her complaint?
4. What else might Ann's supervisor have said as a more complete or appropriate response to her complaint?

CASE STUDY: An Irresistible Job Offer

Ted Mason graduated from a large California university with a B.S. degree in marketing. He was interviewed on campus by a dozen or more national firms and received job offers from several of them after additional interviews at company locations. Ted also talked to the owner-manager of a local San Diego food manufacturing company and was very impressed with both the owner and the work, as it was described to him. The owner of the firm seemed impressed with Ted and invited him to visit their plant and office facilities. After seeing the business plant site and talking with a number of the management people, Ted decided that the offer to begin with the company as a sales management trainee was just what he wanted. The fact that his career with the company would keep him permanently in San Diego was important in his decision, since Ted's father operated a number of sports fishing boats with which Ted helped his father on some of his weekends, mainly because he enjoyed boats and deep-sea fishing. Also, living in San Diego would assure his staying close to his fiancee while she completed her studies at a local college.

Before Ted had given the San Diego firm his final decision, a large national food manufacturer with headquarters in New York called Ted and asked him to fly there to discuss further the offer they had discussed with him on campus. Ted had never been to New York and so, although he did not have a high level of interest in their offer, he saw no reason why he should not accept an all-expense-paid trip to see the big city. When he arrived, he was entertained and interviewed by the top sales executives of the company, which impressed him greatly. The sales department offices on the thirty-second floor of their world headquarters building gave an expansive view of the city and were quite impressive. The vice president of marketing for the firm made Ted an offer to begin in their management training program at a salary fully 30 percent higher than the San Diego offer. He would be in a trainee category for about six months, after which he would be guaranteed a sales management position at the beginning management level of sales supervisor. The vice president asked that Ted give them an answer to the offer as quickly as possible because they had other candidates for the job whom they did not want to take a chance of losing. Ted was highly flattered at the offer and the attention they had given him, and accepted the position. The vice president further explained that while there were two training slots open, one in Los Angeles and one in Pittsburgh, they wanted him to go to Pittsburgh because that slot had been open for the longest period.

Ted found conditions in Pittsburgh to be quite different from what he had expected. The style of life and types of outdoor activities in the area did not correspond to the things he liked to do. Ted was a good salesman, and by working hard he struggled through the six-month training period with no problems being apparent to his superiors. His promotion to sales supervisor placed him in charge of the recruiting, interviewing, hiring, training, and supervising for five sales territories.

Ted first became frustrated and then quite discouraged when after only four months in his new job he found that his sales team was operating below the efficiency of all of the other four supervisory sales teams in the Pittsburgh district. Everything seemed to be falling apart. He couldn't keep his people, he had difficulty finding good replacements, and the morale of his personnel showed in the poor sales record they were establishing. In addition, Ted hated the ice and snow of the cold winters, to which he was not accustomed, and he missed the boats and deep-sea fishing of San Diego.

The real clincher came when he received a letter from his fiancee breaking their engagement and telling him she was interested in someone else. Not only did Ted Mason become disenchanted with his job, but his superior, the Pittsburgh district manager, was also displeased with Ted and his lack of performance since his promotion to sales supervisor. As a result, the district manager passed up an opportunity to give Ted an anticipated merit increase, hoping that this would shake Ted into realizing his need to shape things up. To Ted this was the final blow. The following day Ted wrote his resignation and delivered it to his district manager.

1. What might be the cause of the low level of performance of Ted's sales team?
2. Basically, where did the problem begin? How could it have been averted?
3. Should the district manager accept Ted Mason's resignation? Are there any other alternatives?

APPLICATIONS READING:

The Annual Performance Review Discussion — Making It Constructive

Herbert H. Meyer

Director, Industrial/Organizations Psychology Program

University of South Florida

Tampa, Florida

The personnel program in any production or service organization which employs more than a few hundred people would not be considered as completely respectable if it did not include a systematic performance appraisal program. Under such a program the performance of each employee is appraised and carefully documented at least annually. Moreover, such appraisal programs almost always require that the supervisor who appraises must discuss the individual appraisals with the respective employees.

Typically, such programs have two primary objectives: (1) To provide an *inventory* of human resources talent in the organization, and (2) to *motivate* employees. Motivation is accomplished in two ways. First, the performance appraisal is usually tied into the salary administration program. That is, a "merit pay" philosophy is endorsed under which an individual's pay should coincide with demonstrated performance excellence. Secondly, the feedback discussion of the appraisal should provide an effective source of motivation. Each employee is counseled on how performance may be improved.

In theory, the performance appraisal program appears to be indisputably sound and logical. Yet the program has proved to be an enigma to both personnel experts and line managers. Both the rating process itself and the feedback interview have presented almost insolvable problems in most appraisal programs. There has already been much discussion of various methods to produce more reliable and valid ratings, particularly when tied to a merit pay program.

Even more problematic in an appraisal program is the feedback discussion. Objective evidence has shown that appraisal interviews seldom have the positive effect attributed to them. Some research actually indicates that such discussions often do more harm than good.[1]

These findings lead us to reexamine the theory on which appraisal interviews are based. As a result, I have come to the conclusion that the annual appraisal interview is *not* a psychologically sound procedure. For one thing, the feedback to the individual is poorly timed. In most appraisal programs this intensive, comprehensive feedback comes but once a year. It is certainly a well-

Source: From *Personnel Journal*, vol. 56, no. 10, October 1977. Reprinted with permission of *Personnel Journal*, copyright 1977.

established psychological fact that feedback associated immediately with an act is much more effective than delayed feedback.

An even more serious problem with the appraisal feedback discussion is the fact that it often has a negative side effect on an employee's occupational self-esteem. Our research [2] found that employees were more likely to react defensively than constructively to suggestions for improving performance.

Social psychologists have researched the issue of how people handle threats to their self-esteem and found that a number of unconstructive reactions are typically used to cope with such threats. [3] First, the individual may question the measurement criteria used or he may minimize the importance of the activity. Another undesirable response to threats to self-esteem is the tendency to demean the source.

The potential negative effects of threats to self-esteem in appraisal interviews are minimized by the fact that, typically, managers make few discriminations in their ratings. Almost everyone receives an above-average rating.

A Better Way

Despite all of the problems with appraisal interviews cited here, it does seem that an annual review discussion between supervisor and employee could serve some constructive purposes. Employees do want to know how they are regarded and what the future might hold for them in the organization. The problem is to design a format for accomplishing this which the average manager can use without a great deal of training, and which is not demeaning to the person being assessed. We think we have found the solution to this problem.

We started by formulating some specifications for a constructive annual discussion between manager and employees. The first of these, and perhaps the most important, was to minimize the authoritarian character of the interaction. The usual appraisal feedback procedure, where the manager discusses *his* or *her* ratings of a subordinate, is a highly authoritarian process. There is no doubt about who is the dominant person. Submissive behavior is appropriate for the subordinate. For this reason, the appraisal interview procedure is becoming more and more anachronistic in today's culture. Young people, especially, are likely to reject authoritarianism. As a solution to this problem, we felt that the discussion must be structured in such a way that the two parties participate more as equals.

Secondly, we felt that if the two parties were to participate as equals, both should prepare for the discussion. The employee, as well as the manager, should think through in advance, and possibly even make notes, about concerns or issues that he or she would like to discuss with the manager in this interview.

A third specification, which follows from the first two, is that the interview format or process should be structured in such a way as to insure *two-way* communication.

A fourth objective for the new procedure was that threats to the individual's self-esteem should be minimized. If an individual is to be effective on the job, he or she must have high occupational self-esteen. This does not mean that needed changes in behavior or performance should not be discussed. However, it does mean that discussions of such issues should be problem oriented and not personalized. Unless an individual really is a misfit in the job, it is important that he or she really thinks that his or her performance is good.

A fifth specification for a constructive annual discussion is that it should not incorporate a "report card" type of rating form. Grades on a form of this kind are not only likely to be threatening to the subordinate, but also to have a demeaning effect. The report card emphasizes the subordinate's dependent status.

A final specification for the procedure is that the manager should not try to cover all issues or aspects of the job in a single interview. A constructive outcome of a discussion of this kind is more likely to result if the manager focuses on just one or two issues or problems. To attempt to cover all aspects of the job, with suggestions for performance improvement or behavior change in a number of areas, is an unrealistic goal for a single interview.

The Discussion Format

Based on the above specifications, we designed a format for an annual discussion which we thought might be more constructive than the usual appraisal interview. As indicated in the specifications, the first step in the process is to notify the employee that a discussion is scheduled. The employee is invited to prepare by thinking about his or her role in the organization, how individual contribution could be enhanced, and what kinds of plans or aspirations he or she has for the future.

In the discussion itself, the manager will usually start by again reviewing the purpose of the discussion. However, it is important that following this opening statement, the actual discussion of issues be started by giving the initiative to the interviewee. Specifically, the manager might start this discussion by asking, "How do you feel things are going on the job? What kinds of concerns do you have?"

We have found that this is the only way to insure that there will be genuine two-way communication. If the manager starts by expressing his or her own point of view about the employee's performance of their working relationship, the interview almost invariably develops in a predominantly one-way communication pattern.

It is only after they have discussed the employee's topics, concerns and suggestions that the manager's viewpoint should be presented. This might include a general impression of performance. For example, the manager might say "I've been very pleased...," or "I've been somewhat disappointed in the way things have been working out...." Certainly a manager should take this opportunity to

---

Figure 1

Performance Review Discussion

Employee's name _____

Date of discussion _____

Introduction
  Put employee at ease.
  Purpose: mutual discussion of how things are going.

Employee's view
  How does he/she view job and working climate?
  Any problems?
  Suggestions for changes, improvement?

Supervisor's view of employee's performance
  Summary statement only.
  Avoid comparisons to others.

Behaviors desirable to continue
  Mention one or two items only.

Opportunities for improvement
  No more than one or two items.
  Do not present as "shortcomings." Keep it work-related.

Performance improvement plans
  Plan should be employee's plan.
  Supervisor merely tries to help and counsel.

Future opportunities
  Advancement possibilities?
  Future pay increase possibilities?
  Warning for poor performer.

Questions
  Any general concerns?
  Close on constructive, encouraging note.

Figure 1 Performance Review Discussion

commend the employee for significant accomplishments, and especially for improvements that might have been made on the basis of previous discussions or coaching.

The manager can then introduce the discussion of opportunities for growth or improvement in job performance. Many times the most effective way to accomplish this is to ask the employee to take the initiative here. It is much easier to react to, and perhaps to expand on, plans that someone has for changing performance or behavior than it is to make such suggestion directly. The odds of the individual's self-esteem being threatened are certainly much less if this approach is used. In either case, the manager should try to maintain a problem-solving, rather than a blame-placing approach. The focus should be on future opportunities and plans rather than on past failures.

A natural closing topic of discussion will be what the future might hold for the individual. However, in many organizations this may not be a relevant topic for many people. In a very stable organization, for example, there may be little chance of advancement for many employees. To bring up the topic each year would probably be more threatening than constructive for such employees. On the other hand, for the high-performing employee with obvious potential to advance, a discussion of possible future opportunities and self development plans might be very important to the motivation and retention of that individual.

Figure 1 presents an outline which we prepared for the supervisor to be used as a guide to both preparing for and conducting the discussion. The supervisor will find it helpful to make notes in advance relating not only to the topics or issues to be discussed, but also regarding the strategy to be used in introducing each of these topics or issues. Note that the form does not require scaled ratings of any kind.

The primary purpose of an annual discussion along these lines is not performance feedback and coaching. Performance feedback and coaching must be a day-to-day activity. Effective coaching must be associated immediately and directly with the performance at issue. This annual discussion is designed to open communication channels and to develop a better working relationship between the two parties involved. It is especially valuable in providing a formalized method of insuring *upward* communication. The manager can learn how employees view the work situation and what their concerns are.

A Test of the Procedure

This approach to the performance review discussion has been used successfully in several organizations with a variety of employees, from assembly line workers to engineers and managers. Invariably, both the managers and employees like the procedure much better than the more traditional rating-form approach to appraisal.

An ideal opportunity for a more objective test of this discussion procedure arose at a new plant. The personnel staff at that plant had planned to introduce a new appraisal program for hourly employees. Their program conformed to the traditional format—that is, ratings in critical dimensions of the job. Since the plant was composed of two large buildings where similar manufacturing operations were performed, it seemed like an ideal situation for an experiment. Therefore, we decided to introduce the traditional program in one building and the new approach, described here, in the other building. An attempt was made in each case to provide the training supervisors would need to carry out the respective programs effectively.

After the two programs had been in effect long enough for all employees to have been appraised, a survey was carried out to measure their reactions to the appraisal programs. This survey showed that reactions of employees who experienced the new approach were significantly more favorable than the reactions of employees in the building where the more traditional appraisal program was used.

For example, employees in the building where the new approach to appraisal was used were more likely to say that:

1 Their supervisor recognized and appreciated their work
2 They got answers to their own questions
3 They had an opportunity to participate in the discussion
4 They had received help in performing their job better
5 Judgments the supervisor made about their work were accurate
6 The discussion increased their feeling of pride in their work

Supervisors who used this recommended approach to the performance review discussion also reported, in almost every case, that they like the procedure better than rating programs they had used in the past. Many said that they especially liked the fact that they did not have to assign and discuss numerical grades in various aspects of job performance.

Providing for Administrative Needs

Many personnel administrators insist that numerical grades of some kind must be assigned to each of the employees in the organization. They maintain that such grades provide a systematic basis for administrative decisions which need to be made relating to the status or treatment of individuals.

The most common administrative purpose of performance ratings is to implement a merit pay plan. Most organizations use a pay plan at least for professional and managerial personnel which provides for differential increases to individuals depending on their performance ratings. However, there is no reason to believe that a merit pay program could not be administered without necessarily assigning numbers or grades to the performance of individuals. As a matter of fact, in almost any organization there are factors which influence the size of salary increases granted to individuals other than just performance level achieved in the previous year. Decisions regarding amount of salary increase to be granted, and reasons for the size of increase involved, can certainly be communicated to an employee without necessarily attaching a specific number or grade to the employee's performance level. This decision might be communicated in the annual review discussion recommended here, or in a separate discussion, depending on the timing of the increase, the manager's preference, or similar considerations.

Another administrative need for which appraisal information is likely to be generated is to facilitate manpower planning. Here, again, qualitative information rather than qualified grades or classifications can be recorded for this purpose and discussed with the individuals involved. As a matter of fact, experience of personnel specialists has shown that qualitative information in the form of written out performance or behavioral descriptions on appraisal forms usually proves to be of greater value for manpower planning purposes than the grades or ratings assigned to employees.

In most organizations, promotions to higher-level positions are rarely based on the performance appraisals which managers record as a part of the annual rating program. In almost every case, more comprehensive information is obtained on the qualifications of candidates relating to the specifications for the open position. The opinions of many people in the organization, other than the individual's immediate manager, are likely to be sought. Moreover, in many organizations today "assessment center" type of programs are used to provide more detailed and objective data for making promotional decisions than is typically revealed in the documented annual appraisals.

When we consider an even more critical personnel decision, the decision to demote or terminate an employee, many personnel administrators have insisted that we need systematically recorded annual appraisals to protect the organization against discrimination suits. However, it is very doubtful that a subjective judgment of the supervisor or manager, regardless of how precisely this judgment is categorized, will be accepted in court if the manager is accused of bias. In fact, experience to date has shown that such ratings are not accepted as unbiased in discrimination cases.[4]

To be accepted in a court of law, decisions to demote or terminate an individual will undoubtedly have to be backed up by objective performance evidence. This kind of evidence will also have to be recorded, and should be communicated to the respective individual at the time of occurrence—not on the occasion of the employee's anniversary date when his or her performance review is scheduled. Whether the supervisor judges performance to warrant a "2" or a "4" or "poor" or whatever, will be immaterial in court in most situations. On the other hand, specific descriptions of performance failures, preferably backed by objective data, are much more likely to be accepted. This kind of documentation will be necessary to substantiate critical decisions like terminations, whether or not the organization has a formal program for annual performance review.

Many of the problems that we have had with appraisal programs appear to stem from the fact that we try to achieve too many objectives with a single program. Some of these objectives are incompatible. For example, we may expect the same program to provide the kind of detailed and candid data needed to make hard administrative decisions, and at the same time expect the manager to use such data in a supportive manner to stimulate improved performance. This often proves to be an impossible task: either the data get distorted so that the message is palatable, or the feedback is so threatening to the individual that the results are more negative than constructive.

Appraisal to be effective must be an *ad hoc* procedure. We must use different approaches to satisfy different objectives.

With the approach described here, we have concluded that an annual review discussion can be constructive if we set relatively modest, although important, objectives for it. Admittedly it does not provide for all appraisal needs. It does appear, however, to serve one important need very well—that of opening communication channels between manager and employee. This is likely to be much more than is accomplished with programs that are designed to serve a much broader range of needs.

References

1. See, for example, Meyer, H. H., E. Day and J. R. P. French, Jr. "Split Roles in Performance Appraisal," *Harvard Business Review,* Jan-Feb. 1965.
2. Ibid.
3. See, for example, Sander, Alvin. "Research on Self-Esteem, Feedback and Threats to Self-Esteem," in Zander, A. (ed.) *Performance Appraisals: Effects on Employees and Their Performance.* Ann Arbor, Mich: The Foundation for Research in Human Behavior, 1963.
4. See, for example, Layer, Robert I. "The Discrimination Danger in Performance Appraisal," *The Conference Board Record,* March 1976.

Questions on Reading

1. Why does Herbert Meyer conclude that the typical annual appraisal interview is not a psychologically sound procedure?
2. What are the general specifications that the author suggests for making the annual appraisal interview constructive?
3. Identify the sequence of steps included in the suggested format for the annual appraisal interview.
4. How does the author handle the possible objection that numerical ratings of performance are not determined by his approach to the appraisal interview?

Directing

One of the most complex of the management functions is directing, or providing leadership. Effectively communicating with people and understanding what motivates their behavior are essential to achieving success in this function. Studies of leadership success and supervisory effectiveness enhance our understanding of the personal and procedural factors that make successful management direction likely.

Chapter 10 is concerned with basic concepts in the communication process: the types of symbols, organizational barriers to communication, the structure of communication networks, and the possible patterns of communication in small groups. The last two topics are related to the process of organizing, as well as to that of directing.

Some of the basic findings of psychologists regarding human motivation are summarized in Chapter 11. Included is a discussion of the categories of human motives, motivational conflict, and reactions to personal frustration. In Chapter 12, on the other hand, we turn to industrial applications of motivation theory. In addition to considering the often misunderstood relationship between morale and productivity, we report the results of studies of motivation in industry.

Chapter 13 is concerned with some of the approaches that have been used in studying leadership success and the role of the leader in terms of various organizational climates and leadership styles. Included also is the leader's use of power through disciplining inappropriate actions. The contents of Chapter 14 are more specifically oriented toward the work of the first-level supervisor in terms of the supervisor's role in the organization and the supervisory methods that have been found to be effective. Particular attention is also given to employee resistance to change and how such resistance can be overcome.

Part 4

10 ADMINISTRATIVE COMMUNICATION

- Basic Concepts
- Symbols in Communication
- Barriers to Communication
- Communication Networks
- Communication Patterns in Small Groups
- Review
- Discussion Questions
- References
- Case Study: A Problem in Listening
- Case Study: The Misinformed Supervisor
- Applications Reading: "How to Be a Better Listener" Sherman K. Okun
- Questions on Reading

The process of communication, that is, the passing of information and understanding, is a prerequisite for attaining desired changes in the behavior of subordinates and others in the organization. In previous chapters we have indicated the relationship between the organization chart and the formal chain of communication on the one hand, and the informal organization and its associated grapevine on the other. In this chapter, we begin by defining the communication process in general and identifying the four major elements involved in this process: the *sender,* the *receiver,* the *communication channel,* and the *symbols.* The rest of the chapter builds upon these elements. The section on symbols in communication is concerned with some of the semantic problems in verbal communication, the section on barriers to communication is concerned with some of the factors that impede communication in administrative situations, and the sections on communication networks and communication patterns are concerned with communication channels from the interpersonal and organizational points of view.

Basic Concepts

"Communication" is defined as the passing of information and understanding from one person to another. It is, therefore, an active process involving at least one sender and one receiver. Information and understanding are passed to the receiver, and knowledge of its effect is passed back to the sender in the form of feedback.

1 Of the two persons involved in the communication process, the *sender* is the one who typically initiates the contact for the purpose of passing _____ and _____ to the *receiver.*

information; understanding

2 Two other elements are necessary if communication is to take place: the *communication channel* and the *symbols.* These provide the basis for contact between the _____ and the _____.

sender; receiver

3 In an organization, the various contacts among organizational units and/or individuals can be represented by a system of _____ channels.

communication

4 *Symbols* can be of various types. However, in administrative communication, information and understanding are typically conveyed by the use of verbal _____ .

symbols

Basic Concepts • 303

5 There would be no information flow in the channel connecting the sender and receiver without the use of _____ .

symbols (or words)

6 We have established, then, that the purpose of communication is to pass _____ and _____ from one person to another.

information
understanding

7 Would a discussion between a used car salesman and a prospective customer be a communication situation? [Yes / No]

Yes (The situation conforms to the definition of communication.)

8 The four elements necessary for communication to take place are the sender, the _____ , the _____ , and the _____ .

receiver
communication channel
symbols

9 The success of the communicative effort is based on the extent of new information or understanding achieved by the _____ . Can we *directly* observe the information or understanding achieved by another individual? [Yes / No]

receiver

No (That kind of X-ray machine hasn't been invented yet!)

10 Since the information or understanding within another person cannot be directly observed, the receiver's *behavior* provides the basis for judging the success of a sender's attempt to _____ .

communicate

11 The verbal explanations that the receiver can give and the skills that he can exhibit are both aspects or examples of his _____ .

behavior

12 Even changes in the receiver's facial expression or bodily gestures can be considered as _____ effects.

behavioral (or behavior)

13 *Feedback* is the observation by the sender of the effect of his actions on the _____ of the receiver.

behavior (or actions)

Yes

Yes (though not as much feedback as is available in other situations)

No (although delayed feedback can be available)

feedback

desired

undesired

no

miscommunication

no

14   Consider an executive discussing a new procedure with one of his subordinates. Is feedback available to him in this situation? [Yes / No]

15   Consider a lecture at a professional meeting. Is any feedback available to the speaker in this situation? [Yes / No]

16   Consider a political candidate speaking to an audience via television. Is immediate feedback available to him in this situation? [Yes / No]

17   In a sense, the passing of information and understanding in the reverse of the usual direction, that is, from receiver to sender, is a description of _____ .

18   The sender's efforts to communicate can result in one of three effects, in terms of the receiver's behavior. A *desired change* may occur, an *undesired change* may occur, or *no change* may occur. Successful communication involves the occurrence of a _____ change.

19   Like successful communication, miscommunication involves an effect in the receiver's behavior, but in this case it is a(n) _____ change.

20   On the other hand, *no communication* involves _____ change in the receiver's action from the behavioral point of view.

21   Thus, when the desired effect occurs in the receiver's behavior, successful communication has taken place; when an undesired effect occurs, _____ has taken place; the absence of any effect on the receiver's behavior signifies that _____ communication has taken place.

22   A supervisor reprimands an employee, and as a result the employee vehemently complains to co-

workers about the incident. The immediate effect signifies that [successful communication / miscommunication / no communication] has taken place.

miscommunication

23 A salesman makes a desired sale. This is an example of [successful communication / miscommunication / no communication].

successful communication

24 A supervisor gives instructions to accounting machine operators on how to prevent machine malfunctioning. The following week he notices that the incidence of machine trouble has not changed. This is an example of [successful communication / miscommunication / no communication].

no communication

25 The sender has no way of knowing what effect, if any, his efforts to communicate have had on the receiver unless he provides for _____ in some form.

feedback

26 The presence of feedback provides the basis for the sender to modify his efforts in various ways in order to achieve _____ _____.

successful communication (etc.)

27 Since the success of communication efforts cannot be evaluated without providing for _____, we shall refer to this concept on several occasions in the remaining sections of this chapter.

feedback

Symbols in Communication

The very words that we use can be a source of strength or weakness in our attempt to communicate. *Semantics,* which is the science of language and meaning, concerns itself with the study of communication symbols and their meaning. Not surprisingly, it has been found that words do not necessarily have commonly understood meanings. Certain types of words are especially likely to have ambiguous meanings, and thus may lead to difficulties in communication.

28 The study of communication symbols is included in the science of _____.

semantics

29 Words have been viewed as cognitive maps. From this standpoint, would the "map" necessarily be identical from person to person? [Yes / No]

No

30 Consider the words "grievance," "management," and "work standards." It has been found that union stewards and foreman [agree / disagree] on the meanings of these words.

disagree

31 A staff person from the quality control department has experienced a great deal of difficulty in "getting the message across" to shop foremen. It is possible that the _____ used do not have a commonly understood meaning.

words (or symbols)

32 One of the factors related to the certainty with which a word can be defined is the degree to which it is *abstract,* as contrasted to *concrete*. A word that represents a concept is a(n) _____ word, whereas a word that stands for an object with a physical reality is a(n) _____ word.

abstract

concrete

33 "Table," "car," and "bolt" are _____ words; "struggle," "power," and "progress" are _____ words.

concrete

abstract

34 Successful communication is more likely when a relatively large number of _____ words are used in a message.

concrete

35 However, not all abstract words have equally ambiguous meanings. *Connotative* words point inward and signify aspects of personal experience, which leads to the greatest degree of ambiguity. Abstract words that express an individual's feelings or reactions are thus _____.

connotative

36 *Denotative* words have a strong reference to external events. Therefore, abstract words that refer to factors outside the individual are _____.

denotative

37 Connotative words, then, are directed _____, whereas denotative words point to _____ events.

inward (etc.)

external (etc.)

connotative

denotative

38 The abstract words "beautiful," "stimulating," and "fearful" are _____ words, whereas the abstract words "contract," "management," and "profit" are _____ words.

39 Rank the following situations from highest to lowest (ranks 1, 2, and 3), in terms of the amount of semantic difficulty likely to occur:

3 ____ Message with a high number of concrete words
1 ____ Message with a high number of abstract, connotative words
2 ____ Message with a high number of abstract, denotative words

context

40 When the meaning of a word is uncertain, the *context* provides a *frame of reference* that helps define the word. Semantic difficulty is thus reduced when words or phrases are presented in _____.

increased context

41 As the number of abstract, and especially abstract connotative, words in a message is increased, the length of the message should be [increased / decreased] to provide more _____ as a frame of reference to give the words their intended meanings.

Barriers to Communication

Thus far we have considered the behavioral concepts underlying the communications process and the semantic factors that enhance or impede this process. In addition to taking note of such concepts and factors to improve organizational communication, we should also observe that there are a number of barriers in administrative communication that may have an adverse effect on the process. In this section five such barriers are described: the pressure of time, psychological distance, filtering, premature judgment, and the failure to listen.

42 The *pressure of time* is perhaps often used as an excuse for not communicating with others in the organization, but it is also a real factor affecting the opportunity to communicate. Take, for example, the relationship between a manager and a subordinate. Should

No

every organizational decision made by the subordinate be communicated by him to the manager? [Yes / No]

should

43 The delegation of authority and assignment of responsibility to an individual would suggest that the subordinate should not really try to communicate every detail. However, suppose that certain actions represent exceptions to usual procedures. In order to keep the manager informed such actions [should / need not] be communicated.

time

44 If a subordinate were not to communicate such exceptions, then the coordination of activities in the organization would thereby suffer and the stage would be set for potential embarrassment for the manager or for his subordinate. Thus, the principle of exception can be used as the basis for dealing with the fact that the pressure of _____ affects the opportunity to communicate in an organization.

are

45 In addition to the pressure of time, another barrier to communication in formal organizations is *psychological distance*. From this standpoint, it is suggested that an engineer in the research and development department and an operative employee in the production department [are / are not] likely to have some difficulty in communicating.

more

46 Although psychological distance is to some extent inherent in the different jobs, or roles, occupied by different people, the distance can be exaggerated by unwarranted use of status symbols. The more such symbols of office as private dining rooms, private receptionists, and differing office furniture are used, the [more / less] difficulty is likely in communications between people at different hierarchical levels in the organization.

psychological distance

47 Therefore, the minimal use of status symbols tends to improve organizational communication by reducing the barrier of _____ _____.

48 The third barrier to effective communication

which we consider is *filtering*. The process of filtering involves a biased choice of what is communicated, on the part of either the sender or the receiver. For example, if a subordinate "tells the boss what he wants to hear" filtering is said to have been done by the [sender / receiver]

sender

49 If a subordinate identifies several factors affecting the productivity in a department, but the manager seems to hear and to respond only to those factors that fit his preconceived view of the situation, then filtering has been done by the [sender / receiver].

receiver

50 Thus, the barrier in the communication process by which "selective telling" or "selective listening" takes place, with bias being inherent in the selectivity, is called _____.

filtering

51 The three barriers to effective communication which have thus far been considered are the pressure of _____ the _____ between sender and receiver, and the use of _____ by either the sender or the receiver.

time; psychological distance; filtering

52 Another barrier to effective communication is the tendency that most people have, when listening, toward *premature judgment*. Unlike filtering, premature judgment does not imply selective listening as such. Rather, it implies a tendency to form a judgment based on [excess / insufficient] input.

insufficient

53 Although premature judgment is done by the listener, or receiver, the way that a sender organizes his message may influence the tendency toward premature judgment. For example, if a sender first states that there are four factors affecting department productivity and then discusses all four in greater detail, the initial identification of the number of factors tends to [increase / decrease] the likelihood that the listener will form a premature judgment before all relevant factors are discussed.

decrease

54 Thus, the tendency that most listeners have, to form an evaluation before sufficient information has

premature judgment — been presented, is called _____.

55 Finally, the fifth barrier to effective communication which we consider is the *failure to listen*. Although this factor may seem to be an extension of the barriers associated with the pressure of time, filtering, and premature judgment, what we have in mind in the present context is the attention that a listener should give to *all* content of a message, both emotional as well as factual. From this standpoint, a manager who responds to the facts included in a grievance and ignores an employee's obvious anger [is / is not] really listening to everything the employee is saying.

is not

56 By the very nature of the complexity of the two types of content included in a message, the content which is more likely to be overlooked is that which is [emotional / factual].

emotional

57 Overlooking emotional content would be bad enough in itself, in terms of the effectiveness of the communications process. However, such omission is particularly serious because the emotional content may be the only "real" content of the message. This observation suggests that a supervisor who restricts his attention to the "facts" surrounding a grievance may be [acting appropriately / wasting his time].

wasting his time

58 In situations in which emotional content is prevalent, the listener's strategy should be similar to that employed in nondirective interviewing, as described in Chapter 9 on staffing the organization. Essentially, by encouraging an employee to elaborate further on his problem and to broaden the topic being considered, the listener is more likely to gain an understanding of the [emotional / factual] content of the sender's original message.

emotional

59 The term "empathetic listening" refers to the hearing and understanding of emotional content. Thus, the failure to use empathetic listening is what we have in mind when we indicate that the fifth barrier to effec-

Communication Networks

failure to listen

tive communication in the organization is the _____.

Communication Networks

Whereas a communication channel is the medium by which information and understanding are passed from a sender to a receiver, a communication network on the organizational level is the pattern of contacts among decision centers. Along with the behavioral and semantic factors, the appropriateness of this network affects communication success.

60 The communication situation involving just two persons is the *circuit communication model*. In addition to the sender and the receiver, the circuit communication model includes not only the flow of information to the receiver but also the flow of

feedback

_____ to the sender.

61 Because the model forms a closed circuit, it has been called the _____

circuit communication

model.

62 Construct a diagram for the circuit communication model in the space below, including the sender, receiver, flow of information, and feedback in the diagram.

```
           information
            ↗       ↘
       sender      receiver
            ↖       ↙
            feedback
```

63 Because there are several senders and several receivers, an organization can be viewed as a

communication

_____ network. From this standpoint the organization is represented as a *system of decision centers* that are *interconnected by communication channels*.

64 A system of decision centers interconnected by communication channels is a _____

communication network

_____.

decision
communication

65 A communication network has two important elements: a system of _____ centers, and a number of _____ channels.

part of

66 In Figure 10.1 the communication network portrays [all of / part of] an organization.

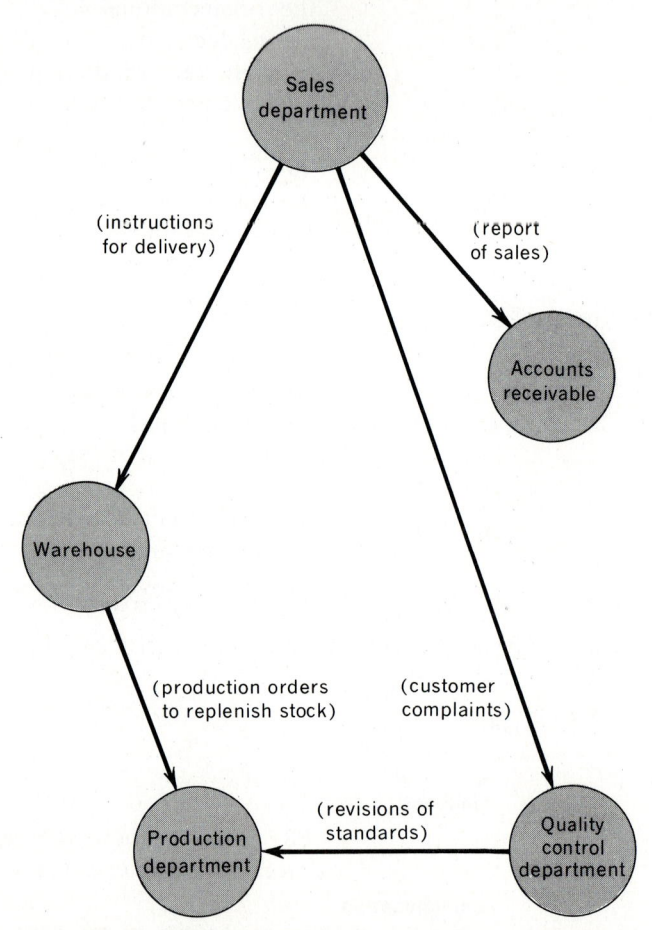

Figure 10.1 A partial communication network.

Five

67 How many communication channels are in the figure? _____ [number]

Five

68 How many decision centers are in Figure 10.1? _____ [number] Which decision center has the

Communication Networks • 313

Sales department	greatest number of outgoing channels? _____
Five (one for each communication channel)	**69** How many feedback loops might there conceivably be in all? _____ [number]
circuit communication	**70** If we were to study the relationship between just two of the decision centers in the figure, say between the quality control department and the production department, ours would be a study that would conform to the _____ model.
communication network	**71** On the other hand, the diagramming of the total pattern of contacts in an organization, which can be used to evaluate or analyze communication flow in an organization, is called a _____
feedback	**72** As is true for the simpler circuit communication model, the sending unit has no way of knowing the effects of its communication efforts unless it provides for _____.
feedback	**73** In organizational terms, *control action* on the part of decision centers is dependent on the availability of _____.
unknown	**74** Without feedback, the organizational effect of earlier decisions would be [known / unknown], and effective control action would not be possible.
control	**75** A delay of feedback to communications efforts within an organization leads to less effective _____ action on the part of decision centers.
delay	**76** A sales manager issues new instructions governing expense-account spending. When he obtains the consolidated reports at the end of the month, he realizes that his instructions were incorrectly followed. In this case, the _____ in feedback has led to slower discovery of the miscommunication.
	77 A supervisor follows the practice of asking subordinates to give their interpretation of assignments that

he has made. He is thus attempting to hasten _____ for the purpose of more effective _____ action.

feedback
control

Communication Patterns in Small Groups

Most of the coverage in this chapter has been concerned with the two-person communication situation, particularly as it is represented by the circuit communication model. Even the communication network itself was viewed largely in the context of studying one channel at a time, along with the associated feedback. In this section of the chapter we describe the results of classic research aimed at evaluating the organizational consequences of different communication patterns, or networks, in small-group problem-solving situations.

78 Figure 10.2 portrays three of the principal communication patterns used by Bavelas and others in a classic study of problem-solving behavior by five-person groups; these are the *circular, chain,* and *central-*

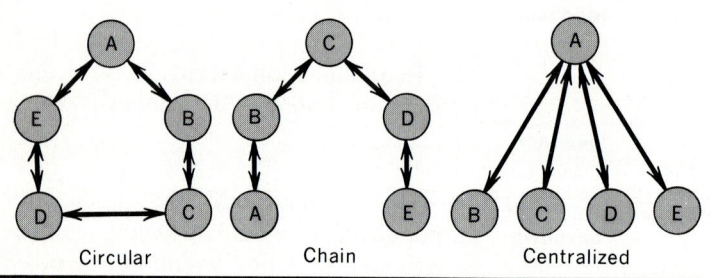

	Circular	Chain	Centralized
Speed (simple problems)	Slow	Fast	Very fast
Accuracy (simple problems)	Poor	Good	Good
Stability of leadership position	None	Marked	Very pronounced
Average morale	High	Low	Very low
Flexibility to problem change	High	Low	Low

Figure 10.2 The influence of different communication patterns on problem-solving performance of small groups. (Adapted from Alex Bavelas and Dermot Barrett, "An Experimental Approach to Organizational Communication." *Personnel,* vol. 27, no. 5, March 1951, pp. 366–371. Reproduced with permission.)

ized patterns. The pattern in which every person has someone "to each side of him" with whom he can

circular   communicate is the _____ pattern.

79 The pattern that is similar to the circular, except that two people find themselves "at the end" of the communication network and therefore can communicate with only one other person, is the

chain   _____ pattern.

80 The pattern in which one person is in a key position because all communications must be with him or

centralized   must pass through him is the _____ pattern.

81 Using these patterns, groups of people were assigned problem-solving tasks in which the information needed to solve the problem was distributed among all members of the group. As indicated in Figure 10.2, the communication pattern which generally was fastest and most accurate for simple problems was the

centralized   _____ pattern.

82 On the other hand, the pattern in which the average morale level was the highest and for which adaptability to a change in the problem was most rapid

circular   was the _____ pattern.

83 Since none of these small-group patterns can represent the full complexity of formal communication networks in organizations, the findings need to be interpreted with some caution. However, as examples of "pure" types of patterns the results indicate that the problem-solving objectives of "speed," as well as

cannot   "flexibility," [can / cannot] be achieved by the same pattern.

84 Rather, the results indicate that speed can be achieved at the expense of flexibility, and vice versa, and that *communication patterns should be designed with reference to the objective that is considered most important.* In the case of these experiments we might note that the pattern with the highest speed has the smallest (Essentially, there are four transmitters of information and one decision maker.) [largest / smallest] number of active participants in the final decision process.

85 The pattern that results in the highest average morale level and greatest flexibility in the face of changed conditions is the one with the [largest / smallest] number of active participants in the decision process.

largest

86 As is also indicated in Figure 10.2, a person's position in a communication pattern can determine his leadership role. Of the three patterns, the one in which the leader emerges most rapidly is the _____ pattern, and he emerges specifically at the position identified by the letter ____.

centralized
A

87 The pattern for which the position of the leader is entirely unpredictable is the _____ pattern.

circular

88 As another example of the importance of position in a communication network, refer to Figure 10.3. This could represent a senior corporate officer, A, who communicates with corporate officers C, D, and E only through his assistant, B. Viewed as a communication pattern, the key organizational position in this case is at the one identified by the letter ____.

B (He is the only one with direct access to all information.)

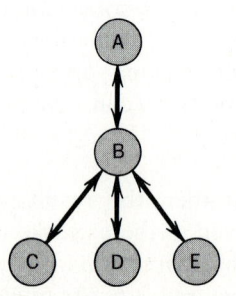

Figure 10.3 A communication pattern in a small group.

Review

information; understanding

89 Communication is defined as the passing of _____ and _____ from one person to another. (Frames 1 to 6)

sender
receiver; channel; symbols

90 The four elements that are necessary for communication to take place are the _____, _____, _____, and _____. (Frames 2 to 8).

behavior (or actions)

91 The ultimate success of a communicative effort depends on the effect it has on the receiver's _____. (Frames 9 to 17)

successful

miscommunication

no communication

92 When the desired change occurs in the receiver's behavior, _____ communication has taken place. When an undesired change occurs, _____ has taken place. Finally, the absence of a change signifies that _____ has taken place. (Frames 18 to 27)

semantics

93 The science of language and meaning is called _____. (Frames 28 to 31)

concrete
abstract

94 Words that stand for objects with a physical reality are _____, whereas words that stand for concepts are _____. (Frames 32 to 39)

connotative

denotative

95 Words that point inward, or describe inner experiences of the sender, are _____, whereas words that refer to externally oriented concepts or objects are _____. (Frames 35 to 39)

abstract
connotative

96 The words that are most difficult to define precisely are those that are both _____ and _____. (Frames 32 to 41)

time

psychological distance

97 Among the barriers to communication which were described, the opportunity to communicate is limited because of the pressure of _____. The extensive use of status symbols is not conducive to enhancing communication because of the associated increase in _____. (Frames 42 to 47)

98 The "selective telling" or "selective listening" that may take place during communication describes the barrier called _____ *filtering*. The tendency that listeners have to arrive at evaluations before all relevant information has been presented is called _____ *premature judgment*. (Frames 48 to 54)

99 The barrier referred to as the failure to listen identifies the failure to use empathetic listening during the communications process. In turn, this indicates that in addition to the factual content of a message the listener should also be alert to the _____ *emotional* content. (Frames 55 to 59)

100 A sender, a receiver, a flow of information to the receiver, and a flow of feedback to the sender are included in the _____ *circuit communication* model. (Frames 60 to 62)

101 "A system of decision centers interconnected by communication channels" defines a _____ *communication network*. (Frames 63 to 71)

102 Timely and effective control action on the part of the decision centers in an organization is dependent on the availability of _____ *feedback* to their communicative efforts. (Frames 72 to 77)

103 The small-group communication pattern which has been found to be the fastest and most accurate for simple problems is the _____ *centralized* pattern, whereas the one with the highest average morale, as well as the most flexibility in the face of changing conditions, is the _____ *circular* pattern. (Frames 78 to 88)

Discussion Questions

1. From the so-called cognitive point of view, communication results in a change in understanding; from the behavioral point of view, it results in a change in performance. Compare these two approaches as ways of explaining what "really" happens during communication.
2. Why is filtering particularly troublesome as a barrier in administrative communication? What can a manager do to reduce this barrier?

3. In the description of barriers to communication it was suggested that not only may an orientation toward the "facts" in a supervisory situation be an incomplete approach, but it may also be misdirected. Do you agree or disagree? Elaborate.
4. What types of words tend to lead to the most semantic difficulty? Why?
5. Comment on the statement, "The circuit communication model is the basic structural element that is included in all complex communication situations."
6. Referring to the major elements that are necessary for communication to take place (sender, receiver, channel, and symbols), give examples of communication failures that can be traced to each of these elements.
7. Describe an organizational situation in which something like the centralized communication pattern might be most appropriate and compare it with a situation in which the circular pattern might be better.
8. From the behavioral point of view, the availability of feedback to the sender is considered to be a key factor affecting the success of communication. In this context, what is feedback and why is it important?

References

Athanassiades, J. C. "The Distortion of Upward Communication in Hierarchical Organizations." *Academy of Management Journal,* vol. 16, no. 2, June 1973.
Bacharach, S. B., and M. Aiken. "Communication in Administrative Bureaucracies." *Academy of Management Journal,* vol. 20, no. 3, September 1977.
Bromage, M. C. "The Management of Communications." *Advanced Management Journal,* vol. 38, no. 2, April 1973.
Cross, G. P. "How to Manage Defensive Communications." *Personnel Journal,* vol. 57, no. 8, August 1978.
Farace, R. V., and D. MacDonald. "New Directions in the Study of Organizational Communication." *Personnel Psychology,* vol. 27, no. 1, Spring 1974.
Gelb, B. D., and G. M. Gelb. "Strategies to Overcome Phony Feedback." *MSU Business Topics,* vol. 22, no. 4, Autumn 1974.
Gelfand, L. I. "Communicate through Your Supervisors." *Harvard Business Review,* vol. 48, no. 6, November-December 1970.
Golightly, H. O. "The What, What Not, and How of Internal Communication." *Business Horizons,* vol. 16, no. 6, December 1973.
Grikscheit, G. M., and W. J. E. Crissy. "Improving Interpersonal Communications Skill." *MSU Business Topics,* vol. 21, no. 4, Autumn 1973.
Hall, Jay. "Communication Revisited." *California Management Review,* vol. 16, no. 3, Spring 1973.
Harriman, B. "Up and Down the Communications Ladder." *Harvard Business Review,* vol. 52, no. 5, September-October 1974.

Hayakawa, S. I. *Language in Thought and Action,* 3d. ed. New York: Harcourt Brace Jovanovich, 1972.

Hoover, D. "Increasing Human Potential through Communicative Effectiveness." *Supervisory Management,* vol. 22, no. 10, October 1977.

Housel, T. J., and W. E. Davis. "The Reduction of Upward Communication Distortion." *Journal of Business Communication,* vol. 14, no. 4, Summer 1977.

Hulbert, J. "They Won't Hear if You Don't Listen." *Administrative Management,* vol. 40, no. 2, February 1979.

Huseman, R.C., et al. "Managing Change through Communication." *Personnel Journal,* vol. 57, no. 1, January 1978.

Inman, T. H. "Effective Management Needs Upward and Downward Communication." *Arizona Business,* vol. 24, no. 5, May 1977.

King, C. P. "Keep Your Communication Climate Healthy." *Personnel Journal,* vol. 57, no. 4, April 1978.

Lorey, W. "Mutual Trust Is the Key to Open Communication." *Administrative Management,* vol. 37, no. 9, September 1976.

McLeod, M. B. "The Communication Problems of Scientists in Business and Industry." *Journal of Business Communication,* vol. 15, no. 3, Spring 1978.

McMaster, J. B. "Getting the Word to the Top." *Management Review,* vol. 68, no. 2, February 1979.

Mayer, H. E. "How the Boss Stays in Touch with the Troops." *Fortune,* vol. 91, no. 6, June 1975.

Mayer, R. J. "Communication and Conflict in Organizations." *Human Resource Management,* vol. 13, no. 4, Winter 1974.

Muchinsky, P. M. "Organizational Communication: Relationships to Organizational Climate and Job Satisfaction." *Academy of Management Journal,* vol. 20, no. 4, December 1977.

Newstrom, J. W., R. M. Monczka, and W. E. Reif. "Perceptions of the Grapevine: Its Value and Influence." *Journal of Business Communication,* vol. 11, no. 3, Spring 1974.

Poole, M. S. "An Information-Task Approach to Organizational Communication." *The Academy of Management Review,* vol. 3, no. 3, July 1978.

Roberts, K. H., and C. A. O'Reilly III. "Failures in Upward Communication in Organizations: Three Possible Culprits." *Academy of Management Journal,* vol. 17, no. 2, June 1974.

Schneider, A. E., W. C. Donaghy, and P. J. Newman. *Organizational Communication.* New York: McGraw-Hill, 1975.

Schwartz, M. M., H. F. Stark, and H. R. Schiffman. "Responses of Union and Management Leaders to Emotionally-Toned Industrial Relations Terms." *Personnel Psychology,* vol. 23, no. 3, Autumn 1970.

Shannon, W. C. "One-Person Communications." *Training and Development Journal,* vol. 32, no. 5, May 1978.

Sussman, L. "Communication: What Are Your Assumptions?" *Supervisory Management,* vol. 21, no. 1, January 1976.

CASE STUDY: A Problem in Listening

In the Cosmopolis Insurance Company, two of the sessions in the fifteen-session supervisory development program are concerned with the topic of communication and its importance in managerial success. Near the end of the first session, Judith Crane, manager of the billing department, volunteered the comment that even though she found the topic to be interesting and agreed that it was important, something vital was missing in the company's training program. "As a supervisor, my problem is that people just don't know how to listen," she said. "With a lot of my people, after I spend a great deal of effort instructing them as to exactly what to do, they're just as likely to be doing something entirely different when I check on their progress later. What we should do is set up a course in good listening and have all our employees take it."

1. Do you agree with Judith Crane that communication can be improved by having people develop better listening skills? Should such a course be offered in the company?
2. In any communication situation, who has ultimate responsibility for communication success or failure? Why?
3. Do you think Ms. Crane is effective as a communicator? How might she improve?

CASE STUDY: The Misinformed Supervisor

Henry Macon, president of the Food Processing Corp., was regarding with acute distress a summary given to him by John Haeningsen, director of personnel. The facts follow in the summary.

Three of the senior staff members in the research and development department have given notice of their resignations. Further, in the course of a confidential survey conducted by Jack Haeningsen, four more have indicated that they are looking for other positions, and three others have expressed serious dissatisfaction with "the way things are going around here."

The Food Processing Corp. was founded in 1933 by Mr. Macon's father as a marketing organization for disposing of excess and surplus food products, mainly potatoes, which constituted a glut on the market during the depressed period of the thirties. The imaginative Senior Macon, realizing the need for new areas to develop in marketing, had hired a research chemist who developed an economical process for converting potatoes into low-cost industrial alcohol. Convinced of the profits to be gained through the sound application and marketing of research, father and son had persevered until, by 1968, they were principal stockholders of a substantial organization which was involved in the production of a large variety of food products with the emphasis still on potatoes, and with marketing activities encompassing military and commercial customers over the entire United States.

The firm employs 1200 people, of whom sixty-five are chemists, engineers, and technicians involved in research and development. William Parsons is assistant general manager in charge of R&D, with over twenty-five years of experience in food-processing research.

Three months earlier, Parsons had promoted Kenneth Bullitt to the position of R&D section chief on military and government contracts. Bullitt was known as a hard-working, hard-driving research chemist who had participated in and directed a series of programs that were brought to successful and profitable conclusion. This was his opportunity to perform as the section chief responsible for an entire group of programs. The promotion of Bullitt, while based on meritorious past performance, was motivated in part by a substantial decrease in government business due to the recent congressional economy wave. Bullitt's new section was staffed by eighteen professional chemists and engineers and twelve support technical workers. The data embodied in Haeningsen's report concerned an incident in this section. It appears that at a regular weekly staff meeting with his people Bullitt made the comment, "When this contract we now have for irradiating flake potatoes for the Air Force is completed in six months, I don't know what we'll do around here to keep you people busy." An early result of this comment was the resignation of three of the staff members, with the additional consequences detailed at the beginning of this case description. Worse, the three engineers who had resigned were well known and respected in the company, and had disclosed the reason for their actions to a number of selected friends. The effect on morale, as well as on productivity, has developed to the point that immediate action is required if further and even more serious consequences are to be averted.

Macon's first reaction was to call Parsons, the assistant general manager of R&D, into his office and order him to reprimand Bullitt and then to have Bullitt either dismissed or at least demoted. Even though the government programs are being reduced, the board of directors of the company has recently decided on increased activity in certain commercial areas, with the result that more research personnel will be needed for the new projects.

1. Was Bullitt correct in communicating his judgment about the prospects for future employment to the people in his section? Why or why not?
2. What should Mr. Macon do about the belief that has developed among many employees regarding the future prospects of the company?

3. What should Mr. Macon do about Kenneth Bullitt and perhaps William Parsons?
4. Are there any changes that Mr. Macon should make with respect to the overall communications system in the company?

APPLICATIONS READING:

How to Be a Better Listener

Sherman K. Okun

Vice President, Folger & Co., Inc.
Management Consultants
Boston, Massachusetts

A recently appointed vice president of operations of a machine tool manufacturer found that unanticipated problems—such as materials shortages, cost overruns, machine downtime, and lost orders—kept cropping up. Evidently, he assumed, the company's reporting system was not providing him with adequate timely information.

He called in the corporate information system's staff and asked them to review his reporting systems. The staff then developed a new set of reports—but he found the same unforeseen problems kept recurring.

The vice president then felt sure that a basic organizational problem was leading to these difficulties. He called in a management consultant, and the consultant soon spotted the trouble. The information the vice president needed was readily available. But it was not being presented to him. The fault lay with the executive, not with the organization. Whenever potential problems were being discussed, the consultant discovered, the vice president quickly began to assess blame instead of calmly seeking solutions.

As a result, no one dared to bring potential problems to his attention.

He was not a listener.

Source: Reprinted with permission from *Nation's Business*, vol. 63, no. 8, August 1975.

Three Conditions to Meet

Communications difficulties are a universal problem in business organizations. All too often, we forget that communicating is a two-way process that involves listening and responding to messages as well as giving them. Too often, real, ongoing communication upward to management is obscured, largely because managers won't or can't hear what is going on.

Three conditions must be met before communications can take place successfully. Subordinates must:

1 Know what their seniors need to hear.
2 Be given the chance to provide this information.
3 Work for people who *can* accept it in a way that will not discourage disclosure.

Remember, reports are just one channel of communication. Only a part of the information executives need can be transmitted in writing. Many facts, nuances, and feelings can't be adequately presented on paper.

Therefore, a manager must be able to obtain information through personal contact. Otherwise, he cannot be fully informed. Thus, an otherwise excellent manager may not be truly effective unless he is a good listener.

When to Listen

Anytime you talk with one or more people, you are in a listening situation. This may be at a private conference with an individual subordinate or at a group meeting, whether a formal presentation is being made or not. It may also occur when talking with people outside the organization, such as a client to whom you are selling or a salesman who is trying to sell to you.

In any of these circumstances, the people with you will have facts, opinions, or feelings that you should know about. Without learning about them, particularly it they come through disguised so as not to upset or contradict you, you will not have accurate, complete information on which to base decisions.

Your staff may have additional information or feelings which, had you been aware of them, might have led you to different conclusions.

At the same time, it should be remembered that listening is not accomplished solely through what is said. How something is said, what is not said, and other nonverbal aspects all provide information.

What to Listen for

Facts, while obviously important, are not the only thing to listen for. Subjective data—thoughts, feelings, and beliefs—also provide important information.

For example, it is necessary to know that a particular sale was lost because of pricing. But it is also important to learn if the salesman did or did not create a relationship with the prospective customer that could result in future sales.

This additional information sometimes has to be carefully drawn out by an alert manager.

Likewise, you should listen to ideas and opinions. Perhaps a new approach to pricing should be considered in view of the last sale. But the full story will not be told if the person who did not land the order is put on the defensive.

To get all the information they need to hear, managers must create an environment in which subordinates or peers can speak up without fear of reprisal or criticism. Inattention also can quickly dam up communications.

Many managers ask their subordinates for information or opinions. However, they often create situations in which their juniors will not be able to offer facts or opinions fully and frankly. This may happen because the manager, despite what he says, appears to be uninterested. Also, he may react negatively to unpleasant news or make it hard to say what he doesn't want to hear.

Thus, an authoritarian, fault-finding approach by the boss will make it difficult for others to believe that he really welcomes their information.

Even where employees don't feel threatened, additional steps are needed to ensure good communications:

- Create a pleasant, businesslike setting. While you can discuss many subjects in office corridors or in the cafeteria, free flow of business communications should be fostered in a more formal setting. A quiet, comfortable office is one of the best places to establish a good listening environment.
- Minimize interruptions. Limit telephone calls and visits by others as much as possible when trying to hear what a subordinate has to say. In other words, focus on him.
- Pick a good time to listen. Late Friday afternoon, when people are tired or thinking about the weekend, can be a bad time to try to communicate. Fairly early in the morning, when both parties normally are fresh, is often a better choice.
- Break off meetings if the atmosphere isn't conducive to good communications. If you are becoming upset or if there are too many interruptions, it's better to reschedule the meeting. You can learn more when you reconvene than you would if the original meeting fails because of the wrong environment.

When It's Your Turn to Talk

In order to listen, you must respond positively, both verbally and nonverbally, to what is spoken and how it is said. To ensure full disclosure from others, you should:

- Speak understandably, with terminology similar to that of the speaker.
- Repeat statements for clarification.

- Summarize key points for verification.
- Use verbal reinforcers, such as "yes" and "I see."
- Use first name or "you."
- Give information that the speaker doesn't know, when that is appropriate.
- Answer questions frankly when you can. Otherwise, indicate that questions can't be answered.
- Use humor that does not offend.
- Phrase interpretations tentatively so that genuine feedback is produced from the speaker.
- Don't pass judgment on what the other person says.

It is important not to criticize. When listening and afterward, do not downgrade opinions or attitudes. Punishments and rewards should be separated from what's said and associated with performance. You won't learn much, either, if you play the hard-boiled boss and make the speaker play the underling.

In other words, exclude blaming, cajoling, exhorting, demanding, patronizing, straying from the subject, intellectualizing, or overanalyzing.

Then There's Body Language

There are nonverbal actions, as well as words, that can help or hinder communications. These make up the so-called body language of which we've heard so much lately.

Nonverbal actions which assist communications include:

- Maintaining eye contact.
- Occasionally nodding the head in agreement.
- Smiling and showing animation.
- Leaning toward the speaker.
- Speaking at a moderate rate, in a quiet tone.

As with verbal responses, body language can be negative, particularly when used in excess or contrary to your character. If so, it will diminish the flow of information. Thus, you should avoid:

- Looking away or turning away from the speaker.
- Sneering or using other contemptuous gestures.
- Closing your eyes.
- Using an unpleasant tone of voice.
- Speaking too slow or too fast.

Praise, Don't Threaten

Thus, there are many ways you can help or hinder the speaker and, in turn, affect what is presented to you.

If you work at it, you can gradually get your associates to talk more openly. One way is to praise them for being frank.

This does not mean that you should not, when appropriate, voice your feelings about being disturbed or unhappy. But this should be done in a constructive, nonthreatening way.

When he comes across as a real listener, the manager will be in a much better position to establish good communications. When that's done, he can really learn what is going on within the organization and fully use the talents and information of his subordinates. But becoming a good listener is like learning to eat raw oysters. You must work at it.

Questions on Reading

1. What are the three conditions that Sherman Okun identifies as being necessary before successful communication can take place?
2. In addition to the three conditions in question 1, what are several other steps to ensure good communication?
3. What are some of the verbal practices to ensure full disclosure from others?
4. What are some nonverbal actions that can help or hinder communications?

11 HUMAN MOTIVATION: BASIC FINDINGS

- Introduction
- Categories of Motives
- Multiple Motivation and the Conflict of Motives
- Reactions to Frustration and Conflict
- Review
- Discussion Questions
- References
- Case Study: Professional Employee Motivation
- Case Study: The Reluctant Supervisor
- Applications Reading: "Understanding Frustration-Instigated Behavior" Paul L. Wilkens and Joel B. Haynes
- Questions on Reading

Whether in a small informal group or in a large organization, people work cooperatively and enthusiastically because of the personal satisfaction associated with such activity. What kinds of satisfactions do people strive for? Are individuals consistent in what they want? What happens when a person must choose between conflicting goals? What are the different types of individual reactions to frustration and conflict? These are the kinds of questions that we investigate in this chapter.

Introduction Human behavior is seldom random in nature; rather, it is directed toward specific goals, or incentives, in the environment. However, this does not mean that goals control behavior. The goals are attractive only because of the motives they satisfy, which are within an individual. Therefore, an individual's behavior is guided by his motives, whereas goals, which are external to the individual, provide him with the opportunity for satisfying his motives.

goals (or incentives)

1 As illustrated in Figure 11.1, people direct their energies toward the attainment of _____ in the environment.

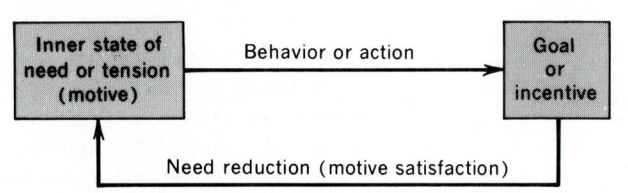

```
┌──────────────┐   Behavior or action   ┌──────────┐
│ Inner state of│ ─────────────────────▶│   Goal   │
│need or tension│                       │    or    │
│   (motive)   │                        │ incentive│
└──────────────┘                        └──────────┘
       ▲                                     │
       └─── Need reduction (motive satisfaction) ──┘
```

Figure 11.1 The process of motivation.

motives

2 However, goals as such are important to an individual only because they provide him with the opportunity to satisfy his _____.

motives

3 For example, an art exhibit does not automatically attract all passersby, nor does an appetizing meal appeal to someone who has just eaten. The effectiveness of a goal or incentive depends on the _____ of the individuals involved.

motives

4 Therefore, it is not the incentives as such that serve to guide behavior; rather, it is the _____ within a person that guide his behavior.

within the person in the environment	**5** Motives are [within the person / in the environment], whereas goals are [within the person / in the environment].
goals (or incentives)	**6** In organizational situations involving adults, the behavior of people is typically guided by well-developed motives; that is, their behavior is directed toward the attainment of specific _____ in the environment.
Unsatisfied	**7** Which motives would be most important in guiding a person's behavior at a particular time, those that are satisfied or those that are unsatisfied? [Satisfied / Unsatisfied]
satisfied	**8** On the other hand, the motives that would have the least influence on a person's behavior are those that are _____.
goals (or incentives)	**9** In summary, we can say that motivated behavior is always directed toward specific _____.
least	**10** The motives that are most important in guiding an individual's behavior are those that are [most / least] satisfied at the time.

Categories of Motives

Since motives exist within individuals and cannot therefore be directly observed, psychologists are forced to make inferences regarding the number and kinds of motives that are associated with human behavior. Because of this difficulty, those working in the area of motivation theory have often come to different conclusions regarding the classification of motives. Based on the observable goals for which people strive, there are three basic categories of motives: *physical, social,* and *psychic.*

goals	**11** When we categorize motives as being in the physical, social, or psychic dimension, we are doing so by inference, because we are actually describing the kinds of observable _____ for which people strive.
	12 The dimension, or category, of motives related to underlying biological needs, such as hunger, thirst,

sexual drive, and the preference for certain conditions of temperature and humidity, is the _____ dimension.

physical

13 In the organizational situation, anything that adds to the physical comfort and security of people is related to motive satisfaction in the _____ dimension.

physical

14 Which three of the following conditions of work are most closely related to the satisfaction of the physical dimension of motives? __, __, and __ [indicate by number]

1, 3, 5

1. Controlled temperature and humidity
2. Pleasant work companions
3. Absence of physical hazards
4. Opportunity to apply new ideas
5. A cafeteria serving good food

15 Since the influence of motives depends on the extent to which they are already satisfied, we would expect that in our society physical motive satisfaction has become relatively [more / less] important during the last fifty years.

less

16 For which socioeconomic group of people would the physical dimension of motivation be most important? [Upper income / Middle income / Lower income]

Lower income

17 Those motives, other than physical, whose satisfaction depends on association with, and acceptance by, other people belong to the _____ dimension.

social

18 For example, being an accepted member of a congenial work group results in _____ motive satisfaction.

social

19 Furthermore, other things being equal, an individual will choose to have membership in a group in which his social status is relatively [high / low]

high

20 Which three of the following conditions of work are most closely related to satisfaction of the social dimension of motives? ___, ___, and ___ [indicate by number]

2, 3, 5

1. Controlled temperature and humidity
2. Pleasant work companions
3. A friendly supervisor
4. Opportunity to apply new ideas
5. Holding a job considered important by others

21 Particularly in determining the influence of an individual's social motives on his behavior, we have to consider not only the level of such satisfaction as *he* perceives it, but also his *level of aspiration*. In other words, the deprivation of social motive satisfaction is the difference between an individual's level of _____ and the individual's perceived _____.

aspiration
satisfaction

22 For example, it is generally difficult for a politician accustomed to a high level of social motive satisfaction to readjust his level of aspiration following an election [victory / defeat].

defeat

23 What is important is not just the perceived amount of social motive satisfaction, but the amount of such satisfaction compared to the individual's level of _____.

aspiration

24 When a level of social motive satisfaction as perceived by the individual is below that individual's aspiration, he tends to work actively toward _____ in the environment that include such satisfaction.

goals (or incentives or things)

25 Beginning in the 1930s, the human relations approach to management was in part a reaction against the assumption that workers strive for economic satisfaction alone. Instead, human relationists have emphasized the importance of interpersonal relationships and informal groups. From the motivation theory point of view, the human relations approach has stressed the

Chapter 11 • Human Motivation: Basic Findings

social	importance of the _____ dimension of motivation as a factor influencing worker productivity.
physical; social	26 The two dimensions, or categories, of motives that we have considered thus far are the _____ and _____ motives. We now turn our attention to the *psychic* motives.
physical social psychic	27 Whereas the behavior of all animals exhibits the influence of the most basic, or _____, dimension of motives and some of the higher animals appear to be influenced by _____ motives, the category of motives that appears to be peculiar to man is that containing the _____ motives.
psychic	28 Goals that are attractive because they add to an individual's self-worth, even though they may not lead to any physical or social satisfaction as such, are concerned with the _____ dimension of motives.
psychic	29 Consider, for example, the person who anonymously contributes his money or personal services to a charitable cause. He receives neither physical motive satisfaction nor social esteem, yet he finds such action personally satisfying. Such satisfaction involves the _____ dimension of motivation.
psychic	30 The employee who corrects a deficiency in a product component because "it is the right thing to do," and not because he expects anyone to know about or reward him for his action, is responding in terms of the _____ dimension of motivation.
1, 3, 4	31 Which three of the following conditions of work are most closely related to the psychic dimension of motivation? ___, ___, and ___ [indicate by number]

1. The opportunity to help others
2. A conveniently located place of work
3. The opportunity to accomplish something worthwhile
4. The opportunity to work independently
5. The opportunity to hold a position of social eminence

32 In recent years, some writers have reacted against the classic human relations emphasis in management because of its main orientation toward the **social** _____ category of motives. From the motivation theory point of view, writers who emphasize the importance of developing men who act on the basis of personal *values,* even when this makes them unpopular, are highlighting the importance of **psychic** _____ motives in managerial behavior.

33 In this section we have considered three dimensions, or classifications, of motives: _____, **physical** _____, and _____.
social; psychic

34 As emphasized at the beginning of this section, **cannot** since motives [can / cannot] be directly observed, the classification of motives described here does not represent the only possibility; we have worked with the minimum number of categories possible.

35 An analysis of human motives that includes more than three categories, and which is frequently cited in management literature, is that developed by A. H. Maslow. As depicted in Figure 11.2, Maslow has dif**five** ferentiated _____ [number] categories of motives.

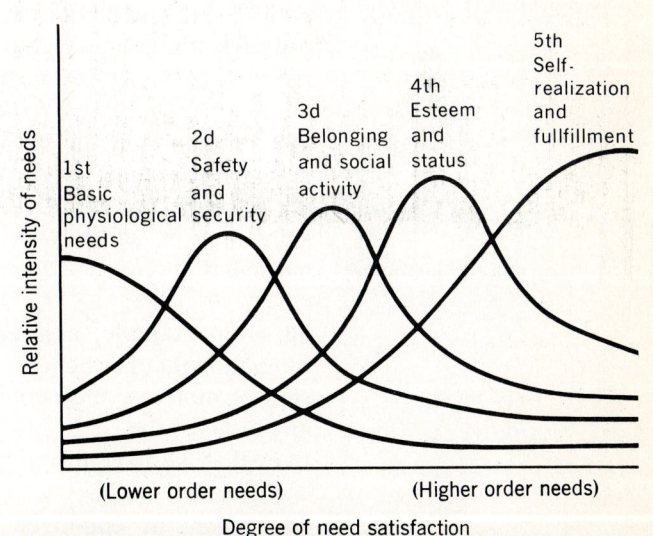

Figure 11.2 Maslow's hierarchy of needs. (Adapted.)

36 As portrayed in Figure 11.2, Maslow suggests that human needs follow a certain order or priority, and this idea is developed further in the next section of this chapter. For the present, we might observe that his two categories, the basic physiological needs and the safety and security needs, are included in the one dimension that we have called the _____ dimension of motives.

physical

37 Similarly, Maslow's belonging and social activity as well as esteem and status needs are included in our _____ dimension of motives.

social

38 Finally, a category of Maslow's that is essentially equivalent to our psychic dimensions of motives is named _____ _____.

self-realization and fulfillment

Multiple Motivation and the Conflict of Motives

We have been referring to examples of motives as if they exist one at a time. Of course, this is hardly the case. The complexity of human nature is reflected in the fact that a variety of motives operate simultaneously to influence an individual's behavior. Furthermore, the fact that some of these motives are incompatible with one another forces an individual to assign priorities and to make choices among these competing motives.

39 Seldom is it the case that a goal is considered desirable because of a single motive alone. Rather, several different _____ from different dimensions may be active when a person works toward a particular _____.

motives

goal (or incentive)

40 For example, although financial incentives are often thought of as being related to the physical dimension of motives, they could represent satisfaction in any or all of the _____ [number] categories of motives that we have discussed.

three

41 When an employee uses his income to buy "necessities of life," the dimension of motivation principally involved is the _____ dimension. When

physical

he purchases status symbols, such as a club membership, _____ motive satisfaction is involved. Contributing to charities and providing for the education of his children exemplifies the _____ dimension of motives.

social

psychic

42 Furthermore, it has been observed that an individual may himself not be aware of the motives that are guiding his behavior; that is, *unconscious* motives may be involved in addition to those that are _____.

conscious (or known to him, etc.)

43 Motives of which the person is at the moment unaware, even though they are active in guiding his behavior, are said to be _____ motives.

unconscious

44 A person who professes no interest in being noticed by others, yet continually wears clothes and does things that attract public attention, may be influenced by [conscious / unconscious] social motives.

unconscious

45 When incompatible motives are simultaneously active within an individual, he may be forced to choose between or among the _____ available in the environment.

goals (or incentives, or objects, etc.)

46 Thus, a person who is having difficulty in choosing personal goals may be affected by incompatible _____.

motives

47 The existence of incompatible motives that are more or less equally influential results in a situation that psychologists have called *motivational conflict*. Thus, motivational conflicts always concern an individual's conflicts [within himself / with those around him].

within himself

48 Considering the simplest situation of just two conflicting motives, psychologists have described three kinds of *conflict* situations, as illustrated in Figure 11.3: the approach-approach, approach-avoidance, and _____ situations.

avoidance-avoidance

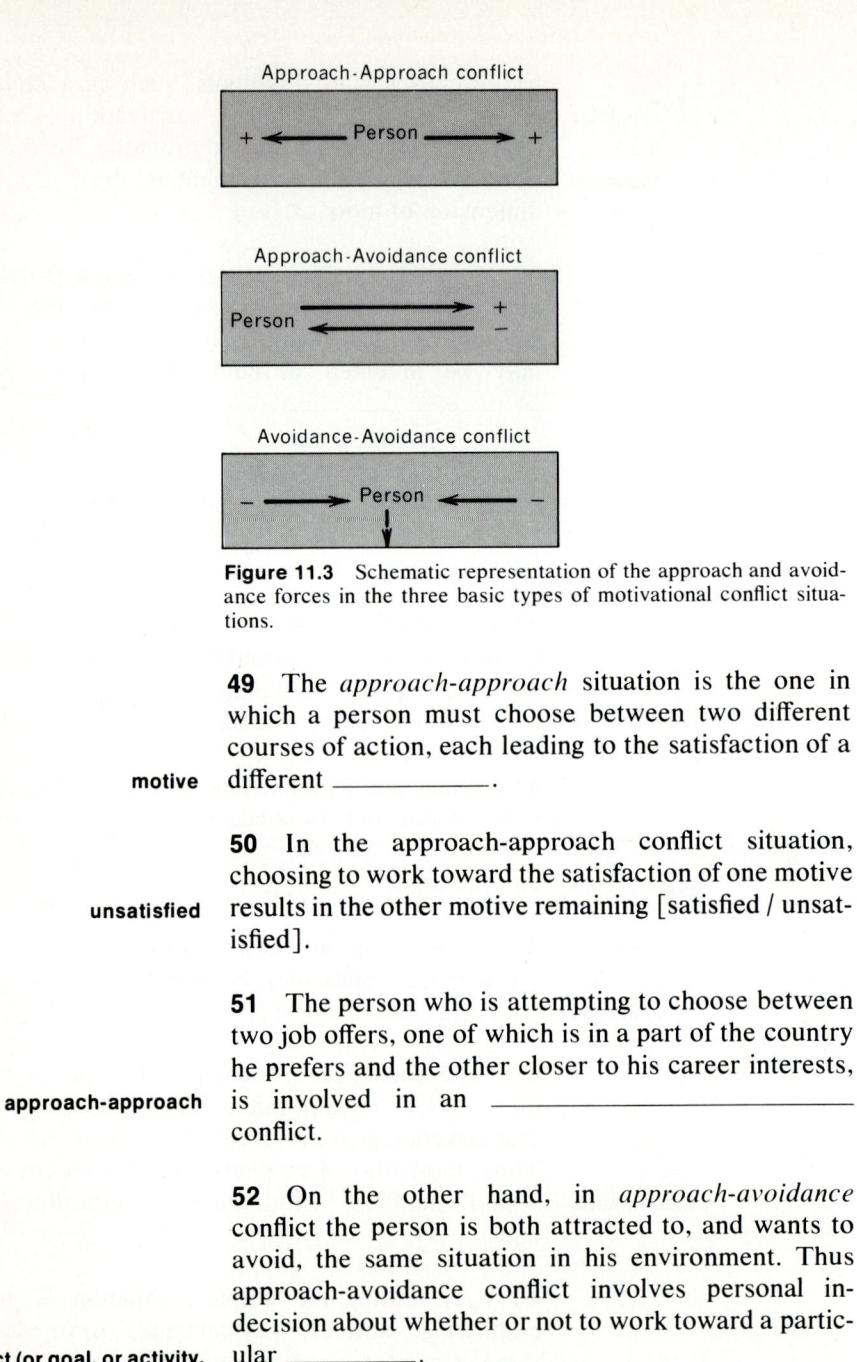

Approach-Approach conflict

Approach-Avoidance conflict

Avoidance-Avoidance conflict

Figure 11.3 Schematic representation of the approach and avoidance forces in the three basic types of motivational conflict situations.

motive

49 The *approach-approach* situation is the one in which a person must choose between two different courses of action, each leading to the satisfaction of a different _____.

unsatisfied

50 In the approach-approach conflict situation, choosing to work toward the satisfaction of one motive results in the other motive remaining [satisfied / unsatisfied].

approach-approach

51 The person who is attempting to choose between two job offers, one of which is in a part of the country he prefers and the other closer to his career interests, is involved in an _____ conflict.

52 On the other hand, in *approach-avoidance* conflict the person is both attracted to, and wants to avoid, the same situation in his environment. Thus approach-avoidance conflict involves personal indecision about whether or not to work toward a particular _____.

object (or goal, or activity, etc.)

53 There is only one situation, or goal, involved in

Multiple Motivation and the Conflict of Motives • 339

motives — the approach-avoidance conflict situation, but there are two conflicting _____ involved.

approach-avoidance — 54 When a person cannot "make up his mind" about a job offer, even though no other job opportunity exists, _____ conflict can be said to exist.

avoidance-avoidance — 55 Finally, the *avoidance-avoidance* conflict occurs when a person is forced to choose between two alternatives, both of which are considered undesirable by him. Being figuratively "between a rock and a hard place" represents an _____ conflict.

No — 56 Because two undesirable alternatives are present in the avoidance-avoidance conflict situation, would you conclude that an individual would choose to remain in such a situation, given a choice? [Yes / No]

is — 57 Unlike both the approach-approach and approach-avoidance situations, in which the possibility of personal satisfaction may cause an individual to remain in a conflict situation, in the avoidance-avoidance situation there [is / is not] typically a desire to *escape*, either physically or psychologically.

avoidance-avoidance

escape — 58 The student faced with the prospect of either failing in a course in which he has no interest or doing more studying is in an _____ conflict. His temporary avoidance of the problem by going to a movie represents an attempt to _____ from the situation.

approach-approach;
approach-avoidance;
avoidance-avoidance — 59 We have considered three kinds of conflict situations in this section: the _____ _____, _____ and _____ situations.

approach-avoidance — 60 The conflict in which only one environmental situation or goal is involved and which results in indecision about whether or not to work toward the goal is _____ conflict.

61 On the other hand, the regional sales representative who is faced with the choice of spending more time on the road or losing some of his accounts is in an _____ conflict situation.

avoidance-avoidance (He wants to avoid having to accept either alternative.)

62 An executive who must decide whether to accept a promotion that necessitates having to move with his family to another city is involved in an _____ conflict.

approach-avoidance (The promotion has both positive and negative features.)

63 Having established that an individual's motives are not necessarily compatible with one another, we now consider the question as to whether there is any pattern in the kind of motives that "win out" in the resulting _____; that is, is there a tendency for the dimensions of motives to follow a hierarchy in terms of their strength?

conflict

64 A. H. Maslow, whom we cited in the preceding section of this chapter in regard to his analysis of five categories of motives, has suggested that motives develop in a certain order and that those categories developed earlier tend to have more strength in situations concerning motivational conflict than those developed later. In terms of his theory, the category illustrated in Figure 11.2 (repeated), which carries the most strength in motivational conflict situations is that containing the _____ needs, whereas the most vulnerable category contains the _____ needs.

basic physiological

self-realization and fulfillment

65 In terms of the three dimensions of motives we have identified and discussed in the preceding section of this chapter, if Maslow's conclusion is correct, the most basic and influential motives would be those included in the _____ dimension, followed by those included in the _____ and _____ dimensions, respectively.

physical
social; psychic

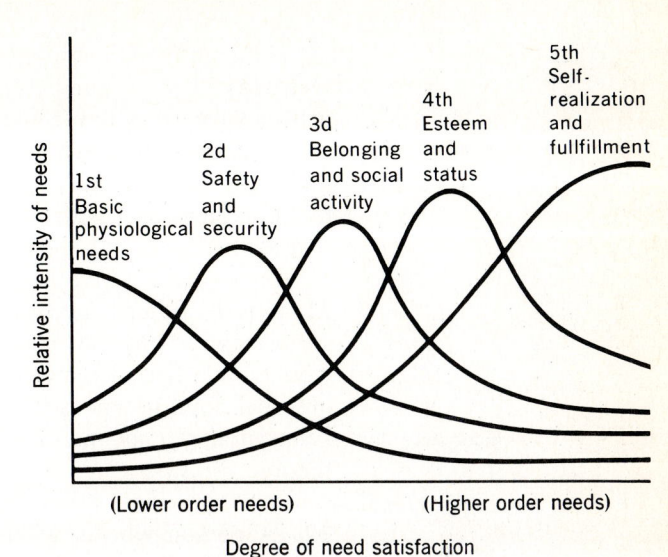

Figure 11.2 Maslow's hierarchy of needs. (Adapted.)

66 From the hierarchical point of view, the development of a higher motive is dependent on the prior satisfaction of those motives below it. Thus, we would expect social motive satisfaction to become important only after the _____ motives have been fundamentally satisfied.

physical

67 Furthermore, we would expect the satisfaction of psychic motives to become important to an individual only after his _____ motives have been reasonably satisfied.

social

68 Similarly, the hierarchical theory suggests that under conditions of stress the satisfaction of motives higher in the hierarchy is given up first. In other words, under conditions of physical threat the category of motive satisfaction that would be given up first is the _____, followed by abandonment of _____ motives.

psychic
social

69 The hierarchical theory would predict that for the extremely hungry person, the questions as to whether he is liked, whether he has status among his associates, and whether he has satisfied his personal ideals would carry [much / little] importance.

little

70 In a study of conditions in hunger-ridden postwar Germany,[1] it was found that the incidence of psychoneurosis was very low. Since the development of neurotic behavior has been associated with frustrated attempts to satisfy social motives, this finding is [consistent / inconsistent] with the hierarchical theory of motivation.

consistent

71 On the other hand, we can observe many apparent exceptions to the hierarchical theory. The artist who puts artistic creation above all else, including physical comfort and social satisfaction, is behaving [consistently / inconsistently] with the hierarchical theory.

inconsistently

72 A person who is willing to give up everything, even his life, for the sake of his values exhibits a behavioral pattern dominated by the _____ dimensions of motives.

psychic

73 Thus, even though motives may generally follow a particular hierarchy, observation indicates that any one of the dimensions of _____ may be dominant in a particular person.

motives (or motivation)

74 Just as some people are most responsive to incentives that satisfy psychic motives, others may be principally oriented toward the satisfaction of the _____ or _____ dimension of motives.

physical; social

Reactions to Frustration and Conflict

Frustration indicates the failure to satisfy personal motives because of barriers to goal attainment. Because personal motives are also not satisfied during motivational conflict, the reactions to conflict are often similar to those observed under externally imposed frustration. One possible reaction to frustration is that the individual will work toward eliminating the barriers to goal attainment. However, a number of other reactions which are not quite so rational are also possible, especially in the face of long-term frustration or conflict. In this section of the chapter we describe the

---

[1] Kilby, Richard W., "Psychoneurosis in Times of Trouble: Evidence for a Hierarchy of Motives," *Journal of Abnormal and Social Psychology*, 1948, vol. 43, pp. 544–545.

aggressive, withdrawal, and *compromise* types of reactions, or defense mechanisms, that are often substituted for effective problem-solving behavior.

75 The nonrational ways of behaving which are described in this section have often been referred to as *defense mechanisms* by psychologists because they serve to protect the individual's feeling of self-worth in the face of continued motivational [satisfaction / frustration].

frustration

76 Thus, ways of thinking and behaving in circumstances of frustration which are not effective problem-solving approaches, are self-deceptive, and serve to protect an individual's self-concept are referred to as _____ mechanisms.

defense

77 The explanation of just how the defense mechanisms protect the self-concept is psychologically complex and beyond the scope of this text. However, the fact that employees (including managers) frequently experience on-the-job frustrations suggest that various defense mechanisms [are / are not] likely to be used in organizations.

are

78 Our description of the defense mechanisms will not be exhaustive, but it will include some examples of the aggressive, withdrawal, and compromise types of mechanisms. As indicated by its title, the *aggressive* type of reaction in response to frustration involves some kind of attack directed [inward / outward].

outward

79 The aggressive reaction may be either direct or displaced. *Direct aggression* is involved when the aggressive response is directed at the barrier to goal attainment or something closely associated with it. As with all defense mechanisms, this behavior does not represent an effective problem-solving strategy. For example, the foreman who "gets mad" at an inspector for rejecting parts manufactured in his department thereby exhibits a [direct / displaced] aggressive response.

direct

80 In *displaced aggression* the aggression is directed toward a scapegoat which (or who) has no direct relation to the reasons for frustration. For example, an employee who develops into an agitator on the job because of marital problems at home has displaced his aggressive response from home to _____.

job (etc.)

81 Thus the first category of defense mechanisms which has just been described includes the _____ reactions, which may be either _____ or _____.

aggressive
direct; displaced

82 The second category of reactions has been called the *withdrawal* type. Withdrawal can be a symptom of a serious psychological problem. However, in the context of the relatively milder defense mechanisms we are considering, two examples are *regression* and *emotional insulation*. When an individual withdraws from the kind of problem-solving effort of which he is capable and turns to less mature behavior instead, _____ can be said to take place.

regression

83 A repairman who hits a sensitive mechanism with a wrench because he's unable to loosen it illustrates the withdrawal reaction called _____.

regression

84 As a withdrawal reaction, *emotional insulation* is somewhat more subtle. By not "exposing" himself emotionally, an individual can often protect an unrealistic self-concept. Thus, the manager who is always very correct in his dealings with others in the company but never extends himself personally and never engages in informal contacts or activities may be engaging in a form of _____.

emotional insulation

85 Thus the second category of defense mechanisms we have described, the withdrawal reactions, includes the reactions (among others) of _____ and _____.

regression
emotional insulation

86 The third category of defense mechanisms includes the *compromise solutions,* so named because they are neither simply of the aggressive nor of the withdrawal type. Of the several reactions included in this category, we shall briefly describe *compensation* and *rationalization*. Achieving a feeling of satisfaction by substituting a different goal for the one that is really desired describes the compromise reaction called

compensation   _____.

87 The manager who prides himself on having his section reports submitted before those of all other sections may be substituting this form of achievement for others that are more meaningful, and thereby he may

compensation   be indulging in a form of _____.

88 On the other hand, rationalization describes the tendency to give related but irrelevant reasons to excuse or "explain away" below-par performance. The employee who always has numerous excuses ready for his failure to achieve job objectives may thus be prac-

rationalization   ticing a form of _____.

89 Two particular forms of rationalization have been described in popular form: the *sour-grape* and *sweet-lemon* rationalizations. The sour-grape rationalization describes the tendency we have to conclude that a goal we failed to achieve really wasn't worthwhile, whereas the sweet-lemon rationalization represents an attempt to identify something good about a situation involving failure. A project manager who says, "It's just as well that we failed to meet the schedule last week, because now we might be able to get some overtime ap-

sweet-lemon   proved," may be indulging in the _____ form of rationalization.

90 The manager who fails to achieve quality objectives and then proceeds to claim that they are really unrealistic and therefore unimportant as objectives

sour-grape   may be indulging in the _____ form of rationalization.

91 In summary, we have considered two examples of the compromise type of defense mechanisms: the reac-

compensation; rationalization   tions of _____ and _____.

92 Two particular forms of rationalization have been popularly described and called the _____

sour-grape; sweet-lemon   and _____ rationalizations.

Review

motives

93 Behavior that is directed toward specific goals in the environment is guided by the individual's _____. (Frames 1 to 6)

least

94 At a particular time, the motives that are most important in guiding behavior are those that are relatively [most / least] satisfied. (Frames 7 to 10)

social

95 Organizations in which camaraderie and esprit de corps are high provide a high amount of motive satisfaction in the _____ dimension for their members. (Frames 11 to 25)

psychic

96 Achievement for its own sake and sacrifice of personal comfort for the good of someone else or for a cause typify the _____ dimension of motivation. (Frames 26 to 38)

unconscious

97 When a person doesn't seem to fully understand or be aware of his own motives, we can describe the situation as including the existence of _____ motives. (Frames 39 to 44)

approach-approach

98 When a person has trouble in choosing between two possible job assignments because of the different type of personal opportunity which each represents, we can describe the situation as involving _____ conflict. (Frames 45 to 51, 59)

approach-avoidance

99 An employee working under a piecework incentive system, who would like to produce more in order to earn more money but would thereby lose the friendship of those in the work group, faces an _____ conflict. (Frames 52 to 54, 60, 62)

avoidance-avoidance

100 The junior executive who faces the choice of either working in the evenings or missing a due date for a particular job assignment is involved in an _____ conflict situation. (Frames 55 to 58, 61)

101 According to the hierarchical theory, the most basic of the three dimensions of motives that we have considered is the _____ dimension. (Frames 63 to 74)

physical

102 We have described three general categories of defense mechanisms as types of unrealistic reactions to frustration: the _____, _____, and _____ types. (Frames 75 to 78)

*aggressive
withdrawal; compromise*

103 An example of an aggressive reaction is _____, an example of a withdrawal reaction is _____, and an example of the compromise type of defense mechanism is _____. (Frames 79 to 88)

*direct (or displaced) aggression;
regression (or emotional insulation);
compensation (or rationalization)*

104 Two forms of rationalization that have been popularized because they are so frequently used are the _____ and _____ rationalizations. (Frames 89 to 92)

sour-grape; sweet-lemon

Discussion Questions

1. It has been said that "man does not live by bread alone." What other kinds of incentives serve to satisfy his motives?
2. Taylor's "scientific management" has been criticized because of its emphasis on economic incentives. In what ways is this criticism legitimate? What factors may have made Taylor's emphasis more appropriate in his time than it is now?
3. The "human relationists" of the thirties and forties demonstrated the importance of noneconomic incentives in the workplace. In their emphasis on social motives what other dimension of motives did they tend to neglect? What was the general nature of the early studies that made such an omission likely?
4. In what respects may managerial indecision be indicative of motivational conflict?
5. What is the general evidence that supports a hierarchical view of human motives? On the other hand, what kind of evidence contradicts this theory?

6. Since "rationalization" may include the construction of rational excuses for failure, how can a manager determine whether an employee is rationalizing or presenting valid reasons for failure?
7. Since motivational conflict represents some kind of conflict between (or among) the motives within an individual, in general how can such conflicts be resolved?
8. A department manager suggests to a section supervisor that the supervisor will have to learn how to motivate his people. What is the general approach by which a supervisor can "motivate" his subordinates?

References

Bekiroglu, H., and T. Gonen. "Motivation—The State of the Art." *Personnel Journal*, vol. 56, no. 10, November 1977.

Dichter, E. *Motivating Human Behavior.* New York: McGraw-Hill, 1971.

Ivancevich, J. M., and J. T. McMahon. "A Study of Task-Goal Attributes, Higher Order Need Strength, and Performance." *Academy of Management Journal*, vol. 20, no. 4, December 1977.

Lewin, K. *A Dynamic Theory of Personality.* New York: McGraw-Hill, 1935.

Maslow, A. H. *Motivation and Personality*, 2d ed. New York: Harper & Row, 1970.

Pate, L. E. "Cognitive versus Reinforcement Views of Intrinsic Motivation." *The Academy of Management Review*, vol. 3, no. 3, July 1978.

Schneider, B., and C. P. Alderfer. "Three Studies of Measures of Need Satisfaction in Organizations." *Administrative Science Quarterly*, vol. 18, no. 4, December 1973.

Steers, R. M., and D. G. Spencer. "Achievement Needs and MBO Goal-setting." *Personnel Journal*, vol. 57, no. 1, January 1978.

Weiner, B. *Theories of Motivation.* Chicago: Markham, 1972.

CASE STUDY: Professional Employee Motivation

The Monroe Company is a company in the machine tool industry whose management group has always prided itself on the high level of employee relations in the company. The company's philosophy primarily reflects the belief of the founder of the firm, since passed away, that the firm's success had to be based on thorough employee commitment to its objectives. The fringe benefits paid by the company are the highest in the industry, and the employee suggestion system has provided a generous financial incentive for suggestions that result in improvements in the company's products or reductions in manufacturing costs. The profit-sharing program, by which the company contributes a fixed percentage of its profits to an employee investment and retirement fund, has also been credited as a major factor in promoting a high level of esprit de corps in the company.

Within the context of this organizational climate, Ron Ohlmann found that in his job as manager of the manufacturing methods department, employee motivation had never been a problem. During the past two years, however, the machine-tool industry has experienced a decline in sales, and the Monroe Company has shared in this decline. In response to market conditions and competitive factors in the industry, personnel reductions have been made in staff groups as well as in manufacturing departments, and merit increases have been largely curtailed. Since company profits were low last year, so was the contribution to the employee profit-sharing fund. Furthermore, the value of the investment fund has itself declined because of falling stock prices.

The general economic "tightening of the belt" within the company has meant that frequently fewer people are available to do the same work. For example, the work load of the manufacturing methods department is not particularly reduced because of lower production schedules but is often increased in certain respects. Ron Ohlmann was gratified at the response of departmental employees during the first several months of economic turndown. A majority of the supervisory and professional employees began putting in extra hours during evenings or on weekends in order to meet departmental commitments and deadlines. Recently, however, Mr. Ohlmann has detected other employee attitudes that he believes are indicative of a developing problem. On three specific occasions he has heard of employee complaints about the overtime work necessary to complete assigned projects. As one of the engineers expressed it, "The company is getting a lot of free labor under the present arrangement, and I don't see any end in sight." Although it is not clear whether the two are related, several engineers have also left the department recently in order to accept job offers with other companies, even though this meant forfeiture of company contributions in their investment fund accounts and even though the salaries they received in their new jobs were not significantly higher.

1. Before the economic turndown, what were the factors, or influences, that led to a high level of employee effort to accomplish the objectives of the organization?
2. In what ways was the motivational climate changed by the turndown in company sales?
3. Should Ohlmann be particularly concerned by the fact that a few of his professional personnel have recently left the company?
4. In the context of the present economic situation what can the company do to improve the motivational climate? What can Ron Ohlmann do?

CASE STUDY: The Reluctant Supervisor

As part of the company's management development program, a group of managers from various functional areas has devoted several class sessions to a study of motivation theory and the relevance of such knowledge to the manager's responsibility for directing and controlling the operations of the organizational unit. One of the participants in the program is Grace Schaeffer, who has been a supervisor in the production department for about a year. During the discussion session, Grace made the observation, "Motivation theory makes sense in general, but there is really no opportunity for me to apply these concepts in my job situation. After all, our shop employees are unionized and have job security and wage scales that are negotiated and are not under my control. The study of motivation concepts has given me some ideas about how to get my children to do their chores and their homework, but it hasn't given me anything I can use on the job. Furthermore, in a working situation we're all dealing with adults, and it seems to me this reward and punishment thing smacks of personal manipulation that just won't go over with people."

1. In what respect is Grace Schaeffer correct in her comment about not having any opportunity to apply motivational concepts in her job situation?
2. What types of incentives for effective performance may Grace be overlooking?
3. What do you think about her concern that the application of motivational concepts leads to the manipulation of people?

APPLICATIONS READING:

Understanding Frustration-Instigated Behavior

Paul L. Wilkens
Assistant Professor of Management
and
Joel B. Haynes
Assistant Professor of Marketing
The Florida State University, Tallahassee, Florida

Successful managers are constantly looking for ways to motivate and direct their subordinates, recognizing that the human element is an integral part of any organization. In order to accomplish the "motivational" aspect of management, it is necessary to gain a clear understanding of why people behave as they do in given situations. And to understand human behavior, the many forms it takes must be recognized.

Source: From *Personnel Journal*, vol. 53, no. 10, October 1974. Reprinted with permission of *Personnel Journal*, copyright 1974.

Goal-Directed Behavior

The vast majority of behavior is basically goal-directed. It is this type of behavior that the manager will encounter most of the time when dealing with subordinates. Goal-directed behavior exists when the individual can proceed toward goal attainment with a minimum of barriers to impede his progress.

The normal behavior pattern is depicted in Figure 1. The individual first perceives the existence of some unsatisfied need. As the awareness of this need increases, tension is created. This tension develops a motive or a reason for the person to seek need-satisfaction. As a result of the tension, the individual searches the environment for an appropriate way to satisfy the perceived need deficiency. Based on past experience and knowledge of the present situation, the individual interprets the needs in terms of a want. A want can be viewed as something which is the result of environmental conditioning. In other words, needs are basic to all individuals; wants, however, determine the specific way the needs will be satisfied. For instance, two individuals may perceive hunger (a basic physiological need). One individual may *want* a hamburger, while another individual may *want* fish. Although both types of food will act to satisfy the need, the different wants are a result of the environmental conditioning which has taken place for each individual. Having perceived a need and interpreted it in terms of a want, the individual then engages in behavior aimed at the attainment of a specific goal. The specific behavior is determined in one of two ways:

1 If the individual has previously satisfied this need through a certain type of behavior, he will have developed an *evoked set*. An *evoked set* comes about through the accumulation of knowledge which is stored in our memory. In other words, if a certain type of behavior resulted in need satisfaction in the past, this information will be stored in our memory. When the individual once again perceives the existence of a certain need, he may evoke the previous behavior pattern from his memory and attempt to satisfy the need by engaging in the same type of behavior as before. [1]

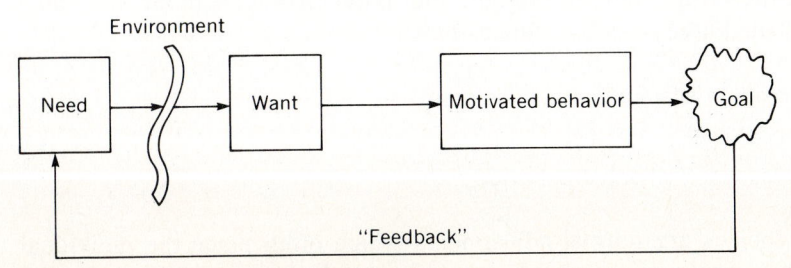

Figure 1 Goal-Directed Behavior Model

2 If the individual is encountering a new or unique situation, he will not have past performance to rely upon. In this case, the individual may engage in a rational decision-making process in the following manner:
  a Determine alternative courses of action.
  b Determine the utility of alternative courses in satisfying the need.
  c Determine the probability of need-satisfaction resulting from each alternative.
  d Select the alternative with the highest probable utility.

Having selected the specific behavior, the individual then works toward the attainment of a specified goal. This goal is something which can be clearly defined by the individual—such as the consumption of specific goods and/or services. When the individual has attained a sufficient amount of the desired goal, this information will signal that the basic need is being satisfied. He will continue to work toward goal attainment until the tension created by the need deficiency is reduced. At this point, another need deficiency is perceived to be most important and the motivational process continues. An example of this total process would be when an individual experiences thirst (a basic physiological need). He enters a restaurant and asks for a Coke (a want); pays for the Coke and begins drinking (specific behavior). He continues to drink until the Coke is consumed (goal) or the goal is reached (i.e., his thirst is quenched and need satisfaction has occurred).

Frustration-Instigated Behavior

Unfortunately, not all behavior follows the normal motivational pattern described above. At times, individuals engage in frustration-instigated behavior. This occurs when the individual perceives that the path toward reaching his goal is blocked in some manner. [2, see Figure 2] As with goal-directed behavior, the individual experiences a need deficiency. This deficiency is interpreted as a want, and the individual engages in goal-directed behavior aimed at satisfying the need deficiency. However, unlike the normal pattern, a barrier arises which tends to thwart his efforts. Barriers can take many different forms—physical, financial, or even psychological (or emotional) in nature. For example, an individual with a psychological barrier might be a person who has convinced himself that goal-attainment is impossible.

Despite the nature of the barrier, the alternatives available to the individual are rather limited. Three possible choices exist:

1 Change behavior in attempt to reach the goal.
2 Change the goal itself.
3 Engage in frustration-instigated behavior.

The first two choices are normal adjustments which often place the individual back on a path to goal attainment. Human beings are very adaptable and in the

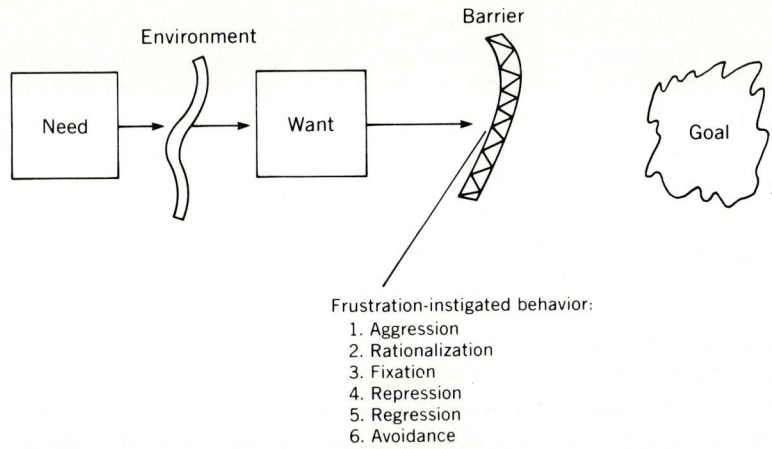

Figure 2 Frustration-Instigated Behavior Model

Frustration-instigated behavior:
1. Aggression
2. Rationalization
3. Fixation
4. Repression
5. Regression
6. Avoidance

vast majority of cases they will change their behavior or goal when they encounter a barrier. It is the third possible reaction to the barrier which should be of concern to the practicing manager.

When an individual perceives that he is unable to satisfy his needs because of a barrier, he is unable to reduce tension and, as a result, he experiences frustration. [3] A student who studies conscientiously every day, only to flunk out of college at the end of his first year, would, indeed, be quite frustrated. Reaching his goal, a college degree, would have resulted in the satisfaction of many needs. However, his inability to achieve this goal means that tension is not reduced (and may even increase), and the individual becomes increasingly frustrated because of his inability to cope with the barrier. People react to frustration in many different ways.

Types of Frustration-Instigated Behavior

There are many different types of defense mechanisms which have been identified by psychologists. Each of them represents a type of frustration-instigated behavior which may involve the following.

Aggression

Frustration may increase to the point where an individual engages in aggressive behavior. Aggression can lead to hostility and a striking out in destructive behavior. One type may be directed against the object or person that is the perceived barrier. For example, the angry worker who hits his supervisor may be expressing aggressive behavior toward the perceived barrier. Another form of aggressive behavior is "displaced aggression." This form is directed at a person or object other than the source of frustration. The worker who is verbally reprimanded by his boss, and then goes home and starts an argument with his wife, provides an example of displaced aggression. Aggression is one of the most common forms of frustration-instigated behavior.

Rationalization

Rationalization occurs when an individual makes excuses for his failure to cope with the barrier. For example, the worker who is unable to accomplish a specific task might blame this shortcoming on poor supervision, poor working conditions, cheap materials, or worn-out tools, rather than admit his own shortcomings which, in reality, may represent the barrier to need satisfaction. This, too, is a fairly common example of frustration-instigated behavior.

Fixation

This type of behavior occurs when an individual continually repeats unsuccessful attempts to reach a particular goal. He exhibits the same behavior pattern over and over again, although experience has shown that it has previously accomplished nothing. According to J. A. C. Brown, common symptoms of fixation in industry are "the inability to accept new facts when experience has shown the old ones to be untenable, and the type of behavior exemplified by the manager who continues to increase penalties" even when this is only making the conditions worse. [4]

Repression

Individuals sometimes repress unpleasant experiences or feelings from their conscious awareness in order to deny their existence. A worker, severely criticized by his supervisor, may be able to "conveniently forget" the experience because it is too painful to remember. Such a reaction enables the individual to temporarily relieve tension by forgetting the existence of a barrier.

Regression

This type of behavior occurs when frustrated individuals give up pursuing constructive attempts to overcome their barriers and regress to more primitive and childish behavior. One of the more common forms of regression, of particular concern to the manager, is horseplay on the job. Although a certain amount of regressive behavior may help to relieve tension in stressful work situations, immoderate horseplay interferes with productivity and may well lead to accidents and injuries. [5]

Avoidance (Noninvolvement)

Avoidance occurs when, after a period of frustration, the individual loses hope of accomplishing his goal and wants to withdraw from reality and thus the source of frustration. This is a common characteristic of people in boring, routine jobs. Often the frustrated individuals resign themselves to the fact that there is little hope for improvement. Specific signs of avoidance are excessive absenteeism or tardiness, a high sick call rate, and high turnover.

It is important to note a couple of points concerning frustration-instigated behavior. When an individual is engaging in this type of behavior, he has stopped trying to make the necessary adjustments which could lead to goal attainment. In other words, *frustration-instigated behavior is not goal-directed and will not result in need satisfaction.* From the perspective of the individual, frustration-instigated behavior helps to relieve some of the tension which has developed as a result of the individual's inability to cope with specific barriers to his need satisfaction. From the standpoint of the individual, frustration-instigated behavior may help to relieve tension brought on by his frustration.

Challenge to the Manager

The knowledge that frustration-instigated behavior is exhibited by all people on various occasions provides the manager with a starting point. Unfortunately, all too often in the past when a supervisor noticed disruptive behavior by one of his subordinates, his typical reaction was, "Joe's irrational behavior is creating so much difficulty in our department that I'm afraid we'll have to let him go." This view of Joe's actions is obviously inadequate. The manager is simply shunting off any responsibility for analyzing the problem and helping Joe to solve it.

In trying to eliminate or at least to minimize frustration-instigated behavior, the manager must first try to identify the barrier which is blocking the subordinate's way. In some cases, this may be easy; in others, especially where the barrier exists primarily in the worker's mind, thorough investigation may be needed.

In many cases, talking privately with the employee may enable the manager to pinpoint the barrier and find ways to overcome the difficulty. Informal discussions with those who are close to the employee may also give some valuable clues for handling the situation.

The next step is to classify the barrier in terms of its potential solution. Some barriers may be removed solely through the efforts of the manager involved, while others may call for a coordinated effort with various staff members.

The final challenge to the manager is the actual removal of the barrier. This is quite possible if he exercises some control over it. For example, counseling with an employee who appears to be noninvolved (avoidance) with his work since having been passed over for promotion, may lead to a number of solutions. To remove this barrier, special training may be arranged which would put the employee in a much stronger position for consideration when the next promotional opening occurs. Another possibility would be to look into the chance of a lateral transfer to an area that will have promotional opportunities in the near future. This will not only help the employee return to goal-directed behavior, it will also benefit the organization through increased productivity and better morale.

A major aspect of effective management is the creation of a climate which is conducive to goal attainment. Employees have needs which must be satisfied, and it is important that they have the opportunity to reach both the intermediate and long-range goals which they have set for themselves. When they exhibit frustration-instigated behavior, they are doing so because barriers exist which prevent them from achieving those goals. By identifying, analyzing and removing the barriers, the manager can help to create an environment which allows the employee to work toward his goals and at the same time toward organizational objectives.

References

1. Joseph A. Litterer, *The Analysis of Organizations* (New York: John Wiley & Sons, Inc., 1965), pp. 23–25.
2. Paul Hersey and Kenneth H. Blanchard, *Management of Organizational Behavior* (Englewood Cliffs, New Jersey: Prentice Hall, Inc., 1969), p. 12.
3. *Ibid.*, p. 13.
4. *Ibid.*, p. 14.
5. Max D. Richards and Paul S. Greenlaw, *Management: Decisions and Behavior* (Homewood, Illinois: Richard D. Irwin, Inc., 1972), p. 147.

Questions on Reading

1. What are the principal components of the goal-directed behavior model? How can this model be used to describe the circumstances resulting in personal frustration?
2. Briefly describe each of the so-called defense mechanisms that represent types of frustration-instigated behavior.
3. What can a manager do to minimize frustration-instigated behavior in the organization?

12 MOTIVATING PEOPLE AT WORK

- Motivation, Morale, and Productivity
- McGregor's Theory X and Theory Y
- The Motivation-Maintenance Theory
- Review
- Discussion Questions
- References
- Case Study: Junior Managers at Universal Systems
- Case Study: Transfer to Another Department
- Applications Reading: "Behavior Modification: A Contingency Approach to Employee Performance" C. Ray Gullett and Robert Reisen
- Questions on Reading

Whereas the preceding chapter presented the principal findings regarding human motivation, conflict, and frustration in general, in this chapter we direct our attention to motivational factors in the job situation as such. We begin by considering the relationship between morale and productivity and indicate why the existence of high morale in an organization does not necessarily mean that people in that organization will be productive. We then describe Theory X and Theory Y as two contrasting assumptions about the nature of human nature which have direct impact on methods of carrying out the managerial function of directing. Finally, we describe the motivation-maintenance theory, a theory of motivation based directly on industrial research, which suggests that high employee satisfaction is not the opposite of employee dissatisfaction but is based on entirely different factors in the job situation.

Motivation, Morale, and Productivity

Since the discovery of the importance of nonmonetary incentives in the Hawthorne studies, described in Chapter 1, particular interest in employee morale has developed. As a result, a number of techniques concerned with morale appraisal have been used in business firms, and the results of these surveys provide a basis for evaluating the effectiveness of a company's human relations efforts. Underlying much of this interest and activity is the implicit assumption that high morale leads to high productivity, and thus to achieve one is virtually to achieve the other. In this section we suggest that individual productivity does not directly result from having the opportunity to satisfy personal motives on the job. Rather, productivity results only when the organizational and personal goals can be integrated, so that accomplishing one type of objective also results in the accomplishment of the other. The general viewpoint presented here will be expanded in the following sections of this chapter, which will give greater consideration to how personal satisfaction *and* productivity can be achieved in an organization.

1 High morale typically has been found to be related to the opportunity a person has to satisfy his motives in a situation. Therefore, providing the means for satisfying personal motives in the work situation leads to

morale   high employee _____ .

2 High productivity refers to successful attainment of organizational goals. In some early research in this field, it was found that employees who were satisfied with their job situations tended also to be more productive. Therefore, it was assumed that high morale leads to high _____.

productivity

3   However, later research findings, which contradicted the earlier evidence, led to skepticism about the assumed relationship between _____ and _____.

morale
productivity

4   Two general motivational methods can be observed in supervisory techniques—*positive* and *negative* motivation. Providing the opportunity for satisfying personal motives is the basis for [positive / negative] motivation, whereas threatening punishment for inappropriate behavior is the basis for [positive / negative] motivation.

positive

negative

5   Control of human activity through the threat of decreased motive satisfaction involves the _____ motivational method.

negative

6   In the diagram below, *P* stands for the person and *OG* for the organization goal. The person is in effect "pushed" toward the organizational goal by the application of the external force associated with [positive / negative] motivation.

negative

⟶ P   OG

7   Because of the threat of reduced satisfactions, in the organization in which negative motivational methods predominate employee morale is typically [high / low].

low

8   Provided that there are some kinds of barriers that keep people in the organization, however, productivity *may* be high in an organization in which _____ motivational techniques predominate.

negative

9   For example, even though he considers conditions poor, the employee who is within ten years of retiring is [likely / unlikely] to leave an organization.

unlikely

360 ● Chapter 12 ● Motivating People at Work

leave

10 However, when negative motivational techniques predominate, individuals with other lucrative job offers will tend to [stay in / leave] the organization, thus depleting the organization's human resources and long-run success.

productivity

11 Therefore, even though the long-run effects result in depletion of personnel resources and human talent in an organization, in the short run the low morale associated with negative motivation may be accompanied by high _____.

morale

12 Turning now to positive motivation, that is, leadership based on reward rather than threat, we see that such methods generally have the *direct* result of raising _____.

productivity

13 If the work situation is such that the individual is able to satisfy his own motives even though organizational goals are not achieved, then high morale, but not high _____, will result.

positive
would not

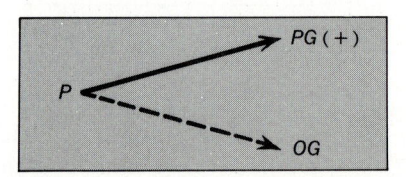

14 In the diagram below, *P* stands for person, *OG* stands for organizational goal, and *PG* stands for personal goal. In this situation involving [positive / negative] motivation, we [would / would not] expect high morale to lead to high productivity.

morale

15 For example, a job situation in which the person is able to enjoy financial security and the company of pleasant working associates independently of his job efforts (at least within certain limits) may *not* result in high productivity, even though his _____ may be high.

high

16 On the other hand, if personal motive satisfaction can be attained *only* in conjunction with, or as a result of, achieving organizational goals, then [high / low]

Motivation, Morale, and Productivity • 361

high — morale *and* [high / low] productivity will tend to result.

17 In the diagram below, *P* again stands for the person, *OG* for the organizational goal, and *PG* for the personal goal. In this situation involving positive motivation, *both* high _____ and high _____ are likely.

morale
productivity

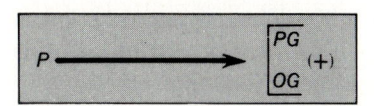

```
P ——————————→   PG
                OG   (+)
```

18 For example, if a person perceives his long-range occupational plans to be consistent with his present job assignment, [high/ low] morale and [high / low] productivity will tend to result.

high; high

19 Through this introduction, then, we have suggested that high morale tends to develop in conjunction with a [positive / negative] motivational climate.

positive

20 However, a positive motivational climate does not necessarily result in high productivity. The two are related when the personal goals of an employee are attained *through* the accomplishment of _____ _____.

organizational goals (or objectives)

21 Furthermore, in the short run, high productivity can also result from the use of negative motivational methods. However, over a period of time this approach results in the tendency for skilled people to [join / leave] the organization.

leave

22 Of course, "real life" situations [usually / seldom] conform closely to just one of the three situations that we have described. However, the relative balance of the motivational factors will be predictive of the kind of employee response that is likely.

seldom

23 Only in the positive motivational method does the manager give active consideration to the motives which underlie the employee's behavior and the goals (or factors or objectives, etc.) _____ in the job situation that might serve as incentives.

24 Because conditions of work and financial arrangements are relatively fixed in many working situations, successful employee motivation on the part of the supervisor typically involves incentives that relate higher-order mainly to the [basic physical / higher-order] needs.

25 The greater success a manager has in "tying together" organizational goal attainment and personal morale goal attainment, the higher will be both _____ productivity and _____.

McGregor's Theory X and Theory Y

In his now classic book entitled *The Human Side of Enterprise* (McGraw-Hill, New York, 1960), Douglas McGregor describes two contrasting sets of assumptions that managers use in attempting to motivate their subordinates toward higher productivity. Called *Theory X* and *Theory Y,* they have been widely accepted as being a convenient and effective way of describing the implications of a manager's motivation theory. Theory X represents the traditional view of direction and control, whereas Theory Y represents the integration of the goals of the individual and those of the organization. The focus of Theory Y, therefore, is much the same as that of our discussion on morale and productivity in the preceding section. However, in this section we highlight the strategy by which this integration of objectives can be achieved.

26 The manager who uses the Theory X approach assumes that the average human being has an inherent dislike of work and will avoid it if he can. Therefore, in order to achieve organizational objectives it is necescoerce sary to [challenge / coerce] most people.

27 In fact, the theory does not directly imply that only punishment or the threat of it will result in effective performance, since positive rewards attached to the job itself could also be motivating. But since the work itself is not considered motivating, the available physical   rewards are assumed to be principally associated with [physical / higher-order] needs.

28 In other words, Theory X suggests that the positive reasons for working are associated with the physical satisfactions purchased away from the job. In a society with a relatively low subsistence level and shortage of employment opportunities this "carrot-and-stick" theory of management would tend to work
well   rather [well / poorly].

29 However, with the higher standards of living and variety of job opportunities in societies that are technically advanced, the physical needs of people are usually fairly well satisfied. In effect, then, this leaves the organization based on Theory X management with
negative   only the [positive / negative] motivational approach.

30 Some further assumptions associated with Theory X are that the average human being prefers to be directed, wants to avoid responsibility, has relatively little ambition, and wants security above all. Again, the implication of these assumptions is that a
cannot   person [can / cannot] be motivated by the contents of the job itself.

31 In the diagram below, S represents the supervisor, P represents the person in a job situation, and J represents the job to be performed. According to Theory X, the job can be described as having a negative valence from the worker's point of view, and thus he tends to avoid job commitment and job responsibility in various direct and/or indirect ways. As indicated in the diagram, the "push" needed to accom-
supervisor   plish job goals comes from the _____.

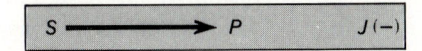

$$S \longrightarrow P \qquad J(-)$$

32 Although Theory X purports to describe human attitudes toward work, McGregor suggests that instead it describes the consequences of the managerial
repugnant   assumption that work is inherently [attractive / repugnant].

33 McGregor suggests that when people are deprived of the opportunity to satisfy higher-order needs that have become important to them, they react in a number of different but predictable ways that are all indicative of personal frustration. Thus, he suggests that the real source of the motivational problems associated with Theory X can be directly related to the nature of the [people / situation].

situation

34 In the past, organizations have attempted to handle the consequences of this frustration without addressing themselves to its cause. Thus a "tough" management attitude represents an orientation toward the [positive / negative] motivational approach.

negative

35 On the other hand, a management strategy based on a "soft" or "human relations" orientation attempts to gain employee commitment by making the job situation pleasant and providing fringe benefits, thus primarily increasing the opportunity to satisfy [physical / higher-order] needs.

physical

36 Of course, the weakness of the soft approach in the absence of any other managerial action is that increased opportunity is given to satisfy needs [through / independent of] job performance as such.

independent of

37 Thus, McGregor suggests that management by direction and control—regardless of whether it is hard or soft—relies on motivational methods that are relatively [effective / ineffective].

ineffective

38 In summarizing the first theory described by McGregor, we can state that the assumption that people are primarily interested in the satisfaction of physical needs, and that the average person dislikes work as such, is descriptive of Theory _____.

X

39 Under Theory X the motivational techniques used can be either positive or negative. However, because basic physical needs are relatively well satisfied in our society today, the motivational techniques actually available by this approach are predominantly [positive / negative] in nature.

negative

Y

40 In his book, McGregor argues that the solution to industry's motivational problems is not hard or soft management as such, but the acceptance of a new set of motivational assumptions that gives prominence to man's higher-order needs. He refers to this alternative set of assumptions as Theory _____.

internal

41 Theory Y suggests that work is as natural as play or rest, and that the average human being does not inherently dislike it. Rather, if a man is committed to the objectives associated with that work, his performance can be effectively guided on the basis of [internal / external] control.

allow individual judgment and choice

42 But how is this commitment to job objectives achieved? McGregor suggests that since the higher-order needs are now the relevant ones for many people, commitment to jobs is increased when the methods and procedures [are carefully prescribed / allow individual judgment and choice].

only partially

43 Similarly, Theory Y further suggests that under the conditions of modern industrial life the intellectual potential of the average human being is being [only partially / fully] utilized.

less

44 McGregor recognizes that complete restructuring of job situations is not possible, and thus we cannot expect to achieve perfect integration of organizational requirements and individual goals. However, to the extent that jobs can be made more meaningful, motivational problems will be [less / more] severe.

higher-order

45 The supervisor who follows the Theory Y approach to management encourages his people to develop and utilize their capacities, knowledge, skills, and ingenuity in accomplishing organizational objectives. This very encouragement provides the opportunity for satisfaction of [physical / higher-order] needs.

not necessarily either hard or soft

46 As described in the preceding frames, then, the Theory Y approach implies that the management method should be [hard / soft / not necessarily either hard or soft].

47 However, since the higher-order needs of employees are typically far from being satisfied, under Theory Y there is greater opportunity for utilizing [positive / negative] motivational methods. *positive*

48 Acceptance of the Theory Y approach does not imply complete absence of external direction and control. It does imply that greater reliance should be placed on [external / internal] control. *internal*

49 Under certain circumstances, such as those for unskilled employees in highly integrated production procedures, the opportunity to apply Theory Y may be limited. Such situations tend to breed motivational problems because there is limited opportunity on the job to satisfy [physical / higher-order] needs. *higher-order*

50 Even with such difficulties, however, the application of Theory Y is enhanced by defining job responsibilities that are relatively [narrow / broad] in scope. *broad*

51 A particular company experience serves as a classic example to support McGregor's thesis along these lines. The concept of *job enrichment* (originally called *job enlargement*), first applied in the Endicott plant of International Business Machines in 1943, is based on the premise that many jobs have been made too narrow and should be broadened in scope and complexity so that the person's overall area of job responsibility is [increased / reduced]. *increased*

52 Specifically, whereas milling-machine operators in the Endicott plant had previously been responsible only for operating the machine as such and setup men had the responsibility of making adjustments for new operations, responsibility for both operating the machines and performing routine adjustments was assigned to the operators. With the increased responsibility, the wage rate for operators was increased, but this cost was more than offset by the reduction in the number of _____ that were required. *setup men*

53 In 1943 IBM's Endicott plant had 3351 machine operators and 207 setup men, compared with 4411 operators and 4 setup men ten years later. Furthermore, management found that employees became more interested in their work, were absent less, did less complaining, and made fewer mistakes after application of the concept of _____ enrichment.

job

54 In recent years there has been considerable interest in applying the concept of job enrichment to automobile assembly operations in this country, and especially in Sweden. Of course, not all production workers desire broadened job responsibilities. But in general, job enrichment provides greater opportunity for the satisfaction of higher-order needs and is thus a particular example of the application of Theory _____ in management.

Y

The Motivation-Maintenance Theory

Another development in motivation theory that has led to a reassessment of the basic assumptions underlying the motivational methods presently used in industry is Herzberg's description of two independent sets of factors that influence job satisfaction and performance. The original research study that led to the formulation of this theory is described by Frederick Herzberg, Bernard Mausner, and Barbara Snyderman in their book *The Motivation to Work* (Wiley, New York, 1959). Many organizational studies have been conducted and many articles have been written based on the motivation-maintenance theory since the publication of this book. Essentially, this theory suggests that two separate sets of factors influence the worker's attitude toward his job. The factors that lead to high job satisfaction and goal-oriented effort—called the *motivational factors,* or *motivators*—are different from the factors that lead to dissatisfaction and discontent—called the *maintenance factors*. The maintenance factors were originally referred to as the "hygiene factors." In order to give greater meaning to these conclusions, in this section we first describe Herzberg's method of research and the data that led to his theory and then consider the implications of the motivation-maintenance theory to the managerial function of directing.

55 In their original research study Frederick Herzberg and his associates at Western Reserve University interviewed 200 engineers and accountants in the Pittsburgh area. They first asked each individual to think of a time during which he felt especially good about his job, to describe the conditions which led to these feelings, and to give an estimate of the duration of time during which these feelings affected his job performance. Of course, in this case the effects on job performance would generally be [positive / negative] in nature.

positive

56 Each individual was then asked to think of a time during which he had developed negative feelings about his job, and again to describe the conditions which led to these feelings and to give an estimate of the duration of time during which these feelings had a [positive / negative] effect on his job performance.

negative

57 In these interviews the researchers found that the individuals identified basically different types of conditions for the positive as contrasted to the negative feelings, rather than naming conditions that were basically opposites. Thus, whereas "recognition" was identified as one of the factors that led to positive feelings toward the job, "lack of recognition" [was / was not] generally identified as a factor leading to negative feelings toward the job.

was not

58 Similarly, whereas "poor company policy and administration" was a factor often underlying negative job feelings, "good company policy and administration" [frequently / seldom] was cited as a reason for positive job feelings.

seldom

59 Therefore, Herzberg concluded that the factors that lead to positive job feelings and associated job commitment and the factors that lead to negative job feelings and dissatisfaction are basically [the same / different].

different

60 The factors leading to positive feelings are the *motivational* factors, and in the original study here described they were found to be the factors of *achieve-*

ment, *recognition, work itself, responsibility,* and *advancement.* The presence or absence of these motivational factors, then, was found to be related to [job satisfaction and commitment / job dissatisfaction].

job satisfaction and commitment

61 On the other hand, the *maintenance factors* included *company policy and administration, supervision, salary, interpersonal relations,* and *working conditions.* Herzberg found that a high level of organizational performance in these areas did *not* result in a high level of satisfaction and positive feelings. However, a low level of organizational concern about these factors resulted in _____.

dissatisfaction (or negative feelings)

62 Figure 12.1 on the following page shows the percentage frequency with which each factor was associated with positive as contrasted to negative feelings toward the job in Herzberg's studies. As indicated in the figure, the factor with the highest percentage frequency as a motivator is _____, whereas the factor with the highest percentage frequency as a maintenance factor is _____.

achievement

company policy and administration

63 Furthermore, in Figure 12.1 we can also note that although each factor we have described is predominantly either a motivator or a maintenance factor, there is some overlap in factors being identified with both positive and negative feelings toward the job. For example, the motivational factor with the highest percentage of mention as a source of negative feelings is _____.

recognition (in this case, the failure to receive recognition)

64 Similarly, the maintenance factor with the highest percentage frequency of mention as a source of positive feelings is _____.

salary

65 Although the identification of factors associated with positive versus negative feelings was thus not entirely mutually exclusive, the percentage frequencies reported in Figure 12.1 indicate [relatively little / considerable] overlap.

relatively little

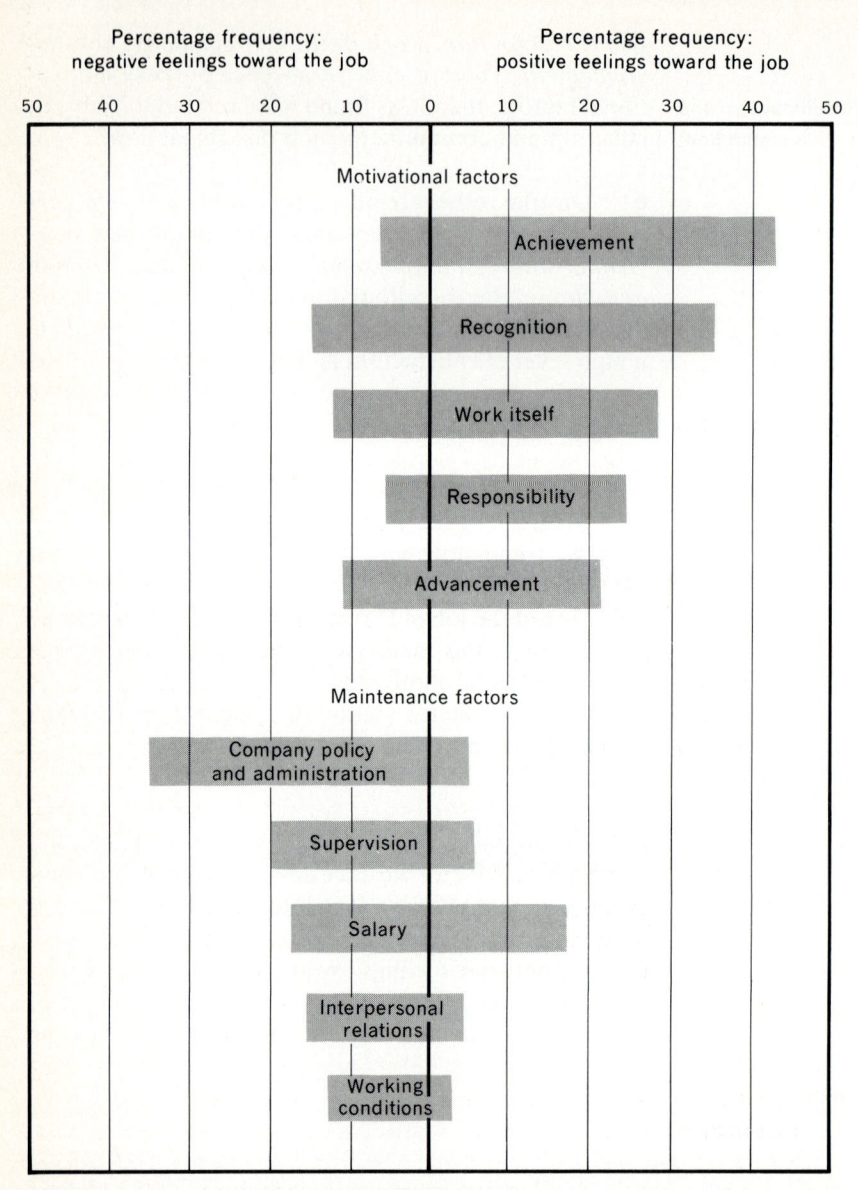

Figure 12.1 Comparison of factors associated with positive and negative feelings toward the job. (Modified from Frederick Herzberg et al., *The Motivation to Work*, John Wiley & Sons, Inc., New York, 1959, p. 81. Used with permission.)

66 Previous to Herzberg's findings, it was generally assumed that employee satisfaction and job commitment were the opposite of employee dissatisfaction and negative feelings toward the job. However, the results of Herzberg's studies indicate that the two [are / are not] essentially opposites.

are not

67 Thus, managerial attention focused on one of these sets of factors reduces negative feelings toward the job but has little effect on the development of job commitment as such. Herzberg refers to these as the

maintenance (or hygiene) _____ factors.

68 Herzberg originally used the word "hygiene" in this context as an analogy to the medical use of the term "preventative and environmental." Thus noncontaminated water [does / does not] prevent disease. It [does / does not] cure disease.

does
does not

69 So also, the hygiene, or maintenance, factors prevent negative job feelings and dissatisfaction, but managerial attention given solely to these factors does

job satisfaction and
commitment (etc.)
not result in _____.

70 Job satisfaction and commitment can be achieved only by directing managerial attention to the

motivational _____ factors.

71 As we mentioned previously, each employee interviewed was also asked to estimate the period of time during which the positive or negative feelings affected his job performance. Although the results were a bit mixed, three factors particularly stood out as resulting in lasting changes of attitude: *work itself, responsibility,* and *advancement.* Thus, the factors as-

motivational sociated with lasting changes were all [motivational / maintenance] factors.

72 Thus far, we have simply named the five principal motivational factors and five principal maintenance factors identified in Herzberg's study. Now, let us consider the types of factors included in each group. Have you noticed anything about the factors that generally differentiates the motivators from the maintenance

(Optional answer; description continues below.) factors? [Yes / No]

73 Referring again to Figure 12.1, note that one set of factors is primarily concerned with things that might be said to "surround" the job; that is, they define the environment, or context, of the job. These are the

maintenance [motivational / maintenance] factors.

motivational

74 On the other hand, the second set of factors is primarily concerned with job content and is job-centered. These factors are oriented toward what happens in the job itself, rather than toward what happens in the job environment. These are the [motivational / maintenance] factors.

job itself

75 Interestingly, when people talk about the sources of satisfaction associated with their jobs, they tend to identify factors in the [job environment / job itself].

job environment (etc.)

76 When people talk about sources of dissatisfaction and negative factors associated with their jobs, they tend to identify factors in the _____.

supporting

77 The study originally conducted by Herzberg and his colleagues has now been repeated a large number of times with a variety of professional and nonprofessional industrial work groups. Some differences in the specific factors have been found, but the maintenance factors have consistently been environmental in nature, whereas the motivational factors have consistently been in the job itself, thus [supporting / refuting] Herzberg's two-factor theory.

more

78 For example, in 1964, M. Scott Myers reported the results of an extensive test of the motivation-maintenance theory at Texas Instruments, Incorporated.[1] During the 1950s the company increased annual sales from $2 million to $200 million while the total number of employees grew from 1700 to 17,000 people. With the growth in the size and complexity of the organization they found that motivational problems become relatively [more / less] important.

broader

79 Accordingly, a random sample of 282 employees was selected and asked the two questions oriented toward job satisfiers and dissatisfiers, respectively. Employees in five job categories were represented in the sample: scientists, engineers, manufacturing supervisors, technicians, and assemblers. As compared with the original study by Herzberg, the sampled employees at Texas Instruments represented a [more specialized / broader] sampling of occupational groups.

[1]M. Scott Myers, "Who Are Your Motivated Workers?" *Harvard Business Review*, January–February, 1964, pp. 73–88.

80 Exhibit 12.1 presents sample "favorable" and "unfavorable" responses to interview questions by incumbents in five job categories. In this exhibit, the kinds of factors that lead to *satisfaction* for employees in different types of jobs are quite [similar/different].

similar (all job-oriented)

Exhibit 12.1 *Sample "Favorable" and "Unfavorable" Responses to Interview Questions by Incumbents in Five Job Categories*

(From M. Scott Myers, "Who Are Your Motivated Workers?" *Harvard Business Review*, January–February, 1964, pp. 74–75. Reproduced with permission.)

Scientist—favorable About six months ago I was given an assignment to develop a new product. It meant more responsibility and an opportunity to learn new concepts. I had to study and learn. It was an entirely different job. I always enjoy learning something new. I had been in basic research where it's difficult to see the end results. Now I'm working much harder because I'm more interested. I'm better suited for this type of work.

Scientist—unfavorable In the fall of 1961 my group would find problems which needed work. We presented them to our supervisor, and he would say, "Don't bother me with details; we are in trouble in this area and need one person for guidance and I am the person." He assigns the problems. He said, "Do what I say whether you think it will work or not." I wouldn't come in Saturday. Made me want to go home and work on my yard. Negative attitude. Killed my initiative because no matter what I came up with my supervisor wouldn't accept it. At first we tried to convince him but finally gave up. Very few gains made in this environment.

Engineer—favorable In 1959 I was working on a carefully outlined project. I was free to do as I saw fit. There was never a "No, you can't do this." I was doing a worthwhile job and was considered capable of handling the project. The task was almost impossible, but their attitude gave me confidence to tackle a difficult job. My accomplishments were recognized. It helped me gain confidence in how to approach a problem. It helped me to supervise a small number of people to accomplish a goal. I accomplished the project and gained something personally.

Engineer—unfavorable In December 1961 I was disappointed in my increase. I was extremely well satisfied with the interview and rating. I was dejected and disillusioned, and I still think about it. I stopped working so much at night as a result of this increase. My supervisor couldn't say much. He tried to get me more money but couldn't get it approved.

Manufacturing supervisor—favorable In September of 1961 I was asked to take over a job which was thought to be impossible. We didn't think TI could ship what had been promised. I was told half would be acceptable, but we shipped the entire order! They had confidence in me to think I could do the job. I am happier when under pressure.

Manufacturing supervisor—unfavorable In the fall of 1958 I disagreed with my supervisor. We were discussing how many of a unit to manufacture, and I told him I thought we shouldn't make too many. He said, "I didn't ask for your opinion...we'll do what I want." I was shocked as I didn't realize he had this kind of personality. It put me in bad with my supervisor and I resented it because he didn't consider my opinion important.

Hourly male technician—favorable In June 1961 I was given a bigger responsibility though no change in job grade. I have a better job, more interesting and one that fits in better with my education. I still feel good about it. I'm working harder because it was different from my routine. I am happier...feel better about my job.

Hourly male technician—unfavorable In 1962 I was working on a project and thought I had a real good solution. A professional in the group but not on my project tore down my project bit by bit in front of those I worked with. He made disparaging remarks. I was unhappy with the man and unhappy with myself. I thought I had solved it when I hadn't. My boss smoothed it over and made me feel better. I stayed away from the others for a week.

Hourly female assembler—favorable About two weeks ago I wire-welded more transistors than anyone had ever done—2100 in nine hours. My foreman complimented me, and I still feel good. Meant self-satisfaction and peace of mind to know I'm doing a good job for them. Once you've done it, you want to do it everyday, but you can't. It affected my feelings toward everyone. My old foreman came and talked to me. I didn't think I could ever wire-weld.

Hourly female assembler—unfavorable For a while the foreman was partial to one of the girls on the line. She didn't work as hard as the other girls and made phone calls. It got to the point where we went to the man over her foreman and complained. We were all worried since we are afraid of reprisals... The girls don't act the same toward each other now because they are afraid. It affects everyone's work. It has been going on for such a long time it's uncomfortable. It is being stopped now by the foreman's supervisor and that girl has been moved.

avoiding dissatisfaction

81   M. Scott Myers summarized the findings at Texas Instruments by concluding that "... work rules, lighting, coffee breaks, titles, seniority rights, wages, fringe benefits, and the like..." were representative of the factors associated with [avoiding dissatisfaction / improving productivity].

motivating employee productivity

82   He also concluded that "... a challenging job which allows a feeling of achievement, responsibility, growth, advancement, enjoyment of work itself, and earned recognition..." was associated with [avoiding employee dissatisfaction / motivating employee productivity].

maintenance

83   The results of these studies do not suggest that maintenance factors are unimportant. The motivation and maintenance factors have different influences in the job situation. Since a person's decision about whether to accept and stay in a job is considerably influenced by such factors as pay and fringe benefits, this type of decision is particularly influenced by _____ factors.

motivational

84   But in a particular job situation, an individual's commitment, or *productivity* decision, is particularly influenced by _____ factors.

```
                              ├┼┼┼┼┼┼┼┼┼┼┼┼┼┼┼┼┼┼┼┼┼┼┼┼┼┼┤
                              Low         Motivational factors         High

                              ├┼┼┼┼┼┼┼┼┼┼┼┼┼┼┼┼┼┼┼┼┼┼┼┼┼┼┤
                              Low         Maintenance factors          High
```

Figure 12.2 Motivational and maintenance factors are independent of one another and are present in varying degrees in any given job situation.

85 Any particular job situation can be described in terms of the motivational and maintenance factors operative in that situation. As illustrated in Figure 12.2, each of these sets of factors [is either present or absent / can be present in varying degrees].

can be present in varying degrees

86 Although most job situations include a mixture of the two groups of factors, a consideration of some "pure types" would help to summarize the implications of the motivation-maintenance theory. For example, a high rate of personnel turnover *and* a low level of job commitment would be typical when motivational factors are represented to a [high / low] extent and maintenance factors are represented to a [high / low] extent.

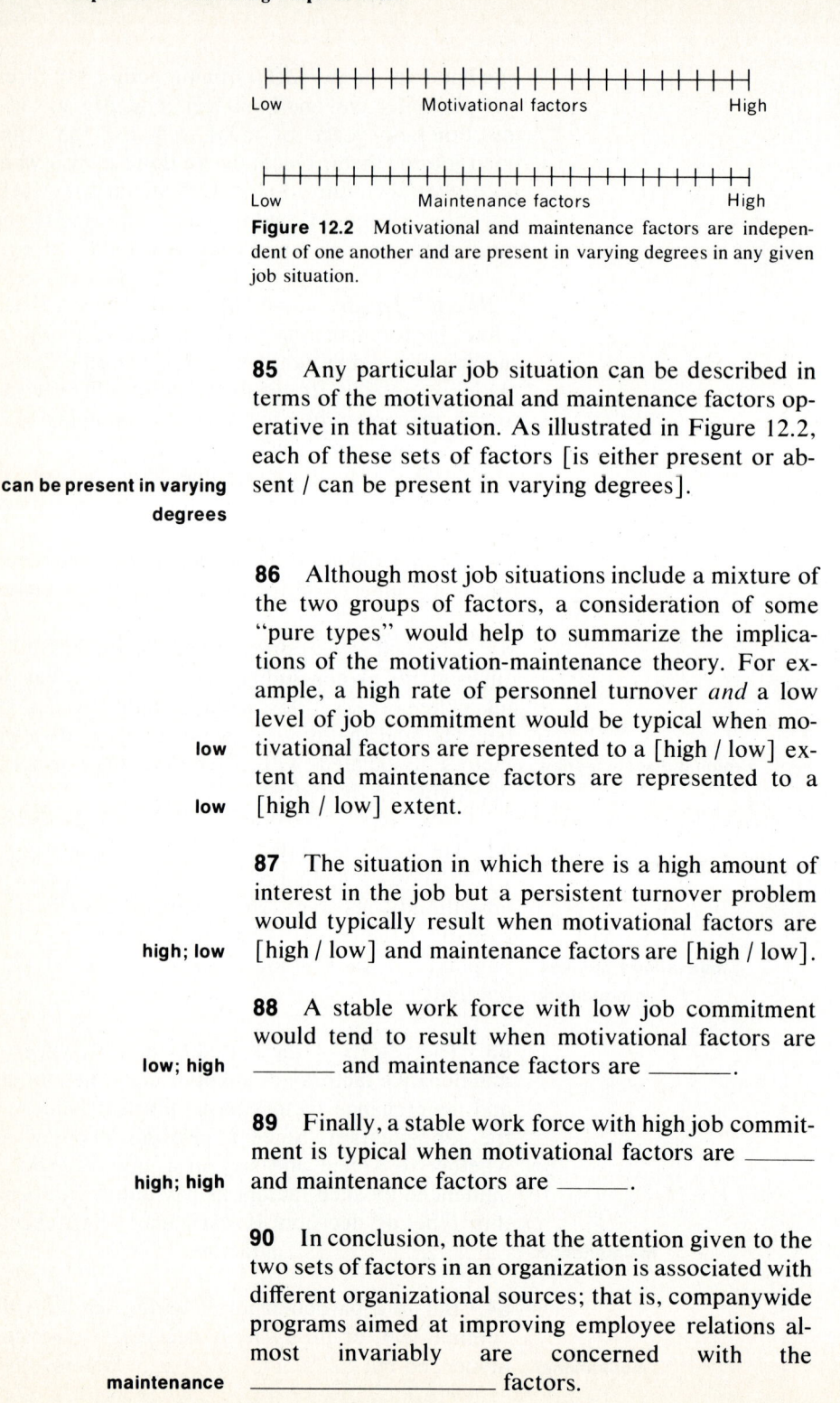

low

low

87 The situation in which there is a high amount of interest in the job but a persistent turnover problem would typically result when motivational factors are [high / low] and maintenance factors are [high / low].

high; low

88 A stable work force with low job commitment would tend to result when motivational factors are _____ and maintenance factors are _____.

low; high

89 Finally, a stable work force with high job commitment is typical when motivational factors are _____ and maintenance factors are _____.

high; high

90 In conclusion, note that the attention given to the two sets of factors in an organization is associated with different organizational sources; that is, companywide programs aimed at improving employee relations almost invariably are concerned with the _____ factors.

maintenance

91 However, the nature of the relationship between a supervisor and his subordinates and the kind of leadership he practices determine the extent to which _____ factors are represented in a job situation.

motivational

Review

positive
morale (but not necessarily high productivity)

92 The approach to motivating individuals which relies on the use of rewards can be described as involving [positive / negative] motivation. This approach almost invariably results in high [productivity / morale]. (Frames 1 to 4, 12 to 15)

low;
can be either high or low

93 Negative motivational methods, based on threat or coercion, result in morale that is [high / low] and in short-run productivity that [is high / is low / can be either high or low]. (Frames 5 to 11)

positive
organizational
personal

94 Both high morale and high productivity can only result in the situation in which there is _____ motivation and an integration of _____ and _____ goals. (Frames 16 to 25)

X

physical
negative

95 The managerial assumption that people basically dislike work, prefer to be directed, and want to avoid responsibility has been called Theory ____. Proponents of this theory assume that man is motivated primarily by [physical / higher-order] needs, and they tend to use [positive / negative] motivational methods. (Frames 26 to 33)

neither of these

96 In considering the hard, or punitive, versus the soft, or human relations, reactions to handling the consequences of Theory X, McGregor suggests that the best alternative is _____. (Frames 34 to 39)

Y

97 The assumption that work is as natural as play or rest, and that higher-order needs are the ones particularly relevant to successful motivation, is called Theory ____. (Frames 40 to 50)

job enrichment

98 A procedure first applied in the Endicott plant of IBM which tends to support McGregor's claims for the advantages of Theory Y is called _____. (Frames 51 to 54)

99 In their interviews with accountants and engineers in the Pittsburgh area, Herzberg and his colleagues found that two separate sets of factors affected job attitude. The factors associated with positive job feelings were called _____ factors, whereas the factors associated with negative job feelings were called _____ factors. (Frames 55 to 65)

motivational

maintenance (or hygiene)

100 Managerial attention directed at the maintenance factors results in reducing sources of employee _____. Attention directed toward the motivational factors tends to result in higher _____. (Frames 66 to 71)

dissatisfaction

job satisfaction (and commitment)

101 A distinguishing feature of the two groups of factors is that whereas the motivational factors tend to be concerned with the [job environment / job itself], the maintenance factors are concerned with the [job environment / job itself]. (Frames 72 to 76)

job itself

job environment

102 Other studies, such as the one at Texas Instruments, have tended to [support / refute] the principal findings incorporated in the motivation-maintenance theory. (Frames 77 to 82)

support

103 Another way of considering the implications of the motivation-maintenance theory is to observe that the decision to join and perhaps remain in an organization is particularly influenced by the _____ factors, whereas the decision to be productive is particularly influenced by the _____ factors. (Frames 83 to 89)

maintenance

motivational

104 From the standpoint of the motivation-maintenance theory, company personnel policies and practices are for the most part oriented toward _____ factors, whereas the leadership techniques of individual managers are directed toward the _____ factors. (Frames 90 and 91)

maintenance

motivational

Discussion Questions

1. Describe the conditions under which positive morale can be associated with low rather than high productivity.
2. Why is the combination of low morale and high productivity generally an unstable or temporary condition?
3. What do you think are the typical employee reactions to Theory X management?
4. What do you think are the typical employee reactions to Theory Y management?
5. Theory X and Theory Y are concerned with the nature of people. How does the nature of the job situation affect the application of these respective theories? What are the implications?
6. Comment on the statement, "When you come right down to it, people will always choose the so-called 'maintenance factors' in preference to the motivational factors, when given a choice."
7. Within the context of the motivation-maintenance theory, how is it possible for an employee to be both "satisfied" and "dissatisfied" at the same time? What are the implications?
8. What can a manager do to increase the number of motivational (as contrasted to maintenance) factors operative in a work situation? What can an organization do along these lines?

References

Alber, A. F. "The Real Cost of Job Enrichment." *Business Horizons,* vol. 22, no. 1, February 1979.

Babb, H. W. "Applications of Behavior Modification in Organizations: A Review and Critique." *The Academy of Management Review,* vol. 3, no. 2, April 1978.

Bagadia, K. S. "An Update on Job Enrichment." *Administrative Management,* vol. 38, no. 2, February 1977.

Beatty, R., and C. Schneier. "A Case for Positive Reinforcement." *Business Horizons,* vol. 18, no. 2, April 1975.

Champagne, P. J., and C. Tavsky. "When Job Enrichment Doesn't Pay." *Personnel,* vol. 55, no. 1, January-February 1978.

Gould, S., and B. L. Hawkins. "Organizational Career Stage as a Moderator of the Satisfaction-Performance Relationship." *Academy of Management Journal,* vol. 21, no. 3, September 1978.

Grigaliunas, B., and Y. Wiener. "Has the Research Challenge to Motivation-Hygiene Theory Been Conclusive? An Analysis of Critical Studies." *Human Relations,* vol. 27, no. 9, December 1974.

Herson, M., et al. (eds.). *Progress in Behavior Modification.* New York: Academic Press, 1975.

Herzberg, F. *Work and the Nature of Man.* Cleveland: World Publishing, 1966.

Herzberg, F. "Motivation-Hygiene Profiles: Pinpointing What Ails the Organization." *Organizational Dynamics,* vol. 3, no. 2, Autumn 1974.

Herberg, F., B. Mausner, and B. Snyderman. *The Motivation to Work.* New York: Wiley, 1959.

Katzell, R. A., and D. Yankelovich. "Improving Productivity and Job Satisfaction." *Organizational Dynamics,* vol. 4, no. 1, Summer 1975.

Keller, R. T., and A. D. Szilagyi. "A Longitudinal Study of Leader Reward Behavior, Subordinate Expectations, and Satisfaction." *Personnel Psychology,* vol. 31, no. 1, Spring 1978.

Kreitner, R. "PM—A New Method of Behavior Change." *Business Horizons,* vol. 18, no. 6, December 1975.

Lahiff, J. M. "Motivators, Hygiene Factors, and Empathic Communication." *Journal of Business Communication,* vol. 13, no. 3, Spring 1976.

Locke, E. A. "Satisfiers and Dissatisfiers among White-Collar and Blue-Collar Employees." *Journal of Applied Psychology,* vol. 58, no. 1, August 1973.

Luthans, F., and R. Kreitner. *Organizational Behavior Modification.* Glenview, Ill.: Scott, Foresman, 1975.

McAdam, J. "Behavior Modification: A Human Resource Management Technology." *Management Review,* vol. 64, no. 10, October 1975.

Meyer, M. C. "Demotivation—Its Cause and Cure," *Personnel Journal,* vol. 57, no. 5, May 1978.

Mikulas, W. *Behavior Modification: An Overview.* New York: Harper & Row, 1972.

Morse, J. J., and J. W. Lorsch. "Beyond Theory Y." *Harvard Business Review,* vol. 48, no. 3, May-June 1970.

Nathanson, C. A., and M. H. Becker. "Job Satisfaction and Job Performance: An Empirical Test of Some Theoretical Propositions." *Organizational Behavior and Human Performance,* vol. 9, no. 2, April 1973.

Near, J. P., R. W. Rice, and R. G. Hunt. "Work and Extra-Work Correlates of Life and Job Satisfaction." *Academy of Management Journal,* vol. 21, no. 2, June 1978.

Organ, D. W. "A Reappraisal and Reinterpretation of the Satisfaction-Causes-Performance Hypothesis." *The Academy of Management Review,* vol. 2, no. 1, January 1977.

Rand, T. M. "Diagnosing the Valued Reward Orientations of Employees." *Personnel Journal,* vol. 56, no. 9, September 1977.

Reif, W. E., and R. C. Tinnell. "A Diagnostic Approach to Job Enrichment." *MSU Business Topics,* vol. 21, no. 4, Autumn 1973.

Roche, W. J., and N. L. Mackinnon. "Motivating People with Meaningful Work." *Harvard Business Review,* vol. 48, no. 3, May-June 1970.

Rosenbaum, B. L. "Understanding and Using Motivation." *Supervisory Management,* vol. 24, no. 1, January 1979.

Rotondi, T., Jr. "Behavior Modification on the Job." *Supervisory Management,* vol. 21, no. 2, February 1976.

Schneider, J. A., and E. A. Locke. "A Critique of Herzberg's Incident Classification System and a Suggested Revision." *Organizational Behavior and Human Performance,* vol. 6, no. 4, July 1971.

Schneier, C. "Behavior Modification in Management: A Review and Critique." *Academy of Management Journal,* vol. 17, no. 3, September 1974.

Skinner, B. F. *Contingencies of Reinforcement.* New York: Appleton Century Crofts, 1969.

Skinner, B. F. *Beyond Freedom and Dignity.* New York: Appleton Century Crofts, 1971.

Starcevich, M. M. "Job Factors Related to Satisfaction and Dissatisfaction across Different Occupational Levels." *Journal of Applied Psychology,* vol. 56, no. 6, December 1972.

Steers, R. M., and R. T. Mowday. "The Motivational Properties of Tasks." *The Academy of Management Review,* vol. 2, no. 4, October 1977.

Steers, R. M., and L. W. Porter. *Motivation and Work Behavior.* New York: McGraw-Hill, 1975.

Truell, G. F. "Core Managerial Strategies Culled from Behavioral Research." *Supervisory Management,* vol. 22, no. 1, January 1977.

Wanous, J. P. "Who Wants Job Enrichment?" *Advanced Management Journal,* vol. 41, no. 3, Summer 1976.

CASE STUDY: Junior Managers at Universal Systems

Toni Miller completed her college work with a major in business administration eighteen months ago. During her last semester at college she was interviewed by a number of company recruiters and was in the fortunate position of being able to choose from among four specific job offers. Based on the opportunity she saw for professional growth, salary level, and company location, she accepted the offer from Universal Systems.

One of the factors that particularly impressed her during her job deliberations was the Junior Management Program (JMP) at Universal Systems. During their first two years of employment, the college graduates in this program are placed sequentially in four different but related job areas for about six months in each location. Based on Toni Miller's interests, it was agreed that her four areas of work experience during this period would be in personnel selection, technical training, supervisory development, and labor relations. Additional features of the JMP included a monthly dinner meeting for program participants which included talks by members of top management and a planned progression of salary increments during program participation.

With eighteen months and three of her four job assignments completed, Toni Miller now feels considerably disenchanted about the program. Further, she feels that she is not alone in her reaction, since a number of the graduates with whom she began the program have either dropped out of it to accept a full-time appointment in one of the areas of their rotational experience or have left the company entirely. She has no complaint with the overall administration of the program, since she has to admit that the company followed through on all commitments made at the time of employment. Rather, her complaint is directed toward the kind of experience, or lack of it, in her specific job assignments.

As an example, the six-month assignment that she just completed was in supervisory development. For the first two months she was given the assignment of compiling information for certain reports required by the personnel and industrial relations division. Since she was aware that the job was previously done by clerical personnel in the department, she was not particularly impressed by the assignment. She discussed the matter with the department manager, who explained that since Toni would be leaving shortly she could not be assigned the kind of responsibility that would require later follow-through. However, the supervisor did reassign her as assistant to two of the professional people in the department, one of whom was a conference leader and the other a program evaluator. As a result, during her last four months in the department she was at least able to get closer to the professional work being done, but she still felt like a "fifth wheel."

1. How would you describe the overall assumption underlying the Junior Management Program?
2. What have been the inadvertent motivational factors included in the program?
3. Can the program of sequenced job assignments be modified to correct its motivational deficiencies? How?
4. What are some alternatives to this type of program?

CASE STUDY: Transfer to Another Department

Ralph Lentini is an electronics engineer who has been with Midvale Electronics since completing graduate studies in engineering eight years ago. During this time he has been employed in the research and development department and has progressed from junior project engineer to project supervisor. In his work as project supervisor he developed the reputation of being an outstanding supervisor in terms of the motivational climate he was able to develop in his project teams. Basically, he set objectives in collaboration with each team member and worked in a consultative capacity with the people in the project, but he avoided specifying the detailed procedures to be followed. Knowing the tendency of research people to get carried away with their own interests, however, collaboration with respect to weekly objectives was the strategy Ralph Lentini followed to keep activities directed toward intended goals. In fact, Ralph was well aware that some of the work being done represented personal interests of various project personnel. But on the other hand, these same people frequently skipped coffee breaks and remained after hours on their own in order to achieve project objectives.

With the phasing out of much of the research and development work in the company, a number of people were transferred to other types of positions. Because of his success in motivating exceptional performance in the project group, Ralph Lentini was assigned as supervisor in the section concerned with assembly of hand-held calculators. Ralph approached his managerial responsibilities with the same philosophy as in the previous position. That is, he informed each person that he was not concerned about the detailed procedure by which work was done, but that he was holding each person accountable for achieving production goals. Further, he indicated that he would briefly review operations with each individual on a weekly basis, but was always available to answer any questions.

Ralph was surprised at some of the employee reactions during his first week on the job. One man indicated that he was glad that Ralph wasn't going to be such a stickler for production as the last supervisor had been, and said that the other supervisor was too rigid about always wanting to see everybody on the job.

The production figures at the end of the week were something of a minor disaster, and Ralph now pondered about what his course of action should be to correct the situation.

1. How would you describe Ralph Lentini's approach to management from the standpoint of Theory X and Theory Y management?
2. What is there are about the two work situations which he supervised which made for the difference in the responses to his approach as a supervisor?
3. What possible differences are there between the people involved in the two work situations which was related to the difference in their responses?
4. What should Ralph Lentini do now?

APPLICATIONS READING:

Behavior Modification:
A Contingency Approach to Employee Performance
C. Ray Gullett
Associate Professor of Management
University of Arkansas
Little Rock, Arkansas

and

Robert Reisen
Administrative Officer
National Bank of Fort Sam Houston
San Antonio, Texas

Source: From *Personnel Journal*, vol. 54, no. 4, April 1975. Reprinted with permission of *Personnel Journal*, copyright 1975.

All "principles" of management are based upon man's conceptions and beliefs about himself. Classical theory, represented by such notables as Taylor, Weber, and Fayol, stressed improvements in productivity and economic performance by providing employees with well-defined and often narrowly structured work environments linked with economic rewards for desired performance. Early human relations theory stressed social satisfactions through cohesive work groups and participation in decision making.[12, 18] Contemporary writers, such as Likert, have continued this tradition in relatively current works dealing with the importance of effective and interlocking work teams.[9] More recently, increased emphasis has been placed on individual autonomy, greater development of a person's talents, and recognition of individual accomplishments.[6, 13] The job enrichment movement and management by objectives have become popular vehicles for implementing these ideas.[1, 4]

Human Needs as an Explanation of Approaches to Motivation

Analyses of both past and current motivational prescriptions often employ the Maslow need hierarchy to explain the rationale behind these prescriptions. Taylor's scientific management has been exhaustively discussed in terms of its tacit assumption that individuals are "economic men" operating at the first two need hierarchy levels. Much of the writings on human relations center on the social needs level, while Herzberg's satisfiers-dissatisfiers concept and McGregor's Theory Y have been compared to the esteem and self actualization need levels.[3] While the formulators of the theories, themselves, have typically made no mention of the hierarchy concept, they, nevertheless, share the tacit assumption with Maslow that a given internal state is the dominant factor determining most employees' behavior at a point in history. Thus, as is true of Maslow's model, these are inner-directed theories of why organization members behave as they do.

But, as others have observed, the problem with human needs lies in our inability to observe them directly.[7] At best, we can only infer their existence through indirect measures. And, perhaps more importantly, we must assume the hierarchy's validity as a way of describing the internal state of most individuals. Even Maslow, himself, had doubts about this. As he explained, "My work on motivation came from the clinic, from a study of neurotic people. The carry-over of this theory to the industrial situation has some support from industrial studies, but, certainly, I would like to see many more studies of this kind, before feeling convinced that this carry-over from the study of neurosis to the study of labor in factories is legitimate."[11, p. 55] In a recent review of the literature of motivation, Miner and Dachler found that need importance varies among individuals. Important variables affecting employee needs, included: span of control, whether one holds a line or staff position, and a person's cultural background. They further concluded that the available evidence either fails to support the need hierarchy concept or it has not been sufficiently formulated to be tested.[14]

On a related note, criticisms of Herzberg's two-factor theory are well known, raising questions as to the validity of his methodology, as well as to the success of the job enrichment prescription on a *carte blanche* basis. And experience has indeed shown that not all employees desire enriched jobs.[15]

The One Best Way to Approach Motivation

Implicit in the need hierarchy schema and in most popular theories of motivation, is the assumption that there is a "best" way to motivate persons in an organization. If one assumes that a given need is dominant in all or virtually all organization members, then payoffs, geared to that need, can be provided as rewards for productivity or inducements to contribute. Thus, scientific management emphasized economic rewards, human relationists stressed social satisfactions, and well-known contemporary behavioral theories put emphasis upon opportunities for self control and development of latent abilities. The need that is stressed is usually linked to the historical point in time of the theory's development.

To an extent, the assumption of a dominant need is undoubtedly justified. In the early years of this century, large masses of workers were unskilled, poorly educated, and primarily concerned with finding and holding a job. In terms of the need hierarchy, they were operating at the physiological and safety need levels. By contrast, today's employees are relatively well educated, more highly skilled and more likely to be secure financially. Unemployment holds less terror than it did in Taylor's time. In today's environment, employees are more likely to respond to management and organization configurations that allow job enrichment, Theory Y management, and management by objectives.

Contingency of Situational Views of Motivation

Clearly, however, a great deal of organizational research has been provided in the last few years that indicates the success of varying sorts of organizational and job configurations.[8, 22, 26] Such factors as type of technology and rate of change in the environment are often major determinants of effective organization and job design. From the standpoint of individual satisfaction, it is becoming clear that not all persons view rewards in the same preference ordering. Intuitively, we can agree with Vroom that, "Lists of motives which are supposedly common to all persons, such as the one proposed by Maslow (1954), fail to do justice to... individual differences."[23]

Vroom's approach to motivation recognized the differences in motives or needs of individuals. By linking motivation to the perceived desirability of various outcomes, the likelihood of these outcomes occurring, as perceived by the individual, and the individual's perception of his ability to influence outcomes, Vroom built a motivational model based on individual differences.[24]

Although theoretically correct, the model shares a deficiency with the Maslow need hierarchy concept: the necessity for determining a person's internal perceptual state to predict his behavior, knowing external contingencies. The model is basically cognitive because as with the Maslow model, it requires the researcher or practitioner to determine individual anticipation. Thus, environmental variables become inner-directed occurrences, assuming varying degrees of importance relative to different persons.

Nevertheless, Vroom's model of motivation broke dramatically with one of the best approaches dominating management thinking and writing since the time of Taylor. By specifically modeling the importance of individual goals and perceptions upon behavior, Vroom moved motivation research in the direction of contingency thinking.

Operant Conditioning and Reinforcement

Independent of introspective and inner directed theories of motivation, operant conditioning has emerged, whose best known advocate is B. F. Skinner. [20, 21] The essence of this approach is that behavior can be changed by the consequences of that behavior. The operant model, unlike other behavioral approaches, avoids concern with the inner motivation of the individual. It does not dwell on man's drives and needs, nor does it hypothesize concerning his aspirations. Rather, it is founded upon the observable; that is, the behaviors or responses which can be seen, measured and modified.

An operant can be described as a "class of responses, the subsequent likelihood of which may be modified by its consequences."[2] Operant behavior refers to any response "the properties of which may be modified by its effect on the environment."[2] The purpose of the operant conditioning process, then, is to develop contingencies of reinforcement that will increase the probability that certain behaviors (responses) will result. These contingencies are the relationships that exist between the occasion upon which a response occurs, the response itself, and the reinforcing consequences.

Identifying Desired Behavior

An application of operant conditioning begins with the identification of desired behaviors of organization members. For programmed and relatively routine work, this task is not greatly difficult. Job analysis, methods and motion study, and engineered time standards may often be employed. Less routine tasks, such as those performed by management and professional employees, become more difficult to define, in terms of desired behavior. Management by objectives offers, however, the potential for identifying desirable end results that members are to pursue. Accomplishment, or lack of accomplishment of objectives, can be evaluated at a later date.

Determining Positive Reinforcers

When desired behaviors are identified, reinforcers must be determined. Positive reinforcers are rewards sought by the individual; negative reinforcers are forms of punishment that a person seeks to avoid. Although some support the use of negative reinforcement, most advocates of operant conditioning maintain that the unanticipated consequences of punishment far outweigh its advantages in influencing behavior. Thus, emphasis is placed, instead, upon the granting or withholding of positive reinforcers.[21]

Potential reinforcers are many and varied, ranging from monetary rewards, to social acceptance, to praise by superiors. Important reinforcers and their potential effect upon behavior are shown in Figure 1. With the exception of such primary reinforcers as water, food and air, external stimuli become reinforcers through learning. These stimuli, such as praise, promotion and tasks requiring

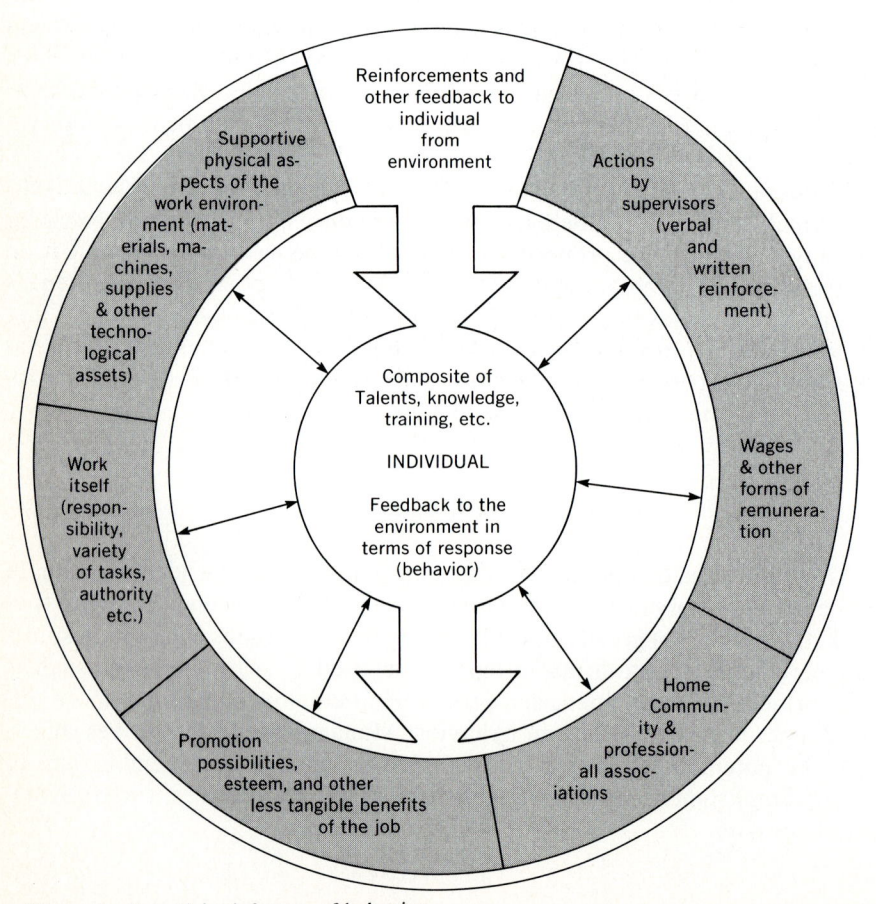

Figure 1 Potential reinforcers of behavior.

complex responses, are called secondary reinforcers. Almost all the rewards used in organizations are secondary in nature.

Two limitations are placed on the effective use of these rewards: their availability in the organization and the extent to which organization members will work to achieve them. Not all jobs, for example, lead to promotions or wage increases. However, when these rewards are available, some employees may be unwilling to work harder to achieve them.

The task then becomes one of identifying those available rewards which employees will work to achieve. Most theories of motivation have predetermined what employees want (i.e., enriched jobs or more money) and thus circumvent this issue. The operant approach, however, emphasizes controlled experimentation to determine which rewards best reinforce desired behavior. Lower error rates, higher work volume, and fewer absences are examples of positive responses to one or more reinforcers.

Effective reinforcers are thus identified through trial and error. At Emery Air Freight, where positive reinforcement has been used with striking success, the point is made this way: "The best test (of a reward's effectiveness): observe the behavior after a reward is offered. Does performance change? If not, try another reward."[17, p. 171] Implicit in this approach is the lack of prejudgement concerning the desirability of one kind of reward over another that is often made in other motivational approaches.

As soon as effective reinforcers are identified, the frequency of their availability should be determined. Rewards can be offered in a number of sequences: continuous, fixed ratio, variable ratio, fixed interval, or variable interval. These sequences are summarized in Figure 2.

The choice among these schedules of reinforcement has a profound effect upon the rate of response and its immunity to extinction. For example, continuous reinforcement works well during a learning period, when a person is acquiring new

Schedules of Reinforcement

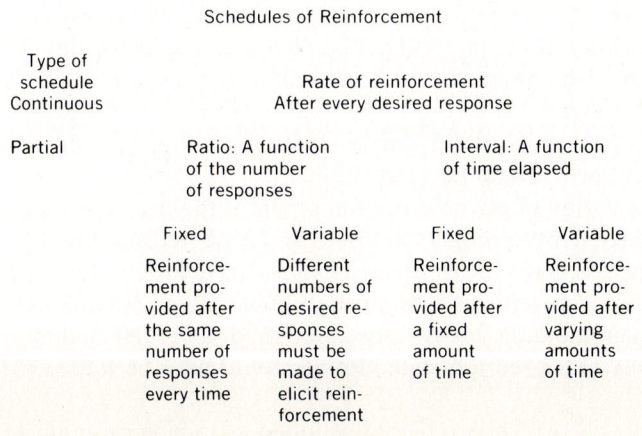

Type of schedule					
Continuous		Rate of reinforcement After every desired response			
Partial		Ratio: A function of the number of responses		Interval: A function of time elapsed	
	Fixed	Variable		Fixed	Variable
	Reinforcement provided after the same number of responses every time	Different numbers of desired responses must be made to elicit reinforcement		Reinforcement provided after a fixed amount of time	Reinforcement provided after varying amounts of time

Figure 2 Schedules of reinforcement.

knowledge. The principle of feedback, utilized in programmed instruction, is an example of continuous reinforcement.

For teaching complex tasks, the shaping concept is often used. Here, initially complex material is broken down into smaller modules. By reinforcing the successful completion of these relatively simple responses, which do not in themselves accomplish the ultimate objective, we enhance the probability of moving behavior in the desired direction. In one such approach, a bed frame manufacturer used the shaping concept to train hardcore unemployeds to produce finished bedframes. As each part of the job was learned, rewards were granted until the entire job cycle was mastered.[19]

As soon as desired job behaviors are learned, non-continuous reinforcement schedules are more effective for maintaining the desired behavior. Both the fixed and variable ratio and interval schedules summarized in Figure 2 are non-continuous. Variable ratio schedules often provide the highest behavior rates. Here, a reinforcer is provided after an average number of responses. For example, a supervisor might praise a worker's performance on the average of once every twenty non-defective units produced. While the average would be set at twenty, praise might occur after the completion of thirty, twenty-five, fifteen and ten units.

Variable schedules of reinforcement may allow previously non-effective rewards to stimulate productivity. Paychecks, for example, while non-continuous, are fixed interval, occurring weekly, monthly, or after some other predictable period of time. The provision of pay on a predictable interval schedule may reinforce only the picking up of the paycheck at the end of the period. Thus, more performance based monetary rewards such as bonuses, commissions, or special awards may be more effective in linking monetary payments to level of productivity. Praise may become more effective when not linked only to annual or semi-annual performance appraisals.

Perhaps the best known success of positive reinforcement is at Emery Air Freight. To improve larger container utilization, which stood initially at 45%, management instituted a checklist program, whereby a worker checked a sheet each time he used the larger container for shipping. At the end of his shift the worker totaled his usage to determine if he had achieved the 90% goal announced by the company. Employees who showed any increase in usage were praised by supervisors and regional managers. The result was that, in a number of the company's offices, usage rose from 45% to 95% in a single day. Savings were estimated at $44,000 a month or $520,000 a year.[25]

One interesting application of position reinforcement is the use of a lottery by a hardware store's management to reduce tardiness and absenteeism. Employees with perfect attendance records were given chances in a lottery for cash prizes. Employee tardiness and absenteeism dropped dramatically as a result.[16, p. 396] The bed frame manufacturer, previously mentioned, awarded points to employees who successfully mastered job skills. Points could later be traded for various prizes.[19]

At the managerial level, two researchers developed a training program to teach supervisors how to use positive reinforcement. Supervisors were taught how to define employee problems in terms of observable events, how to measure the frequencies of behavior, how to determine the probable stimuli that evoked the behavior, and techniques of positive reinforcement to change employee behavior in the desired direction. As a result of the training, participating supervisors increased their effectiveness ratings by a minimum of five per cent with significant cost savings to the company.[10]

In a non-industry experiment, a researcher gave a group of 106 children a series of addition problems to perform each day for five days. At the end of each day one group was praised for its performance. A second group, matched with the first in age, sex, and initial performance, was publicly reproved for its performance. A third matched group was ignored, but allowed to observe the praise and reproach given the other groups. A control group was also tested in a different room and given no feedback whatever. The results after five days show the praised group with the most improved performance, followed by the reproved group, the ignored group, and finally the control group. While some evidence is provided here for the value of negative reinforcement, positive feedback shows a stronger relationship to productivity improvement.[21, p. 217]

In another experiment, four researchers offered small cash payments to workers in a Mexican manufacturing plant for each day they arrived at work on time. A control group that was not allowed to participate in the program showed an increase in tardiness over the test period.[5]

Although operant conditioning through positive reinforcement has shown promise for modifying behavior in organizations, problems in implementation, nevertheless, exist. Most of the experiments reported have occurred at the operative level, where desired behaviors are relatively easy to identify and reinforce. At managerial and professional levels, role complexity greatly complicates the task of identifying desired behaviors and developing appropriate behavior modification techniques. As mentioned previously, management by objectives offers promise at these levels.

A second problem with behavior modification involves conflicting reinforcements. While management may be capable of granting or withholding certain desired rewards, there are, typically, other desired reinforcements which are largely, or totally, outside of management's control. As Figure 1 points out, home, community and professional associations provide rewards and punishments for certain behavior. Social rewards from co-workers may be granted or withheld on the basis of behaviors contrary to formal organization goals. Thus, the problem of providing proper reinforcements to induce desired behaviors widens in scope. To design an effective program of positive reinforcement, the possibility of reinforcers outside the direct control of management must be acknowledged. In some instances, these reinforcers may conflict with organizational goals and may thus nullify, or reduce, the effectiveness of organizational rewards. Where possible, these reinforcements should be made compatible with organizational rewards. One interpretation of the success of Scanlon plans is the combination of monetary rewards and work group approval provided to those whose suggestions for improving productivity are accepted.[16, p. 394]

A final, but perhaps short-term, problem is unfamiliarity of practicing managers in the theory and practice of operant conditioning. Not only are the majority unfamiliar with techniques of reinforcement, they are also unfamiliar with methods of observation of responses. For the most part, management thinking continues to analyze behavior on the basis of internal states, such as those in the Maslow need hierarchy. When a person exhibits inappropriate responses, the tendency may be to rely on theories that try to explain behavior in terms of internal motivations. Dealing with the behavior itself, rather than theorizing about motivations that caused it, would appear to be both more practical and more effective in many instances. Widespread acceptance and understanding of operant conditioning is, however, a necessary precondition to its use in most organizations.

Several suggestions can be made for the implementation of the operant approach. A necessary beginning is the identification of desired performance at all organization levels. This is especially critical for positions above the operative level. Just what is "good performance?" And just as important, when it has been defined, how will we measure it? Management by objectives may often be useful in answering these questions.

Further, our managers must be trained to better understand the relationship between a worker's behavior and the environmental influences which influence it. They should be more attuned to recognizing the relationship between changes in responses and fluctuations in the work, peer group, or supervisory contingencies.

Programmed learning techniques should be applied to training programs wherever possible. Not only are they highly reinforcing to correct responses, they have proven to be one of the fastest methods of instruction, while freeing supervisors to attend to other operations or problems.

Design of compensation plans which operate on variable schedules should be encouraged. Stable periodic payment/bonus plans are not conducive to increased performance. As mentioned earlier, there are many lottery and bonus programs available to management. Their application is limited only by the lack of creativity or imagination of the manager. And these suggestions are meant to neither eliminate nor minimize the value of such practices as employee participation or varied and more complex job content. But as with other rewards, they should be used selectively if there is evidence that employees will respond positively to them.

Finally, we need to convince ourselves of the value and utility of the operant approach to motivation. It has proven its usefulness, but it can only succeed if we study it, understand it, and have the courage to apply it. No change of any kind can be instituted in business, today, which lacks the conviction and support of its management. And this can only be achieved through an understanding and acceptance of the tangible benefits provided by operant conditioning.

For many persons, behavior modification, or operant conditioning, has evoked feelings of mistrust, fear of the loss of individuality, and other negative reactions. Since time began, however, modification of people's behavior has been our way of life. During the socialization process, in our learning institutions, in business organizations, everywhere, we are changing or trying to change the behavior of others. Much of this effort is misguided and, in the end, produces little tangible benefit.

Operant conditioning takes these efforts and improves upon them. Instead of a rule-of-thumb approach, the operant approach stresses goals, achievement, and direction. It stresses the utility of effort; the avoidance of nonconstructive or inappropriate behavior. It is philosophically compatible with contingency theories of management, offering varied rewards that best suit the situation.

The concept of behavior modification is still in an embryonic stage of development. There are, however, indications that it will progress. The observations and suggestions made here will hopefully provide some insight for those who wish to pursue the subject further. With proper utilization, behavior modification may be an important means of implementing a contingency approach to organizational behavior.

References

1. Carrol, Stephen J. Jr. and Josi, Henri L. Jr. *Management by Objectives.* New York: Macmillan, 1973.
2. Catania, Charles. *Contemporary Research in Operant Behavior.* Glenview, Ill.: Scott, Foresman, and Company, 1968.
3. Donnelly, James H. Jr., Gibson, James L., and Ivancevich, John M. *Fundamentals of Management.* Austin, Texas: Business Publications, Inc., 1971.
4. Ford, Robert. *Motivations Through the Work Itself.* New York: American Management Association, 1969.
5. Hermann, J. A., de Montes, Ana I., Dominguez, B., Montes, F., and Hopkins, B. L. "Effects of Bonuses for Punctuality on the Tardiness of Industrial Workers." *Journal of Applied Behavior Analysis* (6, 1973): 563–572.
6. Herzberg, Frederick. *Work and the Nature of Man.* Cleveland: World Publishing Company, 1966.
7. Hicks, Herbert G. and Gullett, C. Ray. *Organizations: Theory and Behavior.* New York: McGraw-Hill Book Company, 1975.
8. Lawrence, Paul R. and Lorsch, Jay W. *Organization and Environment: Managing Differentiation and Integration.* Boston: Division of Research, Harvard Business School, 1967.
9. Likert, Rensis. *The Human Organization.* New York: McGraw-Hill Book Company.
10. Luthans, Fred and Lyman, David. "Training Supervisors to Use Organization Behavior Modification." *Personnel* (Sept.-Oct. 1973): 38–44.
11. Maslow, Abraham. *Eupaychian Management: A Journal.* Homewood, Ill.: Irwin/Dorsey, 1965.

12. Mayo, Elton. *The Human Problems of Industrial Civilization.* New York: Macmillan, 1933.
13. McGregor, Douglas. *The Professional Manager.* New York: McGraw-Hill Book Company, 1967.
14. Miner, John B. and Dachler, H. P. "Personnel Attitudes and Motivation," in P. H. Mussen and M. R. Rosensweig (Eds.) *Annual Review of Psychology* (Vol. 24, 1973).
15. Morse, John J. "A Contingency Look at Job Design." *California Management Review* (Fall 1973): 67–73.
16. Nord, Walter R. "Beyond the Teaching Machine: The Neglected Area of Operant Conditioning in the Theory and Practice of Management." *Organization Behavior and Human Performance* (4, 1969): 375–401.
17. *Positive Reinforcement.* Emery Air Freight System Performance Department, 1970.
18. Roethlisberger, Fritz J. and Dickson, William J. *Management and the Worker.* Cambridge, Mass.: Harvard University Press, 1939.
19. Schneider, C. E. "Behavior Modification: Training the Hard Core Unemployed." *Personnel* (May-June, 1973): 65–69.
20. Skinner, B. F. *Beyond Freedom and Dignity.* New York: Bantam Books, 1971.
21. Skinner, B. F. *Contingencies of Reinforcement, A Theoretical Analysis.* New York: Appleton-Century-Crofts, 1969.
22. Thompson, James D. *Organizations in Action.* New York: McGraw-Hill Book Company, 1967.
23. Vroom, Victor H. *Motivation in Management.* New York: American Foundation for Management Research, 1965.
24. Vroom, Victor H. *Work and Motivation.* New York: John Wiley and Sons, Inc., 1964.
25. "Where Skinner's Theories Work." *Business Week* (Dec. 2, 1972): 64–65.
26. Woodward, Joan. *Industrial Organization: Theory and Practice.* London: Oxford University Press, 1965.

Questions on Reading

1. In the authors' view, what is a basic difficulty associated with approaching motivation from the standpoint of human "needs"?
2. How does the contingency approach to motivation differ from the traditional need-oriented approaches to motivation?
3. As contrasted to the need-oriented approaches to motivation, what is the orientation of operant conditioning?
4. What is a "positive reinforcer"? How can positive reinforcers be identified in an organizational setting?
5. How do the schedules of reinforcement relate to learning and behavior?

13 LEADERSHIP

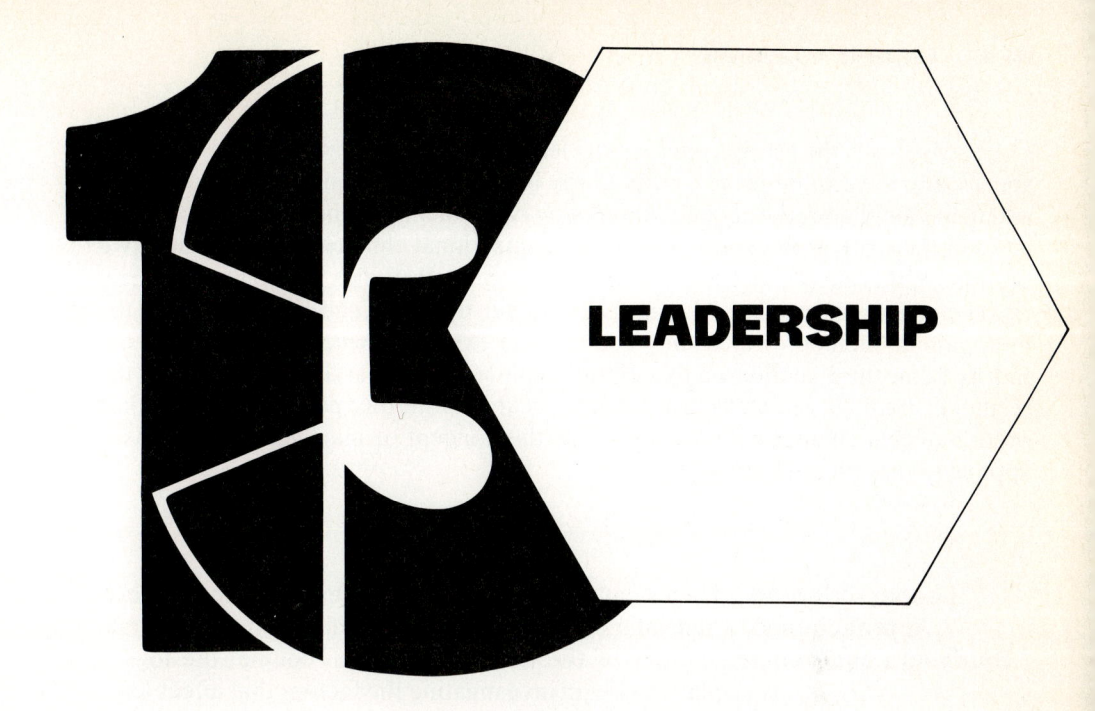

- Leader-Oriented Approaches to Studying Leadership
- The Organizational Climate
- Leadership Styles
- The Contingency View of Leadership
- Managerial Power and Disciplining
- Review
- Discussion Questions
- References
- Case Study: A Change of Supervisors
- Case Study: A Matter of Overtime
- Applications Reading: "Leadership Styles: Which Are Best When?" Alan Weiss
- Questions on Reading

Most of the early studies of leadership effectiveness were directed specifically toward the leader, particularly in regard to personality characteristics and behavior. Later, the scope of interest was broadened to include the characteristics of the work group and the overall organizational climate. Thus, the first two sections of this chapter are devoted to leader-oriented studies and to the organizational climate respectively. Managers also differ from one another in terms of the motivational methods which they use and the extent to which they delegate authority. The third section of this chapter, on leadership styles, summarizes the results of both classic and more recent research from this perspective. The last section of this chapter is concerned with the concept of managerial power as it applies to disciplining employees.

Leader-Oriented Approaches to Studying Leadership

Historically, attempts to explain the basis for successful leadership have focused specifically on the characteristics of the leader. This is, of course, the logical place to begin investigating the factors that affect leadership success. Over the years, the "great-leader" approach, the trait approach, and the behavioral approach have been developed as ways of studying the leader. Of these, the great-leader approach is least sophisticated, since it suggests that successful managers are innately competent leaders who are "born rather than made," and that the basis for their success cannot be uncovered by studying successful leaders.

1 The assumptions that a leader and/or leadership behavior cannot be analyzed and that "a leader is a leader" are consistent with the _____ approach to studying leadership.

great-leader

2 Would organizations following a great-leader approach tend to emphasize executive selection, executive development, or both in their personnel programs? _____

Executive selection (since they assume that leaders are "born and not made")

3 In contrast to the great-leader approach, the *trait approach* assumes that successful leadership is correlated with the personality characteristics of the appointed leader, and that these can be systematically studied. Thus the trait approach offers a basis for dis-

Leader-Oriented Approaches to Studying Leadership • 397

leadership (or managerial, etc.)

covering the factors underlying _____ success.

4 Analyzing such personal characteristics as integrity, promptness, and dependability and attempting to relate these characteristics to executive success involve the _____ approach to studying leadership.

trait

5 The number of traits studied may vary from as few as a half dozen to twenty or more. Would this diversity in the number of traits investigated make it easier or more difficult to compare different studies that have been done from the trait point of view? [Easier / More difficult]

More difficult

6 The absence of a commonly agreed-upon set of executive traits makes comparison between and among studies difficult. Another difficulty is the definition of traits. For example, the trait "honesty" can relate to truth telling or to the property rights of others and hence has [only one / more than one] possible meaning.

more than one

7 A number of years ago *Fortune* magazine asked seventy-five high-ranking executives for definitions and opinions of various executive qualities. The definitions given for "dependability" included 147 different descriptive statements. Exhibit 13.1 on the following page presents the categories of meanings represented by these statements. As indicated, there were _____ [number] different definitions given for the trait of dependability.

twenty-five

8 In addition to the absence of a uniform set of traits to be studied and ambiguity in the _____ of traits, difficulties in *measuring* the traits have also been encountered.

definition (or meaning)

9 Traits are measured by quantifying the opinions of people regarding the traits of a leader. There is a long history of rating-scale development that parallels the development of the _____ approach to studying leadership.

trait

Exhibit 13.1 *Categories of meanings given by executives for the trait "dependability."*

1. Is thorough, steady, reliable, consistent
2. Does complete successful job, gets results
3. Follows orders, seeks approval, carries out assignments
4. Uses good judgment in decision making
5. Is honest, trustworthy, conscientious; keeps promises
6. Needs little or no checking up
7. Is punctual; meets schedules
8. Overcomes obstacles and pressures
9. Accepts full responsibility, does job
10. Is frank, unevasive, courageous
11. Behaves predictably
12. Inspires confidence
13. Is cooperative
14. Is devoted to duty and company
15. Considers others
16. Does more than he has to
17. Does his best
18. Is adaptable to leadership
19. Has good personal habits
20. Asks help if needed
21. Learns from mistakes
22. Has satisfactory substitute
23. Works like his superior
24. Uses initiative
25. Is self-disciplined

Adapted from Perrin Stryker, "On the Meaning of Executive Qualities," *Fortune*, vol. 57, no. 6, June 1958, p. 189. Reproduced with permission.

10 People's opinions are not entirely objective but contain an element of *bias*. This tends to make different descriptions of the same individual [consistent / inconsistent].

inconsistent

11 Accordingly, contemporary developments in rating-scale techniques have been focused on distilling the valid part of a rater's description while attempting to eliminate the part representing the individual's _____.

bias

12 Although the uncovered importance of specific personality traits has varied from study to study, three general trait areas—intelligence, communication skill, and the ability to assess group goals—have been found to be related to _____ success in a variety of situations.

leadership

13 Thus, in comparison with other members of the group they lead, leaders tend to be more intelligent, have better _____ skill, and have a higher ability to assess group goals.

communication

14 It is important that the general leadership characteristics occur in combination in order to be associated with leadership success. All three of the trait areas have to be involved: _____, _____ skill, and ability to assess group goals.

intelligence
communication

15 Thus a leader's low communication skill, for example, [can / cannot] be offset by possession of higher intelligence.

cannot

16 To have a high likelihood of leadership success, the person must be high in the three trait areas compared with [people in general / other group members].

other group members

17 To summarize these findings, the three general trait areas that have been found to be related to leadership success in a variety of situations are _____, _____ skill, and ability to assess _____.

intelligence;
communication;
group goals

18 Thus far we have considered two leader-oriented approaches to studying the basis for leadership success: the _____ approach and the _____ approach.

great-leader
trait

19 A third leader-oriented approach, the *behavioral approach*, shifts the emphasis from an analysis of the leader's characteristics to an analysis of _____ _____.

what the leader does
(leader's methods,
behavior, etc.)

behavioral

20 Observing the relative amount of executive time spent on such activities as planning, motivating, and communicating is consistent with the _____ approach to leadership analysis.

No

21 Observing executive activities yields information about what they do. Does it necessarily yield information about what they *should* be doing? [Yes / No]

unsuccessful (etc.)

22 In order to pinpoint the executive activities that differentiate the successful leader, the activities of the two following kinds of leaders, or executives, need to be compared: those executives considered to be successful and those executives considered to be _____.

leader (manager, etc.)

23 Although identifying the most and least successful executives appears to be a relatively straightforward task, in practice the existence of other factors that affect organizational success makes it difficult to assess the relative influence of what the _____ does on organizational success.

activities (or behavior, etc.)

24 Most writers have based their descriptions of successful leader behavior on their general observations and experiences in a variety of managerial situations. It is only recently that carefully planned and controlled observations of executive _____ have been carried out.

success

25 In order to relate differences in executive behavior to differences in executive success, we need to have reliable measurement of their behavior on the one hand and reliable measurement of their _____ on the other hand.

The Organizational Climate

Although most studies aimed at discovering the basis for leadership success have focused on the leader himself, attention has also been directed at the organizational climate in which the leadership position exists. Research evidence indicates, for example, that the one person who most influences a leader's pattern of behavior is his direct organizational superior.

26 The way that a manager leads is most importantly influenced by how his _____ leads.
superior

27 In a study of first-level supervisors at International Harvester,[1] for example, it was found that the supervisor's leadership style was influenced more by his own organizational superior than by a comprehensive training program in _____ methods.
leadership (managerial, etc.)

28 The general purpose of the leadership training course at International Harvester was to help develop a higher level of a human relations orientation at the foreman level in the company. The results of a questionnaire administered at the beginning and end of the course indicated a significant increase in human relations attitudes, thus providing evidence of program [success / failure].
success

29 However, because the researchers wanted to determine the effects of the program back in the plant, they conducted follow-up studies with those foremen who had completed the course earlier. Figure 13.1 on the following page summarizes the results of the studies in the plant in terms of both human relations _____ and _____.
attitudes; behavior

30 As indicated in Figure 13.1, in comparison with the untrained foreman those who had completed the human relations course were [higher / lower] in both human relations attitudes and behavior.
lower

31 Thus, based on the results in the plant, the training program appeared to be generally [successful / unsuccessful].
unsuccessful

32 On the basis of further analysis of the results the researchers concluded that "... if the old way of doing things in the plant situation is still the shortest path to approval by the boss, then this is what the foreman re-

---

[1] Edwin A. Fleishman, "Leadership Climate, Human Relations Training, and Supervisory Behavior," *Personnel Psychology*, vol. 6, no. 2, 1953, pp. 205–222.

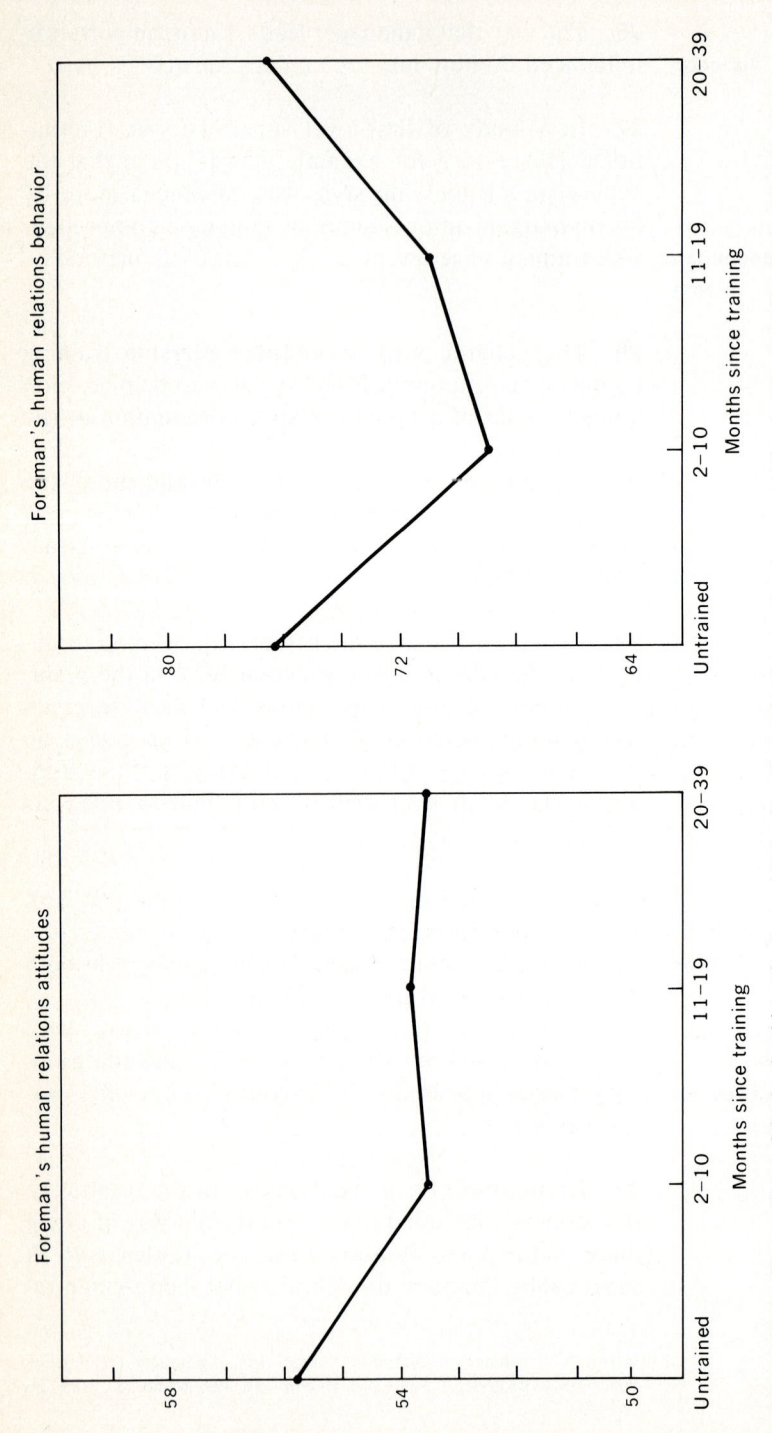

Figure 13.1 Comparison of the leadership attitudes and behavior of untrained and trained groups of foremen back in the plant. (Modified from Edwin A. Fleishman, "Leadership Climate, Human Relations Training, and Supervisory Behavior," *Personnel Psychology*, vol. 6, no. 2, 1953, p. 214. Used with permission.)

ally learns." In other words, the primary influence on the foreman's attitudes and behavior was that exerted by [the training course / **his immediate superior**].

33 Thus, this would suggest that in order to change a "leadership climate" in an organization, we need to *begin* such development and modification at the [supervisory / **top management (and then work with each level below)**] level.

34 We need to begin at the top of an organization in attempting to change leadership climate because the influence on leadership methods extends from [**above** / below].

35 In addition to the leader's relationship with his own supervisor, his relationship with other managers and staff specialists also affects his **leadership (etc.)** _____ behavior.

36 For example, if a manager has had previous difficulty with a particular staff department, he is likely to supervise the work of those of his subordinates who have extensive contact with that department in a manner [similar to / **different from**] that of other subordinates.

Leadership Styles

Overall leadership style can be considered from several points of view, two of which are covered in this section. From the standpoint of the motivational method used, leadership can be positive or negative. From the standpoint of the delegation of authority, leadership can be centralized or decentralized. In a classic study of leadership methods, the authoritarian method was extremely centralized, the free-rein method was extremely decentralized, and the democratic method was between the two in terms of the amount of authority delegated to members of the group. Following a description of this classic study, we conclude this section of the chapter by presenting a more recent approach to describing leadership style that includes consideration of the motivational method used as well as the extent of shared authority.

37 From the standpoint of the motivational methods used, positive leaders emphasize the use of positive motivational methods, and negative leaders tend to use _____ motivational methods.

negative

38 As described in Chapter 12, on motivating people at work, positive motivation involves the possibility of [increased / decreased] motive satisfaction, whereas negative motivation involves the possibility of [increased / decreased] motive satisfaction.

increased

decreased

39 The manager who motivates people by offering them greater satisfaction of their own motives when they work toward the organization's goals is utilizing _____ leadership.

positive

40 The manager who motivates people by explicitly or implicitly threatening punishment of some kind for noncooperation is using _____ leadership.

negative

41 In which leadership climate would the employee tend to "look for a way out" of the situation? _____

Negative

42 Of course, seldom is an actual leadership style completely _____ or completely _____. However, the relative balance between the two determines the motivational climate operating in an organizational unit.

positive

negative

43 Another dimension of leadership style or pattern is the extent to which the leader centralizes or decentralizes decision-making authority. The leader who shares decision-making authority with subordinates tends toward [centralized / decentralized] leadership.

decentralized

44 In a classic study of leadership style,[2] *authoritarian, democratic,* and *free-rein* methods were compared in their effects on group behavior. Which style

---

[2] Kurt Lewin, Ronald Lippitt, and R. K. White, "Patterns of Agressive Behavior in Experimentally Created Climates," *Journal of Social Psychology*, vol. 10, no. 2, 1939, pp. 271–299.

authoritarian	represents the extreme of centralized decision-making authority? _____
Yes (to the extent that people in general tend to respond similarly to leadership methods)	**45** The studies concerned different leadership styles of adult leaders in boys' clubs. Would the effect of the leadership styles on the boys' behavior have any relevance to leadership in adult organizations? [Yes / No]
Free-rein	**46** Which leadership method would involve complete freedom for group or individual decision making, with little or no leader participation? [Authoritarian / Democratic / Free-rein]
Democratic	**47** In which leadership method would all policies be a matter of group discussion and decision, but with the active assistance of the leader? [Authoritarian / Democratic / Free-rein]
authoritarian	**48** The leadership method in which the leader determines all policy himself and assigns specific work tasks to each group member is the [authoritarian / democratic / free-rein].
authoritarian free-rein democratic	**49** Of the three leadership methods studied, maximum centralization of authority was represented by the _____ method, maximum decentralization of authority was represented by the _____ method, and considerable, but not complete, decentralization of authority was represented by the _____ method.
democratic; authoritarian	**50** Although all the results of these studies cannot be completely presented here, several of the differences in the boys' behavior are worth noting. In terms of both quality and quantity of work, the free-rein leadership method was inferior to both the _____ and _____ method.
	51 On the other hand, the highest level of productiv-

ity per se was not found under the democratic leadership method but rather under the _____ method.

authoritarian (Thus research findings may not always conform to our personal biases.

52 Because there is considerable freedom of group expression, but with the coordinating presence of leader authority, the greatest amount of originality in work was found under the _____ method.

democratic (not free-rein, as many might expect)

53 Perhaps because of the high degree of control over individual behavior, the greatest amount of discontent was expressed under the _____ form of leadership.

authoritarian (which, finally, would be expected on the basis of "common sense")

54 Submissive behavior, with some loss of individuality, was most marked in the strongly centralized _____ situation.

authoritarian

55 The leadership style that resulted in the greatest number of group-oriented remarks and the greatest degree of friendliness was the _____.

democratic

56 Summing up, a greater degree of aggression, submission, and productivity characterized the _____ group; a greater degree of friendliness and originality in work characterized the _____ group; and a greater degree of disorganization, nonproductivity, and play-oriented behavior characterized the _____ group.

authoritarian

democratic

free-rein

57 The conclusion that when a leader ceases to lead, disorganization in group behavior results is suggested by the findings associated with the _____ method.

free-rein

58 The conclusion that strong centralized leadership can promote high productivity is suggested by the findings that are associated with the authoritarian _____ method. It should be added, however, that all the boys who dropped out of club activities during these experiments did so while they were in the authoritarian climate.

59 The conclusion that participative leadership methods are especially valuable when innovation or creativity is one of the "products" desired of the work group is suggested by the findings associated with the
democratic _____ leadership style.

60 As an example of more recent interest in leadership style, Exhibit 13.2 on pages 408–409 is adapted from a technique developed by Rensis Likert, director of the Institute of Social Research at the University of Michigan, to help businessmen analyze the management style used by their companies. Of the styles described in this exhibit, the one in which managers have the lowest level of confidence in subordinates is
exploitive authoritative the _____ style.

61 In comparing the management styles in Exhibit 13.2 with the three styles in the classic study by Lewin, Lippitt, and White, it is useful to recognize that no "free-rein" style is included in Exhibit 13.2. Rather, two of the leadership styles in the exhibit are authoritarian in orientation, with the difference being largely in the motivational climate which exists in the organization. Thus, the two styles in Exhibit 13.2 which are authoritarian in orientation are the
exploitive _____ authoritative and the
benevolent _____ authoritative styles.

62 Similarly, two of the management styles included in Exhibit 13.2 tend toward the classic "democratic" styles, with the difference being the extent of delegation and participation by group members. These are
consultative; participative the _____ and _____ styles.

63 The management style in Exhibit 13.2 in which upward communication tends to be "censored for the
benevolent authoritative boss" is the _____ style.

	Exploitive Authoritative	Benevolent Authoritative	Consultative	Participative
Leadership				
How much confidence is shown in subordinates?	None	Condescending	Substantial	Complete
How free do they feel to talk to superiors about job?	Not at all	Not very	Rather free	Fully free
Are subordinates' ideas sought and used, if worthy?	Seldom	Sometimes	Usually	Always
Motivation				
Is predominant use made of (1) fear, (2) threats, (3) punishment, (4) rewards, (5) involvement?	1, 2, 3, occassionally 4	4, some 3	4, some 3 and 5	5, 4, based on group-set goals
Where is responsibility felt for achieving organization's goals?	Mostly at top	Top and middle	Fairly general	At all levels
Communication				
How much communication is aimed at achieving organization's objectives?	Very little	Little	Quite a bit	A great deal
What is the direction of information flow?	Downward	Mostly downward	Down and up	Down, up, and sideways
How is downward communication accepted?	With suspicion	Possibly with suspicion	With caution	With an open mind
How accurate is upward communication?	Often wrong	Censored for the boss	Limited accuracy	Accurate
How well do superiors know problems faced by subordinates?	Know little	Some knowledge	Quite well	Very well

Exhibit 13.2 A rating form for analyzing management style.

Decisions	At what level are decisions formally made?	Mostly at top	Policy at top, some delegation	Broad policy at top, more delegation	Throughout but well integrated
	What is the origin of technical and professional knowledge used in decision making?	Top management	Upper and middle	To a certain extent, throughout	To a great extent, throughout
	Are subordinates involved in decisions related to their work?	Not at all	Occasionally consulted	Generally consulted	Fully involved
	What does decision-making process contribute to motivation?	Nothing, often weakens it	Relatively little	Some contribution	Substantial contribution
Goals	How are organizational goals established?	Orders issued	Orders, some comment invited	After discussion, by orders	By group action (except in crisis)
	How much covert resistance to goals is present?	Strong resistance	Moderate resistance	Some resistance at times	Little or none
Control	How concentrated are review and control functions?	Highly at top	Relatively highly at top	Moderate delegation to lower levels	Quite widely shared
	Is there an informal organization resisting the formal one?	Yes	Usually	Sometimes	No—same goals as formal
	What are cost, productivity, and other control data used for?	Policing, punishment	Reward and punishment	Reward, some self-guidance	Self-guidance, problem solving

(Adapted from *The Human Organization: Its Management and Value* by Rensis Likert. Copyright 1967 by McGraw-Hill Book Company. Reproduced by permission of McGraw-Hill Book Company. No further reproduction authorized.)

64 The management style in which goals are established by orders from above, but after discussion with subordinates, is the _____ style.

consultative

65 Finally, the management style in which control data are used for self-guidance rather than for external control is the _____ style.

participative

66 In using the chart in Exhibit 13.2, each answer is regarded as a rating on a continuous scale from the left to the right of the chart. Likert has found that most executives with whom he has consulted rate their companies in the second and third categories, that is, under the _____ and the _____ styles.

benevolent authoritative
consultative

67 Executives who have used this chart have also indicated their belief that companies generally do best when they have profiles well to the right on this chart, that is, in the direction of the _____ style, and that companies do worst with profiles positioned to the left, that is, in the direction of the _____ style.

participative

exploitive authoritative

The Contingency View of Leadership

The preceding coverage in this chapter regarding the leader, the group, and the organization suggest that successful leadership is dependent on something other than a particular pattern of leadership traits or behavior. Successful leadership is the result of an interaction between the leader and his subordinates in a particular organization. Thus, the leadership style that is successful will differ according to the organizational situation. Years of research by Fred E. Fiedler at the University of Illinois and his colleagues have resulted in a so-called "contingency view of leadership." As described in two major books[3] and many research articles, the success of a leadership style is contingent upon the three organizational variables of leader-member relations, task structure, and leader-position power.

---

[3]Fred E. Fiedler, *A Theory of Leadership Effectiveness,* New York: McGraw-Hill, 1967; and Fred E. Fiedler and Martin M. Chemers, *Leadership and Effective Management,* Glenview, Ill.: Scott, Foresman, 1974.

68 Describing first the three organizational variables upon which leadership is contingent, if there is acceptance of the leader by the group and ready compliance with orders, then "leader-member relations" can be described as being [good / poor].

good

69 The variable of "task structure" indicates the extent to which a specific method of job performance is required. Thus, a research and development group would represent a relatively [structured / unstructured] situation.

unstructured

70 "Leader-position power" indicates the extent of power assigned to the position occupied by the leader, particularly in regard to promotions, pay raises, and the like. Thus, relative to other organizational situations the power of a leader in a military unit is [high / low].

high

71 What Fiedler set out to do was to find the relationship between the three organizational variables just described on the one hand, and appropriate, or successful, leadership behavior on the other hand. The particular facet of leadership behavior studied by Fiedler is the extent to which leadership success depends on being *employee-oriented* as contrasted to being *task-oriented*. Thus, Fiedler hypothesized that the extent to which a leader should be employee-oriented in his managerial behavior is contingent on the variables of leader-member relations, task structure, and _____.

leader-position power

72 In his initial attempts at reviewing the results of many studies, systematic contingency relationships were not obvious. Then, however, Fiedler arranged the organizational variables on a continuum from "worst" to "best," from the standpoint of the leadership challenge involved. Refer to the horizontal axis of the schematic diagram in Figure 13.2. The extreme left end of the scale represents the "worst" leadership situation: the one in which there are poor leader-member relations, an unstructured situation, and weak leader-position power. The extreme right end of the scale represents the "best" (easiest to manage) situation: the

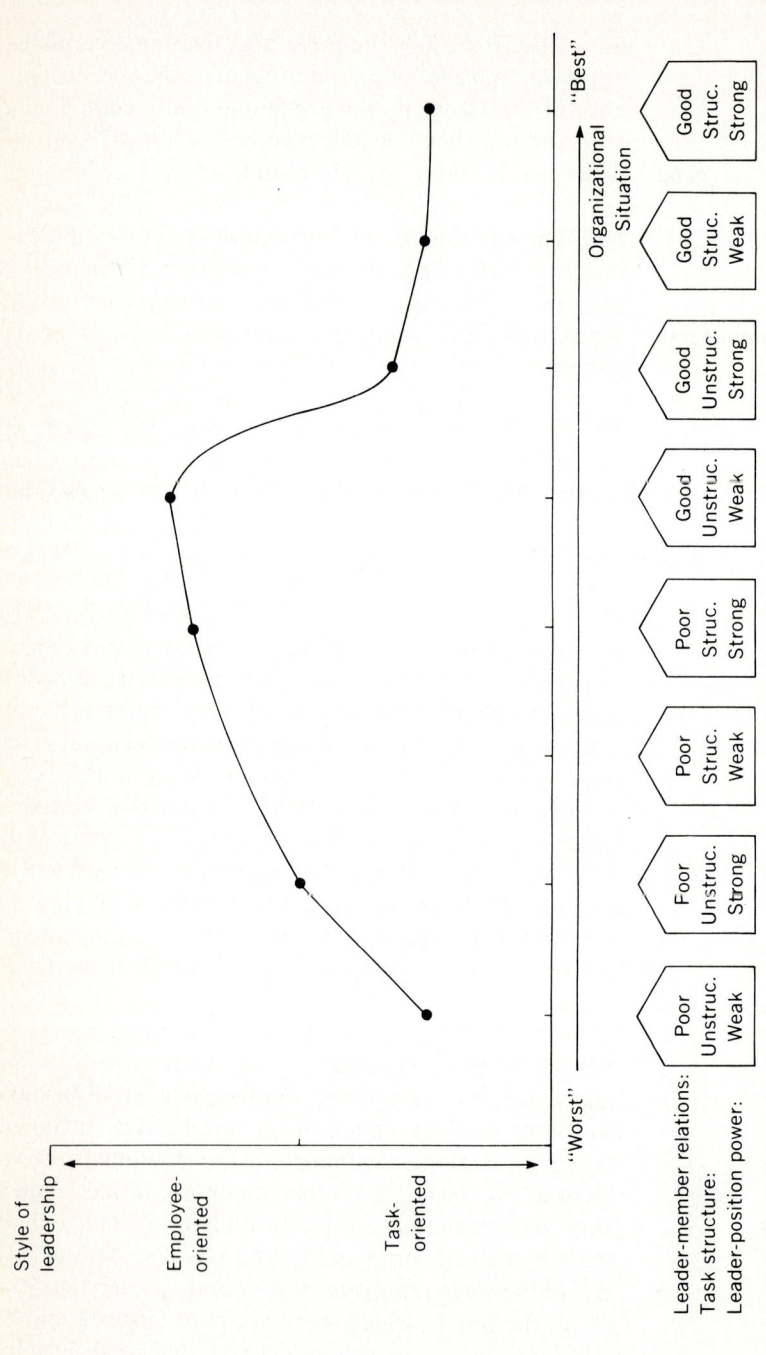

Figure 13.2 Schematic diagram illustrating the contingent relationship between the organizational situation and the required leadership style. (Adapted from Fred E. Fiedler, *A Theory of Leadership Effectiveness*, p. 146. Copyright 1967 by McGraw-Hill, Inc. Used with permission of the McGraw-Hill Book Company.)

one in which there are [good / poor] leader-member relations, a situation which is [structured / unstructured], and [strong / weak] leader-position power.

good
structured
strong

73 The vertical axis of the schematic diagram indicates the extent to which leader should be employee-oriented in order to be successful. The curve entered on the graph represents the smoothed results of many studies. What is particularly interesting in that the relationship between the organizational situation and the appropriate leadership style is represented by a [direct linear relationship / a curvilinear relationship].

a curvilinear relationship

74 Referring to Figure 13.2, it is ironic that the organizational situation which is "best" and that which is "worst" both require a leader who is primarily [employee- / task-] oriented.

task-

75 The necessity of a task-oriented leader in the "worst" situation is recognizable. But as it turns out, task-oriented leadership is also appropriate in the "best" situation, such as a cohesive military task group with a specifically defined mission. Referring to Figure 13.2, we can observe that as an organizational situation improves somewhat from the "worst" combination of organizational variable, then an increased [task- / employee-] oriented leadership is required. However, when the situation is organizationally quite good, then an increased [task- / employee-] oriented leadership is required.

employee-

task-

76 Through his careful definition of organizational variables, Fiedler was able to demonstrate that there is a systematic, though not simple, relationship between the organizational variables and leadership style. Thus one can say that the required leadership style is *contingent* upon the _____.

organizational situation (or organizational variables)

77 Thus, the successful leader is not a blind follower of a particular leadership method, or style. Rather, such a leader chooses the style which is appropriate based on the particular organizational _____.

situation

Managerial Power and Disciplining

Managerial power includes the ability that a manager has to provide rewards and to inflict punishment. Whereas the coverage in Chapter 7, in the section on power and politics, was concerned with the degree of influence that a person has to "get things done" in an organization, in this section we consider the concept of power as it is applied in the context of disciplining subordinate personnel in an organizational unit.

78 As indicated in the introduction above, the ability to provide rewards or to inflict punishment is included in the concept of managerial _____.

power

79 Although the use of power can have a positive (reward) or negative (punishment) connotation, in this section we give attention to several principles that should be followed when disciplinary action on the part of a manager becomes necessary. Thus, the material in this section is concerned with how the manager uses his power to [reward / punish].

punish

80 One of the principles associated with the use of disciplinary power is that such actions by the manager should be consistent. This implies that if an area is designated as a "no smoking" area any employee observed to be smoking there should be disciplined [regardless of previous infractions / only if he has violated rules before].

regardless of previous infractions (but the specific disciplinary actions may vary)

81 Thus, the principle of disciplining which indicates that organizational rules should apply to all employees, regardless of their status, is the principle of _____.

consistency

82 Another principle associated with disciplinary action is that such action should be taken only when there has been *forewarning*. In this respect, a relatively new employee who has violated operating rules unknowingly [should / should not] be disciplined.

should not

83 The principle which makes it necessary that the manager inform each employee of all operating rules and practices so that the employee is in a position to

Managerial Power and Disciplining • 415

forewarning

know which actions are appropriate and which are inappropriate is the principle of _____.

84 In addition to consistency and forewarning, the concept of *fairness* indicates that the penalty included in a disciplinary action should be equitable with respect to the nature of the offense. From this standpoint, discharging an employee with several years of good service because he failed to call in that he was sick would probably be considered [fair / unfair].

unfair

85 Because all employees in the organizational unit will judge whether a penalty was equitable, and not just the individual employee being disciplined, it is particularly important that the principle of _____ be adhered to in such actions.

fairness

86 Thus far we have considered three principles that should be followed in conjunction with using managerial power for disciplining inappropriate behavior or performance: _____, _____, and _____.

consistency
forewarning; fairness

87 A fourth principle that should be followed in applying disciplinary action is *promptness*. If an infraction of organizational rules has occurred, the effectiveness of the disciplinary action in terms of influencing employee behavior is enhanced if the action is taken within several [days / weeks].

days

88 However, the principle of promptness does not necessarily indicate that the disciplinary action should be "immediate." Consider the emotional states of the manager and of the employee in a disciplinary situation. The principles of consistency and fairness are more likely to be followed if disciplining action occurs [immediately / after a "cooling off" period].

after a "cooling off" period

89 Finally, when reprimanding an employee the manager should strive to arrange for some degree of *privacy*. In general, congratulations and rewards should be given publicly and reprimands should be discussed in private. Of course, the main reason for this is the psychological effect of being reprimanded in front of one's fellow employees. That is, an employee is more likely to acknowledge his mistakes and to change his behavior in the future if the reprimand and the associated disciplinary action are discussed in [private / public].

private

90 In addition to the principles of consistency, forewarning, and fairness, two other principles which should be used when disciplinary action is necessary are the principles of _____ and _____.

promptness
privacy

91 The principles which we have considered are summarized in Table 13.1. The attention here devoted to disciplining is not to suggest that a manager should rely on his power to discipline as a primary basis for improving organizational effectiveness. But any manager, and particularly one who is newly appointed, is likely to be "tested" by subordinate personnel in his enforcement of organizational policies and may therefore find it necessary to use his power to _____ with appropriate awareness of the principles involved.

discipline (or punish)

Table 13.1	Principles Associated with Taking Disciplinary Action
	Consistency
	Forewarning
	Fairness
	Promptness
	Privacy

92 In reference to the coverage in the section of this chapter on the organizational climate, primary reliance on disciplinary power in an organizational unit would result in a motivational climate that is predominantly [positive / negative].

negative

93 The use of discipline can help to prevent or discourage repetition of undesirable patterns of behavior if applied in conformance with the principles discussed in this section. However, the appropriate behavior is more likely to replace the undesirable pattern, and to do so more rapidly, when the desired behavior is _____.

rewarded (etc.)

94 Further, we also noted some consequences of authoritarian leadership methods in the section of this chapter on leadership styles. If the desired job performance should include individual initiative and creativity then the motivational climate must be predominantly [positive / negative].

positive

Review

great-leader

95 The leader-oriented approach to studying leadership which is predicated on the assumption that the successful executive is a person of outstanding ability who would have been successful in any situation is the _____ approach. (Frames 1 and 2)

trait

96 Difficulties in defining and measuring personality characteristics of leaders are problems encountered in conjunction with the _____ approach. (Frames 3 to 11)

intelligence
communication skill
ability to assess group goals

97 In comparison with other group members, successful leaders tend to be high in all three general trait areas of _____, _____, and _____. (Frames 12 to 18)

behavioral

98 Shifting the emphasis from what the leader is to what the leader does is consistent with the _____ approach to studying leadership. (Frames 19 to 25)

his supervisor (etc.)

99 In the evaluation of the leadership training course at International Harvester it was found that the most important influence on the foreman's attitudes and behavior came from _____. (Frames 26 to 32)

organizational climate (or situations, etc.)

100 A comprehensive study of leadership would include not only consideration of the leader himself, but also the _____ in which leadership is taking place. (Frames 33 to 36)

101 In terms of overall leadership style as related to motivational methods, the use of rewards is emphasized by the _____ leader, whereas the use of threat or coercion is emphasized by the _____ leader. (Frames 37 to 42)

positive

negative

102 Another facet of leadership style is the extent of centralization or decentralization of decision-making _____. (Frame 43)

authority (etc.)

103 In a classic study of leadership style, the three following leadership methods were used in boy's club groups: _____, _____, and _____. (Frames 44 to 49)

authoritarian
democratic; free-rein

104 In this study of leadership style, a greater degree of disorganization, nonproductivity, and play-oriented behavior were characteristics of the _____ group; a greater degree of aggression, submission, and productivity were characteristics of the _____ group; and a greater degree of friendliness and originality in work were characteristics of the _____ group. (Frames 50 to 59)

free-rein

authoritarian

democratic

105 In a more recent approach to describing leadership style in business organizations, Likert has devised a rating chart in which the most highly centralized method is called the _____ _____ and the most highly decentralized method is called the _____ method. (Frames 60 to 67)

exploitive authoritative

participative

106 In his studies of leadership effectiveness, Fred Fiedler of the University of Illinois has demonstrated that there is a contingent relationship between the required leadership style and the organizational variables of _____, _____, and _____. (Frames 68 to 72)

leader-member relations;
task structure;
leader-position power

107 In the studies by Fiedler, "leadership style" refers to the extent to which the successful leader is

employee   _____-oriented as contrasted with being
task   _____-oriented. (Frame 73)

108 The studies by Fiedler indicate that there is a systematic, but not simple, relationship between the organizational situation and required leadership style. For example, for both the "worst" and the "best" organizational situations the leadership style which is

task   required is primarily _____-oriented. (Frames 74 to 77)

109 The process by which managerial power is used to enforce conformance to organizational rules by punishing inappropriate performance is called

disciplining   _____. (Frames 78 and 79)

110 Of the principles that should be followed in conjunction with taking disciplinary action, the one which indicates that the rules should apply to all personnel

consistency   regardless of rank or status is _____, the one which indicates that the rules should be made

forewarning   known is _____, and the one which indicates that the punitive action should be equitable is

fairness   _____. (Frames 80 to 86)

111 The principle of disciplinary action which indicates that such action should come as soon as possible after the violation of rules is

promptness   _____, and it has been found that a reprimand is most effective when it is discussed

privately   [publicly / privately]. (Frames 87 to 90)

112 In general, the managerial power to discipline should be used sparingly, because desired behavior and performance are best encouraged, or reinforced,

rewards   by the use of _____. (Frames 91 to 94)

Discussion Questions

1. In what sense are the trait and behavioral approaches to studying successful leadership "two sides of the same coin"? How are the two approaches essentially different?
2. In addition to the characteristics of a particular leader, what general factors in

an organization influence the way in which a manager attempts to lead his subordinates?
3. What are some implications of the classic study of leadership style conducted by Lewin, Lippitt, and White? What are the limitations of the study?
4. As indicated by the analysis in Exhibit 13.2, the "participative management" style has a number of apparent virtues. By reviewing the contents of the chart with respect to this management style, identify the reasons why this style would not be considered desirable by some managers.
5. Using the chart devised by Likert, describe the managerial climate in the organization in which you now work or have recently worked. Do you think the climate could be improved? How?
6. Discuss both the specific and the general implications of the contingency view of leadership style developed by Fred Fiedler.
7. Why should a manager minimize his reliance on his power to discipline? What are the alternatives in a situation in which many infractions of the rules are taking place?
8. In general, why is it best to "praise in public but reprimand in private?" Under what circumstances would it be appropriate not to follow this rule?

References

Barrow, J. C. "Worker Performance and Task Complexity as Causal Determinants of Leader Behavior Style and Flexibility." *Journal of Applied Psychology,* vol. 61, no. 4, August 1976.

Barrow, J. C. "The Variables of Leadership: A Review and Conceptual Framework." *The Academy of Management Review,* vol. 2, no. 2, April 1977.

Bons, P. M., and F. E. Fiedler. "Changes in Organizational Leadership and the Behavior of Relationship- and Task-Motivated Leaders." *Administrative Science Quarterly,* vol. 21, no. 3, September 1976.

Butler, D. C. "Improving Management Practices through Leadership Training." *Public Personnel Management,* vol. 8, no. 2, March-April 1979.

Chaney, F. B., and K. S. Teel. "Participative Management—A Practical Experience." *Personnel,* vol. 49, no. 6, November-December 1972.

Crane, D. P. "The Case for Participative Management." *Business Horizons,* vol. 19, no. 2, April 1976.

Davis, T. R. V., and F. Luthans. "Leadership Reexamined: A Behavioral Approach." *The Acadamy of Management Review,* vol. 4, no. 2, April 1979.

Donnelly, J. F. "Participative Management at Work." *Harvard Business Review,* vol. 55, no. 1, January-February 1977.

Downey, H. K., J. E. Sheridan, and J. W. Slocum, Jr. "Analysis of Relationships among Leader Behavior, Subordinate Job Performance and Satisfaction: A Path-Goal Approach." *Academy of Management Journal,* vol. 18, no. 2, June 1975.

Evans, M. G. "Leadership and Motivation: A Core Concept." *Academy of Management Journal,* vol. 13, no. 1, March 1970.

Fiedler, F. E. *A Theory of Leadership Effectiveness.* New York: McGraw-Hill, 1967.

Fiedler, F. E. "The Contingency Model—New Directions for Leadership Utilization." *Journal of Contemporary Business,* vol. 3, no. 4, Autumn 1974.

Fiedler, F. E., and M. M. Chemers. *Leadership and Effective Management.* Glenview, Ill.: Scott, Foresman, 1974.

Flowers, V. S., and C. L. Hughes. "Choosing a Leadership Style." *Personnel,* vol. 55, no. 1, January-February 1978.

Frew, D. R. "Leadership and Followership." *Personnel Journal,* vol. 56, no. 2, February 1977.

Green, S. G., D. M. Nebeker, and M. A. Boni. "Personality and Situational Effects on Leader Behavior." *Academy of Management Journal,* vol. 19, no. 2, June 1976.

Greiner, L. E. "What Managers Think of Participative Leadership." *Harvard Business Review,* vol. 51, no. 2, March-April 1973.

Halal, W. E. "Toward a General Theory of Leadership." *Human Relations,* vol. 27, no. 4, April 1974.

Hand, H. H., M. D. Richards, and J. W. Slocum, Jr. "Organizational Climate and the Effectiveness of a Human Relations Training Program." *Academy of Management Journal,* vol. 16, no. 2, June 1973.

Hellriegel, D., and J. W. Slocum, Jr. "Organizational Climate: Measures, Research and Contingencies." *Academy of Management Journal,* vol. 17, no. 2, June 1974.

Hill, N. "Self-esteem: The Key to Effective Leadership." *Administrative Management,* vol. 37, no. 8, August 1976.

Hill, W. A. "Leadership Style: Rigid or Flexible?" *Organizational Behavior and Human Performance,* vol. 9, no. 1, February 1973.

House, R. J., and T. R. Mitchell. "Path-Goal Theory of Leadership." *Journal of Contemporary Business,* vol. 3, no. 4, Autumn 1974.

Hunt, J. G., and L. L. Larson (eds.). *Leadership Frontiers.* Kent, Ohio: Kent State University Press, 1976.

James, L., and A. Jones. "Organizational Climate: A Review of Theory and Research." *Psychological Bulletin,* vol. 81, no. 12, December 1974.

Karmel, B. "Leadership: A Challenge to Traditional Research Methods and Assumptions." *The Academy of Management Review,* vol. 3, no. 3, July 1978.

Krishnan, R. "Democratic Participation in Decision Making by Employees in American Corporations." *Academy of Management Journal*, vol. 17, no. 2, June 1974.

Martin, R. G. "Five Principles of Corrective Disciplinary Action." *Supervisory Management*, vol. 23, no. 1, January 1978.

Murray, T. J. "More Power for the Middle Manager." *Dun's Review*, vol. III, no. 6, June 1978.

Oberle, R. L. "Administering Disciplinary Action." *Personnel Journal*, vol. 57, no. 1, January 1978.

Palmer, W. J. "Management Effectiveness as a Function of Personality Traits of the Manager." *Personnel Psychology*, vol. 27, no. 2, Summer 1974.

Powell, G. N., and D. A. Butterfield. "The Case for Subsystem Climates in Organizations." *The Academy of Management Review*, vol. 3, no. 1, January 1978.

Pritchard, R., and B. Karasick. "The Effects of Organizational Climate on Managerial Job Performance and Job Satisfaction." *Organizational Behavior and Human Performance*, vol. 9, no. 1, February 1973.

Richards, S. A., and J. V. Cuffe. "Behavioral Correlates of Leadership Effectiveness in Interacting and Counteracting Groups." *Journal of Applied Psychology*, vol. 56, no. 5, October 1972.

Scanlan, F. K. "Managerial Leadership in Perspective: Getting Back to Basics." *Personnel Journal*, vol. 58, no. 3, March 1979.

Schneider, B. "Organizational Climate: Individual Preferences and Organizational Realities." *Journal of Applied Psychology*, vol. 56, no. 3, June 1972.

Schneider, B., and R. A. Snyder. "Some Relationships between Job Satisfaction and Organizational Climate." *Journal of Applied Psychology*, vol. 60, no. 3, June 1975.

Schriesheim, C. A., J. M. Tolliver, and O. C. Behling. "Leadership Theory: Some Implications for Managers." *MSU Business Topics*, vol. 26, no. 3, Summer 1978.

Stogdill, R. M. *Handbook of Leadership: A Survey of Theory and Research.* New York: Free Press, 1974.

Stogdill, R. M. "Historical Trends in Leadership Theory and Research." *Journal of Contemporary Business*, vol. 3, no. 4, Autumn 1974.

Waters, L. K., D. Roach, and N. Batlis. "Organizational Climate Dimensions and Job-Related Attitudes." *Personnel Psychology*, vol. 27, no. 3, Autumn 1974.

Weihrich, H. "How to Change a Leadership Pattern." *Management Review*, vol. 68, no. 4, April 1979.

Zaleznik, A. "Managers and Leaders: Are They Different?" *Harvard Business Review*, vol. 55, no. 3, May-June 1977.

CASE STUDY: A Change of Supervisors

As supervisor of the communications section in Aero-tech, Inc., Ralph Jones had the reputation of being a hard-nosed boss who demanded strict adherence to his instructions and placed great emphasis on the use of formal, as well as informal, control methods. When he was first appointed as supervisor two years ago, a considerable amount of discord developed in the communications section as a result. As a matter of fact, during the first six months of his appointment eight of the fourteen engineering and technical personnel in the section either transferred to other jobs in the company or left the company itself because of dissatisfaction with his methods. However, just about the time that John Dorfman, manager of the research and development department, was considering removing Jones as supervisor, the problems in the section subsided as the remaining members and those he hired accepted his style of leadership. Although he encouraged participation of his subordinates during the planning stage of a project or program, once he made procedure and scheduling decisions, he expected strict compliance on the part of the communications section personnel.

During his tenure as supervisor Ralph Jones reduced project personnel costs associated with the communications section by 10 percent while meeting all time schedules for program completion set by the manager of research and development and by the project managers. He had the reputation of running a tight and efficient operation. Largely because of this record of accomplishment he was offered what he described as an irresistible managerial opportunity with a competing firm in the aerospace industry, and after two weeks' notice left the company to accept that position three months ago.

At first John Dorfman assumed that he would promote someone from within the communications section. However he found that no one had really been Jones' assistant or understudy, and that no one in the section seemed particularly desirous of going into supervision. After two weeks of search, the research and development manager was able to arrange the transfer of Tom Yarborough, then supervisor of the command systems section, to the vacated position. In turn, Yarborough had one of his subordinates take over supervision of the command systems section. Yarborough was regarded as a highly competent supervisor, and although this transfer did not represent a promotion for him, he saw it as an opportunity to gain a greater diversity of experience.

Tom Yarborough was a strong proponent of management by objectives. He believed in making all task assignments in terms of the objectives to be accomplished and leaving it up to the personnel involved to formulate the necessary procedures and methods. He was available for consultation regarding job problems, but the personnel in the communications section found that he avoided becoming involved in the detail of the work. After his first month as supervisor, it was obvious to John Dorfman that things were not going well in the communications section. Two scheduled completion times for tasks assigned to the section had been missed, and the progress on one or two others was possibly also behind schedule. In discussing the situation with several of the key employees in the section during a coffee break, the department manager learned that it was the consensus of the men in the section that Tom Yarborough didn't understand the work he was supervising and was not acting as a supervisor. He refused to specify how goals were to be accomplished and then held individual employees responsible when specific tasks were not completed on time. As a result, the personnel in the section were frustrated by the very absence of direction on his part and doubted that Yarborough was capable of providing the direction even if he wanted to do so.

1. How would you describe Ralph Jones' approach to management in terms of leadership style?
2. Was the employee reaction to Jones' methods predictable? Why?
3. How would you describe Tom Yarborough's approach to management in terms of leadership style?
4. Was the employee reaction to Yarborough's methods predictable? Why?
5. What should Mr. Dorfman do about the present situation in the communications section?

CASE STUDY: A Matter of Overtime

As was typically the case during the closing of the books at the end of the fiscal year, it was necessary to have a number of the employees in the accounting department work beyond the usual office hours so that the end-of-year reports could be prepared on time. As the 5 o'clock hour approached, Joan Zayle, the chief accountant, noticed that two of the employees got ready to leave the office to go home. She therefore called them over to her desk.

Zayle: "You are supposed to be working overtime tonight until about 9:00 P.M."

First employee: "Why, no one notified me that I was supposed to work."

Zayle: "I told both of you the first day of the week about working tonight."

Second employee: "This is the first I have heard of it. I received no written information."

Zayle: "No written message is necessary. The fact that I told you is sufficient."

The employees returned to their desks and started working. At 6:30 P.M. Joan Zayle stated that she was going to the coffee shop down the street for a quick dinner and asked the two if they wanted to join her. They indicated that they did not, so she went to the restaurant alone. When she returned about forty minutes later, the office was deserted.

When the two employees reported for work the next morning Joan Zayle told them they were fired. They went to the industrial relations department and appealed the action. Based in part on the lack of a written record of the assignment to work overtime, the industrial relations manager reduced the firing decision to a two-week layoff. Joan was fuming. Not only had she wasted much of the day in the appeal proceedings, but she was now in the position of having two vacant positions for which she could not hire replacements during this particularly busy time period.

1. At what point did the problem described in the case description really begin?
2. Was the disciplinary decision to fire the two employees appropriate? Why or why not?
3. Should the industrial relations manager have the authority to overrule a manager's decision regarding disciplinary action? In this respect, what mistake did Joan Zayle make?
4. What is likely to be the nature of the relationship between Joan Zayle and the two employees when they return from the two-week layoff?

APPLICATIONS READING:

Leadership Styles: Which Are Best When?

Alan Weiss
Director of Client Service
Kepner-Tregoe, Inc.
Princeton, N.J.

Did you ever wish that all the experts would get together and decide once and for all which leadership style is the best? Then you would never have to worry about such matters as whether certain subordinates are mature enough to handle more responsibility or whether committees can come up with the best decision. You'd simply use the method the experts deem best.

But management isn't that neat and simple. Some leadership styles will work for people with aggressive personalities but flop when used by introverts. Some theories are workable under ordinary circumstances but may not be feasible when time is limited. There is no "perfect" method of leadership. Instead, leadership style depends very much on the individual situation—particularly where time pressures are great.

Our research on leadership is based on the work of Dr. Victor H. Vroom of Yale University and his associate, Dr. Phillip W. Yetton of the Manchester Business School in England—work discussed in their book *Leadership and Decision-Making* (University of Pittsburgh Press, 1973). Following their lead, we can separate potential leadership styles into five categories (the letter-and-number labels are arbitrary):

AI—This style is characterized by completely independent action. Using available information, the leader solves the problem or makes the decision alone.

AII—The leader resolves a situation alone but does go to other people to gather needed data. In gathering this information, the leader may or may not divulge the purpose of the questions. In any case, the people supplying the data play no role in analyzing the problem or making the decision.

CI—In this style, the situation is explained to each person providing data. Their opinions are solicited, but the leader retains the final decision—which may or may not reflect the influence of those who have been consulted.

CII—Here, the situation is explained, data provided, and alternatives proposed in a group setting. Information is exchanged among group members. The final decision is the leader's, and it may or may not reflect the group's influence.

Source: From *Supervisory Management*, vol. 21, no. 1, January 1976, © 1976 by AMACOM, a division of American Management Associations. All rights reserved.

GII—Information is shared and ideas exchanged in a group. Collectively, group members try to resolve the situation. The leader is a chairperson or coordinator facilitating the flow of data; he may or may not try to influence group consensus. However, the leader accepts and implements whatever conclusions the group reaches.

Similarities and Distinctions

The similarities and distinctions of these five styles are illustrated in Exhibit 1.

As we move from **AI** toward **GII**, we can see several things occuring:

1. The nature of the problem or decision is disclosed to more people.
2. Involvement moves from "provides data" to "recommends."
3. Group ownership of and commitment to the solution increases. Consequently, the more a leader uses **GII**, the better off he or she is, right? Wrong—because there is a fourth factor operating as we move toward the right in the exhibit:
4. The time required to arrive at a decision increases. So the question, then, is at what point should time efficiency properly dissuade a leader from involving others to too great an extent? There are some specific ways to determine that.

The most effective style of leadership is always dependent upon the situation. And in all situations there are many variables that affect the quality of and/or commitment to the decision being made. For the purposes of determining what constitutes acceptable behavior in a given situation, we have isolated seven "situation variables." Think of these as factors that determine the points in Exhibit 1: Who is involved, what is the nature of the involvement, and who makes the decision.

	AI	AII	CI	CII	GII
Who is involved	Leader	Leader and others individually	Leader and others individually	Leader and others in group	Leader and others in group
Nature of involvement	Unassisted decision	Individuals respond to specific questions	Individuals provide data, recommendations, one-on-one	Group shares data and analyzes	Group shares data, analyzes, and reaches consensus
Who makes decision	Leader	Leader	Leader	Leader	Group

Exhibit 1 *A comparison of leadership styles.*

The Situation Variables

1. *The quality requirement.* Does it make a difference which course of action is adopted?
2. *Adequate information.* Does the leader have sufficient information to make a high quality analysis alone?
3. *Structure of the situation.* Does the leader know exactly what information is missing and how to get it?
4. *Commitment.* Must others be committed to the solution in order to implement it successfully?
5. *Acceptance of a decision by the leader alone.* If the leader were to make the decision alone, would he or she receive the support of those responsible for its implementation?
6. *Goal congruence.* Do subordinates—especially implementors—have the same interests and/or goals as the organization in resolving the situation?
7. *Conflict over alternatives.* Is there likely to be conflict or disagreement among subordinates over the possible alternatives?

These variables lead to various rules that provide a leader with a feasible set of behavior roles for any situation. For example, by combining the variables concerning quality (#1) and goal congruence (#6) we can develop this rule: When quality is important *and* there is a lack of goal congruence between those implementing the decision and the leader who represents the organization's goals, then: Eliminate the **GII** approach.

Since **GII** is the behavior mode that calls for the group to make the decision—and we have established that there is a quality requirement—the leader cannot afford to relinquish the decision-making prerogative. Why? Because there is a strong possibility that the group's alternative would not meet organizational objectives. Hence, the leader is faced with **AI, AII, CI, and CII.**

If we were now to apply another rule: When quality is important *and* the leader does not have enough information to resolve the situation alone, then: Eliminate the **AI** approach. Since **AI** calls for the leader alone to make the decision, and his information is insufficient to make that decision, we eliminate that mode of behavior, leaving us with **AII, CI and CII.**

For the sake of our example, let's suppose that no other rules apply. That means that our feasible range of behavior is **AII, CI, and CII.** The leader who desires maximum time efficiency can opt for **AII**, since it involves no group participation and is totally leader-controlled. If, however, the leader has subordinate development as a high priority (perhaps the leader wants to ensure that others are capable of doing his or her job) then **CII** would be more appropriate. **CI**, of course, provides a compromise.

If we place the seven situation variables on a decision tree and use the vertical lines as "yes/no" points, we can construct a vehicle for selecting feasible leadership styles. (See Exhibit 2.)

Applications Reading • 429

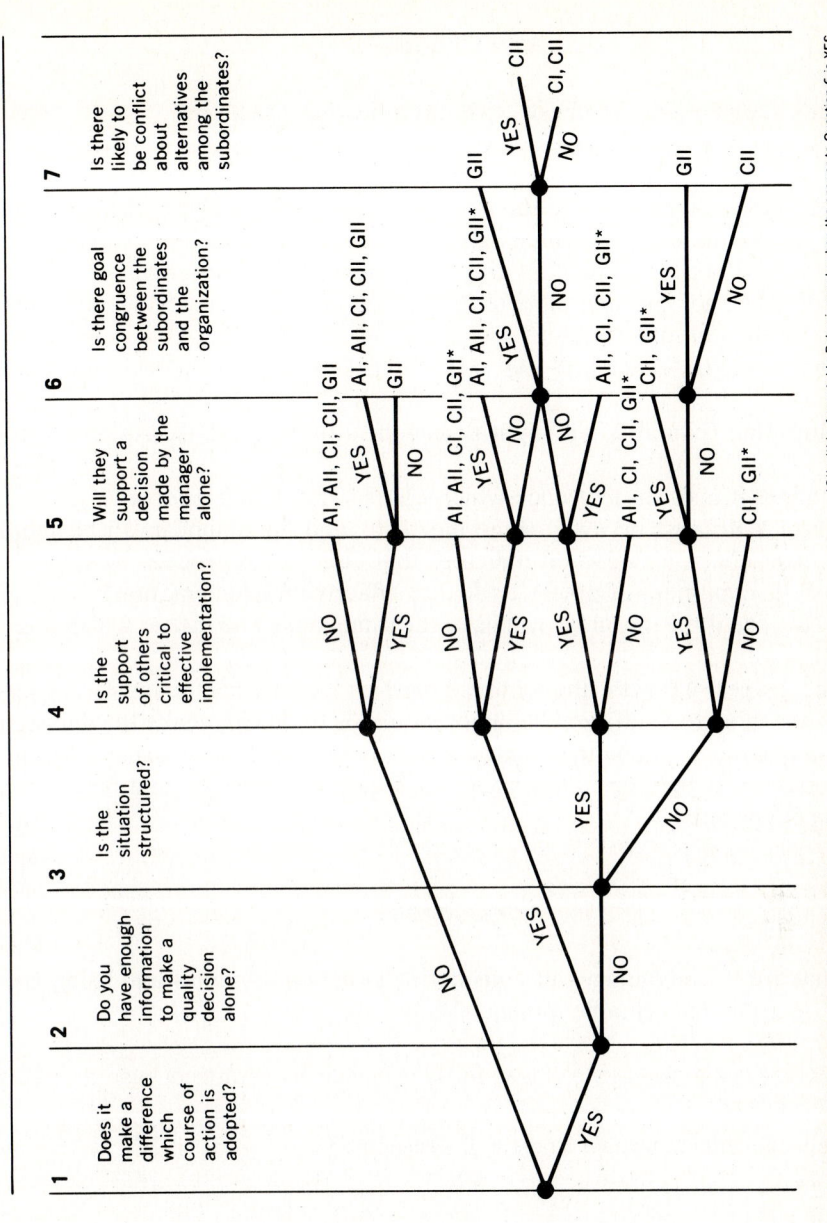

1	2	3	4	5	6	7
Does it make a difference which course of action is adopted?	Do you have enough information to make a quality decision alone?	Is the situation structured?	Is the support of others critical to effective implementation?	Will they support a decision made by the manager alone?	Is there goal congruence between the subordinates and the organization?	Is there likely to be conflict about alternatives among the subordinates?

Decision tree branches:

- YES (Q1) → NO (Q2) → NO (Q4) → AI, AII, CI, CII, GII
- YES (Q1) → NO (Q2) → YES (Q4) → YES (Q5) → AI, AII, CI, CII, GII
- YES (Q1) → NO (Q2) → YES (Q4) → NO (Q5) → GII
- YES (Q1) → YES (Q2) → YES (Q3) → NO (Q4) → AI, AII, CI, CII, GII*
- YES (Q1) → YES (Q2) → YES (Q3) → YES (Q4) → YES (Q5) → AI, AII, CI, CII, GII*
- YES (Q1) → YES (Q2) → YES (Q3) → YES (Q4) → NO (Q5) → YES (Q6) → GII; NO (Q6) → YES (Q7) CII; NO (Q7) CI, CII
- YES (Q1) → YES (Q2) → NO (Q3) → YES (Q4) → YES (Q5) → AII, CI, CII, GII*
- YES (Q1) → YES (Q2) → NO (Q3) → YES (Q4) → NO (Q5) → CII, GII*
- YES (Q1) → YES (Q2) → NO (Q3) → NO (Q4) → YES (Q6) GII; NO (Q6) CII

*GII within Acceptable Behaviors only when the answer to Question 6 is YES.

Copyright © 1973 by Kepner-Tregoe, Inc. All Rights Reserved.

Exhibit 2 *Feasible leadership styles.*

You Choose

Let's suppose you are faced with the following situation:*

Your responsibilities have been increased so that you are to be away from your desk for about 12 hours a week, broken into four-hour sessions on three different mornings. You can choose the mornings you are to be away, but you must make a firm commitment as to which they will be for the coming month. When you are away, you will be out of touch with your subordinates. Their demands on you are unpredictable, so it is impossible to foresee the mornings on which you will be needed more than on others.

What mode of leadership—**AI, AII, CI, CII,** or **GII**—would you choose? Why?

Consulting Exhibit 2, we might assess the situation in this manner:

1 Does it make a difference which course of action is adopted?

—No. You must be away three mornings and none appears to be more desirable than others. The exhibit indicates that you should proceed to step 4.

4 Is commitment of others critical to effective implementation?

—No. The three mornings will have the same impact no matter which three are chosen.

This leaves us with the entire range as acceptable behaviors. Consequently, the most time-efficient behavior would be to quickly make the decision by yourself and move on to other things: **AI.** Exhibit 2 leads us to acceptable behavior modes—it is then up to the leader to decide which to use and how much time efficiency is needed.

Advantages

What are the advantages of considering situation variables and using Exhibit 2 to determine acceptable modes of behavior?

1 To recognize that a given style of leadership is neither necessary nor even desirable for all occasions.
2 To determine when to involve others in a decision.
3 To determine whom to involve.
4 To determine how to involve them.
5 To be aware of those leadership skills that must be developed (that is, conducting meetings, assessing recommendations, interviewing, and so forth).
6 To stay cognizant of which mode of behavior is most time-efficient for any given situation.

* Copyright © 1973 by Kepner-Tregoe, Inc. All rights reserved.

If	Participation should	But only IF
1. There is a high quality requirement	Increase	Others have data needed for a high quality decision.
2. The situation is unstructured	Increase	Others have data needed for a high quality decision.
3. There is low goal congruence	Decrease	There is a strong quality requirement.
4. There is a high level of commitment (not merely compliance) required	Increase	Others would not be committed to a decision made by the leader alone.
5. There is a high probability of commitment to a decision made by the leader alone	Decrease	NO CONDITIONS
6. There is a high level of conflict	Increase	Others would not be committed to a decision made by the leader alone.
7. There is a strong need for training or team building	Increase	NO CONDITIONS

Exhibit 3 *A guide for changing participation levels.*

No leader has the opportunity to methodically run through the chart every time a decision is to be made. Its formal use is most appropriate when major and/or repetitive leadership roles occur. However, the situation variables do provide us with some informal trends that are useful to bear in mind on almost *every* occasion when time is critical and there is some question about who should be involved in a decision. These trends are outlined in Exhibit 3.

Conclusions

Several conclusions can be drawn from observing this model at work:

1 Leaders who *feel* they are participative often use a participative approach only when a quality solution is not needed. (Subordinates could decide where to put a soda machine but not whether to change working hours.) Such "participation" is often self-defeating because of its condescending nature.

2. When there is a lack of goal congruence but decisions are turned over to the group anyway, the recommendations are often ignored because they do not meet the leader's (and organization's) objectives. As more and more recommendations are ignored, the frustration level of subordinates grows.
3. Leaders often strive for increased participation for its own sake without realizing the extra time investment required.
4. Leaders who feel that the most time-efficient behavior is *always* an **AI** mode are wrong. If they lack data, then the **AI** mode may produce a poor or inappropriate decision that will require more time to improve or correct later.
5. There is a feasible or acceptable *range* of behavior in most cases. You do not need to search for the "perfect style" of leadership.

Questions on Reading

1. Although the author states that the letter-number labels associated with the leadership styles are arbitrary, it may be useful to interpret **"A"** as "Authoritative," **"C"** as "Consultative," and **"G"** as "Group-Oriented" (or participative). Accordingly, describe the shift in decision-making authority as one moves from the **AI** to the **GII** style.
2. Under what organizational conditions should participation in the decision process be increased?
3. Under what organizational conditions should participation in the decision process be decreased?
4. What are the author's principal conclusions with respect to choice of a leadership style?

14 EFFECTIVE SUPERVISION

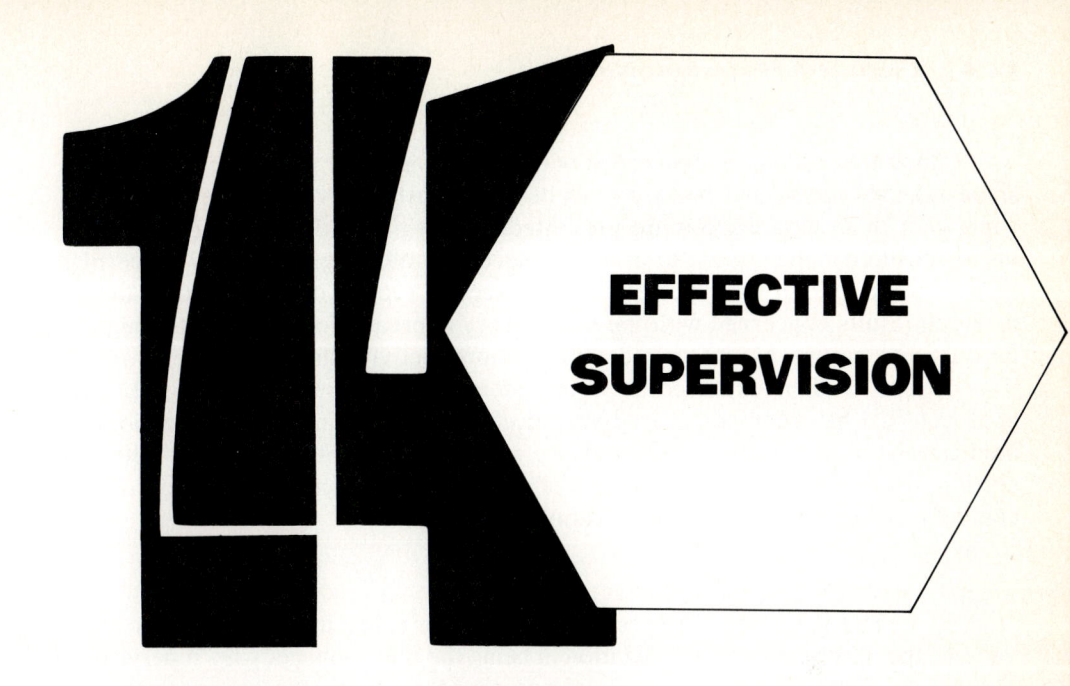

- The Role of the First-Level Supervisor
- Supervisory Effectiveness
- The Managerial Grid
- Overcoming Resistance to Change
- Review
- Discussion Questions
- References
- Case Study: A Change of Supervisory Philosophy at Triflex
- Case Study: An Analysis of Operating Procedures
- Applications Reading: "Rethinking the Supervisory Role" David S. Brown
- Questions on Reading

In this final chapter concerned with the management process of directing, some selected topics and research results particularly relevant to the first-level supervisor in an organization are presented. We begin by describing the supervisor's position in the organization and the several conflicting viewpoints concerning the proper role of the supervisor. In the second section of this chapter, some research results concerned with the supervisory approach found to exist in high-productivity groups as contrasted with low-productivity groups are reviewed. This review is then extended to a consideration of the managerial grid, an approach that has been considered very useful for describing the organizational implications of using various supervisory styles. The chapter concludes with a section concerned with a particular area of supervisory responsibility: that of overcoming resistance to job and organizational changes.

The Role of the First-Level Supervisor

The first-level supervisor is in a unique position in the organization in being the only manager who supervises the work of nonmanagers. Since the ultimate attainment of organizational goals depends on what happens at the operative level, this makes the first-level supervisor's position particularly important. The success of plans and strategies determined by the top management level depends on the supervisor's ability to translate them into action at the working level. In this section we identify several different views concerning the supervisor's appropriate role and consider their implications as factors affecting the supervisor's performance.

1 Throughout this chapter we use the word "supervisor" to designate the first level of management in the organization. Whereas top executives and middle managers in the organization supervise other members of the company management team, the supervisor has responsibility for directing the work of _____

operative employees (or nonmanagers, etc.)

2 In the following list, underline the identifying letters of those position titles that designate supervisory positions.

a; b; c (All these titles designate first-line supervisory positions.)

   a. section head, accounts receivable
   b. supervisor, research and development
   c. foreman, paint shop

3 Therefore, first-level supervisors are located in all the functional areas of work in the organization, including staff, as well as line, components. From this standpoint, both the manager responsible for the work of a group of financial analysts in the company and the foreman on the assembly line are considered to be

supervisors _____ .

4 Most of the studies concerned with the supervisor's work have been done with the first-level supervisor in manufacturing, that is, the foreman. Because the foreman has certain assigned responsibilities for planning, organizing, directing, and controlling, he or she

is appropriately [is / is not] considered a member of management.

5 Although supervisors are now considered members of management, historically there have been a number of different views concerning their proper role in the organization, and the influence of these views is still felt. (Refer to Figure 14.1, on the following page.) The first of these views, which particularly indicates the importance of the supervisory position in the organization, identifies the supervisor as the

key person _____ in management.

6 In terms of the *key-person* concept, from the worker's point of view the supervisor is the direct

top management face-to-face representative of _____ .

7 In the other direction, top management's view of the operative employees is largely based on the kind of

supervisor information passed on to them by the _____ .

8 Thus, because of the supervisor's unique position in the chain of authority and in the communication system, that individual has been considered to be the

key person _____ in management.

9 However, based on the same facts concerning the supervisor's position in the organization, another view of this position is that this individual is the *person in the middle,* caught between the expectations and

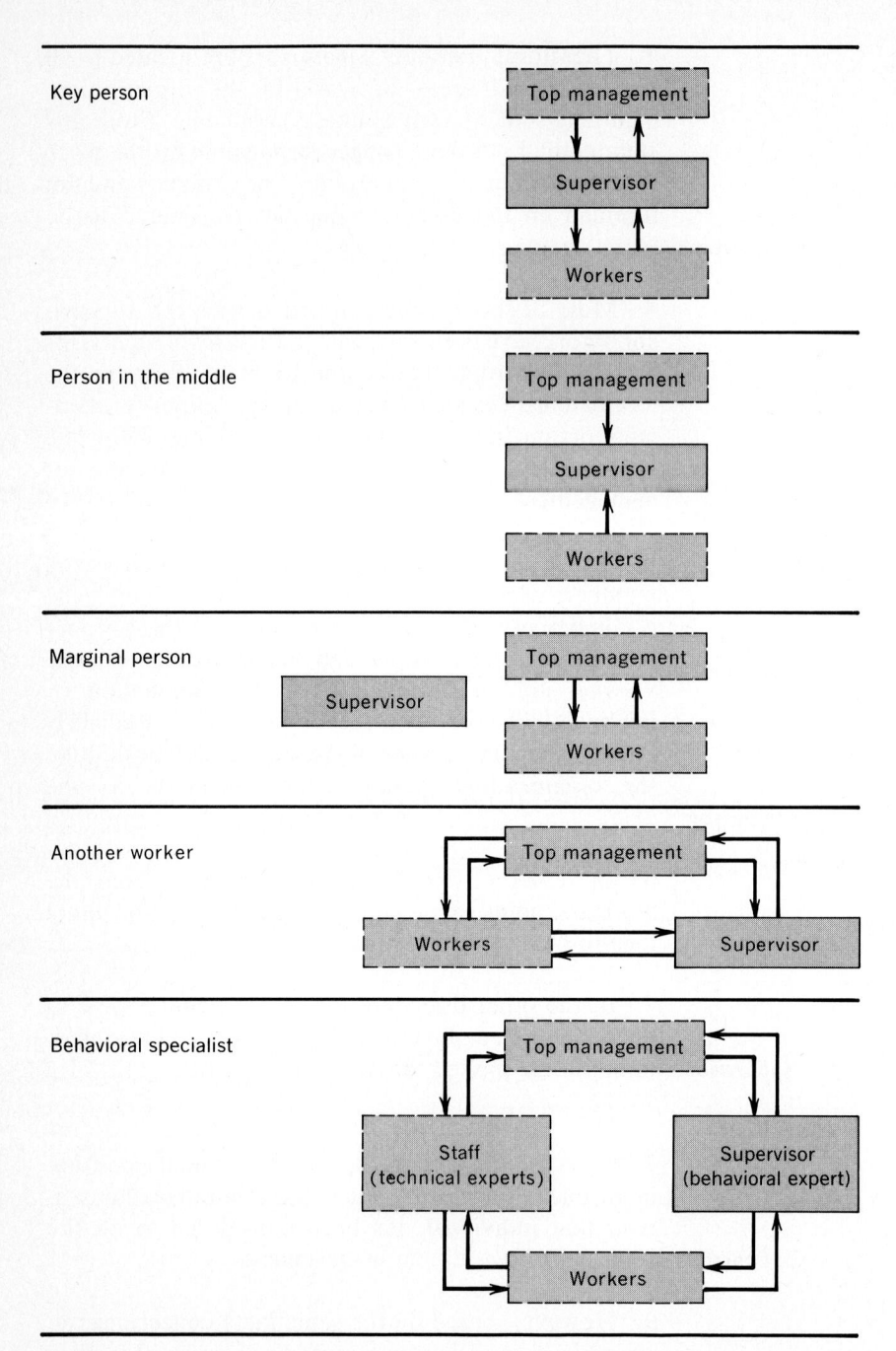

Figure 14.1 Different viewpoints of the supervisor's role. (Adapted from Keith Davis, *Human Behavior at Work: Organizational Behavior,* 5th ed., McGraw-Hill Book Company, New York, 1977, p. 127. Reproduced with permission.)

top management workers	demands of _____ and _____.
key-person	**10** In contrasting the key-person view with the person-in-the-middle view, the one that views the supervisor as being in a strategic position of strength is the _____ view.
person-in-the-middle	**11** The view that takes cognizance of the supervisor's vulnerability to the pressures of competing groups and also the inability of the supervisor to satisfy completely the differing expectations of these competing groups is the _____ _____ view.
management worker	**12** Considering the possible implications of the organizational position from a sociological point of view, the supervisor also can be considered a *marginal person;* i.e., the individual may not be a fully accepted member of either the _____ group or the _____ group.
do not	**13** As is typical of a person with marginal group membership, the supervisor may find that both top management and the workers [do / do not] fully confide in him (or her).
marginal person	**14** Top management and staff specialists typically have extensive contact with one another and a common set of interests, while workers have a pattern of informal groups and perhaps a union. Particularly in automated operations, however, the supervisor may have infrequent contact with other supervisors, thus further adding to the supervisor's position as a _____.
key-person; person-in-the-middle; marginal-person	**15** Thus far we have considered three viewpoints concerning the supervisor's role in the organization: the _____, _____, and _____ viewpoints.
	16 Another view of the supervisor not so prevalent today is that such an individual belongs to *another*

worker group, rather than to management. Until the Labor Management Relations (Taft-Hartley) Act of 1947, supervisors were legally considered to be employees with collective bargaining rights, thus enhancing the likelihood that they would think of themselves as [managers / workers].

workers

17 Although their legal status has changed, many supervisors still think of themselves as being more like workers than managers. Along these lines, both the foreman's previous experience as an operative employee and centralized planning and scheduling in a company tend to [reinforce / change] this viewpoint.

reinforce

18 Both managerial decentralization, by which more authority is delegated to first-level supervisors, and participation of supervisors in management development programs increase the likelihood that the supervisor will identify himself or herself as a member of the _____ group.

management

19 In addition to the key-person, person-in-the-middle, marginal-person, and another-worker views, the supervisor has been considered as the *behavioral specialist* in the organization. From this point of view, the supervisor is not particularly the key person in the operations, but rather one of the many specialists contributing to the organization's effectiveness. The supervisor's specialty is that of dealing with _____ problems on the job.

behavioral

20 The view that the supervisor is primarily a behavioral specialist is particularly likely in the organization that is highly [centralized / decentralized].

centralized (since other types of problems—such as scheduling—are handled by staff specialists)

21 Regardless of the type of organization, however, when supervisors are asked to identify their most important job problems, they almost invariably name such problems as employee motivation and conflicts among people, thereby acknowledging their necessary role as _____ specialists.

behavioral

22 In most organizations the supervisor needs some level of technical knowledge in the areas of work being supervised. However, particularly when detailed schedules and procedures for the department are prepared by technical specialists in the organization, the principal remaining responsibility is that of being the _____ specialist.

behavioral

23 In our review of the different viewpoints of the supervisor's role, both historical and contemporary, we have identified five principal views: the _____, _____, _____, _____, and _____ views.

key-person;
person-in-the-middle;
marginal-person;
another-worker;
behavioral specialist

24 To some extent, all these views apply to the supervisor's position today. However, in order to improve the supervisor's opportunity to do an effective job, the top management of a firm should strive to make the predominant role that of being a _____ in management.

key person

25 From this standpoint, any organizational action that seems to treat the first-level supervisor as a nonmanager or as a member of a "special" group (i.e., neither management nor worker) should certainly be avoided, since these two types of actions would tend to reinforce the _____ and _____ views of the supervisor's role, respectively.

another-worker
marginal-person

26 Being a member of management who is in a key position with respect to the work of operative employees, the supervisor also needs to develop as a behavioral specialist and will often find himself or herself in the position of being the person in the middle. In spite of this, the supervisor's opportunity to do an effective job and to develop self-confidence is reinforced when top management treats the first-level supervisor as a fully accepted member of the _____ group.

management

27   The particular strategy or practices that a firm should follow in order to accomplish this objective is, of course, dependent on the company situation. What is required is true top management acceptance of the supervisor as a manager, rather than the use of any given set of techniques. That thousands of first-level supervisors joined a union—the Foreman's Association of America—before they were redefined as members of management by the Labor Management Relations Act of 1947 indicates that up to that time, at least, many firms were [successful / unsuccessful] in integrating foremen into the company management group.

unsuccessful

Supervisory Effectiveness

Of course, all the preceding chapters in this part of the book on the management function of directing are relevant to developing effective supervisory practices. Since a large number of supervisory problems concern motivation, Chapter 12 on motivating people at work is particularly applicable. In this section we briefly review the results of an extensive series of studies of supervisory practices conducted by Rensis Likert and his colleagues in the Institute for Social Research at the University of Michigan.[1] Their findings are consistent with the motivational principles discussed in both Chapters 11 and 12. They contribute to our understanding of motivation and supervision by describing actual patterns of supervision associated with high-production and low-production units in industrial organizations.

28   The studies of supervisory practices which we describe were conducted in several public utilities, an insurance company, an automobile manufacturing company, a heavy-machinery factory, a railroad, an electric appliance factory, and several government agencies, thus representing a relatively [narrow / broad] industrial sample.

broad

29   In evaluating supervisory effectiveness two major criteria were used: (1) the productivity per man-hour

---

[1]The results of the original series of studies are reported in detail in Rensis Likert, *Motivation: The Core of Management,* Personnel Series, no. 155, American Management Association, New York, 1953.

or some similar measure of the organization's success in achieving its productivity goals, and (2) the job satisfaction and other personal satisfactions derived by employees. The very fact that these two criteria are separately stated suggests that the researchers began with the premise that they [are closely related / might be independent of one another].

might be independent of one another

30 And as a matter of fact, in comparing high-productivity and low-productivity sections within companies, Likert found little relationship between employee attitude toward the company and productivity as such, although absenteeism and turnover may have been affected. As indicated by the data in Table 14.1, whereas 37 percent of the employees in the high-productivity sections had a high level of satisfaction with the company and 24 percent had a low level of satisfaction, in low-productivity sections the percentages for high and low levels of satisfaction were ____ percent ____ percent, respectively.

40
20

Table 14.1 Attitude toward the Company and Section Productivity

Attitude toward company	High-productivity sections	Low-productivity sections
High	37%	40%
Average	39%	40%
Low	24%	20%
	100%	100%

31 Until these studies were completed, it had been a common managerial assumption that developing a favorable employee attitude toward the company will result in increased productivity. The findings reported in Table 14.1 [do / do not] support this assumption.

do not

32 An indirect measure of employee attitude toward the company which is sometimes used is the extent of participation in company recreational activities. To the extent that there is any relationship at all, Table 14.2 indicates that the absence of participation in company recreational activities may be associated with the section being [high / low] in productivity.

high (72% of those in high-productivity sections never participated)

Table 14.2 Participation in Company Recreational Activities and Section Productivity

Participation	High-productivity sections	Low-productivity sections
Frequently	8%	7%
Occasionally	20%	34%
Never	72%	59%
	100%	100%

33 In contrast to these findings, Likert found a marked relationship between the kind of supervision received and productivity, as well as personal satisfaction. In this phase of the studies, supervisors who emphasized work-oriented planning and control procedures in describing their jobs were designated as being [employee- / production-] centered, whereas supervisors who emphasized the interpersonal nature of their jobs were designated as [employee- / production-] centered.

production-

employee-

34 For example, a supervisor might describe his job by saying: "I try to consider each man's strengths and weaknesses and how the men work together before I make any job assignments. When possible, I try to assign a man to the kind of jobs he likes best." This pattern of supervision would be considered _____ centered.

employee-

35 Another supervisor might indicate: "I have to get employees to produce, and my main tool is the efficiency chart. With this chart I am able to plan ahead and give attention to the work areas that are behind." This pattern of supervision would be considered _____ centered.

production-

36 When the approach to supervision was compared with the associated employee productivity, as indicated in Table 14.3, the high-production sections tended to have supervisors who were _____ centered.

employee-

37 Rather surprisingly, then, the supervisors who indicated that they gave primary emphasis to production

Table 14.3 Approach to Supervision and Section Productivity

Approach to supervision	High-productivity sections	Low-productivity sections
Production-centered	14%	70%
Employee-centered	86%	30%
	100%	100%

low   tended to be in charge of sections that were [high / low] in productivity.

38 Further evidence along these lines, as well as an indication of the reasons behind these results, is given by the observed relationship between closeness of supervision and section productivity. As reported in Table 14.4, high-production sections were inclined to
general   have supervisors who employed _____ supervision.

Table 14.4 Closeness of Supervision and Section Productivity

Supervision	High-productivity sections	Low-productivity sections
Close	10%	67%
General	90%	33%
	100%	100%

39 Likert found that production-centered supervisors tended to supervise closely, that is, in terms of specific procedures to be followed rather than in terms of goals to be achieved. Based on the results of these studies, this pattern of supervision is associated with
low   [high / low] section productivity.

40 However, we might well challenge this conclusion by asking whether "cause" and "effect" might not have been reversed. After all, is it not possible that supervisors of low-production units find it necessary to be production-centered and to employ close supervision because their people are not productive, rather than the other way around? In terms of the results we have presented thus far, might this conclusion be
Yes (The data do not   equally valid? [Yes / No]
indicate direction of
causation.)

41 Because of this question of cause and effect, in one of the companies participating in this research project the supervisors of several high- and low-productivity sections were switched to see whether the supervisory approach or productivity would change. The result was that the basic supervisory approaches associated with the two types of supervisors did not change, but the productivity of the sections did change. The former low-productivity sections showed marked improvement with the employee-centered supervisors, whereas the former high-productivity sections slipped somewhat, indicating that [supervisory style affects productivity / productivity affects supervisory style].

supervisory style affects productivity

42 The employee-centered approach with its general, or goal-oriented, supervision does not imply a lack of concern about productivity. Rather it indicates that the supervisors of high-productivity sections recognize that productivity is accomplished by [procedures / people].

people

43 On the other hand, supervisors of low-productivity sections tended to look at employee-centered methods as being a luxury and something to be indulged in [before / after] achieving high productivity.

after

44 Thus far, we have considered the effect of supervisory methods on productivity. The other criterion of supervisory effectiveness in these studies was the level of employee morale. Again, the supervisory approach used did influence employee morale, and, as for the productivity findings, morale was highest in sections with _____ centered supervisors.

employee-

45 Figure 14.2 reports the activities of the supervisors of high- and low-morale groups as seen by their subordinates, in terms of percentage frequency of mention. For the relatively impersonal functions of enforcing rules, arranging work, and supplying material, the supervisors of high-morale groups, as contrasted to low-morale groups, [did / did not] differ substantially.

did not

46 As was true for the productivity results, it

Supervisory Effectiveness ● 445

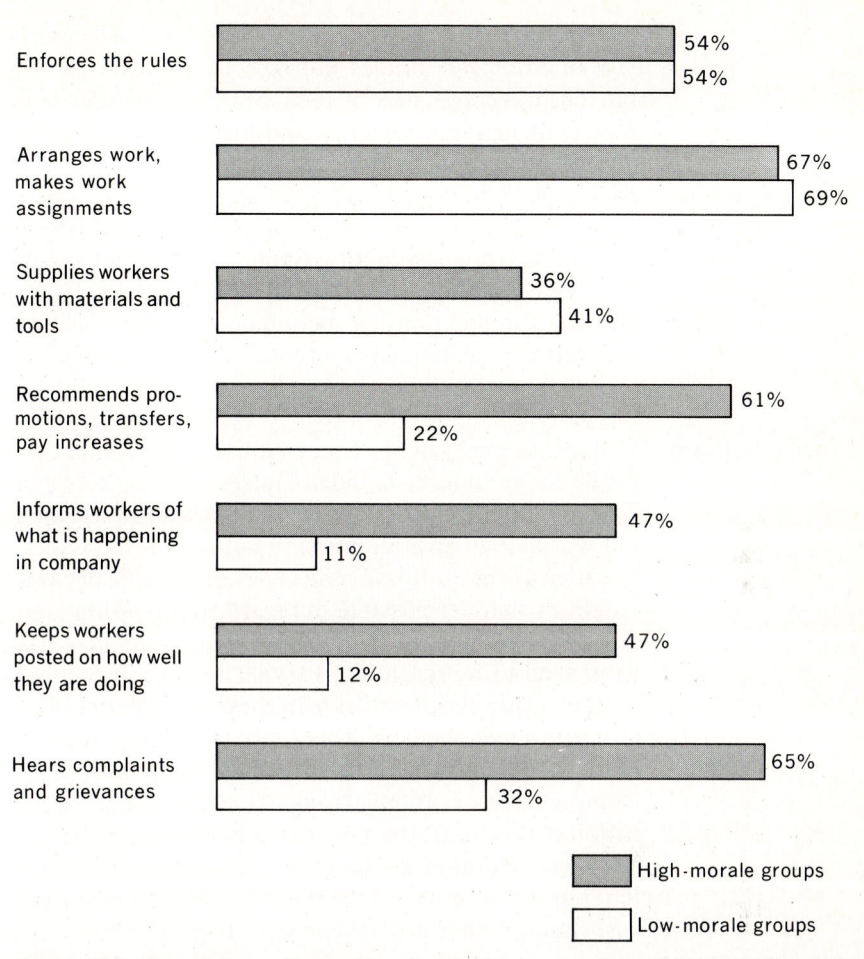

Activity	High-morale	Low-morale
Enforces the rules	54%	54%
Arranges work, makes work assignments	67%	69%
Supplies workers with materials and tools	36%	41%
Recommends promotions, transfers, pay increases	61%	22%
Informs workers of what is happening in company	47%	11%
Keeps workers posted on how well they are doing	47%	12%
Hears complaints and grievances	65%	32%

Figure 14.2 Descriptions of supervisors' activities by members of high-morale and low-morale groups. (Adapted from Rensis Likert, *Motivation: The Core of Management,* Personnel Series, no. 155, American Management Association, New York, 1953, p. 9. Used with permission.)

wasn't so much what the supervisors of low-morale groups did, but what they didn't do that influenced the morale of their sections. What they failed to do was to give adequate attention to the _____ elements in the work situation.

human (or employee, etc.)

47 As an example, whereas only 11 percent of the employees of low-morale groups reported that their supervisor informs the men about what is happening in the company, in high-morale groups the percentage of

47 employees mentioning this was ____ percent.

48 Although there were other results of the University of Michigan studies not directly relevant to our present coverage, one of their principal findings was that both high productivity and high morale of work groups is more likely when the supervisor's approach to his job is _____ centered.

employee-

49 In the research report, employee-centered supervisors gave attention to individual employee needs [instead of / in addition to] the impersonal planning and control responsibilities inherent in their positions.

in addition to

The Managerial Grid

In the University of Michigan studies it was found that the effective supervisor did not make a choice between giving attention to production as contrasted to people but was able to give attention to both of these factors. In order to clarify the several types of supervisory orientations that are possible in regard to the production and people factors in the job, the *managerial grid* has been used to represent the varying degrees of emphasis that a supervisor can give to these two factors. The grid was developed by Robert R. Blake and Jane S. Mouton and was first described in their book *The Managerial Grid* (Gulf, Houston, 1964). Since publication of this book, the system has been widely applied and reported on in the literature. The general characteristics of this grid and the number-designator system associated with it are described in this section.

50 Figure 14.3 presents the managerial grid, with a description of five supervisory approaches entered on the grid. The two numbers identifying each approach indicate the extent of concern for production and people, respectively. Thus a "2,7 managerial style" would represent a relatively [high / low] concern for production and a [high / low] concern for people.

low
high

51 Of the five managerial approaches described on the grid, the one that would most likely lead to a high level of production, *as well as morale*, is the ____ style.

9,9

52 After first considering the characteristics of the other four approaches briefly described on the grid, we

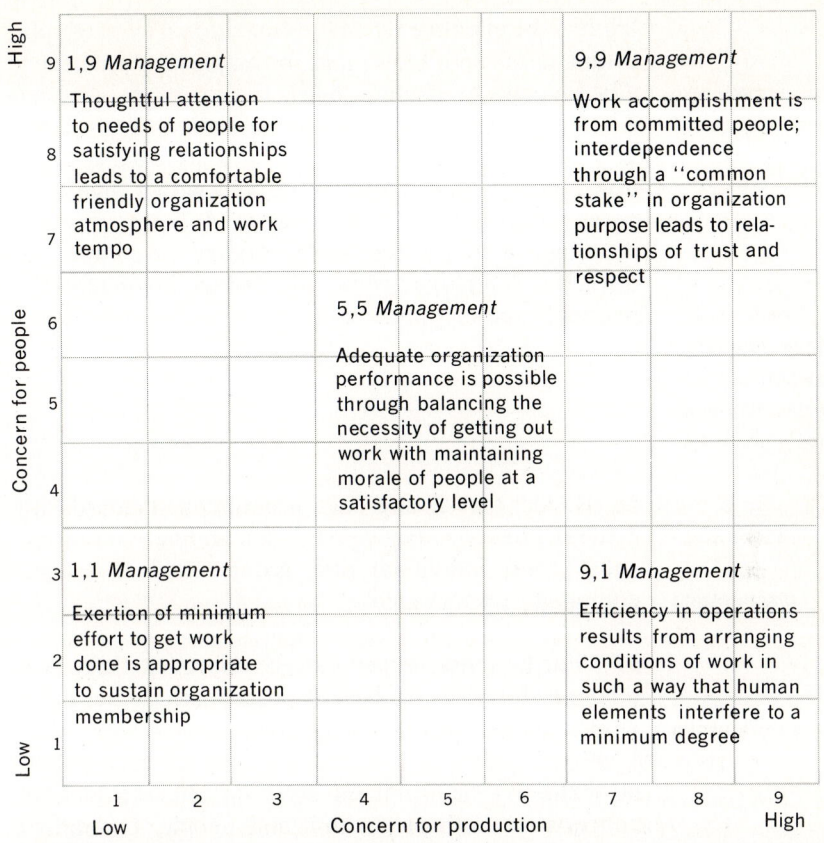

Figure 14.3 The managerial grid. (From Robert R. Blake and Jane S. Mouton, *The Managerial Grid*, Gulf Publishing Company, Houston, 1964, p. 10. Copyright Gulf Publishing Company; reproduced with permission.)

Concern for people (vertical axis, Low 1 to High 9); **Concern for production** (horizontal axis, Low 1 to High 9).

- **1,9 Management**: Thoughtful attention to needs of people for satisfying relationships leads to a comfortable friendly organization atmosphere and work tempo
- **9,9 Management**: Work accomplishment is from committed people; interdependence through a "common stake" in organization purpose leads to relationships of trust and respect
- **5,5 Management**: Adequate organization performance is possible through balancing the necessity of getting out work with maintaining morale of people at a satisfactory level
- **1,1 Management**: Exertion of minimum effort to get work done is appropriate to sustain organization membership
- **9,1 Management**: Efficiency in operations results from arranging conditions of work in such a way that human elements interfere to a minimum degree

production
people

shall then consider the implications of the grid and its use in developing a 9,9 supervisory approach. We begin by considering the 9,1 supervisory style, in which there is a high concern for _____ but a low concern for _____.

is not
low

53 Under the 9,1 style people are regarded as instruments of production, and emphasis is given to the use of formal authority. As a result, the full development of employees generally [is / is not] attained, and employee morale is typically [high / low].

54 However, employee reaction to the 9,1 approach is not universally negative. The approach is most likely to be effective when the educational level of subordinates is [high / low] and the employees are generally [aggressive / submissive].

low
submissive

55 In contrast, the 1,9 supervisory style describes a low concern for production coupled with a high concern for people. As applied to Likert's studies, described in the preceding section of this unit, this describes [employee-centered / production-centered / neither] type of supervision.

neither (The employee-centered supervisors in those studies also displayed concern for production.)

56 Under the 1,9 approach production standards are generally described as being ["demanding" / "reasonable"] and individual and group conflict is [encouraged / discouraged].

"reasonable"

discouraged

57 Furthermore, under the 1,9 approach there is a tendency for goals (as well as procedures) to be set by [the supervisor / the work group].

the work group

58 The 1,1 management style describes a lack of concern for both production and people. Overall, it implies that the supervisor has a [high / low] level of involvement in his job.

low

59 The supervisor who uses this approach tends to see himself as a message carrier between managerial levels and among the individuals at his organizational level. By this approach, the likelihood that an error in decision making will be attributed to him is [high / low].

low (One way of avoiding mistakes is not to make decisions.)

60 Consistent with his tendency to avoid situations in which he might expose himself, the supervisor who follows the 1,1 approach tends to [welcome / avoid] contact with higher-level managers.

avoid

61 Of the three managerial styles we have considered thus far, the one in which the supervisor has decided

	that "people come before production" is the ____, the one in which "production comes before people" is the ____, and the one in which the supervisor avoids any true managerial commitment is the ____.
1,9	
9,1	
1,1	

62 In the middle of the grid, the 5,5 managerial style identifies the supervisor who has moderate concern for both production and people. However, his attitude is that optimum production and optimum morale [are / are not] possible simultaneously.

are not

63 Therefore, the 5,5 supervisor finds it necessary to combine a level of concern for people with that for production so that a kind of workable balance is achieved—one that results in [optimum / acceptable] productivity and [optimum / acceptable] morale.

acceptable
acceptable

64 Historically, the hostile and antagonistic reactions to 9,1 management produced an overreaction toward the 1,9 direction in many organizations. The subsequent swing of the pendulum has frequently resulted in the search for a *balance* by adopting the ____ approach.

5,5

65 Finally, of the several managerial approaches identified in Figure 14.3, the one that is based on the assumption that there is no necessary and inherent conflict between the organization's production requirements and the needs of people is the ____ approach.

9,9

66 Since the 9,9 supervisory approach assumes that people have a need to be involved and committed to productive work, employee participation in work planning is [encouraged / discouraged].

encouraged

67 Put the other way, this means that through individual and group contribution and accomplishment both high ____ and high ____ are achieved in the organization.

productivity; morale

68 Of the five supervisory approaches we have considered, four of them implicitly or explicitly assume that there is an inherent conflict between productivity and morale. The extreme approach oriented entirely

9,1   toward productivity because "that's what people are paid for" is the ____ method. The extreme approach oriented entirely toward human relations because "satisfied people in a friendly group will be productive" is the ____ method.

1,9

69   The approach by which the supervisor tries to "balance" pressure for production with consideration for morale is the ____ method. A supervisor accustomed to a 9,1 approach who runs into employee resistance on the one hand and increased staff control on the other may finally adopt the passive managerial attitude described by the ____ method.

5,5

1,1

70   The approach that presumes a high level of maturity and results in employee involvement and participation in job planning within the context of established objectives is the ____ approach.

9,9

Overcoming Resistance to Change

In addition to organizational responsibility for achieving high production with and through a high level of employee morale and motivation, the supervisor has seen the pace of technological progress add an important ingredient of another sort to this job. Technological improvements frequently necessitate changes in work organization, methods, and procedures, and thus they have a disruptive effect on the social organization at the workplace. A common group reaction to this threat of disruption is resistance to the change. Although this resistance is occasionally overt, as in organized restriction of production, more often it involves a subtle withholding of effort, perhaps to "prove" that the change won't work and should be abandoned. In this section we summarize the results of the now classic study by Coch and French[2] which is concerned precisely with this type of supervisory problem.

71   The studies by Coch and French were done in the main plant of the Harwood Manufacturing Corporation, a garment manufacturer located in Virginia. One

---

[2]Lester Coch and John R. P. French, "Overcoming Resistance to Change," *Human Relations*, vol. 1, no. 4, 1948, pp. 512–532.

Overcoming Resistance to Change • 451

of the most serious problems faced on the supervisory level was the resistance of sewing-machine operators to necessary changes in methods and jobs. From the standpoint of organizational objectives, this resistance led to lower levels of _____.

production

72 For jobs in which a significant change had occurred, management found that only 38 percent of the sewing-machine operators recovered to the standard of sixty units per hour. The other 62 percent either became chronically substandard operators or quit employment after the job change. Furthermore, the experienced operators took longer to recover their original level of production than the time required for new employees to reach the same level. The factor directly associated with this depressing effect on production was the job _____.

change

73 Despite special monetary allowances and discussions with the union the problems associated with the job changes continued. The purpose of the research by Coch and French was to find out (1) why people resist change and (2) what can be done about it. Thus, the first necessary step in the study was to devise a tentative explanation, or theory, for [the reason for the productivity problems / the way of solving the productivity problems].

the reason for the productivity problems

74 One possible explanation for the depressed productivity following a change was that the eight-week period required to recover standard levels represented an unavoidable learning phenomenon. Would the fact that new operators achieved standard production more rapidly than those experiencing the change contradict this explanation? [Yes / No]

No (Discussion continues next frame.)

75 If previous job habits tended to interfere with new job requirements, resulting in "negative transfer" from the standpoint of learning theory, we would expect experienced operators to require [more / less] time than new operators.

more

76 To test this possible explanation, employees whose jobs had been changed were interviewed, and time-and-motion studies were conducted. The changed operators rarely complained of "wanting to do it the old way," and the time-and-motion studies showed very few false moves after the first week of change, indicating that negative transfer [was / **was not**] the principal factor in the recovery problem.

77 It was also found that the level of the operators' productivity before the change was unrelated to the extent of difficulty following the change, further suggesting that the principal problem might be one involving [learning / **motivation**].

78 Therefore, Coch and French devised a motivational explanation for the difficulties associated with the job changes. They suggested that the individual's desire to quickly recover the standard production level and incentive pay interacts with the perceived difficulty of the task during the first stage of change, resulting in a condition of frustration. This condition of frustration shared by a number of individuals then leads to several possible outcomes. When the work group is highly cohesive (i.e., the members are psychologically close to one another) and in addition has negative attitudes toward management, the most likely result is [continued effort to recover / **group restriction of production** / individual employee terminations].

79 When the work group is highly cohesive and has positive attitudes toward management, the most likely result is [**continued effort to recover** / group restriction of production / individual employee terminations].

80 When the people in the work group are not particularly friendly with one another, i.e., when the group is not cohesive, the most likely result of the job change is [continued effort to recover / group restriction of production / **individual employee terminations**].

81 Therefore, the divergent results of successful recovery on the one hand and organized restriction of production on the other hand are both associated with work groups that are _____.   *cohesive*

82 However, Coch and French suggested that *two* factors were necessary to attaining a high proportion of successful recovery: the work group has to be _____ **cohesive; positive** and has to have _____ attitudes toward management.

83 With this tentative explanation in mind, the researchers suggested that the extent of individual and group *participation* in planning the job change would affect both cohesiveness and attitudes. At this point in the research, then, Coch and French were addressing themselves to [why people resist change / **what could be done about resistance to change**].

84 Although they studied a number of work groups under varying conditions, three basic types of conditions were designated in order to test the effects of participation. In the *no-participation* condition employees did not participate in planning the job change, but an explanation of the change and the reasons for it were given to them. In the *participation-through-representation* condition, selected operators from the group worked with supervisory personnel in planning the necessary changes. In the *total-participation* condition all members of the group participated in planning the change. In terms of their underlying theory, the researchers predicted that the condition most successful in achieving recovery in productivity would be the _____ **total-participation** condition.

85 Figure 14.4 summarizes the results of these studies. Note that production figures are indicated for periods both before and after the job change. Before the change, production levels for the three types of groups were [**about the same** / markedly different].

86 After the change, however, employees working under different conditions of participation differed markedly in productivity. The most successful groups were those working under conditions of _____ **total participation** _____ .

87 Still in Figure 14.4, we see that the least successful group, and the one in which there is an apparent re-

454 ● Chapter 14 ● Effective Supervision

```
— — — Total participation
- - - - - Participation through representation
——— No participation (control group)
```

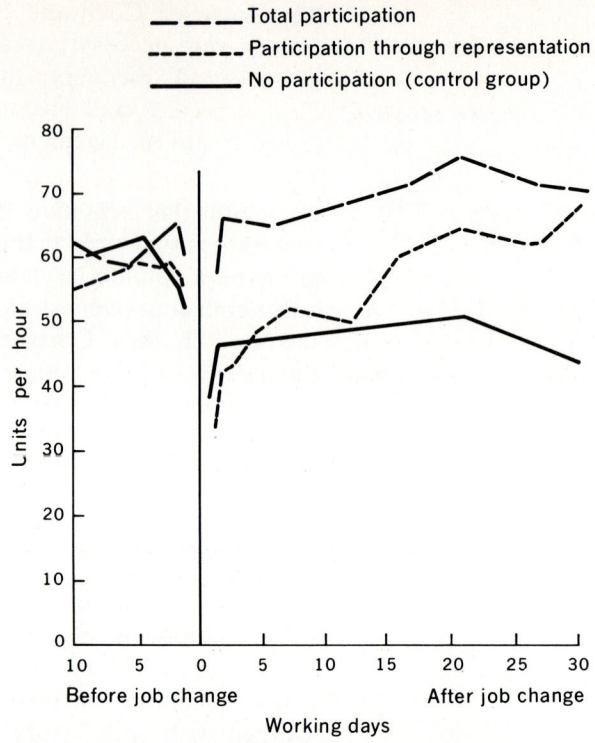

Figure 14.4 Conditions of job change as associated with productivity after the change. (Adapted from Lester Coch and John R. P. French, "Overcoming Resistance to Change," *Human Relations*, vol. 1, no. 4, 1948, p. 523. Reproduced with permission.)

no-participation

striction of production at about fifty units per hour, is the _____ group.

do not (Rather, the conditions of change accounted for the differences.)

88 The researchers also assigned the same people to different conditions of job change and found the results to be the same as those reported in Figure 14.4, thus conclusively demonstrating that differences among the people [do / do not] account for the observed differences in recovering productivity.

participation

89 Overall, the studies at the Harwood Manufacturing Corporation demonstrated that one solution to the employee resistance often encountered during job change is that of providing more opportunity for employee _____ in planning the change.

90 Of course, this approach cannot be applied as an isolated technique, but, rather, it must be applied as part of a management philosophy oriented toward assigning [more / less] authority and responsibility to employees at the operative level.

more

91 However, note also that in the studies at the Harwood Manufacturing Corporation employees working under the total-participation condition had the authority to determine [what the changed objectives should be / how the changed objectives were to be achieved].

how the changed objectives were to be achieved

Review

92 Of the several viewpoints regarding the supervisor's appropriate role, the one that considers the position particularly important because it represents the link with operative employees in the organization is the _____ view. The viewpoint that this organizational position makes the individual vulnerable to pressures from "both sides" is the _____ view. (Frames 1 to 11)

key-person

person-in-the-middle

93 The viewpoint that the supervisor's position results in the individual being accepted neither as a manager nor as a worker is the _____ _____ view. To the extent that a supervisor identifies himself or herself more as an operative employee than as a manager, that supervisor is in fact expressing a belief in the _____ _____ view. (Frames 12 to 18)

marginal-person

another-worker

94 The view suggesting that the supervisor's primary role is that of being a specialist in handling "people problems" is the _____ view. (Frames 19 to 27)

behavioral specialist

95 In the studies of employee productivity and morale conducted by Rensis Likert and his colleagues at the University of Michigan, the effects of two kinds of supervisory approaches were studied. These were the _____ centered and _____ centered approaches. (Frames 28 to 35)

production-;
employee-

96 One of the principal findings of the studies was

that low-productivity sections tended to have production-centered supervisors. Further, in terms of the direction of cause and effect, it was concluded that [productivity affected the supervisory approach / the supervisory approach affected productivity]. (Frames 36 to 41)

the supervisory approach affected productivity

97 As defined in the University of Michigan studies, employee-centered supervisors gave attention to the [human / impersonal / human and impersonal] components of their jobs. (Frames 42 to 49)

human and impersonal

98 In the managerial grid, the approach by which the supervisor gives full attention to production rather than to people is designated _____ management, whereas giving extensive attention to people rather than to production is designated _____ management. (Frames 50 to 57)

9, 1

1, 9

99 The supervisor who fails to stress either production or human relations and regards himself or herself as a kind of communication link rather than as a decision maker is practicing _____ management, whereas the attempt to balance a concern for production with that for people is designated as _____ management. (Frames 58 to 64)

1, 1

5, 5

100 Of the supervisory approaches described on the managerial grid, the only one that presumes no inherent conflict between the goals of achieving optimum production and optimum morale is the _____ approach. (Frames 65 to 70)

9, 9

101 In their studies of employee resistance to change at the Harwood Manufacturing Corporation, Coch and French concluded that the relevant explanation primarily concerned employee [learning / motivation]. (Frames 71 to 78)

motivation

102 Further, they suggested that two conditions had to exist to make successful adjustment to job change most likely: the work group has to be _____ and the group members need to have _____ attitudes toward management. (Frames 79 to 82)

cohesive

positive

**total
participation**

103 In testing their proposed solution to the resistance-to-change problem, Coch and French designated three conditions under which the job change took place; the employees that were consistently superior in adapting successfully to the change were those working under the so-called _____ _____ condition. (Frames 83 to 91)

Discussion Questions

1. In your view, how has the role of the first-level supervisor in manufacturing firms changed in the past twenty years?
2. Do you think that the first-level supervisor is or should be considered the key person in management? Why?
3. In what type of organization is the first-level supervisor most likely to be thought of as being primarily a behavioral specialist? Why?
4. What's all this nonsense about encouraging supervisors to be employee-centered? After all, aren't they (and other employees) being paid to get out the production?
5. In Likert's studies, production-centered supervisors were concerned about production as such, whereas employee-centered supervisors combined an interest in people and production. Why do you suppose Likert does not report any finding for supervisors with a concern for people but not production?
6. How has the managerial grid helped to identify the implications of various types of supervisory practices?
7. Discuss the key elements associated with achieving a successful change in procedures of work, assuming technical feasibility.
8. In terms of the objectives of the respective studies, how did the studies conducted by the University of Michigan group and those carried out at the Harwood Manufacturing Corporation differ? In what respects are the results of the two series of studies similar?

References

Anthony, T. F., and A. B. Carroll. "Preventing Supervision from Becoming an End-of-the-Line Job." *Personnel Journal,* vol. 56, no. 6, June 1977.

Archer, E. R. "Delegation and the 'Dirty Hands' Syndrome." *Supervisory Management,* vol. 22, no. 11, November 1977.

Begosh, D. G. "So You Want to Be a Supervisor." *Supervisory Management,* vol. 23, no. 2, February 1978.

Benson, C. A. "New Supervisors: From the Top of the Heap to the Bottom of the Heap." *Personnel Journal,* vol. 55, no. 4, April 1976.
Blake, R. R., and J. S. Mouton. *The Managerial Grid.* Houston: Gulf, 1964.
Blake, R. R., and J. S. Mouton. "What's New with the Grid?" *Training and Development Journal,* vol. 32, no. 5, May 1978.
Boyd, B. B., and J. M. Jensen. "Perceptions of the First-Line Supervisor's Authority: A Study in Superior-Subordinate Communication." *Academy of Management Journal,* vol. 15, no. 3, September 1972.
Carroll, A. B., and T. F. Anthony. "An Overview of the Supervisor's Job." *Personnel Journal,* vol. 55, no. 5, May 1976.
Cascio, W. F. "Functional Specialization, Culture, and Preference for Participative Management." *Personnel Psychology,* vol. 27, no. 4, Winter 1974.
Coch, L., and J. R. P. French. "Overcoming Resistance to Change." *Human Relations,* vol. 1, no. 4, August 1948.
Davis, K. *Human Behavior at Work. Organizational Behavior,* 5th ed. New York: McGraw-Hill, 1977.
Evans, M. G. "Extensions of a Path-Goal Theory of Motivation." *Journal of Applied Psychology,* vol. 59, no. 2, April 1974.
Glueck, W. F. "Organizational Change in Business and Government." *Academy of Management Journal,* vol. 12, no. 4, December 1969.
Hammer, T. H., and H. P. Dachler. "A Test of Some Assumptions Underlying the Path Goal Model of Supervision: Some Suggested Conceptual Modifications." *Organizational Behavior and Human Performance,* vol. 14, no. 1, August 1975.
Hershey, P., and K. H. Blanchard. "The Management of Change." *Training and Development Journal,* vol. 26, no. 1, January 1972.
King, A. S. "Expectation Effects in Organizational Change." *Administrative Science Quarterly,* vol. 19, no. 2, June 1974.
Kirton, M. J., and G. Mulligan. "Correlates of Managers' Attitudes toward Change." *Journal of Applied Psychology,* vol. 58, no. 1, August 1973.
Kotter, J. P., and L. A. Schlesinger. "Choosing Strategies for Change." *Harvard Business Review,* vol. 57, no. 2, March-April 1979.
Lorsch, J. "Managing Change." In P. Lawrence et al. *Organizational Behavior and Administration.* Homewood, Ill.: Irwin Dorsey Press, 1976.
Margulies, N., and J. Wallace. *Organization Change: Techniques and Applications.* Chicago: Scott, Foresman, 1973.
Mealiea, L. W. "Employee Resistance to Change: A Learned Response Management Can Prevent." *Supervisory Management,* vol. 23, no. 1, January 1978.
Niehouse, O. L., and K. B. Massoni. "Stress—An Inevitable Part of Change." *SAM Advanced Management Journal,* vol. 44, no. 2, Spring 1979.
Oldham, G. R. "The Motivational Strategies Used by Supervisors: Relationships to Effectiveness Indicators." *Organizational Behavior and Human Performance,* vol. 15, no. 1, February 1976.

Powell, G., and B. Z. Posner. "Resistance to Change Reconsidered: Implications for Managers." *Human Resource Management,* vol. 17, no. 1, Spring 1978.
Powell, R. M., and J. L. Schlacter. "Participative Management: A Panacea?" *Academy of Management Journal,* vol. 14, no. 2, June 1971.
Smith, H. L. "An Empirical Approach to Change." *Supervisory Management,* vol. 24, no. 1, January 1979.
Terry, G. "The Supervisor of the (Near) Future." *Training and Development Journal,* vol. 31, no. 1, January 1977.
Wallach, A. E. "The Man in the Middle." *Personnel Journal,* vol. 56, no. 12, December 1977.
Weiss, A. J. "How to Influence People outside Your Control." *Supervisory Management,* vol. 22, no. 12, December 1977.

CASE STUDY: A Change of Supervisory Philosophy at Triflex

Following a series of executive-level conferences aimed at defining the company's human relations outlook and policies at the Triflex Manufacturing Company, manufacturer of home appliances, a committee of top company officers decided that the supervisory implications of the program should be communicated through the company's management development programs. To ascertain that both supervisors and middle managers interpret the new policies in a similar manner, they have directed the coordinator of management development to include at least two levels of management in all conference sessions.

Generally, the new company philosophy emphasizes the acceptance of employee-oriented motivational methods as an addition to the production-oriented philosophy that has been typical of the company's operations. Accordingly, the management development conferences have included a review of motivation theory, summaries of industrial motivation studies, and the implications of these findings to the effective supervision of personnel.

After two months of scheduled weekly conferences, the top management objective of achieving a consensus at both the first level and middle level of management does not appear to be materializing. Whereas most resistance had been anticipated at the supervisory level, it is actually the superintendents in factory operations who appear most resistant. Although the supervisors' commitment to the new methods is still largely at the "lip-service" level, they have at least indicated willingness to give the employee-oriented motivational methods a try. The superintendents, on the other hand, do not believe that the methods are even relevant to their jobs.

As the superintendents and certain other middle managers see it, the company's interest in employee-oriented methods has the objective of avoiding certain labor relations difficulties which are developing in some of the company's plants. Because of this, both the new human relations policies and the supervisory methods derived from them are oriented toward the operative level, rather than having implications for the supervision of managers. They believe that top management should acknowledge the fact that first-level supervisors are in a basically different supervisory situation from that of higher-level managers, and that it is not only wasteful of time but also ineffective to require managers at higher levels to use methods oriented toward operative employees. They agree that employee-oriented methods are useful as motivational methods, but they believe that anyone in a management position should not need to be motivated as such.

1. Do you agree with the superintendents' point of view? Why or why not?
2. Given the present division of opinion between first-level supervisors and superintendents, what is likely to be the level of success in implementing the new company philosophy at the operative-worker level?
3. In what respects did the top management proceed correctly in attempting to redefine the company human relations policies?
4. What additional things could have been or should be done to achieve acceptance of the philosophy at all levels? Should the same philosophy be applicable at all managerial levels?

CASE STUDY: An Analysis of Operating Procedures

Jane Rauch, in charge of the billing department, was called by the controller one morning and was informed that the company was considering some changes in procedures and methods in conjunction with the planned installation of a new computer system. Therefore, some systems people from the hardware manufacturer wished to study the present procedures and methods being used in a number of departments, including the billing department. Further, the schedule called for the analysis in the billing department to be performed on Monday through Wednesday of the following week. After the call Ms. Rauch informed the three office supervisors of the planned visit by the systems analysts and also posted a notice on the bulletin board which indicated that the visit was related to the planned installation of the new computer system.

Promptly at 8:30 A.M. on the following Monday two computer systems analysts arrived in the department and introduced themselves to Ms. Rauch. They spent a few minutes having coffee and generally discussing the improvements and economies which can result from a more comprehensive use of the capabilities associated with recent technological advances in computers. Jane Rauch then introduced the analysts to the supervisors in the department, and they began their work by talking with the supervisors as well as with senior personnel in the department about the procedures and methods being followed. Ms. Rauch did not pay much attention to the analysts during the remainder of the day, particularly because of some additions to the billing procedure which she needed to implement.

Just after lunch on the second day of their visit in the department the two systems analysts stopped at Jane Rauch's office and asked if they could meet privately with her. After the office door was shut, one of the analysts explained the reason for their meeting by saying, "We're having quite a problem with our analysis in your department. Either we're having difficulties communicating with your supervisors and senior personnel, or else they are deliberately trying to foul up our analysis. The two of us discussed the situation at length during lunch today, and we believe that the confusion is deliberate on their part. The people we have talked with have tried to make the procedures more complicated than they really are by always dwelling on the exceptions instead of describing the typical procedures used. For this reason, we think it would be best for us to terminate this analysis until we can get better cooperation from your people."

1. Assuming that the analysts' diagnosis of the source of confusion is correct, why might the supervisors have reacted as they did?
2. What might Jane Rauch have done differently to avoid the problem that developed?
3. Did the controller follow an appropriate procedure in the way he informed Jane Rauch of the study to be made by the systems analysts?
4. What should Ms. Rauch do now?

APPLICATIONS READING:

Rethinking the Supervisory Role

David S. Brown, Ph.D.
Professor of Management
School of Government and Business Administration
George Washington University

Once upon a time, supervising was simple. The work to be supervised was relatively uncomplicated, subordinates knew what was expected of them, and there was no doubt as to what would happen if their responsibilities were not met.

The supervisor himself was a person with both expertness and experience. He had probably come up through the ranks; he had learned the job the hard way; and because of this expertness and his loyalty to the company, he was chosen for a position of honor and responsibility.

Furthermore, the supervisor was close to those he supervised. When they failed to produce, he was immediately aware of it and could do something about it. He had little to worry about in terms of either union or governmental interference. By and large, he knew he would be supported topside.

This is the way things used to be. But somewhere along the line, something changed. Today most supervisors feel caught in the middle between management and labor and are unsure of the support of either. One consistent complaint supervisors make is that they are bypassed from above as well as below.

What Happened?

The fact is that the decades since the 1930s have seen many significant changes in the supervisor's role. Technological changes have had their impact, but of even more importance than these have been the societal changes that have taken place. Today the supervisor is not only a supervisor; he must be a lawyer, counselor, social worker, training specialist, and "PR" man as well.

Of course, I was overstating my case when I said that supervision was once easy. Being a *good* supervisor has never been easy. But in comparison with some of the requirements that today's supervisor must meet, it was certainly much simpler and a great deal more rewarding to be a supervisor a couple of decades ago than it is now. It is time these operating changes were recognized, and *it is also time for management to stop blaming supervisors for the kinds of problems*

Source: From *Supervisory Management*, vol. 22, no. 11, November 1977; AMACOM, a division of American Management Associations. Reprinted by permission of David S. Brown.

that exist in industry and to develop more constructive approaches to these problems.

Let us try to understand why the supervisory role has become so difficult in modern business. Among the major causes of this decline are changes in the society, changes in the workforce, and changes in the job itself.

Changes in Society

The social pot may have come to a boil in America during the late 1960s and early 1970s, but the fire under it had been there for a long time. The basic American credo—which all of us have so long professed belief in—promises life, liberty, the pursuit of happiness, and, by implication, much else. In addition, we endorse the view that *no one* should be excluded from these promises any more. It is only a question of time before promises become expectations, and now that time has arrived.

Let me elaborate on this statement. In recent years, television and other communications have made available to everyone the values and ideas once shared only by a few. The affluence of the middle and upper classes has been made highly visible to those who do not share it—and there are many people in the latter situation, as national income figures make inescapably clear.

Those who watch television see the many new forms of power available to the have-nots. There is the power of people in the streets, of mass demonstrations and marches, of confrontations, and of work slowdowns and stoppages. If television does nothing else, it reminds the viewer that by being action-oriented, he is only being American. He uses his tongue, his fists, his guns to support his demands. So the approach that overcame the forests, crossed the plains, and breasted the mountains is now being applied to internal problems.

The motor car has also underlined and added to this feeling of Americans' independence and activism. It made it possible for the Okies to go west and for those in the Southern cotton fields to get to the large cities. But it has also done something else. It has provided a mobility to the American population that has deprived it of roots and to a certain degree also of stability. The automobile has become our national "get away" vehicle, with all that this label implies.

But no changes in American society have been greater than those in education. Not only do children stay longer in school than ever before, but they are also the targets of a different kind of education than their elders received. This begins with the basis idea—consistent with American philosophy—that each of us should have the opportunity to develop our capabilities to their fullest. It encourages each of us to discover ourselves, to seek our own way and our own identity. And it often does this with little attention as to whether or not there is any place, once we are "developed," for us to go.

Changes in the Workforce

Paralleling the changes in society, major changes have taken place in the national workforce over the last three decades. The majority of today's workers are white, rather than blue collared. Indeed, the term blue collar has lost much of its original meaning. Many of those who fill what would have once been described as blue collar jobs now resent the classification and, in effect, try to declassify themselves.

Additionally, more than a third of today's workforce are women; nearly 40 percent of all women, in fact, are gainfully employed outside the home. And of those workers entering the labor force in the next few years, the majority will be women. Also, the educational level of those who work for a living is rising. Over 80 percent of those between 20 and 29 are high school graduates, and currently a record eight million people are in college, which presages a much more educated workforce in the future.

One major change in today's workers is that those who will make a career of one job in one organization are clearly in the minority. Figures indicate that approximately 20 percent of all American families change their place of residence each year, indicating a high job turnover rate as well. The 20-year-old—whether male or female—who enters the labor force this year may well be in eight to ten different lines of work before retirement. This places a major burden on training systems.

The workforce of the future can be expected also to include larger numbers of blacks and persons of Spanish origins than in the past. Each will bring his own cultural characteristics to the workplace.

Changes such as these, testifying to the new nature of the workforce, are also a reminder that there are major changes in worker-held values as well. In fact, the "work culture" is a considerably different one from what it was a few decades ago.

Generally, work is seen today in a variety of ways, depending upon those who are looking at it. There are some who regard it as a major life objective; others see it as a means to some other end; still others only think of it as a burden. By and large, Americans still work hard—harder than workers in almost any other country—but they have in recent years become more selective in terms of the things they will and won't do.

These workers' views are shaped by the society in which they live. While it is not easy to generalize about these views, such studies as the Department of Health, Education, and Welfare's task report on *Work in America* (1973) make clear some of the demands that workers at all levels are laying before management:

> What the workers want most, as more than 100 studies in the past 20 years show, is to become masters of their immediate environ-

ments and to feel that their work and they themselves are important—the twin ingredients of self-esteem. Workers recognize that some of the dirty jobs can be transformed only into the merely tolerable, but the most oppressive features of work are felt to be avoidable: constant supervision and coercion, lack of variety, monotony, meaningless tasks, and isolation. An increasing number of workers want more autonomy in tackling their tasks, greater opportunity for increasing their skills, rewards that are directly connected to the intrinsic aspects of work, and greater participation in the design of work and formulation of their tasks.

No one should be surprised by sentiments such as these. The American nation has endured a turbulent decade and a half marked by demands for greater freedom of the individual, a fuller expression of human rights, greater opportunities for personal development, and a larger share of the affluence around us. Never a placid or serene society, we have become increasingly a loud and demanding one. The worker at the lathe or behind the counter is not to be excluded from his (or her) entitlements.

Changes in the Job

Not least among the changes that have affected supervisory practices are changes in the nature of the modern organization. No longer is work performed in traditional ways. Factors having to do with space (that is, distance), specialization, client relationships, and power patterns have all had their effect.

The Distance Factor There is no factor that changes the rules of supervision more drastically than that of distance. Distance diminishes direction, so a subordinate out of sight of his supervisor has a freedom not shared by those who sit at desks or work at machines under his watchful eye. The former may be held accountable for performing a given amount of work (when it can be calculated), but he also has a large degree of freedom in terms of how his work is to be done. This is why so many journeyman jobs, such as mailman, garbage collector, bus driver, and serviceman, are eagerly sought by those who understand their own and society's limitations.

But one need not stop here. There are many other jobs of a higher level that also recommend themselves for the same reason: The holder virtually assures himself of freedom from close or direct supervision. These include sales people, teachers, policemen, and social workers who spend much of their time away from headquarters. Such jobs may have their shortcomings, but they do contain a substantial amount of independence that is not to be overlooked.

The Specialized Job   Those who become highly proficient in the performing of a task earn the right to free themselves from the close and watchful attention of their supervisors. Furthermore, often the supervisor is incapable of providing the guidance that was once given. More often, he chooses to regard the individual's work area as a private domain only to be entered when things go wrong. Some supervisors manage to keep well-enough informed so that they will know what to do in the event of the subordinate's illness or resignation, but they make a point, for good reason, of staying well out of the way.

As examples, the scientist and the researcher have unique roles that earn them the right to be spared traditional supervision. As adjutants, helpers, and apprentices have been added, these people also have acquired some of this independence. The technician is, after all, only a step below the professional.

Jobs that require creativity are similarly minimally supervised: writers, artists, designers, advertising people, planners, architects, media people, analysts, and photographers, to name a few. There are ways of influencing newspaper men and women, of course, but traditional supervisory approaches are usually not among these.

New Processes and Equipment   New tools produce new practices. This is particularly true when new processes are introduced or new equipment installed. Not having established guidelines to direct them, those who are involved with the new systems tend to develop their own. They can be counted on to argue for those guidelines that insure them the greatest independence for individual action.

Special Sources of Power   Power may be acquired and wielded in a variety of ways. It can be acquired by subordinates as well as by superiors and can even be legitimized when so held. That this kind of power is usually spoken of as being countervailing does not make it any less real.

The existence of a union—or even the fear of unionization—is a threat to managerial power. The supervisor may have the legal right to recommend an adverse action but may be persuaded not to do so for obvious reasons. There are many other forms of power that limit the ability of supervisors to do some of the things that are expected of them.

There is, for example, the job with its own constituency. In these cases, the subordinate enjoys such a close relationship with the client that management fears to disturb the situation even when it is dissatisfied with some of the things the subordinate is doing. There are employees with special information about the company or program, information that the company would not like to have end up in the hands of a competitor, the press, or the government. And there are those who do jobs no one else cares to do and, by so doing, free themselves from supervisory restraints.

There is also the disagreeable person who insists on having his own way—and gets it because no one wants to tangle with him. And there is the subordinate with several supervisors who proves the old adage, "Those who work for several bosses work for themselves." Finally, there are the "floating" jobs that elude the controls of the usual organizational system.

Implications for Management

Changes in the workforce such as these are not minor; the whole nature of the managerial system is affected by them. They help to explain why today's supervisor is finding supervision in its traditional pattern so difficult to carry out. Not only is the average employee less willing than ever before to be directed, but the changing nature of the organization has produced jobs that are virtually unsupervisable as well.

Does this mean that supervision as such is going out of style? Hardly. But it does mean that older patterns are being replaced by newer ones that emphasize larger acceptance of individual responsibilities at all levels, including those at the bottom; a greater measure of individual freedom on the job; a fuller appreciation of individual worth and dignity; and the need for improving the quality of working life.

These factors call for something more useful than the usual simple—and simplistic—diagnosis that the root of most personnel problems lies with first-line supervisors. What is really needed is a better understanding at all levels of what is taking place in the minds of the American workforce and a new approach that is intelligent, relevant, and doable. It is of no value to continue to reiterate homilies that have long since outworn their usefulness.

A New Meaning for Supervision

There needs to be, as a point of departure, a better appreciation by management of the supervisory role. Traditionally, the first-line supervisor has been held responsible for whatever goes wrong. This is no longer a tenable approach. What is needed is a rethinking of the supervisory role at *all* organizational levels, because this role, in its traditional form, no longer enhances the work system nor is it really acceptable to those who fill the majority of American jobs. This applies not only to those who are supervised but to those who supervise as well. Being a supervisor is the price one must pay in most organizational systems for "getting ahead." And so it is endured, but it has never really developed.

In the long run, it may be more useful to try to *reduce* the supervisory role rather than "improve" it. This is not fantasy. It can be done. In fact, it is already taking place, as the examples given above of jobs with minimal or no supervision suggest. In some respects, we are already seeing the birth of a new, fifth freedom—*a freedom from supervision*—to go with the traditional freedom of speech, freedom of religion, freedom from want, and freedom from fear. That this has occurred in an evolutionary, rather than in a more dramatic, fashion makes it no less substantial. The cumulation of small changes can often produce effects of a revolutionary nature.

Management has often been an active partner in the process. It has done this by granting increased autonomy to those at lesser levels. It has created profit centers where individuals and groups can pursue their own initiatives. It has developed systems of licensing, jobbing, and subcontracting. Many executives have voluntarily broadened spans of supervision or control, fully realizing that, since supervisors have more people to watch over, each worker will be supervised less closely. Many an executive has learned that the best supervision is often the least.

This even suggests there is a need for a rethinking of the word "supervision" in favor of some more acceptable term for this kind of management. In its present form, the term implies the idea of superintendency, oversight, guardianship, and control, which so many people find objectionable. Certainly a nation that has gained so much from an individualistic ethos can make greater use of it in its organizational systems.

A number of institutions have indeed found other ways of approaching the problem and use terms with fewer emotional connotations. The problem, however, is more than a terminological one; it involves the development of more useful forms of institutional action.

Influence vs. Control

"Are we not more interested," Chester Barnard—the noted executive and writer—once asked, "in influence than in control?" The question answers itself. We seek to extend our influence; this is what management is all about. Control is only a means to such an end, and there are other means that are usually more effective.

The manager, whether he be a high-level executive or a first-line supervisor, will already have discovered as much. But it is an easy idea to forget as pressures mount. When something goes wrong, the lights begin to flash and the bells to ring. The system demands *action*, and action usually takes the form of directives and controls.

What the manager must learn to cultivate are ways by which his influence can be increased. There are many of these. He must understand what his—and the organization's—objectives are. He must understand why they are what they are. He must be articulate in putting them forward. He must be willing to hear what others at all levels have to say.

He must know his people—not only those closest to him but those several jobs away—who are important to the good health of the enterprise. He must be able to generalize from what he sees and hears.

The manager needs to think of himself as someone whose life is involved with learning and teaching. He is, in fact, committed to persuading others that what he seeks is important also to them.

The Need for Training

A further word needs to be said for training. The more one turns away from control systems, the greater will be his need for teaching and training. These are, of course, the functions of helping others to acquire and apply knowledge, skills, abilities, and attitudes needed by the organization. As such, they are management's most important means of achieving objectives.

Training offers many advantages. Most people are eager to learn if they see it is to their advantage to do so. And it suggests personal development. The perceptive employee knows that he can become more valuable because of his training.

Training is essentially nonauthoritarian in its approach, for training is part of a cultural norm. From his earliest moments, the child has been the object of training. He learns from it, and it provides an interesting and welcome variation to the drudgery of a regular assignment.

Training helps the manager, at whatever level, to become a leader rather than a director or supervisor. This is, and should be, one of his major objectives. Opportunities for leadership go well beyond the organizational structure. In fact, the less we emphasize structure, the more we emphasize true personal leadership. Perhaps this is the most important lesson that can come from any study of supervisory practices.

Questions on Reading

1. What are the principal changes in society that have made the supervisory role more complex?
2. What changes in the work force does David Brown describe as making the supervisory role more difficult?
3. How have changes in jobs affected the supervisory role?
4. What kind of supervisory role does the author suggest is now appropriate in lieu of the traditional control-oriented role?

Controlling

The management functions of planning and controlling are closely related; for while planning is concerned with the formulation of objectives, controlling is concerned with ascertaining that the specified objectives are achieved. In this sense, activities in a firm are set into motion as the result of managerial planning and they are "kept on the right track" by means of the control process.

In Chapter 15 we identify the general steps included in any control process and consider several types of managerial techniques or devices, and particularly the budget, that are used for the purpose of controlling. Possible types of human reactions to control procedures are also considered, along with a positive strategy for gaining employee acceptance of control procedures.

Chapter 16 covers Program Evaluation and Review Technique in some detail as an example of a system-oriented control device which has had relatively wide-spread application in industry. As is true for most control devices, PERT is used as a planning tool as well as a control device.

Part 5

13 THE CONTROL PROCESS

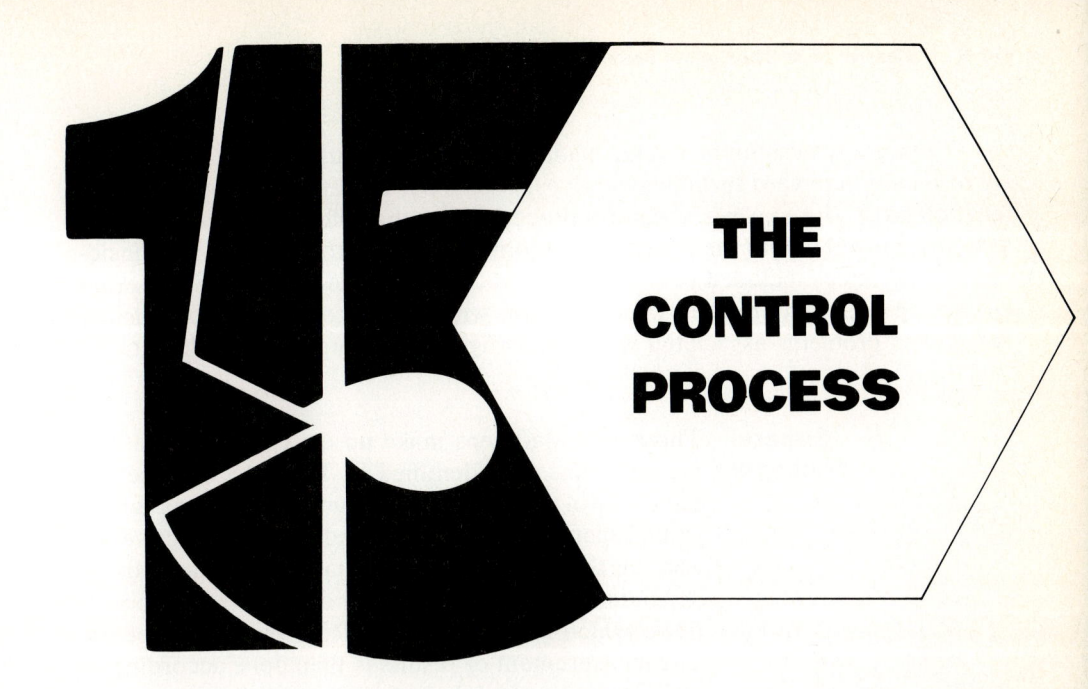

- General Concepts
- Budgetary Control
- Other Control Devices
- Human Reactions to Centralized Control Procedures
- Toward Effective Controls
- Review
- Discussion Questions
- References
- Case Study: Western Office Equipment and Supply Company
- Case Study: Control of In-Process Inventory
- Applications Reading: "Zero-Base Budgeting: Where to Use It and How to Begin" Peter A. Pyhrr
- Questions on Reading

Once any system, be it a mechanical process or a business organization, is set into motion toward specific objectives, events occur that tend to pull that system "off target." A successful control process is one that effects corrections to the system involved before the deviations become serious. In this chapter we consider the basic steps included in any control process, describe the budget and other control devices that are used in conjunction with the process, and also consider the human problems associated with achieving effective organizational control.

General Concepts Three essential steps make up the control process in organizations. As identified in Table 15.1, these are the steps of establishing standards, comparing actual results against the standards, and taking corrective action. Of these, the first step, establishing standards, is dependent on the identification of organization objectives, which is done as part of the planning process. The measurement of results is then done according to the standards which have been established.

Table 15.1 **Three Essential Steps in the Control Process**

Establishing standards
Comparing actual results against the standards
Taking corrective action

standards 1 In the control process, the translation of enterprise goals into specific measurable outcomes, which then become the basis for evaluating performance, constitutes the step of establishing _____.

standard 2 Thus, the level of sales within a department in a retail store is an example of a performance _____.

Yes (And this should be more than a subtraction from total sales, because of the extra expense involved.) 3 In addition to total sales, should the value of returned merchandise be considered in defining a performance standard? [Yes / No]

Yes 4 Should the satisfaction of the customer and his tendency to buy other merchandise in other departments of the store be considered in the standard? [Yes / No]

General Concepts • 475

Yes (In this case, there may be a tendency to carry too much or too little stock.)	**5** Should the quantity of merchandise held in stock be part of the standard used to evaluate departmental performance in the store? [Yes / No]
Yes	**6** Should the standard take into consideration not just the volume of sales but the kind of merchandise sold? [Yes / No]
several	**7** Thus, in defining performance standards we typically find that [one / several] major facet(s) of performance must be considered.
control (or observation, etc.)	**8** Standards can be applied at the level of policies, procedures, or methods. Since entire operations cannot be observed, however, it is necessary to choose certain *points* for the purpose of _____.
control	**9** By definition, a strategic point in an operation that is chosen to be the focal point of control action is called a strategic _____ point.
more	**10** The earlier in a process that a strategic control point is located, the [more / less] likely it will be that deviations can be corrected before the attainment of the organization's goals is affected.
goals (or objectives, etc.)	**11** Strategic control points should be chosen so that the comparisons with the standards at these points are directly reflective of the success in attaining the organization's _____.
strategic control	**12** The standards which are often defined at the _____ points can be of several types. We shall briefly consider *quantity, cost, time use,* and *quality* standards, as listed in Table 15.2.

Table 15.2   Four Principal Types of Standards

Quantity standard
Cost standard
Time use standard
Quality standard

13 Defining expected production volume, sales volume, or the number of people to be employed all involve _____ standards.

quantity

14 Specifying the amount of money to be spent for raw materials or for advertising involves a _____ standard.

cost

15 Setting up a schedule to be followed, or adhered to, in the completion of certain activities involves a _____ standard.

time use

16 The first three types of standards, that is, the _____, _____, and _____ standards, are relatively straightforward in that they readily lend themselves to specific measurement. On the other hand, the quantitative basis for a _____ standard may be more difficult to specify.

quantity; cost; time use

quality

17 Whereas the necessary tolerances for a physical product can be specified in measurable terms, the objective that the credit department should achieve "good public relations," which is also a _____ standard, is harder to specify in quantitative terms.

quality

18 Once the standard of performance is established, the measurement of results at the strategic control points is based on the type of standard involved. Thus, measurement of _____, _____, _____, and _____ may be included.

quantity; cost time use; quality

19 In the measurement of organizational performance, as well as in the definition of standards in the first place, the less tangible quality measurements tend to be relatively [overemphasized / underemphasized].

underemphasized

20 For example, measuring the monthly sales volume achieved by a district sales manager is relatively easy. Measuring his progress in achieving professional development of his sales personnel is [more / less] difficult.

more

21 Along these lines, developing specific cost limitations for travel expenses, for example, but failing to develop any standards for measuring the need or value of the travel in the first place suggests an underemphasis on the measurement of _____ .

quality (or the value of the travel)

22 Not every item at a strategic control point is necessarily measured. The method of *sampling* is often applied in choosing what should be _____ .

measured

23 To the extent that only a portion of the output at the control point is checked and this portion is assumed to be representative of the entire output, the method of _____ is involved.

sampling

24 At the strategic control point, a follow-up is made just for those situations that are [in line / out of line] with the standard. Focusing managerial attention only on those situations that deviate from the standard represents the *principle of exception.*

out of line

25 The restaurant manager who makes a point of checking at random the quality of food being served is applying the method of _____ in carrying out his control activity.

sampling

26 The restaurant manager who investigates the method of food preparation whenever he finds anything wrong or when a specific complaint has been made is following the managerial principle of _____ in carrying out his control activity.

exception

27 The application of sampling [increases / reduces] the number of observations, or measurements, that need to be made at a strategic control point.

reduces

28 Application of the managerial principle of exception [increases / reduces] the number of detailed reviews of procedures that a manager makes in carrying out his control responsibilities.

reduces

29 Thus, the amount of time spent measuring results at strategic control points is minimized by applying the method of _____ , whereas managerial time

sampling

exception

spent in reviewing how results were attained is minimized by applying the managerial principle of _____.

Budgetary Control

Though the process of preparing budgets is associated with the management function of planning, their use is particularly associated with the function of controlling. In order to provide the basis for financial control within the organization, separate budgets are usually prepared for each organization unit within the enterprise for the designated time period. In this section of the chapter we first consider the general characteristics of budgets and then describe five specific types of budgets that can used: operating budgets, cash budgets, appropriation budgets, balance sheet budgets, and variable budgets.

dollar (or monetary; or units that can be converted into dollar amounts, such as man-hours or machine-hours)

30 It has been stated that a budget is a type of plan expressed in quantitative terms. The "quantitative terms" in which budgets are expressed are usually _____ amounts.

establishing standards

31 As indicated in the preceding section, three essential steps in the control process include establishing standards, comparing results with standards, and taking corrective action. In terms of these steps, the preparation of budgets is, in effect, the step of _____.

control
planning

32 The use of budgets to check and correct ongoing expenditures is thus directly a part of the _____ process, whereas setting up the budgets in the first place is part of the _____ process.

cost

33 In terms of the four types of standards described in the preceding section (quantity, cost, time use, and quality), the budgeting process typically involves the use of _____ standards.

34 The use of budgets makes it possible for a manager to compare different organizational units, such as the sales and engineering departments, because of the common basis used for measuring performance, namely, the _____ basis.

monetary (or cost, or financial)

35 However, the observation that budgetary controls may result in an overemphasis on cost reduction and an underemphasis on quality improvement is one of their major [strengths / weaknesses].

weaknesses

36 A general advantage associated with formulating and using budgets is that organizational attention is thereby directed toward the management functions of _____ and _____.

planning; controlling

37 Table 15.3 lists the five types of budgets described in this section. The first specific type of budget is the *operating budget.* An operating budget includes a budget for anticipated revenues and another budget for anticipated expenses. In this context a "sales budget" would be a(n) [revenue / expense] budget.

revenue

Table 15.3 **Types of Budgets**

Operating budget
Cash budget
Appropriation budget
Balance sheet budget
Variable budget

38 In contrast, a budget including an itemization of expected costs would be a(n) _____ budget.

expense

39 Thus, the types of budgets that compose the operating budget are the _____ budget and the _____ budget.

revenue
expense

40 Many products or services experience a seasonal influence with respect to sales. Therefore, the budgeted revenues for different months of the year would be at [the same / different] monetary level(s).

different

41 For firms that are involved in several products

and in several geographic areas, sales budgets by product and by territory [are / are not] required for the purpose of subsequent control action.

are

42 Similarly with respect to the expense budget, the several categories of costs are budgeted individually in order to provide the basis for identifying areas of required control action. Thus, such costs as materials costs, direct labor, indirect labor, overhead, inventory costs, and general administrative costs are generally [consolidated / shown separately].

shown separately

43 The first type of budgeting procedure we have considered, which is directed toward budgeting for anticipated revenues and anticipated expenses, is called the _____ budget.

operating

44 Another type of budget used in business firms is the cash budget. Such a budget can be developed on the basis of the revenues and expenses identified in the operating budget, but with particular attention being given to the anticipated amounts of cash needed during the budgeted period. From this standpoint, a cash budget is principally concerned with the point in time at which merchandise is [sold / paid for].

paid for

45 A cash budget is necessary to assure that an organization will be able to pay bills as they become due. How would it be possible for a company to be operating profitably—that is, for sales to be exceeding costs—and yet not have sufficient cash to pay current liabilities? _____

The sales may result in receivables, in the short run, rather than cash. Also, additional funds may be needed to increase inventories or for additions to capital equipment.

46 If a company anticipates a shortage of cash during an operating period, then early arrangements for short-term borrowing should be made. Along these lines, the condition of the money market should be considered. During the "cash squeeze" accompanying most business recessions, for example, short-term loans are difficult to obtain. In any case, short-term loans generally carry a [higher / lower] rate of interest as compared with long-term financing.

higher

47 On the other hand, if a company anticipates an excess cash position, the financial officer should explore the possibility of obtaining cash discounts from suppliers or consider the use of the funds in short-term investments. Thus, the financial officer generally should try to maintain a [positive / negative] cash balance and should strive to [maximize / minimize] the amount of this balance.

positive
minimize (since excess funds should be "put to work")

48 The type of budget that is concerned with planning for the availability of adequate funds and for the profitable use of any "excess" funds is the _____ budget.

cash

49 In addition to the operating budget and the cash budget, another type of budget is the *appropriation budget*. Such a budget is not concerned with short-term revenues and expenses as such. Rather, an appropriation budget is concerned with the commitment of funds to improve productivity and profitability in the long run. Thus, planned capital expenditures for facilities and equipment [would / would not] be included in such a budget.

would

50 In addition to investments in capital, other expenditures which would be included in an appropriation budget include research and development, institutional advertising, management development programs, and new market development. The feature that all such expenditures have in common is that they are oriented toward improving profitability [within the budget period / in the long run].

in the long run

51 The long-term nature of appropriation expenditures and the fact that limited funds are available for such investments indicate that a careful review of such proposed expenditures is warranted. For this reason, the items to be included in an appropriation budget are

top-management	usually reviewed at the [departmental / top-management] level in the organization.
operating cash; appropriation	**52** Thus far, we have considered three types of budgets used in organizations: _____, _____, and _____ budgets.
assets and liabilities	**53** The fourth type of budget which we now consider is the *balance sheet budget*. Essentially, such a budget represents the intended financial status at the end of the budget period, which is generally the close of the fiscal year. Since attention is directed toward the financial position at a particular point in time, rather than on transactions during a period of time, the items that are included in the projection are [assets and liabilities / receipts and expenditures].
either too low or too high	**54** When the actual balance sheet is prepared at the end of the budget period, a comparison with the balance sheet budget serves to identify needed areas of increased managerial attention and, possibly, the need for special budgets to improve control. For example, such assets as finished goods inventory may be deemed to be [too low / too high / either too low or too high].
balance sheet	**55** The type of budget that can be used to compare actual financial position with intended financial position with respect to a number of specific assets and liabilities is the _____ budget.
inflexibility	**56** Our description of the operating budget was based on the assumption that all expenses should be planned beforehand, and that they should be consistent with a specific sales or production level. If the actual level of operations should differ from that which was anticipated, the use of such an operating budget would lead to organizational [flexibility / inflexibility].
	57 As one approach to combating such inflexibility, the *variable budget* has been developed. By this budgeting method the exact amount budgeted is not specified, but rather it is made dependent on the level

of operations during the budgeting period. Thus, with increases in production volume in a manufacturing plant such a budget would specify [increasing / decreasing] dollar amounts allocated to direct labor.

increasing

58 Would you also expect that the variable budget would identify varying amounts of depreciation on plant and equipment according to production level? [Yes / No]

No

59 Therefore, the budgetary method in which planned expenditures or charges with respect to *variable costs*, but not fixed costs, are tied to the level of operations is called the _____ budget.

variable

60 Figure 15.1 is an example of a variable budget chart that can be used as a planning device and also as a control device. Note that on this chart the fixed costs are at the same level regardless of monthly output, namely, at $_____.

20,000

61 On the other hand, for the range of possible production volumes identified in Figure 15.1 the budgeted *total cost* can vary from a low of $20,000 to a high of $_____.

43,000 (approximately)

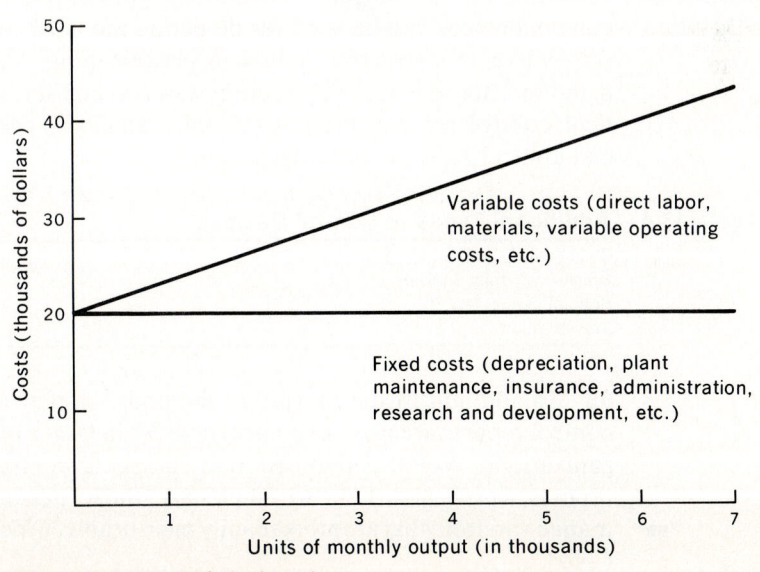

Figure 15.1 Variable budget chart.

62 In addition to perhaps forcing management to study the actual relationships between levels of operation and costs, the principal advantage of the variable budget is that it [reduces uncertainty in costs / allows greater flexibility in the use of budgets].

allows greater flexibility in the use of budgets (The uncertainty is still there, but it can be planned for.)

63 In all, we have considered five types of budgets in this section. The type of budget concerned with anticipated revenues and expenses during a particular period is the _____ budget, while the type of budget concerned with planning for the adequacy of funds during the period is the _____ budget.

operating

cash

64 Allotted funds for long-term investments are involved in the _____ budget, while the intended financial status at the conclusion of a fiscal period is indicated by the _____ budget. Finally, budgetary flexibility, particularly in regard to the direct costs that vary with the level of operations, is enhanced by the use of a _____ budget.

appropriation

balance sheet

variable

Other Control Devices

In addition to the budget, several other types of formal control devices can be used for detecting the need for preventive or corrective action in organizations. As listed in Table 15.4, in this section we consider statistical control reports, break-even-point analysis, special control reports, and internal audits.

Table 15.4   Additional Types of Control Devices

Statistical control report
Break-even-point analysis
Special control report
Internal audit

65 In addition to the budgetary methods, statistical control reports are used as control devices in larger organizations. Would you expect that statistical control reports would also tend to emphasize those performance variables that are more readily measurable? [Yes / No]

Yes

control report

66 For example, a periodic report which provides an analysis of the employee turnover rate is a statistical _____.

67 Because statistical control reports have little meaning unless compared with similar data for previous periods, it is important that they be prepared on a [continuing / noncontinuing] basis.

continuing (weekly, monthly, etc.)

device

68 *Break-even-point analysis* is a second additional type of control _____ used in business firms.

3,000 units

69 Break-even-point analysis involves the use of a chart to depict the overall volume of sales necessary to cover costs. Refer to the break-even chart in Figure 15.2. At what volume of sales will the revenue exactly cover the costs? _____

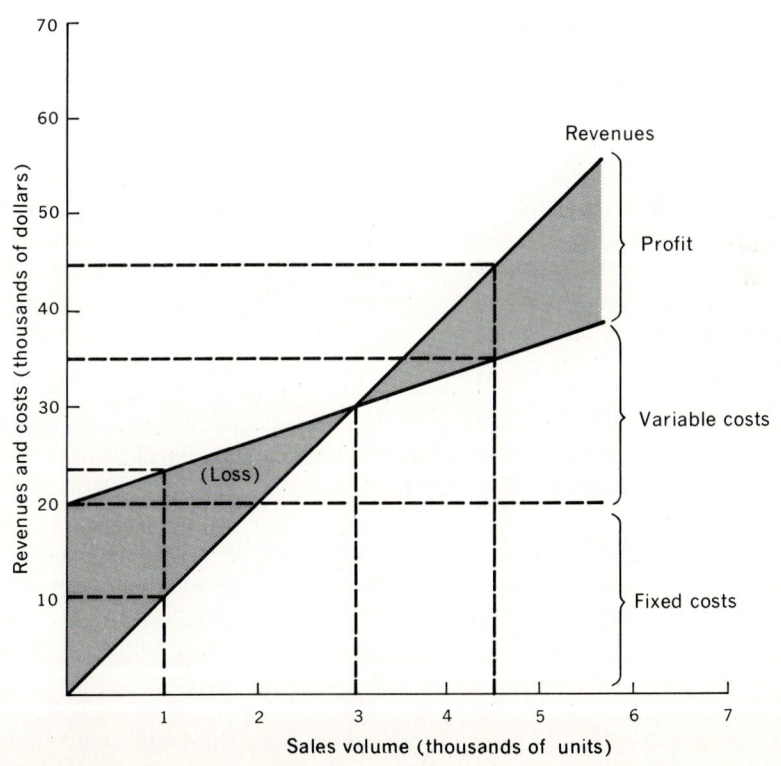

Figure 15.2 Break-even chart.

486 • Chapter 15 • The Control Process

break-even	70 Therefore, in this particular case 3000 units is the _____ point.
sales	71 As you have no doubt noted, the break-even chart is very similar in appearance to the variable budget chart. However, whereas the variable budget chart is used to plan budgets, the break-even chart is used to anticipate the amount of profit (or loss) associated with various levels of _____.
sales revenues	72 Thus, whereas the horizontal axis of Figure 15.1 identifies units of output, in Figure 15.2 it identifies units of _____. Whereas the vertical axis of Figure 15.1 identifies only categories of costs, in Figure 15.2 it identifies costs and _____.
$10,000	73 To exemplify use of the break-even chart, what is the total revenue associated with a sales volume of 1000 units in Figure 15.2? _____
$23,000 (approximately)	74 What are the total costs associated with a sales volume of 1000 units? _____
loss $13,000	75 Therefore, at a sales volume of 1000 units we would expect an overall [profit / loss] in the amount of _____.
profit; $10,000 ($45,000 in revenue minus $35,000 in costs)	76 Similarly, at a sales volume of 4500 units we would expect an overall [profit / loss] in the amount of _____.
profit; loss	77 Thus, by directly comparing revenues and costs at various sales levels, a break-even chart identifies the expected amount of _____ or _____.
statistical control reports break-even-point analysis	78 So far, we have described two types of control devices in addition to the budgetary methods described in the preceding section: _____ _____ and _____.
	79 *Special control reports* are a third additional category of control devices. These reports may or may not contain statistical data, but the distinction from other

Other Control Devices ● 487

noncontinuing
devices is that particular operations are investigated at a particular time for a particular purpose; that is, these reports are done on a [continuing / noncontinuing] basis.

80 The great value of special control reports is that operations appearing to deviate from expected standards are given additional executive attention. This is a direct application of the managerial principle of

exception
_____.

81 A report reviewing present procedures in a particular work area, such as the handling of customer complaints, is an example of a _____

special control report
_____.

82 Finally, the *internal audit* is a fourth additional

control device
type of _____ used in business firms.

83 In addition to an audit of accounts, an evaluation of the application of policies, programs, and methods and the attainment of objectives in a fairly broad area

internal
of operations is included in the _____ audit.

84 For example, the central training department of a large company that directs all subsidiary training units to appraise their own operations annually following a standard checklist of variables is, in effect, conducting

internal audit
an _____.

85 Although the internal audit report may be similar to the special control report, the principal distinctions are that the internal audit report is typically prepared

continuing (monthly, annually, etc.); more
on a [continuing / noncontinuing] basis and is also [more / less] extensive in its area of coverage.

86 In addition to the budget, we have discussed four kinds of devices used in conjunction with the management function of controlling. Included were:

statistical control reports _____ ,
break-even-point analysis _____ ,
special control reports _____ , and the
internal audit _____ .

87 Other than the budget, the type of control device that bears most directly on monetary analysis or the flow of funds is _____

break-even-point analysis _____.

88 The control device that is directly related to the managerial principle of control by exception is the

special control report _____.

89 The control device that is typically used on a continuing basis, and which can be directed at qualitative, or less tangible, results, as well as those that are easily

internal audit quantifiable, is the _____.

90 Would you expect that an executive can come to a complete understanding of ongoing activities in an enterprise and institute appropriate control action through the use of the formal control devices alone?

No [Yes / No]

91 In any organization, personal involvement of the manager with other key people in the enterprise, in ad-

control dition to the use of formal _____
devices _____, is necessary to prevent the manager from becoming isolated from the ongoing operations.

Human Reactions to Centralized Control Procedures

Ultimately, the success of a control system is determined by its effectiveness in getting people to make necessary modifications in their own performance. Although the classical approach to control systems assumes that people will automatically act to correct their own behavior when directed to do so, this does not necessarily happen. Individuals may resist formal control systems for a variety of reasons, some of which are described below.

92 One reason why a control procedure might be disliked is that it tends to disrupt a person's self-image; that is, the focal point of most control reports is to highlight the things that a person has done [well /

poorly poorly].

93 In terms of the influence of reward on behavioral change, it is not surprising that an unpleasant situation, or unpleasant involvement, tends to be [approached / avoided] by an individual.

avoided

94 Assuming that a person accepts the necessity of finding out about, and correcting, his inadequacies, the goals of the control system [need to / need not] be accepted as worthwhile by him.

need to

95 Thus, a failure to accept the organization's _____ is a second reason why a control system may be resisted by an employee.

goals

96 For example, a junior executive who feels that his job is "above the time-clock level" [would / would not] probably resist using a departmental sign-in sheet.

would

97 Even when the employee agrees with the necessity of knowing unpleasant facts and considers the goals of the control systems worthwhile, he may feel that the expected standard of performance is too high and [accept / reject] the control system on this basis.

reject

98 In situations in which it is possible to custom-fit performance standards for each person and this is accomplished, would there be a better chance of reducing resistance to controls? [Yes / No]

Yes

99 For example, as compared with a standard sales quota applied to all personnel, regardless of experience, individual sales quotas based on previous performance are [more / less] likely to be accepted.

more

100 On the other hand, a person may not consider the standard too high but may consider it to be irrelevant to, or at least an incomplete measurement of, attaining the organization's _____.

goals

101 For example, a control device that emphasizes only the importance of current sales volume may be [accepted / resisted] by the sales representative convinced of the importance of developing long-term good will with customers.

resisted

102 Thus far we have considered four reasons why

individuals in an organization might resist controls: a tendency to _____ unpleasant facts, a failure to accept the organization's _____, a belief that the expected standard of performance is too _____, and a belief that the defined standards are a(n) [complete / incomplete] measurement of the attainment of organizational objectives.

avoid
goals
high

incomplete

103 A fifth reason for resistance to controls is that a person may object not to the controls themselves, but to the assignment of control authority to particular groups in the organization. Does an individual typically tend to object to control procedures which are carried out by his own superior? [Yes / No]

No

104 On the other hand, it is more likely that control procedures administered by an outside staff group will be [accepted / resisted] by line personnel.

resisted

105 Finally, just as there are two organizational systems in any firm—the formal and the informal—so also are there two sets of control systems. This implies that a person's work associates are an important source of _____ over his work.

control

106 When informal group norms are consistent with company control objectives, we would expect a high degree of [acceptance of / resistance to] the control devices; when group norms are contradictory to control objectives, we would expect a high degree of [acceptance / resistance].

acceptance of

resistance

107 When the influence of the informal organization is an important factor underlying resistance to control procedures, the problem is best approached by considering how the [individual / group] point of view can be changed.

group (since the group is the source of the resistance)

Toward Effective Controls

Each of the reasons for resisting controls has its counterpart in a line of action that a manager might take to reduce that source of resistance. In addition to this, however, there is a general point of view which, when applied, enhances the likelihood that people will work toward the goals of a control system.

108 First, let us consider that there are three possible focal points in the operation of a control system: *centralized control, personal control,* and *self-_____.*

control

109 Control of a departmental budget by a finance staff is an example of [centralized / personal / self-] control.

centralized

110 The "checking up" and correcting that a supervisor does in his relationship with his subordinates is an example of [centralized / personal / self-] control.

personal

111 The individual who institutes changes in his own work methods after learning that he has failed to achieve desired objectives is practicing [centralized / personal / self-] control.

self-

112 In terms of the personal acceptance of control procedures, it is typically the case that the more intimately a person is involved in the control decisions, the [more / less] likely is it that he will accept them and put them into effect.

more

113 Thus, in terms of the three focal points of control systems, people in our society generally like _____ control best, _____ control least, with _____ control occupying an intermediate position.

self-; centralized personal

114 From the standpoint of classical organization theory, the emphasis has been on the centralized flow of control data toward [top management / the lowest organizational level possible].

top management

115 In terms of the behavioral view of organizational performance, on the other hand, the importance of getting control information to the _____ _____ is emphasized.

lowest organizational level possible (etc.)

control ⟶ 116 From the behavioral point of view, the circuit communication model, described in Chapter 10 on administrative communication, can be directly applied to control procedures as well. From this standpoint, direct feedback of information about results to the person actually doing the work leads to the most timely control _____ action.

decentralization ⟶ 117 In regard to organizational philosophy and structure, an emphasis on self-control is consistent with the organizational philosophy of [centralization / decentralization].

Review
several ⟶ 118 A performance standard for a particular area of operation is typically made up of [one major / several] facet(s) of performance. (Frames 1 to 7)

strategic control point ⟶ 119 A point in an operation that is chosen as a focal point for control activity is called a _____ _____. (Frames 8 to 11)

quantity; cost
time use; quality ⟶ 120 Several types of standards can be defined at a strategic control point in terms of the kind of measurement involved. There are _____, _____, _____, and _____ standards. (Frames 12 to 18)

quality ⟶ 121 A general problem in defining standards and measuring actual results is that the less tangible _____ standards and measurements tend to be underemphasized. (Frames 19 to 21)

sampling ⟶ 122 When just a portion of the output at the strategic control point is checked, with the assumption that this portion is representative of the entire output, the process of _____ is involved. (Frames 22 to 25)

exception ⟶ 123 The amount of follow-up associated with the control process can be reduced by applying the management principle of _____. (Frames 26 to 29)

monetary (or dollar) ⟶ 124 The quantitative units in which budgets are expressed are _____ units. The process of

Review ● 493

planning controlling	formulating and using budgets concerns the management functions of _____ and _____. (Frames 30 to 36)
operating	**125** Of the specific types of budgets considered in this chapter, the type which is concerned with anticipated revenues and expenses during a particular period is the _____ budget. (Frames 37 to 43)
cash appropriation	**126** The type of budget concerned with planning for the availability of adequate funds is the _____ budget, while the type concerned with long-term expenditures and investments is the _____ budget. (Frames 44 to 52)
balance sheet variable	**127** The type of budget that represents the intended financial status at the end of the budget period is the _____ budget. The budgeting method that results in planning and control flexibility by allowing different budgeted amounts for different levels of operation is the _____ budget. (Frames 53 to 64)
statistical control reports break-even-point analysis	**128** In addition to the budget, two other control devices that are entirely oriented toward the use of quantitative information, including the flow of funds, are _____ and _____. (Frames 65 to 78)
special control report internal audit	**129** Of the two types of control devices that may be oriented toward nonquantitative standards, the one that is more limited in scope and is used on a non-continuing basis is the _____, whereas the one that is more extensive and used on a continuing basis is the _____. (Frames 79 to 91)
	130 Six reasons for individual resistance to control systems were discussed. Name three of these. (Frames 92 to 107)
(Refer to frames indicated.)	_____ _____ _____

131 The three possible focal points, or directions, in the operation of a control system are _____ control, _____ control, and _____ control. (Frames 108 to 113)

centralized; personal self-

132 Which focal point in the operation of control systems has the classic approach to organization theory tended to emphasize? _____. (Frame 114)

Centralized control

133 Which focal point in the operation of control systems does the behavioral point of view emphasize? _____. (Frames 115 to 117)

Self-control

Discussion Questions

1. Describe the basic steps included in any control process and indicate how the steps are related to one another.
2. What is the relationship between the management functions of planning and controlling? Between organizing and controlling? Between directing and controlling?
3. Give examples of each of the four types of standards that may be used at a strategic control point. What kinds of measurement problems are associated with each?
4. Discuss the role of budgeting in an organization. What are its strengths and weaknesses?
5. Of the several types of budgets described in this chapter, which two would be of greatest use in a small business enterprise? Why?
6. Discuss the advantages and possible disadvantages of the variable budget. Can it be "overused"?
7. List some specific actions that a manager can take to counteract the various reasons for employee resistance to a control system.
8. Comment on the statement, "People prefer to have control over their own behavior." Do you agree? What are the implications of this statement for the management process of controlling?

References

Adam, E. E., Jr., and W. E. Scott, Jr. "The Application of Behavioral Conditioning Procedures to the Problems of Quality Control." *Academy of Management Journal,* vol. 14, no. 2, June 1971.

Argyris, C. "Human Problems with Budgets." *Harvard Business Review*, vol. 31, no. 1, January-February 1953.

Bales, C. F. "Strategic Control: The President's Paradox." *Business Horizons*, vol. 20, no. 4, August 1977.

Cammann, C., and D. A. Nadler. "Fit Control Systems to Your Managerial Style." *Harvard Business Review*, vol. 54, no. 1, January-February 1976.

Cowen, S. S., B. V. Dean, and A. Lohrasbi. "Zero Base Budgeting as a Management Tool." *MSU Business Topics*, vol. 26, no. 2, Spring 1978.

Emch, A. F. "Control Means Action." *Harvard Business Review*, vol. 32, no. 4, July-August 1954.

Giglioni, G. B., and A. G. Bedeian. "A Conspectus of Management Control Theory: 1900–1972." *Academy of Management Journal*, vol. 17, no. 2, June 1974.

Hofstede, G. "The Poverty of Management Control Philosophy." *The Academy of Management Review*, vol. 3, no. 3, July 1978.

Ivancevich, J. M. "An Analysis of Control, Bases of Control, and Satisfaction in an Organizational Setting." *Academy of Managament Journal*, vol. 13, no. 4, December 1970.

Koontz, H., and R. W. Bradspies. "Managing through Feed-forward Control." *Business Horizons*, vol. 15, no. 3, June 1972.

McGinnis, J. F. "Pluses and Minuses of Zero-based Budgeting." *Administrative Management*, vol. 37, no. 9, September 1976.

Mockler, R. J. *The Management Control Process*. New York: Appleton Century Crofts, 1972.

Negandhi, A. R. *Organization Theory in an Open System*. New York: Dunellen, 1975.

Newman, W. H. *Constructive Control: Design and Use of Control Systems*. Englewood Cliffs, N.J.: Prenctic-Hall, 1975.

Ouchi, W. G. "The Transmission of Control through Organizational Hierarchy." *Academy of Management Journal*, vol. 21, no. 2, June 1978.

Ouchi, W., and M. A. Maguire. "Organizational Control: Two Functions." *Administrative Science Quarterly*, vol. 20, no. 4, December 1975.

Reimann, B., and A. Negandhi. "Strategies of Administrative Control and Organizational Effectiveness." *Human Relations*, vol. 28, no. 5, May 1975.

Searfoss, D. G., and R. M. Monczka. "Perceived Participation in the Budget Process and Motivation to Achieve the Budget." *Academy of Management Journal*, vol. 16, no. 4, December 1973.

Suver, J. D., and R. L. Brown. "Where Does Zero-Base Budgeting Work?" *Harvard Business Review*, vol. 55, no. 6, November-December 1977.

Tosi, H. L., Jr. "Human Effects of Budgeting Systems on Management." *MSU Business Topics*, vol. 22, no. 4, Autumn 1974.

Turcotte, W. E. "Control Systems, Performance, and Satisfaction in Two State Agencies." *Administrative Science Quarterly*, vol. 19, no. 1, March 1974.

Vancil, R. F. "What Kind of Mangement Control Do You Need?" *Harvard Business Review*, vol. 51, no. 2, March-April 1973.

CASE STUDY: Western Office Equipment and Supply Company

The Western Office Equipment and Supply Company is in fact more than a supplier of office equipment and supplies. Upon completing his college studies 20 years ago, Clyde Mueller, who is the principal owner of the firm, was convinced that existing firms selling office equipment in the area in which his firm is now located were not providing essential services desired by the customer. As he saw it, in order to make an intelligent decision about office equipment, an organization needs an analysis of existing office procedures and recommendations for improvement. Accordingly, he established his firm on the premise that an office systems analysis is an integral part of a proposal for equipment purchase. The success of his approach is attested to by the fact that the firm now employs twenty people and grossed over $5 million in sales last year.

Mr. Mueller is general manager of the firm and himself acts as an office systems analyst for selected accounts. In addition, the activities of five other systems analysts are supervised and coordinated by George Hammond, who is the assistant manager and also part owner. Mrs. Betty Huntington supervises the typing pool, which is responsible for typing the recommendations that result from the systems analysts' work in client firms, in addition to performing other clerical services for the organization.

Several months ago the company's scope of operations was broadened to include new geographic areas, and since then a number of problems affecting the preparation of customer recommendations have developed. Previously, Mrs. Huntington had proofread all recommendations before sending them to George Hammond for subsequent distribution to the systems analysts concerned, but with the increase in work load she has had to rely on each typist doing her own proofreading, while she has tried to check the figures included in the recommendations. Of course, questions regarding the accuracy of figures often have to be referred back to the originating analyst. However, with many of the analysts absent from the office for prolonged periods of time because of the expanded territories, confirmation of the figures has been difficult to accomplish.

The analysts have complained to Mr. Hammond both about the increase in the number of typographical and factual errors in their customer recommendations and about the apparent inability of the typing pool to have them prepared when requested. To check on the seriousness of the problem, Hammond kept a tally of the number of customer recommendations sent back to the typing pool for corrections during the past month and found that 80 percent of the recommendations were returned. He also found that the recommendations were being prepared by the day requested, but that their subsequent return for corrections was the principal cause of the delay.

Mr. Hammond has described the situation to Clyde Mueller during their lunch at the club and warned that equipment sales are already being lost because of the delays in the preparation of accurate customer proposals. Mueller expressed surprise, since he has not experienced any difficulty with the customer recommendations prepared for him, which are typed by Mrs. Huntington herself.

As George Hammond sees it, the scope of the firm's operations has obviously outgrown Mrs. Huntington's ability to supervise and control the work performed in the typing pool. He suggests that she be designated as private secretary to Mr. Mueller and that a new supervisor with experience in a larger office be hired to replace her in the typing pool.

1. Would adoption of Mr. Hammond's suggestion probably take care of the difficulties being experienced in the typing pool? Why or why not?
2. What specific changes have taken place in the typing pool as the result of the expansion in the geographic area of the firm's activities?
3. Within the context of the present system, what changes might be made to improve the control system?
4. What organizational changes might be considered to improve the control system?

CASE STUDY: Control of In-Process Inventory

The Rhibler Manufacturing Company is a relatively small firm manufacturing automobile parts and accessories for the replacement market. The company can be described as being highly centralized, in that specialist staff personnel issue quality specifications, cost specifications, and scheduling instructions to each manufacturing department in the company. There are three manufacturing plants, with the largest being located adjacent to the company's corporate office building.

For some time, the controller had noticed that the financial resources devoted to the in-process inventory seemed to be out of line with the known processing and assembly times required for the various items of equipment being manufactured. Essentially, the amount of material being processed seemed excessive in comparison with the amount that could in reality be in an in-process status in the company's facilities. He brought the matter up for discussion at one of the semiweekly sessions of the company's executive committee, and the reaction of the vice president in charge of production was that the controller was "playing around with assumptions and figures that are hypothetical and would only apply to a perfect situation." Further, the vice president for production indicated that the inventory control data show that all the input into the manufacturing plant can be accounted for in terms of the output. During the discussion the controller agreed that there was no question being raised about material being stolen; rather, it just seemed to be taking too long for the material to work its way through the plants. The discussion on the matter concluded with the company president suggesting that the vice president of production review the controller's analysis and take any appropriate action.

Several months after the meeting the company president took a major retail distributor on a tour of the main company plant. In one of the departments the president noticed several crates placed in a corner, which had obviously been there for some time. He walked over to see what they were, and to his surprise he found that they contained a large number of the components assembled in the department. When he questioned the foreman about the crates and why the material had not been shipped out of the department, he obtained a rather hesitant admission that the foreman kept a stock of the various items assembled in the department as a matter of routine. "This way," he explained, "whenever we have a machine breakdown I can use this stock to meet the production schedules, and that helps keep everything moving smoothly down the line."

After the visitor left, the company president called the controller and the vice president in charge of production, and the three of them went through all of the manufacturing and assembly departments in the main plant. In every department they visited they found an inventory of partially or fully assembled components being "held back" by individual foremen. "So that's where the stuff's been hiding," observed the controller. "It looks like we've got some housecleaning to do around here."

1. Assuming that the vice president in charge of production did not in fact know that manufactured items were being "held back," what does this suggest about the adequacy of the control system?
2. In what respects is the practice that the foremen followed appropriate, in terms of achieving organizational objectives? In what respects is the practice that the foremen followed inappropriate?
3. What inadequacy was there, if any, in the overall control system of the company?

APPLICATIONS READING:

Zero-Base Budgeting: Where to Use It and How to Begin

Peter A. Pyhrr
Vice-President of Finance and Treasurer
Alpha Wire Corporation

The profitability crunch forces U.S. businesses to make some agonizing decisions at budget time. Squeezed by rising costs, managers often have to decide between, say, cutting funds for management development or decreasing the allocation for a major research project. How do they make these decisions?

Most allocate their resources by planning and budgeting, although most budgeting decisions tend to be numbers-oriented rather than decision-oriented. Generally managers identify total dollars requested rather than spending priorities, and they start with the current level of operation as an established base instead of reevaluating all programs. Are current programs efficient and effective? What are the alternatives? Should current programs be eliminated or reduced in order to fund higher-priority new programs or to improve profits? These questions are not answered by typical budget procedures in which only a small fraction of the total dollars budgeted receive critical review.

Budgeting from Scratch

One technique, developed by the author while at Texas Instruments, does address itself to these questions. Called "zero-base budgeting" (ZBB), it is used by some 100 companies in the U.S. and is rapidly gaining in popularity. The word "budgeting" in the term "zero-base budgeting" is often misleading, since in many organizations "budgeting" refers to a numbers-oriented process dominated by accountants. However, zero-base budgeting in its correct context refers to a general management tool that companies can use to improve planning, budgeting, and operational decision making. With it, managers can reassess their operations from the ground up and justify every dollar spent in terms of current corporate goals. Instead of staying within the same budgetary structure year after year, they can make major reallocations of resources from one year to the next.

ZBB is applicable to all "actionable or discretionary" activities, programs, or costs. An actionable or discretionary item is an activity or program in which a cost/benefit relationship can be identified, even if that relationship is highly subjective. Zero-base analysis, therefore, can be applied to all administrative (that is, financial, EDP, personnel, and supervision), technical (that is, R&D, engineering,

Source: Reprinted, by permission of the publisher, from S.A.M. *Advanced Management Journal,* vol. 41, no. 3, Summer 1976, © 1976 by Society for Advancement of Management, a division of American Management Associations. All rights reserved.

laboratory, quality control, maintenance, and production planning), and commercial (that is, purchasing, marketing, sales, and traffic) functions.

ZBB cannot be directly applied to direct labor, materials, and overhead (LMO) costs associated with production operations. These are not truly actionable or discretionary costs, because there usually is no benefit from increasing these expenditures. That is, a decision to increase company expenditures for these items does not necessarily bring increased benefits in the form of increased sales, although it does tend to boost production volume. Hence there is not the same simple relationship between costs and benefits with these items as there is with the service and support activities. The amount of resources allocated for LMO usually depends on an engineering study with emphasis on minimizing unit costs, with the budget developed by multiplying units of output by standard unit costs.

Actionable or discretionary costs may make up only a fraction of the total budget of a heavy manufacturing operation; but they represent activities that are usually the most difficult to plan and control, and they offer management the greatest lever to affect profits. Consider these areas of activity that are subject to ZBB analysis and how resource allocation could affect them—and the entire organization:

1. Marketing and R&D programs determine the future course of an organization. If development funds are not adequate, or marketing support is not sufficient to handle expected sales volume, long-term plans for growth may not be achieved.
2. Funding for R&D, capital, industrial engineering, production planning, and so forth can directly affect manufacturing technology and heavily influence direct manufacturing costs.
3. Arbitrary cost reductions in the service and support functions without a full understanding of the consequences can create severe problems, with the cost savings proving minor compared to the resulting production problems and increased direct manufacturing costs.

In any manufacturing organization, actionable and discretionary costs are significant, because they provide management with the leverage it needs for affecting both profits and profitability. The purpose of the ZBB process is to help management evaluate expenditures and make tradeoffs among current operations, development needs, and profits for top management decision making and allocation of resources.

The zero-base approach requires each organization to evaluate and review all its programs and activities (current as well as new) systematically, on the basis of output or performance as well as costs; to emphasize managerial decision making first and numbers-oriented budgets second; and to increase analysis of allocation alternatives. It might be worthwhile to note here that ZBB is an approach, not a fixed procedure or set of forms to be applied uniformly from one organization to the next. The mechanics and management approach differ significantly among the organizations that have adopted the technique, and the process must be adapted to fit the specific needs of each user. However, the basis steps to effective zero-base budgeting are:

1. Identify "decision units."
2. Describe each decision unit as a "decision package."
3. Evaluate and rank all decision packages by cost/benefit analysis to develop the budget request and profit and loss statement.
4. Allocate resources accordingly.

Defining Decision Units

ZBB attempts to focus management's attention on evaluating activities and making decisions related to their continuation. Therefore, the "meaningful elements" of each organization must be determined so that they can be isolated for analysis and decision making. These meaningful elements are termed "decision units" for the sake of terminology.

The decision unit may correspond to a budget unit in those organizations with a detailed budget-unit or cost-center structure. In some cases, the budget-unit manager may wish to separate different functions or operations within his budget unit that are significant in size and that require, in his opinion, separate analysis. In such a case he would identify several decision units for his budget unit.

Decision units can also be defined as major projects, special work assignments, or capital projects. Each organization must determine for itself "what is meaningful." In practice, top management usually determines the organization or program level at which decision units must be defined, leaving it to the discretion of each manager to identify additional decision units if he or she considers them appropriate.

Once management has identified the decision units, it must explain the *decision package concept* to all levels of management and present guidelines for individual managers to use in breaking their areas' activities into workable packages of this kind. Next, it must set in motion a *ranking and consolidation process* whereby the packages sift upward toward the top in such a fashion that the decision packages of less importance are winnowed for top management's study and judgment. Let me now explain these two procedures in more detail.

The Decision Package Concept

The "decision package" is the building block of the ZBB concept. It is a document that identifies and describes each decision unit in such a manner that management can evaluate it, rank it against other decision units competing for funding, and decide whether to approve or disapprove the funding.

The content and format of the decision package must provide management with the information it needs to evaluate each activity. The document must state the goals of the decision unit, the program by which the goals are to be achieved, the benefits expected from the program, the alternatives to the program, the consequences of not approving the package, and the expenditures of funds and the personnel the activity requires.

The key to developing decision packages lies in formulating meaningful alternatives. This involves two steps:

1. **Alternative methods of accomplishing the objectives or performing the operation.** Managers should identify and evaluate all meaningful alternatives and choose the alternative method of accomplishing the objective or performing the operation that they consider best. If an alternative to one currently being funded is chosen, the recommended one should be shown in the decision package and mention made that the current method was not selected.
2. **Different levels of effort of performing the operation.** Once the best method of accomplishing the operation has been chosen from among the various methods being evaluated, a manager must identify alternative levels of effort and funding to perform that operation. Managers must establish a minimum level of effort (which must be below the current level of operation), then identify additional levels or increments as separate decision packages. If appropriate, these incremental levels may bring the operation up to and above its current level.

The identification and evaluation of different levels of effort probably represent the two most difficult aspects of the zero-base analysis, yet they are key elements of the process. If only one level of effort were analyzed (probably reflecting the funding level desired by the manager), and the request from the manager for funds exceeded funding availability, management would have no choice but to do one of four things: It could fund the activity at the requested level, thus reducing profits; eliminate the program; make arbitary reductions; or recycle the budgetary process.

A decision package is defined as "one incremental level in a decision unit." Thus there may be several decision packages for each decision unit. It is these incremental levels that get ranked. By identifying a minimum level of effort, plus additional increments as separate decision packages, each manager presents the following alternatives for top management's decision making:

- **Eliminate the operation** if no decision packages are approved.
- **Reduce the level of funding** if only the minimum-level decision package is approved.
- **Maintain the same level of effort** if the minimum level, plus one or two incremental levels (bringing the operation from the minimum level up to the current level of operation) are approved. (It might be worth noting here that the current level of effort refers only to the level of output or performance, sometimes referred to as a "maintenance level." However, even at the current level of effort, managers may change their method of operation and make operating improvements, so that the current level of effort may be maintained at reduced cost.)
- **Increase levels of funding and performance** if one or more increments above the current level are approved.

The operating manager responsible for the decision unit normally does the analysis of that unit since he is the most knowledgeable about its operation and will be responsible for implementation. However, his analysis will be reviewed by higher management levels and the financial staff. The result of this review may be the modification or the redirection of selected decision packages.

The Ranking Process

The ranking process provides management with a technique to allocate its limited resources by making management concentrate on these questions: "How much sould be spent?" and "where should it be spent?" Management attempts to answer these questions by listing all the packages identified in order of decreasing benefit to the company. It then identifies the benefits to be gained at each level of expenditure, and it studies the consequences of not approving additional decision packages ranked below that expenditure level.

The ranking process establishes priorities among the functions as described in the decision packages. If a company wanted to severely limit its ranking, it could have only those managers preparing packages rank their own packages. However, this approach is obviously unsatisfactory, since it does not offer upper management any opportunity to trade off expenditures among cost centers or other, larger divisions of the company. The burden would be on division managers to establish tradeoffs among industrial engineering, production planning, and maintenance, as well as sales and administrative functions. At the other extreme, one, single ranking of decision packages could be required for an entire company. This ranking would be made by top management. But while this one, single ranking would identify the best allocation of resources, ranking and judging the high volume of packages created by describing all the discrete activities of a large company would impose a ponderous—if not impossible—burden on top management. One realistic compromise (depending primarily on organizational size) might be to stop the formal ranking process at some intermediate organizational level—for example, at the level of the plant manager or profit center. Many companies solve the dilemma by grouping cost centers or profit and loss units together naturally, according to kinds of activity, and producing consolidated rankings for each grouping. Top management will use these rankings to analyze the tradeoffs among profit centers and specifically to compare the marginal benefits of funding additional decision packages against the organization's profit needs.

The difficulty and time consumed in ranking decision packages can be reduced if managers:

- Do not concentrate their time in ranking packages that are regarded as "high priorities" or as "requirements" and that are well within the expenditure guidelines (other than to insure that all cost-reduction opportunities and operating improvements have been explored and followed through). Managers should concentrate their efforts instead on discretionary functions and the levels of effort required to achieve objectives.

- Do not spend too much time worrying whether package No. 4 is more important than package No. 5, but only assure themselves that package Nos. 4 and 5 are more important than package No. 15, and package No. 15 is more important than package No. 25, and so on.

With the decision packages ranked in order of priority, management can continually revise budgets by revising the cutoff level on any or all rankings—that is, it can fund package Nos. 1 through 55 but not package Nos. 56 through 75. This assures that the highest-priority decision packages have been funded. Of course, this means that some of the new high-priority programs have been funded by eliminating or reducing lower-priority, on-going programs rather than by reducing profits.

Detailed budgets are prepared after the corporate budget has been approved. These are done at the budget units when the approved decision packages are returned. Companies using zero-base budgeting hold managers accountable not only for keeping to these budgets but also for the programs and performance to which they are committed in each decision package.

Traditional versus Zero-Base Budgeting

The chart on this page compares traditional budgeting with ZBB. As the chart shows, both budget processes start from some form of long-range planning, during which objectives, goals, strategies, and major programs are defined. During the next phase—budget development—both budget processes develop sales forecasts, from which the costs of direct labor, materials, and overhead are

Traditional versus Zero-Base Budgeting

Budget sequence	Traditional (numbers-oriented)	Zero-Base (management-oriented)
1. Long-term planning (3–5 years)	Objectives, goals, strategies	Objectives, goals, strategies
2. Budget development (1 year) (Actionable or discretionary costs)	Develop sales forecast Establish cost for direct labor, materials, and overhead (using standard costing systems) Estimate costs of current activities Estimate costs of new activities Develop detailed budgets	Develop sales forecast Establish cost for direct labor, materials, and overhead (using standard costing systems) Evaluate current activities and alternatives Identify and evaluate new activities and alternatives Establish priorities
3. Evaluation	Test dollars against goals	Test budget against plan Establish tradeoffs among current operations, development needs, and profits
4. Final product	Finalized budget	Establish budget and operating plan Develop detailed budgets

calculated using standard costing procedures. (These direct costs may be revised later on because of expenditures for such actionable or discretionary items as capital, research, and manufacturing support.)

During this stage of the budgeting process, traditional and zero-base budgeting part company. Under traditional budgeting procedures, management first estimates the costs of current activities. This estimate serves as the base for the budget for the upcoming year; the worth of current activities to the company is not normally evaluated in depth. New activities are considered, and operating managers identify those new programs that can be funded. Detailed budgets are then established for each operation, and the costs of current and new activities are combined into a single budget by charts of accounts.

These detailed budgets are submitted to top management for review and approval. If a budget is rejected, it is returned to the budget unit where the budget-development process is repeated and a revised detailed budget is prepared. Evaluation is not an easy task. Management often is unable to determine whether appropriate actions have been planned or budgeted to achieve established goals. It must test the detailed budgets against dollar goals, and management typically finds that alternatives and lower levels of expense, and their consequences, are not identified.

Under zero-base budgeting, current activities and alternatives are evaluated at the same time as new programs are identified and considered. Operating managers establish their priorities and thereby identify the tradeoffs between expenditure levels and operating needs. New activities can be ranked higher than current ones, and thus new programs can be funded within existing funding levels. Top management makes the final evaluation and funding decisions on the basis of the decision package and ranking analysis.

Using ZBB, top management can readily test the budget against the operating plan, since it is looking at an evaluation in terms of priorities rather than in terms of numbers. It can identify tradeoffs; determine the consequences of alternative expenditure levels; and, based on its evaluation, come up with a new—and better—set of allocations for the upcoming budget year. From its analysis of decision packages, management gets not only a budget but an operating plan, and the budget is a product of operating decisions. (All too often, companies make budget decisions first, and these decisions become a rigid framework within which line managers must make their operating plans.)

ZBB can spotlight problems in the long-term plan—for example, if development funds are not adequate for planned future growth or marketing and operational support are not sufficient to achieve budgeted sales volume. It impacts all planning elements and forces management to make those tough tradeoffs among current operations, development needs, and profits.

Once the budgets have been approved, the detailed budgeting and fine tuning of numbers can be done. (Detailed budgeting is ingrained into budgeting procedures. It's interesting to note, however, that the company that developed ZBB eliminated the requirement for detailed budgets, because it felt that the zero-base budgeting procedures provided all the controls it needed.

Managing the Process

Initial implementation of zero-base budgeting is often done by a task force of operating and financial managers who are responsible for the design and administration of the process throughout the organization. The inclusion of operating managers in the task force is essential, since they are the most knowledgeable about operating needs and problems, will be largely responsible for implementing the ZBB process, and will add credibility to the proposed zero-base implementation plan.

The task force manages the process by:

1. Designing the process to fit the specific needs and character of the organization.
2. Preparing a simple, straightforward budget manual that illustrates the type of zero-base analysis required and explains the decision package and ranking concepts.
3. Presenting the process to management and teaching operating managers responsible for zero-base analysis of a decision unit how to apply the technique.
4. Working with decision-unit managers to improve and expedite the zero-base analysis.
5. Working with middle and top management to review and rank decision packages, compare similar functions across organizational lines, and prepare and finalize the profit plan.
6. Evaluating the process and revising it accordingly.

Step No. 1—designing the process to meet the specific needs and culture of the organization—is critical to successful implementation of zero-base budgeting. Although the basic zero-base concept remains the same, the specific formats and implementation procedures vary from company to company. In designing the system, the following questions should be considered:

- Should ZBB be installed throughout the company or within specific divisions at first, and should the process be implemented the first year on a trial basis?
- What information should the decision package contain, what format should be used in the decision package and ranking forms, and should the format of the forms of different organizational units and kinds of programs be varied?
- How should the review and ranking process be conducted? At what organizational level should rankings be consolidated? How should the actual ranking be done?
- What planning assumptions and guidelines are required?
- How should the process be communicated and administered?
- How much time is needed, and what is the calendar of events, to implement the process?

Conclusion

Texas Instruments launched ZBB in its staff and research divisions in 1969 and expanded its use of the process to the entire company by the following year. The technique has since helped some 100 U.S. companies handle profit, growth, and allocation problems. The reason for its increasing popularity is clear. Zero-base budgeting informs top management about money needed to attain desired program ends by focusing on the dollars needed for the program's accomplishments rather than on the percentage increase or decrease from the previous year's budget. The technique enables companies to identify and compare priorities within and among departments and divisions, and it allows a performance audit to determine whether each activity or operation is being performed as promised and whether duplications of effort among departments or divisions exist. Furthermore, budgets need not be recycled when expenditure levels change; instead, the decision package ranking identifies the activities and operations (decision packages) that should be added or deleted to implement the budget change.

Questions on Reading

1. In considering the applicability of ZBB, what are some examples of "actionable or discretionary" activities and what are some examples of activities that are not in this category?
2. Identify the basic steps to achieve effective zero-base budgeting.
3. Explain the "decision package" concept and its use in ZBB.
4. Identify the specific functions of the task force which is appointed to implement the ZBB process. What kinds of individuals should be in this working group?

16 PROGRAM EVALUATION AND REVIEW TECHNIQUE (PERT)

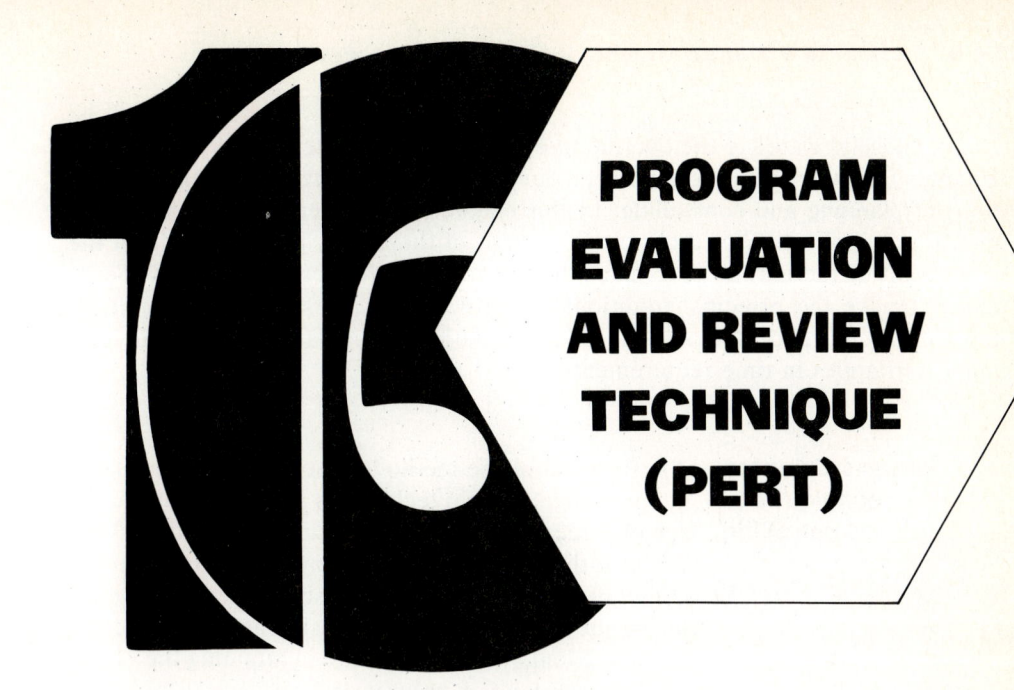

- Systems-Oriented Techniques in Controlling
- Elements of the PERT Network
- Using the PERT Network
- Review
- Discussion Questions
- References
- Case Problems: Program Evaluation and Review Technique
- Case Study: An Unsuccessful Application of PERT
- Applications Reading: "Management Rediscovers CPM" George J. Berkwitt
- Questions on Reading

Closely related to the quantitative decision-making techniques described in Chapter 5, new procedures have been developed as aids in the management functions of planning and controlling. In this chapter, we present the structural elements and application of the most important of these new procedures from the standpoint of the extent of its use: the Program Evaluation and Review Technique. Unlike the principal traditional control devices, this method is oriented toward the control of *time* and thus is particularly applicable to situations involving uncertainties in time requirements.

Systems-Oriented Techniques in Controlling

As is typical of the methods associated with management science, certain techniques in controlling have a systemwide rather than a departmental orientation. Thus, rather than focusing upon the formal components of the organization, system-oriented control techniques highlight the relationship among the activities and events which culminate in attaining the objectives of a project or program.

1 The systems-oriented techniques do not markedly overlap the established control devices, but they provide the kind of information not readily available with the traditional methods. Therefore, when these control techniques are used, it is usually [in place of / in addition to] the control devices described in the preceding chapter.

in addition to

2 Specifically, the systems-oriented control techniques emphasize control of *time*, whereas budgeting, which is the most important traditional control device, is directed toward the control of _____.

cost (or money, etc.)

3 One such technique that has had extensive application in the defense, aerospace, and construction industries is the Program Evaluation and Review Technique (PERT). Consistent with other similar control procedures, it is primarily directed toward the control of _____.

time

4 The Special Projects Office of the U.S. Navy first introduced the use of the Program Evaluation and Review Technique in the Polaris project in 1958. The Navy has stated that because of the use of PERT in this project, the Polaris missile submarine was brought

Systems-Oriented Techniques in Controlling • 511

to combat readiness about two years ahead of the original scheduled date, thus dramatically illustrating the value of PERT in the control of _____.

time (or scheduling, etc.)

5 At about the same time that the Navy was developing PERT in cooperation with the management consulting firm of Booz, Allen & Hamilton, the DuPont Company was concerned with the time and cost required to bring new products from research to production and independently developed a similar technique known as the Critical Path Method (CPM). Like PERT, CPM is primarily oriented toward achieving better managerial control with respect to _____.

time

6 Although the principal traditional control devices, particularly budgeting, are cost-oriented, some of the early methods of production scheduling can be considered as forerunners of PERT and CPM. Of these, the most important is the *Gantt milestone chart*. Henry L. Gantt was a contemporary of Frederick W. Taylor, and thus he is generally identified with the _____ management movement described in Chapter 1.

scientific

7 Figure 16.1 illustrates the general form of the Gantt milestone chart. As indicated, the width of each bar in this chart identifies the total time commitment planned for each _____.

task

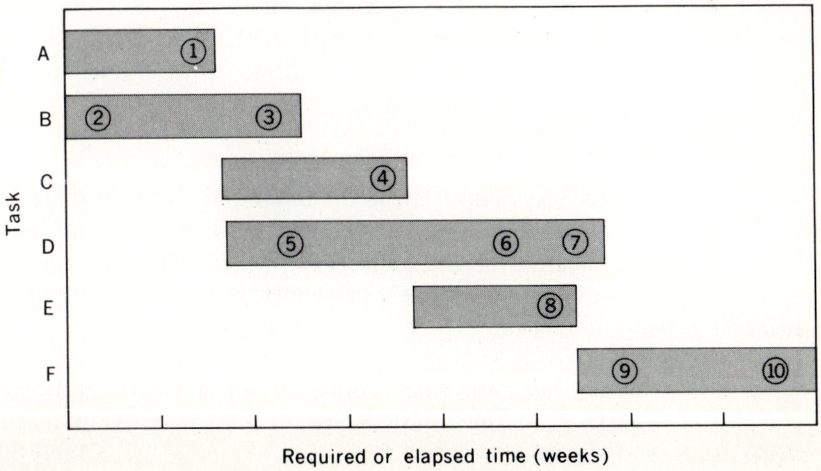

Figure 16.1 General form of the Gantt milestone chart.

8 Furthermore, overlapping bars on this chart indicate which tasks can be worked on simultaneously, whereas absence of overlap indicates that a task has to be completed before the next task can begin. In Figure 16.1, for example, the work on task C cannot begin until task _____ is completed.

A (On the other hand, tasks B and C can overlap to some extent.)

9 The word "milestone" refers to the point of completion of a significant phase of a task. Since these are points at which results can be measured, they are similar to the strategic _____ points described in Chapter 15, on the control process.

control

10 Of course, in this case the milestones are used as a basis for evaluating the project schedule, rather than product quality as such. In Figure 16.1, the milestones within each task are indicated by the _____ entered in the circles.

numbers

11 Furthermore, a milestone cannot be reached until all preceding milestones *within a given task* are completed. Thus, progress toward milestone 3 cannot begin until milestone _____ is completed.

2

12 However, the Gantt milestone chart does *not* indicate the sequential relationship between milestones in separate tasks. As we shall see, such interrelationships *are* indicated by the PERT network. In Figure 16.1, however, is progress toward milestone 8 dependent on milestone 5 being completed? [Yes / No / Uncertain]

Uncertain

13 As contrasted to the limited analysis of interrelationships in Gantt charting, PERT involves the identification of the entire network of activities and associated milestones, or events, which culminate in attaining the _____ of the system.

objectives (or goals)

14 Refer to the sample PERT network in Figure 16.2 on the following page. The first event in the sequence is called "_____" and the last is "_____."

order received; complete unit assembled and tested

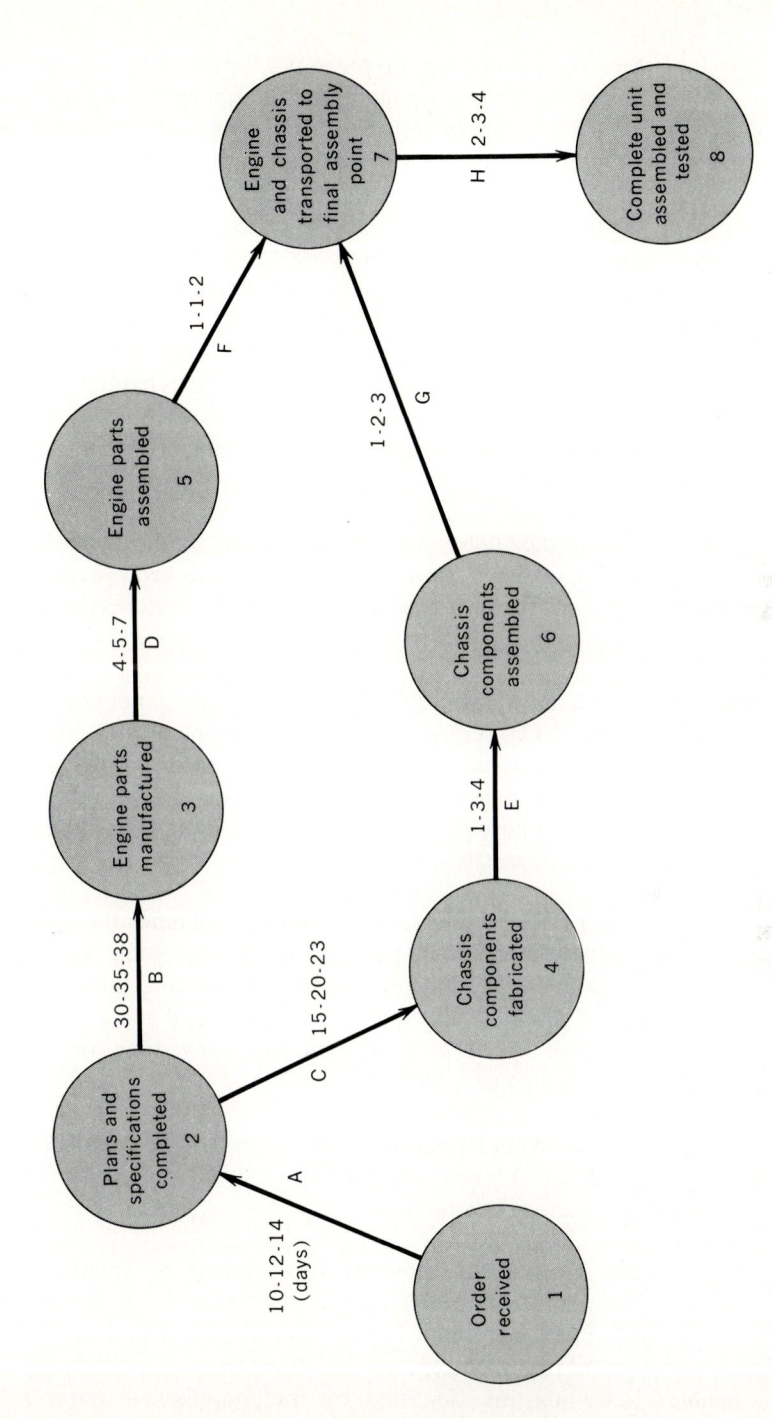

Figure 16.2 A simplified PERT network.

15 In this chapter, we present a fairly detailed coverage of the elements and computational procedure used in PERT. However, the examples will be much simpler than those encountered in actual managerial situations. The typical application of PERT in industry involves hundreds, and even thousands, of events in the PERT network, whereas our sample network in Figure 16.2, for example, has just _____ [number] events.

eight

16 In the following section of this chapter, we present the elements of the PERT network. Thus we shall first cover the [structural / functional] aspects of this technique.

structural

17 In the final section of this chapter we illustrate the use of PERT in decision making and control, thereby emphasizing its [structural / functional] properties.

functional

Elements of the PERT Network

As we have just briefly illustrated, a PERT network is made up of a sequence of events connected by the necessary activities. In Figure 16.2, as in all PERT network diagrams, the events are located within the circles, whereas the activities are indicated by the arrows connecting the circles.

18 In PERT terminology, an *event* signifies the start or completion of a significant step in a project. Notice the kinds of events included in Figure 16.2. Since an event is always the start or completion of some work, does an event as such consume any time or resources? [Yes / No]

No

19 Thus, in PERT analysis an event is distinguished from an *activity,* which *does* involve the use of _____ or resources.

time

20 Events are typically represented by numbers, whereas activities may be represented by letters. Thus, the events in Figure 16.2 are identified by the [numbers / letters] _____ through _____, and the activities are identified by the [numbers / letters] _____ through _____.

numbers; 1; 8
letters
A; H

21 Rather than using letters, we frequently identify activities by the numbers of the two events that they connect: "Activity 3–5" is an alternative way of identifying activity ____ in Figure 16.2.

D

22 Similarly, an alternative label for activity E in the figure would be activity ____.

4–6

23 Thus the basic structure of a PERT network consists of a series of ____ connected by the necessary ____.

events
activities

24 "A time-consuming and resource-consuming element in the PERT network" describes an ____.

activity

25 "A meaningful accomplishment in the program, recognizable as a particular instant in time and not in itself consuming time or resources" describes an ____.

event

26 In a PERT diagram, the events are identified by ____ in the circles, whereas the activities are identified by ____ associated with the arrows.

numbers
letters (or pairs of numbers)

27 The numbers used to indicate the events in a network are not necessarily in a sequential order; rather, the numbers simply serve as labels. From this standpoint, the following diagram [is / is not] a valid example of a PERT network:

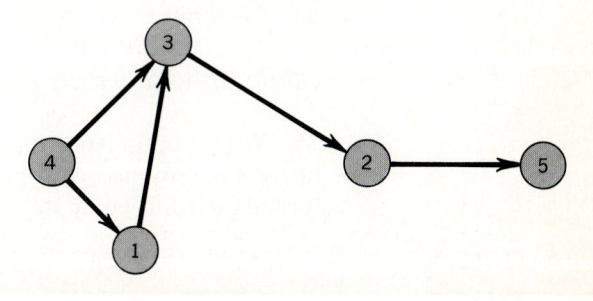

is

28 As we indicated, PERT is primarily concerned with control over time. Accordingly, three estimates

activity (An event does not consume any time.)

for time use—*optimistic, most likely,* and *pessimistic*—are made for each [event / activity].

29 The time estimate which is based on the assumption that everything will go right and has about one chance in a hundred of being realized, is the _____ time.

optimistic

30 The time estimate which would be correct most often if the activity could be repeated many times under exactly the same conditions is the _____ _____ time.

most likely

31 The time estimate based on the assumption that everything short of a catastrophe goes wrong, and which also has about one chance in a hundred of happening, is the _____ time.

pessimistic

pessimistic
optimistic; most likely

32 Accordingly, of the three time estimates given by the supervisor of an activity, the longest time estimate is _____ time, the shortest time estimate is _____ time, and _____ time is between the two.

30; 35
38

33 The three time estimates are sometimes written over the arrows that represent the activities in the PERT network. For activity 2–3 in Figure 16.2 (repeated on the following page), the optimistic time is _____ days, most likely time is _____ days, and pessimistic time is _____ days.

activity

34 Generally, the three time estimates for each _____ are combined into a weighted average, called *expected activity time,* which is designated t_e.

35 Where optimistic time is designated by a, most likely time by m, and pessimistic time by b, the formula used to compute t_e is

$$t_e = \frac{a + 4m + b}{6}$$

This is an estimate of the average time the activity would take if it were repeated many times. The time

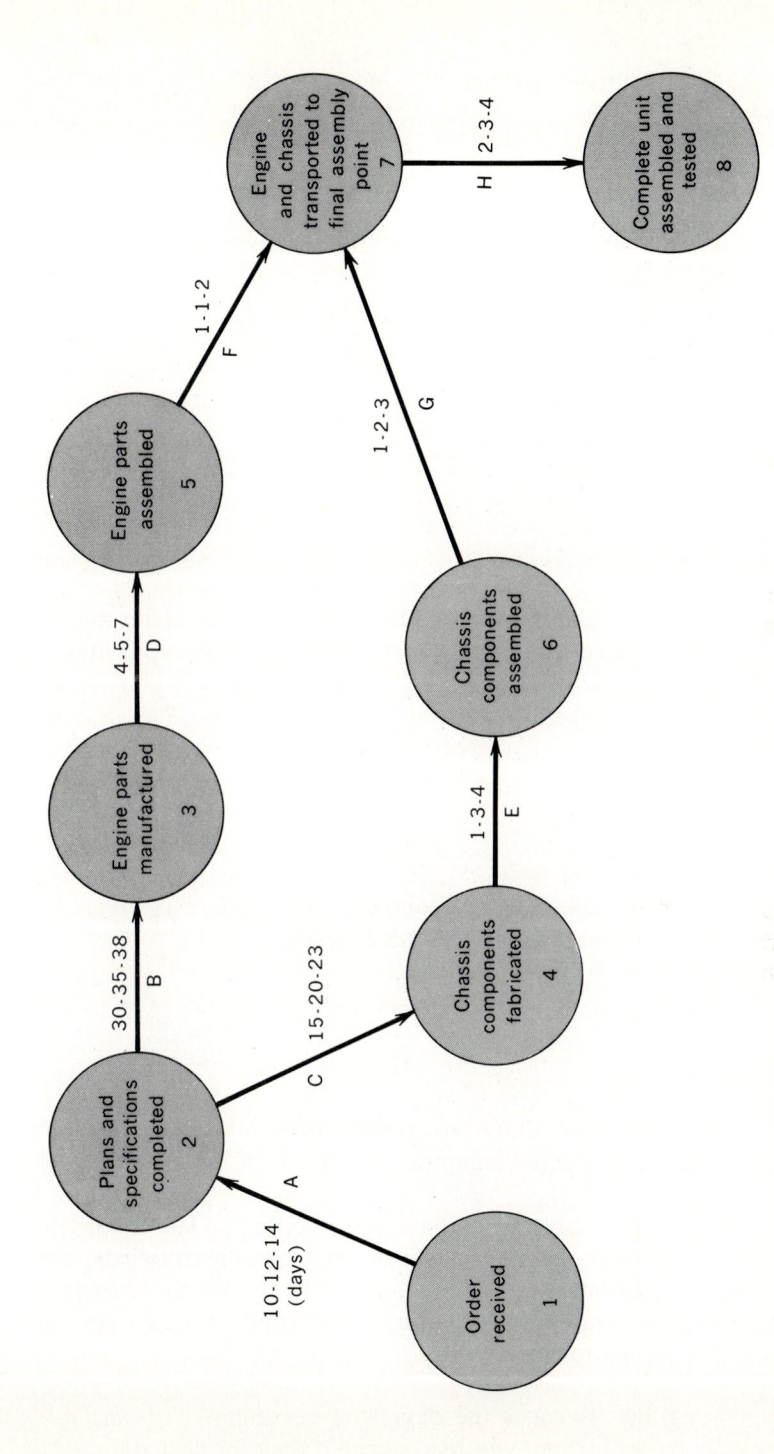

Figure 16.2 A simplified PERT network.

estimate which is most heavily weighted in the formula is the _____ time.

most likely

36 Given the following values for *a*, *m*, and *b*, compute the t_e for each activity, using decimals (to two places), rather than fractions, in your answers:

Activity	a	m	b	t_e
A	4	7	10	_____
B	1	3	6	_____
C	3	4	6	_____

7.00
3.17
4.17

where

$$t_e = \frac{a + 4m + b}{6}$$

37 Using the formula given above, compute the expected time t_e for each of the following activities in Figure 16.2 and post the results below:

Activity	t_e
A	_____
E	_____
H	_____

12.00
2.83
3.00

38 Suppose the following information is given for two activities in a PERT network:

Activity	a	m	b	t_e
K	1	4	7	4.00
L	3	4	5	4.00

Which activity has more uncertainty associated with its expected completion time t_e? [K / L]

K

39 As you may have observed in the last frame, the wider the spread (range) between the optimistic and pessimistic time estimates, the greater the degree of [certainty / uncertainty] associated with the expected time for the activity.

uncertainty

40 Because the degree of uncertainty, or *variance*, associated with the expected time for each activity is

Elements of the PERT Network • 519

also important in PERT analysis, it is calculated using the following formula, in which v stands for variance:

$$v = [(b - a)/6]^2$$

Compute the variance for the expected time t_e when the optimistic time is 1 day and the pessimistic time is 7 days. Do your computations below:

$[(7 - 1)/6]^2 = 1$ $v =$ _____ .

41   Given the formulas $t_e = (a + 4m + b)/6$ and $v = [(b - a)/6]^2$, complete the following table, carrying out your computations to the second decimal place:

t_e	v	Activity	a	m	b	t_e	v
6.00	0.11	1–2	5	6	7	_____	_____
6.00	0.44	1–3	4	6	8	_____	_____
14.67	4.00	2–5	10	14	22	_____	_____

42   For the data in Frame 41, in which of the expected time values would you, as a manager, have the greatest confidence? The expected time for activity

1–2; Because the expected
time for this activity has
the smallest variance
associated with it.
_____ . Why? _____

43   For the data in Frame 41, in which expected time value would you have the least confidence? The expected time for activity _____ . Why? _____

2–5; Because this expected
time value has the largest
variance associated with it.

44   Given the formula

$$v = [(b - a)/6]^2$$

complete the following table for the data in Figure 16.2.

	Activity	a	m	b	v
0.44	A	10	12	14	_____
0.25	D	4	5	7	_____
0.03	F	1	1	2	_____

10 (the sum of the t_e values for activities 1–2 and 2–3)

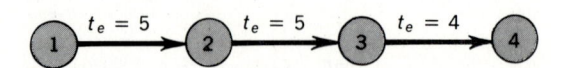

45 We now turn our attention to events rather than activities. The T_E of an event is the expected time for that event to be reached, given the expected activity times in a network. For the network below, what is the value of T_E for event 3; that is, how soon can we expect to arrive at event 3? _____ days.

$$1 \xrightarrow{t_e = 5} 2 \xrightarrow{t_e = 5} 3 \xrightarrow{t_e = 4} 4$$

46 There are often several "paths" through a network that culminate at the final event of the network or lead to particular events along the way. For example, in Figure 16.3, the three paths that lead to the attainment of event 7 are made up of events 1, 3, 4, and 7; 1, 2, and 7; _____, events _____, and events _____.

1, 3, 4, and 7; 1, 2, and 7;
1, 5, 6, 8, and 7

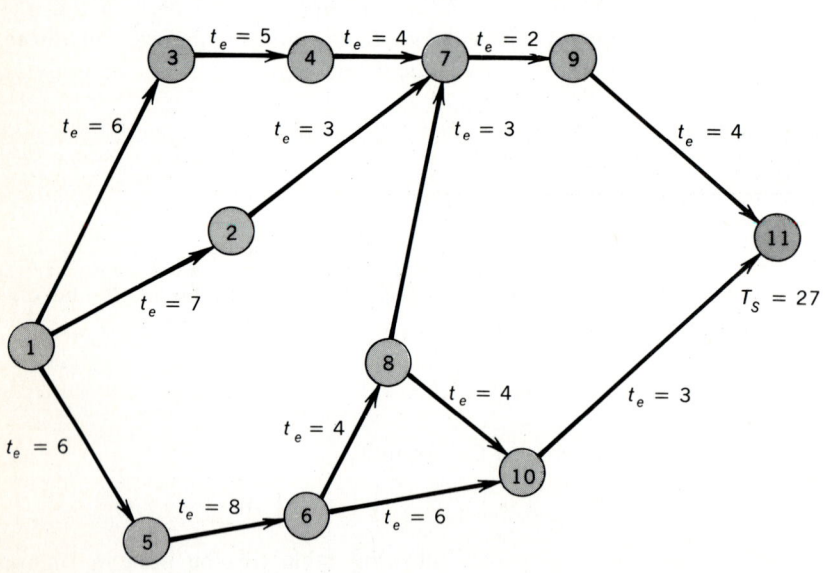

Figure 16.3 A simplified PERT network.

47 *All* the necessary preceding events must be completed before an event can itself be completed. For example, event 7 in Figure 16.3 can be completed

Elements of the PERT Network • 521

only after *all* the events in the three paths that you just identified have been completed. Therefore, when there are two or more paths that lead to an event, the T_E for that event is equal to the T_E in the [least / most] time-consuming path.

most

48 Compute the value of the expected time T_E for event 7 in Figure 16.3. $T_{E(7)} = $ _____.

21 (the addition of the t_e's in the largest time-consuming path)

49 Complete the following table for the events in Figure 16.3:

Event	T_E
3	_____
5	_____
9	_____
11	_____

6
6
23 (via 1–5–6–8–7–9)
27 (via 1–5–6–8–7–9–11)

50 Whereas the expected activity time is represented by the symbol t_e, the expected time to reach an event is represented by the symbol _____.

T_E

51 There are two other types of values associated with events. T_S, the *scheduled time*, is the contractual obligation date for the whole project, or the scheduled completion time for certain major events within the project. Refer to Figure 16.3. What is the scheduled time T_S for event 11, which is the culmination of the project? $T_S = $ _____.

27

52 T_L, on the other hand, is the *latest allowable completion time* for an event so that an entire project is kept on schedule. The T_L for each event must be so established that if every event in a network is completed by this time, then the scheduled time for the project, T_S, will be met. In Figure 16.3, what must the T_L for event 11 be? _____

27 (same as T_S, since this is the final event in the network)

53 In computing the T_L for an event, you must work back from the scheduled completion time of the final

$T_{L(3)} = 11$

event in the network. For the network below, given that the project must be completed in 15 days and that the last activity in the network (Activity 3–4) has an expected time usage of 4 days, in how many days must event 3 be reached for the project to be on schedule at that point? Insert your answer on the diagram.

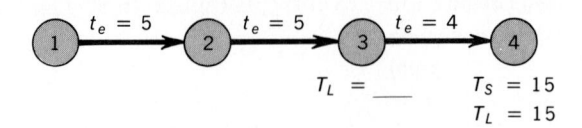

```
    t_e = 5       t_e = 5       t_e = 4
(1) ────────▶ (2) ────────▶ (3) ────────▶ (4)
                              T_L = ___    T_S = 15
                                           T_L = 15
```

54 Thus, to compute the latest allowable completion time T_L for any event, subtract the value of the t_e following it from the value of the T_L of the succeeding event. Fill in the rest of the latest allowable completion times in the following network.

$T_{L(1)} = 1$
$T_{L(2)} = 6$

```
           t_e = 5        t_e = 5        t_e = 4
      (1) ────────▶ (2) ────────▶ (3) ────────▶ (4)
      T_L = ___    T_L = ___    T_L = 11      T_S = 15
                                              T_L = 15
```

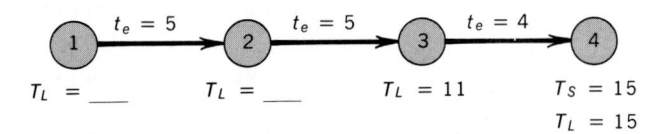

55 Of course, whether or not the latest allowable completion time for each event will be met depends on the value of T_E, the expected completion time, for each event. In the diagram below, insert the value of T_E for each event.

$T_{E(2)} = 5$
$T_{E(3)} = 10$
$T_{E(4)} = 14$

```
  T_E = 0     T_E = ___    T_E = ___    T_E = ___
  (1) ────────▶ (2) ────────▶ (3) ────────▶ (4)
       t_e = 5      t_e = 5      t_e = 4
  T_L = 1      T_L = 6      T_L = 11     T_S = 15
                                          T_L = 15
```

11
10

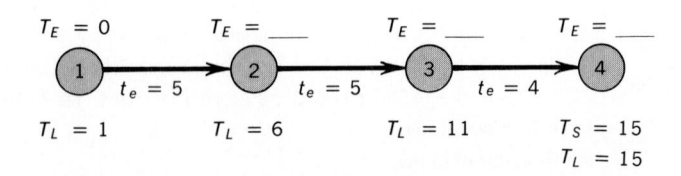

56 Referring to the diagram above, for the entire project to remain on schedule, event 3 must be completed in _____ days, whereas the expected completion time for event 3 is _____ days from now.

57 In computing the T_E for an event, we follow all paths from the beginning of the network to the event in question and choose the addition of the t_e's in the most time-consuming path. In the diagram below, for example, the expected completion time for event 4 is _____ days from now.

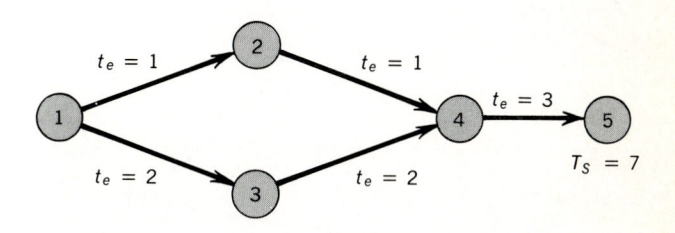

4

58 Similarly, we use the t_e's in the longest time-consuming path in computing the value of T_L by working back from the final event in a network. Thus, for the diagram above, the latest time for event 1, which is the formal beginning of the project, is _____ days from now.

0 (That is, work on the project should begin immediately.)

59 For the last frame, note that unless event 1 is accomplished immediately ($T_L = $ _____), the project will be behind schedule at event 3.

0

60 Complete the following table for the events in Figure 16.3 (repeated on the following page):

Event	T_L
11	_____
7	_____
5	_____
3	_____

27
21
6
12

61 In this section of the chapter we have described the computation of the expected activity time (t_e), the variance associated with the expected activity time (v), the expected completion time for an event (_____), the latest allowable completion time for an event (_____), and the scheduled, or contractual, completion time for an event (_____).

T_E
T_L
T_S

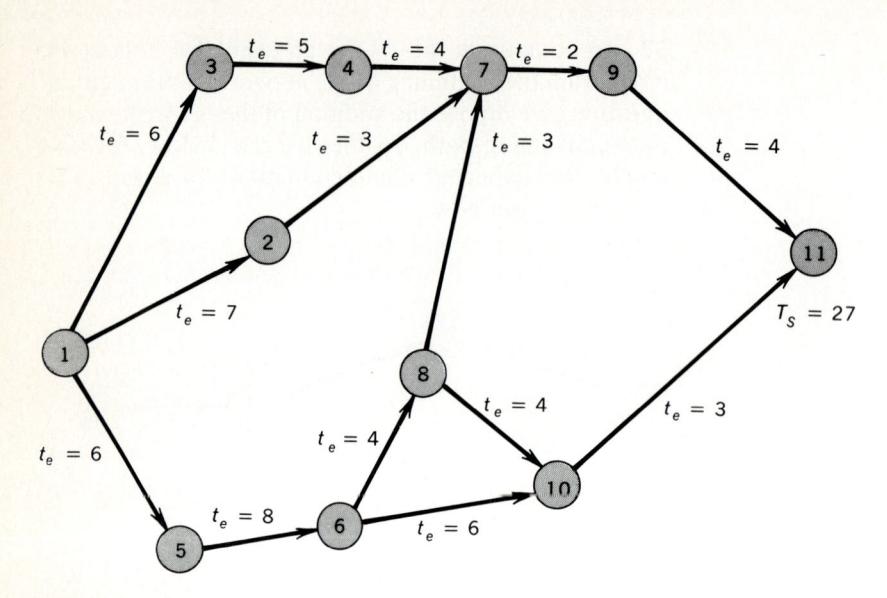

Figure 16.3 A simplified PERT network.

Using the PERT Network

We now demonstrate how the values calculated for individual activities and events are used in overall network analysis and managerial control action.

62 The *slack* associated with an event is a measurement of the excess time available to reach that event. Since it is the number of days (or weeks, etc.) by which the latest allowable completion time exceeds the expected time for an event, the appropriate formula to find the slack for an event would be $[T_L + T_E \,/\, T_L - T_E \,/\, T_E - T_L]$.

$T_L - T_E$

63 For example, if the latest allowable completion time for an event (T_L) is 14 days from now and the expected completion time for the event (T_E) is 12 days from now, then _____ days of slack are associated with reaching the event.

2

64 On the other hand, suppose that the two values just given were reversed, giving us a T_L of 12 and a T_E of 14. What would be the amount of slack associated with this event? _____

−2 days (two days behind schedule)

65 Thus there can be positive, negative, or zero slack associated with reaching an event. From the standpoint of making use of this information, the less slack there is (or the more negative slack there is), the [more / less] *critical* is that event in the project.

more

66 Compute the value of the slack associated with attaining each event in the following table:

	Event	T_L	T_E	Slack ($T_L - T_E$)
2	1	2	0	_____
0	2	5	5	_____
5	3	13	8	_____
−1	4	18	19	_____

67 Referring to the table that you just completed, which event has the most slack time and thus may have excess resources applied to its attainment? Event _____.

3

68 Referring to the table in Frame 66, which event is most critical? Event _____.

4

69 Applying the concept of slack to entire paths, rather than just to individual events, the *critical path* in a PERT network is the one that has the [most / least] slack.

least

70 To put it another way, the path from the first event to goal attainment which consumes the most time is the _____ path.

critical

71 For the network below, the critical path is the one connecting events _____.

1–3–4–5

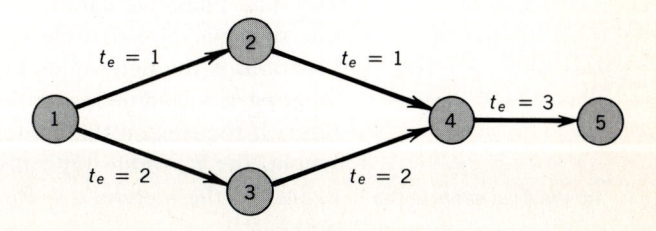

72 Refer to Figure 16.3 on page 524. The critical path for this network is the one connecting events 1-5-6-8-7-9-11 _____.

73 As the name implies, the critical path is critical because a delay in the completion of any of the events in it can result in a delay in achieving the project objective, unless resource or personnel changes are made. Is it possible for there to be two or more equally critical paths in a PERT network? [Yes / No] _____

Yes. Several paths might be at the same minimum slack level.

74 In the following network, both path 1-4-5 and path 1-2-3-5 can be considered critical paths.

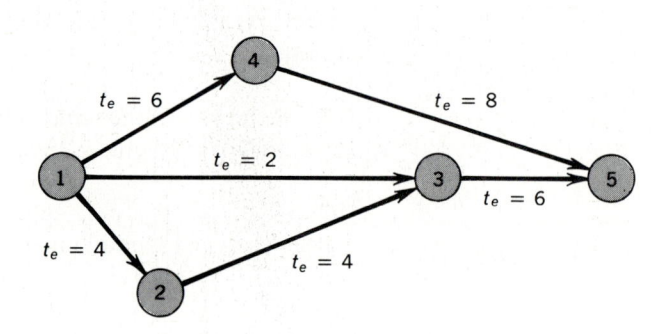

75 Because it directs the manager's attention to those events and activities that are most likely to delay the completion of a project, critical _____ path analysis is valuable as a control technique.

76 The final calculation in PERT analysis, and the one that has considerable significance for the control function, is the determination of the probability P_R of meeting a scheduled completion date for a project. Since it focuses on the completion of the project as a whole, the P_R value typically is calculated [for each event in the network / for the final event in the network.]

for the final event in the network

77 The first step in the calculation of P_R, which is the probability of _____, is to compute the value of Z.

completing the project on schedule (etc.)

78 The formula used to compute Z is

$$Z = \frac{T_S - T_E}{\sqrt{Sv}}$$

where $T_S - T_E$ is for the final event in the network and Sv is the sum of all the variances *in the critical path* of the network. In terms of this formula, can the value of Z be negative? [Yes / No] Explain.

Yes. Whenever a "behind-schedule" condition exists.

79 Find the value of Z for the following network, given the formula

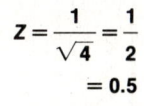

$$Z = \frac{T_S - T_E}{\sqrt{Sv}}$$

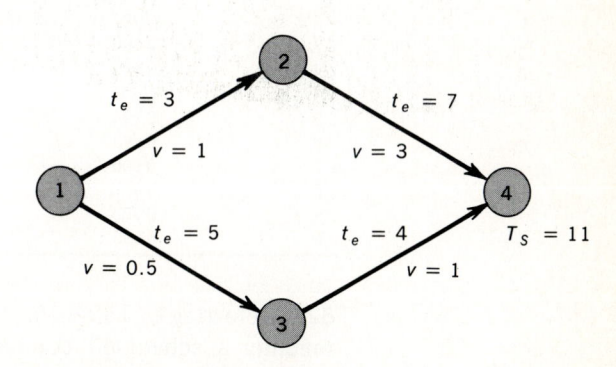

$Z = \dfrac{1}{\sqrt{4}} = \dfrac{1}{2}$
$= 0.5$

(Don't forget that variances are summed for the critical path only.)

80 The second step in the procedure to determine the value of P_R, which is the probability of completing the project on schedule, is to interpret the meaning of the _____ [symbol] value just computed.

Z

0.692

81 The meaning of any value of Z can be determined by reference to the Z table, or the table of areas under the normal distribution curve, which is included in most statistics textbooks. Table 16.1 shown below is a condensed version of this table, somewhat modified to facilitate the determination of P_R values. Referring to Table 16.1, we can see that the value of P_R associated with a Z of 0.5 is _____.

Table 16.1 Table of Cumulative Proportions of Area under the Normal Curve for Various Values of Z

Z	P_R	Z	P_R
0.0	0.500	0.0	0.500
0.1	0.540	−0.1	0.460
0.2	0.579	−0.2	0.421
0.3	0.618	−0.3	0.382
0.4	0.655	−0.4	0.345
0.5	0.692	−0.5	0.308
0.6	0.726	−0.6	0.274
0.7	0.758	−0.7	0.242
0.8	0.788	−0.8	0.212
0.9	0.816	−0.9	0.184
1.0	0.841	−1.0	0.159
1.1	0.864	−1.1	0.136
1.2	0.885	−1.2	0.115
1.3	0.903	−1.3	0.097
1.4	0.919	−1.4	0.081
1.5	0.933	−1.5	0.067
1.6	0.945	−1.6	0.055
1.7	0.955	−1.7	0.045
1.8	0.964	−1.8	0.036
1.9	0.971	−1.9	0.029
2.0	0.977	−2.0	0.023
2.1	0.982	−2.1	0.018
2.2	0.986	−2.2	0.014
2.3	0.989	−2.3	0.011
2.4	0.992	−2.4	0.008
2.5	0.994	−2.5	0.006
2.6	0.995	−2.6	0.005
2.7	0.996	−2.7	0.004
2.8	0.997	−2.8	0.003
2.9	0.998	−2.9	0.002
3.0	0.999	−3.0	0.001

0.500
0.841; 0.242

82 Referring to Table 16.1, what is the probability of meeting a scheduled completion date for a project when the Z value is 0? _____. When $Z = 1.0$? _____. When $Z = -0.7$? _____.

83 Since $T_S - T_E$ is in the numerator of the formula for Z, whenever the scheduled completion date and

0.500 (since $Z = 0$ in this case)

expected completion date exactly coincide, the numerical probability of completing the project on time is stated as (refer to Table 16.1) _____.

84 Although a probability of 0.50 indicates a 50 percent chance of completing the project on time, this is usually considered an acceptable level, perhaps because any minor "slippage" can be offset by the addition of resources to the project. On the other hand, a probability less than about 0.25 usually is interpreted as an indication of considerable risk. Ideally, should we try to eliminate risk by getting P_R to be as close to 1.0 as possible? [Yes / No]

No (See next frame.)

85 Although a manager might feel more comfortable with a very high P_R value because of reduced time pressures, in most instances it is also an indication that personnel or other resources are being used extravagantly, so that high P_R values [are / are not] generally considered "good" by management.

are not

86 Whereas it is taken as an indication of considerable risk when the P_R value is less than _____, a P_R greater than 0.60 is taken to indicate that excess resources are possibly being applied to the project.

0.25

87 What is the value of P_R for the network below? $P_R = $ _____

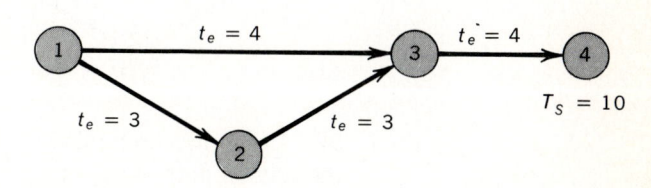

$P_R = 0.500$ (Note that $T_S - T_E = 0$.)

[Network diagram: Node 1 connects to Node 3 with $t_e = 4$, Node 3 connects to Node 4 with $t_e = 4$. Node 1 connects to Node 2 with $t_e = 3$, Node 2 connects to Node 3 with $t_e = 3$. $T_S = 10$ at Node 4.]

88 When a P_R of 0.500 is obtained, is any corrective action usually called for? [Yes / No]

No (except possibly when completion of the entire project is near at hand)

89 Given the following network, determine the value of P_R, using the formula

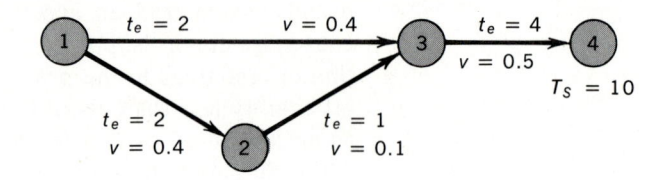

$$Z = \frac{3}{1} = 3.0 \quad Z = \frac{T_S - T_E}{\sqrt{Sv}} \quad P_R = \underline{\hspace{1cm}}$$

$P_R = 0.999$

$t_e = 2$, $v = 0.4$ (1→3)
$v = 0.4$ (3)
$t_e = 4$, $v = 0.5$ (3→4)
$t_e = 2$, $v = 0.4$ (1→2)
$t_e = 1$, $v = 0.1$ (2→3)
$T_S = 10$

90 What kind of corrective action, if any, is appropriate for the situation just described?

Possibly shifting personnel and other resources to another project (etc.)

91 Given the following network, determine the probability of completing the project on time:

$$Z = \frac{-3}{2} = -1.5 \quad Z = \frac{T_S - T_E}{\sqrt{Sv}} \quad P_R = \underline{\hspace{1cm}}$$

$P_R = 0.067$

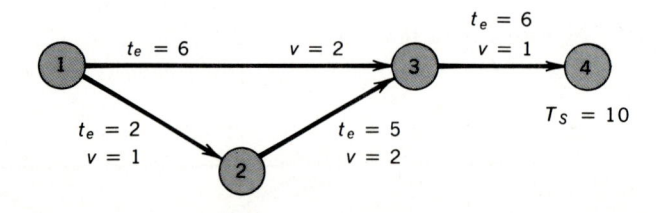

$t_e = 6$, $v = 2$ (1→3)
$t_e = 6$, $v = 1$ (3→4)
$t_e = 2$, $v = 1$ (1→2)
$t_e = 5$, $v = 2$ (2→3)
$T_S = 10$

92 In the preceding frame, which of the activities in the critical path should be given principal attention in attempting to bring the project back on schedule? Activity [1–2 / 2–3 / 3–4]

2–3 (See next frame.)

93 It is tempting to assume that the activity that has the largest expected time can be reduced most. However, the relevant value is not t_e itself, but the

variance _____ associated with each expected activity time.

94 For projects extending over a long time period, thousands of activities and events may make up the PERT network. Under these conditions, would the graphic portrayal of the entire network become unwieldy? [Yes / No]

Yes

95 Accordingly, various summary and detail charts are generally prepared when a great many events constitute a project, and critical paths are identified by computer analysis. However, the basic computational and analytical procedure [is / is not] the same as for the simplified examples in this chapter.

is

Review

96 Systems-oriented control procedures, such as PERT, are mainly directed toward the control of _____. (Frames 1 to 3)

time

97 An early scheduling method that resembles PERT and CPM, but includes no analysis of interrelationships among all of the events, is the Gantt _____ chart. (Frames 4 to 12)

milestone

98 A PERT network is made up of a series of _____, connected by _____, which lead to the attainment of an objective. (Frames 13 to 27)

events; activities

99 The three time estimates for each activity, represented by the symbols a, m, and b, are combined into a weighted average represented by the symbol ____. (Frames 28 to 37)

t_e

100 v is the symbol for the _____ associated with the expected time for each activity. (Frames 38 to 44)

variance

101 The expected completion time for an event is represented by the symbol ____, the latest allowable completion time for an event is represented by ____,

T_E
T_L

and the scheduled completion time for a project is represented by _____. (Frames 45 to 61)

T_S

102 The slack associated with an event is the excess time available to reach an event. It is computed by subtracting the value of _____ from the value of _____ for that event. (Frames 62 to 68)

T_E; T_L

103 The path from the first event to the final event in a network that has the least slack is called the _____. (Frames 69 to 75).

critical path

104 P_R is the notation for the probability of _____. In order to determine P_R, the value of _____ [symbol] must first be computed. (Frames 76 to 80)

completing a project on schedule; Z

105 It is considered an indication of high risk when the P_R value is less than about _____, whereas it is generally taken as an indication that excess resources are being applied to the project when the P_R is greater than _____ for an ongoing project. (Frames 81 to 86)

0.25

0.60

106 Given a project that is behind schedule, it is most fruitful to apply corrective action by trying to reduce the time for those activities with the highest _____. (Frames 92 to 95)

variance (not necessarily those with the highest expected time t_e)

107 Given the following data for the critical path of a PERT network, complete the table below using the formulas provided. (Frames 36 and 37, 41 to 44)

$$t_e = \frac{a + 4m + b}{6} \qquad v = [(b - a)/6]^2$$

t_e	v	Activity	a	m	b	t_e	v
6	1	1–2	3	6	9	___	___
15	4	2–4	9	15	21	___	___
10	4	4–7	6	9	18	___	___

108 For the data above, compute the value of Z given that $T_S = 28$. (Frames 76 to 80)

$= \dfrac{28 - 31}{3}$

$Z = \dfrac{T_S - T_E}{\sqrt{S_V}}$

$= -1.0$

109 Referring to Table 16.1, what is the P_R value associated with a Z of -1.0? $P_R = \underline{\qquad}$. (Frames 87 to 91)

0.159

110 For the data in Frame 107, to which activity in the critical path would you give principal attention in attempting to bring the project back on schedule? (Frames 92 to 93) $\underline{\qquad}$

Either 2–4 or 4–7 or both, since the variances are equal

Discussion Questions

1. Why is the application of PERT particularly useful in the aerospace industry?
2. Discuss the importance of the three activity time estimates for PERT analysis. How might these estimates be made more accurate?
3. What is the value of determining the slack associated with each of the paths in a network?
4. At what value is P_R considered to be too low? Too high? What is the remedial action in each case?
5. In what ways can PERT be used as a planning device? In what ways can it be used as a control device?
6. Discuss the similarities and differences between using the Gantt milestone chart and PERT analysis for project planning and controlling.
7. All the examples of applying PERT have implied the development of some type of product or physical component. Consider how PERT analysis might be used by a bank.
8. One criticism directed at PERT as well as other similar methods of analysis is that the quantitative results are misleading because they are in fact based on judgments and subjective approximations. In what respects is this criticism appropriate and in what respects is it inappropriate?

References

Avots, I. "The Management Side of PERT." *California Management Review*, vol. 4, no. 2, Winter 1962.

Levin, R. I., and C. A. Kirkpatrick. *"Planning and Control with PERT/CPM."* New York: McGraw-Hill, 1966.

Reuter, V. G. "Utilization of Graphic Management Tools." *Arizona Business*, vol. 25, no. 7, August-September 1978.

Sherrard, W. R., and F. Mehlick. "PERT, a Dynamic Approach." *Decision Sciences*, vol. 3, no. 2, April 1972.

Swanson, L. A., and H. L. Pazer. "Implications of the Underlying Assumptions of PERT." *Decision Sciences*, vol. 2, no. 4, October 1971.

CASE PROBLEMS: Program Evaluation and Review Technique

1. A professional society holds an annual dinner meeting at which new members are initiated. The number of people attending this meeting has not varied much from year to year. In addition to the initiation itself, a highlight of the evening is an after-dinner report on the current "state of the profession" by a distinguished practitioner. Using the following events, which are *not* listed in order, construct a PERT network representing the pattern of activities leading up to the dinner meeting.

1. The menu is planned.
2. Certificates of membership for new members are received.
3. Replies and payments are received from present members.
4. Program planning is begun.
5. Prospective members are identified.
6. Invitations are mailed to present members.
7. Invitations are mailed to prospective members.
8. A place for the meeting is established.
9. The dinner meeting is held.
10. Certificates of membership are ordered for new members.
11. A price is established.
12. Replies and payments are received from prospective members.
13. An after-dinner speaker is arranged.
14. A seating arrangement is planned.
15. A date for the meeting is established.

Case Problems • 535

2. Identify the errors in the following PERT network.

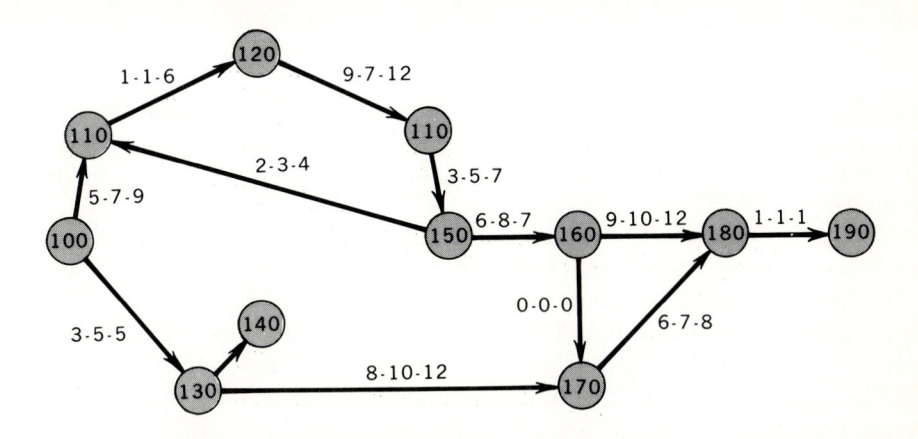

3. Identify the critical path in the network below and compute the amount of slack given that the project is scheduled for completion in thirty months. What can we conclude about the probability that the project will be completed on time? If we are now at event 110, to which activity should we give principal attention in order to accelerate progress toward completion of the project?

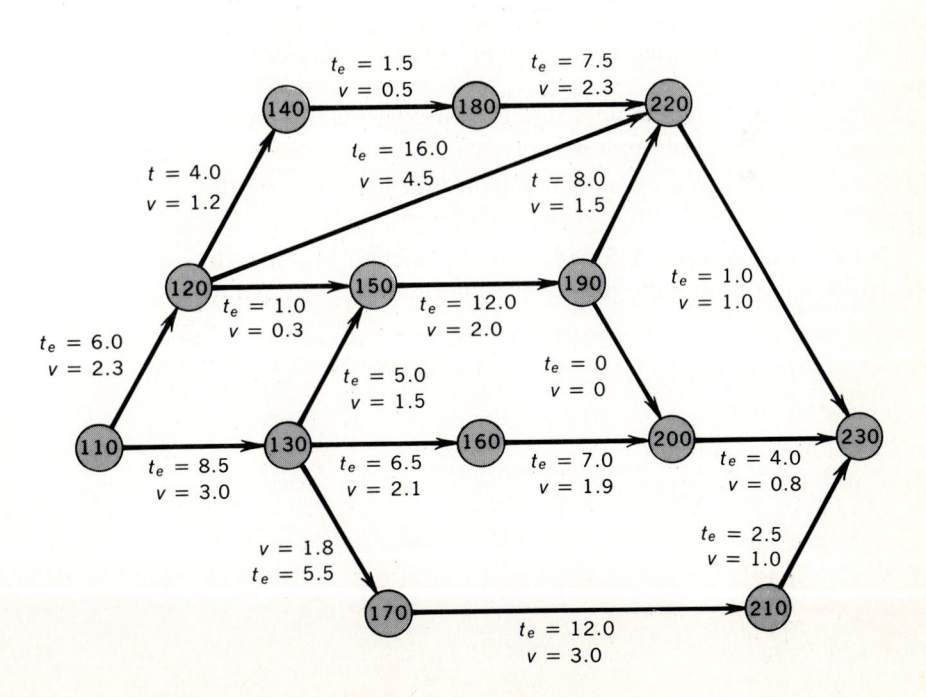

CASE STUDY: An Unsuccessful Application of PERT

For a number of years the Wilson Construction Company has used a modified Gantt chart to help schedule the work activities of the various subcontractors participating in major building projects. After Tom Gadfree, a production superintendent in the company, attended a university-sponsored seminar on PERT analysis, he determined to apply the technique to the next major construction project to which he was assigned.

During the following month an appropriate opportunity presented itself. In conjunction with obtaining the bids from the subcontractors, he also asked each subcontractor to provide an estimate of the optimistic, pessimistic, and most likely amount of time that would be required to do each phase of the work. He then used this information as the quantitative input into the network chart, which he developed based on his knowledge of the interrelationships among and between the various phases of construction.

The following year Tom Gadfree happened to meet Professor Jenkins, who had conducted the seminar on PERT analysis, and the professor asked Tom if he ever got the chance to use the technique. "I sure did," replied Tom, "and I could have lost my job because of it. For one thing, it turned out that all of the time estimates given to me were way low. As a result, the expected time that I came up with for completing the project constituted about 70 percent of the time it actually took. Furthermore, the subcontractors kept slipping back and forth so much in their schedules that I spent a helluva lot of time redrawing that blasted network chart. One tryout of that technique is more than enough for me!"

1. Did Tom Gadfree use an appropriate basis for constructing the network chart in the first place? Why or why not?
2. What errors did he make in obtaining the time estimates for the required activities?
3. What comments might be made with respect to his work in redrawing the network chart during the period of construction?

APPLICATIONS READING:

Management Rediscovers CPM

George J. Berkwitt
Dun's Review

Two years ago, Borden Co. came up with an idea for a new plastic product that would give the company an entree into a $500-million consumer market. In the past, new products at Borden had run the usual gamut of research and development, trial manufacturing, trial marketing, and, finally, if it crossed all the hurdles, full-scale production. Inevitably, the course was strewn with delays, indecision and tangled lines of authority.

But Borden's plastic gadget (the product is still under wraps) is right on target. The difference: CPM. CPM, or critical path method when it is spelled out, is not new. It was developed by a du Pont engineer and a Remington Rand computer expert fifteen years ago. But over the years, it has seen little use outside the construction industry, and its application to corporate management problems was virtually nonexistent. Until a year or two ago, that is. Then corporations, in a continuing search for new, computer-assisted management techniques, rediscovered CPM, and it is now riding a new wave of popularity. Borden's use of the technique to help launch a new business venture is only one of a number of project-oriented functions in the corporation that are increasingly turning to CPM. Among them:

- Marketing. 3M Co. employs a ninety-step CPM network to help in the merchandising of new products. National Cash Register coordinated the introduction of its Century line of computers in 120 cities through the use of CPM. And it has become a standard tool for product launchings at Lever Bros. and Diamond Shamrock.

- Mergers and acquisitions. Many of the gaps and overlaps resulting from the massive combination last year of four railroads to form Burlington Northern were eliminated by CPM. The technique is used for acquisitions by such companies as Fairchild Hiller and Stanley Works. And in CPM's biggest coup so far, it helped smooth the way for the merger of General Electric's computer business into Honeywell.

- Management information systems. Connecticut Bank & Trust, Hartford, used CPM for transferring information into its computers. GE will employ the technique in setting up a new information bank it calls "Management Decision System."

- Staffing and training. International Telephone & Telegraph is in the midst of a CPM-assisted program to train project managers throughout its worldwide network of operating companies.

Source: Reprinted with the special permission of *Dun's Review*, vol. 97, no. 5, May 1971. Copyright 1971, Dun and Bradstreet Publications Corporation.

And the technique is getting an increased play among service companies, too. Hynes & Diamond, a New York City law firm, is using it to trace the most important elements of the contract suits it handles for corporations. And at least two consultants, MDC Systems Corp. of Cherry Hill, New Jersey and William G. Baum of Ardsley, New York are peddling CPM in connection with assignments in cost control and the establishment of maintenance systems.

The technique that is performing all these services is based on an appealingly simple premise: that there is usually just one sequence of activities that is really crucial to the completion of a project. This sequence is called, as you have already guessed, the critical path. CPM relegates all other activities to subservient positions under the critical activities. In practice, the CPM chart can be a linear display of major moves, together with the subactivities needed to accomplish those moves, or it can be a computer program, the only visualization of which comes in the form of printout.

In either case, CPM is providing the answers to a number of seemingly complicated questions in the companies that are using it. Given any activity along the critical path, CPM will immediately indicate what must be accomplished before that activity can be undertaken, which activities will have to wait for the completion of the given activity and which activities can be carried on simultaneously.

It is easy to see why the construction industry has led the way in adopting CPM. With the limited space of the typical urban construction site, materials have had to be made available precisely on schedule: too early and there would be no place to store them; too late and they would delay the entire project. The same stringencies apply to the deployment of manpower and cash. CPM provided the ideal scheduling tool. With it, all material, manpower and cash needs can be assembled under each of the critical stages of the project. CPM, for instance, performed illustriously in coordinating the 4,000 major activities in the construction of TWA's new wing at Kennedy International Airport and in the reorganization of the American Stock Exchange—without disrupting a single day of trading.

Most management projects, of course, are not as readily laid out along a linear path as is a construction project. But with an assist from the computer, corporate planners are learning to use CPM even in complex undertakings such as the new product launching at Borden.

The Borden Chemical Division, where the product is being developed, mapped out the new business venture in three critical path networks, one for each year of a three-year program. For the first year, division planners identified five critical steps: (1) Define the nature of the market and determine its potential. (2) Survey buyers and servicemen in the market for their receptivity to the product. (3) Enter the product-development phase and build a prototype. (4) Refine estimates on market potential. (5) Make a profitability analysis by determining the costs of each of the previous steps.

Holding Open the Options

The principal feature of the critical path of the first year was that it would allow Borden to quit the project with the smallest possible investment if at any stage the product no longer looked profitable. "By the end of the first year," says Henry B. Lange, Borden's director of commerical development, new business ventures, "we knew that we could produce the product profitably. We had the prototype, knew the price and we had a good fix on the market. If any of these looked bad," he adds, "we had the option of closing up shop."

The second year's critical path, leading up to delivery of the product to about a dozen test markets, increased Borden's commitment to the product, but still left open a number of options as to the magnitude of the project. These will be settled as the product is pushed along this year's critical path of broader manufacturing and marketing.

In sum, CPM has provided Lange and the other managers on the project team a graphic view of the entire venture with completion dates, support activities and costs affixed to every stage. And as Lange points out, it has aided one of the most orderly product introductions in Borden's history.

Another company that has turned to CPM to help it get products onto the market is Diamond Shamrock, the large chemical company. Until recently, Diamond, too, had suffered its share of new product fiascos. One problem, as an insider relates it, was that products were announced well before they were ready to go onto the market. As a result, the sales effort was getting ahead of manufacturing, initial enthusiasm among customers was dampened by delayed deliveries and sales targets were missed by wide margins.

"Inadequate organization and planning" was the verdict, so Diamond decided to submit the whole process to CPM. It started with a six-month critical path for a line of sixteen cleaning and sanitizing products. Diamond not only constructed a critical path for the line, it also assigned each stage to a manager, who was then responsible for completing that stage within the established schedule. Like the Borden project, Diamond's critical path also incorporated a number of review points where "go" or "no-go" decisions were to be made for the products. One major review occurs directly after the product-development phase. Another comes seven weeks later, when the first major test marketing information has been assimilated.

In addition to the cleaning products, a number of new products last year were submitted to the discipline of CPM scheduling. "Those that used it," says Whitney Evans, manager of corporate development, "were eminently successful." Evans plans to expand the division's use of CPM "just as rapidly as our organizational resources will permit."

Over at International Telephone and Telegraph, a very different corporate activity is coming under the control of CPM: training and staffing. Last year, the company announced the formation of a task force whose assignment was to "conduct a development program in project management." With ITT carrying on a continuous stream of projects throughout the world, headquarters wanted to sharpen its division's competence in their management.

Task-force director Russell Archibald, who happens to be co-author of a book on CPM-like management techniques called *Network-Based Management Decisions*, has an eight-foot CPM blueprint of the program rolled up in his files. In concept, it is like the spine of a very long fish with the crucial steps in the project—preparation of learning aids, top-management orientation, and so forth—arrayed like vertebrae along the center and the subactivities feeding into it all along the chart. It tells the members of Archibald's team what steps are absolutely essential to the success of the training and staffing program and what must be accomplished to achieve those steps.

Joining GE and Honeywell

Probably the most dramatic use of CPM to date was its service in the merger of GE's computer operations into Honeywell. Because of the vast number of factors, ranging from manpower and physical plant to legal and political considerations, most industry observers believe that this largest-of-all computer mergers would not have been possible without CPM.

"It was a huge job," says Stanley M. Seeds, who as director of corporate acquisitions headed up the merger procedure (he is now controller of information services, Honeywell Information Systems). To coordinate the project, Seeds established in Honeywell's Minneapolis headquarters a "merger war room," whose walls were literally papered with CPM flow charts. The room also was equipped with a worldwide communications hook-up. "We needed to maintain a smooth work flow and tight control," says Seeds. "After all, we were making moves in eighteen countries," he adds.

CPM's role: to stack all the activities that could be performed simultaneously and assign deadlines for activities that had to be performed in sequence. The sequenced activities were those that lay on the critical path. In fact, there was not one but two critical paths. One covered the legal considerations of the merger: the preparation of proxy material, obtaining Securities and Exchange Commission approval, obtaining necessary approvals from foreign governments and the like. The other traced the essential operational moves necessitated by the merger: selection of plants, formation of a product line, organization of a marketing force and the like.

Throughout the merger, the "war room" buzzed with clicking teletype machines, ringing telephones and milling task-force managers (there were fifty task forces in all). Surrounding this cacophony were the CPM flow charts. With push-pin flags marking the day-to-day progress along critical paths, visiting members of top management could immediately determine the status on any segment of the merger.

"We hit the target date for the first phase of the merger right on the head," says Seeds. "I just can't imagine our having accomplished anything this big without CPM."

That sort of endorsement is being heard more and more frequently these days as management rediscovers CPM.

Questions on Reading

1. What is the fundamental premise underlying the use of the critical path method in planning and managing a new project?
2. Why do you think the construction industry has been a major user of CPM?
3. What two separate critical paths were identified when GE's computer operations were merged into Honeywell?
4. In the text, it is stated that network analysis methods such as CPM and PERT are particularly oriented toward planning and control with respect to *time*. Are the several examples of CPM applications in this article consistent with this observation? Cite some of the examples.

Systems Concepts

Throughout this book we have followed the functional approach to management, by which the process of management is described as including the functions of planning, organizing, directing, and controlling. An alternative to the functional approach, and one that has experienced considerable development in recent years, is based on general systems theory. Although the techniques of the systems approach are particularly associated with the development of new planning and controlling techniques, the approach has broader implications in terms of the way that organizational activities are viewed.

Part 6

17 THE SYSTEMS APPROACH TO MANAGEMENT

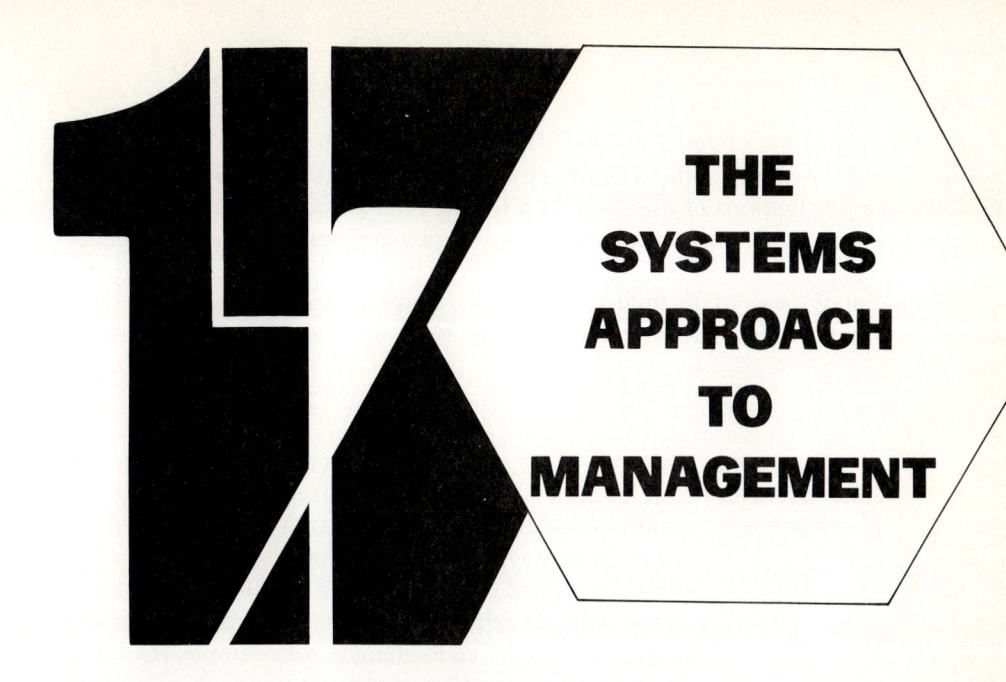

- Systems Concepts and Management
- Program Management
- Computer Information Systems
- Review
- Discussion Questions
- References
- Case Study: A First Experience with Program Management
- Case Study: A Systems-Oriented Manager of Data Processing
- Applications Reading: "Project Management—A New Style for Success" Richard A. Jacobs
- Questions on Reading

We begin this chapter by describing the general nature of the systems approach as it has been applied in the physical and biological sciences and then consider the implications of this approach for the management functions of planning, organizing, and controlling. A particular development, program management, will then be considered as an example of the application of a systems-oriented point of view. In the final section of this chapter we describe the development of computer information systems and their use in enhancing effective management.

Systems Concepts and Management

On the most elementary level, systems analysis implies an analysis of wholes rather than parts. In addition to accepting the assertion that "everything depends on everything else," the systems approach is directed toward discovering and explaining the nature of the multiple relationships among the components of a system. As applied in biology, for example, the focus is on the total organism, and functions such as respiration and digestion are viewed as subsystems within the context of the total bodily system, rather than as isolated processes. In management, the systems approach directs our attention to the total firm as an entity, to an identification of the objectives of that firm, and to the identification of the functions necessary for the achievement of those objectives. In this section we begin by offering a definition of a system in general and then we consider the implications of the systems approach to the management functions of planning, organizing, and controlling and to the related organizational processes of communication and decision making.

1 A *system* can be defined as an established *arrangement of components* which leads to the attainment of *particular objectives* according to *plan*. By the use of italics, we have stressed three principal ingredients in this definition. In analyzing an established system or devising a new system, we should first identify the

particular objectives _____ of the system.

2 The objectives of the system should be identified first because these provide the basis for evaluating functions and relationships within the system. In designing a system, establishing the necessary *arrangement of components* is similar to what we have

organizing   previously designated as the management function of _____.

3 Of course, the identification of objectives is itself part of the planning process. However, when we say that a system is an established arrangement of components which leads to the attainment of particular objectives *according to plan,* we are referring to the necessity of establishing specific policies, procedures, and

objectives   methods by which the _____ are to be attained.

4 Thus, in general a system is an established arrange-

components   ment of _____ which leads to the at-
objectives   tainment of particular _____ according to
plan   _____.

5 Another useful way of considering the meaning of the systems approach in science as well as in administration is to describe how it differs from a nonsystems approach. Sir Arthur Eddington, a noted physicist, has illustrated this difference in his field by the following analogy: "We often think that when we have completed our study of *one* we know all about *two,* because 'two' is 'one and one.' We forget that we still have to make a study of 'and.' Secondary physics is the study of 'and'—that is to say, of organization."[1] By his illustration, Eddington suggests that the study of

in addition to   "and" needs to be done [instead of / in addition to] the study of "one."

6 Thus, the systems approach cannot take the place of the study of specific or molecular processes. However, beyond some point further attention to specifics is less useful for increasing overall understanding than is the study of their relationships. This suggests that

follow   the study of relationships should [precede / follow] the study of specifics.

7 Because the individual scientific disciplines were originally oriented toward research in specific fields, such as physics, chemistry, and astronomy, the later

---

[1]Sir Arthur Eddington, *The Nature of the Physical World,* University of Michigan Press, Ann Arbor, 1958, p. 104.

application of the systems orientation has generally resulted in the need for so-called "interdisciplinary approaches," involving [only one / several] fields of inquiry.

several

8 Similarly, in the area of administrative application the systems approach suggests that a firm's plant location decision, for example, [should / should not] be considered solely as a financial problem.

should not

9 Thus, just as the scientist needs to have knowledge in several related fields in order to be able to apply the systems approach, the manager who wishes to apply this approach needs to be a managerial [specialist / generalist].

generalist

10 Being a "managerial generalist" suggests that as he views the organization as a total entity, the systems-oriented manager [does / does not] need knowledge in specific functional areas, such as finance and personnel.

does

11 Turning now to the implications of the systems approach to some of the management functions that we have studied in this book, we can see that once organizational objectives have been defined, the responsibility for the design of the appropriate system is that of [top / middle / first-level] management.

top

12 The application of the systems approach to business *planning* results in an emphasis on the several major systems that bear upon the adequacy of planning: the *environmental system,* the *competitive system,* and the *internal system.* These are arranged in a hierarchy, with the broadest system being the _____ system.

environmental

13 As contrasted with the competitive and internal systems, consideration of such factors as population changes, anticipated governmental actions, and international developments are included in the _____ system.

environmental

14 On the other hand, consideration of the past,

present, and anticipated actions of other firms in the same product or service field is included in the _____ system.

competitive

15 In addition to the importance of the environmental and competitive systems in the formulation of business plans, particular unique features of the firm itself, including its location, facilities, and personnel, need to be considered as factors in the _____ system.

internal

16 Thus, from the systems viewpoint a hierarchy of three systems impinges on the planning process: the _____, _____, and _____ systems.

**environmental;
competitive;
internal**

17 On the level of planning *procedures*, a planning and controlling technique which focuses on the relationships among the events and activities leading to goal attainment is PERT, as described in Chapter 16. In its orientation on an entire project, PERT is representative of the [functional / systems] approach to management.

systems

18 Developments in quantitative decision-making techniques have also influenced the application of the systems approach to management. As we indicated in Chapter 5, operations research specifically involves a systemwide approach to management decision making and has thus [accelerated / retarded] the development of the systems approach.

accelerated

19 As is true for the planning function, the function of *organizing* has also been affected by the systems approach. Management historians have described three stages in the development of organization theory: the *classical, neoclassical,* and *modern.* The organization chart can be thought of as one of the first "products" of organization theory, and it is thus associated with _____ organization theory.

classical

20 *Classical organization theory* has stressed description of the formal organization structure, hierarchical relationships, span of control, and line-staff relationships. Therefore, of the following two areas of management concern, the one that particularly reflects the classical orientation is [assignment of authority / determining necessary channels of communication].

assignment of authority

21 Whereas classical organization theory can be described as being formal and impersonal in its orientation, *neoclassical organization theory* represents a deliberate effort to modify the theory by including human relations considerations and the influence of the informal organization on performance. The development of the neoclassical position was stimulated by the [scientific management movement / Hawthorne studies], as described in Chapter 1.

Hawthorne studies

22 The two approaches to organization theory which we have considered thus far, both of which begin with the formal organization chart as a point of reference, are the _____ and _____ approaches.

classical; neoclassical

23 On the other hand, *modern organization theory* has extended the modification of the classical theory to the point where the formal structure is not the principal reference point, but rather one of a number of organizational components that need to be considered. Included as organizational components are the individuals, informal groups and intergroup relationships. Thus modern organization theory directly reflects the _____ approach to management that we are considering in this chapter.

systems

24 Modern organization theory has been a topic of interest and discussion among organization theorists for some years. By requiring the manager to have knowledge of the informal and formal parts of the organization *and* their interactions, its application in business organizations has contributed to the concern about developing managerial [specialists / generalists].

generalists

25 The development of modern organization theory has increased managerial recognition of the "and" in organizational relationships. However, the formal organization chart, developed in the context of classical organization theory, continues to be the principal method by which business firms describe their organization structure. The unavailability of a practical "modern organization chart" to represent all the components within the firm has had the effect of [enhancing / limiting] the application of modern organization theory.

limiting

26 Turning now to the management function of *controlling*, we can observe that there are two types of control systems from the systems viewpoint: the *open-sequence* and the *closed-sequence* systems. In the open-sequence system, control activity is initiated on the basis of an information source which is unaffected by the system being controlled. Thus, an example of an open-sequence system is [a home thermostat system / a clock-controlled sprinkling system].

a clock-controlled sprinkling system

27 In engineering parlance, the open-sequence system has been referred to as the *open-loop* system. As illustrated in Figure 17.1, for our lawn sprinkler example the "loop" is open because the amount of sprinkler discharge [does / does not] affect the operation of the timing device.

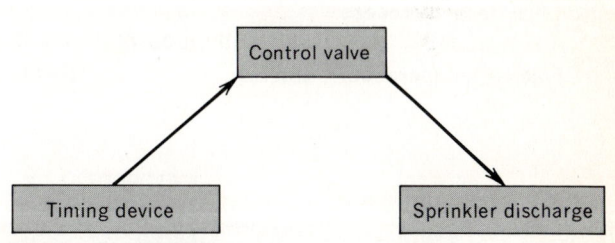

does not

Figure 17.1 An open-sequence control system.

28 In contrast, in a closed-sequence or *closed-loop* system the information used as the basis for control action *is* affected by the system being controlled. Thus, in Figure 17.2 the amount of heat emission [does / does not] affect the thermostat.

does

29 Whereas the timing mechanism is activated by in-

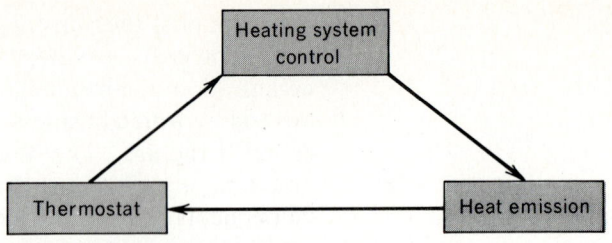

Figure 17.2 A closed-sequence control system.

open-sequence	formation outside the system being controlled, the thermostat system is responsive to the effects of the system output. Therefore, the use of the timing mechanism is an example of an _____
closed-sequence	system, whereas the use of the thermostat is an example of a _____ system.

30 The type of control system that can most realistically be described as being "automatic" is the [open- / closed-] sequence system.

closed-

31 A key feature of an automatic or closed-sequence system is *feedback,* which we also discussed in Chapter 10 on communication. Figure 17.3 illustrates the operation of feedback in such a system. As indicated, the feedback first affects the

correction process

_____, and then through the subsequent corrective action that is initiated, it affects

process (or operation)

the _____ itself.

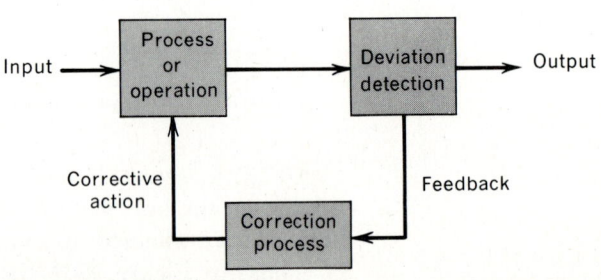

Figure 17.3 Simple feedback in a control system. (Adapted from Harold Koontz and Cyril O'Donnell, *Management: A Systems and Contingency Analysis of Managerial Functions,* 6th ed., McGraw-Hill Book Company, New York, 1976, p. 644. Reproduced with permission.)

32 As general business-related examples, suppose a training manager establishes a technical training course based on historical standards, and the course contents are never changed when the course is repeated. From the systems viewpoint, control of course coverage can be considered [an open-sequence / a closed-sequence] system. On the other hand, suppose the course contents are modified somewhat each time that it is repeated, based on obtaining information regarding the success of previous trainees as well as changing organizational needs. Control of course contents can then be described as constituting a(n) _____ system.

an open-sequence

closed-sequence

33 In general, when system output is controlled on the basis of a comparison between established standards and the output of the system itself, the control system can be described as being an automatic, or _____, system, and the information used as the basis for system control is called _____.

closed-sequence

feedback

34 Turning now to the organization as a whole, in practice the systems approach to management has typically been associated with the organization being conceived of as an information-decision system whose design ultimately affects organizational success. The "organization structure" of primary interest is therefore the one indicating [division of work/ channels of communication].

channels of communication

35 Thus if the firm were to be designed from the systems point of view, it would be based on the needed communication channels in the system. Since established organization charts are based on the division-of-work concept and the description of only the formal communication channels, redefining the organization from the systems viewpoint would require consideration of the formal and _____ components of the organization.

informal

36 Getting back to the definition of a system offered at the beginning of this section, we indicated that it is an established arrangement of components which leads to particular objectives according to plan. As it

554 ● Chapter 17 ● The Systems Approach to Management

communication

has thus far been applied in the systems approach, the arrangement of components is viewed as a [communication / work-group] structure.

37 Figure 17.4 illustrates the design of a basic system. We have not yet described the kind of inputs that enter the processor of the system. The basic ingredients of a process have been identified as being *information, energy,* and *materials.* If the system output is a service rather than a product, the ingredient that might not be included as an input in this case is

materials _____.

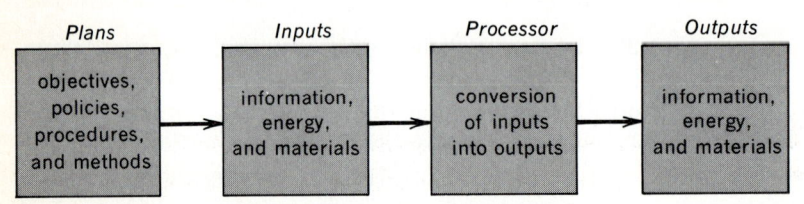

```
   Plans              Inputs           Processor          Outputs
┌──────────┐      ┌──────────┐      ┌──────────┐      ┌──────────┐
│objectives,│      │information,│ →  │conversion │ →  │information,│
│ policies, │  →   │  energy,  │     │ of inputs │     │  energy,  │
│procedures,│      │and materials│    │into outputs│    │and materials│
│and methods│      └──────────┘      └──────────┘      └──────────┘
└──────────┘
```

Figure 17.4 The design of a basic system.

38 Generally, however, all three ingredients—information, energy, and materials—are required as inputs to produce a product or service. Some of the materials may become part of the product and are thus *product materials,* whereas others are embodied in the machines and plant and are *operational materials.* In terms of these definitions, the iron ore shipped to a steel mill is _____ material.

product

39 On the other hand, the furnaces, rolling mills, computers, and other equipment associated with converting product materials into useful outputs are _____ materials.

operational

40 The *output* of a system can also be described as being in the form of information, energy, or materials. The manufacture of automobiles, for example, directly represents a _____ output.

materials

41 The output of an electrical generating station would be described as being a form of _____.

energy

42 Finally, the output of an advisory staff or consult-

information

ing firm, such as a tax consultant, would be in the form of _____.

43 Figure 17.5 is a more extensive representation of a system than the examples we have cited up to this point. As is typical of the current systems-oriented approach, the information and decision processes are particularly highlighted in the diagram. There are, for example, five strategic control points represented in

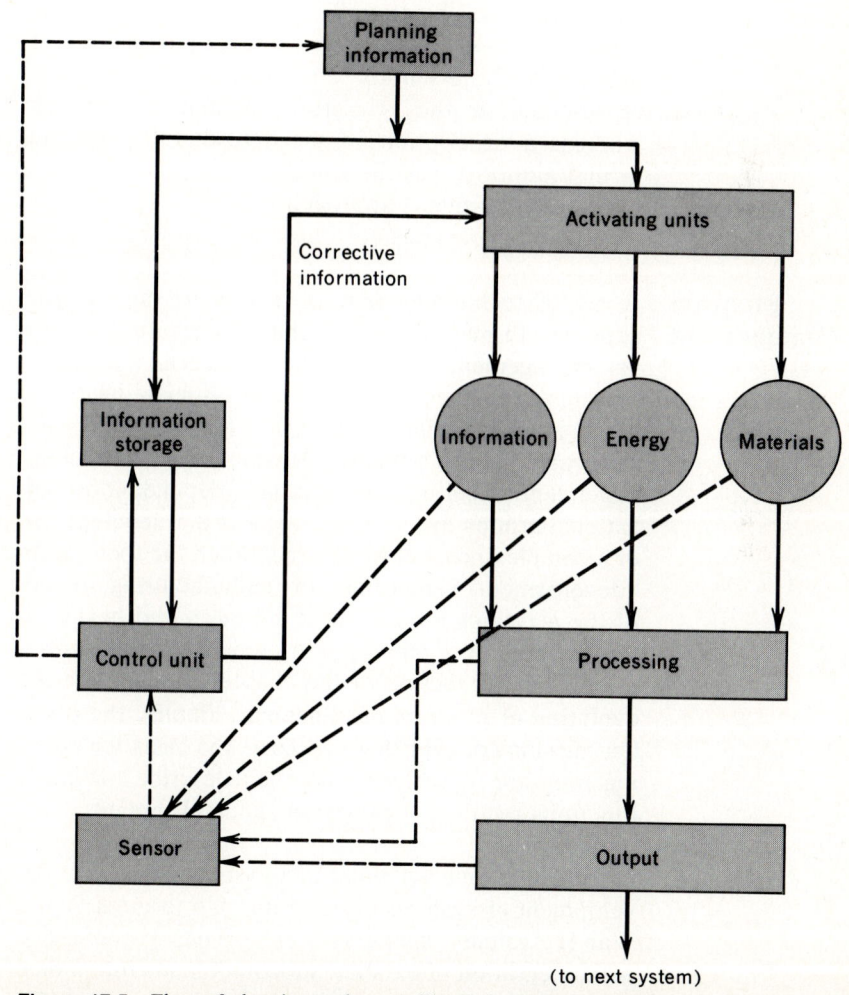

Figure 17.5 Flow of planning and controlling information in a system. (Adapted from Richard A. Johnson, Fremont E. Kast, and James E. Rosenzweig, *The Theory and Management of Systems*, 3d ed., McGraw-Hill Book Company, New York, 1973, p. 125. Reproduced with permission.)

the diagram, the final one constituting a measurement of the final _____ itself.

output

44 As the result of each measurement and comparison at a strategic control point, information is sent to the control and activating units to initiate any needed corrective action. Such information is therefore considered to be the _____ in the system, and the overall system would be described as being a(n) [open-sequence / closed-sequence] system.

feedback

closed-sequence

45 In terms of the overall approach to describing the organization and organizational functions, a description of the information and decision processes is represented by the [classical / systems] approach, whereas a description of the division of work and formal authority relationships is represented by the [classical / systems] approach.

systems

classical

Program Management

A set of techniques that is related to the systems approach to management is that of program, or project, management. Although the managerial techniques of program management have been associated with the development of military and space hardware, they are applicable to any situation in which a number of independently operating but mutually dependent organizational groups are working toward the development of a complex product or service. Since the focus is on "development" rather than on "manufacturing," many of the activities require basic research and hence involve uncertainty regarding the time and cost requirements. In this section of the chapter we describe the evolution of program management, identify the product-mission concept that serves as the basis for defining program objectives, and then describe the basic functions required for mission accomplishment.

46 Program management is an outgrowth of the development of systems engineering. Up through World War II systems engineers were primarily concerned with integration of existing subcomponents into a final product, steady improvement in design, and interchangeability of parts and components. These activities were aimed particularly at achieving [new product development / mass production].

mass production

47 After World War II systems engineers became increasingly concerned with the development of new and technologically complex products. In this context, the technical problems encountered and time requirements of the groups participating in the product development are [more / less] certain.

less

48 The coordination of research and development activities in an environment of uncertainty places a particular premium on the development of timely information flow in the system. From this standpoint, program management represents a blending of both systems engineering and information theory. As such, the overall approach to management that is particularly conducive to improving program management is the _____ approach.

systems

49 The *product-mission concept* has played an important role in the development of program management. In a sense, it is a kind of broader view of the usual product objective. Rather than defining an objective in terms of the desired physical properties of the product, the objective is defined in terms of the mission that the product is intended to perform. One advantage of using the product-mission concept is that preconceptions regarding best product design are [minimized / maximized].

minimized

50 Since designers tend to be influenced by the characteristics of existing products, avoiding design commitments until after the product mission has been defined tends to enhance [continued development of existing products / innovation in product design].

innovation in product design

51 Thus, the approach by which program objectives are defined in terms of product purposes rather than product specifications is the _____ concept.

product-mission

52 We have referred entirely to the design implications of the product-mission approach. In a competitive marketing environment all of the business functions would be oriented toward the product mission as part of a total endeavor. Thus, appropriate methods of advertising and distributing a product [would / would not] depend on the product's defined mission.

would

53 For any development program, five primary functions have to be performed for successful completion of the mission:

1. Perception of need
2. Design
3. Production
4. Delivery
5. Utilization

Using a military problem as an example, not only should perceived needs take into consideration economic and technological feasibility, but the broad initially perceived needs usually have to be made more [general / specific].

specific

54 Since a broad objective may imply several specific objectives, or product missions, these also need to be arranged in order of priority, thus making it feasible to concentrate effort toward the attainment of [arbitrarily chosen / the most important] mission objectives.

the most important

55 Once the *perception of need* is completed, the next step is research and development directed toward *design*. In a new project there is generally a relatively [broad / limited] selection of feasible designs that are evaluated.

broad

56 Following design, the *production* function is performed. As is true for the other functions, the production function typically includes several subfunctions. In this case, these subfunctions include such activities as recruiting manpower, establishing physical facilities, selecting component suppliers, testing and inspection of parts and components, and testing and inspection of the final product. At this stage of the program the problems are concerned with [appropriateness of specifications / coordination of the production subfunctions].

coordination of the production subfunctions

57 *Delivery* is the function of transferring ownership physically from producer to user. This typically includes on-site testing by the [producer only / consumer only / both producer and consumer].

both producer and consumer

58 In military programs the function of *utilization* generally is performed by personnel of the military services. However, need for personnel familiarization and training means that the producing contractors [do / do not] continue to be involved with product functioning after its delivery.

do

59 Returning now to the application of program management within a particular firm, we see that whereas this approach is oriented toward description of the relationship among program subgoals and the overall goal, traditional organization structure is oriented toward describing the functional area of activity within the firm, such as manufacturing and marketing. Program management and functional management are thus [organizational alternatives / two varieties of the same approach to organization].

organizational alternatives

60 Most companies using program management have in fact combined this approach with the existing functional structure. Figure 17.6 illustrates the organization result, which has been called *matrix organization* by some writers. One difficulty with combining the two approaches is that individuals frequently find themselves working for two or more direct superiors: a manager in the functional organization and one or more _____ managers.

program

61 Even though problems like these have been encountered, business firms have generally hesitated to abandon one of these approaches in favor of the other. In addition to the fact that there may be a contractual obligation to use program management in mil-

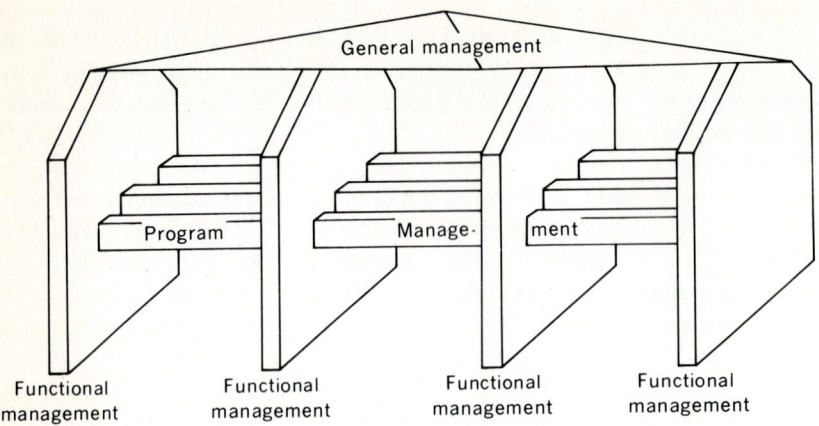

Figure 17.6 Integration of program management within the functionally oriented organization structure. (Adapted from John Stanley Baumgartner, *Project Management*, Richard D. Irwin, Inc., Homewood, Ill., 1963, p. 143. Reproduced with permission.)

         itary and space projects, use of this approach and associated techniques such as **PERT** makes on-
more   schedule program completion [more / less] likely.

62 On the other hand, the unified management of
is not each of the separate activities in the firm [is / is not] attained by use of the program management approach.

63 Therefore the program manager operates as a kind of managerial generalist within the firm and is formally neither superior nor subordinate to the specialized functional managers. This organizational position makes it particularly important that he possess a high
human relations degree of [technological / human relations] skill.

64 Furthermore, although the functional organization has a limitless life span, the program manager's job is finite. Once a program is completed, he and the other program personnel return to their functional departments on a full-time basis or are assigned to other programs. As individuals, therefore, program personnel need to be attuned to the prospect of con-
change tinued job and organizational [stability / change].

65 From the motivational standpoint, it is particularly important that program personnel look at early program completion as a personal success, rather than as "working their way out of a job." For continued success in program management, a company should [frequently / seldom / **never**] terminate employment following successful project completion.

never

66 Maintaining the functional organization within a program-oriented firm provides a "home base" for personnel between program assignments. Thus, even though job changes are associated with program completion, providing overall employment security [**minimizes** / maximizes] the effect of the negative motivational factors in this environment of change.

minimizes

Computer Information Systems

Since the systems approach to business is so closely related to the management of information flow and the making of decisions, developments in data processing have both influenced and been influenced by the systems viewpoint. In our description of these developments we are concerned primarily with their management implications, and not with the technical details of these developments as such. In this section we first review briefly the early developments in data processing methods that led to mechanized data processing. However, the principal part of the coverage will be concerned with the development of electronic data processing. In describing current and future developments in information processing systems, we give particular attention to computer programs, computer software versus hardware, and real-time processing versus batch processing of data.

67 In the data processing field there is a basic distinction between *facts* and *information*. One of the principal purposes of a business data processing system is to screen, collate, and relate the various facts available in a firm in order to develop meaningful _____ for management decision making.

information

68 Other than the collection of the facts as such, in a small business firm the "data processing" may simply involve maintaining a *file* of information. For example, use of the employee time cards, inventory ledger cards, and accounts payable statements may all involve simple _____ maintenance.

file

69 Until the development of *mechanized data processing* (MDP) some years ago, the maintenance of physical card files constituted the principal method of data processing. The needed calculations to update information on the file cards were originally done manually, but they were later supplemented by the use of adding machines and desk calculators to increase the [speed / accuracy / speed and accuracy] of the computations.

speed and accuracy

70 Bookkeeping and accounting machines were also developed to perform calculations, prepare statements, and update records in one combined operation, thus minimizing human errors associated with [original source data / computation and transcription].

computation and transcription

71 A particularly significant occurrence in the history of data processing methods was the development of the punched card as a means of recording information in the 1890 census. Devised by Herman Hollerinth of the Census Bureau, this system permitted mechanical sorting of the cards and thus led to the development of _____ data processing.

mechanized

72 Although the information "stored" on the cards was originally analyzed by mechanical sorting and subsequent counting of cards in each sorted category, during the first half of this century other mechanical devices were developed which made it possible to do such things as duplicate existing cards, update information on an established set of cards, accumulate numerical values, and print statements and summary reports. Pioneered by the International Business Machines Corporation (IBM), such a data processing system was referred to as _____.

mechanized data processing

73 During World War II the electronic computer was developed for application to scientific and military computational problems. The first business-oriented computer installations were completed during the 1950s, thus signaling the beginning of the *electronic data processing* era, or, as it is frequently abbreviated, the _____ era.

EDP

74 The *arithmetic unit* of the electronic computer is an extremely fast calculating machine, performing complex calculations in time measured in billionths of a second (nanosecond). But for business applications there are two other attributes of computer systems that are of greater significance. One is that by the use of a set of machine instructions, or a *computer program*, the computer can perform a sequence of computational and decision-making steps yielding intermediate and final values; the second is that the values can be stored and updated in electronic form within the *storage unit* of the computer information system. Thus, a computer can perform calculations rapidly by use of its _____ unit, follow a series of instructions which are embodied in the computer _____, and store and update information in its _____ unit.

arithmetic

program

storage

75 The earliest applications of the computer in business, and those that are still predominant, were in areas specifically requiring a series of calculations with intermediate and final values. A good example is the application to payroll. Although this may appear to be a simple task at first glance, the need not only to multiply hours worked by wage rates but also to consider overtime premiums, appropriate deductions, and accumulated deductions to date, such as for social security, results in a relatively lengthy set of instructions, or computer _____.

program

76 We have made a point of emphasizing the importance of the computer program because it is in this area that most problems of computer application in business exist, rather than in the technical functioning of the computer as such. Computer errors are generally data input errors or programming errors, rather than equipment errors. For example, if we include the instruction to "deduct $5.60 from gross payroll" as an

can

insurance deduction, but do not first ascertain that the gross figure equals or exceeds $5.60, then the remaining payroll amount [can / cannot] be a negative amount.

77 Early computer programs had to be written in *machine language,* which required the mastery of a symbolic notation system and the use of detailed instructions concerned with internal computer processes, such as the storage of intermediate values resulting from each step of a calculation. A shortage of computer programmers with the necessary knowledge and fortitude to develop programs for business applications was itself a barrier to the feasibility of computer use. During the past twenty-five years the programming task has been simplified by the development of *assembly programs* which translate simpler programming language into the _____ language.

machine

78 Whereas the physical equipment that makes up the computer information system is the *hardware,* the assembly programs and other programs oriented toward simplifying the programming requirement are the *software.* Thus, expanded managerial use of EDP as an information source is particularly dependent on the continued development of computer [hardware / software].

software

79 The pace of the technological developments in the computational speed and storage capacity of computer systems, and in the development of minicomputers, has been so rapid that many computers now in use are considered to be obsolete in terms of [hardware / software].

hardware

80 On the other hand, in addition to the development of assembly programs which simplify programming requirements, libraries of computational subroutines have been developed by manufacturers and users making it possible to construct a program by combining several available subroutines. These, then, represent developments in the area of computer [hardware / software].

software

81 Although steady progress has been made, developments in computer software have not kept pace with those in hardware. The ultimate development in software will presumably be achieved when an executive can make requests of the computer information system in "everyday language," without the necessity of using an individually prepared computer _____.

program

82 The programming languages most frequently used in commercial applications today are FORTRAN ("Formula Translation") and COBOL ("Common Business Oriented Language"). Using either of these programming languages is [easier / more difficult] than using a machine language.

easier

83 To summarize the last few frames, the physical equipment that makes up the computer information system is referred to as the _____, whereas libraries of subroutines, assembly programs, and other items used to simplify the programming task are referred to as the _____.

hardware

software

84 We have already indicated that continued expansion of computer use in business is related to the development of the software. Of the following two general types of business application, the one particularly dependent on the development of software is [a / b].

b

    a. Application to repetitive operations

    b. Application involving a series of unique information requests

85 For repetitive applications the difficulties in programming are frequently offset by the fact that the programs are used repeatedly, whereas such is not the case for the series of unique questions associated with managerial decision-making requirements. From this standpoint, the integration of EDP with the systems approach to management [has already/ has not yet] been completed.

has not yet

86 As contrasted with the use of computer informa-

566 ● Chapter 17 ● The Systems Approach to Management

systems

tion systems in such specialized tasks as payroll and inventory control, integration of the firm's data processing system with the managerial information and decision system would be an application of the _____ approach to management.

87 Finally, there is one other development in computer use that has affected its application in business firms and will continue to be important as the systems approach is increasingly applied in this area. The computer applications we have considered thus far are examples of *batch processing;* that is, facts are collected over a period of time and then periodically processed. When batch processing is used, the records indicate status [up to the present moment / as of the last time data were compiled].

as of the last time data were compiled

88 A development that represents an alternative to batch processing is *real-time processing.* Real-time processing involves updating the master file of information with each and every transaction. In terms of the specialized areas of computer application, real-time processing is most useful for [payroll / inventory control].

inventory control

89 Payroll data are generally needed only periodically, whereas it is a distinct advantage to have inventory records reflect the status to the moment. This kind of perpetual inventory system can be maintained within the context of a computer information system by the use of _____ processing.

real-time

90 Two examples of real-time processing as contrasted to batch processing are the airline reservation systems now generally in use and the SAGE (Semi-Automatic Ground Environment) system used as a continual early warning and air-defense system. In the first case the inputs are reservations and inquiries transmitted from a large number of geographically separated ticket offices, whereas in the latter case the inputs are provided by geographically dispersed radar installations and other data sources. In both cases, processing of data and the compilation of information

with each new input of data   occur [at designated periodic intervals / with each new input of data].

91 The development of real-time data processing makes it feasible to present up-to-the-minute information about a company's operations. This development, combined with further progress in software and minicomputers during the next few years, will increase the applicability of the computer in the total information and decision system in the firm, thus enhancing

systems   use of the _____ approach to management.

Review
components
objectives
plan

92 In general, a system can be defined as an established arrangement of _____ which leads to the attainment of particular _____ according to _____. (Frames 1 to 6)

93 Application of the systems approach to business results in the requirement that executives become

in addition to   "managerial generalists" [instead of / in addition to] having skills in particular functional areas. (Frames 7 to 10)

94 In the area of planning, a hierarchy of three systems is of concern from the systems point of view: the

internal   environmental, competitive, and _____ systems. On the level of procedures, the planning and controlling technique which has been used in conjunction

PERT   tion with the systems approach is _____. (Frames 11 to 18)

95 In the management function of organizing, the type of organization theory concerned with formal organization structure and hierarchical relationships is classical organization theory, and that which represents a modification of the classical to include human relations and informal organization implications is

neoclassical   _____ organization theory. The approach that abandons the formal structure as the principal reference point and considers the relationships among all components that make up the organization is

modern   _____ organization theory. (Frames 19 to 25)

96 In the area of controlling, when a system is controlled by a decision device not affected by system output as such, it is referred to as an

open-sequence _____ system. On the other hand, a truly self-regulating system includes a comparison of system output with standards and uses this feedback as the basis for control action. Such a system

closed-sequence is referred to as a _____ system. (Frames 26 to 33)

97 As applied to business firms, the systems approach to management has typically resulted in describing the arrangement of organizational compo-

communication and decision nents in terms of [work-group / communication and decision] structure. (Frames 34 to 36; 43 to 45)

98 Both the inputs and outputs of a system can be in the form of information, energy, or material. Use of electricity in a system, for example, exemplifies the

energy input of _____, whereas the output that is in the form of a consulting service would exemplify

information _____ output. (Frames 37 to 42)

99 The set of managerial techniques that represents a blending of systems engineering and information

program theory is called _____ management. (Frames 46 to 48)

100 The approach by which program objectives are defined in terms of product purposes rather than product specifications, and which is associated with a number of primary functions beginning with the perception of product need and culminating with product

product-mission utilization, is called the _____ concept. (Frames 49 to 58)

101 Program management and traditional organization structure represent [the same / basically dif-

basically different ferent] approach(es) to organization and management. When program management is used, the program managers in the organization are formally [subordinate /

neither subordinate nor superior superior / neither subordinate nor superior] to the specialized functional managers. (Frames 59 to 66)

mechanized data processing electronic data processing	**102** Whereas MDP stands for _____ _____, EDP stands for _____. (Frames 67 to 73)
arithmetic program storage	**103** In addition to the required input and output equipment, a computer information system performs calculations rapidly by the use of the _____ unit, follows a series of instructions as included in the computer _____, and stores and updates information held in the _____ unit. (Frames 74 to 76)
hardware software	**104** The physical equipment of the computer system is referred to as _____. The assembly programs and other materials oriented toward simplifying programming requirements are referred to as _____. (Frames 77 to 83)
has not yet	**105** In terms of developments to date, we would conclude that integration of EDP with the systems approach to management [has already / has not yet] been completed. (Frames 84 to 86)
batch real-time	**106** When facts are collected over a period of time and processed at periodic intervals, the procedure is referred to as _____ processing. The procedure by which the master file of information is updated with each transaction is referred to as _____ processing. (Frames 87 to 91)

Discussion Questions

1. As compared with the classical approach to organization, which is based on functional specialization, what are the changed executive skill requirements in the systems approach?
2. Is it possible for a particular manager in a particular position to develop as both a specialist and a generalist? In what type of position would development as a specialist take precedence? In what type of position would development as a generalist be particularly important?
3. A chief executive in a pharmaceutical firm, who has a background in marketing, has suggested that the key to his firm's success in planning will depend on

knowledge of the potential market. In terms of organizational objectives in general, why is this an appropriate view? In terms of the systems approach to planning, what considerations might be missing?

4. What are the advantages associated with using an organization chart to describe a firm and its activities? What are the advantages associated with describing the firm in terms of the channels of communication that exist and the locations at which decisions are made?
5. Under what circumstances might an open-sequence control system lead to inappropriate control action? Under what circumstances might a closed-sequence control system lead to inappropriate control action? What are the managerial implications of your observations?
6. In this chapter we have suggested that the authority relationship between program managers and functional managers is usually not clearly specified in matrix organizations. Do you think this condition is inevitable, or is there a way of integrating the two approaches to organizations?
7. In what respects is the systems approach to management an alternative to the functional approach to management? In what respects is the systems approach compatible with the functional approach?
8. What do you think will be the general role of the computer in management ten years from now?

References

Ackoff, R. L. "Towards a System of Systems Concepts." *Management Science,* vol. 17, no. 11, July 1971.

Bonczek, R. H., C. W. Holsapple, and A. B. Whinston. "Aiding Decision Makers with a Generalized Data Base Management System: An Application to Inventory Management." *Decision Sciences,* vol. 9, no. 2, April 1978.

Burack, E., and P. F. Sorenson, Jr. "Management Preparation for Computer Automation: Emergent Patterns and Problems." *Academy of Management Journal,* vol. 19, no. 2, June 1976.

Butler, A. G., Jr. "Project Management: A Study in Organizational Conflict." *Academy of Management Journal,* vol. 16, no. 1, March 1973.

Cleland, D. I., and W. R. King. *Systems Analysis and Project Management.* New York: McGraw-Hill, 1975.

Cook, D. L., and J. C. Granger. "Current Status of Project Management Instruction in American Colleges and Universities." *Academy of Management Journal,* vol. 19, no. 2, June 1976.

Dalton, A. "How Management Information Systems Work." *Supervisory Management,* vol. 21, no. 1, January 1976.

Davis, G. D. *Computers and Information Processing.* New York: McGraw-Hill, 1978.

Davis, J. J. "A Dollars and Common Sense Approach to MIS." *Advanced Management Journal,* vol. 41, no. 3, Summer 1976.

Davis, S. M. "Two Models of Organization." *Sloan Management Review,* vol. 16, no. 1, Fall 1974.

Davis, S. M., and P. R. Lawrence. "Problems of Matrix Organizations." *Harvard Business Review,* vol. 56, no. 3, May-June 1978.

Dunne, E. J., Jr., M. J. Stahl, and L. J. Melhart, Jr. "Influence Sources of Project and Functional Managers in Matrix Organizations." *Academy of Management Journal,* vol. 21, no. 1, March 1978.

Galbraith, J. "Matrix Organization Designs: How to Combine Functional and Project Forms." *Business Horizons,* vol. 14, no. 1, February 1971.

Grimes, A. J., S. M. Klein, and F. A. Shull. "Matrix Model: A Selective Empirical Test." *Academy of Management Journal,* vol. 15, no. 1, March 1972.

Johnson, R. A., F. E. Kast, and J. E. Rosenzweig. *The Theory and Management of Systems,* 3d ed. New York: McGraw-Hill, 1973.

Kast, F. E., and J. E. Rosenzweig. "General Systems Theory: Applications for Organization and Management." *Academy of Management Journal,* vol. 15, no. 4, December 1972.

Kreitner, R. "People Are Systems, Too: Filling the Feedback Vacuum." *Business Horizons,* vol. 20, no. 6, December 1977.

Lucas, H. *Information Systems Concepts for Management.* New York: McGraw-Hill, 1978.

McFadden, F. R., and J. D. Suver. "Costs and Benefits of a Data Base System." *Harvard Business Review,* vol. 56, no. 1, January-February 1978.

Martin, G. N. "Project Management—Pro and Con." *Journal of Systems Management,* vol. 28, no. 11, November 1977.

Philippakis, A. S., and L. J. Kazmier. *Information Systems through COBOL,* 2d ed. New York: McGraw-Hill, 1978.

Rolefson, J. R. "Project Management—Six Critical Steps." *Journal of Systems Management,* vol. 29, no. 4, April 1978.

Schewe, C. D. "The Management Information System User: An Exploratory Behavioral Analysis." *Academy of Management Journal,* vol. 19, no. 4, December 1976.

Thamhain, H. J., and G. R. Gemill. "Influence Style of Project Managers: Some Project Performance Correlates." *Academy of Management Journal,* vol. 17, no. 2, June 1974.

Trenchard, B. "New Data Bases for Management." *Administrative Management,* vol. 40, no. 2, February 1979.

Von Bertalanffy, L. "The History and Status of General Systems Theory." *Academy of Management Journal,* vol. 15, no. 4, December 1972.

Whisler, T. L. *Information Technology and Organizational Change*. Belmont, Calif.: Wadsworth, 1970.

Wilemon, D. L., and J. P. Cicero. "The Project Manager—Anomalies and Ambiguities." *Academy of Management Journal,* vol. 13, no. 3, September 1970.

Wright, N. H. "Matrix Management: A Primer for the Administrative Manager." *Management Review,* vol. 68, no. 4, April 1979.

CASE STUDY: A First Experience with Program Management

Jim Hendrickson has worked with his present employer, a diversified company dedicated to applying the concepts of managerial decentralization, for about fifteen years, ever since he completed his college work in electrical engineering. During this time he has had extensive experience in two of the company's consumer products divisions, and his most recent assignment was as section head of reliability engineering.

Because of the respiratory problems of one of his children, several months ago Hendrickson requested a transfer to the company's aerospace division, located in the Southwest. In requesting the change, he recognized that he had a good deal of work to do in familiarizing himself with the reliability analysis problems associated with aerospace components as contrasted to consumer products, but being just thirty-seven years old, he felt confident that he could make the switch.

In his new position as section head of reliability analysis in the aerospace division he has more direct subordinates than he had in the consumer products division. However, he has found that only about 30 percent of his personnel are in fact working exclusively for him, with the others assigned either full-time or part-time to aerospace programs for which the division is a subcontractor. Consequently, unity of command is the exception rather than the rule, and compared with his previous managerial experience the present situation appears just plain disorganized. In trying to define the appropriate role of the program managers and their relationship with him, he has been particularly frustrated because the program manager positions are not entered on the division organization chart at their actual points of work, but, rather, are simply listed in a box adjoining the chart. In the company policy statement describing the operation of program management, the program manager position is defined as representing the single point of project responsibility to the contracting customer. As to his authority, the release further states that, "The assignment of the program management task is accompanied by delegation of necessary authority to conduct the program with the complete utilization of the technical and supporting facilities of the aerospace division."

Overall, whereas Jim Hendrickson had expected a technical adjustment in his new job, the managerial adjustment has turned out to be the more challenging.

As things stand, he is not at all sure that he is really a supervisor in the same sense as was true in the consumer products division, even though he has about the same kind of supervisory title. As if to bring things to a head, the department manager of engineering support, who is his direct superior, has just sent Hendrickson a memo informing him that the annual performance appraisal reviews for his personnel are to be completed during the next month. Because of the program assignments of many of his men, he really does not feel qualified to appraise their performance. In order to help clarify authority relationships in the division as a whole as well as in his section, Hendrickson has decided to make the following proposal at the next monthly department meeting: that formal responsibility for completing performance appraisals be assigned to a program manager when a man spends more than 50 percent of his time working under that manager's direction during the rating period.

1. What are the organizational advantages, if any, associated with Jim Hendrickson's proposal? How is it likely to be viewed by the other supervisors? By the program managers?
2. What are the organizational disadvantages, if any, associated with proposal?
3. In what way has Hendrickson possibly misconstrued the relationship between himself and program managers and between himself and those of his subordinates who are assigned to program work?

CASE STUDY: A Systems-Oriented Manager of Data Processing

Marilyn Frazier was hired by the communications equipment division of a multiproduct corporation about a year ago to replace the previous manager of the data processing department, who accepted a similar position in a larger data processing facility. The data processing department had been established for over fifteen years and was principally oriented toward such functions as payroll, billing, and inventory control.

Ms. Frazier presented two requests as a condition of her accepting the position: first, that the department be redesignated as the information systems department, and second, that as manager of this department she also be appointed a member of the executive committee of the division, which meets every two weeks with the division general manager to review operations and to serve as an advisory committee. The division general manager accepted both of Marilyn's conditions.

Ms. Frazier has been a long-standing proponent of the philosophy of managerial decentralization and, accordingly, after assuming the department manager position she proceeded to assign specific managerial responsibilities for all the continuing data processing tasks to subordinate personnel in the department. In turn, this gave her the time to devote to her main objective: developing a data base such that all information relevant to the division's products would be integrated within one overall system. It was her contention that such a data base would be instrumental in leading to better decisions in product design, pricing, and marketing, and would thereby lead to improved division profitability. Ms. Frazier was quite aggressive, but not in an abrasive way, and was able to schedule discussions on data base design in several meetings of the executive committee. These discussions culminated in her receiving the approval of the division general manager for the project, with the concurrence of the committee.

Within several weeks after approval of the data-base project was given, the division general manager began receiving informal complaints from the other managers about the amount of involvement of the people in the project. As one manager put it. "Marilyn is as sharp as a tack, and the objectives she described to us and the logic of her proposals are unassailable. But she's got people involved in this thing from all over the division, and I'm afraid she's off on cloud nine. You know, she's kept so distant from the regular data processing tasks that her department has pretty well run itself. Along these lines, I've wondered whether she was really interested in being a data processing manager when she took this job or whether she came in to reorganize and take over the division. In any event, I suggest we reconsider the entire data-base project."

The division general manager took comments such as these under advisement, but as things turned out he never got to act on them. During her attendance at a two-week program in the company's management institute, Marilyn Frazier so impressed several corporate-level managers with her analytical ability and persuasive skills that she was offered a managerial position in corporate headquarters with a substantial increase in salary. After discussion with her husband because of the geographic move involved, she accepted the position with the understanding that she would have a month to help find a replacement and make family arrangements.

1. How would you evaluate Marilyn Frazier's overall strategy in attempting to develop an integrated management information system?
2. Should Ms. Frazier have made known more explicitly her interest in developing a division data base at the time of her employment interview?
3. In what respects might Marilyn Frazier have done a more effective job in her position?
4. What kind of replacement should the division general manager now seek to fill the managerial opening?

APPLICATIONS READING:

Project Management—
A New Style for Success

Richard A. Jacobs
Vice-President
A. T. Kearney, Inc.
Management Consultants
Chicago, Illinois

The complexity of business is increasing at an unprecedented rate. With this increased complexity, the practice of management is undergoing its greatest upheaval in history. A premium is now placed on the multitalented executive who can make decisions about a host of concurrent situations in which no clear-cut answers exist. For example, in addition to conventional problems involving marketing, operating, financial, and competitive situations, today's executive is challenged with the problems of rising fuel costs and diminishing energy supplies; the impact of government regulations on operations; the proliferation of demands for new and improved services; the need to undertake "nonprofit" projects, such as those related to consumerism and environmental protection; and the pressures from all levels in the organization to create more satisfying work and work conditions.

Today's Challenges, Tomorrow's Problems

There are some who believe today's challenges are predictive of several, more significant problems facing the manager of tomorrow. These problems can be categorized in the following way:

- **An increasing rate of change.** The business environment will evolve from today's on-going problem situations to a proliferation of unique, one-time project problems. Even with this, the luxury of "years in the planning" with respect to problem solving will become rare. In many industries, product life and service cycles will shrink. The successful manager will be the one who is quick to recognize an opportunity and deploy the necessary resources to maximize the benefit from the situation.

- **A broader scope.** The magnitude and nature of problems will be more complex. With increasing regularity, problems will cross departmental, divisional, and geographical

Source: Reprinted, by permission of the publisher, from S.A.M. *Advanced Management Journal*, vol. 41, no. 4, Autumn 1976, © 1976 by Society for Advancement of Management, a division of American Management Associations. All rights reserved.

lines. Even the smaller company will be concerned with multinational distribution and operation and the problems of international regulation. Executives will find the conventional, functional organization to be a cumbersome impediment to solving problems in many of these situations. Thus the successful manager will be one who is able to overcome effectively the disadvantages of conventional organization and bring to bear all the unique personnel skills required for finding a problem's solution.

- **A lack of right information.** Tomorrow's manager will be confronted with the capability of acquiring more information than there is time available to digest it. Also, the information will be more difficult to categorize in importance and to present in time for action. This will be due to the dynamic character of objectives and the complexity of control across functional lines. Thus the successful manager will be characterized by his ability to manage and control effectively the information resource.

A New Approach to Management

It is my opinion and that of my company, A. T. Kearney, Inc., that these problems will lead to a new style of management, one calling for the successful executive to cross conventional boundaries and bring together the skills and resources of a team in order to achieve set business objectives. The team concept will maximize the benefits available from a unique opportunity, obtain results in a timely manner, and increase the effectiveness of the personnel involved in a problem-solving effort.

The team concept envisaged will be markedly similar to the successful project management approaches that systems managers are using successfully today when faced with such problems as installing a broad-based company information system. Progressive systems managers have found that, simply stated, "Project management is a means for getting the right things done right." It is a systematic approach to successfully meeting objectives.

Bringing this management style to their companies will provide an unparalleled opportunity for systems personnel, traditionally the leaders in project management. The basis for successful introduction of this style of management, in my opinion, will lie not in the use of the techniques but rather in the training of executive management to plan, organize, and control for project success. Such an undertaking on the part of systems people will not be easy. It will take work, patience, understanding, and, above all else, a management attitude. But it can be done. Consider the case of a major high-technology manufacturer that adopted project management as its approach to problem solving.

A Case in Point

This company has grown rapidly and profitably as a result of new-product introductions, a responsive attitude toward customer service, and innovative manufacturing. Recently, like many businesses, the company's opportunities for higher sales and profits were reduced because of difficulties in acquiring materials, recruiting and developing needed personnel, and so forth. The day-to-day problems of operations created an unprecedented demand for systems assistance and new control information. But the demand for systems assistance was far greater than the resources available. As a result, nearly all the firm's functional managers and officers believed that the systems effort was less than effective in producing results and not fully responsive to the business's needs.

The first step in solving this problem was to educate a management committee. A one-day workshop to air systems problems was held for the president and five user vice-presidents who comprised this management committee and were generally the major beneficiaries of the systems effort. The underlying purpose of the workshop was to "sell" the company's management on the role of executive project management that needed playing and, through practical examples and an explanation of specific techniques, help the executives learn how to play it. The role that needed playing can be broken down into four parts:

1. To evaluate major systems projects, select those deserving development, and place the selected projects in an order of priority most beneficial to the company.
2. To approve the systems plan, identifying the resources required over time to accomplish the projects.
3. To visibly demonstrate management's support of major projects.
4. To track performance and determine if the company is increasing its return on systems investment and getting better service from data processing.

Following is a description of how well the executives performed in their new roles.

Systems Planning

Data processing believed that developing and presenting the systems plan was its responsibility. The role of the company's management committee was to approve the plan. Moreover, in the opinion of the systems personnel, the systems plan, to be effective, had to support the company's long-range plan. But beyond a revenue and *pro forma* financial statement, nothing formal relating to long-range plans was in writing. Consequently the head of the EDP function met individually with the president and each of the five key executives to get them to verbalize the future as they saw it from their own perspectives and needs. During these sessions, specific systems requirements were mentioned by the executives or suggested by the head of EDP on the basis of his discussions with middle management and his judgment of the company's needs.

The data obtained from these interviews were synthesized by EDP into a statement of long-range management objectives. In addition, each kind of major information development project required to support these objectives was described. And, on the basis of the president's input concerning the time frame within which the objectives had to be reached, each information project was charted in Gantt form for executive presentation. The projects for EDP operations improvement were also charted and described in terms of how they would support the overall effort.

With the effort time-framed, the number and types of skills required and the equipment and budget support needed to meet the set objectives were determined. A key aspect of the plan was the staffing requirement for additional systems maintenance personnel so that major development projects could proceed without continual interruptions because of emergency situations.

The next step was to obtain the management committee's approval of the plan. To help each user executive better understand the plan and reach conclusions about it, a workbook was prepared that contained the graphic systems plan and supporting narrative based on EDP's interpretation of the information collected separately from each executive. The workbook also showed alternative plans based on different levels of manpower. In general, the workbook was designed to get the executives to discuss and agree collectively on answers to a series of questions, including:

1. Are the priorities of systems development projects in the proper order to support the overall goal of the business?
2. Should some projects be accelerated, retarded, or deleted? Should others be added? If so, what should their time frames be?
3. What is the proper level of development effort, weighing what is needed and can be afforded against what the organization can absorb in a given time period?

After some discussion, consensus was reached.
EDP gained much from this approach:

1. A common understanding among the users developed as to what the major EDP projects would be and the relative importance of each. In addition to understanding, there was greater individual appreciation of why all projects could not have "first priority."
2. User executives learned why some EDP projects were necessary and how these projects supported the overall company effort.
3. A dedicated systems maintenance group was created that could provide better service in times of emergency without causing delays on major development projects.
4. Management was involved in the decision making.

Project Selection

The fact that a project was included in the systems plan did not guarantee its funding. A vehicle was needed to maintain the systems plan as business conditions changed, to determine specifically the amount of money needed, and to allocate that sum for the start of new projects. To choose and fund the projects to be placed on the "active list" on a quarterly basis, a several-step process was instituted. The first five steps were tied to user-documentation standards:

1. Each key functional executive was given a copy of the systems plan. Consequently he knew in which quarter a project had to start to meet a prescribed finish date. He could accelerate or slow down the plan based on his knowledge of management's thinking concerning overall operating priorities and return-on-investment criteria.

    If conditions were essentially the same as at the last updating of the plan, he could initiate a project requisition in the quarter preceding the scheduled start-up date. He could also initiate requisitions at that time for other significant projects not originally on the systems plan.

2. To initiate a requisition, the user would first prepare, generally with the help of systems people, a proposal documenting the specific objectives of the proposal, its scope, the method of approach to reaching the objectives, and the classification of the work. Projects were classified into three categories:

- **Mandatory.** Those projects that had to be done because of regulatory or statutory reasons, the need to maintain a current critical system, or the need to respond to an important competitive situation.
- **Preferred.** Those projects that were deemed highly important because of a profit, quality, or service situation.
- **Desirable.** Those projects that should be done, provided the economics and other criteria for selection supported the project's choice.

3. Specific measures to quantify the degree to which objectives were achieved were set on all projects. This step was critical to the process. Measures were required not only for tangible projects but also for such nontangible projects as one that surveyed selected customers at various time intervals after purchase to track the nature and magnitude of product failure and the effectiveness of dealer service and maintenance.

4. For projects with tangible benefits, dollar revenues were projected over the life of the project. Such projects had as their objectives cost reduction in functional units of the organization, improved profits through better share of the market or accelerated cash flow, and the prevention of cost default caused by dollars being lost if an existing system were not maintained.

5. Following such quantification, the user placed all projects in a rank-ordered list within each of the three work classifications. A weight was given each item on the list compared with the item in the middle, which was weighted "1"; for example, a project considered twice as important by the user would be given a weight double that of the one with which it was compared, *regardless of the tangible benefits*.

Project ROI

During this process, some projects were dropped or rediscussed with users because they had unrealistic time-constraints. Others were revised or dropped because they required a level of technical sophistication beyond current capabilities or were oversophisticated for either user or systems personnel to work with. Finally, the tangible "preferred" and "desirable" projects were tested against costs, and those that failed a "quick test" (total revenue divided by cost) and failed to meet return-on-investment criteria were dropped.

The projects that passed the quick test were reevaluated using a profitability index, which determined ROI based on the time value of money. A new ranking was developed, and projects were placed on the horizontal row of a matrix-type worksheet on the basis of such factors as logic of development, ROI, and the weight given them by users. The vertical columns of the matrix contained a number of criteria listings—including "mandatory project," "reduction in operating costs," "consumerism," "job enrichment," "competitive pressure," "environmental improvement," "improved quality," and "better service"—that were considered important by the management committee. Some projects were found to fit several criteria types—that is, a check could be placed in several criteria-type columns.

The management committee discussed and confirmed the mandatory projects. It also reviewed and made decisions on delaying some active projects because of changed company situations. With EDP's help, the management committee also placed a weighting percentage on the mandatory column as to its requirements compared with available EDP resources; for example, undertaking all the mandatory requirements would require 30 percent of EDP's management personnel. The remaining criteria-type columns were proportionally weighted by the management committee based on current company priorities, with the total weight of *all* criteria-type columns equalling 100 percent.

Once this was done, EDP computed, based on the matrix, each project's importance and revised accordingly the order of importance. A cutoff was made at the point on the list at which all development resources were accounted for.

Before the final funding decisions were made, the management committee gave the users an opportunity to argue for a change in the order-of-importance listing or for additional resources to undertake more projects. There were often intense discussions about the value of the intangible projects. Of significance, users again were involved in the decision-making process.

Following these discussions, the final projects were selected and placed on the active list, which included all the projects that would commence the next quarter.

Organization for Problem Solving

Visibly demonstrating executive support had been one of the major points of discussion at the initial management committee workshop. The discussion on this point at the workshop had led to the adoption of several unique organizational concepts for problem solving. For example, the management committee agreed that the best people available should be brought together organizationally to help the company meet a project objective. Furthermore, the committee said that the normal functional lines of authority would be dropped during the time an individual worked on a project so the group could be more effectively managed. A third principle agreed on by the committee was that the project organization would be "nonpermanent"; the organization would be dynamic, with individuals with needed skills being moved from the functional organization into the project organization when necessary to accomplish a particular set of goals contributing to the project's objectives. After these individuals completed their assignments, they would return to their functional jobs.

Another principle concerned the role of the "project director." The management committee agreed that he would be the user who was the chief beneficiary of the project. Typically, the project director was a member of the management committee. In certain situations, in which the nature of the major opportunity crossed several functional areas, the president would be the project director. Although the time input might be as little as 15 minutes per week, the responsibilities of the project director were unique and included:

- To complete the project on time.
- To complete the project within budget.
- To ensure that the technical quality of the work was sufficient to realize the objectives set.
- To report on project progress and problems at the management committee meetings.
- To operate the system after completion of the project—that is, "to live with the results."

For the duration of the effort, the project director directly supervised a "project manager," who worked full time on the project. He ensured the project was on schedule by monitoring the efforts of other project team members, and he actually developed the technical design. To help him, a systematic project work approach and a number of planning and control techniques were developed. [These are described in "Putting 'Manage' in Project Management," available at no charge by writing the Research Library, A. T. Kearney, Inc., 100 South Wacker Drive, Chicago, Ill. 60606.]

The organizational concepts developed during the management committee workshop and employed by the company were successful for two reasons. First, they stressed *disciplined user involvement.* Since the project director was made responsible for the project and was aware that his personal performance was being measured, in part, by the success of the project, he worked harder to make the project a success. The other key to success was having *users and systems personnel on the project team*. In this manner, sound technical design evolved, design that was practical for the environment in which the user had to work.

Tracking Performance

The final role played by the management committee was to track performance. Basically the performance evaluation system monitored return on project investment and information service to users. To help the management committee monitor these, EDP prepared for it a series of monthly performance graphs that examined:

- Projects against project goals, based on the specific performance measures established at the time of the project requisition.
- EDP department budget variance.
- Schedule adherence, computed from the number of user reports issued on time compared with the number issued.
- Quality control results, computed from the number of reports issued without error compared with the number of reports issued.

These graphs served as:

- **Excellent communication tools.** Executives could read them quickly and understand them, because they were in a familiar "language."
- **Good control devices.** The graphs highlighted the problems that existed so management attention could be directed where it was needed.
- **Good management relations tools.** They provided vehicles for keeping the important activities of EDP in front of the executive group. Consequently, it was found that, when problems occurred, there was greater and more meaningful participation from the management committee in seeking solutions.

Summary

The company learned that new approaches are needed to deal with the complex, multifunctional problems business is facing and will continue to face in the future. Its executives found that they had more than their traditional roles to play. Team approaches utilizing different skills from throughout their organization were needed and proved more effective than traditional problem-solving approaches employing functional groups.

The company has now successfully applied the project management approach to a wide variety of activities, including the development of a major new segment of the business, the implementation of an improved sales-operations-inventory planning system, the organization of a word processing center, the construction of an environmental protection system, and the introduction and operation of a productivity improvement program for administrative and clerical personnel. In some ways, project management has become the primary style of management for the executive group.

The EDP department has helped the company solve a number of major problems and has taught the management group skills that should help it meet the business challenges of today. It took hard work, patience, and some assistance in training to establish the creditability of the concept. But above all else, it took a management attitude on the part of the systems people. They found that there is a need to get those executives who are typically the beneficiaries of a systems project trained and involved in planning, project selection, and project monitoring. Some of the vehicles that were used to get that involvement and provide project management training included:

- Using a workshop format for the initial communication of the program.
- Helping the company formulate its long-range plans through interviews and analysis.
- Using a workbook format to help the management committee confirm company priorities and establish a systems plan.
- Establishing specific measures for all types of projects so that benefits could be tracked.
- Developing a project/priority, criteria-type matrix to help select projects and assure that the systems plan reflected company priorities.
- Introducing project management organization principles, such as those concerning the role of the project director and the need for a dynamic project team made up of both systems and user personnel.
- Giving the executive group easy-to-read graphs of progress so that performance monitoring could be facilitated.

All of these actions contributed to the results achieved:

- Better return on project investment.
- Higher productivity.
- More stable operations; fewer interruptions and scheduling problems due to emergency situations.
- Better understanding between users and systems personnel.
- Increased management role for EDP.

The direction in which business problems are moving is clear. Project management as a management style for getting *the right things done right* could become the most significant development for solving the unique, one-time project problems we can expect in the future and for distinguishing the successful executive of tomorrow.

Questions on Reading

1. What are several key problem areas that Richard Jacobs identifies as facing the manager of tomorrow?
2. The author states that systems personnel have traditionally been leaders in team-oriented project management. Why do you think this has been true?
3. On what basis are projects ranked in the overall systems plan?
4. What were the principal areas of responsibility of a project director in the company application described in this article?

INDEX

Abstract words, 306–307
Activity in PERT analysis, 514–516
Advisory staff authority, 202–204
Aggression and frustration, 342–344, 353–354
  direct, 343–344, 353
  displaced, 343–344, 353–354
Alternatives, discovery of, in decision making, 112–113
Analysis in decision making, 113–114
Another-worker concept of supervisor, 437–438
Appealed policy, 106
Appraisal of performance, 267–275
Approach-approach conflict, 337–340
Approach-avoidance conflict, 337–340
Appropriation budget, 481–482
Arithmetic unit of computer, 563
Aspiration, level of, 333
Authoritarian leadership style, 404–407
Automatic system, 552

Avoidance-avoidance conflict, 337–340
Avoidance reaction in frustration, 355

Balance sheet budget, 482
Barrier in frustration, 352–353
Barriers in communication, 307–311
Basic policy, 104–105
Batch processing of data, 566
Behavior modification, 384–393
Behavioral approach to studying leadership, 399–400
Behavioral science influences on management concepts, 11–15
Behavioral-specialist concept of supervisor, 438–439
Benevolent authoritative leadership style, 407–410
Bias in interviewing, 267
Blake, Robert R., 446–450
Booz, Allen & Hamilton and development of CPM, 511

Break-even-point analysis, 485–486
Budgetary control, 478–484
Budgets, types of, 479–484

Calculus in decision making, 131
Cash budget, 480–481
Central staff and relationship to line personnel, 219–225
Centralization, 179–182
  advantages of, 192
  (See also Decentralization)
Centralized communication pattern, 314–316
Centralized control, 491
  human reactions to, 488–492
Centralized organization, 176
Chain communication pattern, 314–316
Change, overcoming resistance to, 450–455
Checklist method in performance appraisal, 272–273
Circuit communication model, 311
Circular communication pattern, 314–316

Classical organization theory, 549–550
Closed-loop system, 551
Closed-sequence system, 551–555
Coaching, 276
COBOL, 565
Coch, Lester, 450–455
Communication:
 barriers, 307–311
 basic concepts, 302–305
 channels, 302–303, 311–312
 and function of directing, 13, 48
 and informal organization, 236–237
 networks, 311–314
 patterns in small groups, 314–316
 symbols in, 305–307
Compensation as defense mechanism, 345
Completed staff work, concept of, 202–203
Compromise solutions in frustration, 344–346
Compulsory staff advice, 204
Computer hardware, 564
Computer information systems, 561–567
Computer program, 563
Computer software, 564
Concrete words, 306–307
Conflict:
 of motives, 337–342
 resolving, 251–256
Connotative words, 306–307
Constraints in linear programming, 136
Consultative leadership style, 407–410
Contingency theory, 190
 application of, 197
Contingency view:
 of leadership, 410–413
 of management, 21–23
Control:
 centralized, 491
 personal, 491
 self-, 491
Control devices, 484–488
Control process, 474–492

Control staff authority, 205–206
Controlling, 49–50, 474–492
 systems-oriented techniques in, 510–514
Coordinating, 50–51
CPM (Critical Path Method), 511, 537–541
Creativity in decision making, 112–113
Critical incidents method, 273
Critical path in PERT analysis, 525–526
Critical Path Method (CPM), 511, 537–541
Cultural framework of management, 18–21
Curtice, Harlowe, 179–181
Customer, departmentation by, 169

Decentralization, 179–182
 advantages of, 192–193
 contingency approach to, 189–198
 at General Motors, 179–181
Decentralized organization, 176
Decision making, phases in, 111–115
Decision table, 143
Decision tree analysis, 145–147
Defense mechanism, 343–346
Democratic leadership style, 404–407
Denotative words, 306–307
Departmental policy, 105
Departmentation, 166–172
 by customer, 169
 by function, 166–167
 by number, 166
 by process, 169–170
 by product, 167–168
 by territory, 168
Depth interview method, 264
Diagnosis in decision making, 111–112

Dickson, William J., 15
Direct aggression in frustration, 343–344, 353
Directing, 47–49
Disciplining, 414–417
Displaced aggression in frustration, 343–344, 353–354
Du Pont Company and development of CPM, 511

Electronic data processing (EDP), 562–563
Emotional insulation, 344
Empathic listening, 310
Employee-centered supervision, 442–446
EMV (expected monetary value), 144, 146
Energy in systems approach, 554–555
Event in PERT analysis, 514–516
Exception, principle of, 477–478
Expected activity time in PERT analysis, 516–519
Expected monetary value (EMV), 144, 146
Expected time for event in PERT analysis, 520–521
Exploitive authoritative leadership style, 407–410
External planning premises, 77
External social control, 238

Factual analysis, 114
Fayol, Henri, 7–11
Feasible solution area in linear programming, 138–140
Feedback:
 in closed sequence systems, 552–553
 in communication, 303–305, 311–314
 in motivation, 351
Fiedler, Fred E., 410–413

Filtering in communication, 309
Flat organization structure, 177–178
Fleishman, Edwin A., 400
Forced distribution method, 269–270
Forecasting of sales, 83–88
FORTRAN, 565
Frame of reference in communication, 307
Free-rein leadership style, 404–407
French, John R. P., 450–455
Fringe status in sociogram, 239–240
Frustration, reactions to, 342–346, 350–356
Functional approach to management, 40–43
Functional process, 173
Functional staff authority, 206–211
Functional status, 228–230
Functions:
  management, 40–41
  organizational, 40–41
Future trends in management, 31–37

Gantt, Henry L., 511–512
Gantt milestone chart, 511–512
General Motors and managerial decentralization, 179–181
General policy, 105
Goal-oriented appraisal, 274
Goals in motivation, 330–331, 351, 352
Governmental regulation, 82–83
Grapevine, 236–237
Graphic method in linear programming, 138–141
Graphic scales system in performance appraisal, 270–272

Halo effect, 266

Hardware of computer system, 564
Harwood Manufacturing Corporation, study of resistance to change in, 450–455
Hawthorne studies, 11–12
Herzberg, Frederick, 367–377
Hierarchy:
  of needs, 335–336, 340–342
  of objectives, 74–75
Horizontal growth in organizations, 173–174
Human relations, 11
Humanistic society, 35–36
Hygiene factors in motivation-maintenance theory, 371

Imposed policy, 106–107
Informal organization:
  charting of, 238–241
  functions of, 235–238
Information in systems approach, 554–555
Intermediate departmentation, 170
Internal audit, 487
Internal social control, 238
International Business Machines Corporation and use of job enrichment, 366–367
International Harvester Company, study of leadership training at, 401–403
Interviewing, 263–267

Job enrichment, 366–367
Jury of executive opinion method, 84

Key-person concept of supervisor, 435
Knowledge society, 33–35

Latest allowable time for event in PERT analysis, 521–524
Leadership, 396–417
  behavioral approach to, 399–400
  contingency view of, 410–413
  and disciplining, 414–417
  and function of directing, 48–49
  leader-oriented approach to study of, 396–400
  and organizational climate, 400–403
  styles, 403–410, 425–432, 446–450
  traits, 396–399
Level of aspiration, 333
Lewin, Kurt, 404–407
Likert, Rensis, 407–410, 440–446
Line activities, 200
Line and staff relationships, 199–225
Line-staff friction, 211–213
Linear programming, 133–142
Lippitt, Ronald, 404–407
Listening in communication, 323–327

McGregor, Douglas, 362–367
Machine language in computers, 564
Maintenance factors in motivation-maintenance theory, 369–377
Management by objectives, 74–76, 95–102
Management development, 276–282
Management games, 279–280
Management inventory, 258–260
Management science, 126–131, 154–161
Managerial centralization, 179–182
  advantages of, 192

Managerial decentralization, 179–182
  advantages of, 192–193
  contingency approach to, 189–198
  at General Motors, 179–181
Managerial grid, 446–450
Marginal-person concept of supervisor, 437
Maslow, A. H., 335–336, 340–342
Materials in systems approach, 554–555
Mathematical models, 126–131
Matrix organization, 559
Mausner, Bernard, 367
Mayo, Elton, 11
MBO (management by objectives), 74–76, 95–102
Mechanized data processing (MDP), 562
Merit rating, 268
Methods in planning, 109–111
Methods improvement, 110
Milestone chart, 511–512
Miscommunication, 304–305
Model in management science, 128–131
Modern organization theory, 550–556
Morale and productivity, 358–362, 440–450
Most likely time in PERT analysis, 516
Motion study, 5
Motivation:
  basic concepts, 330–347
  categories of, 331–336
  and function of directing, 47–48
  hierarchical theory of, 335–336
  multiple, 336–337
  negative, 359–360, 404
  positive, 359–362, 404
  process of, 330–331
  relation to morale and productivity, 358–362, 440–450

Motivation-maintenance theory, 367–377
Motivational conflict, 337–342
  and hierarchical theory of motivation, 340–342
Motivational factors in motivation-maintenance theory, 368–377
Motives:
  conflict of, 336–342
  physical, 331–336
  psychic, 331–336
  social, 331–336
  unconscious, 337
Mouton, Jane S., 446–450
Myers, M. Scott, 372–377

Negative motivation, 359–360, 404
Neoclassical organization theory, 550
Networks in communication, 311–314
Nondirective interview method, 264
Normal probabilities, table of, 528

Objectives:
  hierarchy of, 74–75
  management by, 74–76, 95–102
  types of, 68–73
Open-loop system, 551
Open-sequence system, 551–555
Operant conditioning, 387–393
Operating budget, 479–480
Operations research (OR), 15–16
Optimistic time in PERT analysis, 516
OR (operations research), 15–16
Organization structure, 165–198
Organizational functions, 40–41
Organizing, 45–47

Originated policy, 105–106
Out status in sociogram, 239–240

Participative leadership style, 407–410
Patterned interview method, 264–265
Performance appraisal, 267–275, 290–298
Performance review discussion, 291–298
Person-in-the-middle concept of supervisor, 435–436
Personal control in control procedures, 491
Personal staff, 213–214
PERT (Program Evaluation and Review Techniques), 510–531
  elements of, 514–524
  network, 515–517
  use of, 524–531
Pessimistic time in PERT analysis, 516
Physical dimension of motives, 332
Physiological needs, 335–336
Planning, 43–45
Planning environment, 76–82
Polaris project and development of PERT, 510
Policies, 104–109
  and area of work, 107–109
  and organizational level, 104–105
  readability of, 119–124
  and way they are formed, 105–107
Politics in organizations, 243–244
Position description, 261–262
Position rotation, 277
Positive motivational climate, 359–362, 404
Power, 241–244
  and disciplining, 414–417
Primary departmentation, 170
Primary group in sociogram, 239–240

Principle of exception, 477
Probability analysis, 132,
    142–147
    in PERT analysis,
    526–531
Procedures, 109–110
    readability of, 119–124
Product-mission concept,
    557–558
Product or service objective,
    71–73
Production-centered
    supervision, 442–446
Productivity as related to
    morale, 358–362,
    440–450
Profit objective, 69–72
Program Evaluation and
    Review Technique (*see*
    PERT)
Program management,
    556–561
Project management,
    575–584
Psychic dimension of motives,
    334–335
Pyramidal organization
    structure, 177–178

Quantitative approach to
    management, 15–18
Quantitative decision-making
    techniques, 125–161
Queuing theory, 132–133

Ranking method in appraisal,
    269
Rationalization, 345–346,
    354
    sour-grape, 345–346
    sweet-lemon, 345–346
Readability of policies and
    procedures, 119–124
Real-time processing of data,
    566
Receiver in communication,
    302–303
Regression, 344, 354
Reinforcement, 387–393
    schedules of, 389–390
Repression, 354

Resistance to change,
    450–455
Revenue budget, 479
Roethlisberger, F. J., 15
Role, 232–235
Role conflict, 234–235
Role playing, 280
Rumors, refuting, 237

Safety and security needs,
    335–336
Sales force composite method,
    84–85
Sales forecasting, 83–88
Sampling in control process,
    477
Scalar chain, 9
Scalar process, 172
Scalar status, 228–229
Scheduled time in PERT
    analysis, 521
Schedules of reinforcement,
    389–390
Scientific management, 4–7
Selection interviewing,
    263–267
Self-control procedures,
    491–492
Self-realization needs,
    335–336
Semantics, 305
Sender in communication,
    302–303
Sensitivity training, 281
Sequential decision problems,
    145–147
Service economy, 32–33
Service staff authority,
    204–205
Simplex method in linear
    programming, 141–142
Simulation, 134–135
Slack in PERT analysis,
    524–525
Sloan, Alfred P., Jr., 179–181
Snyderman, Barbara, 367
Social control, 238
Social dimension of motives,
    332–334
Social responsibility, 82–83
Socially-concerned society,
    35–36

Sociogram, 239
Software of computer
    systems, 564
Sour-grape rationalization,
    345–346
Span:
    of control, 174–177
    of management, 174–177
    of supervision, 174–177
Special control reports,
    486–487
Specialist staff, 201
Staff activities, 200–201
Staffing, 258–282
Standards in controlling,
    475–478
Statistical control report,
    484–485
Statistical decision analysis,
    142–147
Statistical methods in sales
    forecasting, 86–87
Status, 228–233
Status anxiety, 231
Status symbols, 230–233
Strategic control points, 475
Stress interview method, 266
Supervisor, role of, 434–440,
    461–469
Supervisory effectiveness,
    440–446
Supervisory style, 446–450
Sweet-lemon rationalization,
    345–346
Symbols in communication,
    305–307
System, definition of,
    546–547
    competitive, 548–549
    environmental, 548–549
    internal, 548–549
Systems approach to
    management, 15–18,
    546–567
Systems concepts and
    management, 546–556

Tall organization structure,
    177–178
Taylor, Frederick W., 4–7
Taylor Differential Piecework
    Plan, 6

Technical activities of managers, 41–42
Texas instruments, Incorporated, and test of motivation-maintenance theory, 372–377
Theory X, 362–364
Theory Y, 365–367
Trait approach to studying leadership, 396–399
Transportation method in linear programming, 142

Ultimate departmentation, 170
Unconscious motives, 337
Unity of command, 9
Users' expectation method, 85–86

Variable budget, 482–484
Variance in PERT analysis, 518–519
Vertical growth in organizations, 172–173

White, R. K., 404–407
Withdrawal reactions in frustration, 344
Work simplification, 110–111

Z, value in PERT analysis, 527–530
Z table, 528
Zero-base budgeting (ZBB), 498–507